Praise for *Different o*

'I can see immediately that this is a very valuable book which will be helpful to many other parents and also to many researchers... I think that your endeavour to tell your story from the point of view of self-help is going to be inspirational. I completely agree with you that it is usually in vain when parents wait for experts to tell them what to do and they really do know better themselves – after all, they ARE the experts for their own child. I like the idea that you have included practical points that have proved to be helpful.' **Prof Uta Frith, Institute of Cognitive Neuroscience & Dept. Psychology, University College London**

'This looks to be really great!... I think it is very worthwhile... I am most impressed... you seem to have a very good direct writing style and the content may be slightly different to that you would find in 'professional' books, but that is its strength. It looks as if you are dealing with the range of issues that are omitted from many books but will be of great interest to parents.' **Prof Rita Jordan, Emeritus Professor in Autism Studies in the School of Education, University of Birmingham.**

'I found it very readable and well written, giving not only a detailed insight into the daily life of a child and family affected by both preterm birth and symptoms of Asperger's syndrome but also with many practical approaches and solutions to the situations and problems encountered...' **Dr Frances Cowan, visiting professor, Neonatal Neuroscience, University of Bristol; honorary clinical senior lecturer in Perinatal Neurology, Imperial College, London**

'I like your style of writing and I am sure other parents will find it useful to dip in and out of the book for advice and reassurance... I feel you have done a lovely job with this.' **Dr Carole Buckley, Clinical Champion for Autism, The Royal College of General Practitioners.**

'Thank you so much for sharing these chapters [11, 17] with me. I really enjoyed reading them and feel honoured to have seem them at this stage. Once again I wish you success with what I think is a really great project – the ethos of what you are seeking to do seems spot on and I think your tone of writing fits that really well.' **Dr Penny Benford, Research Fellow, Keeping Children Safe Programme, School of Medicine, Division of Primary Care, Nottingham University.**

'I think it is very good and I have got very engrossed when I have been reading it. You have a very readable style, which will make the book accessible to a range of different audiences. I look forward to the published book... I have enthused about it to colleagues at work, because I think you have so much to say about parenting, not just being the parent of John with autism. You write very well and get a good balance between the theoretical background and your own experiences. I think it is very powerful the way that John is such an important part of the book, giving his perspective on how things were and still are for him. I could elaborate about all sorts of different things I have found interesting and I wish I had read this earlier in my career, because it provides so many insights into the way education makes false interventions, rather than working from the autistic child's strength.' **Cathie Jones, primary school teacher.**

'I'm enjoying reading it in detail – it is so rich. First thing is to emphasise how much I think you have achieved and what a lot of useful, [and recognisable to us] material you have in here. It's great... The introduction is terrific; succinct, concise, and tells you what the book is for... I entirely agree that 'A key feature of the book is John's input', though I think the links you've made between that and what you tried to do as parents are also key.' **Mother of adult twins on the autism spectrum.**

'The overall style is attractive and makes one want to read on. It's quite drawing. The level of detail is about right and the comments from John, in particular, are vital and illuminating... The narrative provides an illuminating perspective on M.'s [our grandson's] development. We are sure it would be so for anyone facing the same situation.' **Prof and Mrs Ian Wand, grandparents of two children on the autism spectrum.**

'On reading the introduction, I found your writing easy to read and follow. The chapters are the same and this is helped by recounting your personal journey... As a simple GP, I always find that the history is the easiest way to engage in a situation. I was very interested in J's voice as well and the way you include it.' **Father of adult twins on the autism spectrum.**

'I loved reading this and I would very much like to read the whole book in its final draft.' **Jane Dobson, teacher and therapist.**

'The whole section [Why Reading Has Been So Important to John] really achieves what you want – making it so clear why reading is so important for John, how his reading tastes developed and matured, what was done to assist this – great stuff!' **Katherine Snape, retired primary headteacher and diocesan schools inspector.**

'Extremely interesting... I think other parents will take courage from your experience and frankness.' **Jessica Atkinson, state registered music therapist.**

'The chapters I have read were captivating and clear.' **Elinor Tolfree, music psychologist.**

First published by Aspie Press in 2016.

Set in Liberation Serif.

A CIP catalogue record for this book is available from the British Library

ISBN: 978-0-9955529-0-6

DIFFERENT OR DISABLED?

A POSITIVE APPROACH TO PARENTING A CHILD ON THE AUTISM SPECTRUM

Dr Charlotte Aldred

Dedication

To John, Lydia and Tony with thanks for all their support.

Table of Contents

Appendices

Introduction

Our son John[1] was born almost 11 weeks early in the 1970s. He had a life-saving operation when he was two weeks old and remained in hospital for a total of 11 weeks. As a child, John had great difficulty relating to and communicating with his peers, coping with change or noise and engaging in both fine and gross motor activities such as writing, dressing and sport. He had very poor organisational abilities, couldn't concentrate (unless he was particularly interested in something) and couldn't copy from the board, spell or take notes. His behaviour could be very challenging. He would have major meltdowns caused largely by frustration or panic and was easily overwhelmed by his emotions. On the other hand he had an excellent memory, possessed an amazing fund of general knowledge, was very articulate, had an engaging sense of humour, a marvellous eye for detail and an extraordinary ability to focus and concentrate for long periods of time on anything he was passionate about.

John was given a Statement of Special Educational Needs at primary school but no diagnoses were made. These days a child with similar characteristics would probably be diagnosed with an autism spectrum disorder (Asperger's syndrome), attention deficit disorder, dyspraxia and possibly dyslexia. Almost no help was provided at the time because no-one seemed to know what to do; we had to find our own way of parenting our 'different' child.

John, who will soon be 40, is a happy, fulfilled and independent adult. He's at ease with himself, lives in his own home (which he paid for himself) and works in a job which he loves and which stretches him intellectually. We are delighted at the way things have worked out; he has found his own niche in the world and achieved his potential. When John was young and we were very concerned about his future we never imagined to what extent things would change for the better and how he would continue to develop throughout his 20s and 30s. However, there was no 'magic cure'. We didn't try to make him 'normal' and he would still be considered to be on the autism spectrum.

This book looks at many aspects of our son's development. It describes the parenting methods we used, the decisions we made with the reasoning behind them, the challenges we met and what (with the benefit of hindsight) we could have done better. A key feature of the book is John's input; his voice can be heard throughout, explaining why he behaved as he did and how the world felt to him. I have also included many quotes from literature in the field which put our experience into a wider context, and have, wherever possible, provided references which could be of use to readers. Although the chapters are designed to be read in any order (with cross references provided to other chapters where necessary), I would recommend that Chapter 1 is read first.

In writing this book I have sought to provide ideas, understanding, encouragement and hope for parents, carers and anyone else coming into regular contact with verbal children on the autism spectrum. Although much more is known these days about children like John (and many more children like him are being diagnosed), there's insufficient funding to provide all the support that carers might require. For this reason a book like mine may be particularly useful. I agree wholeheartedly with Lise Pyles (2002) who wrote:

> For us, the things that helped the most were the things we did ourselves. Most of them were free or cheap. The best things we did were not to wait for others to come to our rescue, and to refuse to believe people who spoke bleakly about our son's future. A positive attitude and persistence can do a lot...

1

Setting the Scene

DIFFERENT, DISABLED, DISORDERED...?

Are people on the autism spectrum different, disabled, disordered or defective and does it matter anyway? When I asked our son John how he viewed himself he replied:

> I've certainly never considered myself disabled, though any objective analysis would surely conclude that I was, from the sheer number of constraints on my life imposed by Asperger's. And I definitely don't consider myself disordered, despite the notable degree of disorder imposed on my thoughts by the ADD [attention deficit disorder]. I tend to think of myself as 'different, thus constrained', due to having to operate in a world constructed without regard for the differences. I tend to use the word 'constraint' a lot with regard to things I don't do in my daily life that others do (keeping pets, driving, going on holidays, etc).

Unfortunately the terms 'disabled' or 'disordered' bring to mind images of people who can't do things as well as 'normal' individuals; this can easily make those so defined feel like second class citizens. However the word 'different' doesn't have the same negative implications and doesn't exclude the possibility of increased as well as decreased abilities. My husband Tony and I have never thought of our son as disabled. Nevertheless we *were* aware that John was very different from his peers. I think Sophie Walker (2012), whose daughter Grace has been diagnosed with Asperger's syndrome, hits the nail on the head when she writes: 'Aspergers is difficult. You don't really fit in the 'normal' world and you don't really fit in the disabled world. You sort of fall through the middle.'

But what is normal? Normal within any culture usually means 'like the majority' and life's rules are typically made by and for the majority. Those who are in a minority may well find themselves in an uncomfortable situation whether they are thought of as disabled or not. Humans are social animals with a strong tribal instinct: they can easily reject those who are different. As Lawson (2003) explains:

> Self-acceptance, self-esteem or self-respect can be problematic in autism and Asperger's syndrome, because the world around us often says that we are odd, strange, difficult, egocentric and social misfits... I am only disabled in a neurotypical [non-autistic] world where my ability is not recognised or utilised.

Tony Attwood, the well known writer on Asperger's syndrome, believes that people diagnosed with Asperger's syndrome are different rather than defective. He goes so far as to say:[2] 'If Asperger's Syndrome was identified by observation of strengths and talents, it would no longer... be referred to as a syndrome.' Many people with Asperger's syndrome prefer to use the term 'Aspie' in order to avoid using the terms syndrome or disorder with their negative connotations. According to O'Toole (2012), for example:

> The label 'Aspie' seems to feel like a better description than the clinical diagnosis; it communicates, without condescension, a very real set of descriptors about

3

commonalities in the ways we think, behave, and interact. Some of those commonalities are helpful to us, some aren't.

There's a fundamental disagreement between those who believe that there's something seriously wrong with people on the autism spectrum (followers of the *medical* or *deficit* model) and those who believe that autism is just an expression of human diversity (followers of the *difference* model). One reason for such differing views is due to the fact that the autistic population is very diverse. As Thomas Insell wrote in *The Four Kingdoms of Autism*:[3]

> Part of the polarization and confusion around autism results from heterogeneity: the diagnosis of autism now applies to a 5-year-old who has no language, a 20-year-old computer science student at MIT who is socially awkward, and a 40-year-old parent who has no interest in social interaction.

Advocates of the medical model believe that it's important to search for a cure for autism and to identify its genetic causes so that it can be eliminated like any other disease. For example, the organisations *Cure Autism Now* and *Autism Speaks*[4] (which merged some years ago) are composed of parents, doctors and scientists devoted to funding research to identify the causes of autism and to prevent, treat and cure it. They fear that describing autism as a difference with unique strengths rather than a severe disability minimises the very real difficulties experienced by so many autistic people. David Wolman describes this point of view very clearly:[5]

> Critics of the difference model reject the whole idea that autism is merely another example of neuro-diversity. After all, being able to plan your meals for the week or ask for directions bespeak important forms of intelligence...

> In the vast majority of journal articles, autism is referred to as a disorder, and the majority of neuro-psychiatric experts will tell you that the description fits – something is wrong with the autistic brain...

> Meanwhile parents, educators, and autism advocates worry that focusing on the latent abilities and intelligence of autistic people may eventually lead to cuts in funding both for research into a cure and services provided by government. As one mother of an autistic boy told me, 'There's no question that my son needs treatment and a cure'.

On the other hand, many people on the spectrum,[6] as well as many psychologists, believe that autism is such a fundamental part of a person that it wouldn't be possible to 'cure' them. They believe that autism is associated with many strengths relative to the 'neurotypical' (that is non-autistic) majority as well as many challenges. In his essay *Don't Mourn for Us*, Jim Sinclair explains:[7]

> Autism isn't something a person *has*, or a 'shell' that a person is trapped inside. There's no normal child hidden behind the autism. Autism is a way of being. It is *pervasive*; it colors every experience, every sensation, perception, thought, emotion, and encounter, every aspect of existence. It is not possible to separate the autism from the person – and if it were possible, the person you'd have left would not be the same person you started with. This is important, so take a moment to

consider it: Autism is a way of being. It is not possible to separate the person from the autism. Therefore, when parents say, I wish my child did not have autism, what they're really saying is, I wish the autistic child I have did not exist, and I had a different (non-autistic) child instead... This is what we hear when you mourn over our existence. This is what we hear when you pray for a cure. This is what we know, when you tell us of your fondest hopes and dreams for us: that your greatest wish is that one day we will cease to be, and strangers you can love will move in behind our faces.

Followers of the difference model also believe that thinking of someone purely in terms of what they *can't* do can be very damaging to their sense of well-being. Again, according to Jim Sinclair:[8]

In the traditional deficit model, autism is defined in terms of deficits – things that are 'wrong' with a person. It then follows that the way to support a person who has all these deficits is to try to fix the things that are wrong, and make the person more like a normal person who doesn't have those deficits...

When people are constantly being treated as if they're defective, criticized for their natural behavior, and taught that they only earn approval and respect by pretending to be something they're not, they're likely to develop a low sense of self-esteem.

If people on the autism spectrum are considered to be different rather than defective, with a set of strengths and weaknesses that isn't the same as those of the neurotypical population, then it's important that the neurotypical majority are educated about these differences so that understanding, acceptance, tolerance and a willingness to make accommodations can be promoted. A belief that someone is different but can still achieve might encourage the use of different teaching methods and the introduction of some environmental changes and supports. The importance of environment cannot be overemphasised: someone might appear disabled in one situation and not in another more suited to their strengths. In the past it was often easier for loners, eccentrics and unusual individuals to thrive; these days, open plan offices, teamwork and the ability to fit in are the norm. Sensitivity to noise and poor social communication skills can make modern working conditions (both at school and in adult life) particularly difficult for even the most intelligent person on the spectrum. As Temple Grandin (2008) notes:

Geeks, nerds, and eccentrics have always been in the world; what has changed is the world itself and our expectations of others within it...

I get worried that today an Asperger's diagnosis may be detrimental to some individuals and hold them back. With greater competition for shrinking numbers of jobs, a person's social capabilities are now looked at as closely as are the person's technical skills or intellectual abilities.

Although most people believe that it's important to help autistic individuals fit into the neurotypical world, followers of the difference model disagree with the therapies that attempt to make autistic people appear 'normal'. As Donna Williams (2006) explains:

There are good reasons for helping Auties [autistic people] cope better in a world dominated by developmentally typical people, but the pure goal of wanting an

Autie to perform a developmentally typical person's version of 'normal' shouldn't be one of them...

If I'm an apple, I don't want to spend years in therapy trying to fix myself up from being what I assume is a failure as an orange...

Indeed many believe it's wrong to try and suppress autistic behaviours (in an attempt to make those engaged in them appear to be more 'normal') as these behaviours are coping mechanisms which enable the autistic individual to deal with the demands of the neurotypical world. Stanton (2000), for example, explains:

[Some people consider] any evidence of autism is... a problem to be eliminated. Even people with high functioning autism rely on a lot of so called stereotypical behaviour such as hand flapping, spinning and rocking to help them concentrate. It serves no purpose to suppress these behaviours. All that happens is that you increase the pressure and the levels of stress.

According to Jim Sinclair,[9] trying to make autistic people conform to a neurotypical pattern of behaviour can be damaging to their mental health:

For autistic people who are very interested in belonging, teaching us to perform imperfect imitations of neurotypical behavior may appear to be successful on the surface, but underneath people are still experiencing all that anxiety and exhaustion and depression and self-hatred. In my experience, the more 'successful' an autistic person has become at emulating NT [neurotypical] social skills, the more anxious and insecure that person is inside. Long-term effects on mental health can be devastating.

Supporters of the difference model also think it's wrong for so much time and money to be spent on looking for a 'cure' rather than providing enough support services to enable autistic people to fulfil their potential and thrive in the neurotypical world. As the authors of the website http://www.aspiesforfreedom.com write: 'Funding for 'cure' research is unlikely to ever produce a result. In the meantime, support services for autistic people are underfunded. This money would be far better used to help existing autistic people.' David Wolman[10] believes that searching for a cure has prevented scientists 'from asking fundamental questions about how autistic brains function'. As he explains:

In the matter of autistic intelligence, Kanner spoke of an array of mental skills, 'islets of ability' – vocabulary, memory, and problem-solving that 'bespeak good intelligence.' Asperger, too, was struck by 'a particular originality of thought and experience.' Yet over the years, those islets attracted scientific interest only when they were amazing – savant-level capabilities in areas such as music, mathematics, and drawing. For the millions of people with autism who weren't savants, the general view was that their condition was tragic, their brainpower lacking...

In his original paper in 1943, Kanner wrote that while many of the children he examined 'were at one time or another looked upon as feebleminded, they are all unquestionably endowed with *good cognitive potentialities.*' Sixty-five years later, though, little is known about those potentialities. As one researcher told me, 'there's no money in the field for looking at differences' in the autistic brain. 'But if you talk about trying to fix a problem – then the funding comes'...

Which of these models do I believe in? As I understand it, autistic symptoms can result from many underlying and complex conditions; the degree to which these symptoms are expressed in an individual varies with genetic predisposition and environment. As a result people on the autism spectrum differ hugely from one another and as such I don't think it's possible for *either* model to apply to everyone. Despite the fact that autistic traits are often enhanced versions of characteristics we all possess to some degree, if they are so extreme that the person is completely unable to fit into the society around them, or if their condition causes them significant distress, then I think they can be considered to be disabled. The profoundly autistic would usually fall into this category and would probably need lifetime care. I would prefer to think of everyone else on the spectrum as different rather than disabled, disordered or defective. Nevertheless I believe that there *can* be definite advantages attached to the treatment of autism as a disability even for the most able individuals. Not only does it make it possible to receive financial support but the recognition that problems exist makes it more likely that appropriate help, accommodations and flexible teaching will be on offer. Acknowledging a child's problems makes it easier for a care-giver to empathise and makes it more likely that help (rather than blame and punishment) will be provided. As John notes: 'I have something which *could* have been a disability but became something more neutral because it was acknowledged and compensated for.'

It's important to ensure that someone considered to be disabled doesn't become handicapped as well, as a result of understanding care-givers providing too much help. This can lead to co-dependency or learned helplessness. As Jim Sinclair explains:

> Another contributor to low self-esteem is being overprotected and 'taken care of' too much, which gives the message that we are incapable of doing things for ourselves. It often becomes a self-fulfilling prophecy because when autistic people aren't given opportunities to learn and try new things, we end up truly being less capable, simply because of the lack of opportunity to develop our abilities...

AN OVERVIEW OF OUR PARENTING METHODS

Although we knew that John found some things difficult, we didn't think of him as someone who had a disease that had to be 'cured'. In fact we had no diagnosis or underlying explanation for any of John's behaviour while he was a child. A key feature of our parenting approach was our attempt (although not always successful) to step into John's shoes and see the world through his eyes and from his point of view, something that one should do ideally for all children. Close observation was crucial: in particular noting what our son enjoyed doing, what he avoided and what caused him to become upset. In this way we learned how to manage his surroundings so as to maximise his happiness and minimise his distress. It's much easier to be patient with a child who's upset if one can see the cause of the meltdown from their point of view. Understanding the underlying problem makes it easier to think laterally and experiment with alternative parenting behaviours in order to avoid a similar situation occurring again. Noticing what really excites one's child makes it much simpler to think of toys and activities that would be enjoyed and would provide a learning opportunity. According to the National Autistic Society:[11]

It is essential to see the world from the standpoint of the child or adult on the autism spectrum. This is a key ingredient in the 'craft' of working with children and adults with autism. We must begin from the position or perspective of the individual and gather insights about how they see and experience their world, knowing what it is that motivates or interests them but importantly what may also frighten, preoccupy or otherwise distress them.

Perhaps as a consequence of our attempt to see the world from John's point of view, we didn't try to change him: we treated him as an individual and allowed him to be himself. We adopted a positive parenting approach, encouraging and developing our son's strengths rather than focusing on his difficulties. According to Gillberg (2002):

> People with Asperger syndrome almost always have major strengths that may, wholly or partly, compensate for the major difficulties. Almost all of the core features of the syndrome have 'positive' opposites.

I think parental attitudes towards their children are really important. Adopting an optimistic yet realistic outlook, which concentrates on what children *can* do rather than what they can't, is preferable to thinking of them as a failure because they are different from others. Encouraging a child's strengths can lead to the development of an expertise which in turn can lead to self-fulfilment, a positive self-image, happiness, friends, hobbies and hopefully a career and independence. Of course it's necessary to accept the individual's weaknesses as well as their strengths but it isn't necessarily a good thing for too much parental effort to go into attempts to change their child into something they can never be. Spending too much time working on a child's deficits/differences can easily damage their self-esteem; better to accept the differences and expend the same time and effort on developing the child's strengths instead. This viewpoint is supported by Ozonoff et al (2002):

> Recognizing and capitalizing on your child's strengths, and helping others to do so too, can go a long way toward making up for his or her areas of difficulty. We've found, in fact, that asking yourself how you can take advantage of the true gifts associated with autism spectrum disorders, or how you can creatively use the unique ways of thinking or behaving associated with AS-HFA, [Asperger's syndrome – high functioning autism] tends to produce many more solutions than strategies that concentrate on attacking your child's weaknesses... Perhaps most important, you help build your child's self-esteem. Success breeds success, and children with AS-HFA who are given opportunities to succeed tend to adapt to the non-AS-HFA world more quickly and completely than those who are taught to view life as one problem after another.

Nevertheless we couldn't, and didn't, ignore those weaknesses that would have made it impossible for John to realise his true potential and thrive in the 'real' world of neurotypicals. Although it wasn't easy (and we didn't always succeed) we tried to imagine which of John's difficulties could lead to long-term problems if they weren't addressed; if we couldn't foresee future problems we left well alone. Having chosen *which* problems to address we had to decide *when* and *how* to approach them; for this a realistic understanding of John's capabilities was crucial. We had no desire to force him to do things he was incapable of: this would have caused him great distress and been a waste of time anyway. John also needed plenty of time to get used to the idea of making *any* change and had to be sufficiently motivated to be prepared to make an effort. With enough motivation John would persevere and work really hard to achieve his objective, whereas failure was inevitable if he couldn't see the point. Our approach was in many ways similar to that of Ross Green[12] which recognises that 'kids do well if they can'. He emphasises the importance of understanding that children's 'challenging behavior occurs when the demands of the environment exceed a kid's capacity to respond adaptively'. He recommends that adults try to understand why and when difficult behaviours arises and then work in collaboration with the child to find a 'realistic and mutually satisfactory' plan of action.

Last, but by no means least, a crucial part of our parenting approach was to help *John* develop a realistic appreciation and acceptance of his own strengths and weaknesses and an understanding of the type of environments that would suit him and enable him to be himself. In this way we hoped that as a square peg he could look for square holes to fit into and avoid the frustration of continually trying to fit into round ones. When one has a clear understanding of one's own capabilities it's much easier to choose a satisfactory pathway through life. It's all too easy for an autistic individual to look around and see what the majority of other people aspire to and then attempt to emulate them, even though this may be totally unrealistic and may lead to frustration and unhappiness. Once John left school his realistic appreciation of his own strengths and weaknesses was a major factor in his choice of career and lifestyle and this has led to happiness and fulfilment; he hasn't wasted time or energy chasing fantasies. Attwood (2006) considers such an acceptance to be an important factor contributing to the success of people on the autism spectrum:

> The person is eventually able to accept his or her strengths and deficits and no longer has a desire to become someone that he or she cannot be: there is a realization that he or she has qualities others admire.

Although all children on the autism spectrum are different, it's to be hoped that there are sufficient commonalities so that some of our parenting approaches (which are described in detail throughout the rest of this book), as well as the lessons we learned, will be useful to others.

2

In the Beginning

PREMATURE LABOUR

It was a beautiful Friday evening and just as the lights turned green the pains started again. As I turned right I clung onto the steering wheel of the car with grim determination, trying to make sure I steered accurately, very conscious of the huge juggernaut on my immediate left. With great relief I parked the car soon afterwards and collected my husband Tony from his evening classes. Fortunately he took over the driving. On the way home my husband became increasingly concerned over my condition and insisted that we called into our local hospital which was still an hour's drive away. I told him that I'd been having strong, regular, abdominal cramps since the late afternoon; I thought they were due to a bladder infection. Even though I looked enormous, it was still nearly 11 weeks before our baby was due and I was quite unaware that babies could be born so early in an apparently uneventful pregnancy. In fact two nights earlier my waters had broken but in my ignorance I hadn't realised what was happening and thought that the baby had moved and was pressing on my bladder. I should have gone straight to hospital as it's very risky to carry on as usual after the membranes surrounding the baby have ruptured: to do so brings with it a risk of infection which I was very lucky to avoid.

We arrived at Casualty around 10.45 pm and the person who booked me in seemed to agree that I couldn't possibly be about to give birth, since 'no-one ever comes in so cheerful if they're in labour'. This happy mood could probably be attributed to the combined effects of wonderful weather, a day spent with a good friend, my normal optimistic outlook and above all total ignorance of the fact that I *was* actually in labour. Shortly afterwards a doctor came to examine me, said that I was 50% dilated, my dates were wrong and I was about to have a five pound baby. Then he disappeared and left me with the midwives.

At 2.10 am on Saturday morning, after gas and air and finally a small amount of pethidine, I gave birth to a lovely little boy whom we called John. I thought he looked perfect but pandemonium seemed to break out immediately. The midwives said that John was very small and there might be two or even three babies in all; he weighed only 1135g/2.5lb, considered to be very small indeed in the 1970s. John was whisked away very quickly and a search was made for the missing doctor. Twenty minutes later I gave birth to an identical twin boy who died soon after birth. So much for wrong dates and a five pound baby although the weight of the two babies combined *was* accurate.

The early delivery was due to the fact that I'm quite small and, as this was my first pregnancy, I'd run out of space for the babies to grow in. If twins had been diagnosed in advance a Caesarean might have been carried out to save both babies.

JOHN'S TIME IN HOSPITAL

After John was born he was taken away immediately and put into an incubator. Because our son was already having breathing difficulties our local hospital (which had its own special care baby unit) decided to look for a London teaching hospital with enough space to take John into intensive care. Given what happened later we were very grateful that this transfer took place, otherwise it's unlikely that John would have lived.

When John arrived at the hospital in London he was given oxygen in a head box for two days because he had mild hyaline membrane disease which was leading to breathing problems. The lungs of very premature babies are immature and there is a significant risk of respiratory distress syndrome which can lead to death; we were warned that the first 48 hours were the most dangerous. John was given a precautionary course of antibiotics and was also treated with phototherapy for jaundice. According to Wikipedia:[13]

> Infant respiratory distress syndrome (IRDS), also called neonatal respiratory distress syndrome or respiratory distress syndrome of newborn, previously called hyaline membrane disease... is the leading cause of death in pre-term infants. The incidence decreases with advancing gestational age, from about 50% in babies born at 26–28 weeks, to about 25% at 30–31 weeks.

In the mid-1970s the mortality figures were probably worse. Fortunately after ten days John had regained most of his birth weight and was doing well; we started to relax a bit. We'd been going regularly to the hospital to see our son and cuddle him for short periods of time. This was a frightening as well as pleasurable experience because it was hard to relax holding such a tiny baby while wearing a face-mask and gown in order to minimise the chance of passing infections on to him. In the incubator John wore nothing except a nappy and socks but when he was taken out for us to hold, he was wrapped in blankets and a woollen hat popped onto his head. As he was too premature to be able to suck, John was fed with my breast milk via a tube going down his nose into his stomach. I'd hired an electric breast pump (which we nicknamed Daisy) from the National Childbirth Trust and my husband was taking the milk into the hospital on his way to work. It was very comforting to know that John and other premature babies in the unit were being fed with it.

One Saturday morning, about two weeks after John was born, we received a phone call from the hospital asking us to come in immediately as John was very ill and they wanted us to sign an operation consent form. It was a terrible shock as we'd seen him the evening before and to our untrained eyes he seemed fine; however, this time when we arrived at the hospital, our son looked terrible. We were told that he had a lung infection which hadn't responded to antibiotics and this, coupled with a blood vessel that hadn't closed (see below), meant that his heart was unable to pump enough oxygenated blood round his body. We were informed that they had to operate on him in order to close this blood vessel. They were unable to tell us what the chances of success might be and so, after signing the form, we went home sick with worry. Fortunately the operation was a great success, otherwise there is little doubt that John would have died. We were told afterwards that this was the first time this particular operation had been carried out in the

UK on such a small baby. John weighed about 1020g/2.25lb at the time of the operation.

Many years later we obtained a copy of John's medical records (see Appendix 1) and were able to see just how ill he'd been. It was quite upsetting reading through these records for the first time. In lay terms, two weeks after birth John had a loud heart murmur, episodes where he went blue and an X-ray indicated pneumonia which did not respond to antibiotics. The next day he had more frequent and prolonged episodes when he stopped breathing and required oxygen. He had signs of congestive heart failure with an increased heart rate and heart size; his liver had also increased in size and he became floppy. He was diagnosed with what is called patent ductus arteriosus (PDA – see below). The PDA was initially treated with drugs but there was no improvement. In fact John continued to deteriorate: he became grey, very floppy, wasn't breathing most of the time on his own and the pneumonia hadn't improved with antibiotics. He 'looked pre-terminal' hence the decision to operate. After the operation John was on a ventilator for 24 hours and needed oxygen in a head box for a further 12 hours. After this he improved a lot, was active, looked pink, his heart size returned to normal and there was no sign of the pneumonia. Absolutely amazing, particularly for the mid-1970s.

Foetal blood circulation is very different to the blood circulation of a baby after it is born. Before birth there is no need for foetal blood to be oxygenated by the lungs as oxygen is received from the mother's placenta. Blood bypasses the lungs via a blood vessel called the ductus arteriosus. PubMed provides the following description of a PDA:[14]

> Patent ductus arteriosus (PDA) is a condition in which a blood vessel called the ductus arteriosus fails to close normally in an infant soon after birth. (The word 'patent' means open)...

> Before birth, the ductus arteriosus allows blood to bypass the baby's lungs... Soon after the infant is born and the lungs fill with air, this blood vessel is no longer needed. It will usually close within a couple of days. If the ductus arteriosus does not close, there will be abnormal blood circulation between the heart and lungs... The condition is more common in premature infants and those with neonatal respiratory distress syndrome.

Although we continued to visit the hospital, we weren't allowed to hold John any more; we weren't too upset, just thankful that he was so much better. However after another week he started to have breathing problems again. During one particular visit we heard John's heart rate slow (from the attached monitors) and saw his breathing stop. An alarm went off, a nurse came and tapped John's feet and then everything went back to normal. This happened more than once during this visit and I found it terribly upsetting, wondering what sort of brain damage these events might be causing. It was some time before I could face visiting John again as I was incapable of handling my feelings of fear and distress while watching him struggle so much to stay alive. Staying at home made it easier for me to cope and not fall apart completely. Fortunately my husband, who is made of tougher stuff, continued to see him when he made his daily trip to the hospital with my milk. After another unsuccessful course of antibiotics the hospital treated John with continuous positive airway pressure (CPAP), which was an experimental technique at the time. They put a face mask on him and let him breathe in air under positive pressure i.e. the air was literally 'pushed in', keeping John's airways slightly open all the time which made it less effort for him to breathe. This technique was very successful and as soon as John was breathing normally I resumed my regular visits. There were no more problems after this and John was transferred (at 5½ weeks old, weighing 1500g/3.3lb) to our local hospital's special care baby unit for 'fattening up'. He was now on mixed tube and bottle feeding and all the milk was still mine.

Once John arrived at our local hospital it was easy for me to visit him every day to see how he was getting on and give him a cuddle. When he was nine weeks old I began to stay all day at the hospital so that I could try and get him used to breastfeeding. In the mid-1970s it was believed, certainly in our local hospital, that it was impossible to breastfeed such a premature baby; I had a real fight with the staff to allow me to try and teach John. Initially they allowed me to breastfeed him for only a minute at a time because they were worried that John would get too tired. They also weighed him before and after each feed to see how much milk he'd drunk. After a week or so John had cottoned on to what he had to do and I was allowed to have longer and longer sessions with him; by the time he came home (at 11 weeks old) he was feeding entirely from the breast. The hospital staff were delighted that such a premature baby could breastfeed after all. They were actively saving for an electric breast pump like the one I'd hired so that all the mothers in their unit would have the opportunity to do what I had done. How times change though. About two years later I happened to talk to someone who'd just been in the same special care baby unit. To my amazement she told me that mothers, who were *not* keen on breastfeeding their premature babies, were now being pressurised by the staff who said that if Mrs Aldred could do it so could they!

Just before John came home he developed anaemia and had to be given a transfusion. Initially I was present when they carried out what should have been a straightforward procedure but I couldn't stay as I found it too upsetting. John was crying and the process took most of the day because the doctors couldn't find a suitable vein. However this was the last intervention and a day later I was delighted to take John home exactly 11 weeks after he was born and now weighing a healthy 2570g/5lb 11oz.

John has an amusing anecdote regarding the marks left on his skin from all the medical procedures he was subjected to as a premature baby. The incident occurred when he was in his teens, walking with his close friend Phil along a road near our home:

> I've only been stopped by the police once. Phil was walking along the road waving a car aerial taken from his junk-heap of a car: they may have thought he'd snapped it off someone else's car, though they never said. So the police stopped us to check us out, and when I tried to intercede, one of them insisted on checking me for needle marks (I suspect my rather slurred and stammery voice didn't help matters). He lit up when he found signs of needle marks on both wrists! Fifteen year old needle marks. Gold star for observational skill, there.

POSSIBLE OUTCOMES FOR VERY PREMATURE BABIES

While John was still in hospital I was extremely concerned that he might be brain damaged as a result of the difficulties he'd experienced since birth. I looked for information about the kind of problems very premature babies might experience as they grew up but found very little in this pre-internet era. All I could find was that some babies had become blind in the past because they received too much oxygen; doctors were fully aware of this problem though and oxygen levels were monitored and controlled very carefully. Things are very different these days. According to Frances Cowan (at the time a senior lecturer in perinatal neurology in the Faculty of Medicine at Imperial College), who was kind enough to review this chapter for me:

> Nowadays imaging the newborn brain using ultrasound has become standard of care, but this was not the case in the 1970s – ultrasound imaging has helped neonatologists and neurologists understand a lot about preterm brain injury – in more recent years MRI brain scans are also done and research shows that the brains of babies born very preterm do develop differently from those born at term even when there is no major problem to see.

The rest of this chapter contains a brief summary of some of the research into the outcomes of premature babies, extracted from the articles and books listed in Appendix 2. I'm quite relieved that I had no idea at the time how far reaching these problems could be; it would have been a source of intense worry.

Premature babies are often categorised for research purposes into the 'Very Low Birth Weight' (VLBW) group weighing less than 1500g at birth and the 'Extremely Low Birth Weight' (ELBW) group weighing less than 1000g. The shorter the length of time the baby stays in the uterus and the lower the birth weight, the greater the risk of disability. Premature boys appear to be more vulnerable than premature girls. John, born nearly 11 weeks early with a birth weight of 1135g falls at the lower end of the VLBW category; however, with all the problems he experienced in the first few weeks after birth it wouldn't be surprising if his outcomes were similar to those reported for smaller babies.

Major disabilities (such as cerebral palsy, blindness, deafness, seizures, hydrocephalus and learning or cognitive disability) are more common in premature babies than in babies that go to term. Even if major medical disability is avoided, many studies have found an increased risk, compared with full-term babies, of a variety of cognitive, visual, motor and behavioural impairments. An increased risk does *not* mean that *all* premature babies will experience all or even some of these difficulties as they grow older but that they are *more likely* to. Cognitive impairments can be quite wide ranging and include those often grouped together by psychologists under the heading *Executive Function* (EF). These EF impairments include difficulties with working memory (the ability to hold information in the mind while working on a problem – important for mental arithmetic, reading and spelling), with planning and organisation and with the ability to focus attention and not get distracted too easily. The ability to inhibit impulsive behaviour may also be impaired, which means these children may act before they think. Problems with mental flexibility and processing speeds may also be found, which can make unexpected change and social interaction difficult to cope with. Children and adults can seem less mature than their peers and may have difficulties processing emotion. Sequencing abilities, learning verbal lists, time management, persistence, reasoning and verbal fluency can all be adversely affected. Quite often problems may not become apparent until the child has to cope with the pressures of school. There may be a lower average IQ, with delays in language development or specific learning problems which can give rise to lower scores on maths, reading, writing and spelling tests. As a result of the above, poorer school performance is likely and the chances of going on to further education are reduced. Behaviour can be affected, in ways sometimes described as 'internalising' (including withdrawal, shyness and anxiety which can lead to depression), or 'externalising' (including hyperactivity and aggression). An increase in both internalising and externalising behaviours is more likely in children born very prematurely. Behavioural problems plus cognitive and motor difficulties can make children extremely vulnerable to victimisation and physical, verbal and/or psychological bullying.

Catherine Limperopoulos and colleagues (2008) found that of the 91 infants they studied, all born with weights less than or equal to 1500g, 26% had a positive result on the Modified Checklist for Autism in Toddlers (M-CHAT). According to the website www.m-chat.org:

> [M-CHAT] is an autism screening tool designed to identify children **16** to **30** months of age who should receive a more thorough assessment for possible early signs of autism spectrum disorder (ASD) or developmental delay.

Similarly Wong et al (2014) found that the scores on the Quantitative Checklist for Autism in Toddlers (Q-CHAT)[15] were significantly higher for the 141 preterm infants they assessed compared with the published scores for the general population, 'indicating greater social-communication difficulty and autistic behaviour'. According to Joan Raphael-Leff, writing in the foreword to Acquarone (2007):

> Babies later diagnosed as autistic are found to have had more complications during gestation and delivery than their normal siblings and others... In addition... infants later diagnosed on the autistic spectrum have a two fold [higher] rate of residence in neonatal intensive care units.

It's well known that environment is critical for brain development during gestation and afterwards. It might be expected that babies who spend the last ten weeks of a pregnancy in an intensive care unit instead of a normal uterine environment (as nature intended) would have some negative outcomes. Life in a neonatal intensive care unit (NICU) will of necessity be stressful, including as it does: loss of physical uterine constraints, feeding via a tube, feeding either with non-maternal milks or feeding at an age when the gut is not designed to be absorbing milk, handling, social contact, noise, increased light levels, interventions and possibly painful procedures and inevitable early exposures to infection. Not an ideal environment for a baby's brain which is developing rapidly in this period. Pre-frontal regions of the brain important for many intellectual functions, such as attention and planning, have been found to be significantly smaller after 10 weeks spent in a NICU rather than a uterus. As Lisa Blakemore-Brown (2002) pointed out:

> Infants who are born very prematurely... are more likely to present with developmental problems relating to the functions of the frontal lobes. Attentional problems and difficulties with social awareness within this group have long been recognised clinically in such populations.

Perhaps surprisingly, Pineda and colleagues (2014) found the outcomes (at two years old), of preterm infants who had spent their neonatal intensive care in private rooms, were less favourable than that of pre-term infants who spent their time in open wards.

In her book *Why Love Matters*, Sue Gerhardt writes about the effect stress can have on a baby's brain:

A baby whose stress (and therefore cortisol) is not kept at a manageable level may eventually be seriously affected. There is some evidence that high levels of cortisol might be toxic to the developing brain over time. In particular, too much cortisol can affect the development of the orbitofrontal part of the pre-frontal cortex... an area which... is responsible for reading social cues and adapting behaviour to social norms.

She also describes the effect early stress has on the part of the brain called the hippocampus, which can become less sensitive to cortisol, making it more difficult for that individual to cope with stress thereafter.

Prematurely born individuals have an increased risk of motor difficulties (a key component of developmental coordination disorder or DCD) affecting fine and gross motor control as well as perceptual and visual motor skills. Poor fine motor control can make it hard to produce fast and legible writing, whilst sporting prowess is severely affected by gross motor impairments. As adults there may be less physical confidence and less participation in physical activity, and according to Hack et al (2002), young adults participated in less risk-taking behaviour. Foulder-Hughes and Cooke, writing in 2003 in the Dyspraxia Foundation Professional Journal, said:

[Their study] aimed to discover whether children who were born very preterm, ≤ 32 weeks gestational age, are at an increased risk of developmental co-ordination disorder (DCD), when compared to children at full term... The incidence of DCD in the preterm group was 30.7% compared to 6.7% in the control population.

A child born prematurely may have hearing impairments and a variety of visual impairments, including problems with visual memory, visual-spatial and visual-motor skills, short-sightedness, a lazy eye, a squint and problems with three dimensional vision. According to Schalij-Delfos and colleagues (2000), 96% of the infants they studied with a gestational age ≤ 31 weeks had some sort of ophthalmological abnormality.

As young adults, those born very prematurely may have a higher mean blood pressure and be more prone to asthma; as they grow older there is an increased risk of heart attacks linked to problems with central obesity, diabetes and atherosclerosis.

It's thought that certain factors may improve the outcome for these very premature babies. It's been found that increased maternal education is correlated with higher intelligence and language functioning but how much is due to genetics and how much to the enriched environment that the child is likely to be exposed to isn't easy to identify. When a baby is very premature there's a risk of poor mother-baby interaction which could mean the mother fails to pay sufficient attention to the infant's developmental needs. This may occur because of the long mother-baby separation while the baby is in hospital which, with the attendant worry and fear, may make mother-baby bonding more difficult. This could be exacerbated by the anxiety and depression that the mother may suffer as a result of the whole experience. In addition the very premature baby could be more unresponsive, may be a less satisfactory social partner and could be more irritable and harder to soothe than a full-term baby.

Parents may not have the resources, knowledge or help to overcome these difficulties. It's been suggested that increased physical contact with the baby, such as carrying him in a soft carrier against the body, can make it easier for the parent to respond immediately to the infant's change in activity and thereby reduce crying. 'Kangaroo' mother care both in the NICU and at home, in which parent and infant have skin to skin contact, is thought by some to aid the development of personal relations and lead to a higher IQ than traditional care. This kind of care was unavailable in the mid-1970s but is frequently used these days.

The *Newborn Individualised Developmental Care and Assessment Programme* (NIDCAP) is another technique that is used sometimes in the NICU. According to the website http://www.winnicott.org.uk/uk-nidcap-centre:[16]

> The NIDCAP is based on observation of babies to find out how they feel, how they are coping with their surroundings and events, and what developmental stage they are at. This allows us to adjust the care to make it more personal, to provide more comfort and appropriate stimulation. Parents are very involved in this process. Low noise levels are maintained, bright lighting is avoided and babies are comfortably nested in their incubators. To help parents feel confident in caring for their tiny, fragile baby we have specialist help to show them how to comfort and communicate with their baby from the very beginning.

In the womb, babies are in a relatively confined space and therefore have something to push against. The 'nests' are designed to provide the premature baby with a similar environment. However, according to Cowan:[17]

> NIDCAP, in its entirety, is not used by so many units in the UK and indeed studies have not proven NIDCAP to be better than standard care in the long term though there is some evidence for better short term outcomes; however such studies are difficult to do, not least because the general principles of NIDCAP have been included in daily care by most units and they have contributed greatly to the recommended standards of good neonatal care today.

Although John doesn't suffer from any major medical disabilities he *does* exhibit many of the characteristics described above, as will become evident later in this book. Of course this doesn't prove that prematurity was responsible for any of John's difficulties as genetic factors can never be overlooked.

3
Food

Food is one of the necessities of life, and mealtimes should be a pleasurable bonding experience. However some autistic children find it very difficult to cope with the social aspects of eating with the rest of the family. In other families mealtimes can turn into battlegrounds, with children refusing to eat what they're given. Picky eating can be a particular issue for some children on the autism spectrum who end up eating a very restricted diet. I was brought up to believe that a well balanced and nutritious diet was essential for good health; I hoped that we could 'train' our children to eat well and enjoy both the taste of food and the social aspects of mealtimes.

BREASTFEEDING

I was feeling quite excited as I left home one autumn evening to go to my first orchestral rehearsal since my son was born. John had been at home for about eight weeks and this was the first time that I was going out without him. I left Tony holding the fort, reasonably confident that everything would be fine, as my husband was used to holding and cuddling John as well as changing his nappies. I'd expressed my milk into a bottle and given it to Tony with instructions to warm it up when John cried for a feed. It was lovely returning to the orchestra and I thoroughly enjoyed my evening, delighted that I was able to resume one of my usual activities. I arrived home in excellent spirits. You can imagine my reaction when I discovered that Tony had spent half the evening trying, unsuccessfully, to persuade John to take milk from the bottle. This was really quite surprising considering that John had been fed by bottle, with my milk, for several weeks in the hospital before he learned to breastfeed. However, now he was used to the breast it seemed as if nothing else would do. This was a very early example of John's lack of flexibility and dislike of change: a rubber teat doesn't taste the same as a nipple, the sucking technique is different and *I* wasn't holding him. So that was the end of orchestral playing for some time until John could last all evening without a feed. If we'd been less ignorant we might have tried giving John my milk from a spoon or a cup but we can't be sure that he would have taken it even then.

Out of curiosity I contacted our local hospital to find out if *they* had experienced any difficulty bottle feeding John at night during those few days before I took him home, when I was breastfeeding him during the day. It was then I discovered that he'd refused to be bottle fed by the staff at night even though it was still my milk. Refusing to be bottle fed proved to be quite a problem though, as I didn't seem to have enough breast milk for John in the late afternoon/early evening. Even though I spent extra time resting, poor Tony still had to walk around all evening with John on his shoulder in order to comfort him until I had produced enough milk. It would have been extremely useful if we could have given John a bottle of formula milk at this time of day so that he wasn't hungry and unhappy. As a result we started him, five and a half months from his date of birth (about three months from his due date), on a small amount of baby cereal so that he wasn't hungry in the evening. Although this was earlier than we would have liked, it falls within the suggested limits recommended for premature babies by the premature baby charity Bliss.

I wonder whether one reason why I had insufficient breast milk was due to the fact that I'd been expressing for such a long time before I was able to feed John myself. Perhaps my body had regulated my milk supply, after so many weeks on the pump, to an inadequate demand. Another possible reason for my difficulties could have been that John, as such a small baby, wasn't able to suck strongly enough to stimulate sufficient milk production. I was completely unaware at the time of any of the techniques that are currently recommended for maximising the milk flow when using an electric pump. These days there is plenty of information on the web about this topic. Googling 'breastfeeding premature babies' or 'breastfeeding preemies' brings up some helpful web sites (see Appendix 28).

Apart from this glitch, John was a good feeder but slow. This didn't matter so much during the day but was less welcome at night when a feed never took less than an hour and a half. At night I used to feed John in the spare room so that I didn't disturb my husband who needed to go to work the following day. I made myself comfortable with a pot of tea and listened to the World Service on the radio. Unfortunately by the time John had finished and was ready for sleep, I was thoroughly awake! Not so good when I only had a couple of hours before John would need another feed. I tried all sorts of things to speed matters up but nothing worked. John liked a nap in the middle of his feed and if I tried to cut this nap short, or tried to put him to sleep after one side only, I would be woken up a few minutes later just as I'd settled into a deep slumber. It wasn't worth it. Fortunately after a few weeks John was only waking up once in the middle of the night rather than twice. I coped during these early weeks by going to sleep in the evening; I could get a couple of hours good sleep before the late evening feed. This would have been very difficult if I hadn't had a partner at home who was willing and able to look after John in the evening. I can't imagine how I would have coped if there'd been two babies to feed. Amazingly, after John had been home for approximately eight weeks, he was sleeping right through the night after his late feed. I felt like a new woman.

Why was I so anxious to breastfeed and why did I spend so long trying to teach my premature baby how to do it? I felt instinctively that breast milk, as the food source provided by nature for young babies, would provide the best nutrients for John. I thought at the time that a premature baby, who's had such a difficult start in life, would be in even greater need of any extra benefits that this milk could provide; however I had no actual evidence for this belief at the time. More recent research has shown that breast milk *is* very beneficial for premature babies. These babies may have immature digestive systems so that breast milk, which is easier to digest than formula milk, is particularly good for them. A premature baby can also miss out on much of the immune protection passed through the placenta from mother to baby during the latter stages of a full-term pregnancy. The antibodies present in a mother's milk can be very important in helping a premature baby fight infection. Breast milk is also thought to improve the IQ of premature babies as well as providing many nutrients that are important for growth and development. As it happens I also found breastfeeding very convenient as we could go out for the day walking or visiting friends and didn't have to bother with bottles; the larder was on tap whenever it was needed.

I found breastfeeding a pleasurable experience because it made me feel very close to my son, a particularly valuable experience given the 11 weeks he was in hospital. I was really sorry when John decided, ten months after he came home, that he wasn't interested in breastfeeding any more. By this time I was only feeding him once a day anyway. This feed took place in our bedroom first thing in the morning because I had a better supply of milk after a good night's sleep. I can still remember John continually pulling away to look at the bedroom door rather than concentrating on feeding properly. It was as if he was trying to say to me: 'Why are you wasting my time breastfeeding instead of taking me through that door and giving me some proper food for breakfast?' Perhaps there wasn't much milk left or the quality was poor.

WEANING

I took a lot of time and trouble over the weaning process as I wanted our son to eat with us and enjoy the same food. I was also convinced that I would never win should I find myself engaged in a battle of wills with a small child. I'd noticed that in the UK, where so much convenience baby food is sold, many young children seemed to dislike the change from baby food to 'real' food. I wondered if this contributed to the beginning of some childhood eating fads. This view is supported by the NHS Start4life project:[18] 'Lots of baby food in jars has a similar texture and taste – that means your baby has less variety early on and may be more likely to be a fussy eater when they progress from baby food jars.' I also believed that food made at home out of fresh ingredients without any additives was far healthier than that made in a factory. I felt very unhappy at the thought of feeding either our baby or ourselves out of jars and packets. I decided to cook John's food from scratch employing the same ingredients that we used in our adult meals. Although I knew this would be labour intensive, I *was* at home all day. I felt that in the long run it would save a lot of time and anxiety if I could ensure that our children were enjoying the same nutritionally healthy food as us.

I've often wondered whether children in France and Italy, where eating good food is such an important part of family life, were weaned onto commercial baby food or did they learn to eat 'real' food as soon as weaning began? I found an interesting blog post by Lacey Bediz headed *Picky Eaters? Look to French children's habits for guidance*:[19]

Living and working at [a] bed and breakfast in France has given me the opportunity to observe eating habits of children who come as guests. The palates, the appetite, the manners of French children would make any chef or foodie ecstatic. *And* a nutritionist, such as myself. I adore the French child's healthy attitude around food. They sit down for a long five course meal and eat all that is offered to them – salads, lamb, vegetables, stinky French cheese and desert!

A meal should be a family bonding experience, a time to connect and share the pleasures of flavor together. Feeding your child separately with different foods creates a picky eater, which continues on into adulthood. I have never met a picky French, Italian or Spanish child or adult.

This point of view is echoed in *French Kids Eat Everything* by Karen le Billon. This book describes how the author moved from Canada to France with her husband and two picky children. As she watched and learned how the French taught their children to eat a wide and varied diet, she gradually improved her own children's eating habits and devised a set of rules that would help other parents do the same. I can strongly recommend this book to any parent about to wean their baby or wanting to expand their picky child's diet.

Although I hadn't read this book, *my* plan was to introduce John *extremely gradually*, in a relaxed environment, to as wide a range of foodstuffs as possible. But how was I going to implement this plan? I didn't have a clue how to move successfully from breast milk, baby cereal and baby rice to real food. I asked my mother how she'd done it, since my two sisters and I were brought up on a well-balanced diet which included wholemeal bread, green vegetables and fresh fruit. My mother came up with some excellent advice. She suggested that I begin by offering John fruit, which is sweet, because he was used to breast milk which is also very sweet. When John was used to eating a wide range of fruits I should then start him on vegetables, starting with the sweetest first. After that I should add carbohydrate foodstuffs such as brown bread, rice, pasta and potatoes, then finally protein foods such as fish, chicken, eggs and cheese. Red meat should be tried last of all. No sugar, honey, salt or anything else should be added, so that John could get used to the strong taste of real food without any additives. In any case it isn't a good thing for babies (or adults!) to have too much salt or sugar. Following my mother's good advice I started the move to real food by introducing John to a *very small* quantity – no more than a mere taste – of mashed banana before his baby cereal. I gave him banana for several days, increasing the quantity gradually as John got used to the taste and was happy to have more. I then introduced a *very small* quantity, again a mere taste, of mashed pear before the familiar banana. I gradually increased the quantity of pear and reduced the amount of banana, again allowing John enough time to get used to the taste of the pear until he was having banana alone on one day and pear alone on a different day. I then introduced a third fruit and then a fourth and so on, always in the same careful way. When we moved onto vegetables I began with one of the sweetest (carrots) and then gradually introduced other vegetables such as swedes, parsnips, peas, marrows and so on, always introducing one food at a time in exactly the same way as I introduced the banana and pear. Today I would introduce sweet potato as an early vegetable but in those days I'd never heard of it. I mashed all the food with a fork and didn't purée or liquidise anything in order to help John become accustomed to the texture of real food. This step by step approach worked really well as there were no sudden shocks. John was never expected to eat a whole meal of something he was unfamiliar with, just a small taste followed by something he knew already and liked. By moving very gradually, introducing each new food separately and never forcing John to have more than he wanted, he learned to associate solid food with pleasure. This technique also enabled me to see whether he was allergic to any foods. The only one I found that caused an allergic response was egg white; even the smallest trace was enough to make John's lips swell up.

Although I was unaware of it at the time, my weaning approach meant that John was introduced to many new foods before the neophobic stage set in. Dr Gillian Harris, a consultant clinical psychologist at the Children's Hospital in Birmingham, described this stage as follows:[20]

> Infants learn to like the foods that they are given as a function of exposure. They learn to like the tastes, then cope with the textures, then recognise the way a food looks, in the first year of life.

Foods that are not seen as safe to eat – and are therefore not recognised as known foods – can trigger a disgust response as early as 18 months old. The neophobic stage occurs in all children at around 20 months of age. Food is rejected on sight because there is a perceptual mismatch between known foods and new foods – or between foods with a slightly different presentation.

Children grow out of the neophobic period over the next three years. Few children show the neophobic response at the age of 5 years. As they grow out of this stage, they usually imitate other children's eating behaviour...

Some children, mainly boys, from the age of 18 months show extreme neophobia. This strong neophobic response is maintained throughout childhood. This response to food is nearly always seen in boys with strong... hypersensitivity. It is also frequently seen in children who are on the autistic spectrum... these children are... less likely to imitate others eating, allow exposure to new foods, generalise their food categories.

Judith Wills, nutrition expert and author of the, *'Children's Food Bible'* and *'Everyday Eating for Babies and Children'*, wrote in a similar vein for Netmums:[21]

Get going as soon as possible with offering them a variety of foods after weaning is established (after the age of 6 months). Research shows that if your child has been introduced to a wide range of foods straight from weaning, they are more likely to accept them. Only 4% of new foods are accepted after the age of two. A delay in offering textured, 'lumpy' foods or chunks of food can contribute to later faddy eating.

It's important that a *new* food is offered *frequently* in *very small quantities* (perhaps just a taste) until the child gets used to it. According to Karen le Billon (2012):

Most children have to taste (rather than simply see) new foods to begin liking them. Research shows that it will take them up to a dozen or more tastes before they consent to eat something new. This is normal.

Naturally there may well be some foods that a child never grows to like and this needs to be respected.

One unexpected problem I encountered, as I tried to spoon-feed our son, was his expectation that the food should arrive in the same continuous stream as his milk. He would scream during the time it took for the spoon to leave his mouth, be filled with more food and get back to his mouth again. As I fed John while he sat on my knee, close to my body and supported with my left arm, I only had one free hand to feed him, so he had to endure the gap in the food supply and I had to endure the screams. I became expert at moving the spoon very fast indeed between plate and mouth! If John had been sitting in a high-chair I suppose I could have had a spoon in each hand; however, I'd started to feed him on my knee so that by moving from breast to solid food he didn't lose the cuddle as well as the comfort of sucking. I thought this would make the transition away from the breast easier. Anyhow I can't believe it would have been good for him if I had shovelled the food in any faster. The screaming stopped when John was about 11 months old and I allowed him to feed himself. Initially he fed himself with his hands and his food was in a suction plate that didn't slip around on the table. The meals consisted either of obvious finger food such as small sandwiches, or of food cooked so that it wasn't too hard and chewy but could still be picked up by hand without falling apart.

About a year after John was born, and as the weaning was going well, we had few qualms about taking John abroad on a camping holiday. As we were camping in a tent and cooking on a small camping cooker in rather primitive conditions with no fridge or freezer, I thought it would be a good idea to take some commercial baby food for John, which I could use safely in this rather unhygienic situation. I bought enough baby food to last for two weeks, perfectly happy to make an exception on this occasion to my usual reluctance to use processed foods. However, even though we used his usual suction plate, John took one mouthful of this manufactured food, spat it out and flatly refused to eat *any* of the flavours I'd bought. Was it the different texture, taste, appearance or smell that caused this reaction? Was it because these were new foods he'd never tried before? I've no idea. I never thought of introducing these convenience foods gradually, in the same way as all the other food John ate, while we were still at home. I assumed that John would be happy to eat them because he'd eaten everything else I'd given him and by this time was eating a very wide range of foods. Out of curiosity I tried the food myself. To my palate they were bland and tasted nothing like the strong taste of 'real' food; I could understand why John didn't want to eat them. John thought his dislike of convenience baby food was probably due to the texture or smell:

> I smelt some convenience baby food in my early twenties (at Jim's: not eating it, just in the same room as Jim's youngest was fed) and was violently sick almost at once. It smelt like a corpse, only worse. Nobody else thought it smelt of anything in particular... but maybe it's changed since the 1970s.

John ate an awful lot of bananas that fortnight. They come so conveniently and hygienically wrapped in their own protective covering! We also cooked our own meals without salt so that John could share our food. This incident makes me suspect that John might have grown into a faddy child if we hadn't introduced him to solid food so carefully. When he was an older child he used to refuse to eat fish fingers and chips when he went to someone else's house, just because he wasn't used to this food at home. It was really quite embarrassing when friends went out of their way to make what they thought would be a favourite meal for a child and then find it turned down in what was probably quite a forceful manner! When John read this recently he described fish fingers as follows:

> They are horrid tasteless floppy things with a vile texture. The texture makes them taste like they've already been eaten. Fish in breadcrumbs, now... And yes, I was certainly forceful in turning down fish fingers (I didn't really grok what politeness was *for* until my 20s, and I'm still very bad at it when I get enthusiastic). I remain astonished that anyone else can eat the things.

If you, like me, don't know the meaning of the word 'grok', it means, according to www.thefreedictionary.com/grok, 'to understand profoundly through intuition or empathy'. It was coined by Robert A. Heinlein in his *Stranger in a Strange Land*.

As John got older and a small amount of salt was acceptable he used to eat the same food as us. We tried to introduce him to as wide a range of food as possible, from traditional English food to pasta and savoury rice dishes. John became particularly fond of spicy foods such as curry which I found quite surprising; I remember how much I hated curry when I first tasted it as an adult. It seemed to burn my mouth and throat and it took ages, starting with the mildest of curries, before I grew to love the taste.

However, John did have one dietary problem. Although he had no difficulty eating hard foods such as apples or raw carrots, it was many years before he could chew meat. He loved the actual taste of meat but it had to be of a soft enough consistency (such as a mince dish or a slowly cooked casserole) so that serious chewing wasn't entailed. So for years we didn't roast or grill meat although John *could* manage to eat roast chicken. This was rather a shame as the rest of us thought that roast joints or grilled steaks were one of life's pleasures. I suppose we could have eaten such food and excluded John but it didn't seem right at the time as he really enjoyed us all eating the same food together. According to Lorna Wing (1996):

> Some children with autistic disorders have trouble with controlling the movements of the muscles involved with chewing and swallowing. They are difficult to wean because they do not know how to cope with lumpy food...

Dyspraxic children may also have oral difficulties, as Ripley, Daines and Barrett (1997) explain:

> The movements of eating and drinking follow a clear developmental sequence from the reflex, suckle/swallowing to sophisticated voluntary chewing...

> The children gradually establish voluntary control over the range of eating and drinking patterns required for increasingly complex food, so by the age of two years, they have mastered the basis of mature eating patterns...

> Dyspraxic babies have difficulties establishing a controlled range of oral movements... They may retain a modified suckle/swallow pattern involving squashing and swallowing food, which may suffice to soften up and break up a considerable range of foods, except meat.

Fortunately by the time John was ten or so he *was* able to chew meat properly after which he loved roast dinners, and mixed grills became one of his favourite meals. John remembers the difficulty he had chewing meat:

> I used to try to chew it like it was vegetables, and that really doesn't work: unless very well done it dissolves into a mass of stringy bits and gets impossible to chew or swallow. It was a long time before I realised that the optimal chewing pattern was different for meat (up-and-down).

As well as slow and careful weaning, I believe there are a few other factors that are crucial when trying to minimise the possibility of having very finicky children. If a child doesn't want to eat their meal then it's important that parents don't worry, or this anxiety will transmit itself to the child who may enjoy the extra attention they receive as a result. Removing the food without a fuss, *not* offering alternatives and not giving snacks or sweet drinks between meals should help to ensure that the child is hungry enough for the next meal. When discussing the use of intervention procedures for autistic children with major feeding problems, Patricia Howlin (1998) wrote:

> Parents can understandably become very anxious lest such programmes result in

their child refusing to eat at all. If intervention procedures are introduced very gradually and without undue pressure, problems should not arise. However, children are likely to be very sensitive to their parents' anxiety over such issues and if they realise that non-eating results in increased attention there is a risk that the problem may escalate... Severe feeding difficulties, once well established, can be notoriously difficult to treat in any child, not just those who have autism, and hence, with problems of this kind, prompt intervention is particularly crucial.

I believe that our weaning methods may have protected John from the eating problems experienced by some children, particularly those on the autism spectrum. Not that I had any idea at the time that my son would turn out to be on this spectrum – a spectrum that hadn't been identified in the 1970s. A particularly strong sense of smell and oversensitivity to the different tastes, textures or appearance of food, may cause children on the autism spectrum to refuse, or have a passion for, particular foods. If the surrounding environment is too noisy or too bright these children may also be unable to eat properly. According to Gillian Harris,[22] the group of children she sees in a feeding clinic often prefer 'beige, dry, carbohydrate' foods with a 'safe' texture; food such as 'bread/toast, dry cereal, crisps, biscuits, fish fingers, [and] potato shapes plus milk chocolate bars or buttons, and yoghurt [with] no lumps.' In her presentation she describes some of the intervention techniques that are used on children in her clinic as well as methods that don't work. A few children on the autism spectrum are known to eat well as toddlers, but as they grow older, become more rigid in their eating patterns and start to refuse the food they used to love. This is a difficult problem that probably needs specialist help. These days there are several useful books and publications on the eating and feeding problems of children on the autism spectrum; a few are mentioned in Appendix 28.

TABLE MANNERS

Over the years we learned not to look too closely at John when he was eating, because the sight was far from attractive. Others, particularly my sisters and parents, thought his table manners were atrocious and didn't hesitate to tell us so. John remembers this clearly: 'I tried to eat 'better' when they were around but it never worked and only made a worse mess (probably because muscle tension blew away what coordination I had).'

Although John's fine motor coordination was very poor, we tried to do as little as possible to help him, only cutting up food that he was absolutely incapable of dealing with. We believed that it was necessary for him to get enough practice – without being pressurised – executing important manual tasks such as these. John found cutlery particularly difficult to use; he needed to stick his elbows out in order to have sufficient control of his knife and fork. As our table wasn't very large this was a bit of an issue when we had visitors; John would be sitting very close to others and would knock into them. We tried to arrange matters so that John was sitting next to one of *us* instead but then the visitors would be sitting opposite John and this wasn't a pleasant sight. For many years (certainly well into his teens), John filled his mouth so full that each cheek bulged with food making him look like a hamster. This certainly can't have made it easy to chew. When there was a tougher piece of meat or gristle in this huge mouthful, John would then have to rush away from the table and get rid of the whole lot. His sister remembers differently: 'Often John didn't leave the table and the whole lot was regurgitated onto his plate actually!' Lisa Kurtz (2008) describes 'overstuffing food in the mouth' as one of the signs of possible oral-motor problems. Fortunately, as John grew older, his coordination improved so much that now, as an adult, he looks reasonably normal at the table although he still eats very fast.

I'm extremely glad we didn't make too much of an issue about John's manners when he was young. I doubt he would have improved any faster and all our mealtimes would have been spoilt. Nevertheless things *were* said at times and as Lydia remembers: 'He did get teased about talking with his mouth full and being a hamster.'

DIET AND BEHAVIOUR

Our children's diet was very broad, including as it did a wide range of fruit, vegetables, protein and carbohydrate foodstuffs. We ate brown bread (home-made for many years) and brown rice and I tried to have fish (including oily fish such as mackerel) on the menu at least once a week. One day per week was entirely vegetarian. My mother always used to say that the wider the diet the better, as this ensured that if any foodstuff was potentially harmful, the exposure would not be too great. Certainly the scares that periodically hit the headlines about particular foods have made me realise that my mother's advice was very wise, even if she didn't follow it herself! We didn't have fizzy drinks or fruit squashes in the house and didn't use ready meals. Hopefully this meant that the children were exposed to few additives and preservatives; even in the 1970s it was thought that certain red and yellow food colourings could lead to children 'bouncing off the walls'. It felt instinctively right to exclude artificial additives from the diet as far as possible and stick to natural ingredients. Unfortunately we didn't have the same awareness of 'organic' food in those days and used all sorts of pesticides when growing our own vegetables.

Would our children have exhibited more challenging behaviour if they'd been on a different diet? It's impossible to say. I suspect that a consistent parenting approach, well understood boundaries and a structure to the day were probably more important than the food they ate. The children knew exactly what was and wasn't allowed and, although they tried hard, they had little success playing one parent off against the other. On the whole I was very happy with most of our children's behaviour; many of John's tantrums had far more to do with fear, panic or frustration and could be managed when we understood the underlying causes. John thinks it was especially frustration and 'sometimes a sense of perceived injustice as I grew older, as well'.

Before the age of approximately seven, John would never tell us that he was hungry and would never ask for food if a meal was delayed significantly. Instead he would get into such a miserable state that, by the time the meal actually began, he was completely incapable of feeding himself or behaving like a rational human being. We had to feed him a few mouthfuls and within minutes he would 'recover', turn back into the happy boy we knew and continue to eat normally as if nothing had happened. We always assumed his blood sugar levels had dropped too much and never blamed him for the behaviour, as it appeared to be completely outside his control. To avoid this behaviour I tried to ensure the meals were on time. A couple of years ago John revealed that he still has problems recognising when he is hungry:

To this day I often cannot tell when I'm hungry. I isolate it by monitoring my own emotional stability and attention span and comparing it against a baseline (itself calibrated by long experience with my normal stress levels in many situations). When my emotional stability crashes and my attention span shrinks to only a few seconds between switches, I know I'm hungry.

A few years earlier, when writing about bodily signals such as hunger, he noted:

I often miss hunger or rather, have difficulty distinguishing it from satiation. I have to think it through: my stomach is complaining: why? how long has it been since I ate? I just spent nine hours hacking on something and didn't eat: OK, that's probably hunger then.

Like most children, John wasn't a perfect angel by any means. There were some occasions when his behaviour at the table was quite obnoxious and threatened to spoil everyone's enjoyment of the meal. I hate unpleasant scenes at mealtimes as these remind me only too clearly of many tense meals in my own childhood when I found the atmosphere unbearable. I used to warn John that if he couldn't control his behaviour he would have to leave the table. If this warning didn't work John would be sent to sit at the bottom of the stairs (which were just outside the door of the dining room) and told to stay there until he'd calmed down and was able to come back and behave in a civilised fashion. It was *not* a 'naughty' step and John was not being punished. No time limits were set and the system seemed to work well. When John felt calm enough he would come back to the table and we would carry on as if nothing had happened. He hated hearing us laughing and talking at the table without him and fortunately seemed to be able to calm himself down: 'I thought of it as a 'calm down' step. What really mattered was probably that nothing was moving in my visual field, that noises were reduced, and that nobody was nearby. Peace and quiet.' On some occasions when *my* tolerance level was low and I couldn't bear to stay at the table with John, *I* left after the warning, instead of him. However I took my meal to the peace and quiet of the bedroom rather than sit at the bottom of the stairs! John hated me leaving the table far more than leaving it himself and as he wrote: 'That was when I *knew* I'd done something wrong.' We didn't have to use either of these tactics often as a warning usually worked. John knew we meant what we said and someone would be leaving the table if his behaviour didn't improve. Although we believed that our children should have as much freedom as possible, it was always within well-defined boundaries. They had to learn to consider other people's feelings and realise that *everyone* in the house was entitled to have their needs fulfilled. We couldn't bear to see children cowed into good behaviour but equally, we didn't like to see them ruling the roost.

Not every meal was a social occasion though; many were what we called 'reading' meals. Although this suited all of us, it was particularly useful for John. All John's aunts remember that he always had a book with him at mealtimes which, as one aunt perceptively pointed out, 'he seemed to escape into if conversation got too much'. John certainly agrees with her analysis, writing: 'That's precisely right. It was a conversation-blocker as much as anything else. You can't close your ears, but if you get absorbed enough you can – just – ignore [the conversation].'

FOOD-RELATED ACTIVITIES

As well as introducing infants very gradually to a wide range of foods, I think it's important that children help with some of the food preparation. It's fun to cook with children, can make them feel very grown up and provides an opportunity for lots of conversation. Before our children went to school I used to bake quite regularly with them. It was really enjoyable for all of us and provided an opportunity to do some practical maths with the children without them realising. We used to weigh the ingredients on a set of plastic bucket scales, one bucket containing the ingredients to be weighed and the other the weights. The children could, with assistance, measure out the ingredients and use the sieve and mixer; they could also lick the beaters without any help at all! As they grew older the children would help in all sorts of ways in the kitchen: weighing, peeling, chopping, stirring, mixing, tasting, etc. Although John was very badly coordinated he still enjoyed helping and the manual practice was excellent for him. Cooking is a wonderful activity for children and carers to share and can help children learn to associate food with pleasure.

While the children were small they watched us grow our own vegetables in the garden. Although they couldn't help very much with the cultivation they enjoyed harvesting the vegetables and watching the 'magic' runner beans grow. As adults they really appreciate eating our home grown produce when they visit us and our daughter is now growing her own vegetables.

Before I went back to work I used to make wine, mainly from kits, but also from other ingredients such as jasmine tea. John was fascinated by the whole process and wanted to help as much as he could. One of his jobs was to suck the wine up through a tube in order to start the liquid decanting from one container to another. He was supposed to spit out the small amount of wine he got into his mouth but he developed a taste for red wine; I used to envisage him as an adult enjoying good food, wine and conversation. How wrong I was! Yes, John really appreciates good food and conversation but he doesn't drink alcohol at all. He gave this up at the age of 11 when his biology teacher made him drink some foul alcoholic concoction they had made in class! Nevertheless he still managed to have a bad experience in his early twenties with alcohol:

> I did get drunk just once, in my early twenties (someone pressed drinks on me at a friend's – I can't remember where any more – and I didn't realise they were alcoholic: they were flavoured enough that the alcohol couldn't be tasted or smelt, at least not by me). Result, after perhaps three small glasses: multi-hour-long panic attack. I don't want *that* again… I don't like the smell anyway.

> Small amounts of red wine would probably be a good idea for health reasons, but I've never got into it, and given my tendency to get obsessed with particular foods this is probably for the best.

As young children, John and his sister enjoyed playing a game called *Tummy Ache*. This was quite an achievement as John and board games were not comfortable companions (see Chapter 12). *Tummy Ache* appealed to John because it was funny, not very competitive and allowed the children to make some choices about the food they could have for their 'meal'. We must have played this game hundreds of times over a period of a few years.

ADULTHOOD

John really appreciates good food and is a pleasure to cook for but when he left home at 18 to go to university and had to fend for himself I suspect he ate really badly for three years. He even admitted to me recently that he went through a one-year-long McDonald's fad but whether that meant this was the *only* place he ate in all year I would rather not know! He says: 'No, it wasn't the only thing I ate but it must have been 40% or so of my meals.'

For several years after leaving university he shared a house with three friends, one of whom, Allie, was an excellent cook. Since then he has been living on his own and his diet is really quite reasonable most of the time. As well as cooking for himself he eats out quite regularly, preferring to stick to the same few restaurants where the food is good and where he feels comfortable. In restaurants John tends to make the same meal choices because he likes them so much, although he does attempt occasionally to force himself to try new things. These days he will even share Indian or Chinese dishes with me (rather than each of us eating a different dish), something he would never do a few years ago. During the last few years, he has learned how to use recipe books, although he often wishes he had an extra hand as his fine motor coordination is still poor. Since John started working from home nearly five years ago he is far less tired and has become quite an adventurous cook. He gets a huge amount of pleasure cooking for visitors to his house; recently he has cooked me some delicious meals.

Although John loves food, sometimes when we are out for a meal his digestive system seems to shut down completely and he can't eat any more. This can happen if the place is too noisy, has a very unfamiliar atmosphere in which John feels uncomfortable, if too much garlic is used in the cooking or if the food is too greasy. This tended to happen quite frequently when John was in his teens and twenties and before he lived on his own and became more familiar with eating out in restaurants. He's still extraordinarily sensitive to the atmosphere around him, not just the noise level but also the whole ambience. On one occasion when John was in his late twenties and after a marvellous week spent as a family in Venice, we stopped for lunch at a recommended restaurant on the way to the airport. This establishment was much more formal than the places we usually ate in and when we sat down at a table, a very unusual menu arrived; even with the help of my phrase book I couldn't understand it. John took a huge dislike to the waiter and the formal atmosphere, hated the fact that we didn't know what the food was and started making a great deal of fuss, saying there was no way he was eating there. He was very upset indeed and went out to the car; his sister Lydia followed him and managed to calm him down. John then spent the whole mealtime reading in the car while we ate what turned out to be by far the best meal of the week. As John recalls:

> Oh, gods, the atmosphere in there. It's the only time I can ever remember actually feeling the walls closing in. Cloying and claustrophobic and stuffy and terrifying. Oh, yes, and *way* too formal, and the waiter kept on trying to anticipate my desires when I just wanted him to *go away*... and let me figure out what on earth to eat in my own good time. I *despise* shops where the servitors dance attendance on the sacred customers: they just stress me out... I don't think I could have eaten

a thing in there, even if it had been the best meal of the century.

To conclude: I believe that very careful weaning, cooking together and making mealtimes relaxed and happy occasions for everyone has contributed to the fact that John, unlike many on the autism spectrum, has enjoyed a wide diet both as a child and an adult and is happy to share the experience with friends and family.

4
Sleep

USING A SLING

It was wonderful having John at home after 11 weeks in hospital; however, I was being driven to distraction by the fact that I could never put him down for a sleep during the day without him screaming blue murder. I couldn't bear the sound of his distress as he was obviously very unhappy so I would pick him up and cuddle him and fortunately this *would* stop him crying. I had to hold him for so long though that I couldn't do anything else all day and even the smallest baby can make one's arms ache after a time.

In the mid-1970s, before much was known about the causes of cot death, we were taught to put babies to sleep on their tummies. Was John very uncomfortable lying on a full tummy after a feed? Did he need to be held close, given the months he'd spent in hospital? There was no soft or furry fleece to lie on in the hospital incubator and Kangaroo Care methods, where babies are held skin to skin against their parents, were not employed at the time. I was aware that in many so called 'primitive communities' mothers carried their babies while they worked. I also knew that the babies of other primates cling onto their mothers while they are small. I realised that this was exactly what I needed to do; in desperation I asked my husband to find something that would enable me to carry John around whilst keeping my arms free. This was in the days before baby slings were widely available; we'd never seen one and didn't even know if such a thing existed in England. Fortunately my husband found one and my problem was solved. John loved the sling and never cried after a feed as long as he was in it. I carried him for many weeks on my front, despite the back-ache that was brought on after a time. I have lovely memories of a warm little body next to mine and looking down to see his sweet face looking up at me. It would take well over an hour before John was so deeply asleep that I could put him down in his crib. I had the cleanest house imaginable as John seemed to enjoy being in the sling while I walked around pushing the vacuum cleaner! I became quite expert at doing most household jobs with this large bulge on my front.

In retrospect, it was a blessing that John spent so much time physically close to me. It helped me form a very close bond with him, something which can be difficult to achieve when there's been a long separation after birth. I'm not sure to what extent I would have been tuned into John's needs and how well I might have coped with the difficulties he faced as he grew older, without the close bond generated by carrying him around on my front in a sling.

WAKING AT NIGHT

I'm rather sensitive to noise and found, quite early on as a mother, that I had to resort to earplugs to ensure that I got any sleep at all at night. Before I started to use earplugs I would wake up whenever John made the tiniest sound, even though he wasn't sleeping in our bedroom. As many of the sounds were nothing to do with crying for milk, I was finding it impossible to sleep for more than a few minutes at a time and was also in danger of thinking that John needed a feed when he didn't. The earplugs were wonderful. I had no problems waking up when John needed feeding because the earplugs didn't stop me hearing a determined cry; what they did block out were the little snuffles and small sounds made by a dreaming baby. Like most people I don't operate well if I haven't slept; a good night's sleep was absolutely essential if I was going to have any chance of being a calm and patient parent. According to Williams and Wright in their book *How to live with Autism and Asperger Syndrome*:

> Sleeping problems are common in children and even more common in children with ASD [Autistic Spectrum Disorder]. These are usually difficulties in settling children to sleep and children waking during the night. When children sleep poorly they are more likely to be bad-tempered during the day and to have more difficulty concentrating. Their parents and carers are also affected by lack of sleep and often become irritable and feel more stressed. Not surprisingly then, poor sleep patterns can lead to parents finding it difficult to cope during the day and can cause problems in relationships between each other and with the child. Finding ways to manage sleep problems are not easy but essential to everyone's well-being.

It seems ironic that so many people have alarms and monitors these days to make sure that they can hear every sound their baby makes, while I was trying to block out all but the strongest cries. In fact in order to reduce cot deaths it's recommended that babies sleep in the same room as their parents for six months; I don't know how anyone gets any sleep at all with a baby so close. As John put it: 'I think your tolerance for noise, like mine, might be a good bit lower than the norm!'

After John had been home for about eight weeks we decided to borrow my godmother's house (while she was away) for a holiday. It was a long and tiring day driving, with a small baby, from the south east of England to Anglesey in North Wales and when we arrived we were absolutely shattered. After giving John a bedtime feed and putting him down to sleep in the spare bedroom we fell fast asleep, relieved to be on holiday after a traumatic few months. The next thing we knew it was morning and for a moment we felt wonderful after a marvellous night's sleep. Then we suddenly remembered that we had a baby and realised that (for the first time since he'd come home) we hadn't heard him all night and I hadn't got up to feed him. My husband Tony and I looked at each other in horror and immediately thought John must be dead and it was our fault as negligent parents. We walked down the corridor to his bedroom with real fear and trepidation; when we looked in his room we were absolutely astonished to find him lying there awake and perfectly happy. Why hadn't he woken us up that night? Was it because his bedroom was quite a long way from ours (at the other end of a long passage) and we'd been so tired that we hadn't heard him, or was it pure coincidence? Whatever the reason, we never heard him cry at night for the rest of that week; even when we got home, where our bedrooms were very close, I never had to feed John again at night.

Up to this point, when John woke at night for a feed, I would always be the one to go to him because he was being breastfed. Now that we realised John was taking in enough milk during his late feed to last right through the night, we changed our tactics. My husband and I agreed that if John woke up in the night in future it would be Tony's turn to go on baby duty. We felt that if *I* went in to comfort John it would be very easy for bad habits to set in because, as far as our baby was concerned, I was a walking larder. I believed that if John had seen and/or smelt me come into his bedroom at night there was no way that he would have settled without a feed. We thought this could easily lead to years of disturbed nights with John being rewarded for waking at night by seeing his mum and being fed. What we couldn't and wouldn't do though, was leave John to cry for any length of time and get himself more and more distressed. So on the few occasions when John *did* have a disturbed night, for example when teething, my husband would go into his room, walk around quietly with John on his shoulder, give him some water and then settle him down. It worked a treat.

JOHN'S BEDROOM

One of my fears, prior to becoming a mother, was finding myself with over-tired, fractious children who were out of control, refused to go to bed or sleep and made our lives a nightmare. For this reason we've always tried to make the children's cots, beds and bedrooms a haven of peace and relaxation and a place they would always be happy to go to. We never, ever, used their bedrooms as a place of punishment or banishment. However John thinks:

> I'm not sure you *can* make a bedroom a place of punishment to someone with Asperger's without packing it with people. It's a place where you can be alone and completely control everything that hits your eyes and ears: how could it not be paradise?

We always had a night-light in John's bedroom when he was very young, as we felt it was less scary should he wake up during the night. However, once John started reading at bedtime, we stopped using the night-light by his bed as he wanted a good bedside light to read by. By this time John also seemed to need absolute darkness for sleeping; as an adult in his own home, he uses black-out blinds. In addition he has a white noise generator in his bedroom to cut down any noise from neighbours and the road. When John lived in rented accommodation, between the years of 18 and 27, he always complained that he slept badly because the curtains let in too much light:

> I can barely remember wanting light at night: I think it was a slight degree of being scared of the dark (or what was out there in it). But one night I tried turning the light off and liked it so much that I never looked back. Living in London with glaring skylight pouring through the window was a real step backwards. The curtains often didn't even reach the edges of the windows!

As our children are less than two years apart in age, we hoped they would play together, would never feel lonely and would learn to share. In order to encourage our children to develop a good relationship, as soon as our daughter Lydia was born we let them sleep in the same room. Although we knew she might disturb John when she woke for a feed at night, we thought it was a risk worth taking; in fact it never turned out to be a major problem. However, when Lydia was small she used to have her daytime naps in a different room from John or she would have been in danger of being hit by flying toys! The strategy worked well and the children spent a lot of time talking and playing together before Tony and I got up in the morning. They shared a bedroom until John started school at the age of five, when we moved them into separate rooms so that he got as much undisturbed sleep as possible. The children spent many years playing *near* each other until their interests diverged radically when they were adolescents. They are still very close emotionally although their interests are very different.

SLEEPING PATTERN

Once John was old enough for demand feeding to stop naturally, we quickly adopted a routine which suited us all. For the first year and a half of his life we let John sleep in late and go to bed late; this is still his preferred sleeping pattern: 'When that pattern breaks down it almost invariably means I'm ill: my sleep cycle goes chaotic then (as well as, obviously, gaining a lot more hours of sleep).' Although this isn't the usual way babies are brought up in the UK, it meant I didn't have to get up early, which I really appreciated. John had a long rest every day after lunch and was very lively and happy in the evening so that he had plenty of time to get to know his daddy. Once we had two children we moved John's bedtime to the early evening.

We always had a long singing and story session both before the daytime rest and every evening before the children went to sleep. It was a calm, pleasurable, leisurely and consistent winding down time before we left them on their own. Even if we were going out in the evening we made sure the bedtime routine was never cut short or hurried and we never left it to babysitters. If necessary we moved everything forward throughout the day; as the children couldn't tell the time, they never realised they were going to bed earlier than usual. We always left toys in John's cot/bed for him to play with before he went to sleep. Although both children were always happy to go to bed and never cried, John never went to sleep quickly, playing with his toys for quite a long time before he dropped off. Sometimes we were aware that John woke up at night, although he didn't cry, unless he was teething or unwell. He played happily and quietly with his toys, unless we were foolish enough to leave a noisy toy in his cot. One night, for example, we woke up with a violent start to hear him blowing his plastic flute loudly. According to John:

> [Waking up in the middle of the night] is quite possibly the standard human sleeping pattern, disrupted in the last couple of centuries by artificial light but common knowledge before then. I know that now my sleep cycle is undisturbed by alarms, I have a segmented sleep pretty much every night.

According to http://en.wikipedia.org/wiki/Segmented_sleep:

> Segmented sleep, also known as divided sleep, bimodal sleep pattern, or interrupted sleep, is a polyphasic or biphasic sleep pattern where two or more periods of sleep are punctuated by a period of wakefulness. Along with a nap (siesta) in the day, it has been argued that this is the natural pattern of human sleep... A case has been made that maintaining such a sleep pattern may be important in regulating stress...

As John grew a bit older he stopped waking up in the night and then slept so deeply that it was years before he was clean and dry at night (see Chapter 7).

As an adult, John commuted into London by train for years and he used these journeys to catch up on his sleep. With train fares as high as they are this is quite an expensive bedroom! After John got home, somewhere between 7.30 and 8.30pm, he worked on the computer all evening, often into the early hours of the morning and then went straight to bed. I found out a long time ago that I can never do brain work late in the evening if I want a decent night's sleep. Either I would be unable to switch my mind off enough to go to sleep or I would dream about the work and then wake up in the early hours still thinking/worrying about it. John doesn't mind dreaming about his work though: 'This happens all the time. It's really useful. The dreams are not purposeless.' John wasn't prepared to give up working and thinking in the evenings. This was the only time he had, apart from the weekends, to tackle the many computer projects he was involved in outside work and to keep up with all his interests. He loved his evening work and if that meant it took a long time to unwind and go to sleep that was a price he was willing to pay. Unfortunately his company then moved from the City of London to Canary Wharf, which meant his journey to work took even longer. He became so tired, going to sleep in the early hours and getting up just a few hours later to go back to work, that he was unable to do much at all in his spare time. The weekends were used to try and catch up on sleep. This finally motivated him sufficiently to find a job that enabled him to work entirely from home and be paid to do the sort of computing he'd been doing as a hobby in his spare time. He works now as part of an international team with the majority of his co-workers living in the United States. This means John can work whatever hours suit him; at last a perfect solution to his sleeping difficulties. The stranger the hours he works the more likely he is to be working at the same time as other members of his team. As John says: 'There *are* strange hours no any more.' He's settled easily into his natural sleeping pattern which means he falls asleep in the early hours of the morning (frequently between 2 and 3am) and then sleeps until late morning, frequently not starting work much before midday. He may well take a long walk at some point during the day and continue working in the evening, which has always been a very productive time for him.

Even when John has tried to go to bed earlier in order to shift his sleeping schedule he has been singularly unsuccessful. It's possible that he suffers from a mild-to-moderate form of what is known as delayed sleep phase syndrome (DSPS) or delayed sleep phase disorder (DSPD). According to Wikipedia:

> People with DSPS generally fall asleep some hours after midnight and have difficulty waking up in the morning... People with DSPS have at least a normal – and often much greater than normal – ability to sleep during the morning, and sometimes the afternoon as well... DSPS patients can sleep well and regularly when they follow their own sleep schedule... Often sufferers manage only a few hours sleep a night during the working week then compensate by sleeping until the afternoon on weekends... People with DSPS can be called extreme night owls. They feel most alert and say they function best and are most creative in the evening and at night. DSPS patients cannot simply force themselves to sleep early... the syndrome is most common in adolescence.

ANXIETY AND SLEEP PROBLEMS

John has never been able to go to sleep easily; once he stopped playing with toys at night he would read for ages in bed. Secondary school was a particularly difficult time in John's life and he had real trouble going to sleep then, because he was so worried about school the next day. Sleep disturbances can be one of the indicators that a child is being bullied but unfortunately John never told us about these worries and I don't think we ever fully appreciated just how unhappy he was. As John wrote to me a few years ago: 'I was unhappy all the time and this didn't stop me sleeping. What stopped me sleeping was stress from constantly going over the worst possibilities for what might happen the next day.'

Martin Kutscher (2005) has written about the relationship between anxiety and sleep problems as follows:

A striking feature of childhood anxiety is that often no one else knows about the problem. In fact, even the mothers of anxious children do not recognise the problem about half the time... Sleep disturbances are an important physiologic window into anxiety disorders. Insomnia (defined as difficulty falling asleep within 20 minutes after your head is on the pillow) is a very frequent symptom.

While John was at secondary school we let him sleep in for as long as he liked at the weekend, in order to catch up on the sleep he went so short of during the school week. Many experts think this is a bad idea as they believe it perpetuates poor sleeping habits. To this day, even when he has nothing to worry about, John has trouble switching off his mind sufficiently in order to go to sleep and can read for a long time in bed: 'Actually this has gradually reduced over the years and is probably no more than fifteen minutes to half an hour these days. I *do* read for an hour or so in between the first and second sleep.' It's characteristic of many people diagnosed with ADHD (Attention Deficit Hyperactivity Disorder) that they can find it difficult to find the 'off switch' when it's bedtime.

In conclusion: John has always found it difficult to go to sleep but carrying him around in a sling when he was a small baby helped. When he was older, playing with toys in his cot/bed and then a few years later reading in bed helped him to fall asleep eventually. Fortunately a calm and consistent bedtime routine ensured John was never reluctant to go to bed as a child. Although he sleeps very deeply once he nods off, John was/is prone to a wakeful spell in the middle of the night.

5
Health

Some of the health issues described in this chapter may be due to autism spectrum disorder, some to prematurity and some may be hereditary. Because everyone is unique, the same combination of issues might not be found very often in other children; nevertheless, some of our experiences may be of interest to readers.

HEIGHT AND WEIGHT

Fortunately everything went comparatively smoothly after John came home from hospital as a baby and his weight, height and head circumference increased steadily (see Appendix 3). After John's very premature birth and all the ensuing problems, he was monitored by hospital paediatricians as well as the local health clinic and health visitor. Although I went regularly to the local health clinic I remember how much I disliked the visits, because they always commented on John's small size. It felt like a personal criticism and I can understand how some people might have been tempted to skip these appointments. I was just relieved that John was gaining weight steadily. Considering how small he'd been to start with, I thought he was doing well. This view was strongly supported by the paediatricians who saw him in the hospital. Did the people in the health clinic realise that there was absolutely no point in making such comments, which can cause worry and distress, if there was nothing anyone could do? Some babies will be larger than average (especially if they're heavy when they are born) and others will be smaller than average. Unless they're suffering from malnutrition or have the kind of medical problem that requires medication (such as a growth factor), children will attain an appropriate height and weight in their own good time. We refused to worry about John's size and four and a half years after his birth, his height, weight and head circumference were all recorded as being in the middle of the normal range and in good proportion. Things are different these days in the UK; a baby's weight is compared with standardised growth charts which show if the weight gain is acceptable.[23] When my daughter took her baby to her local health clinic to be weighed she was given a copy of this chart which showed clearly that her child was thriving and gaining weight steadily.

COLDS AND COUGHS

We were much more concerned that John seemed to have a perpetual cold during his first winter and spring at home. As well as being unpleasant for him, the infections affected John's hearing. On various occasions during this time the paediatrician's notes record:

> Upper respiratory tract infection, red ears and obvious tonsillitis for which he was prescribed Penicillin V... (February)

> An upper respiratory tract infection with residual otitis media [inflammation of the middle ear]... (March)

Another upper respiratory tract infection, and I have had his post nasal space x-rayed. (May)

When John was particularly ill we were very worried about cot death or sudden infant death syndrome (SIDS) and John's ability to keep breathing properly when he was asleep. Although we didn't know it at the time, risk factors for SIDS include prematurity, small birth weight and being a boy.[24] We were always relieved when the worst of the symptoms abated. It was only in the summer of the year after he came home, when he spent a lot of time out in the garden in the sunshine, that he was able to shake off this upper respiratory tract infection and was really well for the first time. 'These days', John says, 'going out in the garden *makes* me sneeze'.

Did he pick these colds up in the college nursery that he attended once a week, from September to March, in the first year of his life? According to John, who has a very jaundiced opinion of schools at the best of times, 'almost certainly. Nurseries and schools are a hotbed of infection so severe that the single most effective thing authorities can do to stop epidemics is to close them all down!' Was John's immune system as such a premature baby so compromised that he was unable to fight off these infections?

After this first year of perpetual colds John stayed cold free for many months and then only succumbed to the occasional cold and cough. When he was eight years old though, he suffered several bouts of bronchitis over a period of 18 months but this also seemed to disappear as he grew older. This was obviously an unpleasant experience as John recalls it to this day: 'If this is the thing where your airways hurt like hell and you cough all the time, I remember it'.

As an adult he became very prone to colds again; these seemed to come on very quickly and were very intense. As these colds stopped him thinking clearly (which he finds essential for his work) he took quite a lot of sick leave when he did little but sleep. Then as quickly as the colds came they cleared up. I often wondered whether John's resistance to the many germs he came into contact with by travelling on public transport was lowered because he didn't get enough sleep. Most week nights his lights weren't switched off much before two o'clock and all his alarms were set for 6.45am. However recently there's been a dramatic improvement. John has been working from home for nearly five years and has experienced very few colds indeed during this time; he can wake up naturally when he's had enough sleep *and* he doesn't have to travel to work.

HEARING

As described in the previous section, John's hearing suffered as a baby due to constant upper respiratory tract infections. Once the colds had cleared up though, John's hearing was found to be satisfactory (see Appendix 4). In fact he seemed to have extremely acute hearing; one had to be very careful indeed not to say anything you didn't want him to hear if he was anywhere in the vicinity. However John didn't seem to hear or be aware of what was happening when he was within a group situation (see Chapter 13). It's as if acute hearing is his natural state but in a group his hearing gets overwhelmed by the general noise. As John explains: 'There's so much background noise that I can't pick up foreground noise at all.'

ALLERGIES

As described in Chapter 3, John was allergic to egg white when he was weaned but this had worn off by the age of two. According to the Mayo Clinic:[25]

> Egg allergy is most common in children. As you grow older, the digestive system matures and allergic food reactions are less likely to occur...

> The same immune system reaction that causes egg allergy can also cause other conditions. If you or your child has an egg allergy, you or your child may be at increased risk of... hay fever.

John started getting bad hay fever when he was 17 and he still gets it every year. In the summer he often can't tell whether he's suffering from hay fever or a cold. Although medication helps somewhat, he's found a very powerful pollen filtration unit to be the best preventative solution:

> More importantly I got an IQAir pollen filter, and since then my hay fever has vanished at home, and has greatly reduced elsewhere for a period of about two days after leaving home's filtered air... My only regret is that it isn't portable.

John's hay fever is at its worst when it starts up each year and before he has turned his filtration unit on or started taking his medication. Before he bought his pollen filter he had some very unpleasant experiences on the train into work which he described to me as follows:

> As near as I can tell I'm allergic to grasses and every ornamental plant you had in your front garden when I was a teenager. It's made me miserable for months every year, but when I started taking high-speed main line trains to work it got much worse: the train acts like a sort of pollen ram, sucking pollen into the carriages and moving it around so I get to inhale all of it. Over the last seven years I've had I think six episodes of severe allergic shock attacks on the train: in two it was just swelling up and some shortness of breath. In the other four I yanked the emergency handle as my ability to breathe went away and the world fell into sparkling darkness, only to come back on the train platform with paramedics leaning over me, having just shot me full of adrenalin. It was all terribly sudden: from normal exploding hay fever symptoms to oops-I-can't-breathe took about twenty seconds. I got an epi-pen because of incidents like this, then promptly lost it.

In the spring of 2012 John sent me the following email: 'It seems I'm allergic to tree pollen now (the utter exhaustion I've been feeling over the last week vanished a few hours after I turned the pollen filter on).' He's promised to obtain another EpiPen, which is self-injectable adrenaline (epinephrine, the emergency treatment for anaphylaxis) but still hasn't done so. He's also said he will switch his filtration unit on when medium to high pollen counts have been reported even if these particular allergens don't affect him. John's father, Tony, also acquired hay fever in his teens but as he grew older the symptoms eased and since he reached 60 he is rarely troubled with it.

During the last few years John has become increasingly sensitive to something in the local anaesthetic given to him by his dentist:

I had an increasingly strong allergic reaction to *something* in the local anaesthetic I was given by my dentist over the last few years. Every time I was given it, a period of exhaustion started about an hour and a half later, and every time it took longer to wear off. Most recently it took over a week, but more worryingly I had increasing difficulty breathing at about the same time as the exhaustion kicked in. The difficulty mounted much more slowly than a hayfever-related attack, slowly enough that I could walk to the doctor's, where they injected me with something to fix it. (Our best guess is that the exhaustion is an adrenaline reaction... and the increasing breathing problems are a response to some breakdown product of the anaesthetic itself.) So I'm not going to be given that local anaesthetic again. As allergies go this is probably one of the less serious ones I could be hit with. Expected future effect on life: nil.

IMMUNISATIONS AND VACCINATIONS

Like many parents we were very unsure what to do about vaccinations. In our case this was partly due to the fact that our son was so small when he was born and had been so ill and partly because, at the time his early vaccinations were due, he always had a cold. We were worried that these vaccinations would cause John harm but at the same time we were also aware that his low immunity meant that he needed the extra protection provided by these immunisations. We also believed that it was important for as many people as possible to be vaccinated in order to minimise the possibility of infection in the population as a whole. In the end we discussed the issue with the health clinic and compromised. As we were particularly worried about the whooping cough (pertussis) vaccine which at the time was considered to be the most likely to have side effects, we only had the diphtheria and tetanus jabs and not the triple vaccine. In those days there was no problem asking for this. Was this a sensible decision? Almost certainly not, because a whooping cough epidemic at the time would have left John very vulnerable, particularly because he was attending a college nursery. What we didn't know then and is really frightening to read now, is that whooping cough is so infectious that any baby that isn't immunised and comes into contact with the disease is likely to catch it. These days pregnant women are advised to have a whooping cough vaccination to protect their babies before they are old enough to receive the vaccination themselves. Even worse is the fact that there *was* a whooping cough epidemic while John was a baby although we didn't know it at the time. According to the Oxford Vaccine Group:[26]

> In 1975 unfounded concerns about the safety of the vaccine resulted in a fall in vaccination rates; only 3 out of every 10 children were vaccinated against pertussis in 1975. This resulted in major epidemics in 1977-79 and 1981-83.

It should be pointed out that (according to the Oxford Vaccine Group) the current vaccine against whooping cough (available since 2004) is far less likely to cause unwanted reactions than the vaccine available in the 1970s.

The polio vaccine was also delayed, because it was believed to be ineffective while a baby was still breast feeding. Once breast feeding had reduced significantly the polio vaccines were administered as well as the second diphtheria and tetanus jabs. John didn't appear to suffer any side effects from the vaccines and so, when he was bigger and stronger and when his younger sister went for her vaccinations, he was also given the whooping cough vaccine.

The measles vaccine was postponed for yet another reason. We were told that the vaccine was grown on egg white; because John was allergic to egg white at the time this injection was due, it was decided to delay it. He was given it a year later when this allergy had disappeared. A list of vaccines and the dates they were administered can be found in Appendix 5.

EYESIGHT

There is a history of poor eyesight on both sides of our family. My sisters wore glasses as children and my husband remembers being too scared to get on the bus, at the age of six, because he couldn't read the number. Tony was very short-sighted (his left eye being worse than the right) and he also had a squint with his left eye looking outwards.

John's medical records show that at six months (from his date of birth) he was 'visually very alert' and when he was four years old his vision was thought to be normal (when tested with Stycar equipment); he didn't have a squint. All photos of John show him without glasses until the age of eight but from eight onwards he was wearing glasses all the time. John became increasingly short-sighted (myopic) as he grew older until his myopia stabilised somewhere between -9.0 and -9.5 dioptres[27] when he was in his early twenties. As a result he's worn glasses with very thick lenses for many years. By the time John reached his mid-thirties his eyesight was sufficiently poor to make him eligible for free eye tests.

When John was eight years old his GP wrote to the consultant ophthalmic surgeon at our local hospital as follows:

> Apart from being very short-sighted, John's mother has become increasingly aware of a variable divergent squint. The right appears to be the stronger eye, in that the left eye is more often the divergent one, but when he concentrates he can focus readily with the left as well.

We were given no advice whatsoever about the squint and it causes John problems to this day, his left eye regularly drifting outwards (exotropia). My husband says he never knows which eye to look at when talking to John! Tony believes that the laziness in John's left eye became apparent at 'about the same time he stopped looking directly at those he was talking to'. Whether John's divergent squint is inherited from his father or a consequence of his prematurity is hard to say. According to Monte Mills, writing in 1999:

> Exotropia [eyes *diverging*] is much less common than esotropia [eyes *converging*] during infancy. Infantile exotropia is rarely an isolated finding, but is frequently seen in association with cerebral palsy, prematurity and other neurodevelopmental conditions…

> In most cases, when exotropia is detected after six months of age, patients have intermittent exotropia… associated with myopia [short-sightedness]

When John's eyes are pointing in different directions he loses binocular vision. He sees two separate images that don't superimpose accurately, giving rise to double vision in the centre of his visual field. Nevertheless when he's reading he seems able to ignore the weaker image from his left eye and perceives a clear image from his right eye. However he's unable to ignore things such as flashing advertisements in his left field of vision on the computer screen; then he's forced to read with his left eye closed. In his previous job, John sat on the 41st floor of a tower block, facing a large window. Because his computer screen (which his right eye was focused on) was small and the light coming through the window (in his left visual field) was bright, the difference between the images was so great that John was often forced to work with his left eye closed. Now that he's working from home, John has two good sized computer screens side by side, both with a black background so that he can work with both eyes open. With concentration, John *can* make his eyes point in the same direction although when he's tired he loses this ability. Then he's unable to prevent his eyes looking in different directions and his drifting eyes lead to drifting double vision. He says he knows this means it's time to go to bed. The problem seemed to be getting worse when he was commuting for about four hours a day and he put this down to the fact that he was very tired most of the time. His eyes are back to their usual state, now that he's no longer commuting. John has adapted well to his lack of eye alignment but it gives him occasional problems with depth perception. For example:

> [The time when] I tried to pour some water out of my filter-jug into a glass, and forgot to move my head around a bit to check the line-up... and the stream missed the glass entirely, as the jug was behind the glass by about 1cm.

John's talked about getting an operation for his short-sightedness and seeking advice about the double vision but he's scared that something might go wrong. He says it's not blindness per se that worries him as 'again *that* is rare (they don't work on both eyes at the same time). What's more common is permanent (major) imperfections in your field of vision. I don't really want that.'

In connection with exotropia, Mills writes that 'correction of refractive error may also help control the deviation'. Although John is unlikely to undergo surgery, he might be prepared to visit a specialist to see if he can be supplied with the appropriate lenses. His usual opticians are unable to provide such a service.

TEETH

Robert and Ann Cobb Lacamera, writing in the *Handbook of Autism and Pervasive Developmental Disorders* (edited by Cohen and Volkmar) note:

> Good dental care is difficult to maintain unless the autistic patient is cooperative... with the introduction of fluoridated drinking water, fluoride oral preparations for home use, and fluoridated toothpaste, the incidence of tooth decay has been decreased. For autistic children and adults, this is important in minimizing corrective procedures, which are psychologically threatening to some patients. Even simple procedures like tooth cleaning and gum treatments by a competent dental hygienist can be difficult.

How true! John really disliked having his teeth cleaned or even examined. While he was young either Tony or I brushed his teeth twice a day but as he grew older we expected him to do this job himself. Once John reached his teens we really couldn't stand over him and watch him do his teeth every day. As a result I suspect the teeth cleaning was very cursory, if it happened at all. He was regularly reminded and would always say they'd been cleaned but had they? Tooth cleaning remained a problem for years, particularly after John left home and I was no longer around to prompt! He would justify his reluctance to clean his teeth by saying that he would be cleaning away protective bacteria and these would do his teeth no harm.

Amazingly the problem was largely resolved a few years ago when I started using an electric toothbrush for the first time and realised how gentle they were. I managed to persuade John to try mine and after he realised how easy it was to use he acquired an electric toothbrush of his own. Since then he has been cleaning his teeth reasonably regularly. Nevertheless he still believes this was a bad move:

> I'm still convinced I did myself considerable harm by starting regular toothbrushing. Since then I've had almost constant dental complaints of one sort or another; sensitive tooth pain, aches under the gum line, there's always something: before then, not a problem. Unfortunately now *S. mutans* is in my mouth I can't get rid of it again.

I can't find any scientific evidence for John's views on tooth cleaning and he's been unable to provide any. As he admits: 'I never said there was a rational foundation for all my beliefs!'

I never realised at the time that the combination of poor motor control (which meant John couldn't manipulate the toothbrush without constantly hitting his gums) and a mouth very sensitive to pain was responsible for John's reluctance to brush his teeth. Hindsight is a wonderful thing; knowing what I do now, I should have given John an electric toothbrush when he was much younger. Looking back, I find it quite disturbing to realise that I hadn't tried to understand the fundamental reasons underlying John's unwillingness to brush his teeth; as a result I hadn't been able to find a simple solution to the problem. I suppose all I can say in mitigation is that these problems seemed relatively minor compared with some of the other issues we faced at the time. On the other hand, if we'd realised just how big a problem oral hygiene would become when John left home, we may have taken this issue more seriously. Lorna Wing, writing in *The Autistic Spectrum*, has some excellent advice:

> Careful and regular tooth brushing is essential. If the child will accept it, an electric toothbrush, if used properly, cleans effectively and also helps the child to become used to the feeling of vibrations in the mouth, which is similar to that of some dental instruments. Regular visits to the dentist are necessary and should begin well before any treatment is needed.

I took some comfort from the fact that, while John was at primary school, he was seen by the school dentist. As I never heard anything from the school dental service I took that to mean that they'd been able to examine John's teeth satisfactorily and found no problems. There was no dental service when John started secondary school so I arranged for him to be seen by *my* dentist. John remembers me going with him for the examination which he found very unpleasant; he recalls making a terrible scene and making me promise not to take him again. According to him:

> [It was] an unpleasantly painful examination (bashing my teeth with something

metal or something like that, ow) and a dentist solemnly saying that I had severe gum disease and would start to lose teeth in the next few years. I lost my first adult tooth, a wisdom tooth, aged 31. I think that dentist could probably be called wrong!

Sally Rogers and colleagues (2012) have some excellent step by step suggestions 'for priming your child for a first trip to the dentist, using pretend play'. I wish I'd thought of doing this as I'm sure it would have made a huge difference. Patricia Howlin (1998) notes that some children are so terrified of visiting the dentist 'that they may suffer severe tooth decay'. She goes on to suggest how 'prior planning and gradual and careful exposure from infancy' may alleviate these fears:

> Firstly families need to elicit the help of a sympathetic dentist... to whom the child can be taken at regular intervals, preferably long before any treatment is required... rides up and down on the chair, being allowed to manipulate the lights, spitting into the basin can all be a source of fun. Later, brief oral examinations should cause few problems, so that by the time any treatment is needed the child is well used to the whole procedure.

I couldn't agree more with this excellent advice. As far as I'm concerned the way dentists treat their NHS patients has improved enormously in the last twenty years. These days they're both gentle in their manner and in the way they treat your mouth. I hope it would be relatively easy to find the sort of sympathetic dentist that Patricia Howlin recommends and to introduce a child to dental visits in the way she describes.

After John's flat refusal to see a dentist again, I was really pleased and relieved when, a few years ago, he took himself off to his local dentist after he had wisdom tooth problems. Some of his wisdom teeth were then removed under a general anaesthetic in hospital. He's been visiting a dentist regularly since then and says he has no fear of them now. John's teeth are actually in a reasonably good condition which he puts down to the lack of cleaning but I think has more to do with fluoride in the toothpaste on the occasions when his teeth were cleaned. How his teeth survived years of drinking diet coke once he left home, I can't imagine. As he wrote: 'I'm amazed my teeth didn't simply dissolve!' Fortunately he has stopped drinking this particular drink. However, his dentist told John relatively recently that he's lost a considerable amount of enamel from his teeth. She thinks this may be due to John grinding his teeth in his sleep as she can see wear marks on them. Although the dentist put a protective cover over the top of his molars, tooth grinding meant that this cover disappeared after a relatively short time. John is currently wearing a special mouth guard at night to protect his teeth from the effects of grinding.

DIGESTIVE PROBLEMS

Even mentioning the topic of autism spectrum disorders and gastrointestinal problems feels akin to entering a mine field. According to Clements and Zarkowska (2000):

> There is controversy and uncertainty as to whether there are some health issues that are especially linked to autism (for example, difficulties in breaking down certain food stuffs such as gluten or casein, gut infections or leakages, difficulties in immune system functioning).

Quite a few children on the autism spectrum appear to have problems with constipation, while many children on this spectrum are known to eat a severely restricted diet. Whether these two facts are connected I'm not in a position to say but it's certainly suggestive. Some parents of autistic children either supplement or restrict their children's food intake and they're absolutely confident that this has improved their children's autistic symptoms. This isn't an approach we've ever tried.

Although I can't prove it, I believe that our children's wide diet (which included a considerable amount of fibre in the form of fruit, vegetables, brown bread and brown rice) was a major factor contributing to the fact that John *didn't* suffer from constipation as a child. However since he's been cooking for himself, he's had a few, severe and prolonged problems with a blocked up digestive system. A few years ago John suffered from an episode of serious constipation which he described as follows:

I had… persistent constipation lasting, on-and-off, for about ten months. I'd blitz it with prescription-only laxatives and the problem would go away only to come back again two weeks later. There was persistent pain from my lower-right abdomen while this went on, particularly when walking. Eventually it cleared up on its own. I suspect something got stuck in my caecum or something like that (they never did a full colonoscopy on me because you can't do that to someone who is constipated!)

Although John didn't suffer from constipation or diarrhoea as a child, he was extremely prone to sudden, severe stomach upsets which always led to vomiting. Although he'd be very sick indeed, it didn't seem to upset him too much. According to John:

It's annoying and unpleasant and the muscle tremors and general weakness afterwards are really quite nasty, but what's the point in being distressed? Once you've been sick, that's it, you're probably better now, and generally I was sick shortly after starting to feel sick, so there wasn't a long horrible period of anticipation. If anything I was glad when I was sick because the worst was over.

It seemed to be more unpleasant for his parents who had to clear up the mess. When possible John would get to the lavatory in time and this was the norm as he got older. Quite unconcerned whenever his stomach was upset, John would stay in bed, eat nothing for over a day and then be back to normal as if nothing had happened. He became an expert at knowing when he could start eating again and how much to eat. To this day I believe these upsets were due to inadequate hand washing after going to the toilet but as a child and adolescent he always strenuously denied this. I believe he now accepts (as an adult) that poor hygiene *can* lead to stomach upsets; as a result he washes his hands carefully both after using the toilet and before cooking. Whether he would now accept that this was the most likely cause of his upset stomachs when he was younger is quite another matter and not one that's worth pursuing! Not so long ago, he admitted:

I used to deny it because it was still happening. However it doesn't happen so often any more. I now suspect it's caused by *either* inadequate hand washing *or* greasy food *or* badly cooked food *or* food I'm not used to.

Surely he doesn't mean my food is greasy or badly cooked given that this happened for many years while he was still living at home! Recently John wrote to me:

Where I used to get violently sick, I now get a churning stomach for no obvious reason which goes away on its own (without being sick), after which I'm simply not hungry for a day. So, just like being sick except without the actual vomiting part. It's nowhere near as common as it used to be (a few times a year, at most). I profess confusion, and given the insane complexity of anything associated with digestion I doubt we will ever have a definitive answer.

OTHER MEDICAL

Many children on the autism spectrum find visits to doctors, dentists and other health professionals very difficult, particularly if the visits have nothing to do with autism. For many years John was no exception. These sessions could be made much easier if all health professionals were aware of the type of accommodations they could introduce to make the visits less traumatic for all concerned. Very useful advice can be obtained from a free leaflet called *Patients with autism spectrum disorders: guidance for health professionals* published by the National Autistic Society (NAS).[28] This is also a useful leaflet for parents to download and read as it might give them ideas to reduce their child's anxiety when visiting a health professional; if necessary, parents could provide a copy for the professionals concerned.

Lack of personal hygiene was possibly implicated in several nasty bouts of impetigo around the mouth which John contracted while he was away at university. According to John, who still doesn't wash his face, this was definitely not the reason:

No, this was during my McDonald's fad year and several other people who ate there regularly got it. Probably someone working there had it (but why the hell was he allowed to work in food preparation with something as infectious as that?)

The impetigo got so bad that eventually John went to the university doctor, even though this was something he was very loath to do on his own. A few months later, he had to go back again; he received medication three times in that month before the impetigo eventually cleared up.

After discovering that he'd never registered with a doctor for the five years he'd shared a house with friends (between leaving university and buying his own house), we realised that John would never get round to it on his own. For this reason, when John bought his first house, we took him along to the local medical practice to register with a doctor. Although I think it's good that John doesn't run to the doctor every time he feels unwell, I used to be concerned that his reluctance to seek medical advice might stop him going soon enough if there was something seriously wrong. I feel less worried now as events have shown that John's instinct for self-preservation appears to be strong enough to ensure he gets medical help should he really need it.

MENTAL HEALTH AND WELL-BEING

Anxiety and depression

John's level of anxiety was brought home to me when, as an adult in his twenties, he compared much of his life to walking along a narrow path with a steep precipice on either side which he could easily fall down if he wasn't careful. Spending time with people he didn't know well, making social gaffes, failing in some task or other, worrying about major anticipated events and fear of any change or of the unexpected, all contributed to a profound feeling of unease and a constant state of tension. As he grew more comfortable with a particular situation because of familiarity, the path would grow wider and the edges of the precipice recede. Tony Attwood (2006) describes this state of near constant anxiety as follows:

> One of the problems faced by children with Asperger's syndrome who use their intellect rather than intuition to succeed in some social situations is that they may be in an almost constant state of alertness and anxiety, leading to a risk of mental and physical exhaustion... There may be intense anxiety or a phobic reaction to certain social situations, or to sensory experiences... or to a change in expectations such as an alteration to the daily school routine.

When John was a child the techniques we employed in order to reduce his anxiety included: sufficient warning and explanation of any impending change, a structured day, allowing plenty of time to read or work on his computer, provision of a calming distraction and, whenever possible, removal of pressure and complete avoidance of the anxiety-inducing situation. Nevertheless, I don't think I ever truly appreciated just how much anxiety John actually experienced as a child. It never crossed my mind that the years he spent biting his clothes may have been a sign of anxiety; I thought they were just another of John's tics (see Chapter 8). Tony Attwood's experience of anxiety in his patients is described in *The Complete Guide to Asperger's Syndrome* as follows:

> We all feel a little anxious sometimes, but many children and adults with Asperger's syndrome appear to be prone to being anxious for much of their day, or to be extremely anxious about a specific event...

> The child can use tantrums, emotional blackmail, rigid defiance and non-compliance to ensure he or she avoids circumstances that would increase anxiety. Another way of avoiding situations associated with anxiety is to retreat into solitude or the special interest. The greatest anxiety is usually associated with social situations, and being alone ensures the person does not make social errors or suffer humiliation or torment by others. The special interest can be so engrossing and enjoyable that no anxious thought intrudes into the person's thinking...

> Having suffered long-term anxiety, the person will become extremely sensitive to any situation that could increase anxiety. There can be a tendency to 'press the panic button' too quickly...

> For some people with Asperger's syndrome, there can be worries about events and experiences that are very unlikely to happen.

The above description reads as if Attwood had seen John as one of his patients and these were extracts from his notes. John agrees with this assessment, although he thinks: 'Tantrums are less an avoidance technique and more a consequence of a failure to avoid.' I'm not aware of John ever using emotional blackmail to avoid doing something but he's certainly prone to worry about events that are unlikely to happen. I still remember how worried he used to be (as a child with an inadequate sense of time and a love of astronomy) about the terrible things that would happen to our solar system in the future.

John is very aware of this tendency:

> You think up some unlikely situation and obsess on it, then it doesn't happen and there's huge relief... but something in retrospect completely predictable then torpedoes you and you haven't prepared for it at all because you were too busy obsessing over the unlikely event.

Lydia (who is 19 months *younger* than John) recalls a fairground ride she went on with John when she was quite young. He really wanted to go on this ride but started panicking because he had trouble trying to get the safety belt on. Then he panicked more, worried about the 'rust around the door', screaming 'we're going to die'. He had a full blown panic attack, crying and shouting during the whole ride. According to Lydia she spent the entire time, which 'felt like two hours', trying to calm him down. This type of incident was (is?) so very typical of John. Something would trigger the incident, such as a problem connected with poor fine motor coordination or sensory overload and then he would notice some detail that most people would never see. This would become exaggerated in his mind until a full blown panic attack was in place. John agrees with this explanation:

> I never thought about it in those terms, but that's precisely it: some subtlety which is *obviously* wrong and *obviously* terribly dangerous... and then if I look at it in a more normal state of mind it's obviously trivial (so the padding is coming away from one safety strap: the strap is still intact, look, it would take a remarkable concatenation of unlikely circumstances for that peeled padding to be the thing that kills you).

John's inability to withstand even a small amount of stress or pressure was first noted at nursery school when he got very upset because the staff tried to make him produce a Christmas card for his parents. According to John:

> I can withstand a lot of stress... but I can't withstand much in the way of *stressors*, because each stressor produces a far larger amount of stress (the emotion) than it does in most people. Or so I speculate.

His infant school teachers found they had to remove the pressure they were applying in order for John to settle down happily. Much later in life, John's employer noted (during an appraisal) that John responded badly when placed under pressure. John said he had insisted they make a note of this 'rather then just randomly marking me down for everything'. Christopher Gillberg wrote in 2002:

> People with Asperger syndrome... seem to panic when subjected to mild or moderate stress or to specific perceptual stimuli for which they have poor tolerance. This is quite often mistaken as a typical panic attack and considered to reflect 'anxiety'. In a sense there is 'panic' and 'anxiety' but both will typically disappear almost instantly if stresses or the unwanted stimuli are removed.

Donna Williams, in her book *The Jumbled Jigsaw*, describes what it feels like to have a panic attack caused by acute anxiety:

> These acute attacks can be like feeling an impending earthquake coming, hearing a tidal wave about to come crashing down on you. They can be like a warning of

a feeling of impending suffocation or drowning. They can be like a compelling physical warning you cannot avoid being alarmed by.

This would appear to be very similar to John's experience of panic:

You know it's coming and that you can't stop it; or you can, but only by removing the stressor: this happens when that cannot be removed, or when, say, it hits you at a time when everyone is asleep, and it's hard to rearrange things at 2am!

Worrying about things that could go wrong, plus a desire to minimise his anxiety levels has made John a very cautious and risk averse person, not necessarily a bad thing. As he explains:

If I'm cautious and risk averse and have vast buffers against things going wrong, I have a reason *not* to be anxious. It's more a pre-emptive anxiety-reduction strategy than a consequence of anxiety: though actually *being* anxious does assist sometimes. I remain cautious now even though I'm not anxious often, because I know that if I were less cautious, the anxiety would return.

I think worrying about what might go wrong and how upset that would make him feel is one reason that he's reluctant to get into an intimate relationship. As he explains: 'The further you climb, the further you can fall, and I am definitely afraid of these heights.'

Intense social anxiety has remained a constant throughout John's life. This seemed to begin in John's second year of life, as evidenced by his intense reaction to the other children he came into contact with in our monthly NCT (National Childbirth Trust) coffee mornings. The reaction was so strong that we had to remove him from that particular situation immediately (see Chapter 12). I can't resist a wicked quote from John regarding the onset of his social difficulties:

Ooh ooh after I was vaccinated!!! Also after I started speaking, after I was born, and after I started breathing oxygen. Thus, an obvious cure for this and indeed for *all* symptoms of autism, and every other disease, is to avoid oxygenated atmospheres. If you do this you will also never get cancer or show any symptoms of old age. MAGIC MIRACLE CURE. Where's my well-paid US lecture tour?

Williams and Wright (2004) describe some strategies that can be used to reduce anxiety, including a calm atmosphere, a quiet place to go to and the use of routine. All of these worked well for John. He was always happy to spend time on his own escaping either into his imagination or into a book. In fact once he could read John was never parted from a book. For most of his school days John kept to himself in the playground, book in hand, often walking around the perimeter or 'bouncing back and forth between two parallel walls... but [this] had the disadvantage of crossing the paths of other people more often... it was a nice way to relax.'

Leventhal-Belfer & Coe (2004) describe various ways that young children cope with social anxiety:

A typical coping pattern that we see in young children with Asperger's Syndrome is avoidance of situations that are socially demanding or not well-structured and have poorly defined rules such as playground activities... As their anxiety rises so does their hypersensitivity to their external environment, leading to their complaints that the space is too noisy, too hot, or too crowded. And in some cases, the children are so overloaded that their behaviour degenerates into a tantrum.

Although John agrees with the above, he's not really happy with the use of the word tantrum under these circumstances:

> 'Tantrum' is a wobbly description for a snapping of overburdened emotional control: it's very much describing the external appearance, not the internal cause. It's not like I ever thought 'oh, let's have a tantrum now'.

Nevertheless I think this *is* a good description of John's behaviour when he was placed in an environment he couldn't cope with. Tantrums occurred quite regularly (into John's twenties) whenever he found himself in situations he couldn't handle. These caused his sister significant distress (see Chapter 19) but she became quite an expert at calming him down after one of his outbursts. Leventhal-Belfer and Coe (2004) describe John's situation accurately when they write:

> Noisy, crowded, chaotic scenes can be overwhelming to some children with Asperger's Syndrome. Situations where the rules are ambiguous or constantly changing (e.g. during recess, birthday parties) can be confusing and anxiety provoking because of the child's rigidity and need for structure. Highly charged emotional situations are also disorganizing for children with Asperger's Syndrome. They can't accurately read and discern the feelings of others and are easily frightened by the strong emotions directed towards them.

Social occasions such as Lydia's birthday parties always provoked intense anxiety and John never wanted parties of his own (see Chapter 12). John's social anxiety was exacerbated hugely by his experiences at secondary school where he had a very problematic relationship with most of the staff as well as being bullied by some of the children (see Chapter 16).

When I asked John recently what makes him anxious nowadays, he said:

> Some major, anticipated event, or more generally anything new I've never done before. This always causes me to be at least anxious enough to disrupt my sleep, even when the event is one that I know has temporary effects, that I'm looking forward to, and that I've done many times before, such as coming up to your house for a holiday. If the event has never happened before, or is in an area where I perceive myself to be weak or have failed in the past, I'll often be far more anxious than that, up to phobic levels of fear: job interviews are a typical example (both giving and receiving).

Some situations (such as moving house, changing jobs or giving a talk) can be anxiety inducing for many people but the intensity of John's anxiety is quite paralysing. For example: he was so nervous about attending the residential field trip that was a compulsory part of his A level biology course that he flatly refused to go even though this meant he sacrificed all the associated marks. Avoidance is undoubtedly an effective way of reducing anxiety. He was also so anxious the first time he had to give a talk as part of his degree course that he ran out of the room soon after he started and refused to go back. He did eventually give some sort of talk as it was compulsory. If he finds the thought of some new situation scary John will avoid taking any action at all unless things get so bad (in the current situation) that the anxiety producing alternative becomes preferable. 'Exactly', agrees John: 'It's a balancing act, and a very unpleasant one, because the anxiety doesn't go away: indeed the lapse of time often adds a time-criticality or lateness component to it that makes it worse.' Even when John is ready to take action he needs a considerable amount of verbal encouragement as well as practical support in order to effect the change. Nevertheless, at the time of writing he *has* been able to move to a new home, start a new job and give some technical talks.

Another source of intense anxiety occurs when there is 'a perceived failure on my part to do something which I know people are expecting me to have done':

> This isn't *always* a cause of anxiety, but if the failure will have significant consequences, or the failure will cause people who respect me to respect me less, or (most selfishly) if the failure will lead to my getting in trouble or other social difficulties, I'll be in a constant state of anxiety until the problem is solved...

> The form of anxiety... has shifted over time. At school I was almost always in selfish mode, 'oops I will get into trouble (again)'. Here and there was the occasional teacher whose opinion of me I cared enough about to get into the 'will respect me less' mode, but that was very rare... At work it's almost always 'will have significant consequences' mixed with 'will respect me less'. The cause of the anxiety is almost always the same: I've engaged in massive prevarication rather than actually getting work done, and now it's too late.

According to John though it would seem that worry and anxiety can also have some significant benefits. They can enable him to achieve a state of hyperfocus and creativity during which he can engage in prodigious amounts of computer-based problem-solving. He describes this anxiety as 'the ultimate goad behind my most extreme bouts of productivity':

> If something is boring but still in my focus and I don't really want to do it, or I'm stuck and sure there's a better way, I'll prevaricate and delay in the hope of finding that better way: but once I get anxious enough about the approaching deadline or about the sheer amount of time I've wasted, the anxiety will power a sort of controlled panic that will get the job done. This is the most intense form of hyperfocus I can get into: in this state, I stop for nothing, not sleep (in this state I can't sleep anyway), not meals (snatched snacks is the most I can do), not anything, and solutions emerge instantly without effort: it's just a matter of typing them in. I have never yet failed at *anything* I've accomplished in this state... and then after it's over, I collapse, and I'm a blurry shivery wreck for the next day or so. Another reason why I don't use it very often. It's exhilarating but not at all pleasant, and the comedown is horrible. I came out of a burst of this at about mid-day today [Sunday], after entering it at about 18:00 on Saturday, collapsed, and woke up about an hour ago, at 19:00. But I've done about a month's work in that single day. Yeah, it's the weekend, but putting the work off would just have made me even *more* anxious... when the work calls, I must answer.

> I've always worried, but it only got really extreme in secondary school, with regular bouts of lying awake at night, unable to get to sleep because of worrying.

(These days I tend to get to sleep OK, but anxiety... shifts into the controlled panic state while I'm asleep and wakes me up at ridiculous times of day, with solutions bubbling in my mind. This was really annoying in the last job, because the place just won't let me in at 5am! In this job, I can just go downstairs and get hacking!)

John's anxiety levels have reduced dramatically since he started working from home in his mid-thirties. I can't remember seeing him so relaxed and happy. 'Is this what life is like for normal people all the time?' wonders John. This improvement is due to the fact that most of John's social contact is over the internet, he's working the hours he chooses, there's a lack of what John considered to be unreasonable external pressure and he can stay in his own calm home environment without the sensory overload generated by commuting and working in a noisy open-plan office. He's in control and many of the things that would make him very anxious can be avoided. He doesn't suffer from persistent anxiety any more though that doesn't mean he's totally anxiety free – but who is? According to John, 'bursts of intense anxiety continue to this day, but there are long non-anxious periods now, which are so very relaxing... if anything my problem is not falling asleep when I'm not anxious!'

I could be wrong but I don't think that John has actually suffered from either a generalised anxiety disorder or depression. The reasons for his anxiety were well founded, based as they were on his experience of situations which had caused him distress and which he hadn't been able to cope with successfully. If the cause of the stress was removed John's anxiety would disappear. However, according to Tony Attwood (2006), generalised anxiety disorder and depression *are* very common in people with Asperger's syndrome:

> Current research indicates that around 65 per cent of adolescents with Asperger's syndrome have an affective or mood disorder. Perhaps the most common is an anxiety disorder... However, the prevalence of depression is also high...

> People with Asperger's syndrome appear vulnerable to feeling depressed, with about one in three children and adults having a clinical depression... The reasons for people with Asperger's syndrome to be depressed are many and include the long-term consequences on self-esteem of feeling unaccepted and misunderstood, the mental exhaustion of trying to succeed socially, feelings of loneliness, being tormented, teased, bullied and ridiculed by peers, and a cognitive style that is pessimistic, focussing on what could go wrong... The depression can lead to a severe withdrawal from social contact and thoughts that, without social success, there is no point in life.

> People with Asperger's syndrome are often perfectionists, tend to be exceptionally good at noticing mistakes, and have a conspicuous fear of failure. There can be a relative lack of optimism, with a tendency to expect failure and not to be able to control events... As the adolescent with Asperger's syndrome achieves greater intellectual maturity, this can be associated with an increased insight into being different and self-perception of being irreparably defective and socially stupid...

> Unemployment has been associated with clinical depression for typical people and this is certainly the case for people with Asperger's syndrome. Depression can

also occur when the person is under-employed – that is, he or she is over-qualified for the job... having a job that is fulfilling and valued can be a preventative measure for a clinical depression.

John is very fortunate indeed that, despite prolonged anxiety and the temperament of a perfectionist who hates to fail, he isn't prone to depression; in fact he remains an enthusiastic, optimistic and cheerful person. John agrees that this is true 'as long as I keep my thoughts away from any consideration of relationships'. I believe one of the reasons John is so happy is that he's been encouraged to devote his time to the special interests for which he's always displayed such a passion. By spending so much of his time reading and computing he has retained a childlike enthusiasm for the world around him. He's also acquired skills and knowledge that have been fundamental to his feelings of self-worth and have enabled him to work in a field that fully utilises his talents. He hasn't felt unaccepted and misunderstood 'since I left school':

> I suspect that if I was focused on something which wasn't such a cooperative activity, something that didn't include *creation* in the same way, that this fate might have befallen me too. Maybe perhaps.

John has never been unemployed or underemployed. If he hadn't found an outlet for his intelligence and creativity, I dread to think what the frustration would have done to his mental health. I believe that concentrating on one's strengths is far healthier than focussing on one's weaknesses. Spending too much time trying to turn into someone else and never really succeeding can be devastating to anyone's self-esteem. John's perfectionist instincts have actually proved to be quite valuable. He has a realistic appreciation of what he *can* do well and also what he can't manage; he doesn't waste time or energy pining for things that he believes are unattainable. On the other hand, as John writes: 'The cost is that 'you are what you dare', and I don't dare much. A lot of those things probably *are* attainable, but I won't risk it.' It's quite possible that John *did* suffer from depression while he was at secondary school although we were unaware of it at the time: 'I suspect that my state during school years would have been considered depressed if I hadn't been so anxious all the time that it masked it.'

Although John still finds attempts to succeed socially mentally exhausting, he doesn't suffer much from feelings of loneliness because 'I *have* the Internet, and while physical presence of other people does dispel loneliness faster, it is almost too much: I tend to get overstimulated, and crash after they leave.'

Emotional overload

Our son was very sensitive to raised voices and got terribly upset if there was any arguing in the house. I don't know whether it was the actual noise generated by the raised voices or the unpleasant atmosphere that he couldn't tolerate but I suspect the latter. John agrees, saying that it felt to him as 'air like ice'. John has always seemed very susceptible to emotional overload and finds it extremely difficult to handle strong emotions in a calm way. Depending on the situation, he will either appear to have no feelings at all or will become very distressed and upset. John writes about his difficulty with handling feelings as follows:

> I think it's more that I don't really know how to express them... I certainly don't

53

feel emotionless, ever! (I have recently started to notice the lack of emotional affect in my speech patterns, but I have no real idea how to fix it.)

John's inability to express his emotions concurs with Tony Attwood's (1998) belief:

A common feature of Asperger's Syndrome is a difficulty with self-disclosure, that is, talking about one's inner feelings. The child may clearly be upset but does not have the ability or words to explain their feelings.

Deidre Lovecky (2004) describes John's behaviour accurately when she writes:

People with AS resemble younger children in their expression of emotions so they look immature. Many still have tantrums well past the age when others have outgrown such extreme expressions of emotion.

Our first Swedish au-pair remembered eight year old John well:

I had no problems in my relationship with John although I had never met such a different, interesting and funny and clever, 8 year old before... He seemed so smart for his age and yet, at the same time emotionally, when he got angry and had his tantrums, he seemed like a three year old... And wow – did he have a temper! It could be scary sometimes when he got really angry, but most of the time he was happy being occupied with his computer or reading books... He was generally good behaved, but also... quite often tantrums, anger and frustrations when people, myself sometimes, didn't understand him or when things didn't go his way. I would say he was mostly obedient... John sure had a temper, easily upset and angry but not for long...

I had very warm feelings for John. He was a lovely and different child that was easy to love... if you could just accept that he was different, had a temper. He was also both caring, soft and sensitive... and it was obvious how much he loved his immediate family.

Attwood (1998) describes several useful strategies that can be employed to help a child learn how to recognise and describe their emotions. He describes one of these as follows: 'A useful visual activity is to draw a gauge or barometer that 'measures' the degree of a specific emotion. The points on that measure can be given numerical values and appropriate words and actions.' I think a technique such as this could have been a helpful way to teach John how to express his emotions in a calm manner. There would have been plenty of opportunity (when reading to John as a young boy) to discuss how some character in the story was feeling and to measure these feelings using an appropriate gauge. It would have been easy to extrapolate this to how John himself was feeling in a variety of circumstances and then get him to volunteer this information on a regular basis by recording his emotions using various gauges. This type of information would have been incredibly useful when John went to school and would have made it much easier for me to appreciate just how difficult he was finding his day. It would have been a really valuable technique to use with John's sister Lydia as well, because she felt that her feelings as the sibling of someone on the autism spectrum were never acknowledged or discussed. Much more detail about Lydia's views can be found in Chapter 19.

An inability to detach himself emotionally meant that John rarely enjoyed films as a teenager or as a young adult because they were too realistic (see Chapter 18).

In his twenties John wrote to me about the waves of feeling that can sweep over him at irregular and unpredictable intervals:

> The most detectable and usual (triggered by stress, unusual changes in routine, lots of people nearby, or nothing at all) is a wave that I call the 'autistic wave'. The symptoms are a sense of utter separateness from the ape-descendants wandering around me (as though I am not even of the same species and can watch them in a quite detached fashion) and from events in the world, an absence of all emotion save for a vague, unlocalised sadness, and an increased intensity of all edges and corners in the visual field... Oddly I see these symptoms in the early stages of illness, too, combined with the usual 'illness tiredness'. I'm not sure why.

When John was eight years old my mother was diagnosed, at the age of 64, with a cancer that had spread. From then on she refused to see the children until she got better. After a couple of months, as it became obvious that she wasn't going to recover and wouldn't see the children again, I had the awful job of sitting down and explaining to them why it had been so long since they'd seen their granny. I also had to tell them that it was likely that they would never see her again. Although I put it as gently as I possibly could, Lydia was absolutely devastated and cried and cried. I was really surprised though that John didn't seem to react at all. They both wrote to their granny and when my father died many years later and I went through my parents' personal belongings I found the letters the children had sent to her at the time. I was really touched to see that she had kept these letters in their original envelopes and had labelled and dated them. What a difference there was between these letters though. Both children wished that she would get well soon but Lydia, aged six, sent a heart-felt letter saying how much she had 'cried because I love you' and included a story and picture about a 'sick granny in hospital'. She put kisses and sticky 'speichel love stars' on the envelope and on the story. Although John signed his letter with lots of kisses most of the content covers topics such as the purchase of a TV monitor for his ZX81 computer (which came without a screen) and the fact that one of the stories he had written at school was read out to the class.

When my father died a few years ago, John was much more upset. When I asked him about this recently he wrote:

> Until my twenties I couldn't ever feel more than numb: an intellectual understanding that 'no, I'll never see her again', but not an emotional one. I knew this was different from what everyone else felt, but to be honest grief strikes me as a horribly overrated emotion and I was happy to not feel it. That seems to have arrived since then: thankfully not enough people close to me die to allow for frequent sampling, but grandpa dying had a much bigger impact. Even then I think that stemmed from an intellectual shift: that all that knowledge and memory are gone, evaporated... So it looks like I have a full emotional palette now, even the nasty self-destructive doomsday emotions like grief. Dammit.

A few months after John wrote this I was diagnosed at a local hospital, also at the age of 64, with a watermelon-sized, malignant tumour which had started on my pancreas. Initially I was told that an operation wasn't possible and chemotherapy and radiotherapy wouldn't work. Fortunately an amazing surgeon at our regional cancer centre *did* have the skill to operate and six years later I'm still doing well. The thought of losing me affected John as profoundly as Lydia and my husband and his relief at my survival was frequently expressed aloud. He certainly doesn't feel numb any more at the thought of the death of someone close to him.

To sum up: Considering John's very difficult start in life he has been very fortunate to experience pretty good health to date. Only anxiety, poor eyesight and hay fever have caused him significant problems.

6
Sensory Differences

I believe the way that John processes visual, auditory and other sensory information is key to understanding some aspects of his behaviour. The human brain receives information from several senses, which include the visual (sight), tactile (touch), auditory (hearing), olfactory (smell), gustatory (taste) and vestibular (balance) systems. The tactile system, which is situated on the skin and even in the mouth, relates to touch and the feel of things, to the experience of different types of pressure, to an awareness of temperature and a perception of pain. The vestibular system, which is situated in the inner ear, is activated by movement. It provides information on where our body is in space and how fast and in what direction it's moving relative to the surroundings. It's one of the factors implicated in maintaining muscle tone and is very important in preserving balance and posture.

Many children (and adults), either on the autism spectrum, with developmental coordination disorder (dyspraxia) or with Nonverbal Learning Disabilities (NLD), have sensory sensitivities that would appear to differ markedly from the so called 'normal' sensory experience. As a result they may encounter significant problems if these differences aren't understood and catered for. Carolann Jackson, president of SAFE and ASAP,[29] speaking at the NAS Professional conference in 2011,[30] said:

> Asperger sensitivities to sight, sound, touch, light, texture, proximity, smell, taste, pain, and temperature are constantly bombarded by everyday situations which neurotypicals rarely notice and are certainly not bothered by. For many people with AS, these intrusions can be *more* distressing and disruptive than those associated with social communication and interaction difficulties. The mere *anticipation* of these unwanted sensory experiences can lead to intense anxiety and panic, resulting in often inappropriate or bizarre behaviours. From my own experiences and those of our members, I believe that these sensory anomalies may be at the root of many of these behaviours.

This agrees with John's experience: 'The social stuff can be avoided and slowly gets better as the years pass. The sensory bombardment never improves (unless the local environment changes).' Sensory-related behaviours are included for the first time in the fifth edition of the *Diagnostic and Statistical Manual* (DSM-5) as one of several diagnostic criteria for Autism Spectrum Disorder.

According to Rubinstien (2005):

> Most children and adults with NLD have only two methods for dealing with sensory overload: they melt down or they shut down. Sensory overload occurs when the brain is confronted with more information than it can handle at one time. Although a meltdown may seem like a destructive act, it is really an act of self defense.

John has used melt-down and shut-down regularly as a way of dealing with sensory overload. When referring to shut-downs or tune outs John wrote: 'I got *good* at this. I could tune out anywhere. I could tune out in the middle of being castigated by teachers (which sent them completely ballistic).' The first time I saw John tune out was in a pre-school gym class; at the time I was really shocked and couldn't understand what was going on. For further details see Chapter 13.

JOHN'S EARLY DAYS AT HOME

After John's 11 weeks in hospital it was wonderful to take him home at last, even though we both felt rather apprehensive about looking after him on our own. However we comforted ourselves with the thought that feeding, bathing, changing and dressing babies, as well as getting them off to sleep *couldn't* be all that difficult because all the other parents we knew had seemed to manage these tasks with relative ease. Unfortunately we weren't so lucky! Whether this was just inexperience and incompetence or whether there were other factors involved is hard to say.

As previously described (see Chapter 4) I was unable to get John to sleep in a crib after his daytime feeds because he wouldn't stop crying but fortunately that problem was overcome by carrying him around in a sling. Was he comforted by being held so closely and firmly? According to John, 'I'm sure I was! A hug from you is comforting *now...*' Fortunately the problem only lasted a few months while John needed a lot of rest. Once he'd settled into a routine of three meals a day and was awake much of the time he didn't need to be held so much. Wrapping the bed-covers very firmly round John as a baby always helped him to go to sleep and to this day he seems to wrap his duvet right round him at night. It wasn't precisely swaddling but not far off. As for his duvet being wrapped around him, John said: 'It cuts down draughtiness and really is more comforting.' I wonder whether, like Temple Grandin (2005), he would have found (or would still find) deep pressure massage relaxing. John suspects that he'd 'find massage relaxing only if done by a machine, though, and [I] really have no idea if I'd like it at all'. Although John enjoys a hug from his mum, he is so physically awkward that he seems to find it difficult to hug back properly. As John explains: 'I just don't want to accidentally put your eye out! It doesn't *feel* awkward like, say, waving does. (I never have a clue what the hell to do there.)'

Nappy changing was quite a problem when John was a young baby. Lorna Wing (1996) wrote that babies who 'later show autistic behaviour' may 'dislike any interference such as nappy changing, dressing and washing'. John disliked all three. Initially nappy changing was a nightmare, with John screaming blue murder every time we laid him down on his changing mat and took the wet or dirty nappy off. I don't know whether it was something to do with the feel of air on his skin (although the house was very warm as England was experiencing a heat wave at the time) or whether he hated being disturbed. The change involved in going from a clean dry nappy to a wet or dirty nappy seemed to cause him no distress whatsoever! Lisa Pyles (2002) had a very similar experience with her son, another John:

John was an easy baby... The only thing that upset John – *really* upset him – was when we uncovered his legs to change his diapers or undress him for a bath. For those few minutes you'd have thought we were abusing him, and nothing would comfort him but covering him up again as quickly as possible.

I used to dread changing our son because I hated to see such a small baby in such obvious distress. As his nappy had to be changed several times a day, I had to find a way to make the process more tolerable for my own sanity. We decided to find a way to distract John during the nappy change in the hope that he wouldn't notice what was going on. We bought a blue plastic bird which sang a song and moved its eyes when a cord was pulled. This toy was only brought out when John's nappy was being changed. We hung the bird close to his changing mat and pulled the cord before we changed him. John was so absorbed watching and listening to the bird that we could change him quickly without any fuss at all! In fact he never cried again during a nappy change; when he was old enough, he loved pulling the bird's cord himself before we changed him. We used the bird until John grew out of daytime nappies. We were amazed, but delighted, at how successful this simple tactic had turned out to be. Distraction was one of the techniques that we found to be particularly useful when parenting our young son. Lorna Wing, writing in her book *The Autistic Spectrum*, notes that 'distraction, such as playing a piece of music, may be helpful' when having to manage a child who gets very upset 'in response to care procedures'. Other useful techniques have been described by Clements and Zarkowska (2000) as 'providing reassurance and avoiding unnecessary exposure' and 'building tolerance of the things that disturb the person'.

CLOTHES

Although John didn't appear to have a strong aversion to any particular clothes when he was a child, he really hated getting *into* or *out of* any clothes. Therefore when he was a small baby we didn't change his clothes more often than necessary, which certainly saved on washing! As John humorously (and accurately!) noted: 'When I grew up I continued this tradition for some years.' Left to his own devices John would have stayed in the same pair of pyjamas for ever, both day and night. Nevertheless he became accustomed to having his clothes changed every day although he never learned to like it. We felt it was an important part of his early education, as we didn't want him to go to nursery school or see other people still in his pyjamas! Eventually John got used to this regime and then, being such a creature of habit, would never dream of going to bed at night with his day clothes on. Until he left home, though, he was happy to slob around for hours in his pyjamas given half a chance. As an adult he grew so accustomed to getting dressed in the morning before he left the house that, although he now works from home, he still gets dressed every day. John thinks 'it probably helps that my house is kept quite cold. I have been known to slob around in a dressing gown when ill, if I think I'm not going to be awake for more than an hour or so.'

Although many children on the autism spectrum find it painful to wear materials that aren't very soft, ordinary clothes have never caused John great discomfort. He still prefers the feel of soft materials, as do I and many others but this has never stopped him wearing ordinary clothes. Like many people though he really disliked wearing a tie at school and fortunately hasn't had to wear one for many years. He also disliked wearing formal clothes to work and hasn't worn a suit for many years either.

John loved the feel of fur as a child. When he was young I had a furry jacket which he loved touching and snuggling up to. We gave him a small piece of fur to hold which he was very attached to and carried around for a couple of years. He still owns it and says he still loves the feel of fur.

It's only since he was 30 or so that John could be taken to a shop to buy clothes without an explosion of bad temper. It's really embarrassing to be in a store with a grown man having a major tantrum like a child but if we hadn't gone shopping with him occasionally, John would have been walking around in ancient, ill fitting clothes full of holes! Interestingly enough he has absolutely no rational explanation these days for this past behaviour as it was a purely emotional response. Even in his mid-thirties John wrote: 'It makes me seriously uneasy even now to pop into a changing room and try things on.' Fortunately he trusts his sister Lydia (who always dresses very well) to go clothes shopping with him. As a result he has looked less disreputable in recent years. 'Not much less', said John: 'Anything looks rumpled after I've put it on.' He's still unwilling to go near clothes shops unless it's absolutely essential. 'Retail therapy' is a truly alien concept to John: 'For me, this would be therapy to get me to like shopping!' Nevertheless things are still improving. I was amazed a couple of years ago when John needed no persuasion to come shopping with me to buy himself some new shirts. There was absolutely no fuss. We looked for shirts together in a big store and John went into the changing rooms willingly. I was half expecting an outburst of shouting to emanate from the changing area but nothing happened. He came out happily, said that all the shirts fitted and then read calmly while I looked for clothes for myself. I couldn't believe it – an enjoyable shopping trip with my son! I think one of the main reasons for John's emotional outbursts in the past was frustration, because dressing and undressing were so difficult; buttons and belts were particularly tricky. Having to try on several sets of clothes one after the other during a shopping trip was just too much to cope with. The fact that he never used to care what he looked like didn't help. Even that has changed relatively recently; John seems to take a bit more care with his appearance these days.

WASHING

We really expected that John would enjoy being bathed when we brought him home from the hospital and were quite surprised and upset to find that he hated the water and just screamed. No amount of gentle talking, smiling and so on made the slightest difference. We tried for several days, hoping he would get used to it but to no avail. In the end we abandoned the daily bath, as babies don't get *that* dirty provided you clean their face, hands and bottoms properly. We didn't tell anyone, family, friends or health professionals, that we weren't bathing our baby every day. We felt they would judge us critically, wouldn't understand the situation and would say we were poor parents. We did bathe John occasionally, either when we were feeling guilty enough or mentally strong enough! To this day, although our baby daughter was perfectly happy having her nappy changed or being bathed, I'm always surprised to see a baby having a bath or nappy change without crying. Our experience left deep scars!

Although John disliked baths and the washing process, he loved playing with water. For many years we exploited this inconsistency. As he grew older and moved into the family bath we used to have a weekly, as opposed to daily, bath time. This was really a playtime in water which lasted for as long as John wanted, which was hours rather than minutes. Over the years it provided many happy hours of concentrated play. John still recalls bath times as a child: 'I have very strong memories of that. Building little empires in drying water in the sloping end of the bath, constructing all sorts of elaborate fantasies using whatever was at hand.'

When he grew older and no longer played in the bath, John's dislike of bathing became obvious again. He took a regular(?) shower of sorts (after frequent reminders) while he still lived at home but once he left home at 18, personal hygiene became a major problem for his family (and no doubt his colleagues). Perhaps not his colleagues, says John:

> Working in computing helped there, in a counter-intuitive and repulsive fashion. I was definitely not the worst BO-wise. Not by a very long way. There are many reasons I'm glad not to be working in an office any more.

It's really sad when you see your son after an absence and rather than hugging and kissing and saying: 'How lovely it is to see you', all you can do is try not to breathe in because of the smell. John always tried to rationalise the situation, saying that his sister and I had an abnormal sense of smell and it was only family members that were so sensitive to the smell of their relatives! In reality I would have thought that our close genetic link would have made us *less* sensitive to his aroma. We would explain that only family members had the honesty to tell him the truth and everyone else was far too polite. That was a concept John appeared to find hard to understand at the time. According to him: 'I'm working with not terribly diplomatic people. Some of them would surely have said something. There's been no change I can perceive in the way I'm treated since that sort of thing stopped.' Some years later though, John acknowledged that his colleagues 'probably couldn't tell because, like I said, I was not remotely the worst of the BO sources in that office'.

Personal hygiene problems would appear to be relatively common in teenagers with Asperger's syndrome. As Christopher Gillberg wrote in his book *A Guide to Asperger Syndrome*:

> At least half of all teenagers with Asperger syndrome whom I have met do not manage personal hygiene in a satisfactory way. They may refuse to wash their hair or to take a shower, complain that the water 'feels strange when it comes into contact with the body'... the mere existence of major hygiene problems in a teenager should prompt suspicion that there may be an underlying autism spectrum disorder.

John used to say that it was much healthier *not* to wash hair as it would retain its natural oils and would become self cleaning after a certain length of time. Unfortunately this never seemed to apply to *his* hair and these days he does agree that 'this was wishful thinking'. In fact one web site[31] describes how you *can* avoid using shampoo and conditioner and get really clean hair but the hair *does* need to be rinsed regularly in warm water. The reasons why the self-cleaning hair system *won't* work are described on another web site.[32] Although John washes his hair regularly these days (because he says that dirty hair makes his scalp feel itchy), he maintains that he never had an itchy scalp before he started washing his hair so often. He says:

> I can't understand how it is that hair unwashed for months used to feel exactly the same as hair unwashed for a day, while now hair unwashed for four days starts to *itch* and if it's been unwashed for two weeks is unbearable. It's not head lice, they don't itch across the whole scalp then all disappear in concert like that. It's some

change in sensory thresholds and I'm not sure I like it.

What can I say except that the dandruff was a sight to behold. He thinks his dandruff is as bad as ever despite the fact that he washes his hair far more often but I would beg to disagree. According to John:

Dandruff clearly has nothing much to do with cleanliness. I've still got dandruff, even though I wash my hair twice a week. Wikipedia says: 'in 2007 it was discovered that the responsible agent is a scalp specific fungus, *Malassezi globosa*'. All shampooing without antifungals does is knocks some flakes off: apparently the effect is to reduce dandruff for only a day or so. (Antifungal shampoo might work, but if so why do I still have dandruff? I've been using antifungals for years. Maybe the fungus has become resistant.)

When John was in his mid-twenties he explained why he hated washing his hair:

The water feels annoying, is almost always the wrong temperature, water in the eyes is most unpleasant, particularly with soap or shampoo attached... and the whole thing is an unproductive use of time in which I can't read, use computers, eat or even think straight. Something to be avoided.

John would also justify his lack of washing by saying that the body is unimportant and only the mind matters. These days he has amended that slightly, saying that the body is important only insofar as it is a means to keep the mind operating. In fact he hopes that in the future it would be possible to keep his mind alive after his body dies. He qualifies this though by saying: 'I'm not a loony about it though, like Ray '260 pills a day' Kurzweil. I *hope* this is possible: Ray has an absolute belief that it'll come to pass and is just trying to stay alive until it does.' A fascinating account of Ray Kurzweil's 'health' regime can be found on Wikipedia.[33]

To our astonishment John's hygiene situation improved enormously soon after he moved into his own house at the age of 27. It's now extremely rare indeed for him to smell, and then not only is he aware of it and very apologetic but there's also a good reason, such as meeting him after work on a hot day. He says: 'If I could have detected it earlier in life I'd have been apologetic then, but I couldn't.' Why did this magical transformation take place? The house he'd rented with friends for several years before he bought his own place had no shower and a horrible bath and I'm sure he never used it. When he bought his own house the smallish bathroom was in a poor condition, there was no shower and John flatly refused to use the rather unsavoury looking bath. The bath was removed and a shower and very large shower tray installed in its place. This meant that he could stand well clear of the water when it first came through the shower head and before the temperature stabilised. The shower was also installed very close to the hot water tank and so it didn't take very long for the water to reach the correct temperature. John was particularly pleased that the temperature dial had a scale on it. This meant that when someone else used the shower and changed the temperature it was easy for him to reset the temperature accurately. I was very surprised to see how cool a temperature setting he used. I remember how often he would complain that in our house (on the temperature settings the rest of the family used) it felt as if the water was burning him. The temperature controls on our showers have never had a scale on them and John was never able to set it to a comfortable temperature. In addition the temperature of the water would drop suddenly when someone else in the house ran a tap and then John complained that the water was now freezing. It's been quite amazing to see what an extraordinary difference John's new shower has made. If only we'd understood just how sensitive John was to water temperature and appreciated that *this* was the critical factor preventing him from showering. We thought John's reluctance to shower was due to manual coordination or psychological problems. John was surprised that we hadn't realised and thought it was a probable explanation for his reaction to being bathed as a baby:

> Sorry, I thought this was not only obvious but something which affected everyone. I know showers/baths *can* be too hot for people, I just didn't realise (until just now) how wide a temperature difference you seem to be able to tolerate.

> Even now I hate showers unless I can get the temperature just right before stepping in, so there is no initial heat/cold sensation at all.

This is an excellent example of the difficulties a carer can have appreciating the actual experience of someone on the autism spectrum and consequently problem solving with them.

I asked John relatively recently why he disliked baths so much. He responded that there were multiple annoyances which he then proceeded to describe in great detail. I can't read his explanation without smiling. It's totally logical and sums up the problems that can arise from acute sensory sensitivity:

> Baths don't seem to be sanely shaped or sized for human beings: either you're barking your knees on the side or you're sitting on the bottom and it is like an infinitely hard mattress. Most uncomfortable. No matter what, most of you is sticking out of the water unless the bath is so full that it's slopping over the side whenever you move. (And I at least move a lot, because it's so uncomfortable.) Getting in involves being roasted piecewise, in a ring up your body. I prefer to leave roasting for my food. (If you put in water cool enough that you don't get roasted, you soon find it's too cold and you have to run more hot water in, roasting one end of your body and making the other end seem all the colder in comparison.) Getting out involves being frozen. It's *boring*, particularly since I don't like to read books in there much because of the (considerable) risk of damaging the book. (I read books anyway, but I'm always worried about the book damage, and it's even harder to find a comfortable position to read in than it is to find a comfortable one to lie in.) There may be more annoyances I can't remember: it's been years since I took a bath.

I can certainly think of one additional thing John wouldn't like and that's the time it can take to run water into the bath. I too remember hating baths while I lived at home as a teenager. The enamel bath felt hard and uncomfortable, the temperature in the bathroom was very cold as we didn't have central heating (or more accurately we couldn't afford to use the central heating supplied in the large draughty vicarages I was brought up in), there was only a small amount of hot water in the bath so that most of one's body was in the cold air and I really disliked the feel of the hard water anyway. Once I left home I found I could really enjoy baths if the bathroom was warm, the bath was made out of a warm material such as plastic and I put plenty of herbal bath preparation into the water which made it feel silky (although according to John that should be 'slimy') and smell nice. John wasn't interested in using any bath oils though and we had a warm bathroom and plastic bath already so there was little I could do to increase his comfort level.

Although John is so much cleaner these days he still doesn't wash his face unless it feels *exceptionally* grimy. As he always uses an electric razor rather than a wet shave, his face feels really horrible to kiss as if there are layers of dead skin cells waiting to be sloughed off! When writing about washing his face John said:

> It feels worse after I'm done than it did before I started. I really dislike the wet-face feeling.

> As one does, I use my hands as temperature test probes while the sink is filling: but temperature sensitivity varies across different parts of the body, and what's the right temperature to the hands is extremely hot to the face. So I have no reliable test probes, and the water that hits my face is almost guaranteed to either sear or freeze me.

As I write this I realise that I also dislike the feel of water on my face. Ever since I left home at eighteen I have cleaned my face, morning and night, with a cleansing lotion. I cannot see John using a cleansing lotion but he has been prepared to use cleansing wipes, at least before he sees me!

Gillberg (2002) recommends introducing a daily personal hygiene routine from a young age:

> It is essential to train people with Asperger syndrome early in life in everyday activities of various kinds... Unless skills in these areas are fostered early, insurmountable problems may emerge in cases with Asperger syndrome. Personal hygiene, in particular, may cause extreme problems, unless a rigorous curriculum is adhered to from early on in development. It may well be one of the most important interventions one can make to implement a curriculum which involves taking a shower (including a hair wash) every day.

John thinks these insurmountable problems 'were surmounted by waiting a few more years for a bit more sensory maturity, and getting a decent shower'. Although I think it's an excellent suggestion, John still doesn't seem to see the point of a rigorous curriculum to promote personal hygiene:

> This is an example of trying to force someone into a robotic routine because they don't have the necessary machinery to use normal sensory cues. Neurologically normal people don't need 'a rigorous curriculum' to keep clean: they just do it when they start to feel icky. I don't see how a robotic routine can possibly have results anywhere near as good.

As for the suggested daily hair wash John couldn't disagree more:

> Daily hair washes? Sheesh. Not with normal shampoo you don't, you'll turn your hair into a damaged frizzy wreck. My problem was never the stress of deciding whether to do that sort of thing: it was remembering to do it at all without some sort of sensory cue.

Perhaps if I'd given John a daily shower and hair wash from a very young age he would have had some sensory cues as he grew older. Pamela Tanguey (2001), when writing about the hygiene issues facing children with Nonverbal Learning Disabilities, agrees that it's important for good habits to become ingrained by adopting a daily routine. She also writes: 'Be sure and introduce the child to the purpose and use of deodorant as soon as it becomes apparent that she needs it.' I think Mary Wrobel (2003) makes a particularly useful point when she emphasises the need to introduce deodorants *before* it becomes necessary:

> Most students with disabilities are not aware of the need to wear deodorant and many even resist doing so because of the change of routine, the wet feeling or the unusual smell. Parents often ask me when they should start this routine with their child. As with most changes, I tell them to start the routine of wearing a deodorant before it becomes a necessity. If a student has a hard time learning to accept new routines, it's always a good idea to start early and take it slowly.

John was 'introduced' to deodorants, but as with washing, mere introduction wasn't nearly sufficient to ensure daily use once he left home! According to John: 'Mere introduction wasn't going to work, something needs to cue me into it or I'll never remember. I have always been cue-driven.'

Despite John's comments, I think (given our experience) that all the above authors have a valid point. If I had my time again I would probably devote more time and thought to John's personal care. Although some people may not agree with me, I think personal hygiene is particularly important for adolescents and adults with 'differences'; its absence can provide yet another trigger for bullying. Parents of young children on the autism spectrum might find a delightful book called *Caring for myself* by Christy Gast and Jane Krug helpful. It includes sections on *Washing My Hands, Getting My Hair Cut, Taking My Bath* and *Brushing My Teeth*.

TEMPERATURE

If John had been very sensitive to the temperature of his environment, it may have been easier for us to realise what an important role water temperature played in his attitude towards washing; however, he's always been extraordinarily unaware of the surrounding air temperature. According to John, there is a perfectly simple explanation for his sensitivity to water temperature and insensitivity to air temperature:

> Air changes temperature slowly. Shower water hitting your skin forces a very rapid temperature change. That's the essential difference. It can easily be a hundred-thousandfold speed difference (a 10°C air temperature change over three hours is quite rare unless you're going outdoors: a 10°C temperature change over a tenth of a second is downright common when shower water hits you).

As England is part of a small island, the temperature can change considerably during the course of a day, depending on whether the sun is shining, how much wind there is, what direction it is blowing in and so on. However John never seemed to notice this. According to Christopher Gillberg, this seems to be quite usual for people on the autism spectrum: 'It is quite common for people with Asperger syndrome and other autism spectrum disorders to be able to tolerate heat and cold at levels that would be completely unacceptable to most other people.' Once John has dressed for the day that's the way he's likely to stay. As the temperature rises and everyone takes off their jumpers, coats and jackets he stays in the same clothes getting hotter and hotter. It's only when someone else remarks: 'Why don't you take off your jumper?' that he becomes aware how warm it is, says 'what a good idea' and removes the garment. To this day John can be working on his computer at home and not realise how cold he has become because the heating isn't on:

> I've never noticed temperature change or similar bodily-state changes very fast; normally it has to wait until someone mentions it to me or until I'm mentally-free enough to check it consciously. (This includes things like my bladder being full or my being hungry or thirsty.) I've been in stuffy offices and not noticed it was hot even though I had a jumper and sometimes even a coat on. As soon as someone mentions it, my overheating or freezing state becomes obvious to me. I notice severe temperature changes, and a temperature so low it hurts or so high it puts me to sleep. In the past I've been hacking away at home and only noticed that the temperature was 2oC and I was wearing only a T-shirt when I started shivering too much to type. My ideal working temperature is 15-17oC.

In the past as winter approached, John usually didn't realise that he should start wearing a coat. One of his aunts wrote to us that John seemed impervious to weather conditions. She remembers him visiting her in his early twenties, on a freezing and very damp day, wearing just a shirt and trousers and without a jumper, jacket or coat! On more than one occasion as an adult he has visited us in the middle of winter without a coat, even though he would be staying for several days and knew we would spend quite a lot of time walking in the countryside. Of course, as always, he has what seems (at least to him) to be a rational explanation for this behaviour:

> If there's ice on the ground it's likely I've just forgotten, but a lot of the time I know I'm going to be walking, so I'll warm up anyway and a coat will be too hot to walk in. So if I'm not going to use it, why go through the roasting inconvenience of getting it up north? (The only way I can get it up is to wear it, and the trains are *warm*.)

There's not much point saying to him that other people take their coats *off* in a warm train! These days we keep a coat here for him so that he always has something warm to wear should he need it. I think he might have improved recently, now that he also lives in the countryside, as he often (but not always) wears a coat when he goes out in the winter. He's still inclined to avoid rain protection though if he has only a few minutes to walk (unless it is actually raining heavily when he goes out), saying he won't get *very* wet. Again John's characteristic logic is evident:

> It's a trade-off: the possibility of getting wet against the certainty of having to drag wet protection around for the whole day. So I don't take wet protection often. I think I've got thoroughly soaked twice in seven years. A good trade-off I think.

It would appear that as an adult he is unaware of temperature and other bodily state changes because he's concentrating so hard on something else. This may well have applied when he was a child as well. There was one incident though, when he was in his late twenties, when high temperatures contributed to John suffering from a sensory over-load and spoiling what should have been a lovely day's sightseeing abroad for the whole family (see Chapter 9). John isn't at all impressed that I should bring up this incident, saying:

> You're never going to let me forget that, are you? It was pretty bloody miserable for me as well, y'know. I didn't just do it to mess up your day (though if I'd known you were going to moan about it for this long, I bloody well would have, sheesh, it was *one day* nearly a decade ago).

HAIR

John has never liked his hair being touched, whether brushed, combed, washed or cut. This isn't unusual for children on the autism spectrum, as Lorna Wing (1996) de-scribes:

> Some of the children resist and have tantrums in response to care procedures, es-pecially hair washing, brushing, combing or cutting. The problem may be sensi-tivity to being touched, resistance to any interference, or it may be due to real fear.

When John was a small child at nursery school, a nurse used to come at regular intervals to check that the children didn't have hair lice. John was the only child who made such a terrible fuss, when the nurse tried to sit him on her knee to look at his hair, that she never succeeded. The nursery school was quite concerned at John's reaction but at the time I thought it was quite possible that his early experiences in hospital had left their mark. He'd been handled so much by nurses and doctors and some of the proce-dures he was exposed to must have been unpleasant. Looking back, I have no idea whether the medical treatment really had any bearing on his reaction to the 'nit' nurse (as she was called) or whether he would have reacted in the same way without these ear-ly experiences. The nit nurse also visited John's primary school and John seems to remember her visits quite clearly and the way she touched his hair:

> If she only touched it I would have had no complaints. She pulled it so hard it felt like it was going to come out at the roots! It took half an hour for the pain to die away. Touching is one thing, yanking is another.

This was definitely one of those occasions when John should have been thoroughly briefed beforehand.

When John was small I always cut his hair, a procedure he tolerated but certainly didn't like. After I started work (when John was six and a half) we found a really kind and gentle hairdresser who would come to our house. John always made a great scene when she started to cut his hair. He hated having to sit still for so long, not that he actually sat particularly still. We let him read for most of the hair cutting session as this was the best way of keeping him relatively calm. When John grew older my husband used to take him to a local barber where they were so quick that he didn't protest too much about going. For years after he left home he continued to use the same barber as before, combining a visit to us with a hair cut. Finding a barber near to his new home was just too much for him at the time. After we moved to the north of England (too far for John to visit us so often) and before he'd found a local barber, John used to turn up with horrendous looking hair which hadn't been cut (or washed) for ages. On one occasion I offered to cut his hair (*after* I'd washed it) as I'd been cutting my husband's hair ever since our move. John let me start and then began fussing and complaining that I was just an amateur and he didn't want an amateur cutting his hair! As far as John is concerned 'hair is a pain source':

> The only people I'm happy to have messing with mine are people with neural links to tell them 'no harder' (that would be me), and people who are good enough that they don't need those links (i.e. professionals in the hairistic field).

We came to an agreement that I would never touch his hair again if it had been cut already when he arrived at our house. The threat of a haircut from me worked, as John describes:

> It's true I put off finding a barber until then: there didn't seem to be any point looking until I had to. After that, well, it was easy: I walked down the road and picked the first unpretentious place that seemed to focus on *cutting* rather than *styling* and used that forever more... I happened to be with Ed, so I had the advantage of a confirmation from him that yes, this place isn't bad.

This quote is so typical of John, illustrating as it does a dislike of fashion and design, probably a desire not to spend more money than necessary on anything related to his appearance, procrastination when he's not sure how to do something and a lack of confidence about some of the simplest things, particularly when they involve interacting with others. After he bought his own house and after some nagging/encouragement from me, John found an acceptable (professional!) barber and always tries to visit him before we meet. A few years ago he wrote that he had no problems having his hair cut these days:

> [But] hair cutting is boring and so avoided until the hair gets in the way of something else (e.g. headphones) or puts me at risk of e.g. having you cut my hair; the razor-on-back-of neck part of getting your hair cut is horrible, but I expect that *everyone* hates that.

These days he also finds that his head itches if his hair needs cutting.

PAIN

John didn't seem to suffer from the pain of teething nearly as much as his sister; she cried a lot as her teeth were coming through. In fact when John was small he didn't seem to feel any pain when he hurt himself. When he fell over he never cried and I, in my ignorance, used to praise him for being such a brave boy. As Tony Attwood (1998) points out, the lack of reaction to pain can be dangerous:

> One of the most worrying aspects for parents is how to detect when the child is in chronic pain and needs medical help. Ear infections or appendicitis may progress to a dangerous level before being detected.

I was really surprised to find, when John was about seven years old, that he suddenly started crying like other children when he fell over. John thinks it's interesting that he didn't seem to feel any pain:

Maybe I just ignored it? I have no real memory of pain when young, even though I have plenty of memories of falling over and things before seven. I'd just look down at the graze and think, oh, it hurts, let's not do that again, and move on. It's almost as if pain didn't have an emotional component at all.

As an adult John wrote to me: 'As far as I know I've always been as sensitive to pain as the next man. I can block it off and ignore it if it's not very intense and it's trying to stop me doing something I care about.'

It did seem strange that, while John was young and apparently not feeling the pain of falling over, he should hate being undressed, washed and so on. This apparently contradictory behaviour seems hard to understand but is pretty typical of children on the autism spectrum. At the time I never thought of John's reactions to touch, temperature and pain as being unusual. Given the complexity of the human brain perhaps it's unreasonable to expect all children to develop in the same way. Acceptance, understanding, tolerance and a willingness to make accommodations and allowances for sensory differences can make life so much easier for children and adults on the autism spectrum.

Light Intensity

When John was about 10 months old (calculated from my expected delivery date), we went on a camping holiday to the Eifel area of Germany, near the Belgian border. It was a wonderful holiday, with glorious weather in a beautiful part of Germany and John was as good as gold. It was lovely to have this family time together without Tony having to go to work. One day we decided to explore a picturesque small town nearby, Tony carrying John on his back in a baby carrier. Everything had been going absolutely smoothly until the moment we decided to look round a large and impressive church. As we pushed the heavy wooden doors open and walked from the bright sunshine into the slightly dank and dimly lit interior, John let out a continuous piercing scream as if he was being murdered. We backed out of the church hastily and the moment we were back in the sunshine the scream stopped as quickly as it had started. After a few minutes we tried again. We pushed the heavy doors open and again, as soon as we stepped inside, John started to scream blue murder. Again we beat a rapid retreat and again he stopped screaming immediately and was his normal happy self. Was it the change in temperature that had upset him with the sudden feel of cool air on his skin? Was the dramatic change in light intensity from bright sunshine to a very gloomy church responsible for John's reaction? He seemed to find something about the sudden change in conditions quite intolerable. Although we hadn't got a clue as to what was going on and why John was so upset, we just solved the problem in as practical and simple a way as possible. We could have abandoned the idea of looking round the church or we could have forced the issue and taken John inside, hoping he would get used to it and stop screaming. However neither of these solutions suited us; Tony and I proceeded to look round the church separately without John.

In general our approach to many of the unusual situations we found ourselves in (as a result of John's personality and behaviour) consisted of identifying a problem, rather than hiding it under the carpet, and finding a practical way round the difficulty even if we didn't understand the reason for the behaviour. In some cases, such as this one, we didn't have to worry about any outcomes resulting from our actions as it didn't really matter whether we went round the church or not. However on many occasions, as well as thinking of simple solutions to the problems we encountered, we also had to think about any possible unintended consequences and make sure we didn't create new difficulties for the future. Some lateral thinking, flexibility, imagination, simplicity and above all not worrying about other people's reactions, were key to our approach to child rearing.

EYE CONTACT

My god-daughter Helen, who was a few years older than John and only saw him occasionally, recalls:

> I could relate to him and I did like him, but I found him a bit strange. He wouldn't smile or make eye contact much or at all. Sometimes grunted rather than using words. Primary age.

Although John made excellent eye contact with us when he was very young, this changed as he grew older and by the time he was 11 his eye contact was very poor. Unfortunately I don't know exactly when this process started or how gradual it was because I was so close to the situation that I didn't really notice anything unusual. My husband became aware of it when John was about eight. Poor eye contact was particularly evident at secondary school, when it became obvious that John was unable to process what the teachers were saying at the same time as looking at them. Unfortunately it's all too easy to assume, that if the person you are talking to doesn't look at you, they're not listening. However in John's case this was far from the truth, at least some of the time. Sometimes his mind *had* gone off on some tangent because of something he'd heard. This became all too obvious when he would pipe up with a question not remotely linked to what the teacher was currently talking about. However, as John noted: 'Only sometimes that meant I *was* listening and had spotted a c onnection nobody else had.' I remember one of his French teachers saying to me (when John was about 12), that the only way he could tell if John was listening and understanding what was being said (in French) was to say something funny and see if John smiled. According to Luke Jackson, who has been diagnosed with Asperger's syndrome and wrote the book *Freaks, Geeks and Asperger Syndrome* as a teenager:

> To find out whether your child or the person you are working with or talking to is listening, the easiest way is to ask them a question related to what you have just said. If they answer and are obviously listening, then personally I think it is irrelevant whether they are looking at you or not.

> When I look someone straight in the eye, particularly someone I am not familiar with, the feeling is so uncomfortable that I cannot really describe it. First of all I feel as if their eyes are burning me and I really feel as if I am looking into the face of an alien... if I get past that stage and don't look away, then whilst someone is talking I find myself staring really hard and looking at their features and completely forgetting to listen to what they are saying...

> Sometimes it is too hard to concentrate on listening and looking at the same time.

John agrees with Luke:

The sensory overload is quite hard to handle. I only get the 'face of an alien' thing ('face of another species', perhaps) when an autistic wave hits. I speculate that this may be a consequence of the overloaded and underdeveloped face-reading system shutting down completely in exhaustion, and suddenly look! I can't read his face at all, not even a little bit! Must be the face of an animal, a cartoon character, an alien, but clearly not a human being.

We never tried to make John look directly at people as we accepted that this was his natural way of interacting. However, when he grew older and we were trying to prepare him for interviews, we did try to persuade him that it was important to look directly at the interviewer when he first met them and shook their hands. It's unfortunate that most people feel uncomfortable if the person they're talking to doesn't look at them directly or stares at them. The former can make someone look shifty and makes it hard to create a rapport; the latter can look rude. Jackson (2002) has some interesting things to say about eye contact:

> Adults seem to make a really big deal of getting people to look at them when they are talking. Apparently it is seen as rude if you don't look at least in the direction of the speaker. This world is full of so many stupid rules! I really hate this one.

John doesn't agree that there are 'so many stupid rules':

> The problem here is that it isn't a rule, it's a neurological tendency tied up with social modelling. It is beneficial to look at someone else's eyes because the muscles around the eyes serve as a hard-to-forge indicator of the other's emotional state (assuming you can read it). Thus, if someone is looking away from you it is often an indication that they are trying to disguise their true emotional state by making it hard for you to read those muscles – thus, shifty. It's not a stupid rule, it's sensible and works – *if* both participants can send and receive those hard-to-forge signals. It's got nothing to do with finding out if people are listening, though: it's a component of the cheater-detection system. (I suspect the relative absence of this system in people with Asperger's may be one reason why we are fairly easy to take advantage of.)

As it happens, John's eye contact has improved enormously in recent years and is unlikely to make people feel *too* uncomfortable although, as mentioned in Chapter 5, the tendency for his eyes to look in different directions can be somewhat disconcerting. John understands this: 'I know I'm seriously put off by it in other people (even much less severe cases), and whenever I see myself in a mirror I wonder how anyone else can talk to anyone who looks that freaky.' John hadn't been aware, until I pointed it out, that his eye contact had improved: 'Yes, looking back, I suppose it has. Reduced social nervousness would be the reason: looking at people isn't so frightening now.'

VISUAL PROCESSING

For some years John, who finds formal clothes uncomfortable, had enjoyed going to work on a Friday in casual clothes. Amazing as it may seem and despite the fact that he was sitting in an open plan office, it took John over a year to realise that (after his firm had been taken over) casual clothes were now being worn by everyone *every* day! He just hadn't noticed. As John recalls:

> It was obvious in hindsight, but I don't normally look at people's clothes anyway (other than to notice that they're wearing some), and since some people wore things like bright red formal shirts, and nobody wore jackets after getting in anyway, the difference between smart casual and suits in areas near the face wasn't that great (and how often do you look at people's legs? OK, normal men probably look at female legs all the time, but the dress code was sexist before: smart-casual for women, suits for men.)

This lack of awareness of what others were doing (or wearing) has been very obvious ever since John was small; as a consequence he's found it difficult to learn by copying others. He never seemed to spend any time watching other people, perhaps because he didn't find it interesting or, as John points out, he may have 'found it overwhelming'. Instead he was always busy concentrating on something mechanical, or a book, or when he was older, on the computer. We became even more aware of this trait when his sister was born and we saw to what an extent she watched what was going on around her and how quickly she learnt by imitating what she saw. It's really not surprising that human beings have remained such a mystery to John. He had great difficulty reading body language and, until relatively recently, had no idea if the person he was talking to was getting bored, didn't understand what he was saying, or was getting annoyed. This is a characteristic attribute of many people on the autism spectrum. It's meant that over the years, due to his lack of observational skills, John has learned far less of practical value from the world around him than might be expected from someone of his intelligence. Rogers and colleagues (2012), who believe that early intervention can promote imitation skills, describe in detail how children on the autism spectrum can be taught these skills:

> Children learn by watching others and doing what they do... Most young children are natural mimics. They copy what they see their parents do; they copy the sounds and the gestures their parents make and the words they say; they even copy how their parents walk and dress. They often favor imitating other children – especially their brothers and sisters, as well as kids who are the same age or a little older and whom they admire...

> Imitation is an especially powerful tool for learning how to interact socially with others. This is because social behavior involves many complex and subtle rules, many of which we haven't consciously thought about...

> We think... that the decreased motivation to imitate may be responsible for a significant part of the delays most young children with ASD show in all areas of development. Imitation is one of the most important skills a young child with autism can learn, because it is such a learning tool by itself and helps children learn so many different types of skills. Children who do not imitate may miss much of the learning that just observing the goings-on in the social environment makes available...

> Fortunately, it's clear from research that young children with ASD can learn to imitate others well and naturally when their own motivation and attention to imitate are increased.

When I asked John recently whether it was true that he had no wish to copy other people, he denied it strongly. Then he added:

[However] others' behaviour generally seemed so incomprehensible, reprehensible or dull that I didn't *want* to emulate them, even if I could work out what they were doing… I emulate those I respect, specifically those behaviours I agree with or admire. Isn't that true of everyone? I just don't respect very many people! 'Peer pressure' certainly has little or no effect on me: the emulation, or not, is a conscious decision.

However he admitted later that this wasn't strictly accurate as it depended on the identity of the peers:

Oh, and I lied: peer pressure *does* have an effect on me: but my peers are a bunch of hackers scattered across the world. At school my peers were a tiny group of friends, not the general mass.

It seemed to me as if conscious imitation of those John respects is something that started relatively recently, perhaps in John's early twenties, and is something that has made it easier for him to get along with others and for them to get on with him. However, John believes he's been consciously imitating others for much longer than this:

I've been doing it for a *long* time, as long as I can remember, but for a very long time there were few people I was willing to emulate, and I had to start with simple stuff and work up to higher-order behaviours.

This certainly makes sense to me because it's probably *only* since John was able to imitate the more complex behaviours of those around him that he seemed to fit in more easily. I know there are situations where John will consciously think: 'What would my father do in these circumstances?' and this will then guide his behaviour. John agrees that this type of emulation 'is fairly recent, probably in the last ten years, as I've become more aware of how worthy of emulation he is in matters of courtesy and morality and general decency and so on!'

I'll never forget the parent-teacher meeting we attended one evening in December, when John was about six and a half. His teacher was very experienced and caring but to our dismay she told us that John was completely incapable of copying anything from the blackboard. He could read what was written but when he took his eyes away from the board, he couldn't remember enough to write anything down. Moreover she'd also discovered that he couldn't spell at all, not even short and simple words such as '*and*' and '*the*'. She'd never met a child who could read well but couldn't spell a single word or copy anything from the board. As there was only one teacher for a class of about 30 children and no teaching assistants or classroom helpers, John was sent to the library to read whenever there were writing activities in the class. As an avid reader this must have seemed like heaven. The fact that other children were doing things he was unable to do hadn't appeared to distress him enough for it to be mentioned to me and so I was completely unaware of what was going on until the parent-teacher meeting. Had he actually noticed what the other children were doing? His teacher had handled the situation so gently and tactfully that John just enjoyed his extra reading sessions in the library. From John's viewpoint:

I recall getting frustrated by not being able to spell, but I didn't mention it because, well, I was reading lots instead. I don't know if I consciously thought 'the teachers will tell Mum if necessary': I don't know if I thought it through that much. There were *books* to read.

The methods we used to solve John's spelling difficulties are described in Chapter 15. During John's pre-school years it was very obvious that he had a problem with certain visual activities. He had enormous difficulty posting shapes into the simple pillar box toy that we owned; this only had a square, circle, triangle and thin letter shaped rectangle to post into. The complex posting toy which we owned, which was spherical and had many more holes of different shapes, was even more impossible for him. Eventually we were able to help him match the shapes by verbalising the task. We described each shape and taught him to find the hole with the same description e.g. a perfectly round circle with no straight edges, a figure with six equal sides, a figure with three sides etc. Of course this was much slower than simply looking at the shape and seeing which hole looked the same but it did get round the problem. Breaking tasks down and verbalising them has been a useful strategy that helped John deal with some of the situations he found problematic. As far as he's concerned, these days 'breaking tasks down and verbalising them is basically my job!' John's problems with recognising shapes easily, made anything to do with jigsaw puzzles difficult. Although we spent a great deal of time doing jigsaws together and John enjoyed this shared activity, he couldn't do even the simplest puzzles on his own. Having a picture to copy or a picture to complete didn't seem to make the jigsaw any easier for him. It seemed to be the opposite of some autistic children who are so good at puzzles that they can do them even when the picture is hidden. One of John's major problems was that he couldn't see how to rotate the jigsaw pieces so as to make them fit the available space. Even when he was 15 years old John did badly on a task in the psychometric WISC test (see Chapter 20) which required the completion of a simple animal jigsaw. He didn't realise that a simple rotation would have dealt with the problem of a leg sticking out of the animal's back! Recently John wrote: 'I still have hopeless trouble with jigsaws. I have to actually physically test-rotate every piece and then visually scan for a possible match. I can't do it mentally at all.' This difficulty is apparent in everyday life. For example, John finds it difficult to recognise when something, such as a pan on the cooker, should be rotated so that the handle doesn't get in his way.

Visual-motor integration, or hand-eye coordination, is also a major weakness of John's. Lisa Kurtz (2006) describes visual-motor integration as follows:

> Visual-motor integration refers to the ability to integrate visual information with fine motor movement. It is the skill that allows the child to anticipate where to place his or her hand in order to catch a moving ball, or how to move the hand in a precise manner to write a letter or word...

> Visual-motor integration is a critical component of early childhood learning... It is the skill that underlies learning to cut with scissors, use a pencil, manage clothing fasteners, and manipulate a variety of toys, and classroom tools and materials.

As a child, John had great difficulty managing all of the above activities. Further details can be found in Chapter 8.

Because of his poor visual memory, John adamantly refused to play any short term memory games. (See Chapter 14.) He also had difficulties with visual sequencing. For example, learning the order of the letters in the alphabet remained a major problem for years after he could read; this made it hard for him to use a dictionary. The sequence of letters in the alphabet has to be learned, as it is quite arbitrary (or as John says: 'Isn't arbitrary, exactly, but it's determined purely by history') and completely lacking in logic. We tried using various toys which ought to have helped him learn the alphabet but in retrospect they were unsuccessful because they tended to rely on good visual skills of one sort or another. As described in Chapter 14, there are methods we *could* have used (if only we'd realised) which *didn't* rely on John's poor visual skills.

When John was about eight and a half he was sent by his school for an assessment at a local children's centre (see Chapter 20). Included in the written report was the following:

His visual sequential memory is at a very low level. This is his inability to hold a sequence of pictures, in the correct orientation, in his short term memory long enough to recall them accurately five seconds later. He also experienced some difficulty copying the abstract designs which although these remained in front of him, he rearranged on the page.

They recommended some visual perception books which I bought and which John enjoyed working through with me. This report certainly explained why John had been unable to learn the alphabet, copy from the board or spell the words he could read so easily.

At secondary school we discovered that he *still* couldn't put pictures in the correct order to tell a story, an exercise that he was expected to do as part of his French homework. When given a set of pictures which depicted a simple sequence of events, such as getting up in the morning, getting dressed, eating breakfast, cleaning teeth, leaving the house, going to school etc., he didn't have a clue how to put them in the correct order. He was diverted by the detail, couldn't see the whole picture, couldn't see that one event led to another and couldn't appreciate the overall story that was being told. This focus on detail and inability to see the whole picture is a feature of many on the autism spectrum; psychologists call the phenomenon *weak central coherence*. I tried to teach John to verbalise what was happening in each picture and think about what would happen before and after each picture, i.e. the order of events. He had to be taught slowly how to do something that most children could do automatically, and although he improved enough to manage his French homework, he never found it easy to put a set of pictures into a logical order. I have no idea if John can do it now that he is an adult but I suspect there is still a weakness as he has difficulty noticing the sequences involved in people's behaviour. John says:

It's distinctly troublesome. I have to laboriously test each possibility in turn: the right answer doesn't 'pop out' as I suspect it does for others. (This is a classic sign of conscious serial versus unconscious parallel processing. The latter is many orders of magnitude faster.)

Lisa Kurtz (2006) devotes a whole chapter in her book *Visual Perception Problems in*

Children with AD/HD, Autism, and Other Learning Disabilities to activities that can be carried out with a child to improve their visual skills. It's full of excellent ideas which I would have been happy to use if I had been aware of them.

The psychometric WISC tests (see Chapter 20) which were carried out when John was both seven and 15, show that at both ages there were very large discrepancies between his verbal and visual abilities. When he was seven, John's Verbal IQ was calculated from these tests as 45 points higher than his Performance IQ and when he was 15, it was measured as 40 points higher. Performance IQ measures, amongst other things, visual sequential, visual spatial and visual motor skills, all of which functioned at a significantly lower level than his verbal abilities. Such high discrepancies are unusual. According to the report produced by the educational psychologist who tested John when he was 15, these are likely to occur in less than 1% of the population.

One very large difference between John and the majority of other children was his almost complete lack of interest in television. The only programmes he ever wanted to watch were either factual or humorous and there weren't many of these. John remembers enjoying cartoons because of their escapist element. Was this lack of interest in the visual medium of television in any way related to the fact that he seemed to be unaware of what those around him were doing? If you do not, or cannot, observe those around you, aren't interested in what others do in real life or can't understand it, watching people on television might hold few attractions. On the other hand, was it related in any way to his very poor visual sequential memory? If you can't remember what you saw a few seconds ago it certainly makes it very difficult to follow a plot. My father, who was once an avid television watcher, stopped watching the box entirely when his dementia grew so severe that he was unable to keep much in his short term memory. John doesn't think this was the problem, pointing out: 'This is I think disproved by the fact that I could enjoy written fiction.' If we'd possessed a video recorder when John was very young, I'm sure he would have watched a few things again and again, like many children on the autism spectrum. In recent years John has started watching boxed sets of DVDs on his computer and is now capable (when he's visiting us) of watching some films with us on television as well. Further detail about John and television watching can be found in Chapter 18.

John wrote to me in his twenties: 'Looking at reflections, bouncing reflections off things, and suchlike is something I've always been attracted by (although the attraction has weakened over time)'. We have a lovely photo of John, aged about 10 months, hunched up on the floor in order to look at himself in the shiny metal surface of our kitchen waste bin. It could be that John's fascination with the appearance of water as a child was connected with the play of light on it as well as with its movement. Perhaps it induced a feeling of tranquillity and calm. Deborah Lipsky and Will Richards, writing in their book *Managing Meltdowns*, describe how sensory stimulation can sometimes be calming for some people on the autism spectrum: 'For some of us the touch of fur or watching running water is calming.' They chose two interesting examples as both of these were particular favourites of John's.

Both our children seemed to love thunderstorms. I remember one night, when the children were quite small and we were staying in the Norfolk fens with their wonderful huge skies, there was an amazing storm. The whole family watched in wonder at the incredible lightning display and neither of the children were frightened. John still remembers this storm, describing it as 'the power of nature unleashed'. To this day John is fascinated by storms and will go outside to get a better view, and yes, he does know that he shouldn't stand under a tree or any other tall object! A few years ago he wrote:

> So I was sitting down hacking... when blue-white light started flicking through the patio doors. Then it started *pouring* in. The storm was here. I stood outside on the green across from the railway line for *half an hour* watching it, with a silly grin on my face. The thunder was continuous and the lightning nearly so; so I certainly didn't need a torch. It's still going on at a reduced level. Amazing.

Although I thoroughly appreciate the extraordinary experience he was having, as a concerned mum I can't help wondering whether he was wearing enough clothing to keep himself dry! As John wrote though:

> Even an unobservant madman like me isn't going to go out in a vertical river without putting on a wetsuit! Unfortunately there was so much condensation inside it and the rain was so strong that I was almost as wet inside as out.

SOUND

Many people on the autism spectrum are sensitive to sound, as Tony Attwood describes in his book *A Complete Guide to Asperger's Syndrome*:

> Clinical observation and personal accounts of people with autism and Asperger's syndrome suggest that there are three types of noise that are perceived as extremely unpleasant. The first category is sudden, unexpected noises... such as a dog barking, telephone ringing, someone coughing, a school fire alarm, the clicking of a pen top or crackling sounds. The second category is high-pitched, continuous sounds, particularly the sound of small electric motors used in domestic electrical equipment such as food processors or vacuum cleaners or the high-pitched sound of a toilet flushing. The third category is confusing, complex or multiple sounds such as occur in shopping centres or noisy social gatherings.

I wasn't aware that John ever had any particular problem with the first two categories of noise; as a young child he seemed to enjoy the washing machine, vacuum cleaner, electric mixer, fireworks and striking clocks. However, John says he finds unexpected noises 'annoying if I'm trying to sleep, and can wake me up. High-pitched squeals of failing bulbs, likewise'. He disliked the sound of barking dogs but I think that was related to a generalised fear of dogs as unpredictable animals that could either bite or jump up and knock him over. The third category of noise though has been the cause of much distress. Although I wasn't aware of any undue sensitivity to sound when John was small, it's possible that his screaming (when he was about a year old) in the presence of a group of similarly aged babies, may have been due to excessive noise levels (see Chapter 12). At the time I felt that it had more to do with the invasion of John's personal space but I could have been mistaken. Once he started school it was obvious that John was easily distracted by the sounds going on in the classroom. He found it difficult to filter out the relevant from the irrelevant. This made it very hard for him to concentrate on what the teacher said when there was other conversation going at the same time. The problem has remained with John to this day; he still 'can't hear people over five other people talking'. For this reason working in an open plan office was very stressful. In recent years John used an iPod with noise cancelling earphones to listen to music while he was in the office. This helped to calm him, aided his concentration and reduced (but didn't eliminate) the distracting effect of telephone calls and conversations around him. For further details see Chapter 13. Attwood (2006) suggests that the use of silicone earplugs or listening to music through a headset can be helpful strategies for those who are very sensitive to noise:

> We are starting to recognise that listening to music using headphones can camouflage the noise that is perceived as too intense and enable the person to walk calmly round the shopping centre or concentrate on work in a noisy classroom.

These adaptations to a noisy environment didn't exist when John was a school boy and would have been of little use in school while the teacher was actually talking. Nevertheless something similar *might* have helped John concentrate when he was young and expected to work at a small table with others. Certainly it would have been worth considering but wearing earphones would have created yet another difference between him and the other children making him appear even more 'weird'. As always each situation has to be judged on its merits and some sort of compromise sought. There is rarely an easy answer and all one can do is one's best in a given situation. I find it fascinating that John seems able to listen to music and read at the same time (something I've never been able to do) but can't listen to a teacher and take notes at the same time. His inability to take notes at secondary school or university was a real problem; he found himself, time and time again, having to prepare for examinations with virtually no notes to revise from.

As a keen science fiction (SF) reader, John used to meet other people with similar interests in a pub in London. However, as he recalls: 'The London Circle SF meeting got too popular recently and is currently meeting in an underground room, a cacophony of echoes: I can't hear a thing.' As a result John stopped going which I thought was a shame; he used to enjoy these meetings and it was the only regular social group he attended. Now that he's moved further away from London he attends a local SF book group which meets every month in a quiet café. Both my son and husband hate crowds, particularly in enclosed spaces such as shops, parties or noisy pubs. In fact both of them will go out of their way to avoid such situations if at all possible. This dislike of crowded places appears to arise from the overall noise level, from an inability to hear what anyone is saying (and thus the impossibility of carrying on a proper conversation) and from a claustrophobic feeling generated by the impression of people pushing in. The whole experience leads to an overwhelming feeling of panic and need to escape: 'I know how I feel about shopping when it is crowded (standard panic oh no... it's-crowds-get-out-of-here constricted feeling: a triggered autistic wave).' Amanda Kirby (1999), writing about children with developmental dyspraxia, describes the problem they may have in crowds:

> The child may not be able to filter out unnecessary sounds... Other children seem to be able to filter out the extraneous sounds and decide which are the most important ones... A child who has dyspraxia may find this very difficult and feel he is being bombarded by sounds.

In the early 1990s I went to an excellent demonstration by Sidney Chu, a paediatric occupational therapist, who was the first person to say that many of John's coordination problems, including his truly dreadful writing, were due to dyspraxia or developmental coordination disorder (DCD). This demonstration attempted, very successfully in my case, to simulate the inability to filter out unwanted noise. A large classroom was arranged so that everyone sat in rows facing the front; in the middle of the rows there was a central gangway, effectively dividing the classroom into two halves. Someone sat in front of each half and read a different story aloud to the people sitting in the rows in front of them, both stories going on at the same time. The audience had to block out the sound of the reader in front of their row of chairs and listen to and answer questions about the story being read to those sitting across the gangway. It was really hard to do and took a lot of concentration. It made one appreciate how difficult and tiring it is if you cannot filter out unwanted sounds.

Ever since he was a child, John has liked background noise in his bedroom at night, at a level that many other people would find very disturbing. He had a pair of gerbils in a large fish tank in his bedroom for many years. The noise they made at night digging tunnels, scrambling around and chewing was such that his friend Phil (who used to stay regularly and slept on the floor of John's bedroom on a mattress) found it really hard to sleep. According to John: 'If I recall rightly, the gerbils were in such a position that they would kick bedding onto Phil as he slept. I can understand finding night-time bombardment a little hard to take!' Our son can still reproduce the sounds the gerbils made and remembers the pleasure he felt knowing that the animals were well and happy. As an adult, John slept for many years with a noisy computer in his bedroom: when he removed it, because it wasn't working properly, the resulting silence meant he was easily woken by noises from outside the house. In order to restore his undisturbed sleep John put a white noise generator in the bedroom, which reduced the noise from his neighbours and from cars going over nearby speed bumps. Perhaps the background noise had acted as a white noise generator. As mentioned in Chapter 5, John's hearing is actually very acute: 'I can hear people talking at normal conversational volume at the other end of the street if the surroundings are quiet enough. Guess why I like fans and music and white noise generators.'

BALANCE

For many years John was unable to sit still on a chair. When sitting at the dinner table he would lean back so far that the chair was on two legs only; this really worried my husband. I think he was terrified that John would fall backwards and hurt himself as well as breaking the chair. Funnily enough I can't remember him ever actually falling backwards. 'No, never', said John:

> The balance was the thing. I don't understand why it scared Tony after he'd seen me do it for such a long time. (It's not as if falling over backwards would do me more damage than I'd done to myself by running into things anyway.)

Interestingly Rubinstien (2005) wrote:

> Kids with NLD have trouble sitting still. Their difficulties with balance, and their need for sensory... stimulation, makes it difficult for them to sit quietly in the

79

type of straight-backed chair traditionally used by families in Western cultures at mealtimes. (Most kids with NLD also lean back as far as they can in any car seat or movie seat.) We have actually had to replace our kitchen chairs twice over a period of ten years because they couldn't take the unnatural angles that were demanded of them during dinner.

As well as tipping his chair back, John would wriggle constantly when he was sitting down. This irritated my husband enormously, particularly if we were going to a play, concert or film when the ability to sit still is quite helpful! John would wriggle even more if he became agitated about something but a firm hand placed over *his* hand seemed to calm him down. If John went to a concert we let him take a book to read; this enabled him to keep still and helped him concentrate on the music. As John reached his late teens he started to wriggle far less and now sits as still as anyone else. As John recalls: 'Every position used to be uncomfortable if I held it for more than a few seconds, but that passed away, and now most positions seem comfortable until my muscles start to cramp.' I remember how surprised John's teachers used to be (when he was 11 and in his new school) to find him suddenly out of his seat and standing by their desk to ask a question. He found it very hard to stay put for an entire lesson and didn't seem to notice that no-one else behaved like this. Fortunately this soon sorted itself out, no doubt with plenty of encouragement from the teachers. On the other hand John 'still can't think hard without walking around'.

I wasn't aware that John had a particularly poor sense of balance but the paediatric physiotherapist who assessed him when he was 21, observed that (amongst other problems) he had difficulties with girdle stability, balance and coordination. As John puts it:

I can balance fine on two legs as long as nothing goes too wrong; if it does go wrong a hand may have to help out too. One leg, forget it; muscle tremors do me in if nothing else does. But balancing on one leg seems like a fairly useless skill to me, anyway.

Nevertheless John learned to ride a bike relatively easily although his control of the machine was poor (see Chapter 8).

When John was young and sitting in a child seat, every car journey of more than an hour or so was marred by the fact that he would be sick. This may have been associated with the workings of his vestibular system although John doesn't think it was anything to do with the motion:

[Our old car] always smelt really strongly of this sort of rotten plastic petrol stench once it warmed up and it made me feel sick immediately. (I'm not sure if it really was petrol. Just *remembering* the smell makes me feel sick. Perhaps the smell was just an illusion *caused* by the nausea, but I've never experienced illusory smells elsewhere... mind you I've never been in another car that smelt like that either.)

Strangely enough, when John started to read in the car he stopped feeling sick even though the car still smelt the same! If I try to read in the car (as a passenger!) or on a bus I feel sick very quickly and I know many people react in the same way. John, though, appeared to concentrate so deeply on his book that he seemed unaware of the relative movement between himself and his surroundings. As described at the beginning of this chapter, the vestibular system is involved in maintaining muscle tone and posture as well as providing information to the body on movement relative to its surroundings. Interestingly enough, as described later in Chapter 8, John's muscle tone and posture have been poor from a very young age.

We never had a trampoline, or access to one, when John was young but like most children he loved bouncy castles. For a few years we *did* have an old spare mattress which both children loved bouncing on. If he was young now I would certainly like John to try trampolining; I suspect he would enjoy it enormously. It would be a good, uncompetitive, form of exercise, excellent for his muscle control and sense of balance. Luke Jackson (2002), diagnosed with Asperger's syndrome, describes rather beautifully how he finds trampolining a good way to chill out after a day at school:

> When it is warmer, I go outside onto our trampoline. We have a full sized one with a massive net around and I often just bounce around or lie there and let the cares of the day fall through to the ground like autumn leaves.

In a similar way, John enjoyed relaxing (with a book of course) in a hammock in the garden on a warm day. Unfortunately the hammock was very old and eventually rotted and fell apart.

SMELL

I don't remember any instances where John's strong sense of smell caused him or us any problems, except perhaps for the smell of the old car. I know he loved the smell of my perfume and clothes and called it a 'mumsy' smell. As he wrote recently: '[I] still do, it hasn't changed, has it? It lasts, too: I can still smell it on the sheets you left me when I moved in (those I haven't used yet), even though that was years ago. (Am I imagining it? Perhaps.)' He's quite right. I've used the same perfume for over forty years and as it is oil based the smell lasts a long time. John couldn't resist pointing out: 'And she calls *me* resistant to change!' At secondary school John recalls: 'I simply hated the smell of hot metal in the metalworking shops... from the grinding wheels I think. I can almost smell it now. I've never smelt anything quite like it before or since.' As an adult he hated the smell of the traffic in London, where he rented a house for several years with friends. When he arrives at our house, which is located in a forest full of larch and Scots Pine, he always comments, as soon as he gets out of the car, on the wonderful smell. The house he lives in now is outside London and near to countryside and he is very aware of the fresh smell of the air there.

John has always had a tendency to sniff his food before eating it. I too have a very strong sense of smell and often smell my food before eating it as I get so much pleasure from the smell alone. I'm not sure to what, if any, extent John copied my behaviour. According to Williams and Wright (2004):

> Some parents say that their children regularly smell their food before eating it, apparently checking that it is familiar. In a recent survey we conducted of the parents of 50 children with ASD, 25% said that their children were influenced by the smell of their food.

What I find very strange is that, despite an apparently acute sense of smell, John could allow *himself* to smell so bad for so many years because of poor personal hygiene.

81

It was as if his dislike of the *feel* of washing was so strong it overcame all other senses; his lack of understanding of how others might react didn't help. It would appear that John is far from alone. Carolann Jackson,[34] when speaking about the impact of sensory issues on people with Asperger's syndrome, said:

> Smell can also affect food choices, and even though certain smells can (like perfume) be overpowering enough to cause vomiting, many Aspies are completely insensitive to their *own* smell. Frankly many of them *pong* really badly.

Commenting on this, John wrote: '[I am] still amazed that this isn't true of everyone. The nose acclimatises so fast… I can detect this sort of thing now, but not via smell: via stickiness and the texture of unwashed hair.'

In conclusion: John's sensory sensitivity (particularly to noise and temperature) provide a plausible explanation for *some* of John's more problematic behaviours.

7
Toilet Related

Although many children on the autism spectrum have no problem learning how to use the toilet and master this skill at a similar age to their peers, some of these children find the move away from nappies problematic. As Maria Wheeler wrote in her book *Toilet Training for Individuals with Autism & Related Disorders*:

> One of the most important skills we need to learn is how to use the toilet successfully and independently... Persons with autism have been reported by researchers as being the most difficult population to toilet train. Many techniques used to toilet train children are not sufficient when used to teach toileting skills to persons with autism.

Compared with the major difficulties some parents and carers have toilet training their children, the problems we had with John were minor, although they didn't seem so at the time.

LEARNING TO USE A TOILET

Although it was easy to teach John how to use a potty during the day, transferring from a potty to the toilet was quite another matter. It seemed as if John had said to himself: 'Why use a toilet when I'm perfectly happy with the potty?' Although we had a child step in front of the toilet, a special seat on it to fit his little bottom and John had watched his parents use the toilet for ages, this made absolutely no difference whatsoever. Telling him: 'Now that you're a big boy you can use the toilet as potties are for small children', or pointing out that all the children he knew were using a toilet, was just a waste of breath. At that age John couldn't care less what other people did, was happy to say so and had no particular desire to please or copy us. I was unable to find a good enough reason to persuade John to use the toilet instead of the potty. I was at my wits' end. As Lorna Wing (1996) pointed out so accurately:

> The trouble is that methods that work with other children are often no use at all with children with autistic disorders. Some of them seem to dislike or even fear the pot or lavatory... The flushing of the toilet may terrify some, though it can fascinate others.

> Resistance to change in an established routine is one of the reasons for delay in toilet training.

Stubbornness and dislike of change were (and still are) fundamental aspects of John's nature. My feeling, over the years, that I was always on the losing side of any discussion with John was repeated countless times in other situations; but John felt *he* was always on the losing side of any discussion also. Racking my brains one day as to how I could motivate John to use the toilet, I had an idea. Even though John was so young, we were aware that motivating him was critical to achieving change. We knew that he loved watching the movement of mechanical objects such as the washing machine and record

83

player and could watch them in action for very long periods of time. So one day I asked John to stand on the closed lid of the toilet and watch. I took the cistern lid off gently (putting it in the bath as this was the only space large enough to accommodate the lid in our tiny bathroom) and then I flushed the toilet. John watched enthralled as the water first rushed out of the cistern and then came back lifting the round float in the process. Then my master stroke! 'Every time you use the toilet I will take the cistern lid off and you can watch me flush the toilet.' It worked a treat. John was so excited by the thought of seeing the loo flush that he used the toilet happily from that moment on. Fortunately I never broke the cistern lid, despite taking it off hundreds of times. Eventually John grew out of the need to watch the flushing mechanism. Last year John wrote:

> I got enthralled by the mechanism all over again a couple of years ago when trying to diagnose the cause of my constantly leaking cistern pipe! I wonder if anyone's ever made a cistern and all components entirely out of transparent materials? A few lights to add appropriate sepulchral glows and it could be a really tacky work of art!

A companion to Marcel Duchamp's 1917 work of art, called *Fountain*, which consisted of a porcelain urinal?

GETTING CLEAN AND DRY AT NIGHT

Although we were successful with daytime potty training and eventually with use of the toilet, our efforts to get John clean and dry at night can only be described as an abysmal failure. It wasn't that John became dry at night and then reverted to wet and dirty nappies; he'd *never* been dry at night. I wake up at night (usually dreaming) if I need to go to the toilet; if I'm extremely tired and sleeping very heavily it might take a nightmare to wake me up. This mechanism didn't seem to be working for John. Once he fell asleep, John never seemed to wake up with the need to go to the toilet and even if he woke up, he was perfectly happy to remain in wet and dirty nappies. For a few years we just accepted the situation but as John grew older we discussed it with him occasionally; however, nothing changed. We did the obvious, such as ensuring that most of John's liquid intake was in the earlier part of the day with no drinks in the evening. We took him to the toilet just before we went to bed when he would usually have a pee even when he was virtually asleep. At this time of night his nappy would be dry but by the time we got up in the morning he was always wet and sometimes had a dirty nappy as well. We didn't know what to do about it. Perhaps if we'd left his nappies off for a long period of time this might have sorted the problem out but when we tried it for the odd night as an experiment, it made no difference. He just wet his night clothes and the bedding instead. We continued to keep John in nappies at night to avoid having to wash both him and his bedding every day, which I would have found rather stressful. There was a real danger that I would have taken my resentment out on John, which would have been so unfair as it wasn't his fault, just his physiology. I still feel guilty when I remember one particular incident that took place when John was about three and a half and his sister about two. I always tried to make no comment whatsoever when I changed John's nappy in the morning but one day I said in an exasperated voice: 'I do wish you wouldn't wet your nappy at night', or something to that effect. To my horror Lydia obviously thought the remark was addressed to her (they still shared a bedroom at the time) and *she* became dry at night from then onwards! Her brother, to whom the remark had actually been directed, stayed as wet as ever at night and seemed quite unaware of, or indifferent to, his sister's achievement. Williams and Wright (2004), who have two chapters in their book devoted to toileting issues, have this to say about children who have never been dry at night:

If your child is under 12, is still not dry at night and never has been, it is most likely that her nervous system has not yet matured enough to control night wet-ting. Using star charts or some of the other mechanisms mentioned will not work in these circumstances because it is not within the wilful control of the child. Re-member, about 5 per cent of ten-year-old boys *without* ASD will wet at night and 10 per cent of five-year-olds… You may have to wait until the child is older and the urinary and nervous systems have matured further. In these circumstances, don't worry.

However we didn't know any of these facts at the time and couldn't help worrying. As John grew older, we suspected that he might be wetting and soiling his nappy in the morning when he first woke up and so we decided to go in to him as soon as he was awake. This policy didn't work though as we were so tired and slept so heavily that we never really heard when John first woke up.

Night-time bed-wetting would have made it awkward for John to stay on his own at another child's house but as the need never arose when he was young that wasn't such a problem. The years marched on and still nothing had changed at night. He was now nearly 10 years old and as he grew older and bigger it became harder to find nappies to fit him. He was far too heavy to lift at night and hard to wake up and physically support for his 11pm walk to the toilet. We were growing increasingly concerned as secondary school and school trips loomed on the horizon. Although as John points out, his refusal to go away on any school trips meant 'that turned out not to be a problem – but you couldn't know that in advance, and certainly couldn't rely on it.'

We felt that we had to take some action. John accepted that something should be done and listened intently when we explained that we would hire a device that would be placed under his sheet and when the first drop of urine fell on it, a bell or buzzer would sound to wake him up so that he could visit the toilet. Although he acknowledged that this was a good idea in principle and understood exactly how the gadget worked, he was absolutely horrified at the thought of being woken up in such a way. You would have thought I was threatening to electrocute him if he ever wet his bed again. Williams and Wright (2004) point out that 'some children on the autism spectrum will not tolerate these devices'. John pleaded and pleaded for me not to hire the device and in the end we came to an agreement that we would stay buzzer free for another two weeks but if he was still wet at night at the end of this time then there would be no more arguments and we would definitely hire the equipment. To my complete surprise, the fear of having the device in his bed was so strong that he was clean and dry at night from then on and we never had to hire the machine. It doesn't feel good to realise that I had resorted (although unintentionally) to fear as a means of achieving a satisfactory outcome but I still don't know what else we could have done. I didn't wish to use medication and in any case I don't know if this would have been appropriate or successful. I was so relieved that the problem was sorted at last and that nobody had become too stressed during the years of night-time wetting. I'm still glad that we used nappies on John at night and thereby avoided the work (for us) and humiliation (for John) that would have been entailed in the daily changing and washing of wet and soiled clothes and bedding. Nevertheless, I've always wondered if I could have used this buzzer technique sooner, perhaps when John was seven or eight. If it was possible for the bell to be in our room rather than John's we could have woken him up when the bell rang and taken him to the toilet at the right time.

USING TOILETS OUTSIDE OUR HOME

When John was about nine we started taking three week camping holidays every summer in France and Germany. Initially John had no problems with the toilets on campsites but this phase didn't last long. Suddenly he refused to open his bowels any more in campsite toilets. According to John that's not quite accurate: 'No. Refused to *go into the room with the loo in it.* That was the fear (well, the room and the loo and the unfamiliarity all at once).' This refusal would go on for days on end until John was in such a terrible state that he was no longer able to eat. With gentle persuasion, which included my husband taking John into the toilets for an inspection, we were able to get him to use the toilets in restaurants. We managed to persuade him that restaurant toilets were more like home toilets rather than public toilets and he certainly knew how to relax in the toilet at home. Fortunately by this time we could afford to eat out sometimes during the holiday rather than cooking every meal in our tent. We can't be sure what caused John's problem but we think it may have been the poor and often very dirty sanitary facilities that we found on some French campsites. From this beginning John seemed to develop a fear of all campsite toilets (even if they were immaculate) and then *all* public toilets. Fortunately there wasn't a problem using urinals.

This fear of using public toilets then prevented John from using the cubicle toilets at secondary school. He had a long bus journey to school and back, leaving the house before eight am and not getting back until after five pm. He would be desperate for the toilet by the time he arrived home and the first thing he would do was rush up the stairs straight into the loo and bang the door shut. (According to John he wasn't desperate: 'I was used to going *days* without, after all. I was certainly *ready* to go, but I don't normally need to go more than daily anyway. It's nowhere near as problematic as it would be if I'd been female.') He would then spend well over an hour in the toilet reading (often aloud) and regularly roaring with laughter. It was John's way of winding down after school whereas many children prefer to watch television. Our second au-pair, who looked after John when he was nine, recalls: 'John loved reading and used to lock himself in the toilet for ages with a funny book. He was into Adrian Mole at this time.' It was fortunate that John *was* able to go to the toilet at home. Children who refuse to do a bowel movement anywhere for a prolonged period of time can have very severe constipation indeed and even stretch the colon.

Even in his twenties, when camping as a family near Venice, John didn't go to the toilet for several days. As these toilets were immaculately clean John was persuaded, with much encouragement from all of us, to stand in a cubicle for some time to accustom himself to the environment. Eventually, a couple of days later, he managed to use the toilet and there were no more problems for the rest of that holiday. Knowing the strength of John's fear in the past and suspecting it hadn't disappeared entirely, we'd been careful to choose a campsite with modern toilets. The toilets on many of the local sites at the time were nothing more than holes in the ground with depressions at the side for feet. As I wouldn't have wished to use these toilets myself for a ten day stay, I was pretty sure that our son wouldn't have gone anywhere near them. John says I was correct, writing to me a few years later: 'I still can't imagine myself using those. Appalling idea.'

The shape and design of the toilet still seems to be important to John. He particularly dislikes lavatory pans that have a flat section above the water level where waste products fall before they are flushed away, something seen quite often in mainland Europe. John says that he's worried that if he produces a lot of excreta it will come into contact with him, something most of us wouldn't like. John has no idea why he developed his fear of public toilets and still admits to 'intense uneasiness around strange loos', although these days, he says he can ignore this feeling. He thinks this is because 'the pointless fear faded with the passage of time and I used more public loos without anything bad happening'. However, he still doesn't go into public toilets located in town centres as he claims they are 'generally utterly disgusting'. I certainly remember a horrible experience in France when the children were young. We'd been wandering round a beautiful old French town (which will remain nameless) and needed to find a loo. We had a very long walk indeed to reach the only public facility and when we got there it was in such an indescribable state that none of us could bear to use it. It's certainly possible that such experiences have left their mark on John although his sister didn't react in the same way. According to John: 'The indescribable state mostly stayed in my mind as a truly disgusting conversational topic, not as a source of fear. (The fear was already there before we discovered that remarkable loo, I think.)'

To conclude: Using a toilet rather than a potty, becoming clean and dry at night and using public lavatories have all been issues at various times during John's life. As it isn't unusual for the parents of children on the autism spectrum to have some concerns related to the subject of toilet training their children, a list of helpful resources can be found in Appendix 28.

8

Motor Related

Motor difficulties can be associated with a variety of conditions, including cerebral palsy, Asperger's syndrome, non-verbal learning disability (NLD), and dyspraxia/developmental coordination disorder (DCD). Motor skills include gross motor skills (such as walking, running, jumping and climbing) and fine motor skills (such as dressing, writing, using scissors and manipulating cutlery). In addition to gross and fine motor skill deficits, John has motor planning difficulties. According to Kurtz (2008):

> Motor planning ability, also referred to as praxis, is the ability to conceptualize, plan, and carry out an unfamiliar motor task or motor sequence. It is different from motor coordination, which refers to the ability to control body movements in a smooth manner.

John wonders 'how much of this is related to my executive-function difficulties with planning *anything*, motor or not?'

Given these problems, it isn't really surprising that (once he could read) John spent most of his spare time with his head in a book rather than kicking a football around. Greenspan and Wieder (1998) describe John perfectly when they write:

> A child with motor-planning difficulties may avoid activities that require motor planning. For example, some children may favor reading because the only action required is turning pages.

PAEDIATRICIANS' REPORTS

Because of John's difficult beginning, he was seen regularly for several years by paediatricians from both of the hospitals that treated him as a baby. The early paediatricians' reports (see Appendix 6) appeared to suggest that there weren't any problems with John's motor development. At eight months John's reflexes were found to be 'present and equal' and he was thought to be 'developmentally normal'. When John was nearly two, a paediatrician said that he displayed a 'lack of co-operation' whilst building a tower. 14 months later he was unable to 'imitate a bridge made out of three bricks'. Problems imitating a sequence of actions (a symptom of motor planning difficulties), as well as poor manual skills, may have accounted for these findings but this wasn't recognised at the time. At 24 months, the paediatrician thought that John had 'more or less caught up with his early developmental delay and he seemed a very normal child'. When he was 32 months, John passed all four elements of the Denver Developmental Screening Test, which included an assessment of his gross and fine motor function. It was only when John was four years old that testing revealed some problems but even then it was thought that he had 'good coordination'. The suggestion that 'this hand/eye coordination problem… may cause problems later at school' proved to be all too accurate. John experienced great difficulties, particularly at secondary school, because he couldn't write fast and legibly; writing in any quantity made his hand hurt. It really makes you wonder how sensitive the Denver Screening tests were. I get the impression that these tests must have been designed to identify really disabling conditions such as cerebral palsy and not to recognise less severe motor problems such as DCD/dyspraxia. John was never referred for additional help and we were never encouraged to carry out any special activities with him to help with his hand-eye coordination.

Despite these paediatricians' reports (which we hadn't seen at the time), it became increasingly obvious to *us* that John had a variety of developmental problems. We found that, from an early age, John struggled to use his hands competently. He always looked awkward and clumsy and couldn't carry out actions such as waving goodbye, blowing his nose or drying his hands. Amazingly, waving goodbye is something he *still* struggles with. Recently he wrote: 'I've actually studied people waving now (via images on YouTube) and I *still* can't do it consistently. It's a really strange motion.'

Given John's early medical history, I was half expecting some problems. It wasn't entirely surprising to find that John had difficulty with many things that other children of his age found easy. However I was grateful that John's motor problems were relatively mild as he didn't have cerebral palsy, a known complication in very premature babies. I resolved to give him as much help as possible at home to overcome any problems that he experienced. John has always been extremely appreciative, commenting in an email: 'And you have! More than anyone could ask for!' Nevertheless I wish I'd been more aware of children's developmental milestones when John was young; I might have tried to obtain additional help for him as a result. A useful guide to these milestones can be found in the book *How to Detect Developmental Delay and What to Do Next* by Mary Mountstephen.

CRAWLING AND WALKING

All the paediatricians' reports say that John had low muscle tone (hypotonic). Not only was I unaware of any of these reports at the time but the concept of low muscle tone wouldn't have meant much to me anyhow. According to Wikipedia:[35]

> The low muscle tone associated with hypotonia must not be confused with low muscle strength... As it is an intrinsic property of the nervous system, it cannot be changed through voluntary control, exercise, or diet.

> True muscle tone is the inherent ability of the muscle to respond to a stretch...

> The child with low tone has muscles that are slow to initiate a muscle contraction, contract very slowly in response to a stimulus, and cannot maintain a contraction for as long as his 'normal' peers. Because these low-toned muscles do not fully contract before they again relax (muscle accommodates to the stimulus and so shuts down again), they remain loose and very stretchy, never realizing their full potential of maintaining a muscle contraction over time.

Despite the hypotonia, John went through all the stages of sitting, crawling and walking at perfectly acceptable ages (corrected for 11 weeks prematurity). He started to roll over at four months, sat with a straight back at eight months, crawled at eight and a half months, pulled himself up on the furniture into a standing position at nine months and walked unaided at 14 months. As for sitting with a straight back, John wrote recently: 'Nobody looking at me slouching in my chair now could believe it.' He crawled perfectly normally, very fast and very expertly; he crawled as much as walked for many months after learning to walk. By 18 months he was walking everywhere as well as crawling up and down stairs. The paediatrician noted that John was immature climbing stairs at 31 months as he used two feet to a step and couldn't jump off the bottom step. Seven months later he was able to climb up the stairs in an adult manner and jump off the bottom step; however, he still came down the stairs two feet to a step.

Given John's poor muscle tone he might have had far more trouble learning to crawl and walk. I believe, although there is no proof, that we did certain things which made it easier for John to learn to crawl and walk. The most important of these was placing him on his tummy to sleep. In those days this was what parents were advised to do but these days we wouldn't be willing to do the same again because of the reported link with cot deaths. We also put John down regularly on his tummy on the carpet. From this tummy down position he developed strong arms and a strong neck by lifting himself up to look around. This must have made learning to crawl much easier. John also enjoyed 'wheel-barrow walking', where he walked on his hands with his legs held by his parents. We never realised how good this would be for strengthening John's upper body. When he reached about five months of age (corrected for prematurity) we thought it would be a good idea to strengthen his legs. We put him on his back on the floor so that his feet could kick the same swinging baby chair that he'd already sat and played in for several months. He loved kicking this chair and learned to time his kick perfectly so that his foot hit the chair at exactly the right point in its travel. Meanwhile he would watch and laugh while the mobiles and sparkly Christmas decorations attached to the frame of the swinging chair moved with the impact of his feet. John also loved using a baby walker because he could chew the frame when he was teething as well as race around like some sort of demon driver.

John didn't wear shoes until he could walk well enough to go out on the pavement. Then I was fortunate enough to have plenty of time to let him walk outside rather than using a push chair. Although I'd never seen anyone else do it, and I know lots of people disapprove, I put reins on John from the very first day we went out for a walk. In the early days, when he was far from stable, it enabled me to haul him up as he stumbled and so prevent him from hurting himself on the ground. I remember the intense pleasure both of us experienced when, for the first time ever, John was able to decide what to touch and explore as we went for walks near our house. The fence, gate, walls, post box, trees and so on became objects that he could feel for the first time while I talked to him about what he was touching. Life in a sling, pram or pushchair is so passive. The world appears quite different when you can choose which direction to go in and what to touch, rather than being moved around by someone else.

John's leg muscles grew very strong as our family has always walked for pleasure; to this day he remains a keen and fast walker. Nevertheless, for most of his life John has looked slightly odd when he walks; he doesn't swing his arms, holding them away from his body in a rather rigid, bent position. Tony remembers that John's posture was fine when he was small, perhaps up to seven years old, but gradually became stiffer as he grew older, walking as he still does without his arms swinging. I was fascinated to discover that this type of gait was described by Gillberg (2002) as characteristic of many people with Asperger's syndrome:

> People with Asperger Syndrome can often be spotted because of their special, indeed sometimes very odd, motor performance. Their gait may be hypotonic, un-

gainly or stiff, often without accompanying arm swing.

As I was slightly concerned that John's unusual appearance (when walking as an adult) would attract unwanted attention and put him at risk of being attacked, I discussed this lack of arm swing with him on several occasions. I also tried (pretty unsuccessfully I must say) to get him to practise moving his arms as he walked. He wrote a few years ago: 'Certainly I walk without arm swing a lot; starting the swing up often feels artificial, and it stutters to a stop quite fast. The swing *does* happen when I'm running though.' I wasn't really aware that John ran often, certainly not as a form of exercise, but according to him 'I used to run *everywhere*. It faded in my mid-twenties as my metabolism slowed.'

Tony Attwood (2006) describes another conspicuous feature of some people with Asperger's syndrome: 'As two people walk side by side they tend to synchronise the movement of their limbs... The person with Asperger's syndrome appears to walk to the beat of a different drum.' When John was younger he seemed incapable of walking side by side. He would walk just in front, weaving from one side to the other, making it hard not to bump into him. It reminded me of the way cats and dogs get under one's feet in the kitchen. Lovecky (2004) observed that people with Asperger's syndrome 'may have difficulty walking in a straight path and so bang into others'. John has always bumped into things as well as people, as he recounts:

> Walking is sort of chaotic. Running into doors and edges of walls and things is most annoying: I've lost count of the number of glasses' frames I've bent that way. It doesn't help that I don't slow down when approaching obstacles.

One interesting observation is the way that hiking seems to make John talkative. John thinks he 'always had the habit of talking while walking – seems to turn the brain on.' Whenever John has to think deeply, for example when working on some difficult computer problem, he will pace around the room muttering. This seems to be in agreement with the work of Oppezzo and Schwartz (2014) who found that walking promotes creativity. I've certainly come across teachers and lecturers who paced a lot while thinking and talking to their students. Lydia finds John's non-stop talking really difficult when we go hiking as a family; she wants to enjoy the peace and quiet of the countryside. So it usually ends up with John and myself walking together, with him doing most (but by no means all) of the talking and Lydia and Tony walking a long way ahead out of earshot!

MANUAL DEXTERITY

The problems John experienced with hand-eye coordination were exacerbated by a small hand tremor. This made all practical tasks difficult and caused him significant problems throughout his childhood, particularly at school. Fortunately his manual skills continued to improve throughout his twenties but this remains an area of weakness and he often wishes he 'had more hands' when undertaking some manual task. In fact he has even gone so far as to say:

> If it wasn't for their short lifespans and lack of language, I think I'd quite like to be an octopus... the living in water bit might make it hard to read books and use computers as well, but I'm sure that could be overcome.

91

The fact that John was always carrying a book and frequently forgot to put it down before embarking on practical jobs only made matters worse! To this day he gets very frustrated, and is still likely to explode in anger, when he struggles with something requiring manual dexterity or when he drops something.

The only professional help John received when he was a child was some occupational therapy (OT) between the ages of nine and ten. A community occupational therapist came into the school once a week but after two terms we received a letter from the occupational therapist which stated:

[John] has made good progress in the areas of Postural Control, Balance and Protective Responses. His motor planning and visuo-spatial skills have also improved along with his general fine co-ordination. I feel that John has reached a plateau in the last few weeks and that it is now appropriate to cease therapy.

We interpreted this as 'we can't help him any more'. It was hard for us to assess what had been achieved as a result of these sessions as there was no communication whatsoever between the therapist and us (apart from this final letter) and we were never asked to carry out any exercises with him to reinforce what was happening in the therapy sessions. Lisa Kurtz (2008) describes the approach of some professionals in the past as follows:

In the past, many professionals have held the belief that developmental coordination problems do not warrant direct intervention because they may be outgrown as the children reach adolescence or adulthood. However, research has shown that this is not the case for most children... While many clumsy children appear less affected as they become older, this is most likely the result of learning to avoid situations that may cause frustration or failure. Failure to provide help for children with coordination difficulties exposes them to the risk of failure in performing school and social activities, frustration and loss of self-esteem, and ridicule and bullying by other children.

Spot on! John certainly suffered from all these side effects of poor coordination while he was at school. According to Sally Payne (2009):

Working with parents is an essential component of occupational therapy with children... The importance of parental involvement in occupational therapy with children who have a developmental co-ordination disorder has long been recognised... A more contemporary view of best practice occupational therapy with children and family is that of family-centred care in which parents become partners in the therapeutic process.

It's to be hoped that parents finding themselves in a similar situation today would have much more involvement with any therapy their child receives, assuming they were lucky enough to get any in the first place. I would strongly suggest that parents do something about it if this involvement is not automatically suggested. Make sure that you know what motor exercises your child has been given so that you can ensure that they're carried out regularly and can provide any necessary help, encouragement or bribery! Ideally the exercises will be fun so your child will enjoy doing them. Amanda Kirby (1999) cautions professionals not to give families too onerous a therapy programme to do with their child as they might not be able to fit this into their busy lives. She also advocates the use of exercises that can be incorporated into the family's usual activities and can be seen more as play than therapy.

As we received no advice we had to find our own ways of helping John cope with the everyday activities that involved manual dexterity. Although we succeeded to a certain extent, I suspect there's much more we could have done if we'd been able to access some of the information that's available these days. The key to those improvements that John made came from my experiences as an amateur cellist. Learning a musical instrument such as the piano, violin or cello isn't easy and the brain and fingers have to learn to do things that don't come naturally to the majority of us. The most effective way of improving one's technical ability on a musical instrument is to choose a task that isn't too difficult (i.e. learn to walk before learning to run), break it down into manageable chunks, find out the most efficient way to work on each of these chunks, practise *little and often* and finally don't put oneself under too much pressure by allowing insufficient time to master the new task. It's no good practising for ages one day and then doing nothing for weeks if one wishes to improve one's musical technique. A short burst of focused activity, repeated regularly, works wonders; the brain/eye/finger connections seem to improve on their own in-between the practice sessions. Knowing what it felt like to struggle with the technical difficulties of playing a cello made it easy for me to appreciate how it felt for John as he struggled with *everything* involving manual control. I realised that I would have to adopt the same practice techniques with John in order to help him with all the day-to-day activities he found so hard and that other children seemed to do so easily. I chose tasks that were achievable, broke them down into small parts, worked out how to do the activity, verbalised it, helped him as often as necessary and allowed plenty of time for regular practice without applying any pressure on him. John wonders now if I was just 'trying to avoid frustration-induced tantrums?' According to Christine Macintyre (2001):

> Children can surprise by how much they can achieve and this is as true of dyspraxic children as any other, although it may take longer and need more effort. Very often, short spells of regular practice can give amazing results, but parents and teachers have to be sensitive as to the best time, i.e. not when the children are too tired for that is self-defeating...

> Practice alone will not necessarily improve performance, for unless the movement patterns are correct, the children will just get faster at doing the wrong thing!

It's important not to waste time working on things that are far too difficult for the child's stage of development as this will be demotivating for everyone. In addition, a child will only be willing to practise something if they can see a reason for doing it, i.e. they are sufficiently motivated. I found it interesting to note that the *Leeds Consensus Statement on Developmental Coordination Disorder* (2006) advocates:[36]

> [Interventions that] contain activities that are functional, based on those that are relevant to daily living and meaningful to the child, parents, teachers and others...
> the intervention should involve the child's wishes as a key part of the process.[37]

Patience and 'picking one's battles' are key. I never did things for John that I felt he could do for himself, even though it took considerably longer for the task to be completed. It was crucial that he was given as much opportunity as possible to practise, if he was to master new skills. I appreciate that this could be very difficult for people with little time but it's worth it in the long run as these methods can be very effective. Once the brain/eye/hand connections are in place the movements become automatic. As Kurtz (2008) writes:

> Repetition is... an important concept in motor learning. New motor skills must be practised, or rehearsed in order to become strong, fluid, and well coordinated. Given enough practice, some movements become so automatic that we are hardly aware of them and need not attend to how well we are executing them.

It's crucial that everything is done in a helpful, positive and non-pressurised way as stress means anxiety and muscle tension and this isn't conducive to learning. As many amateur orchestral players know, a conductor who reprimands his players because their technique isn't good enough will fill them with fear and anxiety and their playing will deteriorate.

These days I would also try to use visualisation techniques where one *imagines* oneself carrying out the activity. It's known that the same areas of the brain become activated as if one were *actually* carrying out the task. I'm not sure though whether John would have been able to use these techniques.

We bought John several toys that would encourage him to practise his manual skills. Some of these were a great success and some were totally ignored. One of the most successful toys was a Fisher Price Activity Centre which we attached to the bars inside John's cot. We spent time showing him what to do and 'helping' him by putting our hand over his until he knew what to do with each activity. He spent hours and hours on his own, over a period of more than a year, playing with this toy until he was able to manipulate all of the devices. The activity centre provided excellent practice for various manual activities such as pressing and turning, increasing both hand strength and dexterity.

In 1982 we decided to buy John his first computer. We thought that using a keyboard and joystick would help John's hand-eye coordination and would be something he would enjoy. John also spent many, many hours playing with his portable electronic 'Pacman', also good for hand-eye coordination. Like many children he was fascinated by electronic games and would have loved the electronic devices available these days. Even as an adult John finds that certain computer games, as well as being a thoroughly entertaining way to relax, provide excellent hand-eye coordination practice. One example is the game 'VVVVVV'.[38]

CONSTRUCTION TOYS

It became obvious to us in John's second year of life (when children begin to stack bricks, do simple jigsaws and so on) that he was starting to lag behind children of his own age. We acquired a variety of construction, hammering, stacking and posting toys, pegboards, threading cards, beads, jigsaws and so on, plus a marvellous collection of bricks. John and I used to spend the best part of an hour a day (before his rest), sitting on the floor in his bedroom, playing together with these toys. He seemed to enjoy my undivided attention but continued to need a lot of help, found all the tasks very difficult and never seemed to improve very much. I verbalised everything in order to make these toys easier for John to use and as he grew older, I also tried to teach *him* to verbalise those activities that he couldn't do automatically. I believe that John had to contend with multiple problems, all of which contributed to the difficulties he experienced with construction type activities. He lacked the fine control and manipulative skills needed for these toys, was unable to plan how to undertake these activities and had difficulties with visual perception. As described previously in Chapter 6, John seemed unable to 'see' which shape went into which hole or how to rotate a piece in a jigsaw puzzle so that it would fit. Rotations in particular seemed to be difficult for him to see, ironic considering the time he'd spent spinning toys or watching things go round when he was young!

From the age of three and a quarter John went (for five afternoons a week) to an excellent local nursery school where they had a wide range of construction toys. John went to this nursery school until he was nearly five but never did anything which involved fine hand control. He spent most of the time playing with water or sand, on the climbing frame or riding around on a tricycle or something similar.

John loved Lego but never managed to do it on his own because of his poor visual-motor skills. As he grew older he was unable to copy the suggested designs that came with the boxes of small or technical Lego, nor could he visualise how the pieces might fit together to make something of his own design. Poor fine motor control also meant that John had difficulty manipulating the pieces. As he recalls:

> It was seriously frustrating not to be able to build nifty things out of Lego (though the problem there was at least as much poor visualization skills: even when I was nine I could see data structures in my head before I built them, but I can't do the same with physical objects).

Nevertheless John really enjoyed making constructions (usually outer space-related) with his father, although Tony did almost all of the actual work. While Tony was putting the Lego together, John would keep talking about the adventures he would have with this new construction. Sometimes Tony would leave John a present to wake up to: a new Lego creation which he made while John was asleep. John loved these presents with a real passion but unfortunately wouldn't let anyone add to them or take them apart to make something else. It's difficult to portray the intensity of the volcanic eruption that would take place if John's precious Lego was even touched!

CUTLERY

Shortly after John started secondary school he asked if he could take packed lunches to school. I agreed to this request provided John was prepared to make these lunches himself. I wanted John to grow up to be independent and as a consequence wasn't prepared to do anything for him that I felt he was (or should be) capable of doing himself. I also had a very strong belief that women shouldn't be skivvies for their families. Although I believed that children should learn how to look after themselves while they still lived at home, I also knew how challenging John would find sandwich-making. At the age of 11 he still found the action of spreading butter on bread really difficult. However I completely agree with Donna Williams (2006) when she writes as follows about the importance of 'tough love' and the dangers of learned dependency:

Tough love is not violence, it is not demoralising forced compliance, it is not being cold and uncaring. Tough love is about walking away sometimes, about not jumping in, about getting on with your own thing… Sometimes, tough love is the most empowering thing you can give someone faced with a struggle, and it can even lead some people to surprise themselves with what they can do when it's 'survival'…

John's dislike of his secondary school meals was so powerful that he was prepared to make his sandwiches, however long it took. Initially he made a week's supply of sandwiches on Saturday mornings and put them in the freezer. At first John found the spreading so difficult, looked so awkward and was so slow that I couldn't bear to be in the same room as him; I found it too upsetting to watch. Nevertheless he was absolutely determined, so I left him to it. With practice, his sandwich-making skills improved enough for him to abandon the Saturday morning sessions and make his packed lunch every evening. As he recalls: 'It was difficult, but it was also enjoyable, because I knew I was getting food out of it. So I overrode the frustration and kept on.' By the time he was in his late teens I think he may have got round the problem by omitting lunch altogether!

Although we'd encouraged John to use cutlery from a very young age, he found it difficult to manage until well into his teens. For several years we made things easier for him by using a plate which was secured firmly to the table by suction. Nevertheless (as described earlier in Chapter 3) he would stick his elbows out at right angles while he was eating, which certainly made things awkward if there were a lot of people at the table. With practice and improved hand control John learned to eat perfectly normally by the time he was an adult.

John also found kitchen utensils very difficult to use, although he enjoyed helping me when he could. I was always able to find something that he could do and eventually he became an expert at peeling potatoes and carrots as long as he wasn't under any time pressure. However, he found chopping fruit for a fruit salad much harder and still finds it quite difficult, saying: 'The fruit is so irregularly shaped that it tends to fly out from under the knife as if it wants to live.'

John's difficulties in the kitchen were not entirely due to poor manual control; motor planning weaknesses also played a significant role. Cooking frequently entails carrying out a sequence of actions in a particular order, something John finds difficult to this day. As his motor control improved with age his motor planning deficits became more obvious. For example, a few years ago, when John (aged 35) was making himself a mushroom and red pepper omelette, I noticed that the eggs weren't whipped properly in the bowl. The reason was that John had tried to whip the eggs *after* he'd added the chopped mushrooms and peppers, rather than before. As I helped him whip the eggs properly (not an easy job with all the chopped vegetables getting in the way of the fork) his response was: 'I always forget this.' I found it interesting to note that this was something John needed to *remember* rather than it being immediately *obvious* that this was the easiest and most logical way to carry out the job. However, according to him: 'Nothing not computing-related is immediately obvious to me, alas'.

DRAWING AND PAINTING

Another special occasion such as Christmas, Easter or Mother's Day and yet another complaint from the nursery school staff about John's behaviour. He seemed to enjoy nursery school and behaved pretty well most of the time, as long as he wasn't asked to make a greeting card or write his name. Then there would be a flat refusal, plus tantrums if any pressure whatsoever was put on him. Did the staff ever realise these activities were quite beyond him? This lack of awareness of the nature, or even existence, of John's difficulties continued to be a problem as he grew up. Teachers, lecturers and managers were misled by John's obvious intelligence, his knowledge and his excellent language skills. As a result they attributed poor performance in other areas to disobedience, laziness and many other unattractive qualities. To a certain extent this is understandable as most people don't exhibit such a large spread of ability. The majority of us tend to assume that intelligent people will find most things easy and people with severe learning difficulties will need help with many activities. That's the underlying reasoning for measuring someone's intelligence by means of a single figure (an IQ) but for people like John the concept of an average IQ is so crude as to be meaningless.

Although the materials were always available at home and his younger sister was very keen on drawing, John's artistic output before he started school was virtually zero. As John put it: 'The very thought is horrifying. *Chimps* are better artists than me.' He showed no desire to use crayons, which was hardly surprising considering the lack of strength and control in his hands and fingers. I never realised quite how much he disliked crayons:

> They're clumsy and unpleasant and slimy and cold and crude and ick. If you're skilled you can do impressive things with them, but it's always struck me as being akin to those people who write whole novels eschewing any use of the letter 'E'. Fine pencils are a much nicer tool... but there my lack of coordination shows me up.

Many children really enjoy drawing and painting and use art as another means of expressing their thoughts and feelings. Perhaps John's inability to take advantage of this medium contributed to his need to talk so much instead.

When John was older, and his fine coordination had improved considerably, he had a friend (Harry) who was very keen on drawing cartoons and comic strips; this undoubtedly had an influence on my son. Between the ages of nine and eleven John produced far more art, often when this friend came for the day and they were having a break from the computer. Our first two Swedish au-pairs (who lived with us when John was between the ages of eight and ten) were very creative and enjoyed making things with the children out of egg cartons, toilet rolls etc. Both children loved doing this and it was certainly something *I* wasn't good at. The au-pairs were obviously very patient with our badly coordinated son, so much so that our first au-pair recalls that John 'did like working with his hands... painting, making things with toilet rolls, egg cartons etc. A creative child as well as intellectual.' Our second au-pair wrote:

> I have still got a home-made Easter card from John that I've treasured all these years, in which he thanks me for giving him 'the drawing bug'. I used to make a

few arty things with them and got him interested in drawing.

As well as the lack of quantity, an obvious feature of John's drawings was a lack of maturity, particularly evident in his drawing of people. He still drew roundish bodies, with no clothes or sign of gender up to the age of nine and a half. Even at the age of 10 he drew bodies very similar to those drawn by the average five year old. I think he became aware that these people looked very unrealistic indeed and from the age of nine onwards discovered stick people. He didn't draw his first house until he was eight years old. That was probably triggered by our recent move into an old house that had three floors and must have seemed enormous to him after the small house he'd lived in previously. Apart from the scrap book which we encouraged him to make when he was five, this house was one of the rare occasions that he drew something which related to the real world around him. Real world pictures included a thunderstorm painted when he was five after we'd all huddled together in the house one night watching the most amazing forked lightning illuminate the sky. He also painted gardens and animals but he never drew dogs as he was scared of them. He preferred snakes, spiders, slugs and snails and once drew a hedgehog which used to visit our garden. Once John could write he would incorporate a lot of writing in his pictures which, from the age of eight, tended to tell a story. I must confess I rarely understood them. These drawings depicted action stories with lots of gruesome incidents including poison, knives, fire and lots of disaster. According to John:

> I wanted something to *happen* in them and the problem was that doing a conventional cartoon with separate panes for each event seemed like so much effort. So I jammed them all into one big picture. This... did not work so well from a comprehensibility perspective.

As John grew older his passion for science fiction stories became obvious in his pictures. These included rockets, spaceships and other interplanetary transport systems. He wrote very imaginative adventure stories at this age and these drawings appeared to originate from the same creative source.

Several authors have described the effect of gender on children's drawings, with boys inclining towards action drawings containing battles and explosions just as in their playing. Girls meanwhile tend towards drawing people with a fascination for the details of clothes, hair, jewellery and so on, again mirroring their play with dolls. These authors also point out that boys of five have less well developed hand/eye skills and coordination than girls, that girls are generally more interested in drawing than boys, and that media in the form of television, computer games, comics and cartoons have a significant influence on children's artistic output.

SCISSORS

Given John's poor fine motor skills, it isn't really surprising that he found scissors extremely difficult to use as a child. By the time he started school at five he was still completely unable to manipulate them. At the time I didn't do anything about this because I thought there were more important things for him to learn and his nervous system didn't seem ready for complicated tasks such as manipulating scissors. However, when I came to pick John up at the end of his first day at infant school, I was met by a teacher who attacked me verbally in a most accusing way with: 'Do you know that John can't use scissors?', as if it was my fault. When I told her I knew that John couldn't use scissors or draw but at least he could read, she virtually said: 'So what?' and ended the 'conversation' by saying: 'I would be worried if I were you.' Unfortunately I was too naïve to say to her: 'So what can you do to help?' and absolutely no advice was offered. What a start to a school career! On reading the above, John said in his typical dry manner:

> What a devastating omission. I'm sure picking up the crucial skill of scissor use in later life will take simply *forever*, much longer than trivial little unimportant things like reading. Only clerks need to know how to read anyway. (Am I using too much sarcasm? The paper should be bursting into flame, not vaporizing. It's important not to overdo these things.)

If I was in the same situation today, I would find the book *Dyspraxia. The Hidden Handicap* by Amanda Kirby enormously helpful. It describes the developmental stages to be passed before a child can use scissors and the basic skills necessary for using them. It also provides tips and activities to help the child practise using scissors. The supplier Special Direct (www.specialdirect.com) has a large number of resources designed to help children with their gross and fine motor skills, including a wide range of differently shaped scissors.

WRITING

Although John carried out a lot of pre-writing exercises during his first year at school, he still had many difficulties when he began writing. He used very large, irregular letters sloping in all directions and had no concept of spacing on the page. For many years he would split words between two lines because he was unable to judge whether a word would actually fit onto one line. John still has these spacing problems as he described recently:

> I still can't do this [fit a word onto one line] because I have no idea how large a word will be because my letterforms are so irregular…

> I'll start writing on an envelope and then realise I've left too much space, or not enough, and it's too late. Pah. Layout is a job for computers!

John's writing improved as he grew older. It became quite reasonable, as long as he was printing slowly (although he said it was 'still painful'); however, he found the move to 'joined up' or 'cursive' writing very difficult. He blames his terrible writing on this transition and has strong views on the subject:

> I don't really see why anyone bothers with cursive writing any more. Virtually everything people read is non-cursive printed work. The letterforms are far clearer with non-cursive writing, so cursive seems like a hack to make things a tiny bit easier for the writers at the expense of all the readers. It makes sense with Arabic or calligraphy, where the cursive flow is actually part of an artwork in itself, but for normal English writing it's a ridiculous 19th-century hangover.

As John found writing so hard to learn in the first place and cursive writing should be much faster than printing, I think it would have been better if John had learned joined up writing from the start. Dixon and Addy (2004) agree with this: 'It is important to introduce cursive writing from the onset.' Although John's school reports would suggest that his writing was fine when he left primary school, this was actually far from the case. Angela Webb, Chair of the National Handwriting Association UK, hit the nail on the head when she wrote in 2008:

> Children need to be able to write both legibly and fluently in order to meet the demands of the curriculum, and pressure on children to develop automatic handwriting skills increases as they age. To date, the emphasis of handwriting teaching in schools seems to have been on accuracy of letter formation and neatness of presentation. However whilst both these aspects of handwriting are important, research evidence shows increasingly that clear presentation is not enough... In order to write well, children need to be able to handwrite fluently *and fast* and they need to be able to sustain this fast writing over time, without experiencing undue fatigue.

John couldn't do any of these things when he started secondary school. Handwriting issues caused him huge problems because he couldn't write legibly and fast, and pain in his hand also meant he couldn't write for long. As a result he handed in very little homework and what he handed in looked a mess, as if he'd taken no care and spent very little time on it. Not surprisingly this didn't endear him to the staff. John explained the reason for his lack of written output at school:

> Writing was so cumbersome and painful that unless something was critically important I just didn't bother to mention it: and of course an answer that only mentions critically important stuff looks like a rather poor answer... nowadays my problem is the opposite: I babble on in print for too long.

To this day he presses so hard that his hand hurts after a time and he has to stop. When he tries to write fast the writing is very spindly, uneven, squashed up and extremely tiring and difficult to read. As John says: 'I can't imagine anyone enjoying reading my handwriting. Even I have trouble.'

Lois Addy's article *Handwriting and Dyspraxia*[39] has some excellent suggestions for the dyspraxic child who has poor handwriting. Meanwhile Martin Kutscher (2005) recommends a variety of treatment approaches such as: '[The] liberal use of a laptop... [Providing] the student with alternate ways of getting notes: a copy of a peer's notes, a copy of the teacher's notes.' If only! John's secondary school had little understanding of his difficulties and for many years refused to supply any practical help whatsoever. Copy a peer's or teacher's notes – you must be joking!

John, the perfectionist, was acutely aware of the poor appearance of his work. One evening (when he was 11) I went into his bedroom to kiss him goodnight and found him sitting in bed reading the first holiday essay that he'd been allowed to do on a computer. He looked up and said with a happy grin: 'This is the first piece of work I've done that looks good.' Although I shared his pleasure I was also quite upset to realise how unrewarding he must be finding a good deal of his life at school, as so much time was spent writing. I find it quite fascinating to see the effort that John has put into learning how to use very complicated typesetting software (called LaTeX) which produces beautiful, book quality typescript. He's proud to be able to produce really high quality output, much better than most of us who use the usual word processing packages. As he explains:

> [Handwriting] hurt (pressing too hard), everyone else was visibly doing much better, and I didn't know how they managed it. (Even if I didn't notice the other kids, I certainly noticed what they produced!)... Everyone else got instant bonus points for turning in neat stuff, and it felt to me like I was losing them unfairly.
>
> Hence my long-standing interest in computer typesetting... if it promises to give me a new way to turn out attractively printed stuff, I leap at it.

In the early 1980s we couldn't find anyone to help John with his writing or advise us how to help him. Even when John was in his early teens we had absolutely no success when we tried (yet again) to find someone to help him with his writing. All *we* were able to do, once John was able to use a pencil, was to encourage him to use one as much as possible. For a few years he was a devotee of '*dot to dot*' and '*maze*' puzzle books and I'm sure this contributed greatly to an improvement in manual control. However, his writing difficulties, which were still visible when John was seen by a paediatric physiotherapist at the age of 21, were not specifically addressed. As seen in the extracts from her report (in Appendix 7), some fundamental problems still remained, despite occupational therapy and all those years spent learning to write at school. If we'd found someone like this physiotherapist when John was young and he'd been able to visit her for regular therapy sessions, I think this could have made a huge difference to his fine motor skills. This would then have made it much easier for John to cope with the burden of written work at secondary school.

These days I hope (but can't say I'm very confident) that children with writing difficulties would receive more help than we did. Although some good practical resources are available (some of which are listed in Appendix 28), these alone are unlikely to be enough. In order to help children like John it's probably advisable that a fundamental assessment of the underlying cognitive and motor reasons for their writing difficulties should be undertaken by a specialist. Writing is a very complex activity and it's crucial to understand precisely *why* the child is experiencing problems so that an appropriate remedial plan can be devised. This plan should then be carried out by a suitably trained teacher; one size will *not* fit all. Without special training, it's unlikely that the ordinary classroom teacher, or classroom assistant, would be able to provide enough help. If we were in the same position again we would start our research with *The National Handwriting Association*,[40] one of whose aims is to support those who work with children with handwriting difficulties. They run an in-service training programme for teachers and teaching assistants and also run an information service. I would encourage any parent in a similar position to obtain specialised help. Don't give up until you can see that your child's writing is legible and fast enough to cope with the demands of secondary school.

All the above advice is probably unnecessary if the child is allowed to use a computer for all written work, both at school and in examinations. These days poor handwriting isn't the handicap it might have been in the past because computers are so widely used. Email and typed communication are far more common than the handwritten letter. I completely agree with Tony Attwood (2006) when he writes: 'Teachers and parents should not be overly concerned about poor handwriting skills; rather ensure that the child learns to type.' I believe John should have been allowed to use a keyboard at school from an early age (as well as practising his handwriting) because his writing problems masked other areas of difficulty, especially at secondary school. Since he never wrote much we never realised that John had great difficulty laying out a factual essay in a logical and structured way. Pamela Tanguay (2002) provides excellent advice on how to structure a composition, the kind of advice which would have been invaluable to John if we'd been aware that he needed it.

In the past, when application forms or other important documents had to be completed by hand, I always filled them in for John without any scruples whatsoever; I believed his writing wouldn't provide a fair reflection of his ability. Most people would be inclined to file an application form handwritten by John in the waste-paper basket; he would never get as far as an interview. I couldn't see why John should be judged badly for something over which he had so little control and for a skill he wouldn't need after the application process was over. Fortunately times have changed and as John says: '[Application forms] can these days thankfully normally be filled in online.'

REPETITIVE STRAIN INJURY (RSI)

I don't think it's very surprising that frequent computer use, allied to the application of excessive force when typing, resulted in RSI (repetitive strain injury). It seemed to have surprised John though:

> Back in the early 2000s I lived with a severe RSI sufferer and was confident that it would never happen to me, oh no! I was young and stupid and tempting fate: about a year later… I started to get numb fingers in the morning, then increasing pain in tendons after typing a lot: then the pain started to creep in when the temperature got low, then every morning, and eventually it felt like I had red-hot wires running down the back of each hand all the time.

In 2005 John bought himself an ergonomic keyboard and eventually managed to persuade his employers to buy one for him at work. As computer use is critical for John's job and for his hobbies and friendships, it was very fortunate that changing his keyboard has proved to be such a success:

> My RSI is now in effect cured: the only sign remaining is fairly rapid pain onset when typing on normal keyboards. The tingling hands, cold fingers, and constant pain have vanished completely (and they say nerve damage is irreparable!) As a result I'm religious about keyboards in a way I really am not about, say, pollen filters: in my opinion ordinary keyboards are a creation of Satan and nobody who does a lot of typing should use them at all. They're just storing up pain for themselves in the future.

I too suffered from RSI from excessive computer use but in my case it was due to overuse of the mouse. Excellent physiotherapy and abandoning the use of a mouse, by learning the equivalent key strokes, sorted my problems out.

SELF-CARE

Almost everything connected with dressing and keeping himself clean proved to be problematic for John. When a child is very young everything is done for them but as they grow older more and more is naturally expected of them. Most children find it easy to learn how to wash, dress and blow their nose at the appropriate time. It's only when you have a child who has real problems with washing and drying themselves, cleaning their teeth, blowing their nose, combing their hair, getting dressed and cleaning themselves after toileting, that you realise what complex movements are involved in all these activities. Until John was well into his teens he would rub the back of his hands up and down on a towel in order to dry them. He was in his mid-twenties before he learnt how to blow his nose properly, a real annoyance to those around him as he was perpetually sniffing. Perhaps we might have been able to teach John how to blow his nose if we'd been aware of the helpful tips listed in *Dyspraxia. A Guide for Teachers and Parents* written by Kate Ripley and colleagues. Cleaning himself after going to the loo remained a problem for years resulting in rather stained underpants and the use of large quantities of loo paper. These days the use of wipes is often recommended. The problems John had washing himself have been described earlier in Chapter 6 but fortunately these had all been resolved by the time he reached his late twenties. When John was old enough to shave Tony taught him how to use an electric razor, partly because that was what *he* used but also because the combination of badly coordinated teenager and sharp razor didn't seem advisable. As Tanguay (2001) warns: 'Do not allow these children to use a straight-edge razor. Their co-ordination difficulties could cause them serious injury if allowed to use a manual razor.'

I was determined that John would be able to dress himself before he started school, even though he found it very difficult. It's always an uneasy balance between requiring one's child do as much as possible for themselves and not expecting them to do something they find impossible. Key factors enabling John to learn to dress himself were: providing clothes and shoes that weren't difficult to use, breaking the tasks down into small chunks, remaining calm and encouraging, giving him plenty of verbal and practical help, allowing him enough time, never doing the job for him and most important of all letting him practise every day. This was relatively easy for me to do as I wasn't going out to work. As John needed a long time to dress himself, it would have been much more difficult if I'd been in a rush every morning to get out of the house. Williams and Wright (2004) describe three techniques which can be used to help children with self-care – chaining, backward chaining and prompting and fading. Although we didn't realise these techniques had special names, we used them routinely when helping John learn new skills which he struggled with. We were also unaware that these were *standard* ways of preventing the difficult behaviour which can easily arise when a child gets very frustrated with their inability to carry out a particular task. Lorna Wing (1996) points out that physical prompting techniques are the most useful for young children with autistic disorders: '[They] do not learn practical skills by being told how, nor by being shown how, but they may learn by direct experience.' Despite all the care we took, John still found dressing a daily struggle. Velcro, and clothes with elasticated waists, were our salvation as they were much easier to use than buttons, zips, shoe laces or belts. As Tanguay (2001) records:

> Buttons and zippers are incredibly difficult for NLD youngsters to manage. Wherever possible, try to avoid them – buy elastic-waist pants, a jacket with Velcro closures, anything to avoid adding one more complication to her already difficult task of getting dressed...

And always, always, allow plenty of time for her to get dressed.

We bought John a wooden, shoe-shaped toy for him to practise tying laces. Lydia remembers the 'terrible problems John had learning to tie his shoe laces' even with the practice shoe. She also recalls that *she* found it hard but nevertheless 'learned before he did', even though she was younger. Nevertheless we practised together, 'little and often', and only bought John shoes with laces once he'd mastered this toy. Mind you he's never found laces particularly easy to tie and when he got older and stronger he stopped untying his laces altogether, pulling his shoes on and off with the laces still tied! He uses this technique to this day, although he admits: 'I'm a right idiot for doing it because it destroys shoes. Ah well.' Perhaps he should start buying slip-on shoes without laces.

We were fortunate that children at John's primary school didn't wear a school uniform so he didn't have to deal with a school tie or clothes that had buttons. To this day John has clear memories of the troubles he had dressing as a child and recalls going around regularly with clothes inside out and back to front. (I certainly don't have the same memories and can't imagine Tony or myself allowing him to walk around like this.) He told me how hard he found it to know where the head and arms should go and that he would have to try many times before he could get a top on properly. He remembers trying to put his head through the 'head hole' *first* (rather than the waist hole) which seemed logical to him at the time. He still finds shirt cuffs a problem as some of them have buttons that are so small that they hurt his hand when he tries to do them up. In his thirties John wrote: 'My new shirt for Lydia's wedding has cufflinks. I'm going to get someone else to put them on. It still takes me several minutes to do up cuff buttons and I have no *idea* what to do with cufflinks.' Even as an adult he's found it difficult to put belts on and says it 'requires much concentration'. He hasn't worn a tie for a long time and says he never became an expert even though he had to wear one for many years at school. His secondary school wouldn't allow him to wear a permanently tied tie with press studs at the back. This would have made life much easier for him, particularly when changing for games.

For many years after he left home, John's clothes used to live on the floor of his wardrobe because he found it extremely hard to hang them up properly. At least they were out of sight and not lying round his bedroom. He said that he *had* tried to hang up his shirts and trousers but as they always slid off the hangers it didn't take long before he realised he might as well put his clothes on the wardrobe floor to start with! It was quite a strange sight to see a completely empty wardrobe rail with a great heap of clothes on the floor below. According to Tanguay (2001) this was to be expected:

> An early task that many of us try and teach our children is to hang up their coat. However, don't expect the NLD child to be able to hang her coat on a hanger. If she has, or had, trouble with buttons and zippers, she will certainly have difficulty getting a coat or jacket on a hanger. Even if she can wrestle the coat onto a

hanger, it would probably fall off before making it into the closet. Rather than using a closet for a child's outerwear, put up hooks, or use a coat tree, and make sure the child can reach high enough to hang her coat on a hook without help.

What a good idea but we should have done it for trousers and shirts as well. Recalling his attempts to hang up his clothes at home John said: 'It felt like I was battling a Hydra: it had a dozen floppy arms and a long biting metal bit, and I only had two arms. How could I hold the hanger *and* slide the shirt over it?' As he never ironed his clothes for many years after he left home, it isn't surprising that John was hardly a picture of masculine elegance. Recently he *has* been hanging up his clothes and ironing them as well. As he says: 'The feeling that I had far too few hands to do this is mostly gone.' His current technique is to 'hold the hanger at an angle and let gravity take the place of one hand'.

POSTURE

As a young child John had a characteristic way of standing; his back arched in and his tummy stuck out. This, coupled with a complete lack of waistline, made it very difficult to stop his trousers slipping down. Although John looked reasonably tidy when he left for school in the morning, he always looked a mess by the time he came home, with his shirt hanging out and everything generally askew. Recently I found out (from *How to Help a Clumsy Child* by Lisa Kurtz) that this posture is characteristic of children with low muscle tone. Tony recalls that John was 'generally untidy, with his shirt hanging out, pullovers bitten around the neck and sleeves, and quite happy having dishevelled hair.'

According to our first au-pair, who looked after John when he was eight: 'He had a bit of a crouch especially whilst walking. His head was often bowed down.' Our last au-pair, who stayed with us when John was 12, remembers him 'holding his hands curved downside, close to his chest; his head looking up and bent on one shoulder when speaking to people.' It was only when John was in his teens that his poor posture became particularly obvious to us. He slouched all the time, with rounded shoulders, head bent, limp wrists and hands clasped high in front of his chest. I hated this posture as I thought it made John look like a victim. I agree with Ripley and colleagues (1997) when they write:

> The awkward gait and unusual, stooped posture of many children with motor coordination problems can also affect how others perceive them. In nature a stooped posture is submissive and may also 'invite' bullying at an instinctive level in some people.

This was indeed an extremely difficult period in John's life when his self-esteem was very low and he was subject to considerable bullying at school.

John became willing to do something about his posture in his late teens, after he'd left school and life was now getting easier for him. I was advised to encourage him to walk around with a book on his head to get the feel of what it was like to walk with a straight back. He practised this for many months and his posture began to improve. There were further improvements in John's posture when he settled successfully into a job as a computer programmer and his self-esteem rose. One of John's aunts said that his general appearance and posture had improved enormously over the years and he seemed much happier to have a hug.

SPORTING ACTIVITIES

Although John really enjoyed physical activity at home, his gross motor skills were far less advanced than those of his peers. If he was to participate fully in sporting activities at school he would have needed lots of additional practice. John said that Victoria Biggs (2005) described it exactly when she wrote: 'Our bodies don't speak the same language as our brains and the translator is drunk.'

I was delighted, and slightly surprised, that John learned to ride a bike relatively easily; it can be difficult for any child regardless of their coordination. Once other children of his age had been using bicycles for some time, we let John start with stabilisers attached to his bike. These gave him the feel of balancing and controlling the bike and also gave him confidence. When he was ready and willing we removed the stabilisers and then held the back of the seat very securely. We gradually loosened our grip as we felt John's balance improve until he was riding on his own. Nevertheless, although he didn't fall off, John's bike control was poor; he would ride too fast, couldn't take one hand off to signal and his road sense wasn't good. In fact his cycling always looked rather manic and out of control. He seemed to lack an appreciation of danger and failed his cycling proficiency test at school when he was 10. We used to go out cycling as a family when John was in his teens but we were always worried when he went cycling off ahead of us. Unfortunately the roads where we lived were very dangerous because of the volume of traffic; I was unhappy with either of the children going too far on their own.

Now that we live in glorious countryside John rarely wants to cycle with us. Cycling in our hilly locality, John says, 'requires me to balance most of my weight on my wrists, and they can't take it for prolonged periods any more.' John believes that the problem is due to borderline RSI which (as described above) he manages to keep under control by using good quality ergonomic keyboards and taking regular typing breaks. It's probably a good thing that John doesn't cycle on his own because of his poor road sense:

> As far as I can tell road sense on a bike requires you to pay attention to about a dozen things at once, half of which are in your peripheral vision (thus blurred into invisibility for me), while also maintaining your balance *and* trying to enjoy yourself as well. Seems rather impractical to me.

For those parents whose child is struggling to learn to ride a bike, Christine Macintyre (2001) offers some useful advice:

> First the bike has to be small enough so that the child can place two feet firmly on the ground and the frame has to be sturdy enough to give real support. If not, the control demands may be too great. Then the child should sit astride the bike and propel himself along a flat, even path for grass tends to be too bumpy or sticky. Once the child is confident that he can keep the bike upright, then move to a gentle slope which flattens out and do the same again. Do not try to put the feet on the pedals – rather lift the legs a little way keeping them ready to stop.

> Only when this has been achieved should the child worry about the pedals... Some children will need to look down to see where their feet are before they can

place them on the pedals so adults should offer them some physical support at this point. Still keep on a gentle slope because this will provide just enough momentum. There should be enough distance for the bike to travel in a straight line so that there are no steering problems at this stage.

I've always loved sport, particularly ball games, and wanted my children to share my pleasure. For this reason I spent plenty of time with them, when they were small, practising throwing and catching. We played with balloons and large plastic bats in the house, threw rings over hoops and practised throwing balls into a bucket. Despite all the practice at home, John's paediatrician reported that at four and a half he had 'passed the gross motor section of the Denver Screening test, but couldn't catch a ball yet'. Tony Attwood (2006) emphasises the importance of parents practising ball skills with their children so that they aren't excluded from social games in the playground:

> From an early age, parents need to provide tuition and practice in ball skills, not in order that their child becomes an exceptional sportsperson, but to ensure that he or she has the basic competence to be included in the popular ball games of peers.

Great in theory; in practice, despite all our efforts, John's skills lagged so far behind most of his peers that he never joined in playground ball games and as far as I'm aware never had the desire to do so. When he was with his peers John only enjoyed participating in activities he was good at, not in those where he would be seen to be a failure. Nevertheless John *was* happy to join in family sports activities, probably because he was given lots of encouragement, the activities were suitably tailored to his skill level and he was never made to feel inadequate. We played cricket and badminton on our camping holidays and we owned a table tennis table and table football from the time John was about eight. He enjoyed playing table tennis but didn't play well. As his motor skills have improved with age so has his table tennis and these days John plays a good game of table football.

I used to take John and his sister regularly to the swimming pool when they were young and we all enjoyed the sessions enormously. First the children played in the water with armbands on and then they learned to keep afloat without them. Once they could keep afloat I took them both to swimming classes and when they were older they both had swimming lessons at school. John was a competent swimmer but never particularly good and unfortunately when he was 13 he developed a bad reaction to the chlorine used in the pool. Tony enjoyed swimming too but in the past also had a similar reaction. These days Tony has no problems with the modern chemicals used in our local pool but as yet we haven't been able to persuade John that he might enjoy swimming again.

When John was about eight he went to Judo classes which I'd hoped might help his motor skills. To start with he seemed to enjoy these sessions. However, as the children who started the classes at the same time as him moved on to more advanced activities, he never moved off the 'starter's mat'. As he was overtaken by more and more children, he became increasingly despondent and eventually gave Judo up. Although the exercise would have been good for his coordination, he was unable to benefit from tuition in a large group. I don't know whether John would have been capable of mastering the judo moves, even with one-to-one coaching, as he had such difficulty copying a sequence of actions. Perhaps he would have had more success if he'd been older when he started.

Luke Jackson (2002) is a strong believer in the benefits of martial arts for people on the autism spectrum, even if they find it very difficult to begin with. Writing from personal experience he notes:

> When we first started I found it so difficult. My co-ordination was terrible and it seemed far worse when I stood with other people who just seemed naturally able... the fact that it is so structured and predictable makes it the perfect form of exercise for anyone on the autistic spectrum...

> The moves that we do are all designed to sharpen our reactions, improve our co-ordination, increase our awareness of timing and distance and our flexibility. It seems to me that Taekwondo is custom-made for people on the autistic spectrum.

The combination of poor motor and social skills makes competitive team sports a nightmare for many children on the autism spectrum. John was no exception and found himself completely out of his depth when he started to play rugby (aged 11) at secondary school. As well as poor gross motor skills, John had no idea what the rules of rugby were, something we were quite unaware of at the time. I'm sure the rules had been explained to the class although John is adamant that this wasn't the case. Anyhow he certainly didn't take them in and was unable to learn from watching his peers. One day, very early on in his short rugby playing life, he suddenly found himself with the ball and to his horror everyone fell on top of him trying to grab the ball. He was so shocked by this experience that he spent every game after that watching the ball carefully in order to make sure that he ran in the opposite direction! With time he became an expert in avoiding rugby altogether by losing his sports kit, hiding in the cloakroom and so on. John's attitude to school ball games make interesting reading as they reveal a link between bullying and sport in his school:

> I note that in school team ball games, the other players were playing sport. I was playing survival.

> I knew *my* rules of football and rugby: avoid the other players at all costs, because some of them would like nothing more than to put the boot in a few times while the teacher's sight was obscured (and the other players would help ensure this came to pass). The ball must be avoided even more assiduously, because if you got it everyone charged towards you with murder in their hearts... So if I got the ball (rare indeed), I kicked it at the largest group of approaching people to get rid of it. Fairly often this contained members of the opposing team, but I couldn't *aim* it at one of them, and I could never remember who was on which team anyway, nor did I care: I was too busy tracking the dangerous ones. The classification that mattered was not 'our team' and 'their team' but 'neutral' and 'enemy', and even the neutral members of my team were probably pissed off at being lumbered with a useless player, so couldn't be counted on not to put the boot in either.

> I avoided rugby even more than football: it had all football's downsides, and it had the scrum, which could have been *optimized* for mayhem. A tight group of people out of sight of the teacher in close physical contact... no *way* was I ever going to get in that situation. I'd probably leave it with broken bones or parts missing.

Since I didn't know the rules the only safe way to avoid ending up in the scrum was to simply arrange to be nowhere near, no matter what the rules said or how annoyed anyone got. In the end it occurred to me that I could simply avoid being on the playing field or indeed 'playing' sport at all, by skipping every class. What a relief. As far as I can tell this never did me any harm at all.

[Losing my sports kit] worked for a long time until they acquired a second kit just to make sure I always had one. Very considerate of them, I'm sure: it meant I had to simply not turn up. I don't understand why they wanted someone so plainly un-suited for this sort of thing to participate at all. Was it just petty sadism? What were they trying to *accomplish*? If it was a lasting hatred of team sports, they succeeded, but I doubt it somehow.

A few years later John no longer believes it was petty sadism:

No, it's obvious now what they wanted. *Conformity*. They didn't care if I was any good or not, or if I loathed it after they were done: they wanted me to not rock the boat and do what everyone else was doing. I did tell one rugby teacher once that I didn't have any clue what the heck the rules were, so it was hard for me to follow them – carefully *not* mentioning that I was much more interested in avoiding most of my fellow team members than in the allegedly enjoyable game in any case. He refused to believe me and ripped into me for 'answering back'. Sigh.

From the age of 15, John enjoyed cross country 'running' or more accurately cross country 'walking, thinking and talking'. However on one occasion he got so far behind everyone else that he got lost and it started pouring with rain: 'It took an hour and a half of weary trudging before I found the way back, by which point I was bitterly cold and sick with worry/fear/panic.'

It's sad to think that all those hours timetabled for PE or sport during John's school career *could* have been spent in activities designed to improve John's gross motor skills and provide him with some exercise. What a wasted opportunity. I appreciate there could be problems with staffing but there are always children who are less well coordinated than their peers and hate team sports. It would be great if these PE time slots could be utilised to help *all* these children improve their motor skills, perhaps by em-ploying suitably trained classroom assistants or volunteers. Fun exercise regimes such as those described by Madeleine Portwood (1999) or by Gill Dixon and Lois Addy (2004) would fit the bill. I'm sure John would have benefited enormously if his schools had used similar regimes. Matt Winter (2003) suggests:

Teachers [should] arrange an alternative PE program. Due to their poor motor skills and difficulty with social interaction, team sports are a huge challenge for children with AS. Working on one of these two skills is very taxing for the child and working on both at once can be almost impossible. PE then becomes a time of great stress for both the child and the teacher and often very little is achieved. It is usually far more beneficial for the child to do an alternative PE program when you are doing team sports with the class. A rotation of responsible class-mates can be trained in two-person PE games that help with motor skills and co-ordination... Most people would perceive there to be a stigma associated with being separated from the class like this but for the child with AS it is usually a great relief and far better than the alternative.

MOTOR TICS

According to Gillberg (2002):

Tics are extremely common in Asperger syndrome. In a Swedish population study, 80% of those with definite Asperger syndrome and 60% of those with definite or suspected Asperger syndrome had tics of one kind or another.

It's hard to remember exactly when John's tics started or just how many he had. Almost all John's tics were motor in nature involving rapid, repetitive movements. The only vocal tics I recall are constant sniffing and muttering under his breath but there may have been others which I've forgotten about. According to John, muttering under his breath is 'not a tic, that's thought processes in action'. There seemed to be so many tics and we did our best to ignore most of them. We never thought of going to a doctor or psychologist for help, just accepting them as part of John's growing up. They became obvious when John was about seven, peaked in his teens and largely but not entirely died out in his twenties. Martin Kutscher (2005) defines tics as follows:

Tics are rapid, repetitive actions that just happen to a child. They occur without any prolonged forethought by the child. Typically, tics tend to come and go, and change from one to another over time.

John's tics seemed to come out of nowhere, as he describes:

The urge to tic would come out of nowhere and then vanish as suddenly, and was pretty much impossible to resist (if I was in a situation when ticcing would be bad, e.g. if my current tic needed a hand and both were in use, the urge simply never came upon me at all).

John still remembers:

I had lots of ticcy things: the curled lip thing, the 'quick check to see if my heart is still beating' thing... the twisting hair thing and doubtless many others I've forgotten.

I can block them consciously at any time and they get blocked when I'm concentrating, and I can initiate them consciously.

I was unaware that John could initiate these tics consciously and I'm pretty sure that this *didn't* happen when he was younger. I find it hard to believe that John could consciously stop any particular tic for more than a few minutes. As Kutscher (2005) writes:

It is useless and counterproductive to ask a child to control his tics. It just does not work that way... It certainly is possible for some children to subconsciously suppress the tics temporarily... Tics also tend to lessen when the child is engrossed in an activity, and during sleep...

However, there is little long-term conscious control over tics. The need to tic is irrepressible. It is like the need to breathe: a person can hold his breath for a while, but cannot do so indefinitely. So can people exert control over their tics? Yes and no, but mostly no.

John agrees:

> The need to tic, when in resting state, was (is?) indeed irrepressible, but I'm not always in resting state: concentration does make them go away, as Kutscher says. (This makes me wonder if tics have some close connection to the barely-understood 'default mode network' in the brain.)

The default mode network (DMN) in the brain consists of a network of areas that are typically more active during rest than during active task performance.[41]

The tics I remember most clearly are the ones that caused me the greatest distress because they made John look so odd. I felt these particular tics would attract unwelcome attention and encourage bullying. Trying to stop these tics by making remarks about them was only partially successful and is definitely *not* to be recommended. It's much kinder to ignore the tics and hope they would disappear of their own accord but sometimes it can be hard to resist making a comment. Usually the tic would stop eventually but normally it would be replaced by another one. Therefore what we did was make no comments about those tics that didn't make John look too peculiar and hope that we could transfer the worst looking tics into less strange looking ones! There were two tics in particular that I remember made John look really weird. The first was a strong facial grimace that involved screwing up his nose and mouth as if his glasses were falling off and he was trying to keep them on. It happened many, many times a day and looked truly awful. The glasses *did* fit properly and weren't tending to slip at all, although John thought:

> This one was the only one that had an underlying cause. My glasses really did feel like they were falling off. Maybe they weren't, but they *felt* like they were... and then this converted itself into a tic and I found myself doing it when my glasses weren't falling off at all.

The second tic, which happened in John's teens, involved him putting the back of his hands under his armpits which bunched his school jacket up and made him look rather like an ape.

Some tics disappeared as quickly as they had appeared and some lasted for years and years. I remember him biting his clothes for over fifteen years; he didn't possess a jumper or shirt without a bitten collar and cuffs. According to Eric Schopler (1995): 'One recurring concern of parents of autistic children is that their children destroy clothes by chewing or tearing them.' Whereas we left John to chew his clothes and look a mess, Schopler describes how some parents coated their children's clothes with substances such as Tabasco sauce or liquid soap. These tasted so unpleasant to the child that they stopped chewing their clothes. Although John doesn't have holes in his clothes these days, he still sucks/bites the knuckle on his right index finger so that it has what looks like a large callus on it. Robert and Ann Cobb Lacamera, writing in the *Handbook of Autism and Pervasive Developmental Disorders* (edited by Cohen and Volkmar) note: 'The hands and lower arms often are the sites of callus formation or open lesions caused by biting.' John doesn't 'know if this is actually a tic. It doesn't feel like one: no irresistible urge. I think it's just a deeply ingrained habit.'

Alopecia (that is a loss of hair) was recorded on John's medical notes when he was 16. The alopecia was localised in a small area near the crown of John's head. This was almost certainly due to his habit of frequently 'twiddling' the hair in this location. John thinks this tic 'went away as suddenly as it appeared, about ten years ago. My current bald spot is an actual real male-pattern baldness bald spot. Time marches on for all of us…' Whatever John thinks, I still see him twiddling his hair while he is reading.

To conclude: Many aspects of childhood were particularly difficult for John as a result of a variety of motor deficits. Fortunately these have improved in adulthood and the use of a computer has meant that he has been able to compensate for handwriting problems. When John was young and poor motor coordination was causing him so many problems at school, there was little in the way of literature to help. Things are very different these days and there are many useful books and web sites that parents, carers and teachers can refer to for helpful strategies and ideas. There are also suppliers that sell products (such as special scissors and pens) that can be of assistance to those with motor problems. Some of the books and suppliers that I have found particularly interesting can be found in Appendix 28.

licking fingers?

9
Change

FEAR OF CHANGE

Any change, whether unexpected or expected, has always been a source of great anxiety for John. His reactions were so strong as a child that it was impossible to ignore them; major tantrums were the norm.

One autumn day, when John was eight, I arrived home from work to find our first au-pair (Anna) rather upset and very puzzled. She'd been fetching the children from school for several weeks without any problems but on this particular day John had a major tantrum outside the school gates. When I asked her to tell me exactly what happened she said, instead of walking straight home from school (as she'd always done in the past), she'd started to walk in the opposite direction. Our very sweet-toothed au-pair wanted to buy herself some sweets at the newsagents before she went home. My daughter had no problem with this change in plan but John reacted with panic, fear, shock: the end of the world and more. He screamed and yelled in the street, oblivious to everyone around him. There was no way Anna could go to the shop and she had to do without her sweets. According to John, aged 32:

'Panic, fear, shock: the end of the world and more' is a good description. That's exactly how a change in routine feels. The floorboards have been kicked away and beneath is the abyss of uncertainty.

[As for walking in the opposite direction] I could handle it more easily now, but the emotional response remains the same, and my likely thought patterns are easily reconstructible: where are we going? why? I expected to be going home! I had *plans* (well, OK, perhaps not very firm ones, but I knew what I was going to be doing dammit and it did not include walking in this direction!) At least tell me first! How long will we be going this way? Every footstep this way is a footstep in the *wrong* direction! It's not what we normally do *therefore* it is *wrong,* sliding off the rails to that scary place where anything is possible and most things are bad.

Our au-pair couldn't understand why this normally cheerful and chatty boy should have behaved so badly. She was very anxious to find out what she should do to avoid such a situation in the future. I explained that it was the *sudden* change in plan that had precipitated John's difficult behaviour. He needed plenty of warning before there was any change to his usual routine so that he had sufficient time to get used to the idea. As John the adult says:

I still much prefer lots of warning. It's not essential any more: I don't explode into panic. I just go off on multi-day worry-fests instead (oh, and phone you and worry at you). It's more internal but every bit as unpleasant.

The more of my life [that] is occupied by normal routines, the happier I am. There's still plenty going on, but the change is all in the detail: the broad brush-

114

strokes are known.

I suggested that should a similar situation arise in the future, Anna should tell John slowly and carefully that she needed to do some shopping first and they would go home *immediately* afterwards. She should also make absolutely sure that John understood what she was saying and was comfortable with the situation before she set off. John is 'not sure *slowly* matters':

> *In advance* and *not so fast I miss it* is more the thing. i.e., pretend that it's really important and significant rather than a piddling little change, because to muggins here it is, and give it a corresponding amount of conversational weight.

I said that it might be more sensible for her to do her shopping *before* she picked John up as he was tired at the end of the school day and looked forward to getting home as soon as possible. As John explains: 'I definitely have a much lower tolerance for change when I'm quite tired. Pretty much zero, actually.' Our last au-pair (Monique), who lived with us when John was aged from 12 to 13, remembers:

> [John] getting very upset if we ask him to do something completely new (out of his routine); his fear of heights: as an illustration, one day we went all of us to a horse show in London and even if you informed him days before this event, he was panic-stricken when we arrived at our seats located at the top rows. And after a while you manage to convince him to enjoy his day out…

I had no idea at the time that this was typical behaviour for many children on the autism spectrum, perhaps because there was no such thing as an autism spectrum in those days. Recently John wrote:

> Changes of plan on their own tend to produce irrational surges of anger, I was *expecting* that, and now I have to figure out what to expect *all over again*, you just wasted lots of my thinking time that I could have been using to think about more interesting things without so much as a by-your-leave.

In previous chapters I've described some of the problems we encountered at home when John was a baby because of his resistance to change. This included his refusal to move from breast to bottle feeding or from a potty to a toilet, his dislike of being washed or having his nappy or clothes removed and his flat refusal to eat the convenience food we took with us on holiday. As a child, Lydia was very aware that John found the unfamiliar difficult at times. His dislike of strange public lavatories and his need to go to the same part of museums (such as the dinosaurs in the Natural History museum) are strong memories of hers. She also remembers the small red and white table she used to sit at with her brother and 'how important it was to John that he always sat on *his* chair' which was a different design to hers. In the same way she recalls how 'important it was to him that he sat on the left hand side of the car' although she would have 'liked to alternate' sometimes. She is sure that even now as an adult 'his side of the car is important to him' and he would 'comment if she sat on *his* side'. However, she thinks:

> He wouldn't get angry now, and would be very gentlemanly and let me sit there. He would have got very upset and angry if I'd tried to take his side as a child. Like so many things, it wasn't worth the bother so I just accepted the lack of flexibility.

I think the fundamental reasons underlying John's inability to cope with change are related to the fact that he processes incoming information rather slowly and has poor organisational and planning skills. This is bound to make him feel very vulnerable when things change suddenly without warning. He may take longer to understand what is happening and when he does, he will find it difficult to work out what he should do. Even if the change is expected, John may still worry about his ability to cope in the new situation. It's easy to understand why, under these circumstances, panic might be the outcome. Also, in the past, John's extraordinary powers of concentration (see Chapter 13) meant he got so absorbed in whatever he was doing that to be expected to stop without warning would be a terrible shock, again leading to the inevitable temper tantrum.

How we Coped with John's Fear of Change

Despite John's inability to cope with change and the horrendous tantrums that could result if he wasn't handled appropriately, we actually experienced comparatively little difficult behaviour when he was a child. How had we managed to avoid so many of the behavioural problems that can frequently arise when raising children like John? I believe the most important factor underlying our child rearing approach was our attempt to look at the world from John's point of view. We tried to put ourselves in John's shoes and understand how his mind worked, what gave him pleasure and what distressed him. In this way it was easier for us to provide an environment that met his needs. Key to creating the safe and calm surroundings that John could thrive in was: a consistent and fair parenting approach; clear boundaries; a structured routine to the day; plenty of warning if changes to his routine were to take place and always explaining what was happening or why we were asking for something to be done – a practice that worked well for our very logical son. I believe anxiety and frustration were the main reasons for John's explosions of bad temper. Important techniques that reduced these were: motivation and bribery, rather than threats and force; being sufficiently flexible to avoid involving John in situations that he would find particularly stressful (unless they were really necessary); not disturbing John unnecessarily when he was concentrating on something and never rushing him.

It was crucial to give John plenty of warning when any activity was about to end. Suddenly telling him to stop doing something he was happily absorbed in would have been guaranteed to provoke an outburst of temper. I learned to give John plenty of notice before asking him to start or end any activity, which meant we avoided constant scenes. This approach, coupled with a fairly regimented day, seemed to make it easy for John to cope with a wide range of activities. These techniques are probably helpful for all children on the autism spectrum, as Brenda Boyd (2003) describes:

> Even a minor change often makes the Asperger syndrome child very anxious. Try to introduce any kind of change, even alterations to his schedule, at a time when you are both feeling relaxed, and give him plenty of advance warning if you can.

My husband did things differently and had more trouble looking after John than I did, as he recalls:

> I found John quite difficult at times. I think that if he was involved in something and I wanted him to do something else (possibly having to get something from

116

the shops) he would not cooperate. It was hard for him to realise that other people had priorities that were different from his. I am sure that he would have been happy to stay on his own doing his own thing but obviously you couldn't leave him. It was difficult for Lydia when something she wanted to do was affected by John's refusal to cooperate.

Even now John doesn't like to be disturbed when he is busy concentrating on something. Giving him enough warning that an activity will have to end soon is, according to John, 'essential, even now':

I don't have screaming tantrums but it ruins my mood and stresses me to hell and back and probably makes me into a nightmare to deal with because my limited degree of social modelling only works at all when unstressed.

One of the reasons I love living alone is that I can hack on something and look up and six hours have gone missing.

Children with a Non-Verbal Learning Disability (NLD) also react badly to unexpected change, as Tanguay (2001) explains:

They also have tremendous challenges in 'shifting mental set' – meaning that once the child is focused on something, moving her attention to something else is quite difficult for her. Forewarning and cueing are helpful strategies. If she is engrossed in an activity, and it is getting close to mealtime, let her know that she will have to stop in five minutes. Timers are also helpful for this. Tell her that the timer will go off when five minutes have elapsed, and then she will have to stop what she is doing and come to dinner.

As Tanguay points out, some people find it helpful to use a timer of some sort (such as an egg timer) to make it easier for the child to see when an activity must end. We never thought of it at the time but the use of a timer, provided it wasn't noisy, might have worked splendidly. John doesn't like the idea despite having tried it:

The problem is that I spend all my time being distracted by the timer's inevitable progression, so I end up hardly concentrating. (The only reason my typing-break timer doesn't do this is because it doesn't give me a countdown warning. Originally it did but I ripped that feature out specifically to stop it distracting me.)

Until the incident with Anna, I don't think I'd realised the extent to which our family had adapted to John's needs. It hadn't taken us long to realise that he didn't like to be disturbed when he was concentrating on something, was very happy with routine and had to be given lots of warning, reassurance and time to get used to any change. Of course we got it wrong quite regularly but John's temper and appalling tantrums were so unpleasant that it provided a strong incentive to adapt our behaviour to his needs! Unfortunately we frequently underestimated the amount of information others would need in order for *them* to manage John successfully. As a consequence many of those who had very close dealings with John (such as au-pairs and teachers) had to learn the hard way. Our second au-pair found John (then aged just over nine) so difficult to deal with initially that she nearly handed in her notice. He drove her close to tears with his temper tantrums:

At first I found John extremely hard work and I just thought he was a very naughty, rude and difficult child. Some days he could drive you insane, close to tears, with his temper tantrums, especially if you said no to something he wanted to do or if you had to stop him in the middle of something he was doing. Kicking and screaming on the floor is what I remember on these occasions.

After I spoke to her and explained what was going on, why he was behaving like this and how I handled him, she found things a lot easier and their relationship improved enormously. As she recalls:

Suddenly it all changed. There was a reason for his behaviour. This was the turning point for me. I could now deal with him in a different way and soon found that a humorous approach worked wonders. We really bonded after this and shared a lot of jokes and laughs (even had a snowball fight one day in February without any tears)... We had a lot of fun together even during our walks to and from school. Jokes all the time.

I find this comment really interesting; John hadn't changed, but as a result of different handling, his behaviour had. Stubbornness is a characteristic John is well aware of. As he wrote in an email when he was in his mid-twenties: 'It's only with difficulty I've semi-overcome the wave of unreasonable anger that can sweep over me at times when people say 'no'.' When John was in his mid-thirties he said: 'Waves of unreasonable anger are thankfully very rare these days (possibly due to age-related testosterone level drop?).'

Providing the ideal type of environment for someone like John isn't always easy and requires considerable patience, difficult to achieve if ether adults or children are overtired. Tony and I could get snappy like anyone else particularly if we were tired, so it was always a top priority to make sure that we, as well as our children, had enough sleep. It was one of the reasons we made such a point of making John's bedroom a relaxing and desirable place to be in and never, ever a place of punishment. It was also the reason why we didn't allow the children to come in and wake us up as soon as they woke up. They had to learn that their parents' sleep was very important and they mustn't disturb us until we were awake and our bedroom door was open. These days many parents use a sleep trainer clock to help their children learn when they should stay in bed and when they can get up. The face of the clock looks different when it is night-time (and the child should stay in bed) and day-time. Although this rule might seem a bit harsh to some parents, it worked well for us. It was the *only* way I could find the patience and tolerance to deal with young children calmly. If I'm tired I can't cope with children's noise, however happy, and don't have the energy to organise an interesting day. I found that looking after young children all day was physically, mentally and emotionally draining. I needed to keep fit by eating and sleeping well and having some child-free time and space for myself. Going back to work when both children were at school was really easy compared with looking after children all day at home. As John so cynically notes:

But mothers looking after children are slackers who should be out working. Looking after children is a really unimportant job because it's unpaid. Everyone says so. (At least everyone who is an (invariably male) economic adviser and idiot.

There is no more important job on this Earth.)

Much as I loved my children's company, I can still remember the joy, when I returned to work, of having my lunch or cup of coffee in absolute peace. I could enjoy a real break with no demands being made on me and go to the loo on my own without a child following me!

JOHN'S ROUTINE AS A YOUNG CHILD

A structured routine to the day was a crucial way to reduce John's general level of anxiety because he always knew what to expect. He still feels the same as an adult:

Given the choice between a probable really fun experience which is also very different from anything I've done before, and a day doing just what I normally do, I'll pick the latter every single time. Yes, it means my life is boring and perhaps less memorable than it might otherwise be, but it means I'm not scared or angry or unhappy so often: my emotional state is predictable and peaceful and unstressed. I'm happy to drop little things like foreign travel and normal holidays and a social life in exchange for that.

Sally Ozonoff et al (2002) explain that most children with Asperger's syndrome or high functioning autism 'have a difficult time when their world is not consistent, routine, and predictable':

As parents, therefore, you should always make consistency a priority, in both your overall approach to parenting and through the establishment of family routines and schedules.

John couldn't agree more:

It didn't change when I grew up: as soon as I left home I established new routines by the simple means of keeping on doing whatever I did on the first day, and changing it only very slowly. This fell over with respect to intermittent tasks (e.g. washing bedsheets) but eventually this little wrinkle got fixed. My current environment is ridiculously structured, everything in its place (though often those places are 'on the table where I dropped it'.)

The provision of such a structured routine at home came about by chance. When John was a few weeks old he went, one day a week for six months, to a college crèche while I attended some classes. I learned a lot by watching the trained staff and seeing what they did with the children. Like many parents who haven't had any experience of young children, I had absolutely no idea how I might spend day after day at home with a very young child. Seeing what they did at the crèche and how happy and content the children seemed to be, gave me lots of good ideas. I decided that what was good enough for the crèche was good enough for me and I would adopt a similarly structured day after John stopped breastfeeding on demand.

After breakfast our weekdays started with free playtime; while I did various household jobs, John could devote himself to the passions of the moment without interruption. He would often 'join in' with some of my tasks which gave us excellent conversational opportunities. I then spent some time in the morning engaged in activities (which depended on John's age) such as *Music and Movement* sessions, playing card and other games, teaching him to read and watching schools' TV programmes together. Although it might seem that all these activities were parent led, that wasn't actually the case as they followed the child's interests at the time. Before John went for his rest (which may have been before or after his lunch depending on his age) I spent time playing with him on his bedroom floor followed by singing songs and reading to him. John then had a long rest which I found invaluable because it gave me 'grown up time' on my own which I devoted entirely to studying. After John's long rest and my precious studying session I felt such a sense of achievement that I had all the patience in the world to spend with him afterwards. Until he was old enough to go to afternoon nursery school we would do a variety of fun activities after John's rest which he really enjoyed. These included: visiting friends with young children, swimming, baking, playing in the garden, going to the playground, feeding the ducks, visiting the zoo (where we had a season ticket), going to the library and the weekly playtime in the bath. Although we had very full days, it was really important that we didn't try to pack too much into one day and did everything at a leisurely pace so that we could avoid any rush or panic. This was to ensure John had enough time to practise activities he found difficult such as dressing. I completely agree with Pamela Tanguay (2001) who explains:

> In addition to providing a routine, it is also important to allow plenty of time for her to do what needs doing. Expect that everything will take this child longer, and understand that if she is rushed she is far less able, and far more likely to fly into a rage.

We were quite prepared to adjust our normal routine (at least up to a point) by leaving John out of activities that would be very stressful for him so that life would be calmer and more comfortable for us all. For example, I used to do most of the weekly shopping at the weekend without any children as John hated shops and crowds and would have objected strongly to leaving favourite activities in order to come to the shops with us. This was easy to organise as my husband was happy to look after our children while I went out but it would have been much more difficult to arrange if I had been a single parent. These days shopping on the internet would solve a lot of problems. Although our children didn't go shopping every week, the whole family (including John) went to the supermarket every three months for a major shop. We used to go on a week-day evening early in the week when the supermarket was relatively empty. To avoid any tantrums, the shopping trip always started with a visit to the sweet shop to buy a hard lollipop on a stick. This bribery and corruption worked wonders as sweets weren't nor-mally available at home and these lollies last a long time! We tried to make this outing fun and did it at a pace that John was comfortable with.

Fortunately John's liking of routine helped him settle easily into nursery school. Everything seemed to go reasonably well until Christmas approached and the routine changed suddenly. Not only was the school practising for an end of term performance but the children were expected to make Christmas cards for their parents. John was very upset by the change in routine and reacted explosively, flatly refusing to get involved in card making.

FLEXIBILITY VERSUS STRUCTURE

Although structure and routine make it much easier for someone on the autism spectrum to cope, an over-reliance on routine can also have its downsides, leading to rigidity and a lack of flexibility. For this reason (despite the temptation to go for the easy option and stick to a very strict routine) I felt it was important that John didn't avoid *all* change. I believe that those who find change naturally difficult need even *more* practice to prevent them becoming too rigid in their ways. Therefore, although we tried to accommodate John as much as possible, we also did our best *not* to avoid those changes that would have limited our functioning as a family just because John would have disliked them. In fact we felt it was important for John to be introduced to as wide a range of activities as possible. Although these changes may have been intensely anxiety provoking initially, we gave John plenty of support and with familiarity came a reduction in fear and anxiety. When planning any change in our daily routine, we made sure there was sufficient time to explain to John what we were planning to do and allow him as much time as he needed to process the information and ask questions. He needed this time to think about the proposed activity, get used to the idea and feel confident that he would be able to manage in the new situation. Carol Gray's *Social Stories*™[42] would have been a helpful way to prepare John for any major change but at the time plenty of warnings and explanations had to suffice. One way of encouraging John to undertake something new was to engage his interest so that curiosity and pleasure overcame his fear of change. Motivation and bribery were important if John was going to get happily involved in *any* new activity. If we could find a way to capture John's imagination, we could persuade him to try almost anything new. Unfortunately, despite our attempts not to limit our family experience, Lydia considers that it was still too limited to meet her needs. Her views on this are described in some detail in Chapter 19. As John explains so drily: 'Bringing up neurotypicals is hard, all those demands that they expect you to mind-read from them!'

It's difficult to strike an appropriate balance between creating the sort of ordered life that a child on the autism spectrum is comfortable with and trying to reduce the child's rigidity so they can cope in the outside world. Much will depend on the individual child and the family culture. For example Susan and Scott, writing about their son Colton in *That's Life with Autism* (edited by Ross and Jolly), went much further than us in their desire to stop their son becoming too rigid in his ways:

> One of the things we've never done is keep him on a rigid routine. We totally disagree with that, at least where Colton is concerned. Our life has been total chaos ever since my husband and I met. If our son had to be on a specific schedule he would never survive in our household. The best part of not having a set routine is that it allows him to be flexible with change. Colton has always struggled with transitions – either he wants to continue an enjoyable activity or he doesn't want to do the new activity. I am confident that if we had him on a strict schedule we wouldn't be as able to function as a family.

> Our plans are constantly in flux... Colton used to get upset about minor deviations from routine... Now he can go with the flow and say its okay to him-

self. We've worked with him on it over the years. We tell him we're going to do this but that we've got to do some other things first; so he doesn't freak out when it's been a couple of hours and he still hasn't gotten to do what he wanted to do… he asks appropriate questions instead of throwing a fit.

One of the techniques I employed before John started school, in order to accustom him to change, was to introduce (quite regularly) a complete change from our usual daily routine by going out for the whole day. I always ensured that John was primed (in detail) several days beforehand so that he knew exactly what we would be doing. In this way instead of panicking John was always excited before we went out. A real favourite was spending the day in London. This involved catching a main line train and then using the underground. I think the children would have been happy to go to London just to spend the whole day going up and down the escalators. For as John says: 'A giant clanking machine that you could ride on and nobody complained? How could we *not* love it?' I have a lovely photo of two young children walking from our house to the train station, each wearing a small rucksack carrying their picnic and any treasures they wanted to play with on the journey. Sometimes we went to the National Gallery and then fed the pigeons (something you were allowed to do at the time) or visited one of the other museums or art galleries. We also enjoyed spending time in Regents Park or Hyde Park, where we met friends who didn't live near us. The children knew, because I told them ever so clearly, that if they didn't do as they were told when we went out for the day I wouldn't be able to repeat these trips. Taking two small children on my own to London for the day could have been very stressful if they'd chosen to misbehave in any way. I still have happy memories of these days out and both children always behaved very well and appeared to enjoy themselves. As an adult though, Lydia told me she 'hated a lot of the museums as they were *so* boring'. John meanwhile says he still remembers being told to do as he was told: 'Oh yes did I ever remember that, perhaps too well. I get a moment of 'shouldn't run off without telling mum first' whenever I decide to take a different route anywhere in London.'

Despite our attempts to accustom John to change and to help him experience as much variety in his life as possible, there were some changes that he never learned to tolerate. For example, in all the years he lived at home John never ceased to get upset when we pruned our trees, although we thought he understood that it was necessary and that the trees would benefit and certainly not come to harm. As a result we used to avoid telling him when we were going to prune since warnings and explanations caused a riot even before we started. We did the pruning when he wasn't there to see it, hoping we would get away with it without him noticing what we'd done. Sometimes we did and sometimes we didn't, in which case we had to put up with the inevitable bad tempered outburst. Even in his early thirties John still felt strongly about the issue, writing:

Yes. I don't like seeing trees cut. Still don't… they didn't evolve in the presence of people lopping bits off them, and I've always far preferred the look of trees left free to grow. The natural wild tangled look. (Like my hair only less dirty. Ahem.) … I'd understand it if the branch was about to grow into a window or something, but otherwise the tree looks worse after you're done than when you start! I still can't see how the tree benefits.

By the time John reached his mid thirties he was accustomed to having the shrubs in his garden pruned as some of them were taking over the garden. Unfortunately his soil was so good that the more these shrubs were pruned the bigger they grew!

One of the biggest changes John experienced as a child took place when he was eight and we moved away from our first house, which we'd bought about two years before John was born. Although we loved the house with its south-facing garden, it was quite small. With two growing children plus their friends and our visitors the house felt very crowded and noisy. We decided the time was right to look for a larger house so that we could have a live-in au-pair to look after the children in the school holidays and after school. Six year old Lydia adapted easily to the move and didn't seem to mind where she lived as long as it was with us. John, on the other hand, found the change very hard, even though he liked his new room (which was more spacious) and understood the need to move. He loved his old bedroom (which had been his since he was a baby) and didn't want to leave it. This sadness took several months to disappear, during which time he was a bit subdued. He didn't fuss or complain but he missed his old surroundings and we had to treat him particularly gently. According to John:

> The feeling was definitely a subspecies of grief (though I didn't know that until later). Bizarre in hindsight, but I suppose I get as attached to physical objects as normal people do to other human beings.

With time he settled in completely and we didn't move again until John was an adult and he wasn't living with us any more. On this occasion we moved out of the town John had lived in all his life and went to live in the middle of beautiful countryside in the north of England. Although we'd sold what had been the family home for fifteen years, both John and his sister accepted the situation; it meant they could have a real holiday in glorious surroundings when they came to stay with us. Although John wasn't very upset by our move, he still had some regrets, saying:

> I felt a bit sad that I'd never see the old house again... now I couldn't go back there, ever again. To me that was the event that *really* felt like the end of childhood. Definitely a loss mixed in with that gain. I still dream about the old place occasionally.

John agrees that he was less affected by our second move because he was no longer living with us but I suspect the fact he adapts to change more readily now than he did when he was younger may have been a factor as well.

CHANGE AS AN ADULT

When a child on the autism spectrum grows up, it's to be expected that, like anyone else, their fundamental strengths and weaknesses will remain the same. A fear of change and a liking of routine will probably feature in many of their lives. For example, Wendy Lawson (2003), a writer with Asperger's syndrome, finds change as an adult difficult:

> For many of us, as individuals with Asperger's syndrome, change may mean discomfort, suspicion, confusion and fear. This is perfectly reasonable. When we haven't experienced a particular thing before, how can we know that it will be all right? How can we trust that the outcome will be a good one?

Despite all our attempts to help John become accustomed to a certain amount of change, he still finds it very difficult. In fact his fear of change, whether expected or unexpected, has been a major factor underlying most of his life choices. John needs his environment to be predictable and controllable. This is no doubt why he took to computers in such a big way. Moving house, changing jobs, finding a girlfriend and foreign travel all fill him with tremendous, paralysing anxiety. As mentioned already in Chapter 5, John has described his life as being akin to walking along a track bounded by a steep drop on either side. When he's comfortable with the people he is with, or the situation he is in, then the track grows wider and the edges of the precipice recede. On the other hand, new or unfamiliar situations make the track much narrower. As John describes it:

I have a fear of unexpected change... sudden changes (and attempting to change a planned action of mine certainly counts) bring the borders of the precipice *much* closer and they keep getting closer until I've worked out possible positive and negative consequences of what's suggested.

John tries to control his daily life as an adult by sticking to pretty rigid routines. A few years ago he wrote to me:

I'm definitely routine-bound. I have a routine for going to and from work, a meta-routine when *at* work... changing routines without announcement causes the precipice to shoot closer very fast. The only way I've found to fix this is to have backup routines in case of emergency, and backups to the backups. This doesn't always help, but in a sense simply having routines fail desensitises me to them failing again... (e.g. I can see that nothing goes *disastrously* wrong when I have to take a different tube line in to work.)

John thinks he has a vast amount of 'control-freakery' as he explained to me recently:

It colours every part of my life. Everything from my relentless roll-yer-ownery on my computer systems to my dislike for having the cleaners move things around and my perfectionist drive in some way derive from it... The 'control-freakery' is an attempt to regularize a world such that unexpected/surprising things don't happen; social situations are bad in part because vast volumes of unexpected things are happening continuously and I don't have the mental machinery to understand them as fast as they are happening. Hence, overwhelming. In time some of this machinery gets automated, and I speed up... I only started noticing this in my early twenties!

As John has progressed through his twenties and into his thirties, he's seemed much more relaxed when I have seen him in social situations, although I know he still finds the social scene very difficult. According to John:

I'm a bit more relaxed as long as some people I know are around. Still stressed as hell otherwise, so I pretty much don't go to social events where everyone is a stranger. (Since almost everyone I know is physically remote, this mostly means I don't go to social events. I don't really miss them.)

John coped amazingly well when the bombs went off in London in the summer of 2005, although the rest of the family were very worried about him when we couldn't make contact. As both of our children would have been travelling to work on the underground at the time the bombs exploded, we were very relieved when Lydia rang us to say she was fine. However she was concerned because she'd been unable to contact John. It was several very worrying hours before we were able to make contact with him at work. At that time John didn't have a mobile phone and every time I phoned his work they said he hadn't arrived, which only added to our family's distress. When John eventually answered the phone at work (around midday) he was perfectly calm and didn't seem to appreciate just how worried we'd been. His mainline train never made it into central London that morning because of the bombs. He'd walked for three hours or so to get to work (using the maps on bus stops as his guide), aware of the police cars and sirens everywhere but unaware of exactly what was going on. When he arrived at work he went online immediately to find out what had happened and according to him, I phoned '*seconds* after that. No time for me to call anywhere. You must have been calling constantly.'

John's fear of the unexpected has meant that he is afraid to take risks. As a result he's always been very prudent with money and this (plus the fact he doesn't drink alcohol and spend money on clothes or a social life) enabled him to save for a house deposit at a comparatively young age. As he explains: 'I just expect everything to go wrong. This seems like a rational approach to me, and the consequences if I'm wrong are better than if I took the opposite approach.' He always makes sure he has enough saved in case of emergencies. This stops him worrying about things that might go wrong, such as losing his job. For many years he had insurance to cover this eventuality, even though it's quite unlikely given his exceptional computing skills.

The desire not to waste money has been a characteristic that was obvious from a very young age. I remember how differently both children handled the money we gave them when we went out to a fête or something similar. Lydia would spend every penny but ensure she bought as much as possible for the money, while John would look round, usually spend nothing at all and keep the money. John says he doesn't like to waste money:

> Money is potential choices. If you keep it, you get to make them later, when the choices might be more urgent. (Unfortunately thanks to inflation this doesn't work for very long, but my emotions don't understand inflation and still think it's basically theft.)

John's main discretionary expenditure is on computer equipment, books, Kindle downloads and eating out; clothes are usually an emergency purchase! As John writes:

> I very rarely spend more than the minimum myself (on anything but computer kit). My internal reason for this is as a hedge against catastrophe…

> Still, I don't spend more than the minimum on *each book*: I prefer cheaper books to expensively-bound ones (not just because the latter take up more space). But on computer kit I tend to buy near-top-of-the-line stuff. It's my one luxury.

After finishing university John moved into a rented house and stayed there for five years. It took years of gentle persuasion to get him to agree to leave these rather squalid surroundings which he shared with 'friends' who took considerable advantage of him. According to John though, *my* perception wasn't entirely accurate: 'I think they really were friends. Sure one of them was an exploitative loony, but I think she was like that to everyone: she really did think of me as a friend, and vice versa.' There were three of them in the house, a couple (male and female) and John. Although he was paying half the rent John's bedroom was absolutely tiny, while the couple had a good sized room each. The woman even tried to persuade John to buy the house with her partner, pay half the mortgage and still stay in the tiny room! She was most unhappy when Tony and I tried to explain to her why we didn't think this was a good idea. At this point in time John had sufficient money and income to buy a house of his own and he knew we would give him all the practical help he needed in order to do the actual purchasing; however, he was terrified of the change. The devil you know and all that! He says:

> I also suspected the way certain housemates would react, although I underestimated the sheer violence of it. I didn't expect a threat to report me to the police for imaginary crimes to stop me moving out, for instance. (This only increased my determination to go. Soon. Like yesterday, please.)

John wrote to me after he'd finally decided to buy a house: 'I know I'd have had great trouble accepting the changes if they'd come from anyone but you, but I've pretty much convinced my paranoid soul that your actions are invariably in my best interest.' This move turned out to be the best thing he could have done and he seems to have been happier in this house living on his own than he had been since the carefree days before he started secondary school. Nevertheless John says:

> I was pretty happy in the previous house for some years. Icy explosions from She Who Shall Remain Nameless were relatively rare, and I didn't really *notice* the squalid surroundings until the sodding rats arrived.

After ten years in his own house he has moved again, into a larger house in a more interesting location. He needed very little persuasion indeed to make this move and settled in extremely quickly.

When John finished his degree and the time came for him to apply for a job, absolutely nothing happened. I kept asking him how he was getting on and sent him lots of adverts from the computing press but still nothing happened. As he'd moved with friends into the rented house described above and we weren't going to pay his rent, John's financial situation was becoming critical. Perhaps it should be mentioned at this point that John's degree had been a four year sandwich course which included a year working for a software company in London. They'd been so pleased with John, when he finished his stint with them, they'd told him they would be happy to offer him a job when he finished his degree, should he want to come back. Had he done anything about this offer or applied for anything else? No. Why hadn't he done anything? I think it was due to a combination of factors: not really wanting to go back to the firm he'd been working for as the work didn't grab his attention sufficiently, a lack of confidence in his own ability to do the type of work he was really interested in, a massive fear of interviews plus an inability to organise himself. In the end I had to travel to John's house and sit next to him while he sent the software company he'd worked for previously an email, saying he'd finished his degree and would like to come back to work for them. They responded very quickly and offered John a job. He stayed with this organisation for thirteen years, during which time the company had several changes of ownership and location and also went through a few redundancy rounds. It was John's dislike of change that was largely responsible for the fact that he stayed so long with the same company, despite the fact that he was frequently very frustrated by the way they did things. It took a long time for people at work to get used to John's way of working. In fact it was only after his colleagues adjusted to *him*, allowed him to work in the way he wanted and discovered how much he knew, that John was really stretched and began to enjoy his job. However, the firm's last move meant that he was having to travel about four hours a day which he found exhausting and very unpleasant as it included travelling in the rush hour on the over-crowded London underground. His absenteeism due to illness had increased considerably because he kept picking up bugs on the journey. John's immediate boss said he was willing to let him work partly from home, as he knew John's productivity would go up, but a more senior person in the firm was very resistant to the idea. Although John agreed in principle that he really should look for a new job, he found the reality very difficult to handle and needed a lot of support to help him through the process. It was only because he had so little free time to carry out his own computing projects (now that his firm had moved) and was so permanently exhausted that John could even consider such a big change. He knew how difficult he would find it to handle the whole job search and interview procedure and how stressful it would be to settle into a different working environment with new colleagues and managers and another culture. It was for this reason that he'd never seriously entertained the idea of changing jobs before, although his pay was considerably below what he could have earned elsewhere. Because John has been an exceptionally loyal employee, I think he's been taken advantage of because his employer thought he'd never leave. I think John is being very charitable when he writes:

> I don't think that was entirely intentional. It's just that the working IT world seems to be designed around the idea that you switch jobs whenever you want a pay rise, and the pay scales are structured accordingly.

As for being taken advantage of, I find it rather sad that John says: 'This happens over and over again, but I can mostly ignore it. I just assume that everyone will take advantage of me, because mostly they do.' I think this software house was very short-sighted preventing John from working largely from home and not paying him the going rate. Apparently they had to recruit three people to replace him! Once John updated his CV (with some help from me), put it on the web and let his internet friends know he wanted to leave his place of work, he landed a super job with one of the biggest IT firms in the world. He works entirely from home (an ideal environment for someone on the autism spectrum), the work is much more challenging and interesting, his co-workers are kindred spirits and John earns considerably more than he did in his previous job. As I write this, John has been working for nearly five years with this company and really loves it. It's a joy to see how happy he is living in a beautiful home in a great location, with no commuting and a job he loves.

Given John's dislike of change it's hardly surprising that he's never been abroad on holiday on his own, although he is reasonably happy to come with us. Although I think that John doubts his ability to cope on his own abroad, he puts it rather differently:

> I suspect I could possibly have coped, but the stress would have been high enough that it wouldn't have been enjoyable, and it's having to compete against 'just keep going as I am' which is a high bar to cross because it's nearly zero stress and I do enjoy it.

He was asked twice by his previous employers to go (alone) to Tunis to train some new employees. He refused, I suspect rather vehemently. As John recalls:

> It was vehement enough that it even got through T's [his boss] skull. I was shaking. Nononono no.

> I'd have much less objection now, because while it is more chaotic there, it is less dictatorial, and I now know people there with enough pull to get me out of official trouble if I should land in it. But that's unusual. In general non-democracies are in a 'do not visit under any circumstances' file, which is rather theoretical because I don't go abroad at all, but provides a pre-filter to let me say no to risky suggestions before I even need to agonize over it and eventually say no anyway.

There have been computer and science fiction meetings and conferences abroad that John would have loved to attend but the intense anxiety generated at the thought of going alone stopped him actually doing anything about them. Nevertheless, these days when he *does* know some of the people (even if it's only through on-line contact) and there's an event that he's really interested in and not taking place too far away from home, he will go to it. In fact two years ago John went to his first science fiction conference in London, organised everything himself and was very excited by the whole event. In the same year he also attended a very 'techie' conference in Cambridge and was on a 'high' for some time afterwards as he enjoyed it so much. This is tremendous progress for John as both these events were attended by a large number of people but the fact that they were both on topics he was passionate about and he knew several of the attendees very well, made all the difference. I wouldn't be surprised if sometime in the future John ventures abroad to attend one of these conferences.

Fear of travel without his family goes back a long way. I think some of the reasons John becomes so anxious at the thought of foreign travel are very understandable, as they include poor organisational and planning skills, relatively slow processing of new information outside his areas of special interest, difficulty communicating with others and in particular asking for help, problems reading other people's body language, an inability to speak any foreign languages and a generalised fear of the new and unknown. This would make foreign travel daunting for anyone, especially someone who needs a substantial amount of routine in their daily life in order to feel comfortable and cope satisfactorily. In many ways John's fears are well founded as he can panic quite easily and a calm approach when things go wrong is crucial when travelling abroad on one's own.

Because John seems to be coping with life in general in what appears, at least superficially, to be a competent manner and because we haven't lived with him for many years, it's very easy for us to forget that underneath he is still the same person: prone to fear, scared of change, quick to panic and requiring plenty of warning before any new situation is encountered. A few years ago, when John and his sister came to Spain with us for a few days on a package tour, we were really caught out. In order to save money we'd asked both our children if it would be all right for John to share a twin-bedded room with his father and Lydia to share with me. As they both agreed we didn't think of mentioning it again once the booking had been made. When we arrived at our hotel in Seville, John made the most terrible fuss when he found out what the sleeping arrangements would be:

I haven't shared a bedroom for over twenty years… I have trouble sleeping in rooms where other people are present. I'm not entirely sure why. I go to sleep on the train easily enough, and that's far more crowded than any bedroom could ever be. Still, the emotional response ('oh shit no') is still there. Bedrooms at night are private places, and to this eternal bachelor this means only one person.

We had to explain to John that he could change in privacy in the en-suite bathroom, that he could read in bed for as long as he liked and so on. After the first night, which John survived perfectly well, he made no more fuss about these arrangements but would he be willing to share a room again? I doubt it. The next day John had another major sulk (which lasted all day) because he found the temperature too hot. According to him though that's 'not quite right':

> The key is that I found the temperature too hot but *did not notice,* just as I don't notice major temperature rises and falls in England, if they're slow enough. Here the temperature was high enough to mess up my normal functioning, and I *still* didn't realise…

> I don't think [the major sulk] was entirely [due to] the temperature (although that was bad enough). I think it was just too much change too fast. My mind wasn't working normally: it was like I was halfway into a disease state, intense borders to everything and hearing oddly muted, and obviously my emotional control was shot as well.

Although it was the end of September, southern Spain can still be *very* warm. Rather than walking on the shaded side of the street and putting up with the heat like the rest of us, he grumbled and grumbled spoiling everyone's day in the process. We took him into a shop to buy some cooler shirts but couldn't persuade him to have anything to eat at lunchtime which did nothing to improve his temper. He had to be cajoled, by appealing to his sense of humour, into eating something as we sat outside a tapas bar in the evening. As it gradually grew cooler and as he ate, John's temper slowly recovered and we were able to enjoy a wander round the city at night. By the next day John knew what to expect in terms of heat and we didn't have much more trouble. As John explains: 'It's the difference between theoretical knowledge and practical knowledge. Obviously I knew Spain would be hot, but I didn't know what that *felt* like.'

John's deep-seated fear of change has made him very reluctant to get involved in any intimate relationships. He's very happy with his life as it is and is scared that he would have a lot to lose if he got involved with someone and it didn't work out. He's coping well on a day to day basis on his own, doesn't feel lonely and doesn't believe he could handle the emotional ups and downs that can arise when you share your life with someone else. Couple that with a total lack of confidence that any woman would want to go out with him and no experience whatsoever on the dating scene and it's easy to see why John still lives alone and is still a bachelor. It's *possible* that when Tony and I are no longer around John could feel lonelier and this might make him risk trying to find a like-minded companion but that is pure conjecture.

John's fear of change only appears to relate to social and practical matters though. He doesn't seem to have any fear of intellectual change, positively thriving on it. 'Not so', said John a couple of years ago:

I think I *do* have a fear of intellectual change, but I enjoy defeating this fear because my curiosity is much stronger! New knowledge is always good, even if does prove your old knowledge wrong…

The fear is easily dominated by euphoria at all the neat new ideas. This is a major benefit, because I can exploit the fear part to make me really critical of any new idea: if it survives the critique, it it is probably not crap. New people at my previous workplace were often really put off by this and thought it indicated that I hated them or something, until they got the bugs ironed out and I suddenly flipped into an enthusiastic advocate. (I'm every bit as critical of my own ideas, but because that's internal the poor sods can't tell.)

John always seems to be on the lookout for new ideas in his fields of interest, which is one of the reasons he reads so prolifically and why he's so knowledgeable and such an interesting person to know. As he says: 'I hate change and that's not a joke. That's why I'm working in a field with a fearsome rate of change, of course! Perhaps I'm just a suppressed masochist or something.'

To sum up: John has always found change to be a major cause of anxiety. Routine and sufficient warning when a change is about to occur has helped John to control his stress levels. Although John's fear of change has held him back in many ways, nevertheless he's been fortunate enough to settle into a way of life that isn't so rigid that he becomes bored or lonely but where *unexpected* change is reduced to a minimum.

10
Language

Although the themes of language and communication are often treated as a single entity in the autism spectrum literature (with communication skills frequently described as 'pragmatic' language), I have decided to put these topics into two separate chapters. Language was in many ways one of John's strengths and communication undoubtedly one of his major weaknesses.

LEARNING TO SPEAK

From the moment John came home from hospital I tried to make sure that he was exposed to as much language as possible. I spoke to him frequently, not just when I was changing his nappy or dressing him. One of the advantages of carrying John in a sling on my front was that he was so physically close to me that it seemed perfectly natural to talk to him. However, as John grew older (but before he could speak) it seemed artificial sitting on the floor next to him (while he was playing) and talking to him when he couldn't reply. It felt as if I was talking aloud to myself, something I wasn't used to doing at the time; this has become a much more familiar activity in recent years! I did find it easy to talk to John while getting on with jobs in the kitchen. I put his little chair (with him in it) onto the work-surface near to me where he could see my face easily. Of course this could have been highly dangerous but he wasn't near the edge and I never went away and left him there. Because he was sitting so close to me, I had no problem giving a running commentary on what I was doing and anything else that went through my mind at the time. It certainly meant that John heard a lot of language directed to him from a young age. I also got into the habit of doing housework and other practical tasks *with* the children when they were young, with conversation going on the whole time. I heartily endorse what Rogers and colleagues (2012) say when they write:

> How parents talk to their children has a big influence on their children's language development, and this is also true for children with autism. Parents who talk frequently to their children (face to face, using simple language) about what the children are doing, seeing, and experiencing; who label their children's actions and objects; and who narrate activities as they are carried out help their children talk more and develop larger vocabularies. Parents who use speech mostly to give their children instructions or corrections limit their children's opportunities for language learning. You want to be sure you are talking to your child throughout the day during both play and nonplay activities, and that whenever possible, you have your child's attention when you are talking.

It's natural when you have a child to compare their progress to that of other children of the same age, even if you know they will all develop at different rates. Perhaps because of John's difficult start I didn't do this too often; it only upset me to find that he seemed behind in every way. Nevertheless I couldn't help noticing that John was relatively slow to start speaking. I remember telling myself not to worry as he always

131

did things a bit later than others. Although he wasn't speaking, John seemed very intelligent and alert and appeared to understand what was going on. His hearing had been tested and was found to be reasonable. I was confident that John understood a lot, partly because of his general behaviour and partly because of a simple game that I played with both my children *before* they could speak. It was a very popular game and started in the bathroom as a means of occupying them when they followed me in there. It enabled me to teach them new words and find out how much they understood, long before they could speak. I would teach them a new word by pointing at something (perhaps the window) and saying 'window' several times. Then I taught them to point at the window when I said: 'Where is the window?' They enjoyed this game enormously and I taught them a huge number of words this way. When they were asked where a particular object was, either they didn't know and I could teach them a new word or, if they knew the answer and pointed correctly, they would get lots of praise. It was lovely for me to be able to play such an interactive game with very young children before they could speak. It enabled them to show me how much they knew in a non-competitive and personal way and I found it amazing to discover how quickly they learned the names of things. We used this game inside and outside the house and also when we looked at picture books together. Knowing how much John understood and knowing that children learn to speak at different ages, I hoped he would get round to speaking when he was ready. In any case he'd been babbling for some time when he was on his own in his bedroom. Interestingly enough I never heard him do this when he was with us. It was as if he wanted to practise in private until he was good enough to speak in public. John wonders whether 'being with *anyone* else made me stressed enough to not want to babble? Maybe I got used to doing it in my cot and never varied the routine? (Now *that* I can believe.)' The babbling sounded just like someone practising some sort of musical exercises. He would repeat a short one syllable sound many times and then move onto another sound and repeat that many times but there was no attempt to produce words. As John pointed out, Steven Pinker in *The Language Instinct* writes about the importance of babbling as a precursor to spoken language:

> Between seven and eight months they suddenly begin to babble in real syllables like *ba-ba-ba*, *neh-neh-neh*, and *dee-dee-dee*. The sounds are the same in all languages, and consist of the phonemes and syllable patterns that are most common across languages. By the end of the first year, babies vary their syllables, like *neh-nee*, *da-dee*, and *meh-neh*...

> Why is babbling so important? The infant is like a person who has been given a complicated piece of audio equipment bristling with unlabelled knobs and switches but missing the instruction manual... by listening to their own babbling, babies in effect write their own instruction manual; they learn how to move which muscle in which way to make which change in the sound. This is a prerequisite to duplicating the speech of their parents.

Once John started speaking it was as if some floodgates had opened; they've never closed since. According to Tony Attwood (2006):

> One of the language characteristics of the child with Asperger's syndrome is that he or she may talk too much or too little. Sometimes the child's genuine

enthusiasm for the special interest leads to garrulous speech and questions, a never-ending babbling brook.

'Yes!', agrees his sister Lydia, while John admits, that even as an adult he is 'definitely on the garrulous side'.

VOCABULARY AND GRAMMAR

When John started to speak in sentences it was quite difficult to understand him. This was partly due to his poor diction but also because he reversed his pronouns. We became expert at reversing the pronouns back again and translating. For example when John *said*, 'you want a drink' he actually *meant*, 'I want a drink'. I spent ages trying to correct the pronoun reversal and attempting to explain to John the difference between 'I' and 'you'. All I succeeded in doing was tying myself up in knots in the process and eventually I gave up. It seemed so strange to me that someone whose understanding and use of language appeared to be so good seemed incapable of getting their pronouns right. According to John: 'It's a particularly hard thing to get right, because you don't just have to look at how other people are using language but *how they use it with respect to each other*.' It was quite a long time before John stopped referring to himself as 'you' but suddenly he seemed to cotton on and that was the end of pronoun reversal. I put this away in my memory bank and thought nothing more of it once the problem had resolved itself. I was absolutely amazed to find out, many years later, that pronoun reversal is quite a common problem for children on the autism spectrum. As a possible explanation Lorna Wing (1996) and Bryna Siegal (1996) both point out that many autistic children begin to speak by echoing what they have heard (echolalia) and this can lead to pronoun reversal. I have no memories of John actually echoing parts of sentences back to me although all language learning must include some echolalia because children learn new words from those they have heard. It has also been suggested by many writers that pronoun reversal by children on the autism spectrum is related to their difficulty in understanding the perspective of others, a characteristic called *Theory of Mind*. However, Oshima-Takana[43] has argued:

> 'I' and 'you' are not learned solely through one-on-one interaction, but by observing others interact with each other. The evidence included the fact that second-born children learn 'I' and 'you' faster than firstborns... and that a neural network in simulation learned 'I' and 'you' faster when there were more participants to observe... Though neither of these findings is conclusive evidence in itself, they both support the intuition that there is little to distinguish 'I' and 'you' from proper names if the child only receives input from the primary caregiver.

The latter explanation strikes a particular chord with me as so much of the language John heard when he was young was directed solely at him. This was partly because he was the first child and he and I spent a significant amount of time on our own but also because he wasn't very interested in watching and listening to others. It must have been very difficult for him to realise that the meaning of words such as 'John' remain constant while the meaning of the words 'I' and 'you' change, depending on who is saying them. Our second child, Lydia, didn't have this pronoun reversal problem but then she wasn't on the autism spectrum and paid far more attention to the people and conversations around her.

Although John *did* use language in order to communicate with us and ask for things that he wanted, he was very undemanding and asked for very little. He talked all the time, regardless of whether anyone was listening and particularly enjoyed using long words, the longer the better; I remember 'hydraulic lift' was an early favourite. Many of the words he used when he was young were chosen because he liked the sound of them. John loved, and still loves, language for its own sake in the way someone might enjoy listening to music or looking at a painting or a sculpture. To this day he tends to read aloud to himself when he comes across a passage he thinks is beautifully written. He says he is 'trying to fix things in his auditory memory for longer, and perhaps celebrating the sound of a particularly wonderfully-written passage.'

According to the paediatricians' reports, John had 'lots of words and expressive jargon' at 18 months (calculated from his due date not birth date), at 24 months his 'speech was fluent though I didn't understand it all', while at 32 months it was noted that John's 'language development was very advanced for his age'. When John was 4 years 4 months the paediatrician noted: '[John] passed the language section [of the Denver Developmental Screening Test] with flying colours. In fact his vocabulary is probably rather better than mine!' These paediatricians were probably unaware that Hans Asperger had observed that some autistic children could talk like adults and had a very advanced vocabulary. As he grew older, John's use of language remained extraordinary. His vocabulary was huge, he understood the meanings of the words he used and they were employed correctly. His language was derived largely from books (first those we read to him and later those he read himself) rather than the speech of those around him. As our first au-pair, who stayed with us when John was eight, recalled: 'He had a fantastic vocabulary for his age – very mature. It must have been due to his constant reading.' I thoroughly enjoyed John's mastery of the English language and loved listening to him speak. Pamela Tanguay (2002) noted:

> A sophisticated vocabulary is one of the hallmarks of non-verbal learning disabilities (NLD) and as a result, adults often assume the child is gifted. What is not so obvious is that this particular child is dependent almost exclusively on language, so that her vocabulary is disproportionately developed. The child does not learn from environmental clues by watching other children or adults, or even from experimentation – she tends to use words and labels for everything. Since she relies so heavily on language, it is natural that her vocabulary and language skills would develop more rapidly than other children of the same age.

I think this is a really perceptive statement which may well have applied to John.

If we'd been more knowledgeable, we might have realised that John's sophisticated language might alienate his peers; however, none of the paediatricians we saw mentioned that John's advanced language might cause him problems. John seemed unaware of the kind of language spoken by those around him and couldn't adjust his own use of language accordingly. This made him sound very odd to other children and they tended to steer clear of him. Tanguay (2002) describes the situation perfectly when she writes: 'The NLD child's vocabulary may be so well developed that her peer group is 'put off' by the child's language, because of their inability to understand, or their lack of interest in, what she is saying.' According to John as he grew up nothing changed:

Hey, I sound odd to other *adults*. I've never stopped sounding odd. They get used to it. I'd like to sound less pedantic sometimes, and I can do it, but whenever I stop concentrating it's back into pedantville again.

Even if we *had* been aware of the potential social problems, I doubt whether we could, or should, have prevented John using his native language so beautifully. Such an intervention might have damaged one of John's cognitive strengths without any guarantees that this would have made his relationships with his peers any easier. John is sure that his use of language *did* alienate his peers:

I'm also sure that holding my language back to prevent that slight alienation would have been the worst mistake you could have made. My English-language skills have been a constant joy to me, as well as a career: it's a rare conscious hour when I don't read something.

When John was in his late teens I went through a phase of looking in a dictionary for the meanings of words I was unsure of (when reading), rather than guessing. I wrote the words and their meanings down in a notebook and one day thought I would see how many of these words John knew. Although I was aware that his vocabulary was excellent, I was still amazed that either he knew already, or was able to work out, the meanings of *all* the words I'd struggled with. If he didn't know the word already he deduced it from the roots of words whose meanings he *did* know. He is still very interested in the roots of words and in linguistics in general, sharing this interest with my father who either spoke or read many languages. John enjoyed the invented languages to be found in books such as the Tolkien *Lord of the Rings* trilogy and the *Earthsea* sequence by Le Guin. Although, to be pedantic, John says:

Earthsea actually doesn't have any invented languages in it. It just feels like it should because of its emphasis on names. Le Guin never worked out more than about a dozen words of any of her languages and never had a coherent grammar for them or anything. She just writes about them so well that you never notice.

Although John thinks these languages 'add *depth* to the world' he also says: 'I'm certainly not one of the obsessives who learns and constructs invented languages and translates huge bodies of text into them just because they can.' According to Lydia, John 'doesn't speak Klingon, thank god'.

Although John's use of language was and still is very good, he continues to use certain phrases incorrectly and nothing can get him to change. For example, he will say 'yes thanks' instead of 'yes please' when asked if he would like something. These phrases are a matter of convention and not really based on logic. Quite why John won't change is hard to say, although the fact that he has difficulty copying what others do or say and doesn't seem to notice (or care?) that it sounds odd may be a contributory factor. It's as if John can't remember what to say because it isn't logical or thinks it's so trivial that he isn't motivated to make the effort required to break the incorrect habit. Sometimes it's tempting to believe that John takes a perverse delight in being different but in reality I think he just isn't aware what others do. However, John and I think Lydia may have a point when she noted that it may well appear logical to John to say 'yes thanks':

You say thanks when you are grateful for something and please when you are asking for something. In this situation you're not asking, you are being offered.

John was, and remains, a pedant about grammar. As Attwood points out in his book *The Complete Guide to Asperger's Syndrome*: 'The child's language profile can include highly developed syntax, grammar and vocabulary.' John became obsessive about the use of the apostrophe. He couldn't resist commenting with glee when he saw signs outside the greengrocer's shop such as *'apple's for sale'*; when he was young he had to be restrained to prevent him telling the shopkeeper of his mistake. To this day John cannot stop himself pointing out every occasion on which an apostrophe is used incorrectly, although he maintains it is 'just because it's fun, not because I'm driven to it. Honestly. Really honestly. I can stop anytime I want to. (Oops, sorry, that's 'any time'.)' Lydia does the same and wonders whether it 'was due to John'. I wasn't at all surprised to find out that he'd bought and thoroughly enjoyed *Eats shoots and leaves: The zero tolerance approach to punctuation* by Lynn Truss. Although he enjoyed the book he says it was 'in a guilty way':

> She's *wrong*, dammit. Language isn't something you can codify and freeze in time in the way she thinks you can. It changes constantly. (In particular, punctuation isn't even part of language, but a typographic convention. I was amazed to discover that even something so apparently fundamental as the full stop was less than four hundred years old in its current form, though the *name* 'period' to mean a sentence-ending dot of some kind is over two thousand years old.)

WECHSLER INTELLIGENCE SCALE FOR CHILDREN (WISC-R TESTS)

Because of the difficulties John experienced at infant school (see Chapter 16), he was assessed by an educational psychologist. She tested him with the WISC-R cognitive tests, a brief summary of which can be found in Appendix 8. These tests were carried out when he was seven and a half and were then repeated when he was 15¾. John's test results can be found in Chapter 20 where they are discussed in some detail. Nevertheless it's interesting to have a brief look at some of the results here as they give an independent view of John's language strengths.

The 'Verbal' sub-tests of the WISC-R (which are presented and answered orally) include the following: *Information*, which involves general knowledge questions; *Similarities*, where the child has to say in what way pairs of words are similar; *Vocabulary*, where the child has to define the meaning of words and *Comprehension*, where the child has to answer questions about something they are read. The latter includes questions relating to social comprehension. The (scaled) score for each test has a maximum value of 19 and the mean for a population of UK children would be expected to be about 10, equivalent to an IQ of 100. When John was seven his scaled scores were as follows: *Information* 17, *Similarities* 18 and *Vocabulary* 16; the *Comprehension* test wasn't carried out. When he was 15 the scaled scores were: *Information* 15, *Similarities* 17, *Vocabulary* 19 and *Comprehension* 18. The psychologist, who carried out the test when John was 15, said that he was the only person she'd ever tested that had answered all the vocabulary questions correctly and his verbal intelligence placed him in the top 1% of the population.

LITERAL INTERPRETATION

According to Tony Attwood (2006): 'The person with Asperger's syndrome tends to make a literal interpretation of what the other person says, being greatly confused by idioms, irony, figures of speech, innuendo and sarcasm.' Although it would appear that many people on the autism spectrum interpret language very literally and hate metaphors, similes and proverbs, I've never been aware that this applied to John. I can't remember him taking things particularly literally or having a problem with metaphors; his language comprehension seemed to be excellent under all circumstances. John agrees:

> I've never interpreted idioms literally as far as I know, except for humour value, nor had other language problems. My native language is the sea in which I swim, and rarely causes me any problems at all. It's interpreting the *intent* behind language where I fall down.

On another occasion he wrote:

> I don't think I can remember a time when I didn't enjoy metaphor and simile both. Of course, I also enjoy intentionally *ignoring* similes: it's the same sort of pattern-recognition hack that makes me like puns.

Unlike many people on the autism spectrum, John isn't a particularly visual thinker; this, plus his excellent vocabulary, may be a clue as to why he has no problems with idioms and figures of speech. According to Ellen Notbohm (2005):

> To children with autism, with their concrete, visual thinking, their (often brilliant) associative abilities and, for many, their limited vocabularies, the imagery generated by some of our most common idioms and other figures of speech must be very disturbing. Ants in his pants? Butterflies in her stomach? Open a can of worms? Cat got your tongue?

After mentioning two particularly graphic idioms ('keep your eyes peeled' and 'eat your heart out'), Lise Pyles (2002) goes on to provide some sensible advice regarding children with Asperger's syndrome and the use of idioms:

> There are so many of these expressions, and we use them quite unconsciously. Teachers should avoid them. Our kids already have difficulty with communication, and avoiding idioms is one concrete way to ease the strain. I think they are good to use at home, however. The more chances J... has to hear various figures of speech, the more likely he will absorb them and begin to use them himself. At home he can ask questions or take the time he needs to process them, a luxury he doesn't have at school. I try to drop one or two into my conversation regularly.

John thinks it's impossible for teachers to avoid all metaphors and idioms and admits: 'Occasionally I have failed to detect sarcasm, but this is bound to happen if you can't pick up body language well. I spot the vast majority of instances, I think.'

HUMOUR

One day when I collected John (aged about four) from nursery school, a member of staff said to me: 'Do you realise that John doesn't know his colours?' I asked what made her think this, knowing full well that John had known his colours for a long time. She took me into a store room where there were some bright red, yellow and blue hula hoops propped up against the wall. Evidently John had followed her into this room and when he was asked what colour these hoops were, he'd given completely incorrect answers. I told the nursery assistant that he *did* know his colours but I had the very strong impression that I wasn't believed. In those days it was rare to come across people who thought the mother might be an expert on her own child. Professionals often thought that mothers were biased, hysterical, emotional, irrational people who thought their own children were special in some way or other – which of course they are! As I walked home with John I asked him why he gave the nursery teacher the wrong answers when she asked him what colour the hula hoops were. I was pretty stunned to be told: 'As the teacher asked me a silly question I gave her a silly answer!' I confess I burst out laughing as I thought this was very funny, although I did explain that the teacher had taken him seriously. I guess no one expects a child of this age to give anything but a straight answer to a straight question. Perhaps I shouldn't have been so surprised, because if I was asked to describe John's personality in one sentence, I would have to include his irrepressible sense of humour. As John explains:

> For if we do not laugh, this world will make us cry. I prefer laughter. As a defence mechanism it has one huge advantage over all others: it's *fun*. (Also, laughter is a signal of incongruity, and if you spot patterns as easily as I do, incongruity is everywhere.)

He's always found things to laugh about, even as a baby. The paediatrician's report on John when he was eight months old mentions the word 'chuckling' three times as well as 'smiles and laughs'. My husband remembers the children playing together when they were small and great hoots of laughter coming from them. John's strong sense of humour coloured everything he did (and does) and is such an attractive part of his personality. All the au-pairs I contacted commented (without prompting) on John's sense of humour. Our first au-pair, who helped us when John was between the ages of eight and nine, wrote: 'He was happy and funny... He had a good sense of humour even at that young age. He often made sarcastic and quite grown-up jokes!' It's frequently asserted that people on the autism spectrum don't have a sense of humour but I suspect this may be linked to their difficulties with language and facial expression. According to Tony Attwood (2006): 'Hans Asperger wrote that children with Asperger's syndrome lack a sense of humour, but this is not consistent with my experience of several thousand children with Asperger's syndrome.' John's sense of humour is largely language based and pretty dry. Like many people with Asperger's syndrome, John loves puns and word play:

> As a lifelong lover of language I'm always playing with it, gluing words together or taking them back to their etymological roots and punning on that. Most of these don't get mentioned to anyone else because they're too obscure; a pun on the

Shakespearean meaning of 'to lie' isn't of interest to people who don't know that meaning.

One clever and very typical play on words was made by John some years ago when I asked him to give me his views on Tony Attwood's 1998 book on Asperger's Syndrome. There's a heading in this book entitled *An Idiosyncratic Use of Words* in which Attwood writes:

> The child appears to have the ability to invent unique words (or neologisms), or is idiosyncratic or original in their use of language... This ability to provide a novel perspective on language is fascinating, and one of the endearing and genuinely creative aspects of Asperger's syndrome.

John's response to this was: 'Attwood missed a beat there. 'Idiosyncretic' would have been a nice coinage to throw into the mix, while being nicely self-referential.' I had to look up the word 'syncretic' in the dictionary and was fascinated to see that one of the meanings of the word syncretism occurs in the field of linguistics and very roughly relates to the merging of two different forms of a word into one.

As a young child, cartoons were the only form of television John enjoyed; he watched these with his father and sister. When he was older he explained this was because they were fun, provided a form of escapism and sometimes would have good fantasy or science fiction themes:

> I remember enjoying *'Inspector Gadget'* quite a lot, I think because I spent half my time trying to guess what he'd pull out of his hat next.

> The laws of the cartoon-physics universe were a lot of fun (as were the convenient ways they let people get out of sticky ends).

> And there was, of course, more than a bit of escapism: many of the cartoons I liked had fantasy/SF themes, and the simpler sort of SF *does* have a large escapist element.

As an older child, the only radio and television programmes John liked (apart from scientific ones such as Horizon) were humorous ones such as *Blackadder, Monty Python* and *Hitchhiker's Guide to the Galaxy*. One of his favourite television programmes while he lived at home was *Blackadder* which he loved for the 'sarcasm and creative use of language'. However, according to John, 'I'm not sure I ever saw any *Blackadder* other than series 4. I have very few memories of it. I think it must have been a flash in the pan.' I also remember him watching *Red Dwarf* very regularly and as an adult he recalls that it had 'some unexpected twists' but that he was 'never desperately keen because the plotting was distinctly uninspired.' Nevertheless one of John's friends at the time recalls: 'He introduced me to *Red Dwarf* and *Blackadder* via the episodes that had been videoed at your house. The majority of our time together was on the computer or watching these videos.' I also remember John watching *Mr Bean* with the whole family but I'm not sure he enjoyed it as much as we did. In fact these days he says it is 'something I wouldn't watch if you paid me'. He thinks:

> [The] wincing kind of humour, that comes from someone else doing horribly embarrassing things, was amplified for me because many of them were recognisably exaggerated versions of the way I myself acted!

As a child John possessed radio scripts of the *Hitchhiker's Guide to the Galaxy* (which he described as 'inspired wonderful lunacy') and *Monty Python*. As with everything John does, he became absolutely obsessed with the *Hitchhiker's Guide* and reread the scripts countless times. He would quote great chunks from it, Marvin of the flat voice 'and the ludicrous over-the-top negative attitude' being a particular favourite. John finds:

> Marvin is oddly less funny these days. A *lot* of my co-workers are depressive or bipolar, and every year or so some major or not-so-major free software developer commits suicide. Depression is *common* among smart people... I'm glad I'm not that smart.

A couple of years ago John bought himself the complete boxed set of the satirical *Yes Minister* and *Yes Prime Minister* series. He enjoys the dry humour enormously. Every time I stayed with John I used to watch a couple of episodes with him until we'd seen it all.

From the age of seven or so John discovered that telling jokes was an excellent way of communicating with adults, holding their attention and making them laugh. For a couple of years or so he had a passion for joke books which he read and reread. He must have learned hundreds of jokes off by heart; whatever the subject at the dinner table he always seemed to have a very appropriate and funny joke to contribute to the conversation. I remember asking him how he managed to do this and he said that he didn't plan what to say but the jokes just seemed to come into his head at the appropriate moment. He certainly didn't get this ability from either of his parents who cannot remember a joke (or much else!) from one day to the next. Although John still loves a joke as an adult, he isn't particularly good at remembering them (as he says: 'The focus shifted') and he certainly doesn't buy or read joke books any more. His sense of humour is undiminished though and he subscribes to the satirical magazine *Private Eye*. A family member observed perceptively: '[John] can be very funny in terms of anecdotes and responding to something others have said. His written humour seems sharper than his spoken humour.' John agrees that his written humour is 'sharper' than his spoken because 'I need a few seconds (or sometimes minutes) to polish things, and there's rarely the time in the back-and-forth of a spoken conversation.'

One of John's methods of relaxing at the end of a busy day is to look at some favourite web sites guaranteed to contain humorous content: 'Some of them are intentionally humorous. Some just happen to have a lot of people on them with senses of humour like mine.' He often sends us emails, or reads out to us, items that he thinks we will find funny. Sometimes I must confess I don't see *why* they're funny but I'm sure that's more to do with *my* general ignorance. When I do understand the subject referred to, these communications can be extremely funny.

Taking advantage of John's keen sense of humour was a tremendous help in many a tricky position. If John got worked up about something, making him see the funny side of the situation could defuse the atmosphere quickly. In fact our very stubborn son could even be motivated to do something he was initially opposed to, if one could incorporate a sense of humour into the mix; making John laugh was the easiest way through his defences.

FOREIGN AND COMPUTER LANGUAGES

Tony Attwood (2006) wrote that some people with Asperger's syndrome 'can have a natural talent and special interest in foreign languages… When a person with Asperger's syndrome learns a foreign language, there can be a remarkable ability to pronounce the words as spoken by a native speaker.' Although John can learn a new computer language very quickly, this ability does *not* extend to the learning of foreign languages. He believes:

> I'm not good at learning languages *per se*: what I'm good at is finding regularities and cranking on them. Computer languages are simple things: a few dozen regularities and consistent rules. Human languages are fiercely complex evolved monstrosities at the limits of what humans are capable of learning, and with no obvious rules. There are only three or four major families of computer languages, and once you've learned a couple of each of them, the rest are normally quite easy to learn.

My father (who spoke many foreign languages) used to say exactly the same thing about families of spoken and written languages: if you knew one in a family it was easier to learn another in the same family. John believes that learning a computer language as early as he did (aged six) 'wired something into my brain at some level which doesn't happen so easily if you learn it when you're older'. Interestingly enough my father was exposed to several foreign languages as a young child. It's known that (for most people) it's much harder to learn foreign languages when you're an adult than when you're a child. Maybe a similar process is at work with the acquisition of computer languages. Despite John's lack of confidence and reluctance to speak French when we visited France on holiday, he still managed to get a grade A in both written and oral French in his GCSE examination. He thinks the reason he was so reluctant to speak abroad was 'because I know what it is to be good at a language, and I know I'm not that good at French'.

In conclusion: Although John is on the autism spectrum, his command of the English language has always been excellent. Unfortunately this ability *doesn't* mean John was a good communicator, as can be seen in the next chapter.

11
Communication

'Why are you so fat?' asked three year old John in a loud, clear voice to a very large customer in our local grocery shop. When he didn't receive a reply John just went closer to her and repeated the question even louder, while I frantically tried to stop him talking and apologized profusely at the same time to the lady in question. Unfortunately, instead of brushing the whole thing off with a laugh, she was absolutely furious and shouted at John. Even though I tried to explain to him why she was so angry, I didn't think at the time that John had any idea what I was talking about. However I don't remember him doing the same thing again, so perhaps I was wrong. The funny thing was that I'd consciously delayed talking to him about concepts such as fat, thin, tall, short, pretty and ugly. I had a premonition that John, who loved talking to anyone willing to listen (including strangers), wouldn't understand when, or why, these words shouldn't be used. When I *did* introduce him to these adjectives I tried to explain that these personal descriptions of people shouldn't be used to their face because they might get upset if they were told that they were fat or ugly. It would appear that none of this went in as John couldn't wait to demonstrate his newly acquired vocabulary. This issue still seems to cause John some difficulty if the recent email I received from him is to be believed:

It takes notable mental effort even now. I mean, sure, I know they shouldn't be used, but reasoning out *why* is hard. Why would someone object to being told something they already know?... Alternate interpretation: shattering self-delusion. If she thought she wasn't overweight at all, perhaps hearing the opposite 'out of the mouths of babes' came as a rude blow.

Interestingly enough Tony Attwood (1998) uses a very similar example in his book when he writes:

The child with Asperger's syndrome may notice that a woman in the line at the supermarket checkout is obese, and remark, in his or her usual tone of voice and volume, that the lady is fat and needs to go on a diet.

As Gillberg (2002) points out:

An almost pathological need to always tell the truth is striking in many cases. The child does not appear to understand 'self-evident' social rules, and cannot be persuaded to keep his thoughts ('truths') to him/herself... The problem is that the child with Asperger syndrome does not understand social rules, cannot judge the situation, and is unable to conclude that 'certain things you just do not say in certain settings.' There will always be things that are socially inappropriate in some situations or will be felt to be hurtful in any situation: the child with Asperger syndrome often appears to be blind to such matters.

For effective communication between two people there needs to be an empathy and understanding between them which acts like oil on machinery and enables a fluid two-way process to take place. Both people must want to communicate and then they must be capable of rapidly processing a considerable amount of data from the other person, much of which won't be in the form of words. Although we may take this process for granted, it's very complicated and is something we can all struggle with at times. Peter Myers et al (2004) describe empathy as 'the bedrock of social interaction'. They go on to say:

Empathizing involves two major steps, which both happen at lightning speed: (a) the ability to attribute mental states (such as beliefs, desires, intentions, thoughts and emotions) to other people, as a natural way of understanding them; and (b) having an automatic appropriate emotional reaction.

Psychologists call the ability to attribute mental states and understand someone else's point of view the *Theory of Mind* (ToM). The absence of ToM, sometimes called mindblindness, is thought to be one explanation for some autism spectrum behaviour. In 2006 Tony Attwood wrote:

The person with Asperger's syndrome has immature or impaired... empathy, not an absence of empathy... The person does care, very deeply, but may not be able to recognise the more subtle signals of emotional states or 'read' complex mental states.

That accords accurately with John's point of view:

I think I can do the empathy part a bit: assuming I can correctly read their expression I can do the 'I feel what you feel' part quite well. The problem is the reading of the expression and the construction of the model of what they're feeling.

... most of my emotional reactions to others' emotional states are normal. The hard part is figuring out what their emotional states *are*.

Baron-Cohen and Wheelwright say that people on the autism spectrum 'may pick up the more extreme emotions, but miss the emotions on another's face or in his voice.' This certainly applied to John, as he pointed out rather wittily when he was 28: 'I certainly miss subtle tone of voice cues and non-verbal stuff. Well, I don't *detect* it: I certainly don't often *miss* it in the sense that I care what they're communicating using magic telepathy.' However, by the time John was 34 his attitude to others had changed considerably: 'I very much do care what they're communicating using magic telepathy because there's pretty much no other way to communicate it, and emotional states matter.' Perhaps it isn't surprising that in recent years I have detected a significant improvement in John's communication skills. John agrees with this, writing:

I've got better at tuning my detection of vocal tones, using content to help out (which is fairly new). Still not much visual in there. Still not much eye contact. (Still too overwhelming.)

This chapter looks at some of the reasons why John experienced so many communication difficulties, despite his excellent command of the English language, his need to talk to people and his desire to be part of a group. John thinks:

[This] is the great autistic tragedy. We are not like non-social animals, loners and content that way: we need aloneness but *also* are still social animals with all the drives that come with it, yet social animals who cannot *be* social.

143

NON-VERBAL COMMUNICATION

According to Leventhal-Belfer and Coe (2004) many young children with Asperger's syndrome have 'difficulty interpreting or reading non-verbal clues':

Social communication depends on our ability to read *non-verbal cues*. Having difficulties in this area can lead to many confusions and misinterpretations on the part of the child.

Meanwhile Tony Attwood (2006) points out:

Typical children, especially after the age of five years, are remarkably astute at perceiving and understanding social clues that indicate thoughts and feelings. It is as though their mind prioritizes social clues above other information in their environment, and they have a mental theory as to what the social clues mean and how to respond...

The person with Asperger's syndrome perceives the physical world more than the social world.

This sounds just like John. He certainly didn't prioritise social clues and as a child his interests were focussed almost entirely on the physical world. In fact from babyhood John appeared to be far more interested in things than people. All his attention was given to watching and playing with inanimate objects, particularly if they moved. As he grew older, John's focus moved to books and computers where his interests have remained to this day. Although John has always been happy in the world of facts, ideas and imagination, he admitted recently:

With time I have come to see the world of social interactions as equally potentially fascinating. It's just a largely-closed book to me (and, true, outside my focus: but a lot of factual stuff is outside my focus too.)

He says he has some vague regrets that he's missing out on some of the pleasures that others appear to enjoy in the social world, such as more friends, but not the social world itself.

As a child John's lack of interest in the people around him meant that he didn't learn by observation what the majority of other children pick up so easily. This may well have contributed to the difficulties John experienced reading facial expressions, body language and emotions and to his failure to modify his own behaviour accordingly. Words alone are relatively unimportant in face-to-face interactions. *How* we say something is usually much more significant than *what* we say. The signals we receive all the time from the faces and bodies of others can help us to appreciate how they feel and how they are reacting to us and what we say. John didn't pick up any subtle visual signals and had no idea how anyone was feeling or thinking unless they spelt it out verbally or the emotions portrayed were very strong. Being able to observe these visual signals is one reason why (for most of us) personal contact is such an important part of any friendship. These days John says: 'That matters to me, too, but perhaps less than to other people (how could I possibly tell?)... I don't think I'm different from the norm here: I think you are overstating things a bit.' The content alone of someone's conversation would be far too sterile for most of us to use as a basis for friendship. We also look for things such as warmth and support and for people that make us feel good about ourselves.

As described previously in Chapter 6, John had poor eye contact for many years, looking at the ground rather than the person he was talking to. If he was asked to look directly at the person he was speaking to, he would end up staring at them. This is extremely common behaviour for children and adults on the autism spectrum, as Attwood (2006) describes:

> People who have Asperger's syndrome have two problems in using information from the eyes to determine what someone is thinking and feeling. First, they tend not to look at the eyes as the dominant source of information regarding social/emotional communication and, second, they are not very good at reading the eyes that they do look at.

Several people who wrote to me, both John's peers and friends of mine, commented that John made little eye contact. According to one of my friends: 'My memories of John in his mid teens were that he spoke very quickly, made little eye contact but was understandable.' One of his aunts wrote to me that John 'avoided eye contact and rather hung his head but this has got much better since adulthood', a sentiment I would entirely agree with. Nevertheless, John still finds:

> It's hard for me to discuss things in person with anyone I don't know really well. I've got the stress of real-time interaction and the problem that information I don't fully understand is being transmitted over a channel that it's actively stressful to look at: the conversational partner's face.

John's not sure why he avoids eye contact: 'Is it discomfort... an attempt to keep the flood of incomprehensible signals down?' In his late twenties John wrote to me as follows:

> In the far past, early teenage years and back into prehistory, I used to parse human expressions entirely by looking at the position of the mouth and facial colour, so I spotted when people were red with anger, or beaming: I fairly soon figured out what things like pursed lips meant too. Around my teenage years I started to use eyebrow position as well; but I didn't use eye muscle tension at all. I didn't even realise it was important until quite recently: people said eyes were important, but eyes don't have expressions themselves, it's the stuff around them.

John said it was reading the chapter entitled *Hotheads*, in Steven Pinker's *How the Mind Works*, that finally explained to him 'what it was about the eyes that signalled emotion, why it was so critical and also why it is so subtle and hard to see... But I still didn't know *what* patterns of muscle tension meant what.' He says the marvellous software called *Mind Reading: The Interactive Guide to Emotions*, developed by Simon Baron-Cohen and colleagues (which he acquired a few years ago), is really helping him understand and recognise some of these subtle signals. Tony Attwood (2006) recommends this interactive DVD program as particularly suitable for children and adults with Asperger's syndrome:

> Such individuals can have considerable difficulty learning cognitive skills in the 'live' social theatre of the classroom, where they have to divide their attention between the activities in front of them and the social, emotional and linguistic

communication of the teacher and the other children. With a computer the feed-back is instantaneous; they do not have to wait for a response from the teacher and they can repeat a scene to identify and analyse the relevant cues many times without annoying or boring others. They are also not going to receive public criti-cism for mistakes and are more likely to relax when engaged in a solitary activity. The program is designed to minimize any irrelevant detail, highlight the relevant cues and to enable the 'student' to progress at his or her own pace.

John's own body language always appeared different from his peers, partly because he had such an intense manner but also because he looked physically awkward. He had (and still has) a stiff frame, for many years he had facial and other motor tics and when he's talking with enthusiasm his hands move a lot. The unconscious signals John sent out may well have instigated a poor response in others. At secondary school in particular, bullying was a major problem:

I'm sure if I'd been able to read people I'd have been able to see currents in the mass: people shying away from me, that sort of thing. I'm sure I existed in a sort of 'bubble' in the flow and that others looking for people to attack read this flow and moved toward its source.

However John learned some very useful things from his awful secondary school ex-perience which have helped to protect him since he left home. In his words:

[These were] how to avoid hostile situations by running away; how to detect hostiles at a considerable distance; and the rapid mapping of possible hostile terri-tory and trajectories across it that minimize danger.

Lydia is very aware that groups of lads hanging around in the street will often nudge each other and stare at John. Fortunately John hasn't been attacked so far, something I used to fear. Although John says he detects 'hostiles' and knows how to avoid them, Ly-dia believes that he doesn't even notice them. He insists he *is* aware of the nudges, com-ments and stares, saying: 'Believe me, I notice it too. It happens just walking past them in the street, so I think it must be postural or gait-related. Ah well, adolescent boys are all testosterone-poisoned anyway.' A few years ago though, John *was* unaware of the group of lads that were hiding round the corner while he was trying to withdraw money from a bank machine in his local town. He didn't notice as they crept up on him while he was in the middle of a transaction. They noted his pin number and then forcibly removed his bank card. John went into the nearby Chinese restaurant (where the staff were very kind to him) and used his mobile to phone the police, who came really quickly. Mean-while the gang followed him to the door of the restaurant taunting him; although John told them he'd phoned the police, they didn't leave. Fortunately they didn't attempt to use John's bank card to withdraw any cash, even though they knew his pin number. When the police arrived, these youths still had the card in their possession. I believe they were taken to the police station where they were given a warning. John was followed by this gang several times after this incident but always at a distance: he's never been surround-ed or hurt. He always made sure that he took them for a very long walk and never went back to his house until they stopped following him. They never found out where he lived. John was told recently: 'Two of them are now in jail for armed robbery (they tried to rob a shop or something, I don't know the details). The rest are being... extremely notable by their absence.'

John has spoken in the past about filters coming into play when he communicates with other people:

My understanding is that *everyone* has these: social masks that change the way you act... I just grew them later than everyone else. They're still not entirely unconscious. They don't come into play around you much if at all: family gets to see the default me. Everyone I know *well* does, pretty much, mainly because I can't concentrate on anything else with them on and it's really tiring to use them at first, though less than it used to be. The social masks used to be incredibly conscious entities. I used to have to almost plan significant conversations out in advance, rehearsing conversational forks and so on and hoping I didn't get too far off track, which I always did. Over time I was able to build up standard responses to things I might be asked in specific situations... New bosses at work I treat cautiously as anything, treat them like unexploded bombs... I have to assume they're going to be expecting god-knows-what political stuff and who knows how they'll expect me to act but I can't avoid being a little different!

When I asked him if he used these filters less when he got to know people better he replied:

Partially: partially they sink into my skin, as it were, and become part of the default way I interact with someone: they get automated out of existence for that one person. I start to figure out, a bit, over the years, how to avoid annoying them too much... I feel more comfortable, certainly. Some of these filters (especially the new-boss one) are really hard to keep going: I have to evaluate everything I'm going to say to make sure it's not too undiplomatic, which always fails somewhat when I get excited.

PROCESSING SPEED

In addition to the difficulties he has with non-verbal communication, John also has problems processing *what* people say to him and thinking of a suitable response speedily enough to make for an easy conversation. The problems are multiplied greatly when he's in a group situation. He can't switch quickly enough between different speakers and subjects and there isn't enough time for him to formulate answers that he's happy with. As Tony Attwood (2006) explains:

Typical people are very quick and efficient in using ToM [Theory of Mind] abilities when engaged in social situations. Research has shown that while some children and adults with Asperger's syndrome can demonstrate quite advanced ToM skills, they can take longer with the cognitive processing of the relevant cues and responses than one would expect...

One of the consequences of using conscious mental calculation rather than intuition is the effect on the timing of responses. In a conversation or social interaction, the person with Asperger's syndrome can be slow in processing aspects that require ToM skills...

I have also noted that ToM abilities in children and adults with Asperger's syndrome can be influenced by the complexity of the situation, the speed of the inter-action and the degree of stress. In large social gatherings the amount of social in-formation can be overwhelming for someone with Asperger's syndrome. The person may have reasonable ToM abilities but have difficulty determining which signals are relevant and which are redundant, especially when inundated with so-cial cues.

The time taken to process social information is similar to the time it takes for someone who is learning a second language to process the speech of someone flu-ent in that language. If the native speaker talks too quickly, the other person can only understand a few fragments of what has been said.

John's processing problems in a group are exacerbated by his inability to cut out the extraneous sound and concentrate solely on the person he's talking to; he hears all the si-multaneously occurring conversations equally and is overcome by the noise. To this day he finds noisy and crowded places very hard to cope with and is perfectly capable of rushing out of a social event. When John was 28 he sent me a copy of a moving email (see Appendix 9) in which he attempts to explain to a friend why he'd walked out of a social gathering (where he knew no-one but the host) after less than a minute. John's use of slow, crude, conscious mental models of people, as opposed to the fast unconscious ones used by most of us, are described in detail in this email. According to Gillberg (2002):

[Slowness may be] one of the major reasons why people with Asperger syndrome have such enormous problems in real life settings even with the kind of social un-derstanding that they manage relatively well in the laboratory.

John completely agrees with this saying: 'I'm trying to do things consciously that you've either automated or have entirely hard-wired; of *course* it's massively slower.'

John hated the phone as a child because he couldn't work out what someone had said *and* think of an answer fast enough to make the conversation flow easily. He never phoned people just for a chat. I find it interesting that someone who was pretty unaware of facial expressions still found it easier to talk to someone in person than speak to them on the phone. Perhaps the fact he could see *when* someone was talking helped. John's processing problems seemed to disappear completely when people phoned him up (as they did quite frequently when he was a child and adolescent) asking for help with their computer problems. The authoritative and adult way he would ask the caller questions and then get them to try out various things on their own computer never failed to amaze me. There would be no small talk whatsoever. He was like a different person but in many ways that was precisely what he was when problem solving in his area of expertise.

As John's conversational skills improved in his late twenties so did his use of the phone, although this only applies to people he knows well:

Any others and I can't tell when to stop or start speaking and the conversation degenerates into collisions, awkward silences, and stammering. With people I know well, I can tell when they've left a hole for me to fill up.

He has a land-line and a mobile phone but usually sends text messages on his mobile rather than holding conversations. The only people John talks to regularly on his land-line (apart from his weekly conference calls for work) are his parents and his best friend, who is particularly keen on this form of communication. Some of their conversation is about the computer projects they are working on together but they also talk about science fiction and a wide range of other subjects. When John rings us up there is no 'how are you' etc. to start the conversation. He plunges straight into whatever he wants to tell you as if you'd both been sitting in the same room for the last hour. In reality, though his conversational skills have improved, his processing speed has not; he still dislikes the phone, and doesn't 'use phones unless absolutely necessary'.

Is this difficulty with the rapid processing of visual and aural information the underlying problem responsible for all of John's communication problems? Was the world of human beings too fast, unpredictable and confusing for him to follow as a baby and young child? Did he focus his attention on things he *could* cope with? Moving objects and scientific facts all had a certain predictability about them which John could learn about at his own pace. Unfortunately, because he didn't watch and listen to those around him, John would have found it difficult to learn how to read body language and society's unspoken social rules would remain a mystery. Of course John may well have found technical matters far more interesting than people but it's certainly tempting to think that processing problems contributed to the final outcome.

The results of cognitive testing (for details see Chapter 20) show that John received a high score on the Comprehension sub-test of the WISC-R which would strongly suggest *strengths* relating to social skills and common sense. However in reality, these have been areas of significant weakness for him. It would appear that John's problems with social relationships were less to do with a *theoretical* lack of knowledge about social rules and the decisions that should be taken in real life situations and rather more to do with the practical application of these rules in everyday life. When John was 30 he wrote:

> I do have spasms of reading textbooks on interpersonal relations and conversational grammar and so forth, but that rarely has any direct effect because I can't apply it fast enough: social events fly past so fast that only neural-layer au-tomated stuff can really help, not conscious learning.

As far as I can see, this is why very early intervention (of the *right* sort) can be so crucial. There's the possibility that some of these conscious processes could be convert-ed into automatic ones. Unfortunately getting the intervention right is far from easy; so-cial situations by their very nature are so varied. Following a set of rules will never make up for a lack of intuitive understanding. In fact inappropriate application of these rules can easily make a person on the autism spectrum stand out even more from their peers. Somehow the young child must be helped and encouraged to watch, listen and un-derstand those around them. All possible means should be used to achieve this objective including video and DVDs, books, games, discussion and so on.

CONVERSATIONAL GRAMMAR

Despite John's excellent command of English grammar, he found the rules of conversational grammar very hard to master. As Leventhal-Belfer and Coe (2004) point out:

Pragmatic language (the ability to use words to engage others socially) is the aspect of communication with which children with Asperger's Syndrome have the most difficulty... turn-taking is critical in maintaining a conversation with another person...

Many young children with Asperger's Syndrome do not read the nonverbal cues in others, nor do they register the comments made by others. They will talk endlessly about something and do not move from their topic to another's easily... Children don't typically stick around when they are being 'talked at.' Adults, on the other hand, may spend more time trying to decipher what the child is trying to say. Therefore, it isn't uncommon for these children to be more comfortable seeking adult attention.

As a child John experienced major problems following the usual conversational conventions relating to taking turns and starting and stopping a conversation. Either he would be very quiet or he would do all the talking, unable to let a conversation roll backwards and forwards in a natural manner. Even as an adult, John finds ordinary conversation with people he doesn't know very difficult. In his late twenties John wrote:

Even now, I don't have any social initiative to speak of... my utter ignorance of how to open conversations, how to find out what people might be interested in, and, indeed, my lack of interest in finding any of this out in most cases...

I don't know how to strike up conversations with people I don't know. The best I can do is pull random conversational topics out of the air and try them, and, well, it works inconsistently, and I can't spot any coherence in what works and what doesn't.

How can you strike up conversations with people when you don't know much about them? I guess I could learn, but the problem then is remembering it, when it's so far outside my focus area and I don't even know how to go about learning.

John *has* learned something recently though:

One trick I've used a few times is when I spot someone reading a book I've read. At least that book, and related books, are probably good conversational starters. That's how I got to know Amanda (she was reading *The Mote in God's Eye* I think).

One of the consequences of John's inability to read body language plus his keen desire to communicate his overwhelming passions and interests, was that he 'talked at' people rather than talking and listening in a normal conversational manner. He never recognised the 'glazed' look that appeared in many people's eyes when he was spouting on about something that interested him and never noticed if they didn't understand what he was talking about. There's no doubt that he's found it really hard communicating effortlessly with others face to face. According to John that's an understatement:

Hard? It pretty much never happens. Talking *at* other people, yeah, that can be effortless but largely because I've half-forgotten the other person is there in the rush of ideas. To-and-fro, no, I suck at that. I even suck at that online to a great degree: I can't follow the flow of conversations in realtime. When they hit me they stumble over rocks and get diverted. I suspect part of this is my distractibility coming into play.

As Attwood (2006) so aptly puts it: 'There is a tendency... to talk at length without recognising another person's boredom.' We were certainly very aware of John's tendency to 'talk at' people about his particular interests and completely dominate any conversation but this was difficult to deal with. We didn't want to dampen his enthusiasm and what he had to say was often very interesting. Fortunately, or maybe unfortunately, adults were always very polite and tolerant and would listen to him (or at least pretend to) even if they had little idea what he was talking about.

According to Tony Attwood (1998), Carol Gray found that children with Asperger's syndrome 'often assume that the other person is thinking exactly what they are thinking or they assume the other person was thinking exactly what they said and nothing else'. When John read this at the age of 27 his reaction was: 'Bang on; that expresses exactly what I was thinking until my teenage years, and I still sometimes forget that others can't read my thoughts.' As my psychologist daughter Lydia so accurately pointed out, 'this is ToM in a nutshell'.

It took many years before John started to notice the 'glazed' look appearing in the eyes of those he was speaking to, began to *listen* to others and didn't talk all the time. When I asked him if he knew what was responsible for him noticing 'glazed' expressions he replied:

It slowly came to light. It wasn't a sudden aha! moment, really. It's not the eyes I use, either (how can I when I don't look at them?) It's the lack of response other than 'hm' and sometimes the lack even of that.

He thinks the improvement started when he was about 15, although he thinks he was still 'prone to missing people being bored to death when I was 21. (I know that because I bored M... to sleep once).' By the time he was 27 'nobody was complaining any more: either I had improved or I was just hanging out with equally boring people. I don't know.' I also asked John what made him realise that it can be a good thing to *listen* to others as well as talk. He replied:

That was when I noticed that it was the only way I could tell if they were following what I was saying! Well, first of all you have to realise that what you're saying *can* bore someone to death, and I'm not sure I really grasped this before my teenage years. The one aha! moment I did get was aged fifteen: I'd just bored someone to death babbling about some nifty new software or something and finally I realised that hey! unaccountably this strange person is *not interested* in this! It was a horrifying realisation (mostly because I realised at once how I'd have to gauge interest continuously and how hard it would be to do that). It also made me feel like a complete idiot because I'd known for many years before that everyone has different interests. I just hadn't realised that people caught fire with interest over different things: that the fire wouldn't necessarily spread from person to person.

As far as the family is concerned, there's one exception to John's improved conversational ability and that occurs when we're out walking. As mentioned in Chapter 8, when John walks it's as if he totally regresses to the child who talked *at* you. The floodgates are opened and should I ask him an innocent question about something he's working on, within seconds he will be off and I won't understand anything he's talking about. Meanwhile he appears to be completely unaware of the situation and seems quite unable to stop. Of course he's *theoretically* aware that I couldn't possibly know what he's talking about but that doesn't translate into a simplified explanation. I have to interrupt frequently to ask what 'so and so' means. It isn't helped by the fact that John can't see my face or expression (because we are walking side by side) or by the fact that he is feeling relaxed and just being himself. His sister can't bear 'the onslaught' when we're all together on a walk. She say 'she uses walking as an opportunity not to think' and so makes sure she walks ahead with her dad.

INTERRUPTING

Tony Attwood (1998) describes the tendency for some people with Asperger's syndrome to interrupt or talk over people as follows:

> One of the potentially infuriating aspects of Asperger's Syndrome is a tendency to interrupt. The person has difficulty identifying the cues for when to start talking (i.e. a momentary pause, the end of the topic of conversation or the body language and eye contact that indicate 'your turn'). They may also not appreciate the effect of interrupting on the flow of conversation or the feelings of the other person.

This certainly applied to John, who would get so passionately involved in the topic being discussed he would interrupt frequently. Kutscher (2005) notes that one of the symptoms of ADHD is impulsivity, which includes 'blurting out answers… or interrupting'. Even in his twenties John wrote:

> I still don't know how to determine who is 'next in line' in a conversation. I feel 'lost' in conversations a lot of the time… whatever the cues are that someone's conversational turn is finished, I can't pick them up, or I pick them up a lot more slowly than other people so I never get a turn. This leaves me with a choice of 'interrupt or shut up' and forget what I was going to say.

> I don't think that the problem with me is that I don't know when I'm interrupting, more that if I don't interrupt I'll never get the chance to say anything!

This habit of interrupting wasn't helped by my poor example. I get so carried away and involved sometimes that the words or questions just seem to burst out under their own volition. 'Exactly', says John. However I don't get lost in conversations. I think *my* tendency to interrupt is largely linked with an underlying impatience at the slowness of others to finish what they are saying and an overwhelming compulsion to have my say, either before I forget it, or the conversation has moved onto a different subject and my thoughts would no longer be relevant. I try to bite my tongue and think I've improved a bit with age but those who know me well may not agree! John finds:

> One major advantage of email (correctly quoted) is that one can 'interrupt' at any point, with complete retention of past context, and no disruption to the ongoing conversation itself; as a result, email conversations are actually a lot *more* flexible than direct ones.

He believes proper quoting is essential, which means interspersing the reply to an email at the appropriate places within the original text. He disagrees with the practice (adopted by most people) of putting the 'reply at the top'. He thinks this is 'like listening to a conversation backwards' as one reads the email reply *before* the original email.

John's sister Lydia suffered a lot as a child because John didn't allow her to have any opinions of her own and was always putting her down by pouring scorn on her views. These days John is mortified by his behaviour, writing: 'Sorry sorry! I didn't mean it! It wasn't real scorn. More 'fight back and we'll find the right answer, whatever it is' scorn. Unfortunately perhaps you had to be me to tell the difference. I've never scorned Lydia.' She found it 'hard to get a word in edgeways' and when she was about seven realised that she 'was being talked over and cut off a lot'. She felt that she 'never managed to get a full sentence out'. Only having 'very short pauses in which to speak' enabled her to become 'very good at the quick one-liner'. As Lydia grew older she's made an enormous effort to stand up to John and ensure that he takes her views seriously. It can't have been easy because he's very knowledgeable about so many things and has such a good memory. She 'remembers quite clearly that you would ask him to be quiet and let me say something, but it was very difficult to keep doing it all the time'. She thinks to 'keep stopping him over and over again would have been bad for his self-image'. She also believed that he couldn't help this pressure to speak as it was connected with his impulsivity. Knowing what she does about attention deficit disorder Lydia thinks 'it would not have been fair on him'. John had no idea that Lydia felt that her views weren't being listened to and finds this really shocking: 'Whenever did she think I didn't? Lydia's views really matter: she's one of the smartest people I know and is enormously insightful (plus the whole sister thing).'

CONVERSATIONAL CONTENT

In many ways John's behaviour and understanding of others was what you might expect from someone who came from another planet. He wasn't interested in gossip, never had any social chit-chat and had no idea how to engage in small talk. As he wrote a few years ago:

> The standard human grapevine (people talking to other people in ever-shifting groups) isn't something I've ever been connected to. I doubt I ever will be. I just can't gossip properly: perhaps it requires more of a grasp of conversational grammar? People don't gossip much to me, I don't gossip much to them. I'm not even sure what is discussed. Social information exchange I presume, but when I overhear it it seems to be mostly football… probably this is an artefact of an 85% male office.

There are many reasons though why John feels he *is* part of the social grapevine when his communications are net-based (see Appendix 10). These days John thinks: 'Gossip about people in my social circle is interesting to some degree – of course it all happens over the net except on the rare occasions when we meet up. I don't give a damn about the celebrity of the week.' John always wanted to interact with others but only on *his* terms. This usually meant exchanging information about his interests, at which point he always became positively enthusiastic and hard to stop. A friend of mine, who saw John as a child about two or three times a year, thought:

[He] appeared distant and seemed to be happier on his own rather than mixing with others. Conversation was not forthcoming, but he would respond when spoken to. When he was interested in telling you something he spoke very quickly and with great enthusiasm. He appeared very focussed on some tasks but almost to the point of being obsessive e.g. computing...

According to other friends of mine they described variously:

John was very knowledgeable about science things... he was very single minded about the things he was interested in – he would tell you all about those...

Although John wasn't the greatest 'social' communicator, I always found him polite and good company and highly knowledgeable and intelligent about his favourite subjects – science, astronomy, computers...

He wanted to tell one a lot about his current interest. It was at the same time impressive and exhausting.

John is far from being alone and says: '[These days] I know it's a bad way to converse and have tried to change.' I'm always surprised at the number of adults (particularly men) that I've met who only want to talk about themselves or their passions and show no, or very little, interest in the person they are actually talking to. One of John's aunts wrote that 'he doesn't actually enquire about my life much.' As far as John is concerned: 'How to do this with anyone is a giant mystery. I suspect my life is just too different from non-geeks to even know what subjects to enquire about.' Lydia, on the other hand, says that as John has grown older he *has* enquired about what she's been doing and how she's getting on. John agrees but says:

This is the result of conscious effort to do what is expected, and because I know Lydia likes it, and because I actually do like to know how this person who lived with me for so many years spends her day. It's still mostly a blur to me, though. It's not natural at all: it's all artifice.

Unfortunately, John's highly technical interests plus his inability when he was young to conduct a two-way conversation, made it particularly difficult for him to communicate with the majority of his peers. They weren't interested in science and computers and thought he was weird. This became more and more of a problem as John's specialist knowledge in the field of computing increased; his language became harder and harder for ordinary mortals to understand. All of John's aunts commented on the fact that they had difficulty understanding him because he spoke so fast and because of the technical content of his conversation, particularly when he was talking about computers. For many years John's sister hardly ever knew what he was talking about, as it was so specialist and made absolutely no concessions to the listener. As she recalls: '[He talked] unrelentingly about things that I had no idea about. I could only understand about 10% of what he said! He was super-intelligent and it was intimidating.' In response, John wrote:

[I] always thought of Lydia as the intimidatingly smart one, breezing through exams with stellar marks with hardly any visible effort, getting heaps of qualifications and everything. It doesn't take intelligence to know what I know, just no social life and a lot of focus.

The only time that John's interests were comprehensible to the ordinary mortals around him was the couple of years or so when he was passionate about jokes. This phase died a death as he gradually became more immersed in computers.

The ability and desire to communicate with technical people plus the inability to talk to non-technical people, have remained with John throughout his life to date. Quoting from his appraisal at work (when John was 29) where he was employed as a systems analyst/computer programmer:

> John is excellent at establishing contacts with technically focused peers both within the company and outside... however he needs to tailor his explanation of problems/solutions to his audience. This is particularly true of his verbal communication.

I know exactly what they mean. If I ask John a simple question about his work I get a detailed, and to me, technically incomprehensible answer. He finds it extremely difficult to put himself in the listener's shoes, find out how much they know already and pitch the explanation at an appropriate level. As Lydia pointed out this is related to his problems with empathy and *Theory of Mind*. Nevertheless I think there *might* have been some improvement in recent years. According to John:

> I've *had* to learn how to translate down in the last decade, or nobody other than co-workers could understand me (and in the last job, not even those most of the time).

> There appears to be a division here: either one's interests are boring to others because they are too complex to be comprehensible without background knowledge (e.g. computing) or they are boring to others because they are too simplistic and the patterns are too hidden to be discernible to others (e.g. those lower-functioning autistics who focus on regular things with subtle patterns like railway timetables).

QUESTIONS, QUESTIONS, QUESTIONS

Two very good friends (Malcolm and Rosemary), who studied physics with me at university, remember a particular day when John was about eight or nine when they'd been invited to Sunday lunch with us. They recall that, with our excellent navigation tips and Rosemary's fast driving, they arrived to find all of us still in bed! As Malcolm put it:

> Lydia and John were detailed to entertain us while you got ready to greet the day in a leisurely fashion. John immediately seized control of the situation by asking how aeroplanes worked – obviously Tony had told him that I worked at the Royal Aircraft Establishment – I very soon had the feeling that my answers to his more and more detailed questions were not adequate in John's opinion. What I could not admit to John was that I knew very little about planes since most of my expertise was in the field of electronic warfare and missile defence. His questions were logical and very persistent though occasionally he did not like the answers... I seem to remember that he had several novel ideas for cockpit controls and pilot training so perhaps I should have listened more carefully since I subsequently moved into that area myself. Definitely not a child to be trifled with.

Meanwhile his wife Rosemary, whom I saw quite regularly before John started school, remembers:

> A very restless, inquiring child, always moving and insistently asking questions to which he expected accurate answers. He was not to be deflected when he wanted to know something and not slow to let one know if the answer was found wanting.

Another good friend of mine, Anne, remembers looking after John when he was about three. She wrote:

> He asked a lot of questions and paid careful attention to the answers. These questions were usually of a technical nature relating to inanimate objects and were never personal or emotional. He was particularly curious about how things worked. One example was when he woke me up one morning with the question 'How do clocks work?' He was holding out the carefully disassembled components of my alarm clock!

This account seems quite surprising given John's poor manual skills but I have no reason to disbelieve Anne's account. Even John finds it unexpected, writing: 'I managed to disassemble something in a fashion that could be described as 'careful' rather than 'incompetent'? Amazing.'

John was very chatty with his nursery school staff, as he was with anyone willing to listen, and he never stopped asking them questions. Sometimes this caused a problem, particularly when he kept interrupting during the story telling sessions or when he seemed to be asking the same question over and over again. I remember one instance which occurred when John was four and the nursery school was decorated with Christmas lights. He kept asking the nursery teachers: 'Where does the electricity came from?' They pointed out the socket into which the lights were plugged but John just repeated the question over and over again. When I asked him about this he told me he wanted to know how the electricity got to the socket and where it came from. He was very interested in anything scientific and may well have known more about electricity than some of the nursery school staff. He was certainly blissfully unaware how irritating he could be with his constant questioning. My husband said that John's habit of 'asking me the same question time and time again when he had already been given an answer' annoyed him. I'm not really sure why John repeated his questions so often when he was a child. Was it because the answers he was given didn't provide an explanation that was adequate for his needs? Was it because he wanted to find something to say and couldn't think of anything other than a question? Was it because he didn't listen to the answers or had forgotten the answer he'd been given previously? Perhaps he'd forgotten that he'd already asked the question? Was it comforting to hear the same answers again and again? Maybe all of these were true on different occasions. Temple Grandin (2005) wrote: 'Constantly asking questions was another of my annoying fixations, and I'd ask the same question and wait with pleasure for the same answer – over and over again.' Perhaps John had to ask a lot of questions because he was a very intelligent child with an enquiring mind whose curiosity about the physical world around him could only be satisfied by asking questions. The questions reduced considerably once he became a fluent and avid reader who could find out the answers for himself.

Relationships with Peers and Adults

As a young child, John always seemed very naive and immature socially. He was a lovely little boy, happily absorbed in his own world and blissfully unaware of peer pressure and the complex social world around him. He didn't copy others or observe how they behaved, had little interest in children's programmes on television and played in the presence of others on his own terms. He didn't seem to pick up unspoken social rules, perhaps because of a fundamental lack of interest in other people's behaviour. According to Attwood (1998): 'The child can be indifferent to peer pressure for the latest toys or clothes.' John, when writing about his unhappy years at secondary school, said:

> One cannot feel peer pressure from those one does not consider peers, and I have to say that I felt *anti-pressure* from most of the people at school; i.e. if they were interested in something I'd make sure I wasn't (to stay out of their way, mostly). I don't think I felt much peer pressure from anyone else, though, either; perhaps because peer pressure is part of the social game that I don't understand; is the internal logic 'if I don't do what everyone else is doing I'll never fit in' fear-based? If so I'm *very* glad I never felt it.

In *An Exact Mind*, Peter Myers is said to have 'preferred the company of adults to that of other children [because they were] less frightening – they provided a more predictable, and consequently, safer environment.' When John was a child he also found adults far easier to deal with than children of his own age; adults would make allowances for him in a way that his peers would not and they were sources of information. As he recalls: 'I preferred adults to other children, because I could learn things from them and they didn't keep trying to pressure me into complicated social stuff.' Nevertheless Alice, the mother of Harry (one of John's closest friends at school), found it difficult to communicate with John. She wrote to me about her memories:

> I think it was his inability to communicate in appropriate ways that I remember most – he did not make eye contact with me, he rarely talked to me directly. If asked to do something he didn't want to do, often related to his safety, he would shout or mutter so I couldn't hear him.

She remembers that John did respond to her son and she often resorted to asking Harry 'to try to persuade John to do whatever I needed him to do.'

Although all John's aunts remembered a warm and very affectionate child who got on well with his sister, he was also remembered by one aunt as gawky, shy, clumsier and more socially awkward than other children. Another aunt remembered John as being tense, frustrated and capable of tantrums if teased or thwarted. However, the aunt who mentioned the tantrums used to tease John mercilessly until he could take it no longer. According to John: 'Thankfully this has stopped of late, probably because the one time she tried it when I was an adult, I responded by giving her one warning and then just leaving!' All John's aunts find him friendly, amusing and kind as an adult and enjoy his company.

John appeared to be largely unaware of most of the children in his nursery class and never knew their names. It took a long time for the children in John's primary school to get used to him and even longer for him to get used to them or even become aware of them as individuals with names. His ignorance of many unwritten social rules made him appear different throughout his years at school. This difference was most apparent to his peers, many of whom would shun him (at best), or when he changed schools at 11, bully him. As Tony Attwood (2006) points out:

> Being isolated and not having friends also makes the child vulnerable to being teased and bullied. The 'predators' at school target someone who is alone, vulnerable and less likely to be protected by peers. Having more friends can mean having fewer enemies.

He appeared really odd to many children; 'weirdo', 'mental' and 'spastic' were typical of the names John was called, particularly after the age of 11. Recently he wrote to me:

> The thing about my lack of social comprehension was that it was generally so extreme that... I didn't even realise that I was missing anything. The 'oops, everyone else seems to be telepathic' thing only kicked in when I wasn't oblivious to things like ostracism any more (maybe fourteen, sixteen, something like that? maybe even later.)

Fortunately John was never isolated or lonely at home as a young child because children often came to play in our house. When John grew older, he had a few close friends who shared his interest in computers. As John remembers:

> I did have friends of my own, although even there it's obvious in hindsight that the others fitted together somewhat better than I did: I was always slightly on the periphery of any group. This is even true now, on the net; I prefer to let others have their say first, and frequently they say everything I'd have said, so I end up not saying anything at all. Oddly this is quite different from the way I act off the net. I have no idea why the difference exists.

Attwood (1998) recommends that parents might enrol any children with Asperger's syndrome in clubs in order to improve their social behaviour. John, aged 27, wasn't impressed with this suggestion:

> I think I'd have hated it in club-like things. The few times I went to a youth club it seemed like school only worse; there was *nothing* but the social stuff I was crap at, but withdrawal was similarly not allowed. I shudder to recall it even now.

With the best of intentions we'd enrolled John in a youth club for a trial year when he was at junior school, thinking he might enjoy it and might make some more friends. The club was at the end of the road we lived in and John seemed to go quite willingly without any fuss. When the year was up and we asked if he wanted to rejoin the following year he declined but I'd absolutely no idea at the time just how much he appeared to have hated it. The poor child was just doing as he was told and was obviously used to spending a considerable amount of time putting up with situations he didn't like. I completely agree with Tony Attwood (2006) when he writes: 'If parents arrange social experiences, it is important that the experiences are brief, structured, successful and voluntary.'

John has been driven 'by a hunt for regularities and patterns: by a need to find order in the world' and not by a need to conform. He's always had strong views on what is right and wrong and what he's prepared to do, regardless of what others may think. One friend of mine, whom we saw rarely as she lived a long way away, wrote:

> All I can remember of him is that he was very 'self sufficient' and didn't seem to need any critical input from other people. i.e. he would speak and act without appearing to worry about the reactions of others. Almost childlike innocence I suppose, but not at all embarrassing. Refreshing I'd say. He never did or said anything unacceptable. He seemed blessed with being able to get on with his life without the crippling doubts I have re my interactions with others. Lucky boy! It's the sort of thing that makes him easy to be with. Non-judgemental?... He always seemed to me a lovely boy. I think life would be better if we were all a bit more like him: free of artifice.

John would also like it if people were free from artifice. What a lovely impression John made on this particular lady but unfortunately her views were not shared by many; life would have been much easier for John if that had been the case. Part of the problem was that, as a child, John had no concept of status; he was unable to adjust his tone, manner or language according to the person he was talking to. Family, teachers, people he didn't know at all and children of all ages were treated identically. He would be too friendly to strangers and didn't seem to be aware that they should be treated a little less openly than someone you knew. He would assume that they knew all about him and would talk to them in exactly the same way as to people he knew well. As he grew older he became much more aware of status although he has very strong views about it:

> The emotional systems that respond to dominant individuals definitely work: I don't know when they turned on, probably in my late teens. I suppress them as much as I can because I consider their existence ethically abominable: nothing else in the human make-up has caused as much trouble across the ages as our dominance relationships, and I refuse to participate.

One positive outcome of John's behaviour is the way he treated children younger than himself. He would give them as much respect as an adult, spending time explaining things to them, even if they didn't understand what he was saying. He's always enjoyed playing with young children (if they wanted to play with him) and he can be very patient, although he doesn't think of it as patience, just friendliness. In fact he thinks:

> I'm really impatient, but if someone is plainly struggling then there is no opportunity for me to get impatient: I can watch them trying to learn and try to help out. There's lots for me to do in that situation.

He plays so well with his young niece that, when she was three, she declared: 'When I grow up I want to marry Uncle John.'

RUDE AND NAUGHTY

John's habit of talking to everyone in the same blunt manner meant that adults often thought he was being rude. His inability to recognise other people's body language also meant he didn't recognise the warning signs people give off when they are becoming annoyed. As a consequence, he would blithely continue with whatever behaviour was provoking this reaction, rather than backing off. As Tony Attwood (2006) writes:

> The child appears to break the social rules and does not respond to the warning

signs. If the adult or other child does not know that this behaviour is due to impaired or delayed ToM skills, the interpretation of the behaviour is to make a moral judgement: that the child with Asperger's syndrome is being deliberately disrespectful and rude.

When John was six and a half and his sister nearly five I went back to work and the children were collected from school by a patient and motherly child-minder. She took the children back to her own house until I arrived at about 5.30pm. Everything seemed to be going smoothly until I arrived from work one day to find a crisis. Whenever the weather was good enough, John would be out in the garden, talking to himself and playing happily on his own. The houses were terraced, the gardens narrow and the fences between the gardens very low. On this particular day John had got into a 'conversation' with the man next door, an old fashioned secondary school teacher with a very short fuse. The man had absolutely 'lost it' and bellowed at my son, really upsetting him in the process. I strongly suspect that if it hadn't been for the fence he would have hit John as well. I went next door immediately to have a word with the man, first to find out what had happened and second to say that his behaviour was absolutely unacceptable and on no account was he ever to behave like that again. It turned out that John had just been his normal self and omitted to give the man the respect he felt he deserved. As John read this he recalled:

Oh, gods, the memory's coming back. What a horrible man. In my memory he even *looked* really nasty, but that could be memory playing tricks on me because of the way he acted. In my memory we exchanged about two sentences before he exploded, and one of those was 'hello'. Totally incomprehensible to me, of course.

To John respect couldn't be demanded but had to be earned. He loved talking to adults and always had enormous respect for those who were intellectually outstanding but he had absolutely no sympathy for those who demanded respect by virtue of their age; this caused problems on many an occasion. As John explains: 'Giving people faux respect because they'll get angry if you don't merely demeans the respect you give those you truly *do* respect.' As a child, John spoke to adults as equals, being very honest and direct and saying what was in his mind without editing his thoughts first or considering the impact on the other person. As far as John is concerned, children and adults *are* equal: 'We *are* children's equals. We just know more than they do, but in compensation, they're much faster learners than we are. It balances out. The child is father to the man and all that.' As Hans Asperger wrote (in Frith, 1991):

Autistic children are egocentric in the extreme. They follow only their own wishes, interests and spontaneous impulses, without considering restrictions or prescriptions imposed from outside. They lack completely any respect for the other person. They treat everyone as an equal as a matter of course and speak with a natural self-confidence...

They may demand a service or simply start a conversation on a theme of their own choosing... without any regard for differences in age, social rank or common courtesies.

In response to this John wrote to me recently as follows: 'I've grasped the last of these to some degree, but have absolutely no desire to grasp the first two.' As well as treating everyone the same, John was also unable to judge what tone of voice to use on what occasion and was quite unaware that this was even more important than the actual words used. According to Leventhal-Belfer and Coe (2004): 'Around four years of age children understand that they need to talk differently to their teachers than to a peer or a younger child.' John didn't. As his tone of voice reflected how he felt, regardless of the person he was talking to, it isn't surprising that John was often in trouble for what was considered to be out-and-out rudeness. John's class teacher wrote on his school report when he was nine: 'John has often been downright rude to many of the staff.' The following year a different teacher wrote:

Although John has commanded a considerable amount of my attention and time I shall feel it was well worth the effort if he settles to more acceptable behaviour towards both adults and his peers. There have been definite signs of improvement, but he still sometimes needs to take care with the tone of his voice.

Even as an adult John finds it difficult to adjust his tone of voice to the circumstances:

I still can't. I just talk to them as I'd like them to talk to me. It works with everyone except stuffed shirts, and I've got a lot better at spotting those and avoiding them (nothing will make them into nice people: if they have something useful to tell me, I'll get that out of them and then detach as rapidly as possible).

Curiously, though the way I act towards people of any age has never changed in this respect, people no longer call it rude. The inevitable conclusion is that no rudeness was ever involved: all it ever was was thin-skinned adults being offended because non-adults did not treat them specially because of their age. Sorry, I'm not an ageist and I cannot regard ageism as a desirable thing.

When Ingrid (our second Swedish au-pair) asked her English husband Ben if he remembered anything about John, within seconds he told her:

When we stayed at his mum and dad's house you all came for a short visit and John immediately started running around the house opening all drawers and cupboards and Ben running after him trying to stop him. He just assumed that he was an extremely rude and naughty boy.

John was nine at the time. Ingrid thinks 'this was the way most people reacted and felt when they met John in those days. Once you got to know him though he was the most loving and funny boy.' According to Walker (2012):

There is another label that often comes with that of autism: the naughty child...

One of the first references thrown up by my internet research was a 2010 survey by autism charity Treehouse which found that three-quarters of parents and carers of autistic children polled believed the public thought their child was just naughty. Next, I found a piece of research finding that scores of pupils were being unfairly excluded from school because their autism was mistaken for naughty behaviour.

With age, John has become far more sensitive to someone's tone of voice. There's still room for improvement in his recognition of facial expression and body language but he's working on this with the help of Simon Baron-Cohen's *Mind Reading* software. I don't think John would be considered to be a rude person any more. However, while he was in his last job, John wrote that 'my bosses might disagree. They sensibly insist on vetting stuff that non-technical clients might see, and I entirely agree with this.' John says he engages in politeness 'purely because I see that some of the rules make sense when inverted, and that the others cost little and stop people getting annoyed'. Nevertheless there are occasions when John feels his social skills are still really lacking. When he was 31 we'd been discussing the fact that he should think about changing his job, something we both knew he would find very difficult to do because of his fear of interviews and any change that involves people. He sent me the following email shortly after this conversation:

> Another reason I don't want to hunt for jobs *just* now is that my social ability seems at a low ebb. So far this week I've pissed off just about *everyone* I've talked to and I don't have a bloody clue why in most cases. I suspect if I went to an interview right now most people would prefer Myra Hindley over me!

SOCIAL GAFFES

In 1998 Attwood wrote:

> Errors in social behaviour are due to several factors, in particular not understanding the consequences on the feelings of others, and being unaware of what they are supposed to do or a more appropriate or subtle alternative. Rarely does such behaviour have malicious intent.

John agrees with this, saying:

> I'd say I almost *never* mean to be malicious; if I am, you can tell because it's obvious. Subtle maliciousness is almost certainly unintended. It's hard enough to make friends without throwing them away.

However, John's difficulties reading body language have meant that, until relatively recently, he could easily upset or embarrass me in public by the things he said. His sister Lydia also had the same problem:

> [John] would appear to intentionally embarrass me at times, by revealing something that was private or not quite true (his take on things)… He would embarrass or upset others by saying/revealing inappropriate things and we had to be careful what we told him.

John agrees that he still has a problem in this area because 'even now I can't attach privacy tags to things people tell me'; however, he thinks he has improved somewhat in recent years. Victoria Biggs (2005) writes that people with DCD/dyspraxia 'have a hard time with the concept of 'secret'.' John believes: 'My problem isn't having trouble with the concept of 'secret', it's losing the secrecy tags on stuff I already know, assuming it's not secret, and then whoops.'

As John grew older, he became painfully aware that he was capable of being unintentionally very hurtful at times, because he hadn't picked up the distress signals emanating from the other person. He became very upset if this was pointed out to him because he's a sensitive person who has no wish to cause pain; he hates to make what he calls 'social gaffes'. According to John the reason social gaffes cause him such a problem is that 'if I recognise that I've made them at the time, it feels bad enough that the lesson always sinks in: I *never* make that mistake again. However, I rarely recognise them.' Nevertheless with time he *has* become increasingly aware of making 'social gaffes' which actually means he makes fewer of them. This is one aspect of John's steadily improving social skills as he progressed through his twenties and thirties.

GROUPS AND TEAM-WORKING

As a child, John found it very difficult to cope with group situations such as those to be found in a classroom. The headmaster's contribution to John's Statement of Special Needs, written when John was nearly eight, said: 'The problem centres on his relative inability to adjust to the classroom environment allied to relationship with and attitude to other children.' According to John's school report, written a little later: 'He finds great difficulty in conforming to class discipline.' When he was nine his teacher wrote:

He has exhibited slightly eccentric behaviour which has made him somewhat isolated at play. He has many sympathetic companions who are put off by his occasional pinching, scratching and biting tactics.

John's current interpretation of such behaviour is: 'Leave me in peace why won't you listen to me please just GO AWAY!!!! (possibly also an effective way of ending attempted bullying?)' John was obviously finding it very difficult to cope with other children at times. Things did improve by the time he was 11, his teacher writing: 'I feel John has made big strides forward in his ability to relate to his classmates. We certainly have 'off' days but he has begun to be able to laugh at himself and accept advice more readily.' John had now been with the same children for several years so there had been plenty of time for him to get used to them and vice versa. This was undoubtedly his best year socially at school and I suspect his outstanding Froebel[44] trained class teacher contributed significantly to this improvement. Unfortunately the following year only two children from John's class went with him to his new school; we went back to square one in terms of John's ability to relate to his classmates.

John found working in a team extremely difficult as a child; this required social skills that were completely beyond him. His school report, when he was nine, stated: 'He finds it almost impossible to cooperate with group work', while according to his report when he was ten: 'John makes a limited contribution to group or class activities although with his remarkable general knowledge and vocabulary and ability to write and research information he should be a real asset.' The ability to work in a team remained a problem for many years but from the age of 11 onwards John did begin to participate in class discussions. His school report from that age stated: 'Most articulate and makes very worthwhile contributions to discussion times, learning slowly that others too must have their say.' I think John's ability to work with others improved considerably as he grew older, although group working at university was spectacularly unsuccessful. According to John this was because the other members of his group didn't have sufficient computing knowledge and weren't prepared to listen to him. Although this may well have been the case, what is also true is that John didn't have the people skills to persuade more ignorant team members that his opinions were really worth consideration. In his teens though, John worked successfully on many computing projects with a friend in a 'team' of two. Since he left university he has continued to work with another friend on a variety of projects in his spare time and ever since he started work he's had to work with others. In his previous job John believed that he was a poor team player: 'I effectively reduce it to non-teamwork by taking all the nasty (and interesting) parts for myself!' Now that he is working with equally competent people John's views have changed:

> I no longer believe this: I have been a little duckling on several projects at the new job and it went fine; also sometimes a big duck on other projects at the same time with the same people!

For many years it appeared as if John disliked being part of any group but I don't believe this was actually true. He just hadn't found a compatible group. John has become an excellent team player as long as it's in his field of expertise and he's dealing with similarly expert people. He's always loved helping others and finds that he has an instant rapport with highly technical computer geeks, so much so that they can easily finish each other's sentences. However he still finds it more difficult to deal with non-technical people. To a certain extent I suspect many of us have experienced something similar. We know what it's like to feel really comfortable with close friends and family and how uncomfortable we can feel if we have to spend any length of time with people whose backgrounds, values, tastes and knowledge are totally different from our own.

As described in Chapter 8, John wasn't interested in sport. As for team sports (particularly those where people are just put in any team in a sports lesson), John just didn't 'get it':

> I can't understand why anyone was interested in the success of a team that they were *assigned* to at random unless the task was of intrinsic interest. Sure some people are intrinsically interested in team sports, but I can't really see that *everyone* is so interested. Are the rest just caught up in the mob emotion or something? If so, *shudder*, it sounds horrible.

Tony Attwood (1998) suggests that teachers should encourage cooperative games in order to improve the social behaviour of the child with Asperger's syndrome. John's reaction to this was:

> Cooperative games? Stress city, no thanks. Perfectionism means that unless the game is positive-sum (and has no concept of 'losing'), then any failure will tend to lead to panic attacks/tantrums/abrupt departure. I'm sure that the ingenuity of children could convert even such games into one with the Aspergic on the outside of a little clique.

THE INTERNET

Everything changed once John immersed himself in the internet:

At last, I found the bunch of globally distributed individualistic nutcases I could call *my* people; hackers and sysadmins all. Asocial I may be, but every human needs a group to be part of, I think, and a globally distributed one where your writing is your persona is perfect for me.

For those not in the know, 'sysadmins' are those in charge of an organisation's computer systems. According to John, 'hackers' means highly motivated computer programmers who work for love rather than money. It does *not* refer to criminals trying to break into other people's systems to steal their data or cause other mischief.

Despite his poor communication skills, John has always had some friends; common interests have always been the basis of his friendships. As John's interests don't include popular masculine pursuits such as football or cars, it's been harder for him to find like-minded people. The internet has proved a wonderful means of locating people that share John's interests and ways of thinking. For as Tony Attwood wrote so accurately in 2006: 'The internet provides an opportunity to meet like-minded individuals who accept the person because of his or her knowledge rather than his or her social persona and appearance.' John's thirst for knowledge, enthusiasm, excellent written language and desire to communicate have meant that the internet has literally transformed his life. It's provided him with friends all over the world with whom he communicates whenever he wants. As John wrote:

> The catchment area of the net is near-global; someone on it *will* be someone with interests in common with you! The problem can be finding them... Plus, *age* is undetectable on the net... I guess I'm lucky in that such a high proportion of hacker-types are Asperger's sufferers, or on the borderline; what would be weird behaviour elsewhere is outright expected there, and joy-in-creation unifies us.

With internet communication available in his home, John will never feel lonely or isolated:

> Though I can't cope with large amounts of social interaction at once, without *any* social interaction I'll withdraw into a depressed and lonely cocoon over the course of a week or so; thankfully this never happens any more thanks to the net. I'm still a social animal: I'm just a social animal who's *really bad at it*.

Occasionally, when he's had a major computer failure and can't get onto the net, John is absolutely bereft; he says it's as if a part of his body was missing. This is really a very apt analogy as the internet, for a person with John's communication difficulties, is the equivalent of a hearing aid for a person with hearing difficulties or a walking stick or wheelchair for someone who can't walk unaided.

The internet, where body language and facial expressions are usually irrelevant, has provided the perfect medium for a person happy with words and language but poor at face-to-face communication. In John's words:

> The value of interactions over the net is more than anything that 'you are what you write'; stuttering, slurring, unexpected pauses in conversations are not detectable.

> In email, everyone is autistic: nobody has magic telepathic body-reading skills and the equivalent (linguistic forms and emoticons) I'm very good at picking up on. Email is hugely preferred to face-to-face contact by every linguistically-strong aspie I know, or at least every one who can type well. There's a reason I use a pseudonym: it's because I've always felt like a different person online, and not just as a figure of speech. Same knowledge, same characteristics, different

165

persona – in fact it's the same, but the stress is so much lower that it *feels* different.

Other people in virtuo are fine; I can terminate and restart the interaction whenever I wish, with the other party often not even knowing I've done it (e.g. email) and because email doesn't tend to have all this social crap, but is more often functional or purely interest-based (e.g. long chatty emails); in physico none of this applies and it's really much harder.

Jim Sinclair,[45] one of the founders of Autism Network International, describes the importance of cyberspace for those on the autism spectrum as follows:

For those of us who are comfortable with written communication, online contact offers the opportunity to meet and interact with other people while remaining at home in our familiar environments. We don't have to go out into noisy crowded public spaces and risk uncontrollable sensory assaults. We can take in and respond to communications at our own pace, instead of having to keep up with realtime conversation. We can participate in online discussions with large groups of people, and since we're only reading one email at a time, we can keep track of who's saying what. We can catch everyone's input if we want to, or choose which ones we want to read and which we want to filter out. We don't miss out on what one person is saying while we're listening to someone else. It's fairly easy online to filter out input from people we find uninteresting or unpleasant to hear from. And many of the communication pitfalls we encounter in face-to-face communication with NTs [neurotypicals] – being expected to understand nonverbal signals, having people try to read meaning into our own appearance and nonverbal behavior – don't exist in text-only communication. (It still boggles my mind when NT people complain about this as a *drawback* of online communication!)

These sentiments agree with many of Penny Benford's findings in her PhD thesis entitled *The use of internet-based communication by people with autism.*[46] She also noted:

It can be hard for people with HFA/AS [high functioning autism/Asperger's syndrome] to modify their emotional responses...

For some their difficulties were such that it was difficult to express themselves verbally when they were experiencing strong emotions. Online communication provided an easier medium to express themselves at such times...

Several of the interviewees referred to instances where they had unintentionally upset people, or an awareness that others found them too direct in their manner of communication. To some extent communicating online provided more space in which to consider the impact of what one says on the feelings of the other person, as well as distance from the emotional responses of others...

Tony Attwood (1998) points out that for many people with Asperger's syndrome 'there is often an eloquence that is remarkable in written or typed form'. According to John though:

It's not my eloquence in typed/written form that's remarkable, but my *lack* of it in speech. I often feel that I can only truly communicate in written English; the

166

simplistic conventions of spoken English are like a straitjacket, and the requirement to construct sentences entirely in memory is terribly confining.

I thought that John's difficulties with social rules didn't apply to the etiquette of the
net which he seemed to adopt easily. It seems I was mistaken, as John explained to me:

Hah. Talk to Adam about the hazings he gave me... to get me to understand those
conventions. They're not complex but it took several weeks and a good few harsh
words before I grasped them. (Adam, more than anyone, gave me my net persona.)

For those, who like me don't know what the word 'hazing' means, it can be defined
as a term used to describe various rituals and other activities involving harassment,
abuse or humiliations used as a way of initiating a person into a group. In retrospect
though, John believes 'hazing' is perhaps too strong a term: 'No harassment, abuse or
humiliation was involved. Well, perhaps a little light shaming if I failed to 'get it' soon
enough.' According to Benford: 'Unintended social transgressions might be prevented
because of the rules and moderation within many online groups'.

A few years ago John told me that he'd learned a great deal about the two- (or multi-)
way nature of a conversation from the internet, where 'lurking and overhearing
conversations is easy: I know orders of magnitude more about most of the people I know
there than I do about most of the people I work with.' Lurking on the internet is
discussed further in Chapter 17. Lydia says she can have an interesting conversation
with John when they go out for a meal in the evening and that he will enquire about
what she is doing and listen to her opinions to some degree. This is certainly a far cry
from those years at home when Lydia was constantly put down by her brother who
always knew more about everything and would never listen to her. He still isn't very
good at social chit-chat but as long as the conversation has some meat to it, he can listen
and accept other people's views, even though he still enjoys a jolly good argument. The
improvement is really quite astonishing. After meeting John again a few years ago when
I had my 60th birthday party, my old friend Malcolm observed:

John appeared to have changed remarkably, becoming a personable young man
with a good deal of charm and at least the appearance of empathy. He was good
company though still very focussed on his own interests. His sheer enthusiasm for
his subject in general and the historic development of computer hardware kept us
going through several long walks through the local countryside. Again I felt I was
being outpaced in more than the physical sense.

His wife Rosemary wrote:

[When John was young] I think it was his single minded pursuit of what he
wanted, without regard to what other people were doing or saying, which was the
most noticeable difference to an outside observer. I have to say that as he grew
older this changed progressively and meeting him again as a young adult he
shows much more social grace and interaction with other people. It is more
comfortable for those around him.

Recently I became aware that John belongs to a very supportive online community.
As described in Chapter 9, John had, after 13 years in the same job, overcome his fear of

change sufficiently to enable him to consider looking for a new job. He informed his online community of fellow geeks where to find his CV on the web and asked them if they had any ideas as to where he might look for a job. Not only did several people come back with excellent improvements to John's CV but this approach led directly to the offer of the perfect job. John has now been working very happily for this company for five years. I doubt that such a satisfactory outcome could have been achieved in the absence of the internet.

LYING

We were astounded to hear from John's teacher (at a parent-teacher meeting) that eight year old John had called her 'a stupid old cow' in front of the whole class. We were even more amazed that we hadn't been informed at the time so that the issue could have been dealt with immediately. Although we'd worried how John would get on with this particular teacher (see Chapter 16), it was now the end of the school year. As she'd never been in touch, we'd naïvely assumed that everything was fine. We were very surprised to hear that she'd experienced major problems with John throughout the year. This teacher told us that she'd sent more than one letter home with John; he'd obviously read them, realised he would get into trouble and never given them to us. We told her that we'd never received the letters and asked why she wasn't surprised not to receive a reply from us. Apparently John had told her that we were too busy to answer and she'd believed him! She'd made no attempt to send any letters via the postal system nor had she tried to contact us by phone. Maybe John's comment was all too accurate, however his behaviour was quite unacceptable on many counts. Not only was his rudeness something I suspect he knew wasn't acceptable but this was the first time we became aware that John was lying. However, John said he 'didn't really consider them lies':

> The goal was to keep the teacher happy so she wouldn't make my life hell. In order to do that, one figures out what she wants to hear and tells her. She's happy, I'm happy, winners all round. This desire that reality should also conform was most unfair: since I couldn't *make* it conform she was essentially punishing me for not being able to change reality to conform with her impossible desires. Telling her what she wanted to hear without regard for reality was much simpler, as long as you only considered the next five minutes.

Although children on the autism spectrum are not supposed to be untruthful, children with ADHD are known to lie quite frequently. According to Barkley et al (1990) (as quoted in Kutscher (2005)): '49% of kids with ADHD lie (vs 5% of typical children).' Our son practised and almost perfected the art of lying during the year with this teacher. He'd found a coping strategy which meant he avoided getting into trouble over things he had or hadn't done. John reckons: 'For a long time, it *worked*. Perhaps I shouldn't have generalized and tried it on people other than that horrible teacher, but generalization is what children *do*.' During a general discussion about what he'd learned at secondary school, John included: 'Minimization of unpleasant and boring tasks by any means possible, including evasion and outright lying. I think I used this quite a lot before, but it really came into its own here.' John's inability to understand how others view such behaviour meant that lying became a long term problem. It went on for years and years and to this day I can't always be sure if John's telling the truth. According to John:

I lied because they blamed me if I told them what they wanted to hear and it wasn't the same as reality, *and* they blamed me if I told them what was real. Most unfair, what was I to do? At least if I told them what they wanted to hear they were happy with me for a moment. So you see, it was quite a rational choice really, if you don't understand why people prefer to be told the truth...

He had absolutely no awareness how despicable and distasteful others find dishonesty and those that engage in it. As an adult John claims:

I have an intellectual understanding of it now, but only from observing the reactions of others (mostly in fiction), though there seems to be a lot of lying in politics and high finance too. Perhaps the problem was not lying, but lying while not a CEO [chief executive officer]?

Because of John's motor coordination difficulties, problems concentrating, poor organisation and planning skills and so on, he was often getting things wrong. As far as he was concerned lying worked most of the time; he wasn't told off and hence avoided a lot of confrontation and unpleasantness. According to John anxiety was at the root of his lying:

Back in the far past it [anxiety] was the cause of almost all my lying, because my anxiety levels when I'd lied to someone were normally lower than the levels when I'd admitted to failing to do something. Why this might be, I'm not sure: I knew lying was wrong, but I suspect that I was reasoning that if the lie was about something relatively unimportant or had a reasonable chance of never being detected, the benefit in reduced anxiety and (often) reduced time spent doing boring out-of-focus stuff outweighed the costs. (I realised that people would remember past lies and adjust their opinion of me based on that, but, before my university years, most people other than you had an opinion of me that could hardly get lower anyway. I then overgeneralised that into 'everyone has a really low opinion of me, therefore I can and should lie to everyone if there is any benefit at all', which is obviously faulty reasoning!) This was faulty reasoning for another reason, of course: once a lie was detected, the consequences generally caused me much more anxiety than I'd have had if I'd just owned up to whatever-it-was in the first place. But that was further in the future... by that time something else would have gone wrong and I'd be consumed with worry over that instead.

In an email written to me in his thirties, John tried to rationalise his reasons for lying and said that he lied not only to avoid punishment but also 'to avoid disappointing you':

The ethics of lying in this area are a knotty question. Is it more ethical to disappoint someone by telling the truth, or to spread a little happiness by lying to them about something unimportant? – and I *still* have trouble believing, emotionally, that anything relating to me could ever be important to anyone else. Thus, lying about such things must be unimportant too: so it spreads a little temporary happiness for no loss, and by the time they realise it's wrong they will probably not care, and I'll have probably gaffed in some other way before then, and I just want to get through the next school day. I've always been good at rationalizing excuses for keeping on doing the same things I was doing anyway.

However, John's lying tactics certainly didn't work *all* the time. There were many occasions when one lie would lead to another until he landed himself in the most appalling difficulties. A few years ago he wrote:

> I have now come to the conclusion that since I can't tell when little white lies become huge steaming black ones, simply telling the brutal truth all the time is preferable. I try to temper it occasionally, but fall back on plain truth-telling whenever possible. Of course my boss hates *that* whenever the truth is not what he wants to hear, but I consider that his failing, not mine.

John was never a very good liar anyway since he couldn't remember what he'd said and the lying was very blatant. As John admits: 'I'm utterly pathetic at full blown lying.' He agrees that he had a problem remembering what he'd said, but felt 'the payback (people don't get angry with me! People are happy!) was so large that I kept trying. After all, I wanted people to be happy, even if I *had* screwed up again, so that meant hiding the screw-up.' John estimated that lying worked about 90% of the time and was therefore worth it. Cold logic, a complete disregard for the views of others and a lack of comprehension of social rules made it very difficult for us to deal with this issue. John says he didn't take into account the views of others:

> I wasn't thinking that far ahead, just to the effect on their emotional state of whatever it was I was planning to lie about being disclosed (often that I'd lied about something else). Often the start of a chain of lies was something to save a bit of effort on my part, maybe avoid a bit of really unpleasant homework and get something actually interesting done, and from then on it cascaded.

I think John got away with so much lying because most of us are largely honest and assume others are too. As he got older I *think* I got better at detecting his lies by assuming that when I asked him a question about something he didn't want to do he wouldn't be telling the truth and therefore asking for proof. For example, if I asked him whether he'd done his homework and he said 'yes' then I would ask him to show it to me. If he was lying there would be an immediate explosion of temper and that was always the give-away that he'd been caught out! Apparently John thinks I *did* become better at detecting his lies: 'Oh yes. I mostly got out of the habit in the end because you were spotting all of them. You used 'trust, but verify' as well'. Tony Attwood (2006) agrees that lying can become an issue for the family. As he writes: 'The person with Asperger's syndrome may not realise that the other person is more likely to be offended by a lie than by any apparent misdemeanour.'

According to John:

> I generally forgot this, and it became obvious to me all over again only once I was entangled in yet another chain of lies... in the end I came to the conclusion that all this mental effort and worry for such a piddling reward was just inefficient. So I switched to telling the truth all the time. This didn't work too well either. I remain unclear where the balance lies.

John also lied to avoid admitting that he was in the wrong, whether or not he would have been punished:

> I definitely *do* find it hard to admit being in the wrong, and such admissions

almost invariably *do* follow large amounts of internal resistance and simulation to see if I can rephrase the question so as to have been in the right. I think that this may be part of the reason for my once-near-constant lying. It's much less frequent these days, taking the form almost entirely of saying things are finished which aren't, quite, yet, in order that people not think I am slow or because I've been getting distracted and want something to beat myself back into action.

According to Attwood (2006): 'Another characteristic associated with Asperger's syndrome is that the person does not know when he or she would be expected to tell a 'white lie', making a comment that is true but likely to cause offence.' Victoria Biggs (2005) advises her readers: 'Do not tell lies – unless someone asks you if they look fat or wonders if their eye make up is horrible. Then be economical with the truth.' John's predictable reaction to this was:

Er. Yeah, i.e. don't tell lies *unless* they're socially-expected ones. And how do you recognise those?

Why not tell the truth here? If you lie about it, she'll go out with horrible eye make up on, and everyone *else* will get a negative reaction. Surely she'd prefer to change it to something not-horrible... what? no? oh.

Unfortunately in our culture some lies are considered acceptable and others are not and most of us have no difficulty distinguishing between these. To someone like John, who finds it difficult to see things from another person's perspective, it appears as if some lies are '*mandatory* and most others are forbidden. The difference remains somewhat elusive.'

ASKING FOR HELP

In the past, John has found it almost impossible to ask for help, even when he was really struggling. During the two years he was studying A level physics I asked him frequently whether he needed any help and he repeatedly assured me that everything was fine. Then suddenly one day at the end of May, just a few weeks before he took the exams, he had a major panic attack and said he couldn't do any of the physics and that had been the situation for the previous two years. Unbelievable! He thinks 'this was a slight panic-induced exaggeration on my part'. Fortunately there was still enough time for me to go through the fundamentals with him and he passed with a reasonable grade. At university we had a similar problem. Although, at the beginning of his computer science course, John and I had been to see the person who was supposed to help students with special needs, it turned out to be a complete waste of time. She expected *him* to go to *her* if he had any difficulties but he *never* went back even though several serious situations arose during his time at university when her intervention could have been very valuable. A friend of ours said that her autistic son 'wouldn't ask where one course was when he couldn't find the lab in his first year [at university] and missed the whole course. No one spotted it until his exam results!' Again Tony Attwood (2006) has something useful to say on this subject:

At a very young age, typical children realise that someone else may have a solution to a practical problem and that others might be interested and able to help. This insight into the thoughts and abilities of other people is not automatic for children with Asperger's syndrome. When presented with a problem, seeking guidance from someone who probably knows what to do is usually not a first or even a second thought. The child may be sitting or standing next to someone who could obviously help but appears 'blinkered' and determined to solve the problem by him- or herself.

Attwood also writes: 'Children with Asperger's syndrome can be reluctant to seek help because of a fear of being considered stupid or annoying the adult.' As far as I can make out there are several reasons why John found it so hard to ask for help in the past: he didn't like to lose face by admitting he didn't understand or know how to do something, he preferred to learn by trying to work things out for himself and he found it stressful having to interact with people when asking for help. As John discovered in his first job, asking for help was difficult:

Sometimes the people I asked exploded at me (because they were doing something else and I didn't realise that if they said nothing, it meant 'not now'). So asking people for help was like stepping into a minefield: I never knew if they'd explode, and if they did it would disturb my equilibrium and ruin the whole day. Much better to struggle through on my own. I learnt more, too.

When he was 30 John also wrote:

I must not make it seem that there is anything that I do not know. I'm slowly getting over it. Also, I prefer to try to figure things out on my own in domains that I want total understanding of, because I know that I'll learn something even from the false starts and wrong turnings. I can also get so absorbed in a problem that I don't notice that I'm surrounded by people I could ask for help! Finally, it meant interacting with people and that's often annoying enough.

A few years later John thought:

I'm getting a bit better, but it still seems both presumptuous and scary to ask for help, much more effort than, say, spending several hours to days trying to solve the problem myself. (Also, I invariably learn more that way. I'm not sure my long-suffering managers agree that this is a good tradeoff, though.)

Recently John has become much better at asking for help, both at work and at home. He thinks there are several reasons for this improvement:

As I learn more I become more aware of just how much more human knowledge there is, even in factual domains, than I can ever amass. So rather than try to learn everything by trial and error I'm asking people for help in domains where I don't want to learn absolutely everything, and concentrating on specific areas a few at a time until I learn them in enough detail to be able to answer any question posed immediately. Then I move on to other areas. If it gets an annoying problem out of the way, I can jump on to something else, and I'm always under crazy time constraints. Mostly it's because I've realised that even if I don't learn from *this* problem, there's an endless sequence of them down the line waiting for me, and if I spend ages on this one problem I'm going to have to wait longer before I encounter the juicy ones further on. Also I finally generalized from my own case and realized that people almost never dislike being asked for advice.

Victoria Biggs (2005), in her book on coping with dyspraxia, was very grateful that she'd been brought up to ask for help; she felt this had helped her to be independent. When reviewing her book for me in 2006 John wrote:

> I'm not sure if explanations that 'you should never be ashamed to ask for help' would help with me. It's just stating the obvious, but it doesn't make the fact that asking other people for help is *much more stressful* than puzzling away to try to solve whateveritis, even if the puzzling might take an hour or so and the asking-people might take five minutes.

This reluctance to ask for help is a trait shared by my husband and I suspect by quite a few men! If I'm lost, when travelling by car to a strange place, I would stop at the nearest garage or ask someone walking along the street how to find the required destination. My husband used to prefer to keep driving regardless, in the hope that the situation would magically sort itself out. He's improved over the years though and will ask for help readily if he's lost – at least if he's with me! John too has gradually improved as he came to realise, that just as *he* likes to be asked for advice, so others might also like to be asked for help. As my psychologist daughter said: 'Asking for help allows others to feel close to you, with studies finding that, when asked for a favour, the person asked likes the asker more.'

VOCAL CHARACTERISTICS

Many of those who came into contact with John found his speech difficult to understand: it was extremely fast, especially when excited; he mumbled and his diction was indistinct; there was a certain flatness in pitch; the content was highly technical; there was some odd pronunciation and he tended to use unusual (but correct) words in day to day conversation. One of his peers said that when John was of primary school age 'sometimes he grunted rather than used words' and another remembered that he 'used to mumble a lot'. In Christopher Gillberg's book *A Guide to Asperger Syndrome*, the author describes the unusual vocal characteristics of many individuals with Asperger syndrome: 'There appears to be a deficiency in the auditory feedback system such that the person with Asperger syndrome may not actually hear that they are speaking too loud or too low.' When commenting on this book in his late twenties, John wrote:

> I stumble over words (when I think faster than I speak); I've certainly got flat prosody, unusual pitch, and volume that starts a conversation properly adjusted and then doesn't change even if the situation changes, except if I get excited when it rises but never falls again without conscious attention. I'd say I certainly *hear* that I'm speaking too loud or fast or what-have-you, but that this is prioritised low enough that it never makes it to conscious awareness. If this feedback is supposed to happen without conscious intervention, then, yes, such a system doesn't seem to exist in me at all.

According to Tony Attwood (2006):

> The prosody and especially the vocal tone of speech can be unusual, with some children and adults with Asperger's syndrome having a 'flat' vocal tone that is

perceived as monotonous. The speech characteristics can include problems with volume, being too loud or too quiet for the context... The fluency or delivery of speech can sometimes be too rapid, particularly when the person is excited or talking about a special interest.

One of John's aunts wrote that he 'had a staccato way of speaking' and in her teens, John's sister became aware 'how odd he sounded: stilted, as if making an announcement':

> His voice did not have a natural flow and rhythm: did not have the natural pacing that speech takes, slowing up at certain points, pausing and speeding up at certain points, that other people have in their speech. It sounded very unnatural, as if there was a pressure to talk and get everything out at once... without a pause.

John is aware of his stilted speech: 'I can hear this, too. I have no idea how to fix it. I can recognise it in the speech of others I know to have Asperger's as well.'

Very fast speech

Lydia never noticed how fast John spoke when she was a young child, probably because she lived with him and she (and I) also speak quickly. She remembers the au-pairs, and then later her boyfriends, pointing out how rapidly John spoke. Our poor au-pairs, who came mainly from Sweden or Finland and spoke excellent English, were horrified to find they couldn't understand John at all when they arrived. By the time they left us they understood John easily, highlighting to them how their mastery of spoken English had improved! As John recalls:

> I remembered feeling happy when they started to understand my horrible slurred speech. It always started with new au-pairs not understanding me and I had to keep repeating myself until they understood. I remember it always started out with a sort of battle.

All of John's aunts commented on his rapid speech and one, who has a hearing problem and has to wear a hearing aid, was quite reluctant to stay with John a few years ago because she found it so hard to understand him. In fact the visit went splendidly and she was pleased to discover how kind and attentive John had been and how well he'd looked after her. I've always had to ask John to slow down and speak more distinctly, when he's stressed and panicking or when he's excited and enthusiastically explaining something to me, because I can't understand a word he's saying. He never complains and just starts again more slowly. Maybe as I get older I also need my ears syringing! The incredibly rapid speech may well be related to the speed of John's thoughts. However it could also be due to John's poor short-term memory (see Chapter 14) which means he feels compelled to get any information out as fast as possible before he forgets it. John agrees with the latter, saying: 'Now *that* is undeniably true. I *will* forget whateveritis almost at once, no matter how important it is, unless I speak it aloud or type it in or something.' The rapid speech, combined with an intense and enthusiastic manner, have combined to make several people (on meeting John for the first time) think he was taking the drug 'speed'!

Flat intonation

As well as speaking too fast and very indistinctly, John tends to talk in a flat voice, without the changes in pitch and emphasis many of us would use. This makes it much harder to concentrate on what he's saying and tends to make one 'switch off' when he is spouting on about something or other, offering the occasional 'mm... mm' without actually taking anything in. I wasn't really aware of this monotonous voice while John lived with us because I was so used to it. It was pointed out to John, for the first time in his early twenties, by the housemates he was living with at the time. Since reading about 'prosody' in autism, I've also become more aware of John's voice but find it much easier to hear the flatness of his speech when I talk to him on the phone. In fact when he first answers the phone his voice sounds quite 'dead' and only when he knows who he's speaking to does it get some 'life' into it. According to John: 'That's because 90% of the calls I get on that line are marketing robots (Telephone Preference Service, my foot). There's no point being nice to a tape recorder.' Many of us speak in a different voice when we answer the phone if we don't know who's at the other end but usually the voice is just formal and unrecognisable rather than flat and lifeless. However John's voice is by no means flat all the time and the monotone can disappear when he is feeling enthusiastic about something. His sister, who *had* noticed John's flat speech while he was still living at home, thought it rather ironic that he was so aware of flat speech in others. Apparently there was a teacher in secondary school that John said sounded like a robot and sent him off to sleep. John also loved mimicking Marvin (in the *Hitch Hiker's Guide to the Galaxy*) whose voice was hilariously flat and monotonous.

Loud volume

Lydia was particularly aware of the volume of John's voice and remembers everyone staring in restaurants as John's voice got louder and faster. His voice can become very loud when he's excited and this is particularly noticeable when he's in a public place. I'm afraid I don't set a good example as my voice tends to be rather louder than I would like on occasion. When John and I are together my daughter and husband, with their nice quiet voices, would be happy to disown us! However it's very hard to change the volume control when one becomes enthusiastic about something as it seems such an intrinsic part of one's personality. John and I do the best we can, don't worry or fret about it and, when prompted, try to turn the noise level down a bit. My mother, who was also an enthusiastic and determined person, had a loud voice too. Perhaps there's a genetic factor at play or perhaps this is just a matter of upbringing. Some friends of ours remember a birdwatching visit to a wonderful bird reserve in Welney, Norfolk, UK:

> We all went to the bird reserve and moved from hide to hide trying not to disturb other watchers or the birds. Our group tendency to point and whisper was not copied by John. His natural exuberance could not cope with our hushed tones and brief silences. He seemed to find our restricted conversation uncomfortable. It was as if he felt a primal need to maintain the flow of verbal contact, at normal rate and volume, whatever the circumstances.

Incomprehensible pronunciation

One of the side effects of learning new vocabulary from reading rather than listening was that John frequently mispronounced words altogether or put the stress on the wrong syllable. Tony Attwood (2006) notes that some children with Asperger's syndrome may pronounce words as they are written rather than spoken because they 'learned language more by reading than listening. There may be stress on specific syllables that changes the expected pronunciation.' This was a *very* common occurrence until John was in his early twenties but still happens occasionally. For example, when he was 30 John pronounced the word 'an*a*thema' as 'anath*e*ma'. When John was younger the mispronunciations were so frequent that occasionally it could be difficult to understand what he was actually trying to say. As he grew older it made us laugh as we asked him to *spell* some words in order to understand him. Luke Jackson, who as a teenager with Asperger syndrome wrote *Freaks, Geeks and Asperger Syndrome*, has the same difficulty:

> I like the English language and like learning new words and speaking correctly. One thing about the way I speak is very strange. Even though I read perfectly well and understand the meanings of masses of words, it seems that I pronounce a lot of them wrong... I am always being laughed at for it. When I was writing this, I was wondering why and all I can think is that people with AS don't spend as much time listening to other people carefully and get more of their vocabulary from books.

I agree with Luke. It's easy to understand how this could happen as English has such inconsistent pronunciation. Any one could struggle to know how to pronounce a new word if they hadn't heard it before.

Stammer

Since his teens John has stammered when he tries to explain something complicated at the same time that he's trying to recall the relevant facts from memory. The reason for this may be due to a relatively poor working memory; this is discussed in more detail in Chapter 14. Although this has never caused John any embarrassment he does find it 'annoying, because it only seems to kick in when I'm discussing something complex.' Attwood (2006) notes that 'some adults with Asperger's syndrome are prone to stuttering when anxious' and this certainly applies to John. He used to find teleconferences at work particularly difficult. He thinks:

> This is because they're invariably sprung on me at no notice so I have no time to prepare my thoughts and have to organise things on the fly... I have no sensible clues to gauge the state of remote participants on the phone, so if I want to say something I'd better start talking *now* and think as I go → stammer, and I'm nervous as anything because I've rarely even heard of the people I'm talking to... because most of the participants write English perfectly well but speak it only with a very, very strong Tunisian accent (and much stammering and 'uh'ing).

These days John has a weekly teleconference as part of his current job and as a result finds they 'are not so bad now':

They're routine, nobody else is quite so bad at spoken English as the Tunisians I was talking to then, and *everyone* has trouble figuring out when it's safe to talk. Maybe we should just start saying 'over' at the end of what we're saying?

TALKING TO HIMSELF

For as long as I can remember John has talked or muttered to himself. Ever since he was young he could be heard in his room (or on the loo) engaged in such excited conversations (with accompanying laughter) that you could have sworn there was someone with him. When he was young, John spent a considerable amount of time (when he wasn't reading or on the computer) playing in his own imaginary worlds and he would regularly talk during these games. Tony thinks this behaviour (which really disturbed him) may have been prompted by John's long running relationship with his imaginary friends Stiggy and Flower (see Chapter 12). As he recalls: '[When John] started to talk to himself. I would tell him that he was doing it and he would reply that he knew and then went on as if it was a perfectly natural thing to do.'

Sometimes, particularly when he was on the loo, John wasn't talking to himself but reading something aloud which he thought particularly funny or liked the sound of. Reading aloud seems to help John retain huge portions of books he likes in long term memory. In fact talking aloud is a technique John has consciously used since he was in his teens to help him improve his short- term auditory memory and help him organise his thoughts. This is particularly useful for John as his visual memory is so poor. John says he still talks to himself and 'always will, essential part of thought. I can't understand how anyone can think without it.' I've often seen him (as an adult) while he's thinking deeply about some tricky computer problem, pacing around the room gesticulating with his hands and talking/muttering to himself the whole time. He wrote recently:

> I'm always muttering away to myself, and my work hits a wall if I'm forced to stop: but it doesn't have to be audible to anyone else... I've always had a problem with volume control, or rather volume *monitoring*, so it creeps up slowly.

When John was young, it was often possible for us to recognise the warning signs of a major meltdown or tantrum. He would become increasingly agitated and restless and start muttering to himself. As he grew older John continued to mutter when he got upset or frustrated. I remember a former housemate of his getting intensely annoyed at this habit. Although John, the adult, often managed to control what might have turned into an enormous tantrum when he was a young child, he was unable to keep his angry thoughts to himself or to verbalise them in a controlled manner to the person who was upsetting him – hence the angry muttering. In *The Complete Guide to Asperger's Syndrome*, Tony Attwood writes:

> Another characteristic of children and some adults with Asperger's syndrome is to vocalise their thoughts... A characteristic of all young children is to vocalise their thoughts as they play alone or with others. By the time they start school however, they have learned to keep their thoughts to themselves...

> There may be several reasons for this behaviour. First the child may be less influenced by peers to be quiet, or less concerned at being different. The vocalisations may also have a constructive purpose or be reassuring... It is important to find

out why the person talks to himself. It could simply be developmental delay or a means of organising his or her thoughts, improving comprehension and providing comfort.

I'm not entirely sure why it's important to understand why a person talks aloud to themselves if it causes no harm to anyone else, is fulfilling some deep seated need and is probably beneficial to the person concerned. There's no reason why we should all behave in the same way. What's needed is to educate people to be more tolerant of difference. I can understand though that it might disturb children or adults sitting nearby but that's no worse than the continual noise that disturbs the person with sensory sensitivity in the classroom, workplace, and many other public places. However my daughter thinks my approach 'is idealistic...! A two-pronged approach is best. I think that anything that marks one out as different/a target is a risk... and it might be important to address it. It can scare others if they think you're mad!'

Fortunately John no longer looks quite so unusual if he's seen muttering to himself as he walks down the street thinking, because lots of people are talking aloud as they use their mobile phones. This probably reduces the chances of him being attacked for being different. John agrees: 'For this alone I could love mobile phones. They made everyone as weird as me!'

WHAT COULD HAVE BEEN DONE DIFFERENTLY?

I'm sure more could have been done to help John with his communication skills when he was young if there'd been the current understanding of autism spectrum conditions. However, in those days there was a lack of awareness that children who appeared to be very articulate might actually experience communication problems. Unfortunately it was all too easy for us parents to underestimate, or completely forget about, John's lack of social skills. This was partly due to the fact that we were so used to him 'being different' and partly because we rarely observed him in the type of social situation (with his peers) that he struggled with the most. In fact I can remember being rather shocked, on walking with John around the grounds of his secondary school, to find him shout/yell a greeting across a really large quadrangle to two boys walking on the other side. The boys, who must have been at least 40 metres away and deep in their own conversation, looked up surprised but returned the greeting politely. I couldn't really believe what I'd seen as the behaviour seemed so socially inappropriate. John was now in his mid-teens and yet he hadn't seemed to realise that this sort of greeting only takes place if people are physically near. Perhaps he was proudly showing me that he actually knew their names? Gillberg (2002) points out:

> [Many children with Asperger syndrome] have problems judging appropriate physical distance when communicating with other people. They will come up too close or stand too far away from the person they wish to address or communicate with in other ways.

I'm sure if I'd been a fly on the wall throughout John's school days I wouldn't have been so shocked; I would have become accustomed to John's socially naïve behaviour with his peers.

Speech and language therapy (SALT) might have been a helpful way of teaching

John some of the rules of conversational grammar. Whether this would have been accessible on the NHS is quite another matter as speech therapists usually have such long waiting lists; a child who is very articulate, although unable to hold a proper two-way conversation, may not be considered a priority. The report *make school make sense*, produced in 2006 by the National Autistic Society, concluded: '38% of children in mainstream schools who need SALT do not get it.' However access to a SALT *can* be gained if this is mentioned specifically in a Statement of Educational Needs. It follows that any parent whose child is on the autism spectrum and manages to get a Statement of Educational Needs should do their best to ensure that access to a SALT is specifically mentioned.

These days I hope a child like John would receive a plan at nursery school to help him understand social rules and improve his conversational skills. Appropriate help at school may still be wishful thinking though. The NAS report *make school make sense* notes: 'Parents say the biggest gap in provision is social skills programmes.' As Leventhal-Belfer and Coe (2004), who devote a chapter in their book *Asperger's syndrome in young children* to social skills groups, point out:

> Small group settings provide a wonderful opportunity to practise *conversational skills,* such as *turn taking, staying on topic,* finding areas of *shared interest,* and learning ways to *enter into play or a conversation topic with a peer.*

Although social skill groups are probably an excellent idea I believe great care has to be taken when 'teaching' children with Asperger's syndrome social skills 'rules'. Unless the child *really* understands why and when a particular behaviour should or shouldn't be used, the intervention may cause more harm than good. According to Howlin (1998):

> The rules of social behaviour are not easy to define. If such rules do exist they are highly complex, and constantly changing according to the social context. This is particularly so when dealing with more complex and subtle social skills. Knowing how to make friends, recognising how other people are feeling or thinking and being able to react appropriately, are fundamental human aptitudes; they are not rule-based skills that are acquired through teaching... no two social situations are absolutely identical, and unless the child was able to *modify* learned skills in order to meet the demands of the new situation, training of this sort will only have a limited impact... Teaching new skills, or correcting errors in situ, is far more likely to be effective than teaching in the relative isolation of a 'social skills group'...

> Some rules are probably best never taught at all. Insisting that a child should 'look at people when they talk to you', for example, is likely to lead to them staring fixedly at every one they meet, which is far more disconcerting than someone who makes only fleeting eye contact...

> A rule that works well in one setting may not work in another situation or with another person.

A few years ago my husband and I went on a one-day field trip which began with everyone (all strangers) meeting in a car park. One young man in his early thirties immediately came towards us when we joined the group, shook our hands and introduced himself by giving his name. He then proceeded to do the same thing as others joined the group. Very polite but unfortunately *not* the way people in the UK usually behave; this behaviour immediately made him stand out as different. It looked as if he'd been *taught* to introduce himself this way. Andron (2001) makes precisely the same point when she writes:

> [Because children on the autism spectrum] cannot see the situation in context we run the risk of them misapplying the rules and looking even more odd because of this. The children who learn the skill of 'greeting' appropriately are a prime example. The rule is to say 'hello' when you come in and 'good-bye' when you leave. What happens is that they develop a routine that requires them to say hello and goodbye to each individual in the room, without getting the contextual cue that a 'good-bye everyone' would be more appropriate. Many children who have come from structured behavioral programs learn to greet and introduce themselves in a rote manner. Every time they enter a room they walk up to each child and say, 'Hello, my name is…', even if they have played with the same child week after week.

This inability to see a situation in context, to see the whole picture rather than the detail, is often a problem for those on the autism spectrum and is called by psychologists the theory of *weak central coherence*. Dr Vermeulen[47] believes that the inability to use context spontaneously is at the core of the way people with autism perceive the world. What should be done then if it's so difficult to teach social skills to children on the autism spectrum? Andron again:

> We must always be aware of the issues related to theory of mind and weak central coherence. We must always help them to understand the cause and effect of situations. We must always explain the reasons behind what we are asking them to do. We must always help them to understand the 'theory' behind what we are requesting. We need to make use of their strength in scientific enquiry, but then help them see where there are flaws in their conclusions. We must always help them to see the whole that is the result of the parts. This is best done in naturalistic settings, where they can experience various situations and observe the results of their actions.

Despite all of the above, I still think it's possible that attending an appropriate social skills group when John was young might have made his secondary school years less traumatic. The opportunity to *practise* conversational skills in a therapeutic environment would have been invaluable. Tony Attwood (2006), for example, recommends the use of social skills groups in order to 'practise new skills in a controlled and supportive environment'. John thinks this is a good idea which would probably have helped him but feels it could have been hard to retain his interest. I think it's particularly important that parents or carers keep in close touch with the progress of such a group and the skills that are being taught. Social skills groups on their own are unlikely to be sufficient in the real world without opportunities to practise in everyday situations; for this parents and carers are crucial. Ozonoff, Dawson and McPartland (2002) emphasise the importance of the home: 'Many of the principles and techniques used in typical therapeutic groups can be used by parents at home. In fact, social skills groups are much more beneficial if supplemented by follow-up at home.'

As well as social skills groups, school interventions that could have been very helpful to John include a trained aide in the playground and classroom and the introduction of a well-run peer intervention programme such as a 'buddy system'[48] or Circle of Friends.[49] Matt Winter, a primary school teacher himself, writes in his book *Asperger Syndrome – What Teachers Need to Know*:

> The rest of the class can be an invaluable support to the child with AS if managed correctly. Remember that you, as the teacher, must model how to respectfully interact with the child. Carefully choose people to be buddies in difficult situations. This can take the form of buddies who work with the child at certain times of the day, buddies to help them in the playground, or buddies for them to go to if they are feeling stressed out. Take time to talk over with buddies exactly why it is that the child needs their support and that they are being trusted with a very important task. Let them know they can come and see you any time if they don't know what to do.

> Make sure you check in regularly with the buddies to see how often the child is making use of them and if they need any help. You will need to encourage the child to see these buddies when you first start this... Always reward the buddies for their good work.

This author also has some valuable advice about the type of things a teacher's aide or assistant could do. These include showing the child how to become more organised, giving extra tuition where necessary, helping the child to do prescribed exercises to improve motor skills and using social stories to help the child understand the feelings of others in the class. As Winter says:

> The teacher aide should always be working to help the child become more independent and be teaching her coping strategies, rather than becoming someone the child relies on and who rescues her...

> Where possible get the teacher aide to work with the child both individually and as part of a group made up of a *cross section* of the class. This is important for the child's self-esteem.

A friend of mine (the mother of adult autistic twins) also pointed out: 'It's crucial that the teaching assistant has the right mindset and empathy with the child on the autistic spectrum as well as some training and expertise.' The type of help described above might well have helped John understand how to relate to the children in his class. It's one thing being supported and helped by parents but they don't go to school with their child and don't see what sort of difficulties the child is experiencing with their peer group.

If I had my time again I would also try and address John's poor communication skills myself; that's assuming I'd actually realised that such a problem existed. This wouldn't be an attempt to make him like everyone else but rather a desire to make it easier for him to understand and relate to those so different from himself. In the book *Hitchhiking through Asperger Syndrome* by Lise Pyles, there is a very useful appendix which lists a variety of things a parent or carer could do to improve their child's social skills. For as she writes so wisely:

> Children with Asperger Syndrome learn social skills intellectually rather than in-
> tuitively. Conscious and helpful teaching is key...

> It's easy (but a trap!) to turn social skill goals into a negative checklist of behav-
> iors to be corrected. Don't fall for this. The idea is NOT to make life easier for the
> parent. The idea is to make life easier for the child. Try to make it fun using
> games, charades, jokes, cartoons, movies, storybooks, field trips etc.

Unfortunately I never realised that John wasn't learning how to read body language
and facial expressions as a child and had no idea what problems this would create for
him as he grew older. I assumed that everyone learned these skills automatically as they
developed. My ignorance was partly due to the fact that John was my first child (so I had
no older children to compare him with) but also due to a complete lack of knowledge
about typical child development. Obviously I can't be sure whether I could have made
any difference if I *had* realised but I suspect that teaching John regularly (while he was
young) what others pick up unconsciously, would have made some difference. He may
have been able to automate these learned skills and thereby use them fast enough to
make it easier to cope with social situations. I think this teaching should have been
begun well before John started school because we had much more time together and it
was easier to motivate him to do what I wanted at that age. This view is supported by
Attwood (2006) who has a very interesting point to make regarding the difficulties
people with Asperger's syndrome have learning social language:

> If we consider social language to be rather like a foreign language to people with
> Asperger's syndrome, then we may find that if we teach and encourage social
> language at an early age, children with Asperger's syndrome may eventually
> speak this 'second language' like a native.

By the time I tried to improve John's social skills it was too late. I remember buying
him a small book on communication skills and body language for his Christmas stocking
when he was in his teens. He was completely uninterested in the gift and flatly refused
to read it. Meanwhile my daughter (who later became a clinical psychologist and had excellent communication skills already) was upset that I hadn't given *her* the book which
she promptly appropriated and read.

How would I go about teaching John when he was very young? One of the first
things I would do is buy the delightful DVD called *The Transporters*,[50] which features
eight different vehicles each with an actor's face on the front. As the User's Guide
explains:

> [The DVD was designed] especially for children with autism spectrum condi-
> tions... who find it hard to recognise facial expressions of emotion.

> ... the idea behind *The Transporters* is to help children to learn about emotions in
> a way they will enjoy. For a child who doesn't naturally want to look at faces or
> people... here's a world in which the only human faces that appear are 'grafted'
> onto beautifully predictable, attractive vehicles. Suddenly, people's faces are an
> object of interest...

Each episode of *The Transporters* focuses on one key emotion, which is presented in different contexts throughout the story. This central emotion is expressed by more than one character, to allow children to explore the expression on different faces...

The DVD is organised so that episodes featuring more basic emotions, understood by younger children, appear first.

The DVD, which can be used for children from about the age of two, has 15 five-minute episodes plus 30 quizzes. The excellent booklet accompanying the DVD is very helpful, suggesting all sorts of questions that a parent or carer might ask their child after they have watched an episode together; it also suggests a variety of other activities that deal specifically with emotions. As well as watching the DVD together I would encourage John to watch the episodes on his own as many times as he wished. I would also talk about people's expressions in the many books I read to John and ask him what he thought the people were feeling and how they were showing it. I would explain how people *show* what they feel by their appearance and the signals they send out as well as by *what* they say and the way they say it. I would help him to recognise the importance of the eyes and mouth in sending out these signals. After John had thoroughly absorbed the contents of *The Transporters* DVD I would buy the DVD-ROM called *Mind Reading: The Interactive Guide to Emotions*, already mentioned in this chapter. It's an amazing piece of software in which six actors portray each of 412 emotions by means of video and audio clips. The 412 emotions are divided into 24 groups, and users can test themselves in a variety of ways. I believe this DVD-ROM and *The Transporters* DVD would have been of enormous benefit to John if we had used them during his childhood.

If I had my time again I would also learn how to use the technique called *Social Stories*™,[51] a concept originally developed by Carol Gray. Tony Attwood (2006) explains how *Social Stories*™ work:

Social Stories™ use positive language and a constructive approach. The suggestions are what to do rather than what not to do. The text will include *descriptive sentences* that provide factual information or statements, and *perspective sentences*, which are written to explain a person's perception of the physical and mental world. Perspective sentences, which are one of the reasons for the success of Social Stories™, describe thoughts, emotions, beliefs, opinions, motivations and knowledge. They are specifically included to improve Theory of Mind abilities.

John's Theory of Mind abilities weren't good and he thinks the perspective stuff in Carol Gray's Social Stories™ is critical. He believes that a major reason he didn't do a lot of the 'social-glue stuff' was that he couldn't see the point of it. Learning to see other people's point of view via a social story might well have made a significant difference to John's ability to get on with his peers, particularly if we'd started using this approach when he was young.

As well as all the work required to help a child on the autism spectrum cope with the world of neurotypicals (NTs), it would be excellent if the NTs, who are supposed to be so good at communicating and putting themselves in the place of others, learned to understand the world of those on the autism spectrum. In reality, the average NT child is probably only good at understanding children like themselves. Lipsky and Richards (2009) hit the nail on the head when they wrote:

> NTs frequently misinterpret an autistic person's action or reaction as a lack of caring what another person is feeling. The irony is that NT individuals who show no empathy towards autistic individuals judge autistic people as having no empathy. This is the real test of empathy: to understand the world of someone unlike you.

To conclude: Although we didn't help John nearly as much as we could have done with his communication skills, it's been a delight to see how much they have improved as an adult. I find it particularly fascinating to discover how much John learned from watching others interact on the internet. Resources that could help parents and carers improve their child's communication abilities can be found in Appendix 28.

12
Play

Play forms a crucial role in any child's development. According to Ives and Munro (2002):

Play for most children is a natural, enjoyable activity... Through play, children learn skills of negotiation, turn-taking and socialising. Relationships with peers and siblings are strengthened through play opportunities.

The stages of play usually progress from children playing alone, to playing alongside others, then to playing with one other person and finally playing in a group. There are many types of play, including physical, sensory, construction, creative and imaginative. John's solitary play was very imaginative but given his poor communication skills it's not surprising that play with his peers was limited. He could play happily with one other person, if they had a strong common interest (usually computer connected), and with a very small group if they knew each other really well. However John couldn't cope with large groups of children and hated birthday parties.

SOLITARY PLAY

John was a very happy little boy, never bored and always busy playing on his own with great intensity and concentration for long periods of time. As he wrote recently: 'And nothing whatsoever has changed. You might call this 'lack of development', I call it finding what made me happy early on.' All *I* had to do was to make sure he was provided with the things he needed to play with, although as he grew older his play was limited somewhat by his poor motor skills. Before John went to nursery school at the age of three, I used to play with him every day before his rest. We played with a variety of stacking, posting and construction toys and when I left his bedroom I placed these toys at the end of his cot. I hoped to give him the opportunity to practise these activities and develop his fine motor skills. Silly me! In reality the moment I left the room John took the lid *off* the plastic pillar box (designed as a posting toy) and then had a wonderful time dropping each component of every toy we'd played with into the pillar box, in order to hear the sound it made as it hit the bottom. Then he tipped the pillar box up and threw the toys round the bedroom! Good throwing practice I guess and certainly a lot easier and much more fun for John than using these construction toys in the way the manufacturers intended! In retrospect I'm very glad that John had plenty of time to play on his own, without interruption, so that he was able to use these toys in the way *he* wanted rather than the way an adult might have thought appropriate. I'm sure these activities were satisfying some deep seated need as they provided enormous pleasure for many months. After John's rest was over we always tidied his room up together so that we could repeat the whole process the following day.

As well as playing for hours and hours with his beloved Fisher Price activity centre, which was attached to the sides of his cot, John was fascinated by all sorts of objects which moved in a repetitive way or made an interesting noise. Soft toys were completely ignored when John was a child, although now he's an adult he has some lovely soft toys on his desk, including an otter, a sheep and some birds! According to John: 'This is a geek tradition.' Williams and Wright (2004) say that some children on the autism spectrum enjoy playing with toys with repetitive movements or watching the spinning of fans, while Simon Baron-Cohen (2004) says boys enjoy 'playing with toys that have clear functions – things with buttons to press, things that will light up, or devices that will cause another object to move.' As a toddler John loved watching clothes spinning round in the washing machine and records turning on the record player. His fascination with mechanical devices such as clocks, and the combine harvester to be found in the Science Museum, will be described in more detail in Chapter 13, which includes a section on special interests. John's godfather Philip, who doesn't have children of his own, recalls:

> John was probably about five or six when you visited us here. Like any excited and inquisitive youngster, he ran around the house and discovered the kitchen television. We noticed his concentration was immediately focussed on the operation of each of the controls. He was evidently fascinated by the resulting visual effects of changing the settings of each one. The sound and pictures were totally ignored, but his ability to control the varying colour effects appeared to be totally absorbing.

When John was given a portable electronic game called *Pac-Man* he played with it endlessly. He didn't have a PlayStation, which was probably just as well as I suspect he would have become quite an addict. 'Strongly agreed', says John. As it was, every time we travelled to mainland Europe on board a Sally Line ferry he used to spend the *entire* two hour journey from Ramsgate to Dunkirk standing on his own by the games machines, just watching older people play. John showed no desire to play himself, for as he wrote recently about the people he watched:

> Not only did they have money (there was no way I was going to spend actual *money* on that sort of thing even if I had any), I knew I could never be remotely as good at any of the games as the people I was watching. In South Korea, watching (*very* good) players play computer games has become a major spectator sport in the last few years, and it's spreading.

John was given a computer of his own when he was about seven years old, which he took to like a duck to water. As computers and reading, both solitary activities, have always played such an important part in John's life, each of them has been given their own chapter in this book.

When he was about eight years old, a continuing pleasure in watching things move led to John's interest in ants, slugs, snails and worms. This interest hasn't completely disappeared, as John wrote relatively recently:

> Even now I can get randomly obsessed with them when I spot them in the garden. I spent three hours last weekend just watching a lovely big spider rebuild her web after I broke it opening the shed door. (Amazingly, the guide thread did not break, even though it more than quadrupled in length when I opened the door. Amazing substance.)

John spent ages studying ants in the garden while they followed a particular path along the edge of a flower border next to a wall. In his mid-thirties John said:

I can still remember exactly where their nest was, buried under next door's foundations. I used to trace them to their destinations and watch them lug things back. The size and variety of things they chose to pick up was bizarre. I still have no idea what they did with most of them. (I mean, small stones and pieces of brick? Why? Were they reinforcing their nest walls with brick?!)

Lydia remembers John collecting slugs in a jar and the slugs escaping into the kitchen, which she thought 'was disgusting'. To which John responded:

Oops. Did I forget to put the top on? (I recall agonising over whether I should put a top on, since it might suffocate them or something. After several escape incidents I settled for putting a top on and punching holes in it.)

At the time Lydia thought this interest 'was just boys'. When we went on family hikes John was always on the look-out for slugs, the bigger and fatter the better. In fact he had the whole family looking out for slugs. As he recalls:

The more bizarrely coloured they were and the faster they could move, the happier I was. It was the gastropod foot and tentacles (and to a lesser extent the radula)[52] that really fascinated me: the tentacles were so *responsive*, and the lovely rippling motion of the foot was fascinating to watch.

Like many children, John enjoyed keeping some carnivorous plants in pots on the kitchen window sill but none of these seemed to live for very long.

For many, many years the medium that gave John the most enormous pleasure was water. At nursery school, when the children were inside, he spent most of the time playing with water on his own. I can understand the endless fascination this provided as water makes a lovely sound and can be made to move in a variety of ways without the need for good manual skills. At home, indoor water play was confined to the weekly bath which (as mentioned in Chapter 6) lasted for hours rather than minutes. This play included pouring water into/onto a variety of objects and watching what happened. For several years John's favourite activity in the garden was walking around spraying plants (and people) with water sprays and water pistols, talking to himself the whole time. As he grew older John loved finding a stream to walk in when we were hiking. Like many children, John thought puddles were wonderful and made for stamping in.

We took the children regularly to play in some of the parks in our neighbourhood, where John really enjoyed climbing and going down slides. When he was small he liked being pushed in a swing but when he was older and capable of swinging on his own it wasn't a favourite activity. John may have found it too physically demanding for what he calls 'the meagre reward'. Unfortunately our nearest park didn't have a slide or climbing equipment but this didn't stop John enjoying himself. While his sister was busy swinging, he played happily in the sand that was provided to cushion children if they fell off the swings. John would be talking away to himself while playing some imaginary games in the sand, always on his own, and always totally absorbed and happy. He remembers that a lot of the fun 'was just watching the collapse properties of heaps of sand, building little pyramids and watching the collapses'. Solitary imaginary games were the norm, John explains, because 'it's hard to pull other people into imaginary games. The characters have their own life inside your head and they can't really jump into other people's.' The most important thing I could do was make sure I had a book with me when we went to the park, so that I didn't rush the children and let them play for as long as they wanted. I believe that allowing children sufficient time to play as they wish is one of the secrets to a calm, happy and peaceful existence as well as encouraging powers of concentration.

IMAGINATIVE PLAY

Many authors suggest that children on the autism spectrum have problems with pretend play and imaginative games, although it's acknowledged by some that imaginary play often improves with age. Leventhal-Belfer and Coe (2004) point out some play-related warning signs or 'Red Flags' that children with Asperger's syndrome may exhibit:

> The concrete re-enactment of scripts from videos, TV shows, books; obsessive interests in one or two play themes... play... at a much younger developmental level than their vocabulary and wealth of information would suggest.

Although John understands running scripts through his head, he 'can't imagine ever re-enacting them'. According to Ives and Munro (2002):

> More able children may enjoy creative play and show some capacity for invention and learning through role play. Certain children may create elaborate fantasy worlds which seem at odds with an impairment in imagination. Closer inspection of the creation may reveal the specific rules and regulations imposed by the child.

John considers rules and regulations essential 'because... without restrictions and limits, you can have nothing to strive for, and what is play if not imaginary striving?' Meanwhile Tony Attwood (2006) writes:

> The play of the child with Asperger's syndrome can also be based on characters and events in fiction, but may be qualitatively different in that it is usually a solitary rather than a shared activity. It may be an exact re-enactment with little variation or creativity, and may include other children, but only if they follow the directions of the child with Asperger's syndrome and do not change the script. The interaction is not as creative, cooperative or reciprocal as would occur with typical peers.

It seems to me that none of these authors' descriptions fit John exactly, except for the fact that his imaginary games *were* usually a solitary activity and his play was possibly at a younger developmental level than that of other children of the same age. John *did* play imaginary games occasionally with a few good friends, particularly around the ages of nine and ten, but the ideas for these were often suggested by *others* or were developed together. I think he kept *his own* imaginary worlds very private and never tried to impose rules and regulations on others, a concept he finds 'quite horrible'. According to John, although his imaginary play was triggered by books he had read, he always invented new scenes. In his words: 'Re-enaction is boring.' When I asked him if he repeated the same scenes over and over again he replied: 'I can't *remember* the old scenes well enough to re-enact them, so it was always invention. Sometimes elements would repeat.'

Attwood's writings (2006) appear to describe John much more accurately when he describes the tendency to internalise thoughts and feelings as one of the compensatory strategies that can be used by young children with Asperger's syndrome who realise they are different from their peers. He writes:

[These children] use imagination and a fantasy life to create another world in which they are more successful...

[They] can develop vivid and complex imaginary worlds, sometimes with make believe friends...

In their imaginary worlds with imaginary friends, children with Asperger's syndrome are understood and successful socially and academically. Another advantage is the responses of the imaginary friends are under the child's control and the friends are instantly available. Imaginary friends can prevent the child from being lonely... Having an imaginary friend is typical of the play of many young children and is not necessarily of clinical significance. However, the child with Asperger's syndrome may only have friends who are imaginary, and the intensity and duration of the imaginary interactions can be qualitatively unusual.

John was certainly more successful in his imaginary world and 'in my teenage years, less persecuted (or every bit as persecuted but I could fight back... or run away)'. From what I can gather, although he can remember few details, John says he was usually (but not always) the successful leading character (that is, the protagonist) in the imaginary plots that made up his vivid and intense fantasy world. However, according to John:

[The protagonist was] not necessarily successful. Oh no. Particularly in the later worlds I made sure there were a lot of reverses so that I could keep the world going! For successful imaginary play, the long-term status quo rules!

When John was younger, he was endowed in his imaginary life with the good manual coordination he was lacking in real life. As he wrote: 'I've always been well-coordinated inside my head!' In this way he was able to be 'more successful' in his imagination than in real life, just as Attwood describes.

As John grew older and started reading science fiction, more and more of his imaginary life was triggered by books that he'd read, although they weren't based on actual characters in these books. As John said: 'They were extrapolations of science fiction almost entirely. Computer games don't have nearly enough depth to them.' One of his fantasy worlds, which involved an unpleasant bureaucracy called the *Authority* and lasted for many years, was triggered by *The Moon Is a Harsh Mistress* by Robert Heinlein. When John started secondary school and experienced serious problems with both pupils and staff, he used his imaginary worlds to enable him to 'get back' at his tormentors in a variety of ways that he was incapable of actually carrying out in the real world. According to John though, his tormentors in this fantasy world 'got back at me quite a lot as well. It wasn't all roses, particularly not in the Authority universe. We were at *war*.' This imaginary world gave John enormous pleasure and may well have been the main reason that he was able to continue going to school without any fuss. It was a very good coping mechanism under the circumstances. Interestingly enough, John was never *socially* successful in any of his imaginary worlds:

I think I was either alone or a pariah or undercover in some way (and thus lying to everyone all the time) in all of them… The rebel cell in the Authority world (four people, all operating under false names starting with the letter 'J'…) was, well, we weren't friends, we were *forced* into our present position by hatred of the Authority, and never got on well at all.

Although superheroes provide considerable entertainment for many children, none of John's games involved heroes with supernatural powers. According to John, overcoming problems by supernatural means took all the fun away. He preferred to overcome adversity by means of clever ideas:

In at least two imaginary worlds I was radically nonhuman… but so was everyone around me. If you're the AI [artificial intelligence] of an unmanned trading starship you don't have superpowers just because you can exceed lightspeed if everyone else can do the same thing. (At least twice, that drive broke down and I was stuck crawling from one world to another at sub-lightspeed, expected arrival in 2000 years or so, how will you get out of *this*. Less superpowers, more, um, sub-powers?)

For several years John had two imaginary friends, Stiggy, his right hand and Flower, his left hand. He remembers that the name Stiggy came from the book 'Stig of the Dump' by Clive King but he can't remember where the name Flower came from. They were wonderful companions as they were always with him, accepted him unconditionally, understood all his ways and provided friendship and companionship without John having to understand body language, social rules or any of the other stuff he couldn't cope with. John always had someone to talk to who responded in a way he could deal with. I remember him having wonderful three way conversations with his friends on long journeys in the car, conversations which would entertain both his parents and his sister. Lydia, now a clinical psychologist, remembers them clearly:

I think Stiggy was the right hand and was naughty, loud and funny – a bit of a pain! He had a harsher voice than Flower, who was softer, gentle and always bore the brunt of Stiggy's mischief. They did interact! This was when John was quite young – perhaps early school age? You could say he was expressing two aspects of his personality that he was having some difficulty integrating. It was very interesting that he was able to express himself in this way.

I would interact with Stiggy in the car as he was next to me and was mischievous, tickling etc.

As an adult, John told me that he knew as a child that Stiggy and Flower weren't real. Although the whole family accepted John's imaginary companions, he never expected them to be fed or have a separate place at the table. He considered that 'Stiggy and Flower were… poorly-separated both from me and from each other (they had different personalities, but pretty much a shared memory and views)'. John also told me that they appeared mainly at bedtime when they used to keep him company at night until he went to sleep. I thought these conversations stopped once John was reading well enough to read himself to sleep. However I was wrong. Stiggy and Flower apparently 'came out after the light went off' for some years after this. Kevin Healey (2008), who has written a biography about his life as someone on the autism spectrum, used a similar device to help him overcome the stress of school:

> I needed to find a way of relaxing during school time. I started to use my right hand as a puppet doll; his name was Smeaker. He became my close friend and was with me wherever I went... Smeaker used to talk with me. I kept him hidden under my school table... Smeaker made me happy when I was sad during school time.

Further insights into John's imaginary life can be found in Appendix 11 where it can be seen that an increasing interest in world politics, as well as computer games, science and science fiction fed a very active imagination. Imaginative scenarios are still used intermittently as a coping mechanism when John feels 'paranoid and set-upon!' John didn't want to tell me about imaginary scenarios that are *still* intermittently active because 'it might spoil them. That happened when I told someone something ongoing when I was about fifteen: all the fun leaked out of it right there and then.'

I think employment of an imaginary life, in order to 'improve' or at least alter one's actual existence, is probably far from unusual and is probably responsible for the enormous success of the computer environment 'Second Life' and the beings called avatars. John doesn't wish to have anything to do with these virtual worlds though because he believes his poor social skills would cause him as many difficulties in these worlds as in the real world. 'It's got the same rapid-reaction-time stuff that I'm so bad at in the real world. I gaffe enough in blogs and usenet, and there I have long periods to consider responses.' At least he's in total control in his own imaginary worlds and doesn't need to be particularly conservative.

Once John started reading he was never parted from a book; this fed both his thirst for knowledge and his imagination. His school reports bear this out: his first report (when he was eight) says that John's 'wide vocabulary is displayed in imaginative writing'; the following year's report, that 'his comprehension and creative work are often excellent'; and when he was 10 the report says 'his written stories are entertaining, imaginative'.

Many children on the autism spectrum take great pleasure in lining up their toys when they are young and/or enjoy collecting. John never lined up his toys and tended to collect information and books rather than toys but he *did* have a collection of marbles. The purpose of the game of marbles is to defeat your opponent and acquire their marbles but from John's remarks I don't think he played with marbles this way:

> I never really knew anyone else with marbles. What on earth are you supposed to *do* when 'playing marbles' anyway? Run them into each other? Where's the fun in that? (Running one marble into a collection of others, that's interesting: you can get very odd effects if you spread out the collection enough. It's sort of like glass billiards.)

Marbles featured as characters in one of John's imaginary games, each marble having its own personality. Further details can be found in Appendix 12. Although I remember having favourite marbles as a child, they didn't possess personalities of their own. According to John:

> It's clear that, social skills or no social skills, the typical hyperactive human

'agency detector' is fully functioning in me. Totally random insensate physical objects have agency and do things because they *want* to.

John's play and ideas may have been very different from the majority of children of his own age but they were certainly not lacking in imagination and creativity. What *is* true is that most of John's imaginative play was solitary rather than social but that's to be expected given his difficulties with social communication. Although John ticks all the boxes for an autism spectrum disorder he does *not* lack imagination as such; instead, he could be said to lack *social* imagination.

SOCIAL PLAY WITHIN THE FAMILY

John was an affectionate and smiley baby and child and loved to be carried around in a sling when he was very small. Unlike some children with autism, who hardly react to their parents or don't like being held, our relationship with our son was physically and emotionally close, loving and mutually satisfying. I can't remember though whether he ever indicated as a baby that he wished to be picked up by holding out his arms. The absence of this behaviour is considered to be one of the early markers for autism. I didn't notice anything unusual but this *was* my first child and I knew nothing about children at the time.

Although John loved to play on his own, he also enjoyed playing with his parents and with his sister. One of John's favourite toys as a baby was a small rubber bear which we called *Peep-O-Bear*. This bear made a satisfying noise when squeezed and was responsible for much laughter from John when we played *Peep-O* with him as a very young child. By the time John was five months old his hand movements were coordinated enough for him to have no trouble grabbing his Dad's glasses or nose when he was being carried, activities which provided endless pleasure, at least for John. I made sure I never wore a necklace!

John loved his little sister and I don't remember any jealousy. They were very close as young children and spent a lot of time together. When Lydia was old enough to sit up unsupported in her cot, we often went into their shared bedroom in the morning to find John sitting opposite her in the same cot, talking and showing her things. It was so sweet.

Although both children played largely on their own in their weekly bath, there were exceptions. One of these was the game called 'Waves', a description of which is definitely not necessary. I had to impose strict limits on this game or the floor and the ceiling below would have been soaked. Lydia remembers a game called 'royal tangles' which was apparently played when their father was supervising bath time, although he doesn't remember any of this. Apparently Tony would go out of the room and the two children would intertwine their limbs and Tony would then come back and try and untangle them! Although *my* memories of the children in the bath are of really independent play it's interesting that Lydia remembers them 'playing together properly in the bath, perhaps because John loved playing with water so much.'

Lydia also remembers how much they 'both loved the fire' in our cottage and how they would 'tell each other what they could see in the flames'. On the way home from a stay in the country, when John was about six or seven, Lydia recalls the two of them sitting in the back of the car and 'imagining the car headlights behind us were monsters'.

192

As she puts it: 'John really got into that one.' As he wrote recently, car headlights *are* monsters. 'They are! Can't you see it? The body is just visible behind the terrible glow of the eyes, all teeth and fangs and long sharp claws.'

Lydia says she remembers that she loved playing on John's bedroom floor and 'wanted to be in the same room as him, with the gerbils'. Less happily she recalls the day John found a mallet and hit her on the head with it. When she asked why he'd done it, he said that he'd wanted to see what would happen. According to John (the adult):

What happened was that I learned not to try that again. I actually tried hitting myself on the head with the mallet first and thought it felt interesting, but I think I must have used more force the second time. Oops?

(No, I really don't know *what* the heck I was thinking. I knew that hitting yourself with things hurt: did I think that perhaps the mallet was different? Why?)

Lydia thinks we didn't realise what had actually happened as we laughed at her when she said she could still walk! She recalls that sometimes John wanted to get involved in her games but when she was playing with her Barbie dolls 'he would do stupid things such as want to introduce robots!' Lydia says 'she was a bossy little sister' and wouldn't let him play 'Barbies with robots'! According to Lorna Wing (1996):

Sisters and brothers, especially if they are of an age at which they are willing and eager to play, also become important to a child with an autistic disorder. Often, the sibling leads the child with an autistic disorder into all kinds of activities in which they would not otherwise engage. The fact that the child is mostly or always a passive partner does not matter. The experience of play is of benefit.

John has really good memories of playing with his sister although there was 'always the sensation that I didn't quite know what she was doing'. When Lydia was older she remembers playing computer games such as *Olympic Winter Games* and *Popeye* with John. She said 'he interacted really well on the computer' and they 'had great fun'.

When John was small my husband and I spent a lot of time in the garden digging out borders, creating a terrace with walls and steps, putting in paths and a trellis and so on. The garden looked like a building site for quite a long time but John enjoyed the activity enormously, especially all the rides in the wheelbarrow. As young children, John and his sister often played together in the garden, on the simple home-made climbing equipment and in the paddling pool. John particularly enjoyed water pistol fights with his sister and father. Lydia remembers them playing a bit more *together* outside but otherwise doesn't remember playing together so much, more alongside each other. John's cousin Sarah remembers the fun she and her brother Hugh had playing with water in our house:

We once had a water fight in and around John and Lydia's bedrooms. Lydia for some reason had lots of syringes and we filled them up and squirted the boys with them. Unfortunately for us, the boys filled a carrier bag with water and flung it at us. I remember some of the water getting on the bookcase by the bottom of the attic stairs and thinking this was all rather exciting. John subsequently (quite recently) informed me that they got into trouble for this!

According to John: 'I thought of it but didn't have the courage to do it. Hugh's implementation! and yes, oddly we did get into trouble for causing a flood, not really much of a shock.'

My husband engaged in plenty of rough and tumble play with the children which John really enjoyed. When the children were small they loved riding on Tony's back while he crawled around the floor on his hands and knees. As Ives and Munroe (2002) wrote: 'The majority of children with autism gain obvious pleasure from physical play with a parent.'

Sharing

As well as romping with his children, Tony made lots of Lego models with John. As mentioned in Chapter 8, John wouldn't let anyone else touch the Lego, including his sister Lydia. I think she would have liked to build some Lego models but she never got the chance as John wouldn't share. As an adult he thinks he *would* have let her use some spare Lego but I think he's wrong. According to John the adult:

> I don't think I'd have objected to her using the unused bits. It was taking apart one of Tony's wonderful creations that would have been simply appalling. They were one of a kind and I could never put them back together again. Tony plainly loved making them as well.

All credit to Lydia that, from a very young age, she understood John so well and cared for him so much that she didn't want to make an issue out of it. She seemed to sense what things to avoid in order not to upset her brother; as most of their interests were very different, she had plenty of other things to play with that he was completely uninterested in. If she'd been equally passionate about Lego, each of them would have needed their own supply. In retrospect, I think I took the easiest and quietest way out and should have found a way of insisting that Lydia had some Lego of her own; however, I'm not sure I could have coped with the continuous tantrums that would have ensued if I'd expected John to share. As it was there were very few quarrels between them. Lydia has vague memories of occasions when John wanted 'things that were hers' and also 'certain things that were just his and she was not allowed to touch or use'. She 'just let him get on with his own stuff' but remembers that 'he used to kick up a stink over certain things, but it wasn't really a problem'. I don't think we would have been able to make John share the few things he was most passionate about without the most enormous amount of upset and tension in the house. I still believe the tantrums and unpleasant atmosphere that would have been created if we'd forced him to share the 'special' toys would have made such a policy quite counter-productive. The intensity of John's passion was such that it didn't seem as if he was capable of sharing. He didn't seem emotionally or psychologically ready and wouldn't have understood what was going on. According to a recent email from John:

> There is *still* no change there. I *know* I'm a wild control freak in some areas: I know it's not an attractive quality... but it ties up with the fear-of-change so it's unlikely ever to moderate.

> I'm not sure I'd have seen it as 'sharing', more 'someone is taking away *my* time with $THING'. The other person would barely have factored in.

We certainly encouraged him to share anything he was less passionate about and that was never a problem. I think John has grown up to be a very kind and generous person, willing to share *almost* anything. Although speaking about his *work* he wouldn't entirely agree: 'Say rather that I'm willing to let people *see* almost anything. I retain very strict control over things I can modify: nobody else gets near them.'

Board Games

Although I tried to play board and card games with both children, John and board games could spell fireworks. As a consequence Lydia really missed out by not playing these as a child with her brother. She recalls that 'if things were not going his way he would throw the board in the air and ruin the game for everyone. He couldn't cope with the unfairness of not winning.' There weren't many games that John could play to the end. Even if he tried to join in, it wouldn't be long before there would be an almighty outburst of fury and, before you knew what was happening, John would tip the board up. 'I grew out of *that* in the end (by learning when not to play at all), although it was an effort.' John's lack of understanding of social rules and total unawareness of, and lack of interest in, what others thought of him (except if they thought he was stupid), meant that he felt no remorse at all in flying into a temper and turning the board upside down to end the game if he was losing. I'm sure he didn't mind waiting for his turn but there were all sorts of other frustrations inherent in the games that he was quite unable to handle, even though he tried. I will never forget the *only* time I played *Snakes and Ladders* with John and his sister. Initially he really enjoyed the game because he was winning and then, just before he got to the top of the board, he landed on a big snake that took him back to somewhere near the beginning. The shock of this sudden reversal in his fortunes, given his difficulty in coping with change unless he'd been sufficiently forewarned, was enough for him to throw a huge tantrum, tip up the board and refuse to play the 'stupid' game ever again. John still thinks 'it's a stupid game'. If I'd spent more time warning him about what could happen things may have turned out differently but I have my doubts, as he was so intense about everything he did and took everything to heart so. He couldn't think to himself that this is a fun game of chance, sometimes you win and sometimes you lose and it doesn't matter anyway. Games of chance demand a flexibility and speed of response that someone like John (who finds any change difficult to cope with) couldn't muster. You could see the frustration build up slowly in any game where John perceived something to be unfair until, like a volcano, the top would blow. Recently John wrote: 'Eventually my self-monitoring developed to the point where I could detect this myself and simply quit the game before I exploded.' That might be true but it's more likely that John would be reluctant to participate in the game in the first place. Amanda Kirby (1999), when describing children with developmental coordination disorder, wrote: 'The child who has DCD often has problems with understanding the rules of the game and what it means to win and lose. He may be overenthusiastic when winning and distraught when he has lost.' Lydia remembers that John would crow when he won some game against her – not a pleasant characteristic. John's views regarding his understanding of the rules of games and his feelings about competition in general are interesting:

I understand the rules of the game perfectly well…

Competitive games feel as if the universe is biased against me: a system of formal rules in which one person can succeed yet another cannot makes no sense. It's like finding that gravity works for your sister but not for you. What's also aggravating is knowing that I *could* have succeeded if only I'd done something else, but not being able to go back and fix it!

Lorna Wing (1996), when writing about children on the autism spectrum said:

When young, most of the children have no concept of winning or losing and board games give the opportunity of teaching this. The trouble is, if and when they do learn, they may become very upset or angry and have a major tantrum if they lose. Board games at home with the family can be useful to teach at least a show of good grace when losing, if the nerves of everyone concerned can stand living through the learning process.

Spot on, and *my* nerves couldn't stand it! To this day Lydia won't play *Monopoly* because of the tantrums she remembers.

In addition to games of chance John couldn't cope with games that demanded skill if he felt he was far less skilled than the other participants and therefore didn't have an equal chance of winning. This is perfectly understandable, for as Schopler (1995) writes: 'No one likes an activity in which there is no chance of success.' Unfortunately John's sister was both very competitive and extremely good at all sorts of games and so for many years John flatly refused to play games such as *Connect 4* with her because he thought he would always lose. After finding a version of *Connect 4* on the internet (which he practised many, many times), John discovered a winning strategy which meant he had a proper plan of action rather than a hit and miss approach based on visual skills. As a result he's become a very good *Connect 4* player; he usually beats me and wins as often as Lydia. According to Amanda Kirby (1999): 'Some traditional games are now made for the computer, such as '*Scrabble*' and '*Yahtzee*', and this allows the child to learn the rules and practise his skills before playing with others.' If I had my time again I would encourage John to become competent at more games by playing them on his own on the computer so that he would eventually be able to join in with the rest of the family. This would have been good for Lydia because she would have loved to play board games with her brother. John still won't play *Scrabble* although his word knowledge is superb. He finds it hard to visualise how a random set of letters can be juggled to create a word. His sister is, yet again, extremely good at this game. These days, Lydia said: 'John won't play at all if he doesn't think he can do well. This is more acceptable [than having a tantrum].' I'm afraid there were times when we used to get irritated and annoyed when John wouldn't participate in some game or other but we never forced, only encouraged, him to join in. In any case it was virtually impossible to force John to do anything he didn't want to do. According to John: 'This also hasn't changed. If you don't have a good reason to get me to do something, why should I do it? This probably drives my bosses to distraction.' A few years ago we were given the game *Articulate* which Tony and I played with Lydia and her husband. John didn't have the confidence to join in at first but was happy to watch. However within a short time he realised that this was a game he *could* play, not surprising considering it demands good language skills. He joined in, played very well and we all enjoyed a hilarious evening together. It was lovely having John join in with the rest of us with no fussing or upsets.

However there were some board games that John *would* play as a child. Lydia recalls John 'playing other games if they were not competitive or random. If they were funny or just fun to play, but where there was no strong feeling of competition. He *did* take turns.' I agree with Lydia that John didn't have a problem taking turns as he'd been used to this from a very young age indeed. However he couldn't bear to lose, hated to do things badly and couldn't cope with anything that he thought was unfair. Fun games, such as *Jumble Sale* and *Tummy Ache*, that were amusing and whose rules we adjusted so that they didn't feel overly competitive in any way, were never a problem. I suppose we could have used these games as an opportunity to show that there's nothing wrong with losing but I was too much of a coward. I also suspected this would have stopped him playing these games altogether, which John agrees with 'without a doubt.' In any case I don't think John would have believed there was nothing wrong with losing. As he said not long ago: 'This is self-evidently false or people wouldn't care if they won. You can't simultaneously say that winning is better than losing, but losing is not worse than winning.' When I asked John recently about his current attitude to losing games, he said:

> Yes. I'm happy to lose, but not if I can't undo what I did wrong and try again. Restarting at the start again seems like such a waste of time. I guess this shows that I don't (emotionally) get the point of playing competitive games with other human beings.

When asked how he felt about losing games of chance he replied: 'Losing there is just annoying. Of course I don't like being annoyed and most games of pure chance seem sort of pointless to me.'

SOCIAL PLAY WITH PEERS

We were the first to arrive at Anne's house for our regular monthly coffee morning. We were six mothers who went to the same National Childbirth Trust (NCT) classes before the birth of our first babies. We'd continued to meet, with our babies, once a month in each other's homes. John and I had been going ever since he arrived home from hospital and it was always a relaxing and enjoyable morning. However on this particular day, about a year after we started going, things turned out very differently. For a few minutes before the other mothers and children arrived all was well. John played perfectly happily on the carpet alongside Anne's child, Bill. When the other children and their mums arrived and the noise level inevitably rose, all hell broke loose. John started screaming at the top of his voice as if he was being murdered. He was inconsolable and I had to pick him up and put him with some toys in a nearby room on his own. He stopped crying immediately and carried on playing happily. I left him there and went back to chat to the other mums, very puzzled and rather concerned. When all the children had gone I brought him back into the sitting room and he continued to play quietly alongside Bill. The following month we met in someone else's house and exactly the same thing happened. Now I was really worried. Unfortunately we didn't have access to a professional whose opinion I trusted and I couldn't find any help in child-rearing books; before the internet and search engines, helpful information about almost anything was very difficult to find. John's behaviour was a real puzzle since he hadn't been kept in isolation at home with his parents; I'd never seen anything like it before. Friends and their children came regularly to our house and we went frequently to visit other families in their homes. Moreover, John had been going once a week to a crèche at a local college where I was studying, although these visits had stopped a few months before this incident because my course had finished. There'd been no problems whatsoever at the crèche and John had been perfectly happy at previous NCT coffee mornings. The only difference now was the other babies were becoming more interactive, invading John's personal space and wanting to communicate. As Lorna Wing (1996) explains:

> In typical development, interest in other children is evident by the end of the first year. Young children with autistic disorders in the aloof group are indifferent to or alarmed by their companions in playgroup, or nursery school.

As I saw it we had three options: carry on as if nothing had happened, avoid all social situations where there were several small children so that John wouldn't become so unhappy, or somehow find a way for John to get used to the presence of others of his own age without being so overwhelmed that he had to scream. We decided to try the last option because we were really worried about the long-term consequences should John continue to be unable to cope in a group. Although the easiest option may have been to remove John from any social situation that stressed him, we felt that the risks were too great. We feared that John would still be unable to cope with children when he was due to attend nursery and then primary school. Allowing John (aged one) to get used to other children *en masse* for just half a day a week seemed much kinder than moving him at the age of five from splendid isolation into full time school. Therefore in the September of his second year of life, we enrolled him at a local nursery for one morning session a week. John settled in remarkably well, the routine of the nursery helping as well as the fact that each week he saw the same caring staff and the same children. He knew what to expect and didn't have to cope with too much change. Apart from story, music and snack time, John spent the whole morning, when he was indoors, pushing toy cars around on the floor. When the weather was good he loved playing outside on the climbing frame or on the toy vehicles. Although John never interacted with the other children or made any friends, he didn't scream and, as far as I'm aware, never screamed again in the presence of other children. We were happy with these small steps as it meant he was now capable of tolerating other children around him. We were able to resume our NCT coffee mornings without any more problems. Ives and Munroe (2004) support this kind of approach when they write: 'How can children with autism be taught to play more effectively? The first stage for many children is teaching them to tolerate other people being near.' The ability to cope with groups of people, often not of one's own choosing, is an essential component of successful school attendance and most jobs. Children need all the practice they can get learning to manage effectively in such situations. We felt that it was particularly important for children, who appeared to have difficulty relating to their peers, to get *extra* practice dealing with groups if they were to have any chance of leading a full and independent life. Although school was difficult for John, particularly in his teens, I doubt that he would have been able to cope, either at university or at work, without the lessons he learned as a child at school. John is less sure about this:

> I'm not so sure the lessons I learned as a teenager (how to evade hostiles and analyse groups to isolate the dangerous members...) were useful, except inasmuch as they now have me twitching in fright whenever people get annoyed with me.

Nevertheless I would certainly make the same decision again if I was in a similar situation, although these days I would hope to have some input from experts with knowledge about children on the autism spectrum.

When *I* was a child, friends never came to our house to play or for a meal and I never invited anyone to stay overnight. My family didn't encourage it. I don't think I noticed this when I was at the local primary school, as I had great fun playing with friends in the street and (when we were older) in the local park. When I started secondary school though I was very aware of our lack of hospitality. As I went to a different day school from everyone else in my primary school class and my new school was quite a long way away, I was quite lonely at times because I couldn't invite my new school friends home. Because of my experience as a child I was determined that *my* children would feel free to invite their friends round to play or stay overnight.

Initially friends of mine came regularly to our house with their young children and we would visit these friends in their homes. Whenever visitors with children came for a meal we tended to put all the children on a separate table where our children could act as hosts. This was partly because our dining room table was rather small but also because it was so much fun for the children. The noise of laughter and talking that used to come from their table easily matched that from the adults' table. As the children grew older they made their own local friends. I was happy for the children to have a considerable degree of freedom when they played, provided they learned to be reasonably responsible, didn't damage our belongings and tidied up when they'd finished. As a result, both children had a nucleus of friends who had virtually grown up with them, seemed like an extended family and who were used to John and his ways and didn't exclude him. John was always happy to have plenty of social activity in the house and I have very pleasurable memories of 'presiding' over the table at lunch time with the children and their young guests all chatting away merrily. An old friend Polly wrote to me:

> I remember the children being very welcome and free to play wherever they wanted at your house... I certainly have no memory of any tantrums or anything like that.
>
> I think Lydia was very lively, and John was much quieter, and would often be involved with some fairly intricate play.

As a young child, John's play was usually in parallel, rather than together, with the other children. Lydia, however, was often the centre of the play activity. (There were exceptions to this, such as those friends who were as happy as John to play with slugs and snails.) John would hover on the periphery, near enough to hear what was going on but not actually joining in, happily playing on his own and always talking. Lydia still remembers how much she loved it when John's friends came round to the house as they all played together. She told me:

> Even around the age of eight, John would often be on the outside, on his computer commentating on what was going on. He would go in and out of the play area, but never in the middle of it whereas I was always in the middle of it.

This situation is similar to that described by Leventhal-Belfer and Coe (2004) when they wrote about children with Asperger's syndrome: 'They may look like they are engaged in very rich thematic play with their peers, but if you listen carefully they are often playing next to another child and not with them.' When writing about the diagnosis of Asperger's syndrome, Tony Attwood (2006) notes:

> [The importance of having a diagnostic assessment that] includes an examination of the child's abilities in a range of social situations, such as when playing with friends, parents, siblings or peers, and in new social situations. The signs of Asperger's syndrome are more apparent when the child is playing with peers rather than parents or an adult such as the examining clinician.

It was many years before John moved from playing alongside other children to playing *with* them. At this early stage he didn't seem to have any need to have friends and seemed perfectly happy whether he was on his own or whether there were other children around. I totally agree with Williams and Wright (2004) that 'typically, children with Autism Spectrum Disorders prefer to play on their own' and with Tony Attwood (1998) who writes: 'The young child with Asperger's syndrome does not seem motivated or know how to play with other children of their age... They seem quite content with their own company.' Nevertheless I believe that the open house we operated may have made it easier for our son to learn how to interact (on his own terms) with other children. In fact I think that without this input from local children our son may never have learned what it meant to have a friend and could have been very lonely as he grew older.

We were very lucky that the back garden of our first house, where we lived until John was eight, faced south and was consequently very sunny for most of the day, at least when the English weather was good. Before the children started school, and after that in the holidays and at weekends, the garden acted like an extra room and the children played and ate outside whenever they could. There was sufficient space on the terrace for four small children to go round on tricycles, little cars and other such vehicles, several of which we'd bought from our favourite second hand shop. John liked having friends around and was very happy for other children to use any of the wheeled vehicles except his red, sit-in pedal car. He was passionate about this car, playing with it for hours on end until he grew too big to get into it any more. He loved this car with such an intensity that the children, who all knew him very well, seemed to accept the situation just as they accepted John as he was. Lydia remembers one little girl though who was 'really bossy and managed to kick John out of the car (more than once) and ride in it for a really long time, John muttering darkly while she did so'.

John didn't seem to go through the stages of friendship described by Tony Attwood (1998) but started to make good friends in his own time, when he was ready and when he found other children who shared his interests. He was about nine years old when he found children who seemed to enjoy his company and at this age he seemed capable of sharing and playing *with* them. He has never been without at least one close friend since then and in recent years he told me: 'I would get lonely if I had no real friends, but I can cope with just one.'

Our first house was opposite that of a very close friend of mine who became one of Lydia's godmothers. Two of her children were close in age to our children: a girl, Clare, who was the same age as John and a son, David, who was three years younger. Until we moved house, all four children spent an enormous amount of time with each other. Clare remembers John 'making noises like a machine':

> It was obvious he loved machines and he seemed to spend most of the time talking about them and playing with them. I remember him being sweet but hav-

ing extreme/disproportional reactions to things. I think he found it impossible to control his negative feelings. I remember he used to scamper around and used to mumble quite a lot which made what he said hard to understand.

Clare's aunt remembered John's 'inability to control his disappointment after receiving a Christmas present he didn't like, saying: 'Not another book about animals'.' Meanwhile David, a very sociable boy, remembers:

> ... sitting next to John watching him play computer games and not getting a go; I was probably too shy to ask.

> He was strong for his age and I remember him hurting me when we were playing, but I knew at the time he did not mean to. I think he did not know his own strength.

> I remember he was very quick to change his mood and he could get very angry because of this and perhaps because of the age difference I was always a little wary.

> I remember him getting a present from my mum. I can't remember if it was a Christmas or birthday present but I do remember him not liking the present and getting upset. I was shocked at the time by his reaction. I think this is an early memory.

> I always regarded him as different and he would play different games to that I would have played with my other peers.

> He seemed happiest playing on his computer and I remember him showing me how it worked.

When we moved to our second house, John and Lydia made good friends with Sam and Alison who lived in the same street. Alison was in John's class at school and her brother was two and a half years older. Sam wrote to me at length about his memories of playing with John as a child. An abbreviated version follows:

> The occasion I remember most clearly... involved us playing between our two houses. The background was that out of Lego I had built something on the theme of the Space Shuttle... One afternoon John and I were playing with Lego and we ended up playing with this... we went through loading, crew embarkation and countdown (the procedure was on a check-list) with John observing and assisting, easily grasping the 'commercial' and 'technical' sides of the operation as we continued. The launch was a great success as I recall, in spite of a minor technical problem. I don't remember exactly how this ended, but I do remember it being a very enjoyable afternoon...

> When John and I did things together we seemed to concentrate on things that were scientific or technical, I seem to recall. We used to talk about the marvels and horrors of deep space and the nature of the universe – at the time I seem to remember that a relatively new idea was that the universe folded back upon itself. We wondered how this was possible and, if so, what was outside it? How were we to understand 'nothing' in the most literal terms? (I still don't.) We looked for answers in a Patrick Moore book, 'Travellers in Space and Time', which I recall

we read parts of together on at least one occasion.

I love this account as it shows how well John could interact and cooperate *provided* he was sufficiently interested in what was going on. It also demonstrates that John didn't have a need to take over and dominate to make things happen his way. I think John was probably about 10 years old at the time. Both Sam and John remember the bike club they formed with Lydia and Alison. John recalls:

> ... playing with Alison and Sam outside, behind houses and near garages – Sam had a silly bike called Chitty Chitty Bang Bang which kept going wrong – he was far too big for the bike – we all took bikes and cycled around – I was really happy and enjoyed it but can't remember any details.

Alison recalls being great friends with John and Harry from the age of nine or so and playing together both at school and at home. She sent me a long and deeply felt email in which she describes the 'important role that John played in' her childhood:

> I remember John... as having been one of my best friends at a time when I was relatively happy...

> We would play together with Harry in the playground... I don't remember all the games we played. I remember playing marbles a lot... All three of us liked science. I don't remember the objective of the game we played, but I think John particularly enjoyed making silly noises while he was dashing around, and this made me laugh. We used a lot of imagination – I think space and aliens might have featured somewhere too. I got the impression that much of the fun John was having was going on in his own head and we weren't privy to the best of it. I remember him going round the school outside of lessons, even when he was by himself, in his own world which seemed anything but dreamlike; rapidly uttered conversations and dramatic action between more than one person were often enacted as part of his games.

> One memory which I have always treasured was the flying of food bags. I don't remember which one of us started it (it wasn't me, but I quickly caught on), but we used to get used sandwich bags and attach string to them with a paper clip. On a windy day you could fly them like a kite and we would spend the whole lunch hour doing this. It was a bit like having a pet on a lead and we would talk to the bags and try and tempt them down with the offer of chocolate drops etc. It was all very daft, but one morning we arrived in the playground to find nearly every child flying a bag on a piece of string; bags of all shapes and sizes! It's the only time I think I've ever been involved in setting a trend...

> I will always look back with fondness on the time that we were good friends... John had his problems, but he didn't judge me on my ability to play games, how I talked or what I looked like, and at that age when you are finding your way with other people that is very very important. It's what real friendship should always be about... My friendship with John also confirmed what I had been brought up to believe; that its not just O.K. to be different, its good, that you shouldn't judge people superficially and that you should always stand up for your friends. Not that I was any kind of saint, I'm sure I treated John pretty badly, I could be bossy

PLAY

and I think I probably bossed him about quite a bit. I'm sorry for that! The fact was that people came to regard me as someone who had 'taken John on' and was responsible for him in a way which implied he was not capable of looking after himself. That could have encouraged me to look down on him in a way which he didn't deserve, and I hope I didn't do that.

John agrees that the last two years in junior school (years 5 and 6) were also his happiest school years and considers that Harry, Phil and Alison were 'real friends'. Unfortunately there was little contact between John and Alison after they left junior school as they both went to different secondary schools. If John hadn't passed the entrance exams to his private day school he would have gone to the same mixed comprehensive as Alison. They may well have remained friends and this might have made both their lives easier at secondary school.

Once John became proficient on the computer this interest became the basis of several close friendships which he maintained from about the age of eight until he left secondary school. The close friendships with Harry and Phil, for example, lasted for many years and both were built around the common interest of computing. I think common interests are by far the best way of helping children on the autism spectrum to acquire friends. Parents can really make a difference if they can find other children who enjoy the same things as their child and invite them to their home to play. There's much more likelihood to be some interaction between these children than if children without common interests come round to play. In addition to spending time on the computer, John and Harry spent a considerable amount of time designing elaborate adventure and role playing games. Apparently one game involved a player spending a day at school trying to stay alive. John roared with laughter as he told me that he suspects that if it had been sold, 'every teacher in the school would have sued me for slander'. Both Phil and Harry spent a great deal of time in our house but never at the same time.

As Phil grew older he also enjoyed clubbing with Lydia and her friends. I still remember John hovering around the edges watching while Lydia and a group of friends took hours getting ready to go out. These teenagers came into our house (which always seemed to be the base of activities) looking like normal human beings and emerged some time later looking quite unrecognisable, with amazing hair styles and clothes. When I asked John recently if he would have liked to participate and whether he resented Phil leaving him, John was quite emphatic about his dislike of clubbing:

If he enjoyed that sort of horrible alien stuff, that was fine with me: I always knew he was gregarious... It's a close approximation to hell. An environment optimized for massive widescale social interaction and male/female interactions between people who almost certainly share none of my interests, listening to music I find at best nonmusical, and the whole thing so crammed with people and flooded with irrelevant stimuli that I think it would drive me out in under a minute. *Shudder*. I prefer my social interaction to be quieter, slower, and at a distance!

More recently John wrote: 'I suspect I'd enjoy some of the music now... if it were played about 40dB quieter!' I asked John a few years ago how he felt when Phil became involved with a girl and then became less committed to their computing projects.

'Less committed' is not the word. He *vanished*. Completely. It wasn't just from me; he'd vanish from home as well, and, he said, from everything else he normally did, all at once. It was more like a phase change than romantic involvement... I understood it well enough to understand that I didn't understand Phil's taste in women at all and to get annoyed about the waste of time and the fact I couldn't swap ideas with anyone until Phil recovered (sort of like recovery from a debilitating disease).

John, aged 35, amended the above when he sent me an email dated February 14th:

Bwahaha. Hark at the man who'd never fallen in love. Romantic involvement *is* a phase change, if a temporary one (so I write, alone on Valentine's Day as always). I can completely understand vanishing like that now (though I'd never dare do it).

Not such a close friend, but still a very regular visitor to our house, was another boy, Nigel, the son of someone I'd met when we were both attending National Childbirth Trust classes. He wrote the following to me:

My first strong memory was when we came over to your New Year's Eve party. I think it was in 1987. I remember thinking it was good to see John again. I remember us and a few others having a pillow fight and getting feathers everywhere.

My main memories are from then, until I lost contact with him in around 1998 approx. I would say that he was a friend and I enjoyed our time together. It was great that we had some common interests especially computers and sci-fi.

In the times we spent together during secondary school age we'd often play computer games together which I always enjoyed...

He was always very enthusiastic and very knowledgeable about computers, and was often keen to quote or read out sections from various humorous or sci-fi books he had.

He often communicated at quite a technical level (especially about computer things) and from what I remember he would talk quite quickly and not have a great deal of eye-contact. I think maybe he found it easier to communicate to those with similar interests or technical understanding...

I remember that spending time at your house seemed quite different to mine, in that in some ways things were more relaxed and seemed to have less rules. He would sometimes comment about the fact that my mum seemed quite strict.

We often had pizza when we were getting our own lunch at your house, and one time I remember we'd forgotten to take the plastic wrapper off, so there was a strange plastic burning smell when it started to cook.

I have some memories of visiting him while he was at ... [university]. Again it was mainly time on his computer. I remember waiting for him at his room in hall (we'd missed each other so I'd gone there), and someone in his hall told me he was known as The Professor – presumably he had a reputation of being very brainy and techy!

John found Nigel's mother (a secondary school teacher) really hard to cope with at the time and still remembers her clearly:

> She was way, way, way too strict. I remember mealtimes as decidedly overcooked and unpleasant food and really formal. I didn't eat much because I was so stressed out. She was always in school teacher mode – her attitude to managing children was to lay down rules that must be followed, regardless of how reasonable these rules were or any reason behind them. I didn't have tantrums there but came pretty close. I managed to control myself because I realised that Nigel had to cope all the time with these rules (poor sod) and it made me feel so much better realising that I didn't have to. I had something reasonable and sane waiting for me at the end of the day.

As our children grew older, their friends stayed regularly overnight at weekends and during the holidays. Even though our second house was large and there was more than one spare room that friends could have slept in, they normally preferred to sleep on a mattress in the same room as the child they were staying with. Our children's bedrooms were at the far end of the house with two doors and a corridor between their bedrooms and ours but that didn't stop us being woken one night (about one in the morning) to the sounds of loud laughter and excited talking. We made our way to the source of the noise, opened the door of our daughter's bedroom and found both our children, with the two friends that were staying overnight, having a marvellous midnight feast! They were shocked to realise they'd woken us up as they'd managed to keep these midnight capers a complete secret from us until then. After telling them to keep the noise down as we had to go to work the next day, we went back to bed. As far as I'm aware these midnight feasts continued but we were never woken up again. Lydia remembers these midnight feasts clearly and how much John enjoyed them. As she recalls:

> The preparations were a lot of fun. The idea came from St Clares and Malory Towers. We had crisps, Pepsi, sweets etc., and set our alarms for midnight. We probably got away with a few before we got caught!

Food was always an important part of our socialising and the children were just carrying on this tradition in their own way; however, I can't help noticing that the food consisted of all the unhealthy stuff that wasn't a usual part of their diet!

I'm not really surprised that I didn't realise just how socially inadequate John would turn out to be in situations where he was expected to interact with children that he didn't have a close relationship with. At home and in the homes of friends his behaviour didn't seem too unusual. Children seemed to enjoy coming to the house to play and John obviously enjoyed friends coming round. However I think the parents of John's friends may have found it more difficult when he went to their houses to play. Perhaps I forgot to spell out how to manage him successfully. I suppose my only excuse is that I was trying to make everything seem as normal as possible and therefore tried not to single John out as needing special attention. Big mistake! As Alice, the mother of John's closest school friend Harry, recalls:

> These were memories from junior school. I still remember the famous trip to... zoo, where he would not stick with me and the other children. He kept wandering off often talking to himself. He lost his glasses that day if you remember and you were cross about it. I was more relieved at having got him back in one piece.

Another occasion I lost him completely was when I took them all to the theatre...
When we went to leave at the end of the performance he was nowhere to be seen.
Thinking he may have gone to the car, I took the other children there, but John
was not there. I left the others in the car and went back to the auditorium. John
was there screaming that I had walked off and left him – I never did find out
where he had been.

Away from family and friends John had far more difficulty fitting in. As John specu-
lates:

> I had problems with people I didn't know well because not only could I not model
> them, but at that stage I couldn't even *tell* that I couldn't model them; the model
> that ended up being used was I suspect a more or less distorted copy of my own
> self-model ('cos you have to start with a model of *someone*, and which model is
> more accurate than your model of yourself?). Amazingly this totally failed to
> predict anything useful about their reactions and only annoyed them. I suspect it
> works better for normal people, because they really *are* enough like those around
> them that self-models can provide a reasonably good initial stepping-stone.

From the emails I received from those peers of John that we only saw occasionally
(because they lived a long way away), John was easier to deal with when he was
younger. Once he became fascinated by computers they found it more difficult to interact with him if they were not into computers to the same degree.

There was one unpleasant incident at home which occurred when John was about
nine or ten. Our second house had two garden sheds, so we helped the children make the
larger shed into a clubhouse. We removed all the dangerous gardening tools and chemicals, hung curtains at the windows, put posters on the walls, installed a table and chairs
and so on. Some local children (that *our* children hadn't had contact with before) immediately started coming round to play in the clubhouse. Unfortunately it wasn't long
before they became very unpleasant to John and as Lydia remembers 'excluded him a
lot'. She recalls that she was so upset by their behaviour that she 'wanted to end the
gang and got very upset and told Mum and Dad'. We immediately stopped these children coming round to the clubhouse any more. According to John:

> This was classic clique-formation behaviour, with me on the outside as usual.
> This was my first real exposure to this sort of group crystallisation. Unfortunately
> it would not be my last. This was the first chill zephyr, harbinger of the Arctic
> blast that would howl at [secondary school].

The immediate reaction of children who'd never met John before was quite striking. I
remember the day when John was about eight and our family went to a flying display,
aircraft being one of my husband's strong passions. Tony was watching the planes and I
was watching the children who'd gone into the playground provided on the site. John
and Lydia were soon joined by other children and in what seemed like seconds to me
Lydia went off to play with the other children and John was left on his own. I was quite
upset by this and amazed at the speed with which these children reacted to John. He
seemed perfectly happy to be left on his own though, no doubt talking aloud to himself
and in his own imaginative world. Normally I was shielded from experiences like this
because I didn't see John at school. At home or in my friends' houses all the children

were used to him and he to them.

Birthday Parties

Before John started school his friends were really the friends he'd made because of *my* relationship with their parents. He was therefore invited to birthday teas/parties but I don't think he got involved in any formal games. As Nigel's mother recalls in an email sent to me: 'I do think back to a birthday party of Nigel's… John was far more interested in the workings of a clock (possibly the one with turning gold balls) than the party games we were trying to get him to join.' According to Lorna Wing (1996):

> Most young children with autistic disorders do not understand the point of birthday parties and do not participate if parents invite other children and there is no point in trying to make them take part. Older and more able children may like to go to parties although they may join in very little.

John wasn't invited to parties as a school child, a typical situation noted by Tony Attwood (1998). It appeared to me that the lack of party invitations didn't cause John any distress as he seemed quite unaware of his exclusion and would have refused to attend if he *had* been invited. According to John though, at some point in time (perhaps in secondary school?):

> I knew that those around me were having parties and I went to some lengths (right up to hiding and outright refusing: I didn't realise then that refusals could be considered an insult) to ensure that nobody ever invited me.

The only children's parties he went to were his sister's and John found these an enormous strain. We adapted quite a few of the games so that John could join in the celebrations and not spoil everyone else's fun with crying and tantrums. Nevertheless, he recalls: 'I often tended to end up [in the bedroom] trying to recover after an emotional meltdown. I don't know why I didn't just stay there. Yes, it would have felt lonely, but less unpleasant than doing the opposite.' He would have been horrified at the thought of a party of his own. Many traditional party games, such as *Musical Chairs* or *Pass the Parcel*, have an element of chance which John couldn't cope with. In *Musical Chairs* John would get very upset because each time the music stopped someone would be 'out' as a chair had been removed. We had to comfort him and never forced him to play. Greenspan and Wieder (1998) may well have identified the reason why John found so many games difficult. According to them:

> If your child has trouble with motor-planning or visual-spatial processing problems she may have trouble with games because games require sequencing. Games that involve the body (such as musical chairs), that require taking turns, and that have three or four steps are particularly difficult.

As described in previous chapters John had difficulties with motor planning *and* visual processing. *Pass the Parcel* was a problem because only one person received the present wrapped up in the centre of the parcel. However we adapted this game by putting a sweet between each layer of paper and fixed it so that the parcel stopped with him quite early on in the game. Lydia still remembers great parties when she was young although she recalls quite clearly that we 'had to put something between each layer [of

Pass the Parcel] as John would get so upset if he did not win… there was also a problem with the chocolate game'. I still remember how tense and upset John became when the 'Chocolate' game was played. A bar of chocolate was put on a chopping board in the middle of the floor with a knife, a fork, a large pair of Wellington boots, gloves, a scarf and a silly hat nearby. The children sat on the floor in a circle round the board and a shaker with two dice in it went round the children in turn. Whenever anyone shook a double six they went into the middle of the circle, put on the clothes and started to attack the chocolate with the knife and fork. They carried on eating the chocolate until the next child shook a double six when the clothes were transferred to the new child who could then cut into the chocolate themselves. Lydia recalls that 'time seemed to speed up when I went into the middle as it took so long to get dressed that it seemed as if another double six came round very quickly'. Because of the sheer randomness of the game one child could end up eating quite a lot of chocolate before someone else threw two sixes, while some children ate none. John couldn't bear to see this despite the fact that we'd promised everyone a piece of the same chocolate at the end of the game if they hadn't eaten any already. John says he can barely remember the details of the chocolate game 'but the mention of it raises my stress levels, even now'.

He seemed to enjoy (or was at least able to play without a tantrum) *some* party games, such as *Sardines,* to a certain extent. This is the version of *Hide and Seek* where the finder joins the person they were looking for and the next finder joins *them* until everyone is squashed into some small space. A simple game, without a competitive element, no motor or visual skills required and funny as well, was the perfect game for John.

To conclude: John played very happily on his own for long periods of time as a child and also enjoyed the company of his sister. He was happy as a young child playing alongside children who came regularly to the house and as he grew older he made close friends with a few children who shared his interest in computers. However he found groups of children that he didn't know well very scary and had to learn to cope in their presence. He never got used to parties or board games, hating anything that was competitive or depended on chance.

13
Concentration

People on the autism spectrum can possess extraordinary powers of focused concentration, often called hyperfocus. This ability to concentrate very deeply on topics of interest can result in what some call 'obsessions' or 'fixations' but I prefer to call 'special interests'. Whether the possession of 'special interests' is considered to be an asset or a deficit is a matter of debate. One might expect that someone with such powers of concentration would do well at school. Unfortunately the ability to focus on topics of interest can be associated with an inability to pay attention to matters that are of little interest, a feature that is sometimes called distractibility.

FOCUSED CONCENTRATION

According to John:

> I use 'focused concentration' in homage to Vernor Vinge's *A Deepness in the Sky*, which featured a particularly horrible dictatorship (the 'Emergency' or 'Emergents') which had found a way to effectively enslave normal human beings by turning them into custom-built autistics, focused endlessly on whatever tasks the slavemasters wished. The Focused were explicitly modelled as a more extreme version of autistics: I don't know anyone with Asperger's who's read it and didn't identify with them.

Wendy Lawson (2010) suggests that the ability to hyperfocus is at the heart of what it is to be autistic. Hyperfocus, or 'being in the zone', can lead to outstanding achievement. According to John it's one of his objectives in life to be in this state, despite the fact that he finds it very tiring. He describes the impact of 'being in the zone':

> Hyperfocus is critical to my working life... in hyperfocus I can think seemingly tens of times faster than normal: the entire project is visible at once as a network of interlocking relations, and the necessary changes are just instantly evident. I spend... only about 10% of my time in hyperfocus... (It's exhausting, to start with... I spent about 30% of today in hyperfocus tracking down some critical bugs and I'm shattered.)

John goes on to describe what distracts him from this remarkable state:

> Light, human voices, and sudden changes in background sound can easily jolt me out of the otherwise robust hyperfocus state. Distractions such as being lethally hungry, thirsty, terribly cold, or exhausted I am not likely to notice until something else distracts me.

It's hardly surprising that making children switch suddenly to another activity while so deeply engrossed can, at the very least, be really hard for them to cope with and, at the worst, provoke real anger. It could certainly contribute to the difficulties experienced by people on the autism spectrum when dealing with sudden change. As Deidre Lovecky

(2004) wrote:

> Because children with AS (Asperger's syndrome) hyperfocus, it can be difficult for them to leave ideas or material they find interesting to work on other things. When gifted children with AS engage in their favorite pastimes, they enter into a state of flow. Whether these are creative or not, leaving them appears to be painful... the child has difficulty letting go of what he or she is already focused on to do something else. Shifting attention is especially problematic when going from a preferred activity to a nonpreferred one... however, difficulty shifting can occur even between preferred activities. It's the stopping and starting that's the problem.

John completely agrees with Sainsbury (2009) when she writes: 'I could not switch my attention from one subject to another by an act of will; it seemed to take a sort of 'mental wrench' to manage it at all.' At secondary school John really disliked the continual change of subject every forty minutes. It didn't suit his learning style at all. Mel Levine (2002) thinks: 'Changing classes every fifty minutes may limit how well students are able to consolidate much of what goes on in class.' Levine quotes a teacher who said:

> Sometimes I marvel at how our students do it, proceeding like drones from one class to the next with no letup. As soon as they get into the groove in one subject, it's time to switch tracks completely. We're almost teaching them not to get too involved in anything, how to disengage rather than how to engage.

John's intense preoccupations have been an intrinsic part of his life since he was very small and we've frequently encouraged them as they made him so happy. We found his enthusiasm for these passions most engaging. He enjoyed playing with particular toys or watching certain objects for very long periods of time, often over many months if not years. We didn't stop or interrupt these activities if at all possible, as we felt that the ability to concentrate was something to be encouraged. As John explained relatively recently:

> Only with much concentration and time can hidden patterns emerge, and the feeling when they slot into place inside your head is so wonderful that I wouldn't give them up for anything: it's the highest joy in my job and spare-time activities both, and I can't see anything displacing it from that position.

Although we were unaware of it at the time, I think John's paediatrician believed this to be a poor way of bringing up a child. In a letter written to our family doctor when John was three, she said (referring to me): 'I think she lets John do as he wishes, without any pressurising. This is why I think that the structured environment of... nursery will probably be good for him.' As described in Chapter 9 we had a very structured routine at home but a lot of 'free' time was also built into the day for John to do what he wanted, without any pressure and with plenty of warning when this time was coming to an end.

John was a few months old when we first became aware of his exceptional powers of concentration. He used to sit in a small chair which was suspended from a metal frame to which we'd attached mobiles, sparkly things, rattles, bells and so on. When his hand moved involuntarily it would hit something which would either move or make a sound.

We'd rigged up this arrangement so that John had something interesting to look at and wouldn't get bored and miserable. John loved this chair and was so absorbed that we could be out of sight in the next room (which we were decorating at the time) and he wouldn't appear to notice our absence. We knew he was all right because we could hear rattles and so on and could even tell which hand he'd moved by the different sounds made by the attached gadgetry. Even when we walked into the room he was sitting in, either to check up on him or to go through to the kitchen, John seemed entirely unaware of us, never looked up and carried on playing in the chair. Even then we thought this behaviour was slightly unusual but we were delighted to have such a happy baby who displayed such powers of concentration. As he was our first child I don't think we realised *how* different this behaviour was from the majority of other children. It turned out be a very characteristic aspect of John's personality. Some months later, John played so much with his Fisher Price Activity Centre, which was attached to the bars of his cot, that all the colours wore off and some parts of it no longer worked. He literally tested it to destruction. We took some time before buying a replacement because it was quite an expensive toy. However, we argued that even if John grew out of it quite quickly we had another baby by this time and we expected that she would also get a lot of fun from it. As it turned out we were wrong; the purchase turned out to be a complete waste of money. John *did* grow out of it rapidly and our daughter played with it a few times and then grew bored with it.

John's fascination with things that moved had an unexpectedly beneficial outcome. When he was about 19 months old his sister Lydia was born. I needed to find something interesting to occupy John while I was breastfeeding in order to minimise any feelings of jealousy and stop him disrupting my feeding time with the new baby. While I fed Lydia on one side of our bed John stood on the other side listening to nursery rhyme records on our record player and watching the records go round. He kept perfectly still throughout the whole side of an LP (which lasted about thirty minutes) and seemed oblivious of the fact that I was feeding his sister. I was absolutely delighted and to be frank quite amazed at the success of my diversionary ploy. I suspect that the sight of the record spinning round and round may have been of more interest than the nursery rhymes themselves. If that was the case the modern alternatives might have been far less successful! These days I guess I would use Thomas the Tank Engine DVDs or something equivalent.

For more than two years, roughly between the ages of four and six, John was fascinated by clocks. If we went out for the day as a family to visit a town, we had to watch John like a hawk, or before we knew what had happened we lost him, only to find him with his nose pressed to the window of the last clock shop we'd passed. We frightened ourselves quite badly on more than one occasion when this happened. Meanwhile in our hall at home we had an old, rather attractive, long clock with a door which could be opened to reveal the pendulum. The clock chimed every hour and had to be wound every 24 hours by opening the door and pulling the chain so that the weight rose from the bottom to the top of its travel. Every school day, as soon as John got home, he would go into the dining room, drag a chair into the hall and place it in front of the clock. He would open the clock door and then stand on the chair watching the minute and hour hands go round for over an hour. From John's perspective:

> If that was all it did it would have been much less interesting. You could see its tiny motion whenever the pendulum ticked, then a tiny fall back, and the size of

each depended on which way the hand was going.

This was how he spent his 'winding down' time after school which most children would spend in front of the television. This was one of the few instances I remember my husband expressing concern over John's behaviour. He thought it was abnormal and quite disturbing, something which John finds rather surprising, writing as he did about his father: 'Mr. Thick Books of British Aircraft Registries thought that? The irony, it burns.' At the time I felt this behaviour was satisfying some need, even though I'd no idea what this could be. I also felt that John would eventually grow out of this passion in his own good time, which he did. I suppose I might have been more concerned if he'd looked at the clock every waking moment of the day and hadn't done anything else. However he had plenty of time for other activities, particularly as he didn't watch television. We still have this clock and recently I asked my son to open its door and see if he remembered how he felt when he stood in front of it as a child. As John opened the door he remembered the special smell inside the clock, which he described as 'midway between wood shavings and the smell of old books', and the feeling of anticipation and excitement as the hour approached. There would be a whirring sound and while the clock chimed John would watch the chain and weight move rapidly and noisily downwards. Perhaps unsurprisingly, John had no trouble whatsoever becoming extremely proficient at telling the time.

A typical example of the intensity and passion behind John's focused concentration – and his need to spend far longer than most people on the things that attracted him – could be seen during our visits to the London Science Museum. When I first started visiting this museum with John as a pre-school child, we used to concentrate on the children's section, where there were lots of buttons to press and things to watch; however, I also liked to have a quick stroll around other parts of the museum. One day, when John was about three years old, we came upon a working combine harvester. For quite some time after that he had absolutely no wish to see anything else in the museum and would stay watching this piece of machinery for at least a couple of hours. As John wrote a few years ago: 'I still know exactly what it looked like and a lot of how it worked, twenty-eight or so years later. I'd have been happy to see other combine harvesters, as long as they were exactly the same as that one!' I'm embarrassed to recall that I used to leave John alone watching the combine harvester while I took Lydia around other parts of the museum. I popped back now and again to check how John was getting on. Sometimes I would find him explaining to some adult who was looking round the museum, how the machine worked, as if he was a museum curator. I was surprised to find that John remembered that 'one of the people who assembled that machine for display turned up once, and we had a nice talk about the way the bits fit together and what related machines are like! (At least I liked it.)' At the time I didn't think anything of leaving him there as I believed him to be absolutely safe and that nobody or nothing would ever get him to shift from the machine. John would have screamed the place down if anyone had even suggested it. Although, as John pointed out: 'That curator could probably have got me to move by promising a look at similar things backstage, but nobody else could.' In retrospect I'm horrified that I could leave such a young child alone in a public place and that no one ever said anything to me. Perhaps things were different then. According to John: 'It was a *museum*. Museums are special places, away from the world: nothing bad can happen there.' Nevertheless, instead of taking both children on my own to the museum during the week while my husband was at work, we should have taken the children together at the weekend. While one of us walked round with Lydia, the other one could have sat down with a book for a couple of hours in the vicinity of the combine harvester. What I couldn't do was take John to the museum and expect him to be satisfied with a few minutes at each exhibit like other visitors. He would have created a terrible scene. Eventually he grew out of this combine harvester passion but my friend Jane (who was a trained scientist like myself and also had young children) mentioned another difficulty connected with a visit we all made together to this museum:

> I remember a visit to the Science Museum, and I think that John couldn't have been more than seven at the time, maybe younger, when we were listening to those things like telephones that give information about the displays. He was annoying Lucy [her daughter] and Lydia by insisting on listening to the telephones first and on hearing every word, so we would have to stay by one display for ages waiting for him to finish. He would get very worked up about things if he didn't get his way.

From John's point of view: 'I wasn't trying to stop other people from listening, I just wasn't going to wait! As for skipping bits, no way!'

SPECIAL INTERESTS

When he was young, John's passions changed relatively often, although as an adult he can still feel a remnant of some of the old feelings. For example, he still feels the shadow of an urge to walk *in* a stream rather than by its side on the footpath. He was also adamant, when he was 27 and looking for a vacuum cleaner for his new house, that he had to have one that allowed him to see the contents whirl round and round. I admit I was slightly surprised but was even more taken aback when my husband said that he felt the same! However as John grew older, things changed. As he describes:

> My focuses used to change every couple of years, but by the time I was ten some had congealed and have never changed since... I'm not sure how many interests I once had; I know that it's been a fairly constant 2.5 since my teenage years and rose to perhaps 3.5 in my mid-20s.

He goes on to describe 'computing and science fiction as deep interests, science in general as semi-deep and, since my early twenties, politics and economics as semi-semi-deep'. The two long term special interests of reading and computing are described in chapters of their own as they've played such an important role in John's life. He agrees with Gillberg (2002) that his interest patterns are narrow but thinks they've widened as he's grown older. Tony Attwood, writing in Kutscher (2005), describes John accurately when he says:

> The focus of the interest invariably changes, but at a time directed by the child, and is replaced by another special interest that is the choice of the child, not a parent or teacher. The complexity and number of interests varies according to the child's developmental level and intellectual capacity. Over time there is a progression to multiple and more abstract or complex interests... In the teenage years the interests can evolve to include electronics and computers, fantasy

213

literature, science fiction... All of these mirror the interests of peers, but again, the intensity and focus is unusual. There can be a natural ability to understand computer languages, graphics and advanced computer programming skills.

According to John:

An interest must be complex enough that its driving principles are not immediately evident, but not so complex that its driving principles are completely obscured (e.g. social interactions). Obviously this sweet spot moves over time.

My son has very clear views on the way that someone with narrow, focused interests should be treated. He wrote the following a few years ago when he was 30, in response to someone on the internet who wanted advice about one of their students who had a diagnosis of Asperger's syndrome:

If he's anything like the aspies [someone with Asperger's syndrome] I've known (mostly undiagnosed but obvious to me at least), he'll have voracious interests in specific domains, which can vary per individual and over time without obvious cause: I know I've added history, politics, molecular biology and psychology to my list of focus areas in the last ten years: why those subjects? I have no clue. The domains will almost certainly be complex, factual, and capable of endless variety on some level. (This seems to me to be a *major* difference from people with full-blown autism, who can focus on virtually anything regular, a classic example being train timetables. I don't know many people with Asperger's who'd get hooked on something as *closed* as that, and they'd generally want more dimensions to the complexity. It happens, but generally the focus seems to be in areas where things are *going on*, changing from day to day in (small and controllable!) ways, or failing that large enough to absorb for a long time: e.g. classical Western orchestral music, which has enough complexity to absorb anyone for a lifetime. However I'm not aware of any studies being done in this area and this may be inaccurate, the result of selection bias on my part.) In *young* aspergics, virtually anything may seem complex enough to focus on for a year or two. I focused on our ancient grandfather clock for a year between the ages of four and five, staring with endless concentration at it for an hour or more every day, smelling its lovely scent of extremely aged wood. It faded when I could tell the time and understood every tiny detail of the peculiar rattles and clonks that battered device produced, and could predict them in advance for an entire day... Whether these choices of focus area were triggered by frustration at not being able to do something obviously crucial, or were entirely arbitrary, I have no idea. My mild fascination with the behaviour of snails was hardly useful, but lasted for ten years, and didn't so much fade as *shift* into an interest in molecular biology which I don't have enough time to feed... Inside a focus area, interest, enthusiasm, and memory are boundless and effortless. Outside them, interest is minimal (I find it hard to stay awake in discussions too far outside a focus area) and memory is fleeting at best. This makes it damned hard to *learn* about the areas I'm weak in: I can't remember them! I'm not sure if there *is* a way to deal with us outside our focus areas. I'm not sure if there's a way to deal with *anyone* outside of topics they're interested in (I'm the wrong person to ask about *that*): it's just that the interest is more... focussed with Aspergics... I'd be inclined to say that if you're trying to deal with him outside his focus area, you're almost doomed from the start. Even he probably can't modify his focus areas consciously, and he might not be able to express what makes them so fascinating. Performance outside those areas is likely to be weak to nonexistent (he's spending no time on it because it's so uninteresting, and there are far too many interesting details elsewhere, and it can't be important compared to the focus anyway).

HYPERFOCUS ON SPECIAL INTERESTS – PROBLEM OR ASSET?

According to Kristine Barnett (writing in *The Spark: A Mother's Story of Nurturing Genius*), her son Jake was diagnosed as autistic when he was two and wasn't expected to read. As he didn't seem to be improving in his special education classes, she took the brave step of removing him from these classes and keeping him at home:

> Why is it all about what these kids can't do? Why isn't anyone looking more closely at what they can do?...

> But while I couldn't claim to fully understand Jake's passions and interests, neither could I justify discouraging those interests just because the rest of us didn't understand them, or because they didn't match up with some so-called normal template for childhood development. If we wanted to help Jake, we had to stop focusing on what he couldn't do...

> I set up new routines for Jake. But instead of constantly pushing him in a direction he didn't want to go, drilling him over and over to get his lowest skills up, I let him spend lots of time every day on activities he liked...

> The more we learned about Jake, the more I realized how fortunate it was that we hadn't taken away everything he'd been using for self-stimulation in those early days. The cereal he'd dump out onto the kitchen floor? He was figuring out the volume of the boxes...

> It was incredible to realize that all this potential had been there the whole time. My beloved boy hadn't been missing after all. He'd just been working. And now that we were beginning to understand what he was capable of, it was even more terrifying to think about how much might have been lost...

> Our strengths and skill sets are there, right from the beginning, but they need time and encouragement to flourish.

As a result of her approach, Jake's extraordinary talent for maths and physics was allowed to flourish. By the time he was five Jake was able to attend mainstream kindergarten and then he 'began taking college level courses in maths, astronomy, and physics at age eight and was accepted to university at nine.' At 15, Jake was the youngest student to be accepted into the Perimeter Institute for Advanced Theoretical Physics in Waterloo, Canada. At 18, he is studying for a PhD at the same institute.

Although some parents and professionals regard the ability to focus so intently to be an asset, others consider it to be a major problem that needs to be addressed. As Adams and Mesibov (2003) explain:

Most of the parents and professionals who work with people with ASD have both positive and negative views of special interests. Some view them positively because they might represent an area of real strength and skill... The other side of these narrow interests is that they are very specific and often irrelevant to effective functioning in the real world. In addition, they can exacerbate negative behaviors, including repetitive questioning, interrupting others, and egocentric social interactions.

John believes his ability to hyperfocus 'is utterly essential for virtually everything I do. I do sometimes wish that I could *decide* to hyperfocus on something, rather than its being decided for me by some unconscious agency.' Tony Attwood (2006) wrote that in his opinion the ability to hyperfocus 'is a trait that can be a great advantage to society' and 'people with Asperger's syndrome are natural experts', views I completely concur with. Rather than ban or limit the special interests of a child on the autism spectrum, I think that the ability to concentrate so deeply should be encouraged, the child helped to broaden their range of interests over time and their skills and talents gently nudged towards topics that could provide them with future employment. John agrees passionately with my views, the thought of banning special interests being totally abhorrent to him:

> What a *horrible* idea. Forbidding the things you're good at isn't going to make you better at anything else, it'll just make you depressed and frustrated and probably disruptive and eventually good for nothing. If you banned me from doing the things I was focused on (perhaps on the grounds that obsession is *per se* bad), I'm not sure there'd be a lot left of me.

I find it very strange that the focused interests of many on the autism spectrum can be frowned on while the same focus seen in people training to be top flight musicians or athletes is encouraged and supported. Dedication and hard work are essential to reach the top in all competitive fields regardless of talent. It would appear that some work areas are more acceptable than others. As Boyd (2009) notes: 'A special interest in some area of sport, art or music for example is more socially acceptable and is more likely to be nurtured and encouraged.'

I really dislike the terms fixations and obsessions, with their critical overtones and implications that these characteristics are not a good thing. Obsessions imply something unreasonable which has taken the person over in a harmful way and if not removed entirely should at the very least be severely rationed. This is certainly a view held by some who believe that all human beings should behave in a similar ('normal') way and have a wide range of socially acceptable interests. They think that those who display a very intense focus on a limited number of topics are defective in some way. John wrote to me recently as follows:

> Ah, hyperfocus. I've been in it for most of two weeks now, longer than ever before by some margin. It can be quite disabling when it lasts for this long – it's still exhausting, for starters, but when you have this many ideas bubbling up you can't sleep. But ye gods has it ever been productive. Looking back at the last two weeks I'm not sure you could say that my obsession with getting the problems worked out... has been entirely rational nor entirely good for me (I'm blurred and shivery now it's over, like I'm coming out of a long illness or something). But it

was so very much *fun*, and now it's done the world is a tiny bit better for it, and I can't think of a better way to spend a working fortnight than doing that, even if it did sort of leak into and take over my spare time and dominate my thoughts during my sleeping hours and weekends as well.

I could not possibly have spent this long in hyperfocus when I had to commute every day.

The medical model of autism considers people on the autism spectrum to have a disorder, one of whose symptoms is defined as restricted interests. The new *Diagnostic and Statistical Manual of Mental Disorder* (DSM-5) cites the following as one of the possible criteria to be used when diagnosing autism spectrum disorder:[53]

Highly restricted, fixated interests that are abnormal in intensity or focus (such as strong attachment to or preoccupation with unusual objects, excessively circumscribed or perseverative interests).

This definition implies that the kind of focus exhibited by those not on the autism spectrum should be considered as 'normal' and that exhibited by those on the spectrum abnormal. I find this quite disturbing, implying as it does that one type of concentration is good and the other is not and should therefore be corrected if at all possible. Clare Sainsbury, a young writer with Asperger's syndrome, wrote in her book *Martian in the Playground*:

All too often, obsessions are seen as pathological symptoms, which interfere with whatever the teacher is trying to teach and so need to be suppressed. I feel that this is an extraordinary waste of motivation and energy, particularly given how hard it can be to motivate children with Asperger's in other respects.

John, who thinks Clare is a 'soul mate' after reading her book, commented passionately on the use of the words 'pathological symptoms' when referring to special interests:

Anyone who sees them this way is an inhuman moron. They're the centre of the pupil's life, they're a source of endless motivation, and they're almost always centred around learning something complicated; teachers should be treating this like gold dust. (Having anyone of any age interested in learning to this degree is rare enough.)

Luke Jackson (2002), a teenager with Asperger's syndrome, wrote in his book *Freaks, Geeks and Asperger Syndrome*: 'When people hear the word 'obsession' they automatically think that it is something negative or bad. That's why I prefer the term favourite topic or subject.' John definitely doesn't agree with Luke's preference:

[This phrase] isn't strong enough. 'Favourite' topics aren't automatically learnt after a single exposure: 'favourite' topics don't rivet your attention where all else is fog; 'favourite' topics don't structure your entire life to such a degree that you don't *care* what unrelated things may be discarded in the process. Everyone has favourite topics: most people do not have focuses.

Luke went on:

Q: When is an obsession not an obsession?

A: When it is about football.

How unfair is that? It seems that our society fully accepts the fact that a lot of men and boys 'eat, sleep and breathe football'.

In fact Adams and Mesibov (2003) were very surprised to find (when they compared the interests of a small group of university students with a group of people with high-functioning autism or Asperger's syndrome of similar age and intellectual functioning):

> The differences between the groups were not as great as we had anticipated. It was not that the participants with ASD had broader and more commonly held interests, but rather the interests of our university students were narrower, more specific, and more idiosyncratic than we had thought... there were a few small differences in the categories of interests.

In particular the students were more interested in sports. As John wrote though:

> If these were American university students I can understand that. University sports are a religion over there to a degree that is quite incomprehensible to anyone from the other side of the Atlantic. The entire university often seems to exist merely as an appendage to the sports program.

Is it possible that parents and teachers worry, criticise, get annoyed and even seek professional help just because they don't understand or share their autistic child's passionate interest in something? As Luke says:

> Sometimes I think that a parent may want to stop a fascination or fixation because it is bugging them. As I have said, these are not the same as compulsions, which can take over someone's life. They are ways of feeling in control and ways of relieving stress. There is also one fact that many people seem to overlook – we actually love the things we talk about.

John doesn't believe there is such a clear cut differentiation between focused interests and compulsions. 'The difference is, if anything, merely one of degree, not kind. What's *wrong* with having your life taken over by some interest, as long as it doesn't impede survival?'

It may not be the actual topic of interest that parents get worried about, rather the intensity with which it is pursued. This can be so great that it can, if parents aren't careful, dominate the whole household. However, as John points out: '[Intensity] is not unusual in adults expert in some field. Why is it considered pathological in children?' According to Christopher Gillberg (2002):

> It has to be said that it is not the interest in itself, but rather the character of the person's relationship to the interest, that is the problem. The individual with Asperger syndrome so engrosses himself in the interest that it becomes tedious, often painfully so, for other people. So much time, energy and thought are spent on it, that there is little or no time left for anything else.

Not surprisingly John's views don't agree with Gillberg's:

Ah. So the harmful part is that it's *annoying to others*. Foolish me, assuming that the presence of harm to the patient was the point. Annoying to others? Must be a pathology.

I might also point out that *anyone* sufficiently expert in *any* field, when communicating with people who he thinks are equally expert, is likely to be borderline incomprehensible to anyone listening in. (Not just intellectual fields: they all have their own jargon. Some non-intellectual fields are famous for it, e.g. cricket and baseball). The only difference with autistics is that we often talk like that to non-experts because we can't judge the knowledge levels of other people well. *That* is where effort should be exerted, not at quashing the expertise.

I certainly engross myself in interests as described; but luckily this is fairly common in the SF [science fiction] field, and downright obligatory in the computing field (you've got to exhibit monastic dedication if you're going to learn enough). So it's a *feature* for me, *not* a problem.

As far as I'm concerned, as long as the essential things in life are carried out (such as eating, sleeping, homework, chores etc.) and the child's interest doesn't completely dominate and take over the family's way of life, why should it matter if all the remaining time is spent engrossing oneself in a particular subject? If that bores others, tough luck! John couldn't agree more. Obviously boring other people isn't the way to make friends but that problem will probably disappear if one can find people who share the same passionate interest. As Clements and Zarkowska (2000) state:

> It is important to ask whether the behaviour itself poses a real problem… We have to think very carefully about whether we should leave the behaviour alone or whether it is really to the person's advantage for limits to be set and the behaviours curtailed. It is important to be clear what the person should be doing instead… There will be no success in just setting out to *stop* a behaviour.

Many authors agree that should these interests be of *danger* to anyone, it's important that they are stopped.

We'd become so accustomed to John's ability to play with objects of interest for very long periods of time that we were really surprised to find that Lydia, as a young child, would only concentrate for a short period of time on one thing before she wanted to try something new. Many years later we found out that Lydia's behaviour was actually typical of very young children. I remember hearing Professor Gary Mesibov (who was director of the TEACCH programme at the university of North Carolina) using an excellent analogy to explain these differences. He imagined a flashlight (torch) that can be set either on a narrow intense beam (the child on the autism spectrum) or adjusted to have a wide diffuse beam (the neurotypical child), both of which are useful in different situations. This description fits our children perfectly. John had (and still has) the intense focus of a narrow beam of light, excellent at picking out small details and studying things in great depth, while Lydia had the wide focus of a diffuse beam of light. Some psychologists call the narrow focussed feature '*weak central coherence*'. The world is definitely a richer and more productive place by having both types of people in the population. Those with a narrow and intense focus and an ability to pursue a subject with passion have been responsible for many scientific breakthroughs and enormous creativity in many fields. In fact writers such as Michael Fitzgerald (2004) and Iona

James (2006) believe that autobiographical and biographical evidence suggests that many outstanding individuals, past and present, (including scientists, mathematicians, composers, artists, authors and philosophers) could be described as being on the autism spectrum. Fitzgerald believes:

> Asperger's syndrome provides a plus – it makes people more creative. People with it are generally hyper-focused, very persistent workaholics who tend to see things from detail to global rather than looking at the bigger picture first and then working backwards, as most people do.

However, in *An Exact Mind. An Artist with Asperger Syndrome* (a book of beautiful drawings by Peter Myers), Simon Baron-Cohen and Sally Wheelwright wrote that Peter's art shows: 'The autistic mind not only has excellent attention to detail, but the global whole can be envisaged just as well as the local parts. In this sense his art refutes the central coherence theory.' John agrees with this, writing:

> Indeed, I design programs by envisaging the whole and spotting regularities in that whole which can be implemented 'once and only once'. I can certainly see the whole: but the whole is made up of details, and they all must be right: so naturally one spends more effort, in the end, on the sum of all the parts than on the whole.

POTENTIAL BENEFITS OF SPECIAL INTERESTS

I think we've been very fortunate that John's amazing powers of concentration, focus and attention to detail have been harnessed to activities that have provided him with pleasure, a means of keeping himself calm, intellectual challenge, creative fulfilment, friends, hobbies and employment. John is very grateful that we didn't attempt to ration his access to his special interests and indeed offered him things we thought he would enjoy and would be good at. Most of his long term passions, such as science fiction and computing, arose from materials that I deliberately introduced when he was young. John maintains that his special interests play such a crucial role in his life that 'I'm damned glad that you didn't try to reduce or eliminate any of mine, except to make sure that e.g. I got my homework done sometimes!... Broadening the interest is the only thing that I'd consider *right*.' Obviously a child cannot do what they want *all* the time as they have to learn to fit in with the rest of the family. Setting boundaries is just as important for a child on the autism spectrum as for any other child. Nevertheless, allowing children to spend plenty of time doing what they are good at and enjoy, while subtly broadening these interests and skills, can boost their self-esteem and confidence and with a bit of luck they will mature into fulfilled and happy adults.

Many adults on the autism spectrum suffer from depression. I have no idea to what extent depression in autistic individuals arises from a genetic vulnerability. However I can't help wondering whether the likelihood of suffering from depression is increased by a lack of self-esteem and fulfilment which could arise from continually feeling like a square peg trying to fit into a round hole. Surely concentrating on a person's interests and strengths, so that these can really develop, would make those on the autism spectrum feel good about themselves and make it more likely that they could find a place in the world where they feel truly valued for what they can do well? I think that trying to turn a person into something they're not is, in the long term, a risky business. Which is better – the person who is proud of what they do and who they are and who has been encouraged to pursue their natural interests and talents, or someone who has been constantly discouraged from being themselves and therefore failed to develop their natural strengths?

Tony Attwood (1998) gives several reasons as to why the phenomenon of special interests occurs. He believes these are: to facilitate conversation, to indicate intelligence, to provide order and consistency, as a means of relaxation and as an enjoyable activity. John has plenty to say about this:

> I don't think I've *ever* got interested in something 'to facilitate conversation' or 'to indicate intelligence'; if something I'm interested in has that effect, well and good, but it's not important. The order-and-consistency stuff is a big reason for my interest in computers, and the relaxation stuff for my interest in SF [science fiction], but in both cases that's only part of the explanation, I think. Both of these rapidly became a way for me to *exploit a strength* as well – fluency with language (and also my near-intuitive understanding of certain aspects of computer operation). It's always enjoyable doing something you're good at, so this is self-reinforcing. (This may be one reason why those interests have never faded. I can't see how e.g. collecting Smarties tops is self-reinforcing; neither is reading the grandfather clock, at least not past a certain point. But there's no limit to improvement in English, nor to the amount one can learn in the CS [computer science] field – at least, if there is a limit to the latter the human race is nowhere near it yet.)

I certainly agree with John's assessment. One of the reasons he was so happy when he lived at home (and now, in his own place), was that he could spend enough time engaged in activities that he could do well, that gave him great pleasure and were very relaxing. I'm sure he could never have coped with the stress of school if he hadn't been able to wind down so effectively at home. It goes without saying that the school holidays were always far more enjoyable than term time! John says:

> One of the things I hated about secondary school was that worry about the next day and especially homework was always intruding, preventing any long periods of wind-down, even at weekends (as they hit me with even more homework then, often eating many hours and ruining an entire day).

The calming effects of engaging in a special interest and how this can be exploited are described by Clements and Zarkowsa (2000) as follows:

> Try to schedule the hobby for times of predictable stress or intervene early in the build up of stress to divert the person... Try not to give access to the special interest immediately after something unacceptable has been done. This runs the risk of directly reinforcing unacceptable behaviour.

Sensible comments, I would suggest. On *very* rare occasions we had to stop, or at least threaten to stop, access to the computer if John's behaviour was totally unacceptable or if he was deliberately disobedient. He agreed that this was probably the only punishment that would be effective and he readily accepted the consequences when he knew he'd over stepped the mark; however, we used this technique *very* sparingly. I would agree with Tony Attwood (2006) when he says:

> Some parents have used removal of access to the interest as a punishment for mis-behaviour or tasks not completed. While this strategy can be an effective component of a home-based behaviour management program, it could become a trigger to agitated behaviour if the child cannot tolerate denied access. I recommend that there is some caution regarding removal of access to the interest as a punishment, as other strategies may be more successful, and the interest should remain a positive aspect of the person's daily life. Preventing access to one of the few pleasures in the person's life will invariably be resisted.

I think it's much better to use the special interests as a reward after a child has spent time doing necessary things that they don't want to do, such as homework.

Dean Beadle (2008), a young man with Asperger's syndrome, has some interesting observations to make about the potential benefits of a child's special interests:

> Often, a big issue for parents and carers of autistic children is trying to understand what their children are thinking... I'm sure if you were to analyse an autistic person's special interest, you will develop an understanding of them that you had never gleaned before. On another level, showing an interest in a child's obsession can help a parent to enjoy a level of communication that had seemed unachievable before. Looking at it in this light, a child's special interest is actually incredibly useful.

I agree with this whole-heartedly. The key to my insight into John's needs was via the clues presented by his obvious interests; in order to motivate him to do *anything* these fundamental interests had to be harnessed. By so doing we have a very happy and fulfilled son who (though still on the autism spectrum) is capable of living and working independently in a neurotypical world.

Employment

When John was in his teens we were very conscious that his lack of eye contact, in-tense manner and absence of small talk would mean that he would make a very poor impression at job interviews. We felt that *outstanding* computing expertise was necessary in order to compensate for these weaknesses. We hoped that employers would be prepared to turn a blind eye to some social eccentricities if the employee's skills were really valuable. Temple Grandin (2008) and Tony Attwood (2006) stress the importance of channelling special interests in such a way that they can provide employment, a strategy which has certainly turned out to be successful for John. His fascination with computing from a young age has meant that the expertise he acquired has enabled him to be employed as a computer programmer/analyst/software engineer ever since he left universi-ty. As Hans Asperger wrote (Uta Frith, 1991):

> We see here something that we have come across in almost all autistic individuals, a special interest which enables them to achieve quite extraordinary levels of performance in a certain area... Able autistic individuals can rise to emi-nent positions and perform with such outstanding success that one may even con-clude that only such people are capable of certain achievements. It is as if they

had compensatory abilities to counter-balance their deficiencies. Their unswerving determination and penetrating intellectual powers, part of their spontaneous and original mental activity, their narrowness and single-mindedness, as manifested in their special interests, can be immensely valuable and can lead to outstanding achievements in their chosen areas. We can see in the autistic person, far more clearly than with any normal child, a predestination for a particular profession from earliest youth. A particular line of work often grows naturally out of their special abilities.

Ozonoff, Dawson and McPartland (2002) wrote in a similar fashion:

Parents of children with high-functioning autism spectrum disorders often lament their child's single-mindedness about certain subjects or interests – usually to the detriment of necessities such as school-work, chores, and personal hygiene. But the very same tendency for focus makes these children diligent students of the subjects that intrigue them and very high achievers in those area.

We can certainly relate to this, as homework and personal hygiene were certainly contentious issues for many years. In fact as a means of acquiring knowledge, school was in many ways a waste of time for someone like John. As he recalls: 'Some of the classes were fascinating (e.g. English, parts of the sciences) but others I can barely recall. The lifetime spent in those classes was wasted.' In fact John was a natural student but only when the subject matter fascinated him. Once he was interested in something, time spent on the subject was of no concern and he would pursue the topic in far greater depth than any school would expect. However, if he wasn't interested... I completely agree with Tony Attwood's (2006) comment:

Much of the knowledge associated with the interest is self-directed and self-taught. The interest is chosen because of some aspect that is appealing or important to the child with Asperger's syndrome and not because the activity is the latest craze and the child must have the 'currency' of popularity. The interest is often a solitary and intuitive activity, pursued with great passion.

This was what John found 'so strange... during the dotcom boom and afterwards... For the first time ever one of my obsessions had exploded onto the global stage and got *everyone* obsessed!' The importance of John's special interests and some idea of their intensity can be gleaned from his words when he wrote, in his late twenties: 'I've never had an interest in any human that's as intense as my interest in learning in my interest areas. A good thing too; I'm not sure if the other party would survive it!' After becoming *very* attracted to a female friend in his thirties he had to admit:

This hasn't been true any more (if only for a few months). And I *hated* it. It was so clearly an irrational distortion of my normal thought patterns. It was like having a traitor in my skull, but this traitor was *me*... perhaps it would have been less horrible if reciprocated, but I still can't imagine that.

Friendships

Tony Attwood (2006) points out that special interests can lead to friendships as well as employment. He writes: 'One of the common replies of typical children and adults to the question 'What makes a good friend?' is 'We like the same things'; shared interests can be the basis of friendship.' Indeed John has had very close friendships since he was a child as a result of a common interest in computers and then science fiction. For many years he's also been able to make friends over the internet with those who share his interests. Fortunately this has saved him from being lonely, even though his social skills were such an area of weakness. I totally agree with Gillberg (2002), who writes as follows about the importance of finding out the special interests of a child on the autism spectrum:

> Children with computer skills and interests have recently become 'more acceptable' to their age peers. Many boys and girls without autism spectrum disorders share their computer interest, and so there is sometimes a very good basis for positive long-term interactions. There may be other special interests (e.g. chess, or playing an instrument) and these may well form excellent 'common ground' on which some individuals with Asperger syndrome, eventually, find a 'friend'. It is therefore of the utmost importance to try and find out which special skills he/she is good at.

Patricia Howlin (1998) suggests that teachers help to develop an autistic child's special skills as this may make it easier for them to be accepted by their peers:

> In that normal children will be more willing to tolerate a peer who is 'different' if he or she has some special abilities it is important to try to develop such skills as far as possible. With guidance from teachers, children can be helped to use these skills in order to foster social interactions or to increase their acceptance within the classroom.

When thinking about the problems he had making friends at school John wrote: 'I can't really understand how anyone could consider mere similar age enough of a reason to make friends with someone.' Similarly, John has never had any desire to join any organisations or make friends with people *just* because they're on the autism spectrum. Again Gillberg (2002) has the following relevant comments to make:

> People with Asperger syndrome (and other high-functioning autism spectrum disorders) seem to be more dependent than other people on spending time with those who share their interests, and have about the same level of intelligence and overall functioning. I have often been surprised by their frank statements that they cannot 'tolerate' those who are not like them, or that they can 'just tolerate' others, but only if they are not expected to converse or interact with them.

PERFECTIONISM

As well as the ability to focus so intensely on topics of interest, another aspect of John's character which explains much of his behaviour has been his perfectionist approach to anything he undertakes. According to Attwood (2006):

> The learning profile of children and adults with Asperger's syndrome can include a tendency to focus on errors, a need to fix an irregularity and a desire to be a perfectionist. This can lead to fear of making a mistake and the child's refusal to commence an activity unless he or she can complete it perfectly.

This is a very accurate description of John's learning profile. He's indeed a perfectionist, an attribute which can be considered both a weakness and a strength. It's admirable to try and do something as well as possible and is a trait shared by many creative people who aren't satisfied until their work of art or musical composition is 'perfect' in their eyes. John believes that it's essential to be a perfectionist if one is to become a really good computer programmer:

> This is also one reason why the number of bugs other people find in my code is exceptionally low (it was about an order of magnitude below anyone else at the last job, despite the complexity of the code I wrote being about an order of magnitude higher than anyone else's): because I feel actual physical shame when people find that I've done something wrong, I go over it again and again, combing every last potential problem out, before I let it go. Classic perfectionism, but why? Personal identification with one's work, and shame when it is found to be faulty.

Nevertheless John admits that 'the gap between that and perfectionism interfering with task completion is narrow; I know I have dozens of things littering my disks that I won't release yet because they're not quite right.' The perfectionist can lose all sense of proportion about the task in hand, forgetting and no longer interested in its original purpose and unaware of time constraints. The task takes on a life of its own and must be completed 'perfectly' regardless of anyone or anything else. Any attempt to intervene and seek a compromise so that the job is finished quickly (but not to the perfectionist's exacting standards) can be met with frustration and anger. This perfectionist trait, although leading to John's undoubted expertise in the field of computing, has also caused him many problems since he left home. It was amazing that he actually received his degree in computer science as he had enormous difficulty finishing his large third year project and handing it in. He buried his head in the sand, completely forgot, or didn't care that this project only existed as part of the degree and kept wanting to make improvements as he felt it wasn't good enough. The words 'compromise' or 'good enough' can definitely be a red rag to a bull as far as John is concerned. In his words: 'Only perfect is good enough, and that just barely!' Nevertheless, I think that after many years working for a commercial software house, which had to make a profit, he has (with great reluctance) found a way of coping with a lack of perfection on occasion. As John said, this software house is 'full of kludgers':

> I can cope with lack of perfection, but only by deciding to fix whatever-it-is later. I can't decide not to fix something which is wrong without losing all interest in the entire area (it becomes sort of spiritually contaminated: the feeling of disgust is just like you get when asked to eat contaminated food).

Lorna Wing (1996) points out that 'children with autistic disorders are especially liable to be upset by failure'. As a child John was reluctant to start any task he thought he couldn't do well. This certainly caused some problems at school. When he was nearly nine his teacher wrote about John's mathematics:

> Occasionally he makes up his mind that a topic is too difficult before even giving it a try. He hates to be wrong and tends to hold back unless he is sure of success, making his progress seem patchy when in fact it is steady.

The following year a different teacher wrote: 'He determinedly makes up his mind what he will and will not do.' Perhaps, as a child, John was struggling so much that he tried to minimise his sense of failure by giving up when he thought something was too difficult for him. The situation was exacerbated because John was well aware how many things he did badly because of poor motor, visual and organisational skills, a most frustrating situation for such a perfectionist. I can certainly understand why he felt the only way of coping with situations when he felt out of his depth and thought he would look stupid, was to refuse to participate at all. It's not surprising that John disliked giving those around him yet more opportunities to see him fail. We felt very sorry for John although he can't really understand why:

> My being bad at most things is not a misfortune that overcame me, it just is, built in from the start. You might as well feel sorry that I can't dive to 3km and hunt squid. (Is it different for things that most people can do, if I'm an exception who cannot? I suppose that makes sense.)

I don't think we had any idea of the problems that could arise from John's need to do things well as this is a character trait that parents and schools try to encourage; it's also a fundamental characteristic of my own personality. I think it might have helped John if I'd taken Attwood's (2006) advice and used *Social Stories*™ 'to explain that we learn more from our mistakes than our successes; mistakes can lead to interesting discoveries, and an error is an opportunity not a disaster.' However at the time Carol Gray hadn't published her work on *Social Stories*™, the first publication date being 1998. John says that he always knew that one learned from one's own mistakes:

> It's one reason why I asked for help so rarely, because I learnt more doing it myself. But it was and remains important that nobody else can see me going wrong! (Why? Search me, it's emotional, it doesn't need to make sense.)

Fortunately as John grew older his attitude towards errors changed. Instead of being too scared to begin something new, he uses his errors in order to improve his knowledge and skill. He's still aiming for perfection but in a much more positive way. The artist Peter Myers, who has Asperger's syndrome, wrote in 2004: 'I am an imperfect perfectionist, which is really annoying... The desire to achieve perfection, which is never achieved, drives one on to greater efforts. Satisfaction, is knowing when to stop.' In response to Peter's words John wrote:

> 'Imperfect perfectionist' is a perfect phrase. I hereby steal it. Satisfaction is indeed knowing when to stop: i.e., never. One can never be perfect: there is always more to do. (So much more!) Even if I was the best hacker [computer programmer] on Earth (which I'm not, by a long way), I'd still have many improvements to make.

Although it goes against all his instincts, these days John knows that sometimes you have to stop, quoting an apocryphal phrase in software development: 'There comes a time in the course of any project to shoot the engineers and put the damn thing into production.' With the passage of time and the recovery of his self-esteem and inner confidence (after the destructive effects of secondary school), John has adopted a very sensible approach to coping with things he finds difficult. Describing what it is like to live with patchy abilities, John wrote:

> It's led to a sort of fatalistic perfectionism, which you'd think was a contradictory philosophy. In areas where I know I'm capable, everything must be perfect and flawless (it never is, but it's a good goal to aim for). In others, merely not fouling things up too badly is enough, and what will be will be.

DISTRACTIBILITY

Unfortunately John's amazing powers of concentration and need to do things perfectly are accompanied by a tendency to become easily distracted. John's distractibility, or lack of attention, arises from both external and internal sources. His ability to distract *himself* has proved to be the most problematic. John really dislikes the fact that his mind is often distracted from the task in hand by his own thoughts darting all over the place. As he says: 'The concentration deficits themselves have, as far as I can see, no upsides and are seriously annoying a lot of the time.' Complex music seems to smooth his thoughts out somewhat, stopping them leaping all over the place. 'They still leap, but the leaps are more controlled: if not on the subject, at least in the same direction as my train of thought was already going!' Hans Asperger, writing in 1944 (Uta Frith, 1991), described an autistic boy as being 'particularly prone to being distracted, that is, distracted from within. This type of distraction impairs the performance of many autistic children.' Until John is deeply immersed in an activity of real interest his thoughts can dive all over the place:

> Even without external distractions... my attention flickers without my control all the time unless I am hyperfocused, once a minute or more (when under extreme social stress, every couple of seconds). It's not that I can't pay attention to something boring: it's that my attention will flicker away to something else soon *no matter what*, and if I'm not intrinsically interested in the subject, it won't flicker back again (any more than it would normally flicker to something boring).

Unfortunately any job has times when the work can be boring; this is particularly troubling for John, who is then plagued by distracting thoughts. As he describes it:

> It's like someone whispering in your ear about something *much* more interesting that you could be doing, every ten seconds or so. (Of course I don't actually have anyone whispering in my ear, but there's no way to accurately simulate loss of attention!)

He has to find an approach to the work which excites him so that he can concentrate properly. That means he often tends to work on several things at once, diving from one topic to another until the subject he is supposed to be working on interests him enough, or his boss puts sufficient pressure on him, to complete the task in hand! In practice, John has often found that he does his best work when he's tired. Tiredness seems to suppress distracting thoughts and makes it easier for him to concentrate.

The first time I became aware that John had a problem paying attention was at his first pre-school gym session, which I thought might be an enjoyable way to improve his gross motor skills. Mothers were allowed to stay and watch the class. I remember the children all sitting in a circle on the floor and the lady in charge asking them to stand up.

Everyone stood up except John, who seemed to be in a world of his own and appeared not to hear her. This happened repeatedly during the session. The demands on the children weren't difficult and John could do the actual tasks but unless he was addressed by name he seemed completely unaware of what was going on. He didn't seem unhappy or stressed but sat staring at the floor as if his mind was on other things. The whole incident was a real shock to me as I'd never seen anything like it and couldn't understand what was going on. It was particularly disconcerting because John seemed to be an alert and intelligent child, with excellent powers of concentration, who had no problems following my instructions. However the situation at home was virtually one-to-one and quite different from being in a group of people you don't know.

'Inattention' is one of the characteristics of attention deficit disorder but can also be a problem for many diagnosed with Asperger's syndrome. In fact Tony Attwood (2006) noted: 'Studies have suggested that at least 75% of children with Asperger's syndrome also have a profile of learning abilities indicative of an additional diagnosis of Attention Deficit disorder.' John doesn't agree that his behaviour at the gym class was anything to do with inattention. 'I'm not sure I can call a conscious shutting out of the world 'inattention'. The attention deficit that I really notice is frequent jumps of attention, an inability to focus.' Whatever John thinks, his behaviour in the gym *was* an early indicator of what turned out to be a long term problem. He had significant problems in school concentrating on the subject being taught unless he was really interested in it. This didn't endear him to his teachers, who attempted to do something about it. From John's point of view:

> What was really frustrating to me later was that teachers assumed that they could just tell me to pay attention and I would. This to me is like being told 'fall asleep right now!' It's not under conscious control. I can consciously choose to attend to something, but the system which switches attention away to something else is not under conscious control... I can attend to something boring when asked, for maybe as long as seconds, before something else more interesting appears or my attention wanders to some other more interesting thought. And stopping that is like stopping breathing. The only way to stop it is to genuinely be more interested in the original thing than in any likely distraction.

Clare Sainsbury (2009) had a similar experience:

> I have never been able to control what I attend to, or pay attention to something on command... and my school reports regularly criticised me for 'refusing' to pay attention to subjects which did not interest me.

Even if he *was* interested, John's thoughts would regularly go off at a tangent, which the majority of teachers found very trying. He was making links between the subject in hand and other related information, which was (and still is) the way his mind works; this has led to an amazing long-term memory where every fact is linked to other facts (see Chapter 14). As John says: 'Finding the links is one of the best feelings I know... It's certainly irreplaceable in my field.'

Despite the pre-school gym experience, it was still a complete surprise to find that John had problems concentrating at primary school, given his extraordinary powers of focus at home. Here however, John's time was spent doing things he enjoyed and he had a lot of individual attention. At school (in a class of about 30 children) he was expected to concentrate on a topic of the teacher's choosing which he may have found boring. John's Statement of Special Needs, produced when he was seven, described 'weakness of concentration' and 'difficulties with... concentration'. John's first school report, received when he was eight, noted that 'he is too easily distracted and requires individual attention – far more than I can give him to complete or succeed in any given task.' Two years later another teacher wrote about his mathematics: 'But all too often he wastes time, his mind leaping to other irrelevant interests.' John still doesn't truly understand what this teacher meant, saying: 'Even now the phrase is hard for me to grasp. How can an interest be 'irrelevant'?' In his final primary school report yet another teacher wrote:

> [John] is still difficult to keep on task when working on investigations. He will suddenly see other connections which set him off at a tangent, but I have given him the opportunity of exploring these possibilities and invariably task one is accomplished.

When writing about gifted children with attention deficit hyperactivity disorder Lovecky (2004) observed: 'They are easily distracted by material that is tangential and they are apt to go off onto tangents that are interesting.' According to Gillberg (2002), the above scenario also seems to be very typical of the behaviour of children with Asperger's syndrome:

> Attention deficits are extremely common in high-functioning autism spectrum disorders (including Asperger syndrome), and this often leads to a lack of interest in many school subjects. Achievement in these subjects is consequently affected, and it is quite common for highly intelligent individuals with Asperger syndrome to be severely underachieving.

I was pretty horrified to find out from John (aged eight), that if he was bored in class he would read a book under the desk. His feelings on the subject can be summed up by his recent comment: 'Reading is good, right? Being bored out of your head so you can't concentrate on anything is bad, right?' Not an attitude any school teacher would approve of, I suspect. I've no idea whether his teacher knew that he was reading under his desk or whether she was particularly tolerant. In fact he told me recently that this habit remained with him for years both in primary and secondary school. He read under the desk whenever he found the lessons boring, either because they were going too slowly or because he knew the subject matter in great detail already. Very occasionally it was because the lessons were incomprehensible due to lack of attention in previous lessons! As John recalls:

> I have definite memories of getting in trouble for reading *other* books under the desk while I was meant to be working on other things. It didn't stop me though, it was just like reading under the covers!... only I kept on getting caught. It never really occurred to me that the teacher could tell the difference between someone writing and someone reading by just looking across the room.

While he read he would keep one ear open in case the lesson became interesting. As Christopher Gillberg (2002) points out:

> Individuals with Asperger syndrome are often thought to be 'daydreamers'... At-

tention to what goes on in the environment appears to be minimal. Oddly enough, he/she may suddenly demonstrate that all senses appear to have been 'on' all the time... It is as though the individual with Asperger syndrome were the sufferer of some kind of 'on/off-state' during which attention about what goes on in the environment is switched on only for brief periods of time, and it is during these seconds that astute observations are registered.

John's experiences seem to back this view up:

The 'daydreamer' stuff was certainly true of me. What tends to happen is that the information imparted is either literally boring, or I've heard it before or can easily predict it from what I already know. The 'attention on/off state' stuff is also very true; I've never been able to control where my attention points, or its intensity (it's mostly on 'high'). I'd say that there's constant low-level monitoring of what goes on in the external world, and that if it gets interesting my attention can be redirected there very fast (this is in a sense a general human trait; if something's about to eat you it helps to notice that it's there); however, this monitoring isn't conscious, and refocusing of attention is also not often consciously controlled. The searchlight is on automatic.

I can see that difficulties in paying attention can prove to be a real problem for children and their teachers and understand why so many children with attention problems are put onto medication. As Brenda Boyd (2003) writes:

Attention problems can cause a lot of problems for the child, especially if they are not recognised and understood. At school he may well under-perform and be considered less bright than he really is, or he can seem lazy and uncooperative.

John says he wouldn't like medication though. He believes it would blunt his creative thoughts and the pleasure he derives from getting 'into the flow' when he is working intensely and in a focused way:

Distractibility and hyperfocus are opposites and I have both. I don't think I'd want to give up the distractibility if it meant I lost the hyperfocus; it's too useful (and too addictive). The hyperfocus entirely compensates for the distractibility when it matters.

I don't know if medication designed to increase attention span (such as Ritalin) would have this downside but it *does* have some side effects. One of these is a possible increase in tics, which were a considerable problem when John was a child. According to Attwood (2006):

Several adults who have been prescribed medication to treat anxiety, depression or problems with anger management have described how the medication has 'lifted' their mood, but 'flattened' their enjoyment of the special interest.

As an adult John *does* use medication of a sort, i.e. caffeine, in order to help him concentrate. 'I'm a serial caffeine abuser! I have bursts (a few weeks long) of eschewing all caffeine, but that's entirely to make it have more of a hit when I get back onto the coffee trail!' He also admits:

I've used marijuana five or six times, because it *does* have substantial positive effects on concentration in moderate quantities. The effect on attention is similar to that of getting very tired, only more intense; the external world drops away, my short-term memory seems to expand, my thoughts seem to speed up slightly, and jobs that'd normally take several hours of hard thought can be finished in twenty minutes or so. When I come down from that sort of intensity of work I am of course exhausted… It might be that being tired enough would have most of these effects, but unfortunately I think I'd fall asleep long before; also, tiredness eventually frays my chains of thought apart, destroying my ability to think logically entirely.

As well as lack of attention due to internal sources, John can also become very distracted by external noise (e.g. people talking) and finds it very hard to block this noise out. From John's perspective his distractibility at primary school was perfectly understandable. 'The noise! The constant activity! How can *anyone* concentrate there?' As mentioned in Chapter 6, being able to listen to music through earphones at appropriate times at school (i.e. *not* when the teacher was talking) *might* have helped John considerably. It has certainly helped him as an adult as it reduces the impact of external noise. While he was in his previous job he recalled:

Any external distraction instantly breaks my concentration… Of course work is open-plan, so distractions are absolutely incessant… My only solution when not hyperfocussing is earplugs, MP3 players, or something of that nature, and even that doesn't work well.

John has used noise cancelling earphones for years. At one time, whenever he had to think really hard, the only quiet place that he could escape to at work was the toilets. Now that he works from home, which is very quiet, he's far more productive. It's not so much that it's quiet, says John:

More to the point, all the noise sources there are *under my control*. The only sound I can't stop is the computer fans, which are constant thus not distracting. If I want music or the sound of rain or dripping water or monastic chants I can have them, with or without headphones, and nobody else will care.

To conclude: John's wonderful powers of focused concentration and his perfectionist streak are characteristics he really values as they enable him to produce excellent work as an adult computer programmer. However his perfectionist streak has also caused him a variety of problems both as a child and as an adult. Unfortunately, if John isn't interested in a particular topic he is easily disturbed by distracting thoughts over which he has little control. As his concentration is also broken easily by external noise, John's achievements at school and university were very patchy and did not reflect his abilities adequately. With maturity has come an improved ability to handle both his distractibility and his need not to be seen to fail.

14
Memory

It's with some trepidation that I devote a chapter of this book to the subject of memory as it's a particularly complex topic, the understanding of which is in a great state of flux due to the large amount of research effort being devoted to it. I've done my best to avoid technical detail and keep my descriptions of various forms of memory as simple as possible and hopefully this won't invalidate what I have to say. I felt that it was important to write about the undoubted impact on John of a long-term memory that is particularly good and a short-term or working memory that is a weakness. Many authors have commented on the fact that people on the autism spectrum have exceptional long-term memories, especially for facts connected with their special interests.

LONG-TERM MEMORY

According to the New Scientist,[54] long-term memory can be divided into *implicit* or *procedural* memory (the memory for processes such as riding a bike) and *explicit* or *declarative* memory (memories we are aware of and can describe). *Explicit* memory itself can be separated into the memory for facts (*semantic* memory) and the memory for events (*autobiographical* or *episodic* memory). Long-term memory is vast and the memories in it last for a very long time. It can be thought of as a great storehouse into which new information is regularly lodged. Unfortunately because the store is so large it can be difficult to retrieve this information at a later date. As Levine (2003) describes it:

> Long-term memory is a seemingly limitless repository for preserving knowledge, skills and life experiences... the great long-term memory challenge is to store information systematically, to put it where we are most likely to find it later...

> The best way to remember something is to change it, to transform the information in some manner. If it's visual, make it verbal, if it's verbal create a diagram or picture of it...

John's long-term memory for facts has amazed us for as long as we can remember. According to him:

> I never realised there was anything unusual about it until I was in my twenties. I remember sometimes thinking in my teens that a lot of people around me had really bad memories, but didn't extend this into realising that mine was particularly good.

John seemed to be able to retrieve facts from memory with ease whenever he wanted and he certainly understood what he remembered. A school report when John was 10 mentions his 'remarkable general knowledge' and this is corroborated by the results of the psychometric WISC-R tests which he took at the age of seven. According to Kaufman (1994), 'exceptionally good long-term storage capacities' are indicated where there are high scores for the *Information, Vocabulary, Similarities* and *Comprehension* Tests. As described in further detail in Chapter 20, John's scores were particularly high in these tests. From a young age, his passion for factual books combined with an amazing memory, made him so knowledgeable that whenever anyone in the family wanted to know some fact, the first reaction was to 'ask John'. These days (particularly because John doesn't live with us) we would usually use Google instead. John is an enormous fan of Google, which he calls 'the greatest distributed memory aid the world has ever known'.

Words

As mentioned in Chapter 10, one of the earliest things we noticed, soon after John started speaking, was his ability to remember long words and use them appropriately. In fact he loved these words so much that he would always choose the long, erudite word in preference to the simple word commonly used in everyday speech. According to John:

> I think this is why I like a lot of the books I read, as well: they tend to do much the same, often as a stylistic convention. (The TV series *Babylon 5* is much the same, probably as a result of the theatrical background of almost everyone involved.)

> This can be done badly, though. Stephen R. Donaldson is a particularly bad example: he writes like he's swallowed a thesaurus, but uses half the obscure words he uses wrongly, and pays no attention to context. Brushing your teeth does not merit long and complicated words! (But the true master of inappropriate use of obscure words in the SF field is the immortal Lionel Fanthorpe.)

I never really understood where and how John learned so many of these words and how he understood their meaning so accurately that he was able to use them in their correct context. It seemed unlikely that these words came from the children's books we read to him which would have used relatively simple language. Did we use some of these words ourselves or did he have one ear open while he was playing and I was doing jobs in the house with Radio 4 on. 'Of course', writes John, who then goes on:

> Pinker points out in *The Language Instinct* that until puberty we learn approximately one new word every two hours, day in, day out, often extrapolating meaning and use correctly and remembering it perfectly after a single hearing, even if we don't use it until decades later. That figure ignores time spent asleep, so it's actually more like a word an hour. For over a decade. Humans are awesomely good at learning their native language.

Once John started reading everything he could lay his hands on, his vocabulary increased exponentially and it rapidly overtook mine. I loved listening to him speak because he used the English language so beautifully. However, as described previously, it was also one of the many things that created a barrier between him and his peers.

When John was between the ages of seven and nine he had a passion for joke books which he read and reread many times. For this reason he remembered vast numbers of jokes perfectly. As mentioned in Chapter 11, this meant that John was excellent company at a meal because, whatever the topic of conversation, he could always remember an appropriate joke. Although still possessing a wicked sense of humour, John grew out of this passion for joke books. These days he quotes chunks of poetic writing from science fiction books instead, which do not necessarily have quite the same appeal. John believes:

> A lot of the quotes I make you probably don't notice, because I don't mention that they're quotes, but just drop them into conversation where they would fit anyway. It doesn't matter that nobody else notices them! (On the net, someone is certain to notice them and almost certain to point it out!)

Ever since childhood John has frequently read aloud and he's always had a prodigious ability to quote chunks of text, something I've never been able to do. Even as an adult he loves the sound of words and language and when a passage in a book particularly appeals to him he can be heard reading it aloud so that he can hear the full beauty of the words and commit them to memory. For example he wrote to me recently:

> When one encounters lines like this, one just has to read them aloud, to appreciate the music in the syllables (written on encountering an old friend for the first time in ten years, terribly changed): 'His eyes went deeper and darker than ever I had seen, his pupils twin abysses, blackness unending; around them his irises constricted in rings, shadow-shifting, oceanic depths reflected in a thousand wavering lights.' (from *Kushiel's Avatar*, by Jacqueline Carey). I often babble nifty pieces of dialogue to myself, as well, but that's automated and mostly unconscious. Reading stuff like the above aloud, that's conscious, to help fix the stuff in memory.

According to John though, *Kushiel's Avatar* 'is very definitely *not* a book I read when I was a child'. John said he also read aloud 'because the language in that bit is excellent, or because it's a high point and I want to, I don't know, make it seem more real'. When I've asked John whether he 'sees' the text in his mind's eye or hears the words when he quotes so extensively, he says that neither happens; the words just come out all together in a large chunk as if the playback button was pressed on a recording machine. He also said: 'I can rarely remember continuous chunks longer than a couple of sentences – but sometimes remembering those sentences can trigger memories of the next sentences.'

Techniques for improving long-term memory

I really envy John's ability to memorise and wish I'd been able to acquire it. I find detailed facts extremely hard to remember just by reading them once and I rarely find the time to reread things because of all the other activities I choose to fill my time with. Perhaps I too could remember more if I constantly reread books and didn't spread my time and mental energy so widely and thinly. John has always been able to devote a huge amount of time to reading because he minimises the time devoted to activities outside his special interest areas. He frequently rereads books or those parts of books that he enjoys the most. This helps to fix the text in his memory. John agrees that the sentences he can quote come from books he's read many times. When asked if he could quote from a book he'd read just once he replied:

> No, I couldn't! If the book is excellent, but it's rare, and there are usually small mutations to the text, so if I want to get it *right* I have to look it up. (If it's remembered because the language is excellent, I generally do want to look it up.)

One key to John's excellent memory for words seemed to be his love of the way they sounded which then provided sufficient motivation for him to repeat them frequently. Repetition, or rehearsal, is known to move information from short-term memory and consolidate it in long-term memory. Levine (2003) has some interesting things to say about this:

> School policy makers should consider that long-term memory works best when there's sufficient time for consolidation. This does not occur when you partake of social studies for forty minutes followed by algebra for forty minutes, then English for forty minutes, and immediately thereafter physical education. Switching from one subject to another pretty much prevents the consolidation of the one that preceded it. Class periods should be longer, and there must be consolidation time.

One of the things John really disliked about secondary school was the constant change of subject every forty minutes. However John believes:

> [For me] proper consolidation of new information so I can derive new facts from it pretty much only happens during sleep. I can't learn for more than a few hours without getting exhausted, probably a cue that I need to sleep now to assimilate what I just learnt. The school day was *far* too long for that, particularly when you threw homework in at the end. I'm amazed I ever remembered anything I learnt at school.

I'm not entirely sure that *all* of John's attention problems (as described in the previous chapter) were a bad thing. Some of his teachers would get annoyed when John piped up in a lesson with a question that seemed to be completely unconnected with what they were talking about. They complained that he would go off on tangents when he was supposed to be focusing on topics set by them. However, John pointed out that this didn't apply to his English teachers at secondary school 'because they got the connections almost at once, every time'. Although I have no evidence to back up my theory, I think these tangents resulted in the creation of crucial connections between new information and existing knowledge; they provide clues as to why John has such a remarkable memory. According to Levine (2003), if new facts are linked to as much pre-existing, readily accessible knowledge as possible, this may well make it easier to access these new facts in the future; the greater the number of connections the larger the number of potential access routes. Attwood (1998) discusses the tendency of those with Asperger's syndrome to 'make irrelevant comments' and writes: 'It seems as if the child says the first thought that comes to mind, unaware how confusing this can be for the other person.' In 2006 Attwood also wrote:

> The reason for this feature remains elusive, but may be associated with a tendency to be impulsive and less able to formulate a logical structure or sequence for the statement or description, and an inability to consider the perspective of the other person.

John totally agrees that the 'inability to consider the perspective of the other person' is spot on but also explains:

> The 'irrelevant comments', at least when I make them, tend to have been trig-

gered by a multi-stage internal thought process taking me from something being discussed (perhaps minutes ago) to the 'irrelevance'. I've started to quash expressions of these regardless of interest because it's occurred to me that there's no chance that anyone else can have had the same thought process, nor that they can reverse engineer it from my comments, mind readers though they are.

What John does so effectively is to link everything he reads, even if he is skimming a text, with the knowledge he has already. He looks for patterns and connections all the time and is always actively thinking when he reads, rather than adopting my rather passive approach to reading. I think his knowledge is wonderfully connected into a meaningful whole which can be accessed at many points. When describing his learning method, he says: 'Relating everything I learn to my existing knowledge is fundamental.' To this day John makes me feel most inadequate, because he cannot understand how I can read something and then forget it. My limited knowledge seems to be well hidden in individual silos which aren't connected and which are hard to open. I think our educational system has encouraged my shallow approach to learning, which can lead to good results in the short term but fails to educate in the broadest sense of the word. However, according to John:

> It is possible to go too far the other way. Frank [John's closest friend] gets no pleasure at all from rereading, because he remembers everything he reads perfectly. I don't, so rereading is a continuing pleasure.

Exams and learning

John should have done really well at school and in exams because of his excellent long-term memory and his love of learning. However he was a square peg in a round hole when it came to the educational system. Learning for its own sake was a real pleasure but he wasn't interested in doing well in exams or in studying topics of no appeal to him. In fact he would go further than that, saying: 'Anti-interested in exams, more like. If there's an exam in a subject it makes me less interested in it and less likely to learn it.' Exams and John definitely weren't natural companions; in secondary school he took hardly any notes and found revision an alien concept. He's never been able to knuckle down and learn something *just* in order to answer a question in an exam. As he wrote to me on one occasion:

> Part of the problem with having a memory that inhales things I'm interested in perfectly is that I never had any motivation to do any revision. If I didn't remember whateveritwas already, I wasn't going to remember it after rereading it, either.

Motivation and interest were, and still are, critical to whether John learns and remembers something. If these are present he will find all the patterns and make all the connections for the new information to become fully integrated with the knowledge he possesses already. If he isn't interested in a particular topic he may be able to cope with it if he can find a different way of thinking about it that excites and motivates him but if he can't do this then he will do the absolute minimum and learn nothing. Unfortunately exams never motivated him. However as an adult, John says:

> I'm always knuckling down and learning something intrinsically boring in order to get something done at work. The difference is simply that I'm interested in the

end result (or, at the very least, am interested in the end result being as near perfect as I can make it, or in making people happy with the end result). Exams... you spend time writing them, they're seen by one or two people who don't care how well you did or even know who you are, and who are marking lots of other exams too, and then they're reduced to one number and thrown away. What a waste. Yes, I know that number is the ultimate purpose of the whole exam, but it still feels far too much like a waste of effort to spend any effort on.

John described his attitude to learning and school very clearly when he wrote:

It's just that I've never been focused on school-work... It's obvious that some people can focus on the mostly-boring hash of unrelated gunge that is school-work, but there's no way I could. (Some subjects were fascinating, but even there, um, what purpose does homework serve exactly? With a few very limited exceptions, like maths, practice doesn't make perfect for me. Either I know it instantly and forget it only over years or it'll never go in.)

Photographic memory

Many writers refer to the fact that the long-term memory of some people on the autism spectrum is so good it can be thought of as a photographic or eidetic memory. John certainly cannot do this:

I have a phonographic memory for the written word, not a photographic one! It's not eidetic, but it's probably as close as you can get without actually *being* eidetic: I can remember in arbitrary detail if I know I'm going to need to do that when I read the original, but don't generally try.

Rote learning

There appears to be some disagreement between authors about the ability of people on the autism spectrum to learn facts by rote, 'parrot fashion'. For example, Christopher Gillberg (2002) wrote: 'About one-third of my patients with Asperger syndrome have exceptionally good rote memory skills', while Clare Sainsbury (2009) wrote:

Problems with attention may also be connected with the common problems that children with Asperger's have with rote memorization (learning times tables, for example). This is often particularly baffling and frustrating to teachers given that our memories are often excellent... especially when it comes to accumulating facts on a topic that we are obsessed with...

Sainsbury also had great difficulty learning 'foreign language vocabulary by rote'. John too had a great problem learning facts that didn't excite him in some way, had no underlying logic and just had to be learned parrot fashion. For example it took him years to learn the sequence of letters which make up the alphabet; their order is not a matter of logic, just something to be learned by rote. We looked at the usual children's alphabet friezes and books and also did alphabet jigsaws together but nothing seemed to work. In retrospect these were poor techniques for someone like John whose visual memory is poor and who found jigsaws difficult at the best of times. It may well have been easier for him to learn the alphabet if we'd used a song which could have been chanted or sung aloud. The classic ABC song can be found by Googling for 'alphabet nursery rhyme'.

According to Levine (2003):

> Rhythmic games and songs early in life can help reinforce sequential ordering. Songs and rhymes about the alphabet, the months of the year, and other practical sequences are particularly effective. Music, in general, can be a forceful promoter of sequential ordering.

These days a suitably engaging computer game may also have worked. John's inability to learn the alphabet easily meant it took years and years before he could use a dictionary competently, despite being such a proficient reader. However, according to John: 'These days dictionaries are online, so alphabets are unnecessary for this purpose.' John also had problems learning mathematical 'times tables' by heart and to this day he doesn't know them perfectly, despite all the practice at home. Again according to John this is 'another obsolete skill'. It isn't really surprising that John wasn't excited by the order of letters in the alphabet and the product of two numbers. Although he was perfectly cooperative and would readily work on these things with me, this lack of interest seemed to make it almost impossible for him to memorise these seemingly unrelated facts. Just like Clare, John had major problems learning foreign language vocabulary by rote:

> I can't really understand how anyone can do this. It's so utterly different from the way humans naturally learn languages... at the time they were trying to make me do this I, like every other human my age with good natural language skills, was just emerging from a decade-plus-long phase of learning about one new word an hour *without even trying*. Not one of those came from a vocabulary booklet, and I didn't have to write any of them down to 'help' either.

Episodic memory

Some children on the autism spectrum have an excellent *episodic* memory (memory for events). According to Tony Attwood (2006):

> Parents of a child or adult with Asperger's syndrome often remark on their son or daughter's ability to give vivid and accurate descriptions of events that occurred during infancy... Early autobiographical memories can be predominantly visual and of experiences of importance to the person.

John's episodic memory isn't particularly good; he doesn't remember a great deal about events that occurred before he reached secondary school age. As John has a poor visual memory, it wouldn't be surprising that he doesn't retain visual memories of events. Mel Levine (2003) wondered whether the better the episodic memory relating to events in one's life, the worse the semantic memory for factual material. He observed many 'children who display an immense torrent of episodic memory amid a trickle of semantic memory'. John's experience, with his excellent long-term memory for facts and poor episodic memory, appears to support Levine's theory. Nevertheless John thinks his poor episodic memory for past events is partly due to the fact that 'I never refer to them, so they've faded out over the course of a decade or so. This is perfectly normal, and in fact probably optimal behaviour for an information-storage system.'

John is very typical of people with poor social skills, in that he has a poor memory for *other people's* personal events. It was years before he remembered things such as his parents' birthdays and the need to send a card. However, he *has* been very conscientious about our birthdays in recent years, going to a great deal of trouble to try and find appropriate cards. John claims that 'this… is artifice. It requires conscious effort and when I'm ill or stressed it vanishes like a dream.' Nevertheless, however artificial some of John's social behaviour seems to be to him, his family thinks there has been great progress in John's social development as he moved from his late twenties into his thirties. However, even in his thirties John still had no idea where most of the people he had worked with (for over ten years) lived or indeed anything about their private lives or interests. According to John 'even trying to find out would feel creepy to me. This might be a male thing, an autistic thing, or an English thing.' I can't imagine women working in an office for a week, no matter years, without knowing where the person sitting opposite them lived!

WORKING/SHORT-TERM MEMORY

In 1974 Baddeley and Hitch proposed a model of working memory which described a system of short-term memory that allows several pieces of information to be held simultaneously in mind for interactive processing. Working memory has different components including visual-spatial and auditory memory. Whereas long-term memory is vast and the memories last for a very long time, working (or short-term) memory has a very limited capacity both in terms of size and duration. There seems to be some confusion in the literature about the use of the terms short-term memory and working memory, with some authors using these terms interchangeably. I like Mel Levine's (2003) description when he writes:

Active working memory is the place where short-term memory and long-term memory work together. If a teacher asks a student a question, that enquiry enters active working memory via short-term memory. The student then needs to hold that question in place in active working memory while searching long-term memory and doing some reasoning to come up with a response.

It's thought that many people on the autism spectrum, as well as those with ADHD, dyspraxia, dyslexia and other specific learning difficulties, have working memory deficits. John's cognitive test results (see Chapter 20) show large differences between the results of the various sub-tests that make up the WISC-R. In particular he had lower values in the *Arithmetic, Digit Span* and *Coding* sub-tests, all of which include the need to store information for a brief time in short-term memory. John's results suggest that he has a working memory weakness whether the input is verbal or visual, with the latter being significantly worse. This type of deficit is thought to lead to problems with sequencing and to make the acquisition of literacy and numeracy skills difficult. According to Alloway (2009), who has carried out some large-scale investigations into the impact of working memory deficits on school children:

Working memory is critical for a variety of activities at school, from complex subjects such as reading comprehension, mental arithmetic, and word problems to simple tasks like copying from the board and navigating around school…

In screening of 4000 primary aged children in mainstream schools, 1 in 10 was identified as having working memory difficulties. There were several key findings regarding their cognitive skills. The first is that the majority of them performed below age-expected levels in reading and mathematics... I found that their working memory skills, rather than IQ, at 5 years old were the best predictor of reading, spelling and math outcomes six years later...

Teachers typically judged the children to be highly inattentive, and have short attention spans and high levels of distractibility. They were also commonly described as forgetting what they are currently doing and things they have learned, failing to remember instructions and failing to complete tasks...

The final key finding is that children with working memory difficulties take a much longer time to process information. They are unable to cope with timed activities and fast presentation of information. As a result, they often end up abandoning the activity altogether out of frustration.

As John points out: '[Working memory is] critical for every intellectual activity we ever do', not only school activities.

According to Gillberg (2002): 'Dyscalculia (specific problems in mathematics)... may well be over-represented in Asperger syndrome', although he acknowledges that some individuals are 'outstanding mathematicians'. Even at the age of 11, John was unable to do the simplest of additions (such as 2 plus 7) without the aid of his fingers; he only stopped using his fingers after this age because he was allowed to use a calculator. When some people criticise the use of calculators by children and say they should learn to do mental arithmetic instead, they don't realise that there are some children who find doing sums in their head so difficult that they would be seriously disadvantaged if they weren't allowed to use a calculator. According to John: 'If I try doing anything complex with maths inside my head, the numbers get instantly mixed up into a sort of purée and nonsense emerges... If it's symbolic, I can do it. If it involves actual *numbers*, I can't.' When John was much older his mental arithmetic improved considerably because his interest was captured by the sort of short cuts that can be employed to make the manipulation of numbers in your head easier, e.g. adding 9 onto a number is the same as adding 10 and subtracting 1. For example, in order to add 39 (which is 40−1) and 58 (which is 60−2), add 40 and 60 to give 100, and then subtract 3 giving a quick answer of 97. Teaching these methods at school would have been very helpful to everyone, including John.

Although John was reading very well by the age of six (see the next chapter), he was totally incapable of spelling even the simplest words or copying anything from the board. Because John's manual skills were so poor that he'd been engaged in writing *exercises* in class before he was six rather than writing actual words, these problems hadn't been recognised. His experienced teacher didn't seem to know how to deal with a child that could read very well but couldn't spell anything. Although I knew nothing about the workings of short-term memory, it seemed obvious to me at the time that John must have major problems with his short-term visual memory because he was unable to copy words from the board even though he could read them. In the next chapter I describe how I worked around this difficulty and taught John to spell. I suspect that without one-to-one help John might not have learned to read or spell so proficiently.

As a child John was very aware of his weaknesses. As this was coupled with a perfectionist nature and a strong desire to do well, he completely refused to participate in any activities that he felt would highlight his difficulties. For example, one popular memory game is the 'tray-game' where a set of unrelated items are put onto a tray, shown to the children for a short time and the tray then removed. The children have to try to remember what was on the tray. An alternative is to remove one item from the tray while it is out of sight and when it is returned see who can remember what the missing item was. John flatly refused to play this kind of game as he knew he would be unable to remember what was on the tray. This type of activity is sometimes suggested as a way of helping children improve their visual short-term memory or at least develop techniques to compensate for any deficiencies. John remembers this game clearly or at least his reactions to it. 'I always thought of this as a form of torture, and was totally unsurprised when in Pratchett's *Small Gods* it was used as a test by a particularly nasty villain.' Nevertheless with hindsight I think I could have helped John by playing this game with him in private, so no one else would have seen his difficulties. I could have started with only two items on the tray and taught him to say the names of the objects aloud to himself whilst finding a funny way of linking the items, as this might have helped him to remember them. As the number of items grew I could have shown him how these could be mentally sorted into meaningful groups as this can make it easier to remember the items. John thinks:

These techniques might have worked, but I suspect I would have been perfect up to about four items then simply fallen apart, or remembered only a random four. Sorting into groups might have helped, but how would I have remembered the membership of each group?

As described in Chapter 11, John interrupts frequently because he thinks he will forget what he's going to say otherwise. This phenomenon is described by Tony Attwood (2006) who writes:

Another problem with working memory is a tendency to forget a thought quickly. One of the reasons children with Asperger's syndrome are notorious for interrupting others was explained by one child who said he had to say what was on his mind because if he waited he would forget what he was going to say.

Problems holding a great deal of data in his mind, while working with it at the same time, could also be responsible for some of the difficulties experienced by John in social groups. As Deirdre Lovecky (2004) writes:

Gifted children with AD/HD are likely to exhibit social difficulties based on poor working memory in group situations. When playing with one friend, the complexity of the situation is less likely to be as overwhelming as in a group.

The same could be said of children on the autism spectrum.

As described in the previous chapter, John is frequently plagued by distracting thoughts. Distracting thoughts are known to reduce available working memory which is quite a problem given that working memory capacity is already very restricted. Grabbing John's attention in the first place, by making the topic under study sufficiently interesting, was (and is) key to making the most of his working memory. Levine (2003) describes this very accurately when he writes:

[There is an] intimate relationship between short-term memory and attention controls. Needless to say, it's hard to remember something if you're not listening!

Tuning out takes its toll on short-term memory…

Active working memory craves peace of mind. Anxiety infects it like a computer virus. If you're feeling sad and preoccupied, there may not be room for much else in your mind's working memory.

Unfortunately John is extremely prone to feelings of anxiety but whether this increases his working memory difficulties or whether these feelings arise partly as a consequence of these deficits is hard to say. It could be a mixture of both.

As described in Chapter 11, what *seems* to be a very strange side effect of John's relatively limited working memory is his stammer. He doesn't usually stammer in everyday conversation but as soon as one asks him to remember something he's read or to explain something, both of which involve recalling information from long term memory, then he is inclined to stammer. According to John his stammering 'generally gets severe only when I'm trying to explain something verbally which I'm thinking about at the same time'. He remembers stammering in mid-secondary school but *can't* remember stammering in primary school. I too don't recall any stammering when John was young and as an adult he only stammers some of the time. I became particularly aware of John's stammering after he left home. I would ask him to explain something to me which involved him trying to remember certain facts. The first part of the explanation came out quickly (he's a very fast speaker) and then it's as if some part of his working memory ran out of space and the flow of information stalled. He would stop on a syllable which would get repeated several times as he continued to think. It appeared as if he couldn't retrieve facts from his extraordinarily good long term memory at the same time as constructing a full sentence. Maybe that's the same for all of us but in John's case the time gap between memory retrieval and sentence production is large enough to be obvious. In John's words: 'Stopping speaking and starting the sentence again invariably clears it up.' If John would just stay quiet for a moment and think before he started speaking and then if he could slow his speech down sufficiently perhaps there would be less stuttering. Given that social stress can make stuttering worse, giving talks at work hasn't been easy but John enjoys imparting his knowledge and his colleagues just have to put up with a considerable amount of stammering.

Organisation and planning

Working memory can be considered to be one component of something psychologists call *executive function* (EF), whose role in the brain has been likened to that of a conductor in an orchestra. EF is thought to be a property of the frontal lobes. Other components of EF include the ability to recall information, plan ahead and organise, control emotions, pay attention, start and finish a task, shift attention from one thing to another and cope with change. One definition of EF[55] states: '[It is] the cognitive process that regulates an individual's ability to organize thoughts and activities, prioritize tasks, manage time efficiently, and make decisions'. John's inability to learn seemingly unrelated facts in which he has little interest (such as the order of letters in the alphabet) has caused him far less of a long-term problem than the difficulties he has experienced as a result of executive function deficits. John's attention difficulties, relatively slow processing speed, problems coping with change and controlling his emotions have already been described in previous chapters. By the time he started secondary school it also became increasingly obvious that John found it very hard to plan and organise either himself or his work. Oral instructions were, and still are, a waste of breath as they will certainly be forgotten (or not heard), but then this applies equally to my husband. If I want to be sure that Tony will remember to do something, every small detail *must* be written down and as long as my husband doesn't lose the list or forget to look at it, with a bit of luck all should be fine.

From a young age John seemed to be blissfully unaware of the simplest day to day practicalities of life. In fact by the time he was three years old and his sister 18 months, it was quite natural for us to treat her as the older, more responsible sibling. Lydia was the complete opposite of her brother – very aware of what was going on around her and very organised, reliable and efficient. Fortunately while John was at primary school little was expected of him in terms of self-management. He was lucky enough not to have homework, there was no special sports kit to take to school, all his classes were in the same classroom and all equipment such as pencils and so on was provided. So there were no comments about John's difficulties organising himself. When John started secondary school though, his organisation and planning difficulties landed him in all sorts of trouble. In the first two years of secondary school John would frequently turn up to lessons without pencils and other equipment, even if he'd left home with them in the morning; sports kit was lost more often than not. At home we did our best to try and help John organise himself, with colour-coded folders for his homework and so on. Unfortunately not only would he 'forget' to do his homework on time but even when he *had* done it *and* it was in the bag which he took to school, he would then forget to hand it in! John's difficulties were never recognised by the school as something that required assistance, even though he did very well when he was put 'on report'. This was a scheme in which, among other things, the child is monitored closely to make sure they have written the correct homework down, completed it on time and handed it in. However being 'on report' was thought of as a disgrace and the school wouldn't let John stay on it for too long as they wanted to encourage self-discipline. As soon as he came off the scheme the same problems arose again and the teachers were always so disappointed. I totally understand why they wanted to encourage self-discipline but they wouldn't have dreamt of removing a hearing aid from a deaf child because he could manage well when using the aid. At the time, though, none of us knew about executive function and working memory deficits and how these might affect a child's behaviour. I think that if we, as parents, had understood that John's problems with organisation were symptoms of executive function deficits over which he had little control, we could have explained this to his teachers and tried to find ways of helping him that were actually effective. Instead his weaknesses in organisation and planning were put down to laziness, insubordination, lack of taking responsibility and so on, frequently resulting in detentions. When he forgot to go to some of these he received further detentions. We used to dread going to the secondary school parent-teacher meetings where we were made to feel that it was *our* fault that our son was so disorganised. John's experiences were like those described by Dendy[56] in his article *Executive Function… What is this anyway?*:

> Unfortunately students with ADD or ADHD are often punished for executive function deficits such as lack of organizational and memory skills that interfere with their ability to bring home the correct homework assignments and books.

Hopefully after reading this article, teachers and parents will develop more innovative intervention strategies.

These days we might use some of the interesting suggestions to improve working memory to be found in the books written by Deidre Lovecky (2004) and Amanda Kirby (1999).

Unfortunately John had major problems organising his written work as well as organising himself. When he was in his last year at primary school his teacher wrote: 'Written project work is still disappointing, with his undoubted ability to research, he still seems unwilling to assemble the information and present it logically.' This was a real clue to John's problems organising written work, if only we'd recognised it as such. In fact what the teacher thought was *unwilling* was actually *unable* but at the time none of us realised that such an articulate and knowledgeable child had such underlying difficulties with planning and organisation. In retrospect it's obvious that there must be some underlying problem when an able child is incapable of finishing a job properly; we really missed a trick not realising this at the time. I don't think anyone, including a child, sets out to fail; as John says: 'Certainly a raving perfectionist like me never does.' For years John's difficulties organising his thoughts on paper remained hidden because he produced very little written work due to his handwriting difficulties. If the problems had been recognised John could have been taught techniques to help him present his work logically on the page.

John's lack of practicality has also given rise to great amusement at times. When we moved to the north of England and left our grown up children in the south of the country, John (now aged 23) arrived for his first visit (which was to last more than a week) with a rucksack full of books and no spare clothes of any sort! As John remembers it he only forgot his shirts, but I remember differently. On another visit Lydia had to intervene when she saw John getting onto the wrong train which happened to leave on an adjacent platform. According to John:

> This has happened more than once when I'm alone, but thankfully something has always clued me in to my mistake within a minute or two, be it announcements, a seat reserved for someone else or the simple fact that lots of people were getting on to the train at the adjacent platform.

Techniques to improve working memory

Fortunately during his teens John discovered several techniques to improve his working memory and in particular to compensate for his very poor visual memory. As described in Chapter 11, talking or muttering aloud, either when he reads or when he is trying to work something out, enables John to transform the words he sees on the page into words he can hear. Moreover by repeating the words he keeps them longer in his working memory. In recent years John wrote: 'Talking to myself helps me cycle things through auditory memory and is a technique I use constantly at work when I need to free up general short-term memory slots for other things.' As Mel Levine (2003) puts it:

> You can extend the life of data in short-term memory in several ways: whisper it under your breath, form pictures in your mind's eyes, if it is visual you can put it into words... known as rehearsal strategies.

John also exploits the technique of 'chunking' which increases the apparent capacity of working memory. This method, which *groups* words, patterns, concepts or digits together, is used by many people to remember telephone numbers. It's much easier to remember 422 768 531 937 than 422768531937. In a recent email John wrote:

> There's considerable evidence that what makes experts better at things than non-experts is that after many years of practice, they've seen most significant things in their field of study so many times that the chunks they work with grow. There was a study with chess players of all skills up to grandmaster, and it looks like grandmasters can pretty much note entire chessboards as a single chunk: they know the significant features of any board they're likely to see and remember just those, as a unit.

Another technique that's extremely useful in freeing up available working memory is to automate as many tasks as possible. Anyone learning a new skill knows how hard it is to learn more than one new thing at a time and how important it is to practise 'little and often'. Practise helps to make tasks automatic, which means that active working memory is no longer called on to carry out that particular task. As Levine (2003) writes: 'If an ingredient of a task is easy and fully automatic for your child, so she doesn't even have to think about it, valuable extra space is freed up in active working memory.' Provided someone with special needs is given every opportunity to practise those tasks they find tricky, rather than having too much done for them, then with time they will find these particular jobs easier. Levine believes this mechanism is crucial for children as they progress through the educational system:

> So much of what students are called upon to extract from long-term memory needs to be accessible instantly and available for use with virtually no expenditure of mental energy or effort... Most reading comprehension difficulties in middle school stem from a lack of automatic decoding of individual words... Parents can and must help students with delayed automatization. The only answer, I'm afraid, is plenty of drill on the basics.

John agrees: 'Automation is the key to this, and to every other complex problem. There doesn't seem to be any limit to the complexity of problems you can learn to do without thinking, either.'

It's been amazing for us to see to what extent John has continued to develop as he moved through adulthood. As an adult he has become much more organised and reliable by using his computer to make lots of 'To Do' lists. However I think there's still room for improvement, as these lists still consist largely of things John *wants* to do (i.e. computing related) rather than *needs* to do. Things he's less interested in, or involve some form of communication which he is uncomfortable with (such as ringing someone to service his boiler), either don't reach the list, or if they do, stay near the bottom; constant reminders are still required before anything happens. Therein lies the key to so much of John's memory. If he's really interested or excited by something he will remember it but otherwise it goes straight out of his memory, if it ever reaches it in the first place!

These comments were written a few years ago and since then John has moved into his current house. He loves this house and makes sure, without any prompting from us, that everything stays in good working order, which includes arranging for regular boiler servicing to take place. To our delight, John is coping very well indeed in his own home. He lives near shops and restaurants which are open late, all his bills are paid by direct debit, cleaners come regularly to keep his house presentable and all his paperwork is filed away carefully in a filing cabinet. Whenever I come to stay the house looks really clean and tidy, I'm made most welcome and there's usually a delicious meal waiting for me.

To conclude: Reading aloud, re-reading books of interest and consciously linking new information to his existing knowledge have all contributed to John's excellent long-term memory. However, whereas his wonderful long-term memory is an acknowledged asset, John feels that his working memory deficits have a negative impact on his life. As he wrote: 'If I could have one mental upgrade it would not be social modelling ability (that's number two): it would be a much bigger working memory.' This choice is probably a reflection of the fact that intellectual concerns are more important to John than social matters, not surprising in someone on the autism spectrum. Although these working memory deficits resulted in a variety of difficulties at school, as an adult John has settled into an organisationally simple way of life that makes allowances for his executive function weaknesses.

15
Reading and Spelling

The most pleasurable part of my childhood was undoubtedly reading. I loved books and through them I was able to escape, whenever I chose, to another world: a world I found far more enjoyable than the one I actually lived in. I'm eternally grateful to my mother for going to the library every week while I was a child and choosing such good books. It was like Christmas every Saturday as I waited with excited anticipation for her to return from her weekly shopping trip with new treasures from the library. I really wanted my children to derive the same pleasure from reading, although I hoped they would enjoy their home life more. When John and Lydia were young I remember there were times that I longed for the day when they would be able to settle down quietly with a book. This feeling was particularly strong when we took them for country walks. When we stopped for a break, say for a picnic at lunchtime, I yearned for a few minutes peace to read a book but knew this was impossible until the children could do the same.

BEING READ TO

In order to introduce John to books and the pleasure that can be derived from them, we started 'reading' to him well before he was a year old. This initially involved looking at picture books together, talking about what we could see and asking him questions. As he grew older we gradually moved onto story books with more words and fewer pictures. We always progressed at a pace dictated by John's needs.

I knew that children often want the same books to be read to them time and time again; I also knew how difficult I would find this, given my rather low boredom threshold. In order to avoid such a situation, I made sure we had access to a large number of books, both library books and those we acquired very cheaply from second-hand shops, library sales, school fairs and jumble sales. Then each time I read to the children I pre-selected some books and let them choose from my selection. This always included a mix of stories, factual books and rhymes or poems. Both children enjoyed making their choices whilst I was happy with whatever they chose.

We always spent a long time in the library on our weekly visits so that the children could have a really good look at the books in stock before deciding which ones to borrow. As well as looking at books they'd never seen before, both children enjoyed looking again at some of the books they'd borrowed on previous occasions as if they were meeting an old friend. I might make suggestions and find books I thought the children would enjoy but *they* actually chose which books to take home. These visits continued long after I stopped reading to the children.

While John was young enough to have a rest during the day I had two daily reading sessions with him, each lasting about thirty minutes. One took place before his daily rest; the other in the evening before he went to bed. These sessions reduced to one a day when John stopped having daytime rests. They eventually stopped altogether when John was reading so fast that he actually preferred to get on with a book himself rather than be read to. I loved reading to the children and never interrupted these sessions to answer the phone or front door. It was a cosy and relaxing time for us all, an escape from the re-alities of daily life. Whatever happened, I tried to make sure it was never rushed or cut short. If we were going out in the evening we would do everything a bit earlier to make sure the children didn't lose out. I always read to them in their bedroom and afterwards they would be so calm and happy that neither of them ever protested when we left the room and never caused a problem at bed- or rest-time. I think they needed some time on their own after these intensive reading sessions and were probably glad to see the back of us!

Our reading sessions were always totally interactive with John deeply involved, ask-ing questions as well as listening. However the teachers at John's nursery school found it very difficult to cope with his habit of asking questions while a story was being read. The staff considered these interruptions disruptive, feeling they spoilt the flow of the story for the other children. Unfortunately John found it difficult to change his be-haviour. He would have been unaware that he was behaving differently from the other children. I think it took quite a long time before the teachers were able to stop him ask-ing questions. Although I've a great deal of sympathy for his teachers and realise how difficult reading to a group of children must be, it seems a real shame to stop children asking questions and expect them to sit passively while books are being read. Unfortu-nately he wouldn't have been able to save his questions until the end of the story as it is likely he would have forgotten them by then.

How I Taught John to Read

As John grew older his love of books continued to increase. He'd watched me for years as I followed the words on the page with my finger while I read to him, so he was well aware that there was a relationship between these funny symbols on the page and the stories he heard. Nevertheless he hadn't managed to recognise *any* words on the page by himself. As I was keen to ensure that John read fluently for pleasure, I decided to teach him at home. I wanted him to be reading reasonably well and actually enjoying it by the time he started school. I was concerned that boys of this age might easily become bored with the typical subject matter covered by elementary readers at that time; I was really afraid that John would react badly to a repetitive text that was totally unconnected with his interests. I was aware that most teachers at the time John was of primary school age didn't like parents teaching their children to read before they went to school but I thought it would be much easier to teach something as complex as reading in a one-to-one situation because the pace can be adjusted to the child's needs and it's easy to make it fun.

As it transpired, John coped poorly in a classroom situation and may have had significant problems learning to read as part of a group. As described in the previous chapter, John *also* had significant problems with working memory, which Alloway (2009) has shown can be a predictor of poor reading outcomes. John's relatively low scores on the *Coding* and *Picture Arrangement* tasks in the WISC-R cognitive tests (see Chapter 20) would, according to Kauffman (1994), indicate a problem with visual sequencing. He also wrote that children with sequencing problems may 'have serious reading problems, especially in decoding words.' John certainly took much longer than his sister before he could read words reliably and he needed many more repetitions. According to Attwood (2006):

> A recent study suggests that one in five children with Asperger's syndrome have significant problems with reading... from my clinical experience, conventional remedial reading programs have not been as effective with children with Asperger's syndrome as one would expect.

So having made the decision to teach John to read how did I go about it? I knew nothing about the teaching of reading (as my background was in physics and maths) but I came across a book by Glen Doman called *Teach your Baby to Read*. According to Doman it was perfectly possible for very young children to learn to read but the letters must be large enough for their visual systems to handle. I agreed totally with the author that the child mustn't get bored, the learning should be fun and the sessions should always end before the child wanted to stop. However I felt that his method, which involved showing word cards to a child several times a day, would drive me crazy and I would never be able to keep it up. I also thought this method of teaching, however effective it may be, was far from fun. I decided to make up my own games which I could tailor to John's requirements in such a way as to ensure he really enjoyed them. Doman's reading method, which teaches children to recognise by sight those words that are used frequently in the English language, works on the principle so aptly described by Kutscher (2005): 'Teach to sight read commonly used words. This will speed up reading. The first 100 words of Fry's *Instant Word List* make up 50% of a student's reading.' This word list, which is one of countless such lists, can be retrieved from http://www.k12reader. com/subject/vocabulary/fry-words. However, it must be pointed out that teaching to read by sight (Look and Say) is always going to be difficult, if not impossible, for some children.

I bought the *Teach your Baby to Read* kit which consisted of individual words written in large lower case letters on a white background. I introduced the first word, *mummy*, to John when he was about three and a quarter years old but it was obvious pretty quickly that he wasn't ready to read so I abandoned the attempt and put the kit away. I took it out again when he was just four and this time he *was* ready. There was no sitting at a table learning by heart, which John thinks is 'an effective way to make reading deadly boring'. Instead we played games on the floor, which John really enjoyed even though they incorporated lots of repetition. The main aim of the process was to find games he enjoyed for their own sake and to use these as a means of reinforcing word recognition. We only spent a few minutes every weekday morning and always stopped long before John wanted to. I'd been saving our empty cereal packets for a long time and now I cut them open, stuck the large printed words from the reading kit onto the plain side of the packets and then cut the edges of the cardboard to give them irregular shapes. In the first game we played we had to pretend that our dining room carpet had a river flowing through the middle and the cardboard shapes were stepping stones. I chose this particular game because John was passionate about water and rivers. He learned one word at a time by looking at it and repeating it several times. Then I put the word (which had now become a stepping stone) into the river; if John could read it he could jump onto the stone and thereby cross the river. This imaginary river was very narrow when he only knew one word but as he learned more words the river grew wider in order to accommodate more stepping stones. If John had a problem remembering the word I would give as much assistance as necessary by making the sound of the first letter which often helped. If that wasn't enough, I'd continue sounding out the word so slowly that he might get it right even before I finished. Regardless of the amount of help he'd received, John was always able to jump onto the next stone once he'd said the correct word. I never added a new word until I felt all the previous words were absolutely secure. The process went very smoothly and John loved the game. He was delighted to see more and more stones in the water and soon our room was too small for the huge river! I had to add a new game but I still used the 'river' game first with the newer words. In the second game I made a circle on the carpet with John in the centre and *all* the words facing in John's direction. Then I asked him to find a certain word, stand on it and perform a funny action. *I* was getting him accustomed to recognising a large number of written words but *he* was having fun doing all the actions I asked for, the more outrageous the better. These actions involved John in some sort of motor activity such as standing on one leg and making a rude noise, or in an imaginative activity such as pretending to be a large lion and roaring as loudly as he could. He loved this game and looked forward to carrying out the actions, the sillier the better. He was quite unaware that I was ensuring his knowledge of all the words written on the card became secure through repetition.

When we'd finished all the words in the kit, I made up new words and wrote these in big letters in the same size and style as the reading kit. Initially I used words that would appeal to John and would enable me to make up silly sentences that would amuse him. The sort of sentence he would have enjoyed (although I can't remember the exact sentences I used) would have been similar to 'the dinner ate daddy' or 'the mouse ran after the cat'. All childish humour, but then he *was* only four years old. One advantage of writing silly sentences was their unpredictability meant that John was less likely to guess the word from its meaning. His 'reward' was having a good laugh when he got to the end of the sentence; this made him eager to play the game. This type of humour would never have worked with John's sister, Lydia. She'd have thought these sentences really stupid but she did enjoy the 'river' and 'circle' games as much as her brother. Instead of the 'silly sentence' game I played '*Hide and Seek*' with her, a game she enjoyed very much. We would take turns hiding a word although *I* always chose the word to be hidden. When Lydia hid the word I had to find it and then *she* would tell me what it was. When I hid the word Lydia found it and again she told me what it was. She loved this game and it was just as successful at reinforcing her word recognition as the 'silly sentence' game with John. He'd have hated playing *Hide and Seek* as he still can't find things that aren't immediately obvious.

Once John knew how to read a large number of (commonly occurring) words really reliably and could also read the little book supplied with the reading kit, I had to look for some suitable books for him to read next. I found some marvellous Ladybird story books which had a beautiful picture on one side of the page with only one or two simple sentences, in large lettering, on the page opposite the picture. Initially I wrote the words that John didn't know already in the same large letters as before, stuck them onto cardboard and added them to our games. I only used words that are commonly found in the English language and excluded words that would have appeared *only* in that book, such as unusual names. I didn't show John a new Ladybird book until he knew all the words in it and then, to his delight, he found he could read it easily. The sense of achievement was wonderful. I used this technique for several books but as John's core reading vocabulary increased, the activity games died a natural death. However I still continued to introduce any unknown words separately before John was given a new book to read. I wanted him to associate reading books with pleasure and enjoyment, not with a struggle to decipher new words. In reality there were never many new words to introduce as he knew so many basic words already.

Throughout this process I also used the fact that words can be broken down into the smallest language sounds or phonemes (e.g. *s*, *u*, and *ch* for *such*) and always sounded the words out for John, phoneme by phoneme. This method is often called phonics. 44 phonemes are combined in different ways to create *every* word in the English language. As John learned more words he was able, with help, to start sounding out and working out new words from the sounds he knew already. I always covered new words with my hand and exposed them phoneme by phoneme. I totally agree with Martin Kutscher who wrote in 2005: 'Phonics will be essential for the poor decoder. We cannot assume that everyone can teach themselves the rules of phonics.' Richards (1999) insists that dyslexics can learn to read and that a thorough training in fundamental phonological awareness is crucial:

> Phonological awareness is a major component in considering a diagnosis of dyslexia. A phoneme, the smallest meaningful segment of spoken language, is a fundamental element of the linguistic system. Phonemes are important because they make up all spoken and written words... Dyslexia represents a deficiency in processing these fundamental elements.

As John's reading vocabulary increased he recognised many phonemes from words he knew already; I started to introduce new books *without* introducing the unfamiliar words first. John was able to work out how to read new words by covering them up and exposing them bit by bit, thereby building the words from the components he knew already. I gave as much help and prompting as necessary but also encouraged him to use the meaning and context to help him work out what the word might be; I wanted to make sure the text was understood at the same time as it was read.

When John started school I raided the school library, public libraries, charity and second-hand shops, school fairs and so on for lots of extra books to read together. Initially the school needed quite a lot of persuasion to allow John to borrow books from the older children's library. However John really needed to take more advanced books home as his reading was improving by leaps and bounds. I was determined that John would have a variety of books of the appropriate standard so that he didn't get bored and would continue to enjoy reading.

The regular one-to-one attention involved in playing games with their mum meant this learning to read activity was always approached with great pleasure by both of our children. Not only did both of them learn to read well and enjoy reading before they went to school, they also learned to trust me to teach them in a successful and enjoyable way. This meant they were happy, when they were older, for me to help them with any school work they found difficult. In John's case there were many occasions when this proved to be extremely useful.

In retrospect, I think the involvement of motor activity was particularly helpful for John when he learned to read. Certainly as he grew older it became apparent that in order to think John found it very helpful to pace about. In fact he would go so far as to say:

'[It is] pretty much essential, actually. I pace around at work, I always think things up while walking.' There seems to be a powerful link between the motor and cognitive areas of the brain and totally fortuitously this may have been tapped into by the methods I employed when teaching John to read. Various researchers have indeed suggested that there are links between reading disorders and motor disabilities and as Richards (1999) writes: 'Research supports and substantiates the need for multisensory phonics in this population of learners.'

Would I Use The Same Methods Now?

Although the methods I used were very successful I'm not sure I would use *exactly* the same techniques now, partly because of the difficulties John experienced learning to spell when he was at school (see later in this chapter). However I would *still* teach John to read before he started school as I think the one-to-one attention was probably essential. I would retain certain aspects of my original method, such as the fun and games, the involvement of motor activity, lots of repetition and lots of reading to promote fluency but I would place much greater emphasis on phonic decoding from the beginning. Many researchers have attributed poor reading success to inadequate teaching methods and in particular to the lack of a systematic approach to teaching phonics. Reading is such a vital skill for everyone that politics and ideology should not be allowed to interfere with attempts to offer every child the best reading techniques (i.e. full immersion in a systematic, multi-sensory phonics method) suggested by research evidence from around the world. According to a UK education department website:[57]

> Research shows that when phonics is taught in a structured way – starting with the easiest sounds and progressing through to the most complex – it is the most effective way of teaching young children to read. It is particularly helpful for children aged 5–7.

I think John would enjoy the methods employed by *The Jolly Phonics* reading scheme[58] as it looks fun and incorporates actions; I would be very tempted to use this scheme at home. However there are several multisensory phonic schemes available so I know it would be wise to find out what scheme his primary school was going to use and see what I thought of that first. I certainly wouldn't want to confuse John with my choice of reading scheme. If I didn't think John would like the scheme chosen by the school and/or the school was not very successful in teaching children to read, I would be inclined to choose a different infant school.

I would beg any readers whose children are struggling with reading to treat this as a matter of *urgency*. Don't delay. Get immediate, expert, *individual* help for your child and, if at all possible, get involved yourself as well. Kutscher (2005) thinks it's essential to detect reading problems early:

> The 'late bloomer' theory of reading is officially dead; 88% of poor readers at the end of 1st grade [USA ages 6-7] will still be poor readers at the end of 4th grade [USA ages 9-10] – unless there is early, aggressive intervention...

His book gives many suggestions for helping students with reading problems, including the teaching of phonics and the use of sight word recognition for speed and for words that do not follow the phonic rules.

HOW JOHN READS

When John was 17 and taking 'A' Level English, one of his English teachers (at his very academic school) said he'd never come across anyone who could read so quickly and yet take in the content. According to John:

> At that point I would be as good as I ever was at taking in fine factual detail and plotting (including spotting contradictions), which has always felt a lot like programming to me (or perhaps the other way around). Analysis of character and motivation had a long way to go, and I'm only just starting to be able to reliably spot unreliable narrators and figure out what the truth is likely to be.

John taught himself to scan a text extremely quickly and absorb all the main ideas. He reads in a very different way from me and I can do no better than let him describe it in his own words:

> I can't speak for others, but I at least have multiple means of reading, which all come down to one thing: pattern-matching... Virtually all words are read and pattern-matched as whole units... Because this is pattern-matching it's very fast (as fast as memory recall of something you know very well)... Common phrases get pattern-matched as well, so that I don't need to go from letters to words at all: I can go straight to whole phrases. Also very fast... When skimming at moderate speed (as on a first read if I want to get a feel for the general outline before reading the rest, or as on reads where I know the stuff I'm reading is padded, or when locally searching across a couple of pages for something in particular) I sample the starts of most sentences, and skip the rest if it seems to be saying something obvious. When skimming at high speed I sample the starts of randomly chosen sentences... When trying to find where I've read up to in a book I'm rereading for the first time in a long while, I open the book near the middle, skim the start of a sentence, see if I remember it, then halve the portion of the book before or after that point (depending) and keep searching. I did this even before I knew what binary searches were, but that's what this is, and it's accordingly fast: six to ten samples suffice to find my place even in the largest books... some forms of writing provide additional levels of categorization that I can skim on (article headings, and so on)... Rereads tend to involve a lot more moderate-speed skimming over bits I consider 'padding' or less than excellent, then slowdowns in areas I consider good. (On the first read, of course, I can't tell which bits will be padding, but unless it's been many years since I've read a book, I can generally recognize the padding on seeing it.) If I'm short of time or if the book has a lot of padding (sadly common) I'll high-speed-skim or binary search to areas I consider excellent and just read them.

Although John frequently uses an ereader these days, he still reads in the same way. However finding where he's read up to is now much easier as his Kindle does it automatically for him. John doesn't read everything in the same way though. When reading technical magazines or proofreading books, he's 'in maximum pedantry mode, ready to pick things to pieces.' He reads computing textbooks and manuals thoroughly when he first buys them (so he knows what's in them) and then refers to them 'when necessary. The degree of necessity often depends on the quality of online documentation.' The better the online documentation the smaller the need.

WHY READING HAS BEEN SO IMPORTANT TO JOHN

I've no doubt whatsoever that teaching John to read before he started school was one of the most important things I've ever done for him. Reading is an absolutely crucial skill and without this ability many doors would have been closed. I find it terrifying to imagine what life would have been like for John if he hadn't been able to read well. Given the difficulties he has in relating to people, his problems with organization and coordination and his fear of change, an inability to read fluently would probably have meant that John had no outlet for his creativity, intelligence and sociability. He could have found himself a frustrated, unhappy and lonely individual, his life dominated by his weaknesses rather than his strengths. As a result John might have suffered from depression and as he puts it, his life might have been 'dominated by bursts of destructive, frustrated rage'. Certainly in John's case the ability to read well has been like a magic key to a happy and fulfilled life. Reading has provided him with a source of intense pleasure, a means of avoiding stress and of calming down when he gets upset. It's also been an essential requirement for secondary school and the world of work, a means of satisfying John's insatiable thirst for knowledge and a way of accessing the world of computer programming which has led to a career, independence and a lifetime's hobby. Written communication on the internet has provided John with the companionship and friendship of like-minded people and has meant he never feels lonely despite living on his own.

Once John became a fluent reader he was never parted from a book. Victoria Biggs (2005) wrote:

I'm not being melodramatic when I say that for the first two years of secondary school reading was the one thing that kept me sane. Everything was so strange and puzzling back then, and I would retreat into a book and find instant peace.

John couldn't agree more, writing: 'Sanity for me is books, computers, and such things. Books as a place to fall into when the world gets too stressful: computers as a place which would always do only and exactly what I said.' John used books as a means of avoiding the stress associated with contact with other children. This was understandable, given his poor social skills, but didn't help him to integrate or give him the opportunity to observe how other children communicated with each other. John believes that observing other children 'was well outside my focus and too complex to analyse with the tools I then had available. Even if I'd looked, I wouldn't have got much out of it.' Reading to avoid contact with other children started at primary school (although I wasn't aware of it at the time) and continued at secondary school where John used to walk round the edge of the playground reading a book. We discussed the issue on one occasion when John was at secondary school. I suggested that John try to manage occasionally without this prop in the playground as it probably isolated him from others and sent out a message that he didn't want to be with them. I remember John's reluctance to abandon this habit; I think this was too frightening a prospect for him. He remembers the conversation well:

I wondered why you thought it was a problem that I was sending a message that I didn't want to be with people whom I mostly didn't want to be with! It seemed, well, *accurate* to me. I can remember trying half-heartedly to cut down, but it only really cut down when I started to have other things to do instead.

As a friend of mine (with autistic twins) pointed out: 'This seems to be one of the most difficult things to appreciate about these ASD kids/adults. i.e. they really don't want to interact with others a lot of the time.'

Sometimes John's escape into reading has been a real cause for concern. For many years he would read as he walked along the pavement; I was terrified that he would cross the road without looking and be run over. He had to be collected from school until he was 11 and from the bus stop for some years afterwards. This was far longer than other children of his age but his dangerous habit of reading in the street, plus a general lack of traffic awareness and practical common-sense, made it necessary. I thought he'd given this habit up years ago and couldn't believe it when John wrote to me in 2009:

Ended: has it ended? I still do it when not walking too fast to do it safely... I do check periodically to make sure the way is clear, and have never once collided with anything. (Sometimes I have got lost in thought when *not* reading and run into road signs and the like.)

Fortunately he seems to have been safe enough so far. Long may it continue.

Books John Loved and Hated

I thought it would be useful to include some details about John's favourite books in this chapter because they provide an interesting insight into his personality and character, both as a child and as an adult.

Like so many young children John had very pronounced reading preferences and to a certain extent these have continued into adulthood. He loved books that were imaginative, had a 'feel good' factor, were humorous, contained rhymes, or were factual with a strong scientific or engineering flavour. Books with good illustrations were particularly popular with all of us, parents and children alike. He really loved books in which things went wrong for the protagonist or turned out unexpectedly but in which no one got into trouble and everything turned out all right in the end. John probably identified with the characters for whom things went wrong because *he* was so used to making mistakes, knocking things over and generally finding daily life much more difficult and confusing than his peers. I think it made John feel much better about himself and his situation to know that he wasn't the *only* one who could get things wrong. He was also reassured by a happy ending.

Although books in which small things went wrong but everything turned out well in the end were such favourites, it soon became obvious that John hated any books which had a 'baddy' in them or in which someone or something got hurt or killed. I can't help wondering whether this reaction was related in some way to all the procedures John had to endure as a young baby in hospital (some of which would have been very painful). It was definitely connected to the difficulty John had dealing with strong emotions which could easily overwhelm him. This dislike of frightening, or even slightly scary, books lasted for years; fairy tales in particular were very unpopular with John and had to be

255

read separately to my daughter who really loved them. The one exception to this was cartoons; they didn't seem to induce any bad feelings, only laughter. Apart from cartoons, where he knew the characters are 'plainly not meant to represent real human beings', John seemed to get so deeply involved in the story that he couldn't separate make-believe from reality. As he explains: 'Well, *I*-the-intellect could. *I*-the-emotions could not. I seemed to gain this ability in my mid-teens.' He totally identified with the main characters in the book whether they were humans, animals, witches, giants and so on. Violence or upset of any kind seemed to cause huge emotional turmoil; John seemed unable to cope with any fear or suffering endured by the characters in the story. It was all taken personally. As so many children's stories involve a bit of fear and suspense (with 'goodies' winning and 'baddies' suffering in some way), this reaction caused a bit of a problem at nursery school. John would get really upset by some of the books that were read to the children. Sometimes the teachers couldn't understand *what* had upset him. If they described the incident in the book, I could usually work out why John had become so upset. I remember them asking me one day about a book that seemed quite innocuous to them but had made John react very badly. When I asked them to describe the offending passage they told me it was about a dog jumping up to greet someone. John was very scared of dogs at that age and the thought of one jumping up on him, whatever the intent, was just too much. Interestingly enough Tony Attwood (1998) writes: 'Children with Asperger's Syndrome can fear dogs, not because of a fear of being attacked, but the noise of the barking is perceived as too intense and unbearable.' I certainly remember John being scared of dogs barking but he believes that his fear of dogs is due to their unpredictability:

> I can tell what cats will do (and even if I annoy them they can't hurt me badly). Dogs... dogs are deeply embedded in the whole body-language world that I can't read... we have *no* common tongue, but they think we have, and because they don't have language I have no way to tell them otherwise. Cats don't think we have a common tongue, and they're loners, and I understand loners.

Both children were very fond of poetry, action songs such as *Row the Boat* and rhyming books in general. The humorous rhymes of the Dr Seuss books such as *The Cat in the Hat*, with their detailed drawings of funny incidents, were very popular. The children couldn't have enough of these and really seemed to enjoy the sounds of the words in their own right. Once the children were able to read, they wanted to read the poetry aloud to me rather than me to them. I was fascinated by their obvious love of the sound of the words, the pulse and metre of the poem, as well as the rhyming. I suspect a love of rhyme makes it much easier for a child to learn to read because the emphasis is on the sound of the words themselves and not just on the outcome of a particular story. According to Mel Levine (2003), problems with phonological awareness (distinguishing sounds) and phonemic awareness (distinguishing the sounds that make up words) are thought to be the most common reasons why children have reading problems. As he says: 'Early on, affected children demonstrate difficulty rhyming words.' It would seem that time spent with young children on rhymes of any sort would be extremely helpful when they grow older and start to learn to read.

Not surprisingly John, who was so fascinated by mechanical things such as washing machines, clocks and combine harvesters, was particularly fond as a child of any books describing how things were made or how they worked or behaved. He loved the beautiful illustrations and clear explanations in the Althea series which included books such as *How to build a House* or *How to build a Road*. I learned a lot from these as well! John was a glutton for factual books from a very young age. We had many books in the Ladybird *Junior Science* series and Ladybird *How it Works* series, as well as large numbers of Usborne science books, picture encyclopaedias and picture dictionaries. On looking through the books we've kept, I saw an inscription from an aunt wishing him a 'Happy 4th birthday' in the book *How Machines Work* (by Christopher Rawson, 1976, Usborne). At the time it seemed perfectly normal for such a young child to enjoy such technical books but now it seems rather strange. Another Usborne book, *How Your Body Works* by Judy Hindley and Christopher Rawson, was an all time favourite with its fabulous, highly coloured and imaginative pictures. *Tell Me Why* by Arklady Leokum (1982, Hamlyn) was read many, many times from cover to cover. It was the perfect book for the curious child who wants to know everything about everything. John, aged 30, remembered these books (when I showed them to him) with a great rush of pleasure and knew exactly which pages he'd loved so much and why. Like so many children, books about volcanoes, dinosaurs, stars and planets were also early favourites. Although he loved science and astronomy books, sometimes John used to frighten himself as a result of reading about all the violent things that can happen in the universe; he was too young to have a proper feeling for the time-scales involved. According to John: 'Even if you *do* have a proper feeling it's a bit spine-tingling.'

John was given an amazing series of *Insight* magazines (Marshall Cavendish 1981/2) in 98 parts by a friend of mine whose son had finished with them. John read and reread these science magazines, which were written especially for children, many times. He started reading some of my *New Scientist* magazines before he was eight years old. His love of all things scientific has never diminished. His scientific general knowledge is both wide and deep, although he's never worked in this field and his reading is purely for pleasure and interest. John has, for many years, continued to be a regular reader of *New Scientist, Scientific American*, and astronomy magazines.

Once John could read well, he continued to love a wide range of books. Particular favourites were the books about Nigel Molesworth (by Geoffrey Willans and Ronald Searle) such as *How to be Topp*, with their wonderful drawings, schoolboy humour and awful spelling. John found spelling very difficult when he was young; once he'd overcome this hurdle, it gave him enormous pleasure to see and laugh at the terrible (intentional) mistakes in the Nigel Molesworth stories.

Because of John's interest in anything scientific and his love of imaginative stories, I thought that science fiction (SF) might be a genre that he would really enjoy as he grew older. Although I had a small collection of SF books, they were far too advanced for a nine year old. I didn't know which authors to choose nor how old John needed to be to start reading SF but was fortunate enough to find a science fiction aficionado in the computer department at my work who was able to advise me. This colleague, who was passionate and very knowledgeable about science fiction, was glad to help. He advised me to start John on books by Nicholas Fisk which I was able to find in our local library. John loved these books and from then on read more and more science fiction. He remembers being fond of Douglas Hill when he was at secondary school and as an adult he's read and enjoyed a very wide range of science fiction and fantasy books. When

John was preparing to move house in the summer of 2013 we estimated he had about 2500 books in his library.

I asked John in 2010 (when he was in his mid-thirties) to list the books and authors that were his current favourites and tell me what he liked about them. Not surprisingly, given the large number of books he's enjoyed, John found this very difficult. In the end he sent me a very interesting email which can be found in Appendix 13. This email gives a really good insight into the workings of John's mind. It reveals that there are many aspects of a book that attract him, including writing style, dry humour and satire, good characterisation, underlying decency, ideas, plots, world building, history and politics. He can be quite scathing though about aspects of these books that he doesn't like. As he says: 'My model is Mark Twain. Nobody could pan a book like he could.' Six years earlier, in 2004, when asked about the fiction books he read most often and what they have in common, he wrote:

Many have a strong sense of wonder – e.g. Vinge's *Fire Upon the Deep*, Greg Bear's *Eon*, just about anything by Greg Egan;

Many sculpt fascinatingly *different* worlds – e.g. anything by Vinge, Jack Vance, Bear, le Guin;

Many are excellently written in the sense of 'use of English' – e.g. *Lord of the Rings* by Tolkien, the *Kushiel* series by Jacqueline Carey, anything by Le Guin;

Some tug on the emotional heartstrings a lot – e.g. *Eon* again, the *Kushiel* series: I'm not an emotional null and that *is* something I sometimes look for.

There are some similarities between the 2004 and 2010 lists of favourite authors and books but in 2010 John leaves some authors out, either because he doesn't like their recent books or because good characterisation is now more important to him. As he wrote in his 2010 email about authors he was no longer hooked on:

My tastes have matured and they frankly aren't terribly good writers. Most are excellent *plotters*, and back when interpersonal relations were too painful to read about or hard to grasp properly, that was what I was looking for.

There's no doubt that, as John's grown older, his social skills have developed quite remarkably. Books, films (for further details see Chapter 18) and the internet have all played an important role in this development. I'm not sure to what extent this process could have been speeded up artificially by therapeutic interventions. John's views about this are interesting:

I suspect ABA [Applied Behaviour Analysis] programmes and the like are founded on the idea that we learn about human relations by observing them and doing them ourselves, so if we did *nothing else* we would learn faster. Unfortunately there is no royal road to learning: we cannot learn on command, nor can we force those aha! moments when previously hidden connections are exposed. I'm not sure that I was good enough at spotting connections when much younger to have derived some of the stuff I have, nor would I have seen the point. A lot of these programmes also seem to be founded on the idea that we can learn human relations in isolation from everything else, which makes sense from a neurotypical perspective because you have specialized neural machinery to handle them, so to you social relations really *do* stand separate from the rest of the known world, a thing apart. For me they do not: understanding of the webwork of social relations and interactions *descends from* other knowledge, about game theory and psychology and linguistics and politics and cabbages and kings, and you cannot learn about the social relations *consciously* until you understand those more fundamental things. Yes, those more fundamental things are very complex, but I don't need to understand them *completely*, just *enough* to get the gist.

As the friend of mine with the autistic twins wrote: 'Sounds like the intellectual analysis of what might be going on feeding learning rather than the instinctive learning of a neurotypical on social interaction.' There seems to have been a 'right time' for each small improvement in John's understanding of those around him; therefore, when he was ready, the books he read or the films he began to watch left their mark. I think this is true for all of us in the same way that seeds only germinate when *all* the conditions are right. When I asked John recently whether books requiring social comprehension had ever caused him problems, he replied:

To be honest a lot of SF, particularly older SF, didn't require enormous degrees of social comprehension anyway; and even when it does, as long as there's some other element there I could concentrate on that. But things that were purely social in nature were hard to grapple with... some I simply couldn't handle until I was older.

I also asked him whether he'd experienced any problems with social comprehension when studying his 'A' level English texts to which he replied:

Only once. We were given some Austen to read and I only got about five pages in before my interest failed me so hard I couldn't force myself to continue. I was very quiet while everyone else was discussing that. I think it was partly the social milieu (the troubles of financially-imperilled nineteenth-century middling-upper-class women couldn't really be more removed from my situation, or less relevant-seeming), partly the writing style: it seemed terribly longwinded yet also overly simplistic: dammit if something is going to be longwinded I want some flowery elaboration too.

From quite a young age, reading, digesting and virtually memorising voluminous computer manuals became a way of life for John. As a youngster and adolescent he bought lots of popular computing magazines, some of which were full of computer program listings. (See also Chapter 17.

As a child John always looked forward to Sunday when the weekly children's newspaper called the *Funday Times* arrived inside our *Sunday Times* paper. He moved gradually from reading this magazine alone to reading the main newspaper itself. He's very interested in politics and current affairs and subscribes to the *Economist* and *Private Eye*.

I find it really interesting that all John's current interests, be it computing, science, science fiction, humour, politics or current affairs, started before the age of eleven. This long relationship with these topics has given him an enviable depth of knowledge and understanding in these fields, although he says: 'The more I learn, the more I realise I don't know.'

Spelling Problems

When we spoke to John's teacher at the parent-teacher meeting held at the end of the first term in Year 2 (age 6-7), we were really shocked to discover that our son was *still* having serious problems at school. There had been a lot of difficulties initially (which are described in the next chapter) but we thought the school was handling these well and things were progressing smoothly. To a certain extent that was true but the problems the teacher described now were quite unlike anything mentioned before. As described in Chapter 6, John's class teacher had discovered his inability to spell although he was an excellent reader. Early in the term John had asked his teacher to help him spell simple words such as '*and*' and '*the*'. Initially she thought John was joking, bearing in mind how well he read and his keenly developed sense of humour. When she realised that John really couldn't spell these (or any other) words she was very puzzled and concerned. Although a very experienced teacher, she'd never seen anyone like him before and didn't know how to help him. It's normal for children of this age to make spelling errors, as English spelling can be quite illogical at times, but it's very unusual for a good reader to be unable to spell anything at all.

Because of these difficulties John was unable to carry out much of the work expected of him in this class because it involved writing. His teacher told me that John had spent a considerable part of that term in the library reading on his own – something he'd never mentioned to me. I said I would see whether I could help him over the Christmas holidays and asked her to give me a list of the words she expected children in her class to be able to spell. Knowing nothing about primary school teaching, I assumed that the words on this list would be short and easy. I was really surprised to see that the words were not necessarily short, including as they did words such as Christmas, January and February. It then became apparent to me that spelling was not taught, in this school at least, in a logical manner starting 'from scratch' with short and simple words and building up to longer and harder words. The school's approach to spelling appeared to be based on the assumption that when children were able to *read* simple words they would also be able to spell them automatically; there was no need for these spellings to be taught explicitly. Instead the children were taught how to spell the words they would need in order to write their diaries or stories. I don't know how these spellings were taught in the school and they weren't given spellings to learn at home; whatever method was used it wasn't working for John. His apparent inability to spell even the simplest words meant that he was failing completely under this particular regime. I realised immediately that asking John, who couldn't spell '*and*' or '*the*', to learn how to spell Christmas was like asking a toddler to climb Everest. I also suspected that with this sort of tuition he might *never* learn to spell.

Why Couldn't John Spell?

Why can most children spell the words they can read even if the spelling is not completely accurate? Why can many children make a good attempt at spelling words they've never seen just by the sound of the words, making obvious and logical phonetic spelling mistakes? How was it possible for our son to read so well and talk so fluently and *still* not be able to spell anything at all?

In order to read well John had to know how to decipher new words competently as well as recognise familiar words easily. Although he *was* using phonics to read new words and not guessing them, this seemed to be a one way process; he was unable to use his knowledge of phonics to work out how to spell. Using technical phonics language, John was able to decode written words by converting graphemes (that is, the *written symbols* of letters or groups of letters) into the corresponding phonemes (which are the smallest unit of *sound*) and blending them together in order to read the word. What he *couldn't* do was segment a word he heard into its phonemes and then convert these phonemes into the corresponding graphemes in order to spell the word. For example: although John could read the word *shop* he couldn't hear/ imagine the word, break it down into the sounds *sh, o,* and *p* and then convert these sounds into the letters *s, h, o,* and *p*.

How had John found himself in this situation and why isn't it more common? His problems probably resulted from the fact that when I taught him to read, I hadn't done any work on writing or spelling because his fine motor control was so poor that he was unable to use a crayon or pencil. Because of this he didn't get any practise writing the letters whose sounds he was learning. John's working memory deficits, particularly on the visual side (see Chapter 14), may also have contributed to his problems with spelling. If I had my time again I would *definitely* teach John to spell at the same time as teaching him to read. Even though John couldn't write, we *could* have used plastic or cardboard letters. Every time John learned to read a new word he could have practised spelling it by arranging these letters in the correct order. These techniques, plus many more, are part of any good, modern, systematic phonics scheme.

TEACHING JOHN TO SPELL

At this point in time though there was nothing I could do about the fact that John hadn't learned to spell when he'd learned to read. As the school didn't seem to know what to do about this problem, plus the fact that there were at least 30 children in John's class and no classroom assistants, I felt that I had to do something about this situation myself. We couldn't risk our son growing up unable to write with the obvious implications for school and adult life. He would be unable to achieve his undoubted potential and would probably be unemployable. This was really serious and I was very scared. So despite a complete lack of experience, I set out to teach John to spell from scratch. He was happy to be taught by me and trusted me implicitly; when I asked him if he would like me to teach him how to spell he was very enthusiastic. Despite having problems relating to his classmates and being pretty unaware of what they were doing, he was very aware indeed that they were all able to write and he couldn't even begin. I assured him with real confidence in my voice that he *would* be able to spell if he worked with me but it would take quite a long time. In reality I'd never done anything like this before and had no idea whether my approach would actually work; however, I felt it was absolutely crucial that John believed success was inevitable given enough time.

We started our daily spelling sessions in John's bedroom where it was private and quiet and where we wouldn't be disturbed. As with reading, I always kept the sessions short, never spending more than a few minutes a day; we always stopped with John wanting to do more. We worked at a pace that ensured he would always succeed and there was lots of revision and testing so that everything John learned was being continually reinforced. He remained motivated throughout and thoroughly enjoyed our times together, buoyed up by the constant praise and encouragement and by a real sense of achievement as his spelling improved. So how did I do it?

Due to John's inability to copy from the board (see Chapter 6), I reasoned that he had some sort of problem with his short-term visual memory. As a result I decided to use the *sound* of the letters alone (rather than their appearance) in order to teach John how to spell. I began by teaching him the *sound* of the letter *b* (the first consonant), and showed him how to write it at the same time. I got him to listen to lots of words *beginning* with the letter *b* such as *bat, ball* and *baby*, until I was absolutely confident that he could recognise the sound. As I called out a series of words, every time John heard a word beginning with *b* he would write this letter down and if the letter was something else he wouldn't write anything down. We made it into a fun game and, as mentioned above, I paced the game so that John usually got the answer right and so received lots of praise. It seemed to take a very long time for us to get to the second consonant *c*, which he then learned in the same way, with the *b* being revised at the same time. Gradually John learned to recognise the sound of all the consonants at the beginning of words and was able to write them all down. He also learned to recognise those consonants that sound at the *end* of words such as the *t* in *but, cat* and *lot*. Once this part of the process was complete, I taught John all the vowels in a similar way and suddenly he could spell a very large number of three letter words. I still remember the amazement and joy that John felt when he could suddenly write real words. Of course *I* had known what was going to happen when we eventually added the vowels to all the consonants that John knew already; however, *he* hadn't realised what was going to happen and I hadn't warned him that it wouldn't be long before he would be able to spell a lot of words. I had left it as a surprise. His pleasure and pride in what he could do was a real reward for what had seemed like a long, slow process.

After the above stage was complete, John learned the graphemes made up of pairs of letters (a *digraph*) such as *ch, sh, th* and *wh*. Later we moved to examples where two or three consonants sound one after the other, such as *br-, -pr-, spr-, -st-* and *-nt*, or where one doesn't appear to sound at all as in *lamb* and *talk*. We learned vowel combinations such as *ai, ie, ea, ou, ee* and *oo* and I wrote words out underlining these vowels in colour, so that John could see how similar sounding words looked the same. I taught him simple rules: for example what happens if you add an *e* to the end of words like *hat* (to make *hate*) and *fat* (to make *fate*). We looked at simple plurals where you add an *-s* to the end of the word and learned other word endings such as *-ing, -ink, -ong* and *-ed*. After a large number of words with straightforward spellings were mastered, we covered as many irregular spellings as I could think of, such as *ruff* and *rough, where, wear* and *were, their* and *there, pair, pare* and *pear, piece* and *peace, heel* and *heal*, and so on. I started to work through *The Old Fashioned Rules of Spelling Book* (Alan Jamieson, Ward Lock Educational, 1980) with John but by now he was so fascinated by spelling that he read and thoroughly learned most of this book on his own, just for pleasure. It was an excellent book, full of useful rules, many of which I confess I wasn't really aware of at the time. As this book advised:

> By working through this book, you will learn some simple rules, and you will be able to spell many of the words you use every day. Rules and patterns account for over 80% of all English words, so follow these rules carefully.

John says spelling rules can be found these days on web sites such as www.dyslexia. org/spelling_rules.shtml and www.davidappleyard.com/english/spelling.htm. As John's spelling improved I bought a book called *The Essential Spelling List* (written by Fred Schonell in 1979 and produced for W H Smith by Macmillan Education) to test John on his spellings. This was a really useful book in which over three thousand words were graded into six lists for children between the ages of 7 and 12. When John made a mistake I would write out the correct version, underlining the error in colour, and often writing out words that had a similar spelling and underlining the equivalent portion of the word so that he could see the relevant patterns more easily.

When I looked recently at some spelling schemes for children who couldn't spell, all the ones I saw progressed far too fast for John in the early stages. In fact we spent so long working on the letter *b* that I thought it would take years to cover all the consonants! However as we went through the alphabet the process accelerated as John 'got the message' and started to harness his existing reading ability. I think it's absolutely crucial that the tuition pace is correct for the individual child. This is much easier in a one-to-one situation than in the classroom. If it's too fast the child will fail and be discouraged; if it's too slow they'll get bored. It's also essential that the teaching is 'little and often'. This means there shouldn't be a prolonged gap during the school holidays or the child will forget too much.

THE OUTCOME

It took about a year of daily practise for John's spelling to catch up with his peers but then he continued to improve so much that he became one of the best spellers I know. John took (and still takes) enormous pleasure in spotting spelling mistakes, particularly those on public signs or those made by me! Given the difficulties John had learning to spell it isn't surprising that he wrote:

> I certainly took pride in my spelling once I could spell better than almost anyone else. Spelling checkers are for dunces, I can spell 'incorrigible' or 'Acanthostega'[59] with the best of them. (Note that the words don't have to be in English, as long as they are pronounceable!)

To this day he seems capable of scanning a text extremely quickly and immediately spotting any spelling mistakes. Not surprisingly he's proofread several books written by science fiction authors of his acquaintance. According to John:

> I suspect that I could have become a professional proofreader or editor if I hadn't gone into computing. Every editor I know has this inability to miss spelling and grammatical errors, even if they want to. The mistakes 'pop out' without effort: unconscious parallel processing at work.

Interestingly enough, when John wrote by hand he used to make quite a lot of spelling mistakes which he then crossed out and corrected immediately, adding to the messy quality of his work. Now that everything is on the computer he can correct all the typos as he goes along. When I asked him whether the immediate corrections took place because the words looked wrong when he read them, he replied:

> Yes, sometimes: I'll type in a particularly nasty word (like 'mesopharyngeal',

say), and transpose some element, leading to 'mesophanrygeal'. Spotting it... just works, as long as I can see the word in writing (or print, or patterns of phosphors!) I think it's pattern-matching to common elements of English words matched to knowledge of how such elements sound, or something like that. The system's not always right: 'weird' still looks wrong to me and I always misspell it, even though I use it quite a lot.

Weird happens to be one of the exceptions to the rule (*i* before *e* except after *c*) and *I* always hesitate before spelling this particular word. As John pointed out, other exceptions include *eiderdown, height* and *their*. Although John believes his 'spelling is greatly auditory in nature, even when I don't actually know how to pronounce a word', he can't work out how he spells 'any more than I can work out how I walk. It's totally automated'. He also finds it's odd that he has so little memory of being unable to spell anything.

When I started to teach John how to spell, I knew nothing about the plasticity of young children's brains. The transformation in John's spelling has been an excellent example of how the young brain can adapt if encouraged to do so: different pathways have been created in John's brain to compensate for deficits in the existing ones. This is of course why early intervention is always encouraged if children find certain activities difficult. As a general principle, we've found it more useful to find 'another way' round John's problems rather than banging our heads against a brick wall trying to make him do something in the same way, or for the same reason, as other people.

16
School

NURSERY SCHOOL

John never failed to surprise me. At the end of his first term at nursery school I went, as a proud parent, to his first Christmas 'performance'. I arrived early and sat near the front as I wanted a good view. Big mistake! A few minutes before the performance was due to start, all the children filed in and stood at the front of the room. John stood next to the teacher who had her hand on him, no doubt to keep him still and stop him wriggling. Just before the concert was due to start John spotted me and immediately ran over. Nothing could persuade him to rejoin the rest of his class. He was perfectly happy to sit with me and watch the show; he didn't seem to realise that he was supposed to be in it as well and that I'd come to watch *him* in the performance. John was three and a half at the time. He'd been going to this nursery every weekday afternoon for a whole term but compared to the other children he was on a different planet. Peer pressure and doing the same as the other children were completely meaningless concepts to him. According to John (the adult) peer pressure still is:

> I understand it intellectually, but have no emotional grasp of it at all. So other people are doing whatever it is, but that doesn't mean you should do it too without thinking to see if it's right! That way lies smoking and bad fake pop groups and who knows what.

It was as if the other children didn't exist and for many years after this he was pretty unaware of most of them. According to John:

> They existed: they just weren't particularly interesting features of the world. (In hindsight, the mental machinery which parses 'other human beings' into their own unique category had obviously not matured at all. It did, but it took years, and since when it matured it gave me huge heaps of extra stress I'm not sure it was *entirely* a good thing.)

I shouldn't have been as surprised as I was since I knew that John didn't look to see what other children were doing, a trait that had been obvious from a very young age. Nevertheless we were regularly caught unawares by John's unusual behaviour.

The following year I arrived early again for the Christmas concert but this time made sure that I hid at the back of the classroom behind other parents so that John couldn't see me. Most children would become anxious if they couldn't see their parents in the audience but not John. He didn't seem really aware of what was going on. He wasn't excited in any way and felt no sense of pride or achievement in the performance but behaved as if it was just another day at nursery school. Again the teacher stood next to John to keep him still but this time he stayed put, while I stayed well out of sight until the end.

When John was young we were fortunate enough to have several good state nursery schools in our locality, each of which took children from somewhere between the ages of three and four. There were three school terms a year and each child attended either five mornings or five afternoons per week. Most of the mothers I knew seemed keen for their children to go to the morning sessions but I wanted John to go to nursery school in the afternoon. The most important reason for wanting John at home in the mornings was that this was our special time when (as mentioned previously) I used to do a wide range of activities with him. I wanted to continue these sessions in the morning while John was still fresh and alert. I suspected that he would be too tired after a morning at nursery to do anything so intensive in the afternoon. Although John could have taken part at nursery in many of the same activities that he and I did together, he wouldn't have received such personal attention and I wasn't sure to what extent he would cooperate, given his unwillingness to get involved in much at the local college nursery (see Chapter 12). There was also another reason for wanting John to attend the afternoon sessions at nursery school. It could be considered rather trivial but it was important to me. It meant that for two more years the children and I could continue to enjoy leisurely and peaceful mornings without the stress of having to get up early, dress, wash and eat breakfast quickly. I knew this would be the situation once John started infant school when he was five and would continue until he left school at 18; the longer I could put off stressed out mornings the better. The stresses would have been quite considerable given that John preferred going to bed late and getting up late, a characteristic that's remained with him to this day. Moreover he still had great difficulty dressing himself and needed lots of time if he was to do as much as possible for himself. I also had a younger child to look after who was still too young to do much for herself; it was a great relief to postpone frenetic mornings for two more years.

After nearly two years of half a day a week at the local college nursery, the transition to the state nursery at the age of three and a quarter was easy. The nursery school routine suited John well, although he found it difficult when the routine changed for occasions such as Christmas. I agree with Ives and Munroe (2002) that a structured environment was important, as children on the autism spectrum may 'find a noisy and unstructured nursery very stressful to be in'. Although John attended this nursery school for nearly two years, he never interacted with the other children, never knew their names or made any friends. When the weather was good he enjoyed playing outside, either on small ride-on vehicles, in the sand pit or on the climbing frame. Inside, he refused to sit at the tables and do any construction or craft work; he would have a major tantrum if anyone tried to persuade him to make a card for his parents for Christmas or Easter (see also Chapter 8). Apart from listening to stories, joining in musical activities or talking to the staff, he spent the rest of the time happily playing alone with water, deep in his own imaginative world and, I strongly suspect, talking to himself as he did at home. I think he could have played with water all day every day if he'd been allowed to, without ever getting bored. Only recently John described water as 'endlessly mutable, endlessly fascinating, the root of all life'. The nursery school staff were very kind to John and it was accepted that some children were loners and dreamers. They coped well with his constant questions and the occasional emotional outburst when he was asked to do something he couldn't cope with or when he became upset by something in a story. These days I'm pretty sure someone would have commented on John's behaviour, his inability to relate to the other children and his problems with fine motor control; I suspect this would have prompted an assessment of some sort and hopefully some early intervention.

INFANT SCHOOL

There were two state primary schools roughly equidistant from our home. Each one had a separate infant school, catering for children between the ages of five and seven, and a junior school for children up to the age of 11. As we were quite clueless about what to look for in a primary school and what would suit our son's needs best, we choose the nearest school, which also seemed to have a good academic reputation. It's hard enough at the best of times to know how your child will develop and what sort of schooling will suit them but for someone like John, who seemed so different from all the children we knew, it was even more challenging. We had absolutely no idea what his needs were going to be for the next six years or how he would develop.

Fortunately, as John was used to going to nursery school every day and knew that it was a natural progression for all 'big' boys to move on from nursery to 'big' school, he started infant school perfectly happily just after Easter. Like many mothers I felt more bereft than him, although I went out of my way not to show it. However my husband Tony believes that once John started school 'a certain tension crept in and rather more anger and worry became apparent'. Based on personal experience, Tony thinks: 'For children who like both their own and family company and are really enjoying pre-school life, being sent to school is the first crisis in their lives.' According to John though: 'Replace 'crisis' with 'tragedy' and you have my opinion. (It is not entirely destructive, but it must be argued that it has destructive qualities.)' Tony remembers how upset *he* became when he had to start school and believes John may have felt the same.

I've no idea what John achieved in his first term as he brought nothing home. Neither his teacher nor the head spoke to me about John, apart from the first day when I was told about John's inability to use scissors (see Chapter 8). John never told me anything about school and when I tried to find out what he'd been doing all day, he always said he couldn't remember. He had no such problem remembering what he'd read.

While John was in this reception class I started to get concerned about the junior school that he would move up to a couple of years later as it was very strict and old-fashioned. In fact the whole primary school seemed devoid of nurturing qualities. Although the junior school achieved excellent academic results it was largely by making the children spend long periods of time doing rote, repetitive work. I began to realise that our son might not fare well in such an environment. We decided to move him after the one term to the other local primary school which seemed a gentler, more caring place. It was a good decision; John stayed in this school until he was 11 when he moved to a secondary school.

On the surface John didn't seem to mind this change at all, as yet again he hadn't integrated at all into his class, didn't appear to have made any friends or even know anyone's name. This certainly seems to agree with Gillberg's point (2002): 'The majority of those with Asperger syndrome are not troubled by their lack of friends, at least not during the early school years. Gradually, many become aware of being 'odd', 'unusual' or 'different'.' Although John didn't seem to mind going to the new school and never complained, his new class teacher was concerned about his inability to behave appropriately in a classroom situation and his frequent tantrums. I was called in to see this teacher and the head of the infant school. I told them something about John's birth history, the difficulties he's had to cope with ever since and the large gap between his strengths and weaknesses. I also described how we managed to engage his attention at home and motivate him. John's obvious intelligence and general knowledge, excellent command of the English language, logical and questioning approach to new information and advanced reading ability had masked the fact that he also had major weaknesses in many areas that were important in the classroom. Coping in the classroom was really challenging for John because he found sitting still very difficult, couldn't work with other children, was unable to concentrate on things he wasn't interested in or didn't find easy, and was a long way behind his peers in motor activities such as drawing, writing, handicrafts and sport. The situation at school improved enormously after this meeting as his teacher reduced the pressure on him to achieve things he was incapable of. She gave him lots of practice with pre-writing and writing exercises, helped him where needed and generally understood that he was doing his best and if he got upset it was because he couldn't cope. We felt John was in capable hands in this school and didn't have any major worries because his writing skills, although a long way behind his peers, were steadily improving with all the practice he was being given.

As everything seemed to be going relatively smoothly, we were very shocked to hear, at the parent-teacher meeting held in the December of his second year, that John was still having serious problems. As described in the previous chapter, this experienced teacher had discovered that John (although an excellent reader) was unable to copy from the board and couldn't spell at all. Because of these problems he was unable to participate in most of the activities that the other children in the class were engaged in, as these involved writing. A few months after this parent-teacher meeting we received a letter from the head which said:

> Since we stopped pressurising John he has seemed much happier, but there are still areas of concern. I should like to refer him to our educational psychologist in order to have his needs assessed. Then we, and subsequently the Junior school teachers will have a clear idea of how to help him achieve his seemingly high potential.

We agreed to the head's request and this turned out to be the first stage in producing a Statement of Special Educational Needs for John (see Chapter 20).

There were no teaching assistants in his class so the class teacher had to deal with about thirty children at a time on her own; children like John, who needed so much individual attention, must have been a real problem. There were many reasons why John would have been a difficult child to cope with: he was unable to sit still or concentrate for long unless he was engaged on something he really enjoyed; he had a tendency to interrupt whenever he thought of something to ask, regardless of whether this was the topic under discussion or whether this was an appropriate moment to ask a question; his strong will, stubbornness, lack of control of his emotions and tendency to become very distraught would have made it hard to provide correction; he had a lack of respect for authority and lacked awareness of what constituted polite and acceptable behaviour.

JUNIOR SCHOOL

By the end of his second year at infant school John had got used to the children in his class at last and they to him and he even knew some of their names. Now we were faced with one of those difficult moments when a decision has to be made between two equally unappealing alternatives. We discovered that the following term, when John moved from the infants' school to the junior school, the class teacher was a really old fashioned martinet who valued neat handwriting and obedience above all else. We knew she would find our son very difficult to handle and would give him a hard time because his writing was very untidy indeed and there wasn't much of it. We had the option to move him to a parallel class where the teacher was much more understanding and would have encouraged him and made allowances for his difficulties. However it would have meant him starting again in terms of building a relationship with his classmates, a process that was far from easy for all concerned. His current classmates understood his strange ways and were really quite supportive; because John's social skills were so poor we felt this was too important a factor to be ignored. There was also a risk that in a new class John might have been a target for bullies. So given the choice of an inappropriate teacher and existing classmates or a sympathetic teacher but new classmates, we decided to leave him where he was.

As expected John *did* have a very difficult year indeed with the new teacher. She wrote on his end of year school report:

> Spelling and handwriting have noticeably improved, but he still has difficulties with hand control. All written work and art and craft work is very poorly presented and he is too easily satisfied with anything outside his immediate interest…

> Finds difficulty conforming to class discipline. He is too easily distracted and requires individual attention – far more than I can give him to succeed in any task.

As described in Chapter 13, problems focussing and concentrating on topics which don't interest or excite him persist to this day. John *still* has unpleasant memories of his time in her class. In his words:

> This year was a dark blot on my memory, a time of being held in over breaks time and time again to write and write and write *ow ow ow*, the teacher eagle-eyed, noticing if I stopped for even five seconds and snapping at me, but somehow failing to notice that it *hurt*. Apparently tears of pain from a seven-year-old are not worth noticing, or a further sign of slovenliness, or something.

Many, many years later, long after John finished secondary school, we found ourselves sitting behind this teacher at the theatre. It was rather sobering to realise how well she remembered him, the whole experience having left many scars! She would not be the only teacher in John's life who was quite unaware of (or just totally underestimated) the effort required, and the resulting tiredness, when he had to spend any length of time doing something which he found very difficult. It's really not surprising that John gave up so easily before his work reached the standard expected by the teacher. According to John:

> Once anything was written down at all I was happy. Making it look pretty as well was hopeless to even wish for… Of course it was not only unreadable but very short: I normally had far more in my head than I could ever have written down.

As described previously in Chapter 11, John started lying in this class as a way to avoid getting into trouble.

The teacher in John's second year in junior school (age group 8/9) was far more sympathetic, really seemed to like him and wanted to understand him better. We were most impressed that she even went to a computer class in order to have some idea what John was talking about when he went on about his favourite topic. We were far less impressed to find out, from John, that he spent quite a lot of time secretly reading a book under his desk rather than doing whatever he was supposed to be doing. Pretty typical behaviour I'm afraid! This teacher was the first one to comment specifically, in writing, on his uneasy relationship with other children and the staff. We wrote a long comment to this year end report as we were so unhappy that the school seemed unable to communicate with us *during the year* regarding any difficulties that John was having, so that we could work on them together. John was obviously still finding school stressful at times as our first au-pair recalled: 'I never knew in what mood he would be when I picked him up from school. Sometimes he was very happy, other days very upset depending upon what had happened in school that day.'

The third year junior class (children aged 9/10) teacher resigned shortly before term started and the head didn't have time to appoint an appropriately trained and experienced member of staff for the class. He gave the job to the existing remedial teacher and she appeared to have been given little advice as to the academic requirements of this class. Those were the days before the national curriculum and it would appear that teachers could teach whatever they liked. In addition they were having an industrial dispute which involved 'going slow' and not working outside their contracted hours. This meant the parent-teacher meeting had to be held in the crowded classroom during the school day with the children still sitting at their desks – most unsatisfactory. Nevertheless I took time off work to attend the meeting, which took place in the middle of November. There was no children's work of any kind on display except for art work on the walls. I asked to see all John's work books in order to see what writing and maths he had done that term. This was my first opportunity that school year to see his work as the school didn't set homework and so his books never came home. I was astounded and very angry to find that these children had done hardly any maths, English or writing practice since early September when term started; I'm afraid I really lost my cool. It seemed that the teacher had spent the whole time getting them to do works of art for the walls – unbelievable! This, despite the fact that I'd received a letter in October, in response to one of mine, assuring me that my son was doing almost daily cursive writing practice. I wrote a very strong letter to the head, copied to the teacher, saying that I expected children who would be moving up to secondary school in less than two years time, to be doing maths and English *every day* as a matter of course. I also wanted the head to ensure that this teacher knew what the children in her class should be achieving and to monitor her work. Of course the teacher was upset and no doubt I could have been more tactful but my son's (and the other children's) future education was at stake and I wasn't prepared to see my son waste this year at school. This was a particularly important year for John because I was hoping that he would be in a position to take the entrance exams to private day schools early in the following academic year, should we feel that this was appropriate. As it was, his primary school didn't cover enough maths to enable children to pass these entrance exams without some extra tuition, so a year without much maths at all would have been bad news. I had no intention of letting sleeping dogs lie and forcing John to spend the evening doing the work he should have been doing at school; he was very tired by the end of the day and deserved free time to relax by reading and working on the computer. Fortunately this letter and possibly those from other parents had the desired effect and some proper work did take place in the classroom after this. Nevertheless this teacher *still* didn't seem to appreciate the need for John to practise his writing daily, if he was to have any chance of catching up with his peers and sitting any exams. For this reason I felt the need to write yet again, giving some of the background to John's difficulties and stressing the importance of the writing programme. Some extracts from this letter can be seen in Appendix 14. In retrospect it seems quite extraordinary that I should have felt the need to write such a letter to someone who used to be a remedial teacher! Surely most of what I wrote should have been second nature to her but apparently it wasn't or I doubt I would have said what I did. Perhaps I am being unfair and it was the large discrepancy between John's strengths and weaknesses that blinded the teacher to the reality of his problems and the help that he needed. This discrepancy became a major problem in secondary school, where John's obvious intelligence, coupled with his inability to get much down on paper and his chronic lack of organisational ability, led to all sorts of problems.

As usual we turned up to the first parent-teacher meeting of John's fourth and final year at the junior school full of apprehension, expecting to hear about all the problems John was causing and how difficult the teacher was finding him. This fear and dread prior to meeting any of John's teachers lasted until he left school at 18. This was partly due to the pain it caused us to hear about all of John's failures and partly due to the fact that we believed most of his teachers (particularly at secondary school) blamed *us* for his behaviour, although they didn't actually say so directly. Anyhow, to our amazement John's fourth year class teacher said she was having no problems whatsoever. The teacher was Froebel trained and was accustomed to treating each child as an individual. Her techniques suited John admirably; he was very happy in her class and seemed to be part of a really close group of friends, both boys and girls. According to the website www. froebelweb.org/web2005.html:

> The philosophy of education of Friedrich Fröbel, 1782-1852 stresses the respect with which the individuality and ability of each child should be treated; the importance of creating a happy, harmonious environment in which he or she can grow; and the value of self-activity and play as a foundation on which the integrated development of the whole person can be built.

As this teacher noted in her year end report: 'John has made big strides forward in his ability to relate to his classmates.' Unfortunately most of these children went to different secondary schools and the friendships didn't survive the change of school.

John's junior school reports are informative. They describe a boy who loved reading and as a result had acquired an excellent vocabulary and a wide general knowledge; his comprehension, oral and written English were good, he could write imaginatively and had no problems with grammar. What his teachers never pointed out, and possibly never realised, was that John had great difficulties remembering the sequence of letters in the alphabet and consequently was very slow using a dictionary; he was well into his teens before he could use a dictionary competently. The school seemed pleased with the improvements in John's writing (see Chapter 8) over the years but the end result proved to be insufficient for the demands of secondary school. Here there was a requirement to write fast *and* legibly and also to take notes while the teacher was speaking, something John was quite incapable of. He could listen or write but couldn't do both at the same time. As John explained:

> Both require concentration. I had not (and still have not) automated the process of writing: it was much too difficult, required constant conscious adjustment to cope with yet another tiny muscle tremor or 1/10 second coordination failure, and hurt too much. Can *you* concentrate on two things at once when one is painful and difficult?

Although I agree with John that I can only learn one new, difficult skill at a time, I don't think his explanation is the whole truth. He was still unable to take notes when he had the use of a keyboard (where he was very competent) in the classroom. While he was listening and concentrating he couldn't do *anything* else.

The mathematics sections of John's reports mention a few problem areas, such as 'slowness in problem work' and 'rarely works to full capacity', which continued to give rise to difficulties for many years. The reports don't mention the fact that John actually had significant problems with rote maths facts. As mentioned in Chapter 14 he couldn't do simple addition in his head (such as 4 plus 5) without using his fingers, at an age when all his peers had abandoned this type of aid. Despite a lot of extra practice at home, his knowledge of multiplication tables was, and is to this day, insecure. For all these reasons he was delighted when he was given a calculator as it helped him overcome a real weakness and he rapidly acquainted himself with all the calculator functions.

Other comments mentioned elsewhere in the reports include: 'Initially very enthusiastic in topic work, but interest wanes all too soon'; 'Will work on his own when the subject appeals'; 'Is too easily distracted'. As mentioned already in Chapter 14, when John was aged 10/11 his school report stated: 'Written project work is still disappointing... he still seems unwilling to assemble the information and present it logically – the chore of writing is too great perhaps.' Unfortunately it became apparent many years later, when John was using a computer for all writing activities, that he had a real problem organising his work (or anything else) and that this weakness had been masked by his writing difficulties. He wasn't 'unwilling' but 'unable'. There are many aids and techniques available which can help one organise written material but there needs to be an awareness that a problem actually exists. One of the many reasons why a child with writing problems should be allowed to use a computer sooner rather than later is that weaknesses (such as this one) can then be detected and appropriate help provided. If the child finds writing so difficult that they don't produce much written work, then difficulties such as these remain hidden.

Apart from the last two years in junior school, John was very isolated throughout his school days. Attwood (1998) describes John perfectly when he writes: 'At school lunchtimes the child is often found on their own in a secluded area of the playground, sometimes talking to themselves or in the library reading about their particular interest.' John, who had a real need to spend time on his own when he was outside the classroom, wrote as follows about the methods he used to find peace and quiet:

> The corner of the playground or long orbits over the playing fields worked well enough in primary school; in secondary school I could often find empty rooms in

obscure corners, or long walks over the most distant and empty pathways in the school grounds. I think I entered the sixth-form common room twice in two years, after years of wondering what went on in there (the appeal of the forbidden). It was appalling; noisy, crowded, and stark. Back to obscure corners for me.

These days John finds socialising fun but he also finds it exhausting:

Which is one reason why I don't do it much. But I'm not sure I considered it exhausting in my teenage years or before: I didn't really notice the need to do it at all. I'd talk to people if they talked to me, but never really tried to figure out how they thought. I enjoyed breaks because they meant I could go a long way away from anyone else and dive back into one of my invented worlds!

John described the difficulties he experienced making friends as follows:

If you find someone who could be a friend, how could you tell? The school friends I made were nearly all made when they were less than about thirteen, following which their social strategies just got too complex for me to even guess if they wanted to start a friendship (which they probably almost never did). It was perhaps a decade before I got enough of a model together to be able to guess, sometimes, when people might want to say more than hello.

As mentioned already in Chapter 11, 'buddy' systems or 'circles of friends' (methods that can be used to help a child on the autism spectrum relate to their peers) might have been helpful to John both at primary and secondary school but they weren't available when he was at school. As Humphrey and Symes wrote in 2011:

Developing peer awareness and understanding is key if pupils with autism are to be socially accepted. One popular method involves developing a 'circle of friends', where members of the pupil's peer group are used to support them. A key element of this is sensitively-handled disclosure of the pupil's diagnosis, with the hope that other pupils will be more likely to accept the differences they see, if they have been educated about the cause of these differences. This whole-class meeting is regarded as one of the most successful parts of the intervention…

Interventions aimed at improving the social skills of pupils could focus on improving understanding and recognition of emotions, improving their social interaction skills, and the development of conversational skills. Pupils might be taught coping strategies to deal with bullying, how to recognise they are being bullied and who to tell when it occurs.

I was able to make contact with two of the children that used to be in John's class in junior school: Alison, one of the girls that John was so friendly with in his last two years at this school, and Clare, who used to live opposite the first house we lived in but wasn't a particular friend once John started school. Although Clare didn't remember much, she recalled:

At school we must have been about seven years old. He was told off by our teacher and told to leave the classroom. Outside the classroom he banged on the door shouting 'let me in you stupid cow'. I don't remember him being bullied at school as such. I think other pupils were shocked by his reactions and found him entertaining and enjoyed the episodes of him acting up in the classroom.

Alison seems to remember a great deal about her time at this school and considered John to be a really good friend. Her comments paint an interesting picture of John's behaviour at the time and how he was perceived by his classmates:

> I think he had a short fuse and often lost his temper in a quite explosive way and/or got very upset. I remember his face going red and him shouting with little bits of spit coming out of his mouth. The only trouble is I can't remember what it was that usually upset him in the first place. I think it might often have been frustration, either with his own difficulties or even just school in general. I think he was also quite rude, perhaps unintentionally so, and so didn't always engage well with other kids because they didn't take to him at first. Other children did pick on him and call him names, they laughed at him sometimes when they didn't understand his behaviour. I think some of the children might have thought that he was mad or 'mental' and the fact that John couldn't always control what he said or did encouraged them to laugh at him.

Interestingly enough John was either unaware of, or wasn't upset by, the reactions of the rest of his classmates. Alison considered that she, John and Harry were 'in a way... three misfits.' Harry was very intelligent and went on to the same academic secondary school that John went to. John was very close friends indeed with Harry and also with another child, Phil, who was in the year below him at school but also lived locally. John remembers there was also another friend at primary school who used to play with them, a girl called Mary whom he was very fond of. John doesn't remember a great deal about what they got up to but he does recall 'a lot of silly jokes':

> I spent a lot of time trying to make Mary laugh, which was not difficult as I recall...

> Phil and I spent a large part of the third year junior breaks dismantling a large part of a low wall with exquisite care: the mortar was old and crumbling and we were picking it apart grain by grain, no nails or stones allowed, just fingers...

> Phil, Harry and I (and sometimes Alison) had this sort of human-voice-as-instrument improvised-music thing going. Harry came up with it... who knows where he got it from. *That* was a pile of fun (also completely bizarre). The human voice making silly sounds in combination with others is quite a powerful instrument...

John still remembers the fun he had with the flying food bags (see Chapter 12) as does one of the ladies who worked at the school at the time and remembered the pleasure John and his friend seemed to be having in the playground as they watched these bags sail into the air. When John wrote about the social group he was a part of in the last two years in primary school (Harry, Alison, Mary and Phil) he recalled:

> Whenever I tried to do anything at all with any other social grouping it was disastrous. In hindsight I was sort of incohesive even then, often slipping away from the group to do what to others were probably rather strange things like repeatedly walking from one side of the 'thin' front part of the playground to the other, counting footsteps and trying to reach 1km, then 2km... sometimes Harry

would accompany me for conversation's sake (presumably).

As well as these pleasant memories of his junior school friendships, John still has negative recollections:

Of course negative stuff pops out occasionally: staying behind in break copying something out because my handwriting was so bad (?! this makes no sense!), being made to stand in the corner once for reasons that elude me now and probably did then... but I have no idea how frequent these events were. Probably not very: they just survived where nothing else did because they were emotionally intense... The secondary school social ostracism hadn't kicked in, probably more because of changes in the others/the toxic social structure of secondary schools than because of me. So my major worry was messing up school work, which (one presumes by induction) happened all the time. I speculate that quality of handwriting was a major problem, but all I can say is that I still have an emotional response to it.

CHOOSING A SECONDARY SCHOOL

Criteria and choices

This is a difficult time for any parent but in our case choosing the most appropriate school, for a child with such large differences between their strengths and weaknesses, was extraordinarily hard. Should we look for a school that would cater for John's difficulties and help and support him but might not stretch him academically? Should we look for a school that suited John's intellectual strengths but might not be accustomed to children with John's problems? Mike Stanton (2000) describes the problem very aptly when he writes:

Even the special needs culture in mainstream schools is not always amenable to children with autism... They are often too bright for the curriculum available to their autistic peers in special school but too socially naive to get by within mainstream... If they are to be maintained within a mainstream setting that offers a curriculum to match their intellectual ability, then the schools as well as the parents need clear signposts that will lead them to understand and cater for the special needs that arise from our children's autism.

What we wanted was a caring school that would understand and support our son but would also stretch him academically. Temple Grandin, a gifted animal scientist on the autism spectrum, wrote in *Emergence. Labelled Autistic* that she had coped well in her elementary school which had only 13 students in each class and one teacher for all subjects. When she transferred to a large junior high school 'with thirty to forty students in a class and a different teacher for each subject' she found it 'a confusing, traumatic experience'. In fact after two and a half years she was expelled for reacting to name-calling by throwing a book at the child responsible. She then started at a small school, with only 32 pupils, where she could receive a lot of individual attention; this school proved to be a great success. In the ideal school for John, the classes would be small, the strengths and weaknesses of each child would be understood and the teachers would know how to motivate and stretch the children, while helping them with any difficulties.

The school would be very academic and encourage the children to think for themselves. It would also be a day school, as John really needed to retreat to the haven of his home each evening and weekend; here he could be totally himself and relax from the strain of trying to cope with other people all day. Other issues that we had to consider when choosing a secondary school included the attitude of the school to bullying, whether it was to be a mixed or single sex school, the distance from home, the cost (if it was private) and the class size. Unfortunately there didn't seem to be any schools in our locality that met all, or even most, of our criteria. We couldn't find an academic day school with small classes and a pupil, as opposed to subject, based approach. Moreover, because there were several schools in the area, both mixed and single sex, comprehensive and private and all with entry at eleven years of age, John's small group of friends was going to be broken up regardless of the school we chose.

As far as we were concerned, the only realistic choice we had was between one of the local mixed comprehensives, a local boys comprehensive, and a couple of single sex, fee paying, academic day schools where there was an entrance exam and interview. Unfortunately all these schools had classes of about 30 children. Nevertheless, my husband, John, and I went to open days at all these schools, had a good look round and spoke to some of the staff. We would have been delighted for John to go to a local state school, which would have been free, within walking distance of our home and might have had other children from his primary school class. However the single sex state school seemed very regimented and strict and we didn't think this would suit John. The mixed comprehensive had a very nice feeling indeed and may well have provided a supportive atmosphere but academically we felt the school wouldn't have stretched John; he would have been bored, achieved little and therefore not made the most of his strengths. We were particularly concerned that there was no 'streaming' in most subject areas. This meant that in English and History classes, for example, the teacher would have to cater for all abilities; this would certainly have influenced the quality of class discussion, teacher expectations and topics covered. Indeed the history eras covered were very narrow and the English set books far from challenging. The teachers at this comprehensive also taught mixed sciences rather than separate physics, chemistry and biology, which we felt wasn't appropriate for a child who was so keen and knowledgeable about scientific topics. Nevertheless, this school was our first state school choice and the letter we wrote to the local education authority giving the reasons why we wished John to go to this particular school can be seen in Appendix 15. At that time, the allocation of secondary school places in our locality was made on the basis of parental choice. If the schools that were chosen were oversubscribed, then the reasons given by the parents for choosing those schools became decisive. It's interesting that we specifically mentioned bullying under the section headed 'Child's Needs', as well as John's poor coordination, problems coping within the classroom and need for a disciplined, caring and enthusiastic atmosphere.

One of the private schools John was going to apply for was much smaller than the other, which was an advantage but it seemed to cater more for the monied and privileged, rather than the purely academic, which would have been at odds with our family philosophy and John's strong feelings of fairness. The other private school was very large but was divided into houses and into a junior, middle and senior school, each with their own head, which helped to make it feel smaller. Each subject area had its own designated location in the school with current articles from journals displayed on notice boards. There were many specialist teachers qualified in subjects such as physics where there was a national shortage; their enthusiasm and love of learning for its own sake, without any 'dumbing down', was just right for John. He really liked what he saw on the open day and this was the only school he enthused about but there was still the barrier of an entrance exam and an interview to surmount. I'd been coaching John, at the weekends and in the holidays, in the maths he hadn't covered at his junior school and had worked through some past maths papers (available on a sort of black market!) with him. There was no need to do any other work with him. Because we were so worried about finding a suitable school for John, we wrote to the head of both private schools (well before the entrance exams took place) explaining very frankly the strengths and weaknesses of our son as we saw them and to ask the heads whether they felt their school would meet John's needs. Our preferred school sent their admissions tutor to observe John at work in his fourth year classroom and to speak to his class teacher about him, while the other private school did nothing. John then took and passed the entrance exams to both schools. After the interview he was turned down at the smaller school and accepted at his preferred school. John said that the admissions tutor 'then turned into my first year form master. Talk about paying the price for your mistakes immediately!' John was also offered a place at his preferred state school but we decided to accept the private school place believing that it would suit him academically as it was full of very clever children.

Outcome

Unfortunately, although this school was definitely right for John intellectually, most of the teachers were unable to cope with his areas of difficulty. Accustomed as they were to clever children with few problems, they were amazingly ignorant about the so called hidden difficulties that John was struggling with. It didn't appear as if anyone ever thought: 'Why is this child struggling and how we can help him?' If he'd been deaf they would have been happy for him to use a hearing aid and sit at the front of the class and would never have expected him to work hard to overcome his deafness. There was no SENCO (Special Educational Needs Coordinator) during John's years at secondary school and being an independent school, there was no requirement for them to consider his Statement of Special Educational Needs. Moreover there was absolutely no awareness of topics such as dyspraxia, Asperger's syndrome, or attention deficit disorder in secondary schools at that time, so that some of John's difficulties led to the imposition of detentions rather than additional help. As John remembers:

> Most of my teachers, especially in secondary school, didn't even consider that they might have to do anything. My bad handwriting was a sign of laziness and probably moral torpidity, was 'my fault', and therefore they were quite justified in ignoring it except to mark me down harshly for it and its side effects. To this day I don't know how good I actually am at most of the subjects taught at school: all I know is that I couldn't handwrite well or fast enough in those subjects, because that's the only message the teachers saw fit to impart, through grading at least. It's like learning didn't matter if you couldn't make complicated marks with one hand at high speed. It all seems pathetically hilarious now, since my life is filled with learning and a good bit of teaching and mentoring, but entirely without

handwriting. My previous job knew me as the guy who knows everything (and there's a definite drift that way in this job too, after only four months), even though I never wrote any of it down by hand.

I think the school really regretted ever offering him a place, although they never gave up on him and always kept trying to make him take more responsibility for his actions. Apart from an occasional sympathetic teacher, the staff just didn't understand that the difference between John's intellectual abilities and his actual achievements (his inability to take notes, write neatly and quickly, organise both himself and his work so that home-work of a decent standard was handed in on time and so on) was not down to laziness, wilfulness and a desire to be difficult but was due to invisible difficulties beyond his control. John really couldn't understand the teachers' attitude:

I always found this numbingly strange. Why would anyone lazy show it by making such an effort and turning out something so bad? Why would anyone wilfully turn out crap with great difficulty rather than, say, doing nothing at all? If I'd gone on strike I could have understood this, but the harder I tried the more they seemed to complain.

It's not that I wanted to turn out crap. Rather, the pain of writing anything at all, attention deficits, and an inability to edit what I'd already written led to work that took much longer to write than anyone would expect given its apparent quality. It took me an hour to turn out something that most people could do in five or ten minutes, so the staff naturally believed that I'd spent no time on it. (They continued to believe this despite seeing me struggling to write at any speed at all in class. This is harder to forgive.)

Note that the only time in the first few years that I could produce typewritten work it was good enough that it got published in the school mag. – mind you it wasn't good in absolute terms – there's no way anyone *else* would have published it – but still.

Of course what John didn't comprehend was that his teachers were totally unaware how much effort he was actually expending when he tried to do his homework – they just looked at the poor quality end product from the point of view of someone with no writing or organisational difficulties. According to John though: 'If they paid any atten-tion to me in class, they shouldn't have been unaware. It's not as if writing got easier for me when I was in school.' All John needed in order to do well was for his teachers to understand his problems and as a consequence be willing to provide suitable help and accommodations rather than punishment and constant criticism. Myles and Southwick's (1999) approach would have been ideal for John. They suggest that a child who has difficulty taking notes should receive a copy of the notes taken by a peer:

The individual with Asperger syndrome whose organizational skills make it diffi-cult for homework to get home has a homework hotline buddy who helps her re-member what assignments are due.

Adults working with these children should continually ask, 'What can be done to make the environment more understandable for my student? How can I help her be more successful?' It is the ultimate goal to help individuals with Asperger Syndrome understand their exceptionality, complete with its strengths and challenges. From this understanding will come an awareness of the modifications the individual needs in order to be successful. The student with Asperger Syndrome can then be taught to be active in putting into place modifications that will help her demonstrate her skills in a positive way.

What types of accommodation would we have liked for John? The most helpful would have been: to use a computer for copying from the board and doing homework, to have a set of lesson notes from the teacher or copy another child's notes (provided they were good enough) or tape the lesson, to copy the homework instructions from another child or have the teacher check that John had all the information written down. We asked for all these things and were flatly refused! For example we asked the head if John could record his lessons as he was unable to listen and take notes at the same time, no matter take down the homework instructions. The head was adamant that no recorder could ever be taken into lessons. John thinks:

> The tape recorder would have been an excellent way of solving the get-down-the-homework problem, but the teachers were *really* paranoid about being taped, to the extent that several of them asked me if the power brick next to my laptop was a recording device! So taping was right out because of fear-of-being-sued paranoia.

Many of the difficulties John experienced at school were due to the combination of high intelligence and executive function weaknesses. (See Chapter 14 for more details about executive function.) Problems also arose because of a large difference between John's Verbal IQ and Performance IQ (see Chapter 20) and poor motor skills (see Chapter 8). According to Gillberg (2002):

> Clinical experience suggests that executive dysfunction in Asperger syndrome tends to predict a poor outcome as regards education and psychosocial adjustment. In such cases... it is very important to provide external structure in the educational setting, so as to compensate for poor inner structuring skills...

> It is not difficult to imagine that such discrepancies [between verbal and performance IQ]... contribute to other people making severe mistakes in their personal judgements and therefore making unreasonable demands.

> One of the greatest assets of many people with Asperger syndrome is their high intelligence. It is therefore sad to see sometimes how a young adult person with an IQ of over 150 can be completely lost in education settings where there is little outer structure. One of my patients with such a high IQ did well during the school years when the structures surrounding him were almost rigid and school work was checked on every day. At university he has failed completely, mostly because he has been expected to motivate himself and structure his work all by himself.

I think Patricia Howlin hit the nail on the head when she wrote in 1998:

> For children with Asperger syndrome, specialist help, or even sympathy may prove... difficult to find. Indeed, because of their relatively high cognitive ability, and their *apparently* competent communication skills, this group of children is often least well served or understood... Most have to cope in mainstream school

with little or no help. Their parents may be dismissed as over-protective, or too lax, and can find it very difficult to get the support or advice they need. Moreover, the children's good vocabulary, and even their well-developed obsessional interests, frequently give the impression that they are capable of far higher levels of achievement than is actually the case. Others' expectations of their social competence tends to be unrealistically high, and when these expectations are not met the children are viewed as negative, uncooperative, rude and manipulative. Seemingly so close to 'normality', there is constant pressure for them to 'fit in', in ways that would never be demanded of a less able autistic child. This can lead to enormous pressure, resulting in extreme levels of anxiety and stress, which in turn can further impede social progress.

Because of their very uneven profile of skills and deficits, such children may require even more highly specialised help than those with global learning difficulties.

Mike Stanton (2000) also has some very perceptive views on the problems encountered by the more academically able child with autism in the UK:

There is very little provision for able pupils who cannot manage mainstream schooling...

There are specialist schools for children with Asperger syndrome. But they are expensive and few and far between...

Primary schools are more autism friendly than secondary schools. They are usually smaller. The curriculum and timetable are less rigidly confined by the pressures of the public examination system. You spend most of the year with the same teacher in the same room for all your lessons. Perhaps most important of all you do not have to socialize with teenage boys...

We have to recognize that diversity and choice are essential elements if we are to meet the needs of all pupils in an inclusive education system. If mainstream schools are enabled to adapt and take on board the successful ideas developed in specialist educational settings those elements of diversity and choice can be extended to include the special needs of children with autism...

It is tempting for local health and education authorities to opt for 'a one size fits all' solution, a single package that combines administrative and financial convenience. Unfortunately all children are congenitally inconvenient and children with autism are refreshingly normal in this respect. What works for your child might not work for mine and provision, ideally, should be based on the child's individual profile and not their geographical profile.

Children on the autism spectrum and/or with ADHD may not be easy to teach in a large class in a mainstream school; teacher understanding and accommodations are essential. John was no exception, partly because of his attitude to learning and to his teachers. He didn't understand, or if he understood didn't agree with, the unwritten contract that operates between pupils and teachers in any successful school. This contract expects that pupils should work to the best of their ability in *every* subject and should be polite and respect all the teachers, regardless of any private opinions held about them and the quality of their teaching. John had no idea, until he read the previous sentence, that such a thing as an unwritten contract existed between pupils and their school and he has a very strong reaction to the suggestion:

> Clearly unwritten contracts exist, and are fundamental to English law: they're the reason why you have to pay for something before you can walk out of a shop with it, for instance. But no such contract necessarily exists between a pupil and her school as far as I can see. There must be a meeting of the minds for such a contract to exist, and there surely was not between me and my teachers...

> I can see why it makes sense for the *school*, but I can't see why it makes sense for the *pupils*, nor why giving people respect who do not deserve it is considered distinct from lying. As for working to the best of my ability in every subject, sure, as soon as you give me an attention transplant. What each teacher *actually* wanted was that we should give *their subject* precedence over all the others. There was absolutely no attempt to coordinate homework to try to prevent people from being overwhelmed by torrents of the stuff, and if we pointed out that giving us an essay for two days time collided with three other essays due on the same day, their responses were always the same: 'not my problem', or at best, 'do mine first'. Attempting to point out the impossibility of satisfying this constraint for every one of them invariably resulted in explosions of rage, a display of selfish stupidity and wilful blindness that is a nice role model for a City worker, perhaps, but not for anyone else.

According to Gillberg (2002), John's attitude to school is far from unusual for children on the autism spectrum:

> There are often major problems with school work. The teenager with Asperger syndrome sometimes does not realise the importance of good performance at school... It can be almost impossible to convince them of the need to devote more time and energy to school work.

> School problems are very common in Asperger syndrome, even in those who are highly intelligent. Many have great difficulty concentrating on and taking an interest in tasks considered important in the academic world, be it primary school or at the university level.

To this day John still doesn't seem to understand why good performance at school is important, writing recently to me as follows:

> It's seventeen years later and I *still* don't understand the importance of it. I thought we went to school to learn, not to 'perform'. What are we, circus animals?...

> I know why *others* think it is important – because they think the sole purpose of school is to do well in exams. I guess I don't see much point in exams, but this may be bias caused by my specializing in a subject of such youth and complexity that nobody knows how to set examinations that say anything much useful about the people sitting them. Also it's bias caused by my being really bad at exams!

As described in an earlier chapter, John really applied himself when he liked a subject but didn't put in any effort otherwise. According to him:

I was thoroughly uninterested by quite a lot of subjects at school; I couldn't care less if I got a low mark in music, for instance, and even a low mark in French didn't concern me much. (I've known since I was about eight where my strengths lay; what's the point of trying to get good at French when I'd never stand a chance of being expert in it? What's the point of working at a subject only to become, at best, mediocre? There probably is a point to this if you have no particular strengths: better to be mediocre at everything than bad at everything. But if you know perfectly well that you can fly effortlessly in some fields, why go to great lengths to learn to stagger rather than crawl in others, when you could be spending the time soaring?)... In secondary school, though, I found that avoiding sport had no negative consequences I cared about, so I did it all the time... I didn't learn very much useful in secondary education at least. Some things, but probably only a few percent of my time wasn't wasted. But then a major purpose of schools is keeping children out of the way of adults, so I suppose wasting your time until you grow up is what's *meant* to happen.

What a cynic, and definitely *not* an attitude that would endear John to his teachers! 'That's not cynicism, that's rational analysis coming to bleak conclusions...' says John. He believes that his secondary school was the cause of intense misery and it was this experience that coloured his views:

> I'm not very cynical in most areas. If I'm cynical about schooling, it's because it made me so. (Cynical is not the word, anyway. I'm shaking. Even two decades later the rank injustice of that place burns: even now I have nightmares about it.)

Clare Sainsbury (2009) really hit a sensitive spot when she wrote: 'A child with Asperger's may not understand that they are supposed to obey the teacher without discussion, let alone that they are not allowed to correct the teacher's errors.' In response John wrote recently:

> Even now this makes me bristle. Why?... so it's acceptable for a teacher to pass on *wrong* things to a classful of pupils? Most teachers seemed to be happy to have their occasional errors squashed as fast as possible: Mr. W. actually introduced them intentionally to check if we were awake! I did encounter one particular teacher when I was fifteen whose reaction to a single correction of a serious error (an error of 100 years in dating something in history; not one date but a whole series of them, all off by the same amount) was to explode in wrath over 'appalling insubordination', halt all useful teaching for the remainder of the lesson in favour of sitting in silence, and give me a detention. I considered this patent insanity; he was damaging his own teaching and losing an entire hour of lesson time because of shame over a *single typo*? What a poor sad insecure little man he must have been. It was also ridiculously inconsistent given that other teachers at the same school were expecting correction of errors and penalizing you if you *didn't* do so. (I said as much in the detention essay, but I suspect he never read it as he never commented, and if he'd read it there'd have been an explosion to rival Krakatoa emitting dozens of detentions and you'd probably have been called in and would I suspect have agreed with me).

Of course what John hadn't realised (and no doubt others in his class had), was that all teachers are different and the rules that apply to one do not necessarily apply to them all. A depth of social understanding that John would have found very hard to accommodate at that age and possibly even now given the above comments! John's current view is:

> Sure, all teachers are different, but I'd prefer them to go to a bit of effort to establish consistency. Possibly I care more about this than most, with not only Asperger's and SF reading, but also software development *all* telling me that consistency is among the highest of all virtues.

> I did understand intellectually that they might not all have the same desire to be corrected, and so on, but first I could never track that stuff in enough detail to be useful, and secondly how was I supposed to know the explosion would happen before it happened? I suspect there were clues that this person didn't like to be corrected that a normal socially-telepathic person would have picked up on, but I cannot be sure.

I suspect that many of the children in John's class would have noticed the typo also but would have realised that it was prudent *not* to say anything to this particular teacher. John thinks that the typo was so blatant that this is probably true but as he says: 'You know what I'm like with typos. The drive to share them is almost unstoppable, even now.' Myles and Southwick (1999) would consider the above situation to be an example of what they call the 'hidden curriculum'. As they describe it:

> Students with Asperger Syndrome are at a disadvantage because they usually do not understand the hidden curriculum. They inadvertently break the rules associated with the hidden curriculum and either get in trouble with adults or become further ostracised or hurt by peers. As a result, they require direct instruction on the hidden curriculum... Persons with Asperger Syndrome... need to know (a) teacher expectations, (b) teacher-pleasing behaviors, (c) students to interact with and those to stay away from, and (d) behaviors that attract positive and negative attention. Understanding the hidden curriculum can make all the difference to students with Asperger Syndrome – it can keep them out of detention or worse, and it can help them make friends.

According to John: 'I had no idea until now that any such thing might exist. I assumed that my fellow pupils knew this social-telepathy thing before they arrived, or picked it up so fast they might as well have done.' I suspect that if John had received some direct instruction on the hidden curriculum at his secondary school it would have made a significant difference.

The main problem John experienced at this school was the bullying and ostracism, which made these by far the worst years of his life. As John wrote to me a few years ago:

> I know I've *always* found it easier to interact with adults and children than teenagers, which helped not at all in my horribly isolating secondary school. (It was quite like being in jail with a thousand people who hated me for eight hours a day, 180-odd days a year... a jail my parents had to *pay* for.)

> I was being bullied because I was 'different' for all sorts of reasons, because I

didn't have the same interests as the attackers, and because I didn't have the social ability to dodge their fire.

Unfortunately these days the bullying might be even worse as some children can't even escape when they get home; they might have to cope with nasty emails, texts or comments on social media. When Gillberg (2002) wrote about bullying in relationship to children with Asperger syndrome he said: 'This may be open scapegoating or physical aggression, but sometimes it is a matter of silent exclusion. Bullying is probably a much under-rated phenomenon in Asperger syndrome.' Stanton (2000) has some perceptive views about children on the autism spectrum and bullying at school:

A school may be justly proud of its anti bullying policy and caring ethos. Yet when faced with a claim of systematic bullying the school goes onto the defensive, demanding proof, challenging the young person's version of events. Under pressure the person with autism will admit that nobody actually hit him. It was just some silly name calling.

But this name calling can be just as hurtful and threatening as actual violence. Racial abuse of minorities is quite rightly viewed as anathema by education authorities. Schools operate zero tolerance when physical or sensory handicaps are the subject of ridicule and taunts. But the lad with autism is supposed to laugh off the whispered taunts...

Children with autism sometimes imagine they are being bullied or teased when they are not. Their social impairment often leads people with autism to misread the motives of others. But if certain incidents or behaviours are perceived as bullying by them *it is that perception that counts.*

Mel Levine, in his book *A Mind at a Time*, wrote:

Verbal and physical derision or abuse in school should be considered a form of criminal behaviour and punished accordingly. Peer cruelty is unacceptable and a clear violation of kids' rights... A school for all kinds of minds should be a microcosm in which students come to tolerate and respect one another... It should be a place where social conformity and peer pressure are dampened in favour of the celebration and encouragement of healthy differences.

What an ideal to aim for! As one school head said to Mel Levine:

One of my greatest challenges is to do something about the destructive things kids do to one another. Our politicians keep blaming teachers and parents for everything. But no one ever wants to deal with the toxic effects students can have on one another. I'm concerned about the oppressive power of peer pressure.

John agrees that peer cruelty is unacceptable but wonders:

How do you stop it? It's a microcosm of adult relationships in an environment without law... as long as a large number of adolescents are forced together in an environment in which they must make their own societies without adult participation, we'll have just the sort of horrible stuff that burned me, because they pick up their behaviours from their surroundings, and all that is in their surroundings is each other: and this without a fully developed forebrain to constrain extremes of response. Of course this is a profoundly strange and recent development: for all but a few centuries of our evolutionary history, adolescents have been surrounded by *adults*.

However he *does* think mainstream schooling could have worked much better for him:

> If only the teachers had written down what needed to be done in some unambiguous fashion rather than just saying it quickly as the lesson broke up, and if I had somewhere I could go outside lessons to which I could control entrance: i.e. I could keep specific people out (which is less a special requirement than a human right which every adult in a non-totalitarian society possesses as a matter of course, but which apparently society considers teenagers and below don't need, strange that). Is that all it would have taken? A single room? It seems almost too simple...

A safe haven is one of the strategies advocated by Clare Lawrence (2010) who writes: 'It is imperative that the pupil with AS (*Asperger syndrome*) has somewhere where he can go if in need of sanctuary.'

Could we make a better choice these days?

Did we find the best secondary school for John at the time? I really don't know. It's certainly appalling that he was so unhappy at the school he went to but whether he would have been any happier at another school is very hard to say. What would we do now, with hindsight, if we had to make the same choice again for another child with a similar profile? Although we would still want an academic school for a child with a similar intelligence profile to our son, we are much more aware of the bullying issue and the devastating effect it can have on a child; this would be a topic that we would pursue with any school we visited. As John explains:

> Its consequences affect me to this day. I strongly suspect my comprehensive lack of anything remotely resembling bravery and my extreme focus on finding a single safe thing to do and sticking to it originates in... [secondary school] where whenever I stuck my head out someone stamped on it. Seven years of that will have a lasting effect.

We would wish to see what practical steps the school took to help children who have difficulties fitting in socially and who are therefore more likely to be bullied. I would be particularly interested to find out what accommodations the school would be prepared to make for children who have problems writing, taking notes, getting themselves organised and so on, and whether they had a quiet place of safety for the child to retreat to in order to de-stress and calm down. Hopefully John would have an Individual Education Plan or something similar, which would be reviewed every term. Reading books, such as those mentioned in Appendix 28, would mean that Tony and I would be in a much better position to ensure that John had a more positive school experience. I would also heed the plea made by a teacher (writing in *That's Life with Autism* edited by Ross and Jolly) who wrote:

> The biggest thing I can tell parents is to communicate your expectations, needs,

and desires. I cannot stress this enough. If the lines of communication are kept open and you approach the teacher in an open-minded, positive way everyone will benefit. As much as possible try to work together as a team; after all, it is in the best interests of the child. If you want to talk to the teachers, set up an email system, call them, or schedule an appointment. Most teachers are willing to establish a workable system of communication if requested by a parent.

There were occasions that we were tempted to homeschool, as John would have found it much easier to cope in a one-to-one situation. As Attwood (2006) wrote:

The acquisition of knowledge in a classroom requires considerable social and linguistic skills. The difficulties experienced in these areas by children with Asperger's syndrome can impede the understanding of academic concepts.

John would certainly have preferred this option. He far prefers learning on his own, saying: 'Self-directed learning is always much more fun, perhaps because I have complete control over the pace.' However we never tried to homeschool as we felt that John really needed to learn how to manage in a group situation (however difficult he found it) if he was going to be able to hold down a job in the real world and achieve some measure of independence. In addition we wouldn't have been happy staying at home for years on end, didn't have the knowledge or skills to teach him and couldn't have afforded private tutors. It's impossible to be sure how things would have turned out if we'd educated John alone at home but we felt at the time that he would have become even more isolated from his peers and more of an eccentric. We feel that continuing to stay in the real world has taught John so much (although often in uncomfortable ways), has rubbed many rough corners off and has made it possible for him to learn (over many, many years) how to cope with those very different from himself who happen to be in the majority. He's become an independent, fulfilled and happy adult, living a long way from his parents in his own house and with a permanent job that utilises his strengths. However, according to Stanton (2000):

We may have to develop our own system of flexi-schooling. Many of our young people would do better in a campus situation – selecting from the curriculum options on offer plus additional support for social skills, speech and language etc.

One way this could work is via home schooling. Only instead of working at home and seeing your home school tutor one day a week we could set up a home schooling centre...

If there'd been a small group of us with intelligent children with special needs, who could have shared the cost of tutors, I think Mike Stanton's idea of a homeschooling centre could have been *very* successful. John would have had the high teacher pupil ratio he needed, could have been stretched academically, helped to cope socially and hopefully wouldn't have been bullied. I would have been able to continue to work which would have fulfilled me professionally and would have enabled us to pay for the tutors. Lise Pyles, a parent of a child with Asperger Syndrome who has followed several schooling options on three continents, has found homeschooling with sufficient support to be very successful. As she writes in her book *Hitchhiking through Asperger Syndrome*:

As I think about it, it's clear most schools work from the outside in, where everything is planned ahead of time and students are added in at the last minute irrespective of their needs. Rarely is the child considered first and even more rarely are things looked at from the child's point of view. Ideally it should be the other way round.

Homeschooling, to its credit, does it the other way around. Children are at the centre of the process, not as in 'spoiled and catered to' but also not wedged in as an afterthought. They just naturally work from a base of comfort and security with people they most trust and understand. That frees the child then to reach out to other things – geography, astronomy, learning math and whatever else. It is only one of the reasons why many families of children with Asperger Syndrome choose homeschooling, but it's probably a big reason why so many are astounded at the progress their child makes.

Mainstream school for children on the autism spectrum in the 21st century

Has the experience of mainstream school in the UK improved significantly for children on the autism spectrum since John left school in the mid 1990s? I suspect not as much as one would hope. In 2006, The National Autistic Society (NAS) published a report (based on the views and experiences of 1,271 parents/carers) entitled *make school make sense. Autism and education: the reality for families today.*[60] I found this report particularly depressing given findings such as:

In mainstream school only 23% of parents are satisfied with the level of understanding demonstrated by subject teachers, and almost double this figure (42%) say they are dissatisfied...

Over 40% of children with autism have been bullied at school. Children with Asperger syndrome are particularly vulnerable, with 59% of their parents reporting that they have been bullied. 44% of parents of children who have been bullied feel that the school did not take action to stop the bullying...

1 in 5 children with autism has been excluded from school, and 67% of these have been excluded more than once. 16% had either been excluded more than ten times or so many times that their parents had lost count. 24% of excluded children were excluded permanently.

What is particularly dispiriting is that the NAS found: 'When we compare the answers given in this report with those given in 2000, we find that little has changed.' To celebrate their 50th birthday the NAS published a report based on a survey of 8000 people and called *The way we are: autism in 2012* by Kathrine Bancroft, Amanda Batten, Sarah Lambert and Tom Madders. Yet again the bullying and school exclusion statistics are unacceptable. To quote directly from the report:

Unfortunately, 63% of young people with autism have been bullied at school. This rises to 75% when we look at secondary school age, and 82% of young people with high functioning autism or Asperger syndrome. Schools' responses to bullying vary greatly. While some schools have excellent strategies, others do not always recognise the seriousness of the issue...

27% of children with autism have been excluded from school, compared with 4% of children without autism.

The All-Party Parliamentary Group on Autism (APPGA) produced a report[61] in 2012 in which they found:

> 84% of respondents to our survey said teachers are not given enough training to teach and support children with autism effectively. Concerns about training are particularly high among respondents who were parents or teachers of children with Asperger syndrome or high-functioning autism (89%)...

> The vast majority of survey respondents felt that there is not enough support for teachers in the classroom to allow them to teach children with autism effectively...

> Almost every single case of exclusion from mainstream school could have been avoided were staff more aware of children's needs and were there better planning at the school level to support children with autism.

As I write there is a two year, three-tier training programme being developed by the Autism Education Trust, and funded by the Department of Education, designed to improve autism awareness and knowledge in schools.[62] The programme works through regional training hubs. Tier 1 training, which delivers basic autism awareness to teaching and non-teaching staff, is available free of charge to primary and secondary schools. Hopefully, given time, *all* schools will take advantage of this programme and no child on the autism spectrum will have to cope with school personnel who have no idea how to manage them.

To sum up: John's experience in mainstream schools has been very mixed indeed and largely unsatisfactory. Children like him are very difficult (if not impossible) to teach in large classes and bullying has also been a significant problem. Homeschooling with other clever children in a homeschooling centre with a high teacher/pupil ratio would have been ideal. This option would have enabled John to get the individual help and attention he needed while providing academic challenges and enabling him to learn how to manage within a group.

17

The Computer

I believe that one of the most important lessons to be learned from John's development into a happy and fulfilled adult is that the intense and narrow focus that characterises so many children on the autism spectrum is a *strength* that should be exploited. If at all possible this focus should be gradually steered towards something that can provide fulfilment, friends and a career. Although several authors note that people on the autism spectrum often have a real aptitude for computing, I don't think the benefits of this relationship have been emphasised sufficiently. I'm convinced that introducing John to computers when he was young (as well as teaching him to read) has been the main reason why he's such a contented individual whose life isn't dominated by failure. Computers have remained a passion of John's from the age of seven when he first started using them. In fact the depth of John's feelings for his computers can be judged from the intensity of his reaction when anything goes wrong with one of them:

> I suspect this is a perfectly normal human reaction... to one's *children* getting in trouble. If I ever have children I'm going to have a serious refocusing task ahead of me...

> (My computers *are* my dependants. They are perfect slaves and they are absolutely helpless without me. They need regular care and maintenance and if I don't pay attention they'll take my life over. Oh wait, they did.)

Too many adults on the autism spectrum, or with dyspraxia, are unemployed or are working in jobs that don't utilise their strengths. I become quite upset when I think what life might have been like for our son if he hadn't developed his computing skills. These have provided him with a creative outlet, a perpetual intellectual challenge, some companionship and a career. As for John, 'I... try not to think about it. The possibilities for what might have been... are mostly horrible for me. As it probably is for the 85% or whatever it is who are unemployed.' Without computing, I believe John might have been a very frustrated and unhappy individual, unable to find an outlet for his intelligent problem solving mind, probably unemployed, friendless and for all these reasons, depressed as well. Many people on the autism spectrum who find it difficult to cope with the inconsistencies of the world around them would agree with John:

> Computers are an oasis of consistency and controllability in a chaotic and unpredictable world. Sure, *some* people view them as tools to get work done with, and I'm glad that some people who think like that are willing to pay me money to help them do that at the same time as keeping myself sane, but for me they are a wonderfully predictable comfort blanket first and foremost. *Utility* is a very small part of it... Predictability is a huge part of it.

That isn't to say that the path John took is right for *all* children on the autism spectrum but it would probably suit many. As Attwood (2006) wrote: 'Computers were designed by and for people with Asperger's syndrome.'

289

THE EARLY YEARS

I'd been using computers for my research work as a scientist in the 1960s (long before computers were available at home) and realised that John might really take to computing. He was a logical child who loved machines and programming a computer is a very logical process, though John thinks: 'To me it has always felt more like composition, or perhaps flying (like a bird, not like an airline passenger). There's logic in there, but it's subsumed, just part of the flow.' As a result, we bought John his first computer (a Sinclair ZX81) when he was seven years old. This computer, which was launched in 1981 and discontinued in 1983, was one of the first computers to be available in British shops as a small, ready-assembled machine. There was no colour or sound, very little memory, a horrible plastic membrane keyboard (apparently the word Sinclair aficionados use is 'memorable') and no monitor; the computer had to be connected to a television. There was so little memory that programs were loaded via an audio cassette recorder and of course there wasn't any internet access at the time. I was fortunate enough to find several books for children on computer programming in BASIC (the computer language understood by the ZX81), published by the marvellous children's publisher Usborne. These books (like everything they produced) were beautifully illustrated, humorous and very well laid out, with clear ideas and language pitched at just the right level for a young enquiring mind. We started on the simplest book and John immediately took to the whole idea of programming a computer to make it do what he wanted. As he typed in some commands these were echoed back on the television screen in front of him and as John still remembers: 'Just the 'echoed back' part had me hooked, I think. It was like handwriting only it didn't hurt, it was nearly effortless, and it looked a lot more readable.' I can still remember John's amazement and pleasure when he typed in his first very simple program and the computer worked out the right answer. In John's words:

> That high has me hooked to this day. Illegal drugs are *boring* compared to the joy of creation and seeing my creations run, free of me and working nonetheless. OK, free of me and falling over with bugs nonetheless. But all the bugs in there are mistakes on my part: if I made no mistakes, it would work perfectly.

For the first time in his life John was really in control and capable of making things happen, although according to him it would be more accurate to say: 'I could make things happen even before then, but now I could make things go *right!*' Until then John's poor motor coordination meant that everything was a struggle and he never felt in control; even drawing a picture or using Lego were beyond him.

After a remarkably short time John didn't need any more programming help from me as his knowledge was already greater than mine. As John said, a few years ago: 'I've been learning constantly for nearly thirty years since then, and there is *still* so very much more to learn. For a lover of complexity there is no better field.' We started to buy him all sorts of technical magazines and books about computing and with the aid of these he taught himself a considerable amount; undoubtedly this has stood him in good stead to this day. Because the ZX81 was so short of memory John learned to write programs in a very efficient way. These ran as fast as possible whilst using a minimum amount of memory. As John said:

The ZX81 was a lovely little box, more portable than any portable computer made before 1998, as long as you didn't mind the lack of battery or screen when you carried it around. I learned a lot about compact coding techniques on that box.

NEXT STEPS

After a few years we bought John a Commodore 64 which he used until he was 13. He was very unhappy with the programming language on this computer and spent a lot of time writing his own! During this time John acquired many games on cassette, continued to subscribe to several computing magazines and bought quite a few computer manuals. The magazines had large program listings for various games which he would type laboriously into his computer.

When John was 12 we bought our first PC but he found it very inadequate in many ways. Nevertheless he continued to develop his programming skills on it. I used to share this computer with him and remember the occasion when I couldn't log on; John had written a security system which stopped me from accessing the computer at certain times of day! We bought John's first really good computer when he was 15. It was expensive at the time and John and I did our research very carefully. It was quite obvious that computing was going to be John's career and it was important that he had a machine which would allow him to develop his skills fully. This computer was such a good buy that John continued to use it for another 12 years.

John has bought several computers since he left home and has a few networked in his home. He's able to access his computer system remotely when he stays with us, although our home is about two hundred and fifty miles away from his. Wonderful stuff, technology! I rely on him totally for advice when things go wrong on *my* computer, for telling me what upgrades to install and for ensuring that my laptop's security software and virus checkers are kept up to date. His help was invaluable when this book was published on Amazon.

SHOULD COMPUTER ACCESS BE LIMITED?

Quite a few authors, while pointing out that many children on the autism spectrum love computers, also have warnings about rationing the child's access in case the computer becomes an obsession. For example Lorna Wing (1996) wrote:

Computers and computer games are particularly fascinating even to some who have few skills in other areas... The disadvantage is that computer activities can easily become a dominant obsession, so parents should, from the start, impose clear limits on the time allowed.

While Williams and Wright (2004) write:

Sometimes children with ASD [autism spectrum disorder] respond well to information on a computer screen. There are many games and teaching programmes readily available... At one time it was thought that the use of computers would automatically lead to the children developing obsessions about computers and hence would reduce their social contact. In fact, the use of computers often helps to encourage communication as many children are greatly motivated by them and are keen to ask for help and share their enjoyment. It is important, however, to offer several alternative activities and to be cautious about allowing your child too much time exclusively on the computer as obsessions can easily develop.

What does John think about the views expressed by the above authors on rationing computer access?

I sort of see what they're driving at, I think. From one perspective, in which the be-all and end-all is promoting normal behaviour and improving social function even if this damages specific strengths, it makes sense...

However, as you comment further on, I'm not sure I'd have stayed sane and avoided depression without a computer: when all around was homework and horrible teachers and bullying and loneliness, the computer gave me a place I controlled completely and could call my own.

I consider computer *games* completely different here. Games are probably much less of a benison and much less useful than programming, especially programming a system like the ZX81 which was simple enough to grasp in its entirety in a reasonably short time (modern systems are far too complex to grasp in totality in a lifetime: you have to learn small pieces of them instead, and trust that the rest works).[63] In a game, the sense of control is intentionally reduced by the game designers, and most games are in a real sense a closed system aimed at neurotypical players. (A lot of online games aren't such a closed system... but the emphasis in those is on social interaction, because that's what neurotypicals are obsessed with. I don't know if they're a good fit for other aspergics but they certainly aren't a good fit for *me*.)

Some authors advise concentrating on a child's strengths but for children who love computers, limiting access could make it hard to carry out this advice. As John explains:

Computers are so complex that it takes many years of intense effort to get any good at them, in which time they are changing and adding yet more to learn... If you restrict access to prevent obsession you also prevent excellence, it's that simple. The same is probably true in other fields with massive amounts to learn, like mathematics, but at least mathematics doesn't change so fast that if you learn too slowly you fall behind!

My views on obsessions have been described forcefully in Chapter 13, as I think these should, wherever possible, be exploited rather than restricted. I agree though that an obsession which *completely* takes over one's life is (like any addiction) harmful and shouldn't be encouraged. As Luke Jackson, a teenager with Asperger's syndrome, wrote in 2002:

Mum says that something becomes an addiction or obsession when it takes an unreasonable place in your life. If something dominates your thoughts and behaviours to such an extent that the rest of your life is being interfered with, then that is the time to find ways to modify your behaviour and try to 'wean yourself off it'.

Education at home in computer safety[64] and ethics is crucial so that those spending time on the computer understand the difference between right and wrong. It's particularly important that children on the autism spectrum (who can be socially naive) are educated in computer safety so they don't become the victims of predatory paedophiles, scammers, identity thieves etc. on the internet. Naïvety could also mean that teenagers or adults on the autism spectrum find themselves working, perhaps unwittingly, for criminals who use the autistic person's computer skills to engage in a variety of unlawful activities such as the theft of money or business secrets. It's crucial that anyone with advanced computer skills is made fully aware of the potential penalties should their computer interests lead them into illegal activities, such as hacking into military installations. The Gary McKinnon[65] situation is a very sad case in point. There's a real danger that someone sitting in their bedroom working away on their computer can forget that some of the things they are doing may actually be having an impact in the real world. Computer expertise can be thought of as a very powerful weapon and like any weapon, the user *has* to learn to handle it responsibly. According to John:

> The rule I've always followed is that if I'm making changes on another person's system or looking at part of their system which they did not mean for the general public to look at, I need permission. That's not actually what the law says (it's much more ambiguous), but it's sufficient to not annoy people, and if people aren't annoyed they aren't going to throw the law at you. The downside is that this requires enough social nous to figure out whether part of someone else's system is meant to be public-facing, as well as enough technical nous to figure out that what you're doing is on another person's system in the first place. These days computer time or virtual machines are often rented from other organizations (like Amazon's S3) and that makes things even more complicated.

Do *I* think computer access should be limited and if so to what extent? I believe that *if* homework (and anything else that parents want their children to do) has been carried out already, then children should be allowed to use their free time as they think fit, particularly at the weekends and in the school holidays. We all need time to wind down and relax and I don't see why children should be any different. I consider that children who love computers should be allowed as much time and given as much help as possible in order to develop their computing skills as well as time to play games. Is spending time on a computer really worse than hours spent reading, playing chess, sports training or practising a musical instrument or ballet? Why should some skills be encouraged and approved of whereas others are frowned on? It feels like some outdated prejudice along the lines of 'everything was better in the good old days'. As John explains:

> Yeah, well, you know, people who use computers are pathetic geeks. This attitude lasted until the dotcom boom, when everyone seemed to notice that a lot of the pathetic geeks seemed to have become very rich. (A good few of those geeks didn't care very much, but a lot of neurotypicals appear to be fixated on money to a degree that would be considered a pathological obsession if an autistic did it.)

I know that relatively unrestricted computer time goes against the advice of many experts and I'm not rational about this myself; I wouldn't like children spending hours and hours watching television! I agree with Luke Jackson though that television is a very passive activity, whilst computing is far from passive. There are some computer activities (such as watching YouTube videos) which fall into the same passive category as watching television and I wouldn't be happy with unrestricted time on these. However nothing is ever quite so simple. According to Ozonoff et al (2002): 'Many parents report that their child will stay at the computer for hours, not breaking to go to the toilet, to eat or to sleep unless pressurised, and even then with much resistance.' According to John:

> Several reports have come in (mostly from South Korea, for some reason) of people getting so obsessed that they stay at the computer until they die of thirst. This is probably going a good bit too far. Sheer statistics makes it quite likely that I will die at my computer, but I'm not going to die there because I forgot to drink!

I don't think parents should *ever* find themselves in a position where a child is calling all the shots. I definitely wouldn't be happy with a child playing nothing but the same computer game all day every day for years on end. Apparently there have been many occasions when John (as an adult) has been unaware of his bodily functions whilst immersed in some programming project, as he explains:

> Yeah, well, this has happened to me, but simply because I don't *notice* mere biology until it gets fairly extreme, not when the silicon mist descends and time vanishes into the maw of creation unleashed. (why yes, programming *is* a fairly lyrical experience for me. Not for nothing did I compare it to composition!)

As a teenager John really disliked going to the house of one of his friends (Nigel) because his mother was very strict and would limit the time they spent on the computer which made John very angry. According to John though: 'It wasn't the limiting that annoyed me: it was the lack of reason for it, and the horrible way the atmosphere froze whenever she opened her mouth. Homes should not be dictatorships.' In the other houses he visited (and in our house) there was no time limitation, provided homework and other jobs had been done satisfactorily. I suspect some parents would disagree with my approach but I felt it was right for John; he was so happy and relaxed while he was on the computer and his passion for it never stopped him wanting to do other things with us. John was only separated from his computer for a significant period of time when we went on our three week camping holidays in the summer. Although he loved camping, he really missed his computer. However he adapted well to the situation, spending some of his time thinking about and then writing designs for new computer programs on paper.

BENEFITS OF THE COMPUTER – PSYCHOLOGICAL

Computing in its various guises has contributed enormously to John's happiness, although as he points out:

> Note what it's predicated on? The ability to read. Computer programmers are people of words: we read and write (as in 'produce words', not as in 'handwrite') enormous amounts, all the time. If reading and writing aren't nearly effortless, there is no way you can ever get the same benefits from a computer that I did. (You can probably still get certain benefits from computer games.)

As described in later sections of this chapter, the intellectual and creative stimulation that programming provides, the companionship and feelings of belonging that the internet provides and the fact that he has a career that pays the bills and utilises his strengths all contribute massively to John's emotional well being. Given that so many adults on the autism spectrum suffer from depression it makes me really happy that I was fortunate enough to find something that has given John so much long-term fulfilment. I suspect he might have become very depressed during his secondary school years if it hadn't been for the pleasure and respite he derived by using his computer every day at home. John believes: '[The fact] that I survived... [secondary school] without getting depressed suggest that I am depression-proof, at least as long as there is a computer available!' The feelings of control and consequent pleasure that John experienced when he wrote his first simple BASIC program as a seven year old have never left him. So much of what we experience depends on others or on external events; it's very healthy psychologically to feel that one has real control of some part of one's life. In John's case, it's his interaction with the computer that gives him these feelings, whether it's working on some programming project, deciding which newsgroup he will catch up on or who he will communicate with. Penny Benford (2008), writing in her PhD thesis *The use of internet-based communication by people with autism*[66] noted:

> One's success as a communicator depends on how much control one can exert over the interaction. Communication is a complex process and there are many interconnecting levels at which control can be lost.

> Online communication can restore some control to the process of communicating with other people.

As an adult, John also uses the computer as an aid to help him overcome his poor short term memory and his hopeless organisational abilities. This adds to his feelings of being in control and lessens the 'cock-ups' with their associated feelings of panic. John has a computerised 'to do' list, controls his finances on the computer, buys goods and sends himself emails and automated reminders. He also keeps a record of all his internet communications which he can refer to whenever he needs.

If you're unfortunate enough to be in a position like John, where your abilities are very patchy, you will be continually aware of your 'failures' and it's very easy for your feelings of self-worth to take a severe knock. His poor manual skills meant John may have felt like a failure as soon as he started nursery school, seeing other children draw and make things which he couldn't even attempt. By the time John left secondary school at 18 his self-esteem was at rock-bottom where 'it had been for some years'. He began to feel much better about himself when he went to university to study computer science and found that now he was spending his time doing things he was good at. As he said: 'It [self-esteem] recovered fast as soon as I hit university. The combination of the net and doing stuff I enjoyed all the time ensured that.' Like all of us, John's sense of well-being is enhanced by his ability to do something really well. The positive feelings that come with mastering any skill and continually trying to improve are very valuable and provide an important contribution to any feelings of self-worth.

John has always been a very kind person and from childhood he's enjoyed helping others with their computer problems, probably the only area in which he actually felt competent enough to be of assistance. It must have been very rewarding for him to be able to help others in this way. As he wrote: 'I did it because it feels good to do it, and because it's just about the only thing I could do that made people happy.' It was quite moving to see, on the card he was presented with when he left his last job, how many people had thanked him for his help. According to Attwood (2006):

> An interest in computers can be popular with peers and there can be great delight in being sought after for advice or ability to repair a computer 'crash', or to develop a new computer program or graphic. This can provide a rare moment of being genuinely needed and valued by others. A small group of friends can form at school, based on a common interest in computers, and within this group the person can make genuine friends.

John's computing knowledge was the one thing that people actually respected him for and this is bound to have made him feel good about himself. As Ozonoff et al (2002) wrote: 'Helping others is often a very successful way to build self-esteem and self-efficacy.' John agrees with this and says it spurs him on to keep improving his skills:

> This remains true to this day, but I'm happy to be respected for one thing. It just means I have to be really *really* good at it. All this means is that I have to spend much of my spare time learning stuff, which is a pile of fun.

When John writes a new computer program and releases it into the free software community where it can be of use to others, he feels that he has 'made a difference', something that many of us can find hard to achieve. The emotional satisfaction that John derives from the process is revealed in the following:

> It means other people have benefited, and that the code is free and can potentially outlive me. This is every bit as important, I think. The rest of you have immortality through children: I have to aim for immortality through code!

BENEFITS OF THE COMPUTER – SOCIAL

Close Friends

Although children and adults on the autism spectrum enjoy their own company and have difficulties with social communication, they're often quite sociable and want to have friends. It's tragic that many of them find themselves lonely, isolated and misunderstood. John could easily have been in this position but fortunately, because of a shared interest in computing, he's never been lonely despite his poor social skills. In fact John's passion for computing has meant that he's always had a few really good friends; spending time with them has helped him to learn how to take turns and to consider other people's needs. John put it very clearly when he said a few years ago: 'I don't think I've ever done anything with *anyone* in my spare time after I hit secondary school apart from computing. Computers are a universe unto themselves, and quite rich enough for me.' More recently though, John sent me an email in which he said that the above was 'not true any more! SF and (now) sceptic stuff: my friendship with M... is *not* based on computing, for instance.' Tony Attwood (2006) really hit the nail on the head when writing about a child who had a passion for ants:

> Shared interests are a basis for friendship... His peers tolerated his enthusiasm and monologues on ants, but he was not regarded as a potential friend as there

was a limit to their enthusiasm for the topic... By chance another child with Asperger's syndrome lived close by, and also had an interest in ants... When observing their interactions, it was clear that there was a natural balance to the conversation, with both children being able to wait patiently, listen attentively, show empathy and give compliments at a level not observed when they were with their typical peers.

From the age of about nine through to leaving home at 18, John had the same three friends (Phil, Harry and Nigel) that he saw regularly at weekends and in the school holidays. The closest friend, Phil, lived about thirty minutes walking distance away and was in the year below John at primary school. One day, when John was about nine years old, I was working in the front garden when a lady whom I'd never met before walked past our house with her two boys. We started to chat and I happened to mention how keen John was on computing; she said her elder son Phil was too. I invited him into the house to spend time with John on the computer and from then on they were almost inseparable. Phil often stayed the night in the holidays when John was a teenager and both boys spent hours at a time working hard on their large, ongoing, self-generated computer programming projects. John believes his current work is still heavily influenced by the time he spent with Phil in his teens. John says he had the same sort of feelings towards Phil as he would have had towards a brother.

The relationship with the other two boys was different. Harry was also a close friend who was in John's class at primary school and then went to the same secondary school. They lived too far away from each other to be able walk to each other's houses easily and depended on lifts. John and Harry also spent a lot of time together on their own computer projects; these tended to involve Harry's ideas while John did the computer programming. However they also spent time on other things such as 'role playing game stuff, involving miniatures and fiercely complicated rules' all of which would have been initiated by Harry. Harry was a very talented artist as well as a very bright boy and he introduced John to drawing cartoons – the only time John has ever enjoyed drawing. Although computing was the common interest that had enabled these boys to become friends, they were able to enjoy other activities together as well.

Nigel went to a different school and wasn't such a close friend as Phil and Harry. John saw Nigel regularly for many years but not nearly as often as Phil and Harry. When they did visit each other it was usually for the whole day and they both seemed to enjoy themselves a lot. As Nigel's mother recalls: 'When John and Nigel used to spend a day together, both were totally engrossed in the computer. It was difficult to drag them away, even for meals!' Recently John wrote: 'Yeah, it was always fun, but I could never quite relax. I couldn't model Nigel at all, while my models of Phil and Harry were pretty good, at least in our areas of shared interest.' The boys didn't get involved in computer projects but spent their time playing 'arcane and complex adventure games' on the computer. When I asked John whether there were winners and losers and did he get upset if he lost, he replied:

> I didn't get upset. These were generally cooperative adventure games. It was us against nature, or rather us against the developers of the original game. If we lost we tried again and treated it as an opportunity to explore earlier branches we hadn't gone down. I think it's the cooperative part that saves it from being annoy-

ing.

I find this statement really interesting coming as it does from someone who has so much difficulty with social communication.

I never worried whether John was involved in heavy computer projects with his friends or whether he was playing games; I was just pleased that he was really happy and having such fun with a friend. John didn't play games very often with Phil or Harry, just now and again as John put it, 'to let off steam'. These games tended to be joystick driven and were probably quite good for John's hand – eye coordination.

Apart from Harry, John had no other close friends at secondary school and none of his peers were interested in computing. One or two teachers acknowledged John's computing skills and asked him to help them with computer related matters but this was a rare exception. According to Attwood, (2006) things might be very different if John was at school now. That would be wonderful – if true – and would support my feelings that a passion for the computer should be encouraged rather than rationed. As Attwood writes:

> Some teenagers and adults with Asperger's syndrome seem to have a natural ability to understand computer languages and computer graphics, and often have advanced computer-programming skills. The interest is appreciated by peers and there is a distinct teenage culture for experts in computers. Such individuals would have previously been considered as nerds and despised by peers but are now popular as they can access cheat codes, solve computer problems and may be portrayed as the hero, not the 'fall guy' in popular films and television programmes.

While John was at university he made, again via computing, another very good friend, Frank; they are still really close. They have the same sort of really satisfying intellectual relationship that John had with Phil. As John wrote: 'One thing's certainly true: I get on with Phil and Frank in about the same way: ideas flying on all sides all the time.' The way they cooperate over a computer project is interesting. As John says:

> I'm a born critic. With both Frank and Phil, they tend to propose ideas and I tend to try as hard as possible to shoot them down from every direction at once. If they survive *that*, they've probably good ideas, so we implement them. This isn't invariable, but I'd say that I only come up with perhaps 1/3rd of the ideas, and shoot perhaps 4/5ths of them down. I think this is because I tend to shoot my own ideas down before ever expressing them.

I suspect it would be quite entertaining (and probably quite exhausting) to be a fly on the wall listening to John and Frank communicate. As John explains:

> Both Frank and I think much faster than we talk, so we have a habit of listening to the first few sentences of what the other person is saying, extrapolating from there, and then criticising the result. Both of us are learning not to do that so much, because generally there's some new nifty factor in the stuff we hadn't heard that makes our extrapolations wrong, so we're criticising a straw man.

I think it's interesting to examine *why* John is so friendly with Frank and why they have such a close relationship. John has spent, and still spends, a considerable amount of his spare time working on (but not usually finishing) computer projects with Frank, either by phone or over the net. They get on so well that they tend to talk to each other on the phone frequently (at times almost every day) not just about computing but also about science fiction, maths, science and politics. As John said: 'When I got to know Frank… we *snapped* together socially with an almost perceptible click. Our interests are still in near-perfect alignment. I guess it's why we talk so often.' John's relationship with Phil and then Frank was/is very stimulating and it's obvious that intellectual interests unite them rather than personal, social or emotional exchanges. When I asked John what he felt about Frank, he wrote:

> Admiration of mental abilities (it's good that I can hone my own on his, I think); his memory and reasoning skills are amazing, and his knowledge is encyclopaedic – more to the point, is encyclopaedic in a number of areas where *mine is not*, and vice versa, so we complement each other well.

> He's a fascinating fount of ideas (and he has that opinion of me, as well, he says) … I'm a neophile, and Frank can always be relied upon to have new and nifty ideas.

According to John, Frank can be 'terribly dogmatic, often without cause' but John likes Frank's sense of humour, although he finds it 'twisted and somewhat hard to trigger'. It would appear that communicating with Frank can be too challenging for John at times; when I asked him whether it made a difference seeing Frank in person or whether he preferred communicating by phone or over the net, he replied:

> Of course it makes a difference, and it's generally better in person: but at least over the net I can sometimes beg off. Frank can be a bit overwhelming and it's useful to be able to stop for a while and relax again.

> Ultrabright people are like that [overwhelming]. He's plainly much smarter than I am: I often find it a challenge to keep up with him, while he doesn't find it a challenge to keep up with me (or with anyone). It's important to surround yourself with people brighter than you are: it keeps you from getting arrogant and gives you something to aim at.

The Internet

As described above, most of John's friendships when he was living at home were with local boys who shared his love of computing and computers; however, once John started using the internet at university, life changed dramatically. If John had been born in the last few years I'm sure he would have been using the internet long before he left home. However in the 1980s the internet wasn't available at home and in the early 1990s it was far too expensive. Rather than facing huge telephone bills or having fights as we tried to ration John's access to the internet, we decided it would be easier not to have it in the house at all. John suspects that once he left home he would have been lonely if it hadn't been for the net. 'So many of my friends (or at least close acquaintances) are physically remote.' According to Benford (2008), this view was shared by many of her interviewees, because the internet 'had enabled many of the users to find a peer group, such that they could feel validated and less isolated'. As described previously in Chapter 11, there's no doubt that the internet has been a wonderful way for John to find and communicate with like-minded people from all over the world. He's found many 'nerdy' people who think in a similar way to himself, which has been a real comfort to someone who's always found himself so different from those around him. As Benford discovered from her interviews with people on the autism spectrum:

> The internet may also enable them to find and contact others with a shared interest...
>
> It seemed to be a more comfortable and reliable way of going about finding others with a common interest, and establishing communication with them.

John has made genuine friends this way, and although they're usually separated geographically, there can be occasions when they meet. For many years, he's belonged to a network of 'geeky' people that he can grouse to or ask for advice if he has a query about something. Benford (2008) also found that online communication can provide support to people on the autism spectrum:

> There are many factors... which contribute to the supportive role online communication can have for the interviewees: being able to express oneself more easily and open up about feelings and personal issues; the enhanced control one felt over communicating when experiencing strong emotions; the feeling of security due to online anonymity; the potential to find others who have similar situations to one's own; and the therapeutic benefit of getting things off one's chest in text. The support which people obtained online may be from a forum, or from individuals.

However she also found: 'For some of the interviewees online support groups could be quite negative and distressing to participate in'. Fortunately John's participation in the online technical network he belongs to hasn't resulted in such negative experiences. In fact (as described in Chapter 11) this network provided invaluable support when John was looking for a new job. The internet has really enabled John to satisfy the human need to belong to a group of like-minded individuals, something that would have been almost impossible to achieve otherwise. As Benford wrote:

> For many people taking part in a group situation was problematic, but online situations could eliminate some of the challenges faced by people with HFA/AS enabling group participation and a sense of involvement.

John's poor social skills and difficulties with reading body language don't matter so much on the net; he can communicate on pretty equal terms using the medium of written language. Again as described in Chapter 11, John has always found groups very difficult to deal with. This is partly due to the fact that he can't hear properly when there is a lot of background chatter but also because he doesn't process conversations fast enough in order to provide timely and relevant input. The use of the internet and especially email completely overcomes these difficulties. He has as much time as he likes to read what others have said and make a considered and thoughtful response, which can be edited before it's sent. Obviously the sensory issues of too much background noise disappear when you are sitting in your own home engaged in an email conversation. This was something that Benford's thesis also emphasised:

> Another way in which many interviewees experienced a lack of control related to

a struggle with conversational aspects such as pace, topic and the timing of turntaking, particularly in a group situation... Online however there is a sense of having more control over these aspects, and hence more of a voice...

Losing control over a communicative interaction can also relate to problems processing incoming information from other speakers, which can be addressed by the permanent and slower nature of online communication...

For many spoken communication could be overwhelming due to sensory overload or difficulties dealing with too many stimuli simultaneously. This overload was affected by extraneous sensory stimuli as well as the stimuli involved in communication, and was particularly problematical in group situations...

There was a feeling that the internet lends itself to more considered and clearer communication...

The availability of a permanent record online also supports the potential for accurate and efficient communication.

On the internet John is no longer at a social disadvantage: his weaknesses are hidden and his strengths maximised. Wonderful! I really believe that everyone on the autism spectrum should be encouraged to find like-minded individuals on the net so they don't have to feel like social outcasts all the time. Tony Attwood (2006) described the situation perfectly when he wrote:

Genuine and long-lasting friendships can develop over the internet based on shared experiences, interests and mutual support. The internet provides an opportunity to meet like-minded individuals who accept the person because of his or her knowledge rather than his or her social persona and appearance...

The internet has become the modern equivalent of the dance hall in terms of an opportunity for young people to meet. The great advantage of this form of communication to the person with Asperger's syndrome is that he or she often has a greater eloquence in disclosing and expressing thoughts and feelings through typing rather than face-to face conversation. In social gatherings the person is expected to be able to listen to and process the other person's speech, often against a background of other conversations, to reply immediately, and simultaneously analyse non-verbal cues such as gestures, facial expression and tone of voice. When using the computer, the person can concentrate on social exchange without being overwhelmed by so many sensory experiences and social signals.

John says it's hardly surprising that the net suits people on the autism spectrum so much 'given that the founders of the net and its social culture were almost purely geeks, nerds and hackers, and that hackerdom tends to turn you into an imitative Aspergic even if you weren't one already'.

The internet is so important to John that it comes pretty close to air, water and food as an essential lifeline, which he would defend vigorously if its essential freedom was threatened in any way. As he says: 'We'll keep it running despite the huge corporations and governments and their constant depressingly predictable and clumsy attempts to take it over and change it to work 'their way'.' In fact the computer and the internet feel like a part of himself to such an extent, that when his system has broken down in some way, the impact is profound and can lead to feelings of depression:

> The feeling is more like controlled panic until things are recovered, but, yes, if the downtime is long, or I can't work on fixing it right away, the lack of stimulation and constant mental running over recovery procedures and possible damage can get me depressed as well.

However it must be stressed that John doesn't like internet features such as web cameras (where his difficulties reading body language would show) or chat rooms and instant messaging websites which rely on instant responses where his slower processing speed would become apparent. As he explains:

> I do sometimes use them, but if you're expecting an instant response from me you're in for a shock... they're OK for one-on-one conversations, but where a lot of people are involved I tend to not contribute at all, because by the time I've thought of something to say, the conversation has flowed on past it.

The traffic flow is so great on most chat and instant messaging sites that John can't respond fast enough to join in the conversation before the topic under discussion has changed. His feelings agree with those expressed by some of the people Benford interviewed:

> For some the real time nature of chat rooms (compared to email) was such that it was too fast and did not afford sufficient processing time. Being able to take one's time did not seem to be so acceptable or feasible here...

John prefers to use the written word on networks that don't require immediate replies so that he has time to think about what he is going to write and structure it properly. However this situation has changed somewhat in the last couple of years since he communicates regularly (and happily) with the rest of his work team (who live all over the world) via several private IRC (internet relay chat) channels. When a message is typed by one person on an IRC channel it can be seen almost immediately by all those who have access to that channel and happen to be looking at it. John copes well with these IRC channels because the number of messages is very low. He finds 'they're quite useful for quick back-and-forth things, but for anything that requires deep thought they're useless'. John doesn't use any social networks such as Facebook, LinkedIn or Twitter and has no use for virtual worlds such as Second Life, where he believes his poor social skills would be as much of a handicap as they are in the real world.

During his twenties and thirties John's social skills have improved enormously. What I find really interesting is that John says that much of this has been due to 'lurking' on the internet, which enabled him to watch how people were interacting. He could read the exchanges between other people on the net while sitting in his own home in a quiet and stress-free environment. He's been able to 'see' how important it is to listen to others, to be careful how you say things so as not to be misunderstood or upset others, to be polite and so on. However John says it's not as simple as that:

> Most of what I've learned is much more abstruse than that, so abstruse that human learning-by-imitation has kicked in and I can't even describe most of what I learned. Things like the flow of conversations, 'practical conversational grammar' if you will – you can't learn that from anywhere except watching it happen. 'It's

important to listen to others' is a platitude that anyone can say – and it's not much use unless you already know it, because the *real* rule is far more complex: if you actually obeyed the rule as stated you'd never get a word in edgeways and the conversation would roll right over the top of you, when it didn't stutter to a halt because everyone was waiting for everyone else. Seeing under what circumstances it is important to listen to others (and all the rest), and seeing how it emerges from the grammar of conversation in use, is a much more important thing. Because it's that grammar that you really have to fit into. The platitudes are just reminders for people who already know the grammar to pay attention to specific bits of it that neurotypicals often skimp on. (More generally, that neurotypical children and teenagers who know the grammar but don't have much experience in its use often skimp on.)

Benford also found that some of her interviewees had benefited from 'lurking' as she records:

> It is also possible online to 'lurk' and take a less involved role in a group situation, something which could be seen negatively in a face-to-face situation, but which had its benefits for some of the interviewees, enabling involvement at a level suitable to their needs...

> For some of the interviewees, their experiences online had increased their confidence in some of their interactions offline.

Many people on the autism spectrum have derived much comfort from groups whose only common interest is the fact that their members are on the spectrum, but this doesn't apply to John:

> Being on the autistic spectrum isn't really an interest of mine, it's just a property of me, so it's only interesting inasmuch as it's a condition with rather unusual properties and I have an insider's view of it. I'm not that interested in hair colour either even though my hair is coloured, and even if it was coloured tartan it would probably not be a *major* interest. I suspect for those people hit harder with the autism stick than I was, having others with similar problems might let them swap coping strategies and so forth: but I always worked them out for myself (or you worked them out for me, when younger). You might be onto something regarding reduction of isolation, but I suspect that'd have more of a benefit for their neurotypical relatives: after all, it was some time before I even noticed that I was isolated!

> But perhaps I'm talking rubbish. After all, a lot of autistics plainly *do* like this sort of thing...

Despite John's views, I think that if John (and his parents) had been able to access such networks when he was in his teens they could have been very helpful indeed. I suspect they could have reduced both his and our feelings of isolation knowing there were many people 'out there' who shared similar experiences at school. In addition they could well have been a source of useful advice as Sophie Walker (2012) found when trying to help her daughter Grace:

> In despair one evening, I posted a plea for help on a parenting website, asking

how I could protect Grace from the seemingly endless bullying and help her construct more robust friendships. The replies flooded in from parents of children with Aspergers or autism. Many offered practical advice...

Grace, meanwhile, has used the internet to make a friend of her own age who also has Asperger's.

According to Gillberg (2002):

Nowadays, many people with Asperger syndrome have found a forum for contact and communication on the internet. There they can 'chat' – in writing – and interact without having to be literally in personal contact. There are now a number of networks in the field of autism spectrum disorders, and several of these are much appreciated by teenagers and adults with Asperger syndrome. In the future, this way of keeping in contact with other people with autism spectrum disorders will almost definitely develop into an important aspect of quality of life, even for some young children.

Specific Software Applications (Apps)

Finally there are other social benefits available as a result of the marvellous advances in technology in recent years. Unfortunately we were unable to take advantage of any of these when John was young but if he was a child now I'm sure we would find some of them very useful. For example (as mentioned previously in Chapter 11), John has found his ability to recognise facial expressions has improved as a result of using Simon Baron-Cohen's excellent computer software product called *Mind Reading*. There are now a large number of iPad apps which can help even profoundly autistic children communicate their needs to their carers. However it can be difficult to decide which apps would be useful and which would be a waste of money. Autism Apps[67] can provide some assistance as explained on their web site:

Autism Apps is simply a comprehensive list of apps that are being used with and by people diagnosed with autism, Down syndrome and other special needs. It also includes links to any available information that can be found for each app. The apps are also separated into over 30 categories, and the descriptions are all searchable, so any type of app is easy to find and download... Autism Apps links to extensive reviews of the apps written by parents, specialists, and other users usually from first-hand experience. Autism Apps also has links to video demonstrations or video reviews of the apps when they are available.

Other recommended web sites with applications for children on the autism spectrum can be found in Appendix 28.

BENEFITS OF THE COMPUTER – MOTOR SKILLS

As described in Chapter 8, John's fine motor skills have never been good. His writing has always been very difficult and tiring to read and very painful for him to produce. I thought that typing programs into a computer and playing games, some with joysticks and some with keystrokes, would improve John's hand-eye coordination and therefore his writing. Indeed I was happy for John to play games on the computer for this very

reason. However John doesn't think his hand-eye coordination for tasks other than computing was helped at all. In fact he goes as far as to say:

> In hindsight this is like giving someone a bath in the fountain of youth in the hope
> that it will reduce their need for anti-wrinkle cream.

> I think this was the only mistake you made. I got good at typing over many years
> but I'm not sure it really helped anything else. (But then it didn't need to: typing is
> a *much* more important job skill than handwriting. I'm fairly sure it was more
> important even in the 1980s.)

Keyboard skills are a necessity for any youngster these day but for a child with poor
coordination and handwriting, the ability to produce written work on a computer is absolutely vital, as this helps to 'level the playing field'. I also think that allowing children
with poor fine motor skills to use a keyboard earlier rather than later is crucial. As Kirby
(1999) wrote in her book about dyspraxia:

> The child with co-ordination problems may have to learn to rely upon the com-
> puter to produce written work. This can be turned into an advantage, in that he
> may become very highly skilled and could consider this as an occupation for life.

Unfortunately for John, the use of the computer at school has been more about an opportunity missed than one exploited. Difficulties such as dyspraxia weren't recognised
when he was at secondary school, although it was perfectly obvious to everyone that
John had real difficulty writing neatly and in any quantity. John obviously still feels
rather bitter about this:

> They considered it not a sign of difficulty but of laziness. I'd say that all that was
> obvious to them was that I was writing slowly and messily. They didn't consider
> that this might be a sign of a problem I was experiencing rather than a problem I
> was intentionally causing them.

John was expected to learn how to write fast and neatly without any help, something
he was incapable of doing. Once he started secondary school at the age of 11 it would
have been enormously helpful if he'd been able to use a computer to take notes in class
and to write all the essays he was given for homework. John would have been able to
produce a reasonable quantity of work in the allotted homework time. As it was he was
only allowed to do homework on the computer from the age of 15 onwards, after I had a
meeting with the head to put forward a carefully prepared case. The first time he was
allowed to take notes on a computer in class was in the sixth form although I don't think
he took many. If John had been allowed to use a computer right through secondary
school it may well have affected his choice of subjects for GCSE. In particular he might
well have taken history far further than he did. As John wrote:

> There was a crunch of things that had to be thrown out and not followed any
> more, but history would have probably survived that crunch if it hadn't been for
> the 'writing out dictation is all you need' attitude of the teachers.

> Nowadays I know that history isn't all about copying down stuff other people
> have written, preferably without understanding or even remembering it, but I
> didn't learn that in school! I have plenty of memories of the horrible lengthy

dictation sessions in history lessons, but I have no clue what we were actually studying: my attention was captured by getting it all down in time and evading the teacher's wrath should I dare to try to skip a bit and rest my hand.

BENEFITS OF THE COMPUTER – INTELLECTUAL AND CREATIVE

The intellectual benefits of the computer have been multiple: John has been able to utilise his creative abilities and pattern spotting skills to the full, has been intellectually challenged and has, via the internet, been able to satisfy his insatiable thirst for knowledge. I'm sure he'd have been very happy going to a virtual school (if they'd existed when he was a teenager) where the lessons were online and he didn't have to cope with the other children.

Because of John's poor fine motor skills, many creative activities such as drawing, painting, and sculpture would have been unlikely pastimes. However writing new computer programs has enabled John to be as creative as he wants. In the same way that a composer can create a new piece of music from a limited number of notes and an author can write a story or poem from a limited number of letters, so John has been able to make something new from a limited set of instructions. For people with a strong creative bent it's essential that their creativity can be adequately expressed in order to avoid frustration and a host of secondary problems. For John, the computer has provided this outlet.

Computing has also enabled John to indulge his love of complex systems and pattern spotting, a characteristic strength of many people on the autism spectrum. As he puts it:

> *Patterns* are the thing; spotting similarities between things and generalizing from them. This is of course a crucial skill in most areas of human endeavour; it's odd that most people are so bad at it, preferring to learn recipes to be mindlessly repeated rather than map out general rules and work from those. I really wish that more people were better at mapping.

The pleasure John obtains when he spots a pattern in a complex system, is clear from an email he sent me in 2004: '*Why* I like complex systems so much, I don't know: it's one with the burst of joy-in-discovery I get when I spot a new generalization when coding and when I fix a bug.' John uses his pattern spotting skills to learn new computer languages extremely rapidly, something most people can't do. According to John:

> Once anyone's learnt a few computer languages it gets much easier to learn more: but most people never learn enough to get them over that initial hump. One thing university did for me was expose me to enough languages to get me over that hump in every major family of languages in existence!

John believes (although he acknowledges 'without much evidence') his *early* introduction to computer programming 'wired something into my brain at some level which doesn't happen so easily if you learn it when you're older'. He's convinced that these early years made an enormous difference and gave him a 'sixth sense' or intuitive feel for computers and how to make them work efficiently. While he was living at home we often saw him with his head stuck in some technical computer manual, the details of which he seemed to absorb like blotting paper soaking up water. However, as John wrote:

Those manuals didn't help with the sixth sense. They told me, as it were, the vocabulary, and how to put sentences together: but the sixth sense is more about how to combine sentences into paragraphs and paragraphs into an essay. As far as anyone knows, you can only really learn that from experience (whether that be writing a lot of working programs, reading a lot of programs in great detail, or reading a lot of essays).

John is a very intelligent person who likes to be intellectually stretched, hates to fail and doesn't like spending too much time engaged on activities that he isn't good at. To this day a significant part of John's waking hours are spent on the computer. Not only does he have a full-time paid job as a programmer but in his spare time he regularly creates new programming projects either for himself or with a close friend. He's also been involved for many years in the free software and open source communities, where projects are worked on by many people over the internet. Computing has been a rapidly developing field throughout John's life and has provided, and will no doubt continue to provide, as much intellectual challenge as he could wish for. There is always new stuff to learn and new projects to work on, either alone or with others. What more could you ask for? I think John is very lucky to have found something he loves so much and which provides such fulfilment.

For a person as hungry for knowledge as John, the information that can be obtained from the internet has been everything he could ever desire. Whenever he wants to find something out he will always use the net, the perfect solution for someone with an enquiring mind. Meanwhile many of the books John reads or films he watches have been recommended by people he respects on a variety of blogs that he follows.

BENEFITS OF THE COMPUTER – CAREER

Even in times of high employment, anyone who is able to work at something they love is very fortunate indeed. Many people have to work in jobs they don't enjoy purely out of necessity and given a chance they would be happy to give them up. When the employment market becomes difficult, then having a job at all, no matter one that utilises one's training and skills, can become problematic. This is particularly the case for those on the autism spectrum; the social skills required to manoeuvre one's way through the interview process can be quite daunting. The possession of outstanding technical skills and knowledge can be one way into employment as such specialised skills can be all too rare. According to John though: 'Good programmers are not rare (though bad ones are, alas, even less rare). This is one reason why I have to keep my skills up to snuff!' Because the social skills of someone on the autism spectrum are likely to remain a weakness, it's crucial that their technical skills are encouraged and allowed to develop fully. As stated previously, allowing a child to spend as much time as they want on their 'special interests' and gently steering these in ways that will make the individual more employable when they grow up, will help. It was certainly John's technical knowledge which helped him find his first job in a computer software company and not his people skills. In 2006 Attwood wrote:

I have noted that some international companies in the information technology area already have a considerably high percentage of specialist staff with undiagnosed Asperger's syndrome, or at least a very similar personality profile... Adults

307

with Asperger's syndrome may congregate in working environments that need expertise in those special interests associated with Asperger's syndrome. Companies that employ engineers and computer specialists may have more employees with Asperger's syndrome than one would expect when considering the prevalence figures in the general population. These employers may create an 'Asperger friendly and appreciative' community.

I don't think that the company John worked for from the time he left university until he was 35 was at all Asperger friendly; however, they found John's amazing knowledge, enthusiasm and loyalty very useful. Unfortunately (as mentioned previously in Chapter 9), they've also been happy to take advantage of the fact that he hasn't attempted to leave and kept his pay well below the market average for his skills. Nevertheless he's been very lucky to have been employed continuously since he left university in a job that he really liked and which enabled him to pay for his mortgage, rail fares and books. Nowadays he works for a very large American computer company, his salary is more respectable and he's able to work in the ideal conditions for someone on the autism spectrum – that is, entirely from home. One of the reasons John likes working from home is that all his communication (except for the weekly phone conference) is text based via the internet. In his previous office based job, John's boss insisted on a considerable amount of detailed technical information being communicated verbally. John found this extremely difficult. The fact that email is used so commonly these days within many organisations has made life much easier for those on their workforce who are on the autism spectrum.

I wonder though whether John would have become such a good programmer if we'd considered computing an 'obsession' and strictly limited its use?

Yes, because I'd have gone obsessive as soon as I left home. But it would have been too late for me to be an expert by the time I got to the workplace: that takes ten years or so of effort in most fields of endeavour, and at least that long in programming. So I suspect I'd have been doing call-centre work or something horribly unpleasant like that for many years.

To conclude: There's no doubt in my mind that exploiting John's ability to focus so intensely on something that interested him, introducing him at an early age to a topic (computer programming) that I thought he would enjoy and then allowing him as much time as he needed to indulge his passion, was the best course of action I could have taken. I can't imagine what life would have been like for John without computers. They have played to his strengths, enabled him to be part of a social group of like-minded individuals and provided him with a challenging and enjoyable way of earning a living.

18
The Arts

When I was growing up, immediately after the second world war, there was no spare money for going to the cinema, theatre, art galleries or concerts. If it hadn't been for the influence of some of the boyfriends I had in my teens, I might never have realised how much these activities would add to the quality of my life. I discovered that paintings, sculpture, films, plays and concerts broadened one's horizons, provided an intellectual challenge, fed the imagination and nourished one's inner spiritual being. I wanted to offer my children the opportunity to experience something similar and tried to open their eyes in a pleasurable way to the wonderful world of the arts. I hoped that artistic creativity would become a normal part of their lives. According to John:

> It has! The art of computer programming, that is. (It doesn't count as an art only because non-geeks are philistines. There are *lots* of art forms you need to learn to appreciate: this is one. Do I actually believe this? Half-and-half. Mathematical proof is definitely an art, if an under-appreciated one, and so are literature and music: programming is in some ways halfway between all three.)

I thought it best to introduce my children to the arts while they were very young and therefore still willing to do what I suggested; teenagers usually want to do their own thing.

Music

Both my husband and I come from families of musicians going back for generations. In fact I met my husband Tony when we sat next to each other in the cello section of an amateur orchestra in London. Given our musical backgrounds it was only natural that I would introduce our children to music early on. Like many mothers I started singing nursery rhymes to both children when they were very young; singing, clapping and doing the actions were all part of the fun.

While John lived at home he heard a considerable amount of live music in the house as I practised the cello on my own or played chamber music with friends. The music room in our second house was directly below John's bedroom; on several occasions he came bursting into the room (often in his pyjamas) unable to contain himself as he said how much he loved a particular tune that was being played at the time. John says he has lovely memories of lying in bed (before he went to sleep) listening to the sound of music coming through the floor boards. In fact he says that 'music always makes me think of home'.

The first musical activities I remember taking the children to were the workshops put on in London by Atarah Ben-Tovim. The children were quite young at the time: Lydia was three and John five. The three of us travelled to the South Bank by train and underground, each carrying a musical instrument such as a triangle, castanets or a tambourine. Atarah is a flautist with a larger-than-life personality and a marvellous way with children. We went several times because our children loved going to see her and both of them thoroughly enjoyed all the participation. As they grew older we took them to all sorts of concerts for children both locally and in London.

Most of the orchestral concerts that I played in took place on a Saturday night and on Saturday afternoons there would be a final rehearsal. My husband used to take both children (from quite a young age) to listen to these afternoon rehearsals. They provided an excellent opportunity for the children to hear, in an informal setting, 'grown-up' music played by a full orchestra. As long as they kept quiet, it didn't matter if they read, walked around, had a snack etc. It was nice for them to see their mum playing with other people and to see and hear some wonderful music being played live. John says he remembers these clearly:

> On the occasions I forgot a book, I had terrible trouble sitting still, until the music caught me up, and then the time just vanished. (Sometimes it never did catch me up, probably due to changes in my own internal state rather than the music itself, and then I was wriggling the whole time). Even when I took a book I rarely read much of it once the music caught me.

We didn't take John to evening concerts where the audience was in the dark as he wouldn't have been able to read and would have found it impossible to keep still enough. However from his twenties onwards John has been able to keep very still indeed in concerts and no longer reads; he listens intently to the music. In recent years he's taken almost half his annual holiday from work to stay with us and go to all the concerts in the marvellous chamber music festival that operates in our locality. He also makes a point of going to as many concerts as possible where he lives and listens to a great deal of music at home. Music has a very calming influence on him as well as helping him think. In fact he uses different types of music for different types of work. According to Williams and Wright: 'Since the social world is so unpredictable, it can produce a lot of anxiety in children with ASD. Reducing anxiety can be very helpful... calming music may help if not disliked by the child'.

I still remember the first recording (*The Planets* by Gustav Holst) which John loved with a passion as a teenager and which he listened to many, many times. As Lorna Wing (1996) wrote: 'Music can be the focus of a repetitive routine. Most autistic people are fascinated by music and may play the same tunes on records, cassettes, or compact discs over and over again.' During the many years I've played in amateur orchestras, I've certainly come across quite a few excellent musicians that I would consider to be somewhere on the autism spectrum.

We'd hoped that John would be able to learn to play a musical instrument as he seemed to be a musical boy but we realised that his poor fine motor skills might cause difficulties. He started piano lessons when he was about seven with an excellent teacher but made very slow progress (despite working hard) because his coordination wasn't up to it. Our first au-pair wrote to us recently: 'I remember he didn't like the days his piano teacher came, and the lessons often ended in tears. He got angry and frustrated when it didn't go his way!' I don't think I ever realised just how upset he became because John never said anything to me, even though I listened to his piano practice every day. After a couple of years or so John gave the piano lessons up. He couldn't manage to play with both hands together, a difficult enough task even for those with no fine motor problems. The whole experience appeared to traumatise his teacher to such an extent that she flatly refused to teach his sister who was very musical, extremely well coordinated and had already been learning the violin for two years. In retrospect it's perhaps not altogether surprising that poor coordination coupled with a perfectionist personality and quite a temper led to such scenes. Would I do the same again and let John have piano lessons knowing what I do now? I must say that on the whole I would be reluctant to put someone through this sort of stress knowingly but John was very keen to learn at the time so that he wouldn't be the only one in the family not playing a musical instrument. According to John that wasn't the only reason:

> I liked the idea of letting the tunes in my head into the world. Alas, it was not to be, and as my exposure to the musical world increased those tunes faded out. (A good thing too: they were nowhere near as good as what real composers can produce.)

Perhaps I should have been more sensitive to his difficulties and encouraged him to give up sooner, or perhaps he should have started on an easier instrument which required less coordination between left and right hands. I asked John recently whether he remembered anything about these lessons. His overwhelming memory was a terrible sense of frustration. He said he 'could hear the music in his head' but when he tried to make his hands play the right notes at the correct time 'everything went wrong'. He remembers that he had major problems trying to coordinate both hands and the difficulties just increased as soon as he had to use more than one finger at a time, as in chords. He says that he's only very recently, in his thirties after decades of practice, been able to type on the computer keyboard with more than two fingers. I know some people recommend piano lessons to help poor fine coordination in general but John thinks that nothing but his fine coordination for piano playing was helped. He doesn't feel it helped his writing at all.

There were no more music lessons until secondary school when John started learning the French horn. He made reasonable progress and after four terms took The Associated Board grade 2 examination, receiving a merit. The examiner's comments included 'warm tonal qualities' and 'rhythmically alert'. Although John really played quite well, making a nice sound, playing in tune and reading music well, he wouldn't play in any ensembles. By the third year his progress had slowed considerably and he still refused to play in any groups. When I asked John why he wouldn't play with anyone else he said he couldn't bear to be seen to make a mistake in public as that would provoke more unwelcome attention from other pupils. He was picked on so much at secondary school that his confidence was very low and it's quite understandable that he didn't want to put himself, yet again, in a vulnerable position. As one can only play one note at a time on the French horn, it really needs to be played with others in order to play most of the music that's been written for it. I'd been listening to John's horn practice every day and tried to accompany him on the piano. However, as I've never had piano lessons I'm a terrible pianist and couldn't do the piano parts justice. I was beginning to find these sessions quite trying and couldn't really see the point of John continuing if he was never going to play with anyone else and only picked the horn up in order to practise for his lessons with me. I asked John if he would prefer to give the horn up, saying he could always come back to it when he was older if he wanted. He has never regretted his decision to stop playing the horn and has never shown any desire to take it up again.

ART

When John was a young child he loved looking at books that contained bright and detailed pictures. We've always had a lot of pictures on the walls of our house and when he was young, John's bedroom wall was covered with brightly coloured pictures, posters and friezes. As a baby/toddler he would enjoy being held in front of a picture on the wall while I talked to him about it. In fact we used to tell babysitters that if John woke up and was distressed they should either read him a story or hold him in front of any of our pictures and talk to him about them; I'm not aware though that he ever woke up and needed this treatment.

Some years ago John read the book *An Exact Mind* by Peter Myers (who has Asperger's syndrome), Simon Baron-Cohen and Sally Wheelwright. This book contains many examples of Peter's work and John found many of the pictures really fascinating. I got in touch with Peter Myers and bought prints of the pictures John had appeared to like so much. Tony and I planned to have these framed and give them to John for a surprise Christmas present. Although John had a few pictures on the walls of his house, including two large prints of paintings of steam trains, a print of an Escher construction and several prints of penguins (a bird he is particularly fond of), he had plenty of picture-free walls left. However just before Christmas, with his present already wrapped up, John suddenly announced, with impeccable timing and not realising what we'd planned to give him, that he really liked having some quiet places on his walls that were picture-free and where he could rest his eyes. He said he found our walls far too busy. He was 34 years old and this was the first time he'd ever expressed such feelings. I always thought John liked our picture-filled walls but it looks as if I may have been mistaken. According to John:

> The pictures are nice individually, but there are just *too many*. There's nowhere my eye can rest unless I look at the ceiling, and I get the impression that if you could have hung pictures there as well, you would…

Nevertheless we *did* give him the pictures and he seemed to like them. Fortunately he still has plenty of spare space on his walls. No more pictures though!

Although I wanted to introduce my children to original works of art while they were young, I was also aware how easy it would be to bore them so much that they would never want to visit a gallery again. These days I see lots of young children in art galleries and there are often activities for them to participate in or handsets with specially created material for them to watch and listen to. However, in the early 1980s I never saw any children in art galleries and there was nothing catering specifically for their needs. My strategy to avoid 'overkill' in the National Gallery, for example, would be to *start* rather than end at the bookshop. Each child was asked to choose any two postcards of paintings in the gallery and inevitably this meant they looked carefully at many others before they made their final decision. Then we would try and find the original pictures, which in a large gallery usually involved lots of detective work. Of course we stopped occasionally if the children found something they particularly wanted to look at on the way. I would ask them simple questions about the pictures we stopped at such as: 'Can you see what so and so is doing?', 'How many animals can you find?' and so on. I'd encourage them to comment on anything they found interesting, strange, funny and so on. I never bothered with the names of the painters and would only mention the fact that the painter might have lived hundreds of years ago if it was really relevant to something they'd noticed. What surprised me, both then and even now, on the rare occasions we happen to see a painting together, was John's amazing eye for detail. For someone who often appeared to be unaware of what was going on around him it always seemed so strange that he could see so much detail, usually far more than I was aware of. According to John: 'That's because wholesale ignoring of everything is the only way to survive in the world. But pictures, pictures are *meant* to be looked at. So I can turn off the filters.' The first time we went to the National Gallery I had no idea what postcards the children would choose but I can still remember being taken completely by surprise when John (aged somewhere between four and five) made his choices. His postcards were both of women, one a beautiful nude and the other entitled *A Grotesque Old Woman*, painted somewhere between 1525 and 1530 by Quinten Massys. This painting is of an extraordinarily ugly woman which (according to the description)[68] was probably intended to satirise old women who try to recreate their youth, rather than as a portrait of a specific person. According to a National Gallery podcast in November 2008, Miranda Hinkley reported:

> The wrinkled subject of one of the best loved paintings in the show, *A Grotesque Old Woman* by Massys, has horrified and delighted generations of viewers, and famously inspired Tenniel's depiction of the Duchess in 'Alice in Wonderland'.

The contrast between John's two choices of picture couldn't have been greater but in retrospect I suppose one can understand the fascination that the very ugly and hence unusual, might hold for an extremely curious child, however politically incorrect this might be. Or did he find this picture funny? John thinks 'I went for it because the incongruity made it funny – a face balanced halfway between woman, man, and orang-utan.'

The Tate Gallery, which had a lot of modern and contemporary art, was particularly popular with our children. In those days there was just one Tate gallery in London but today Tate Modern would provide a similar experience. I remember John being particularly interested in surrealist paintings; the strange images provided lots of opportunity for discussions about dreams and fantasies. According to John: '[Surrealist paintings] remain interesting to me. Something about the disturbance of senses and the wonderful more-intense-than-life colours in a lot of them.'

Did this early immersion in art actually make a long term difference? It's very hard to be sure but as an adult my daughter often goes to major art exhibitions and has a real love of art. John, like my husband, will only look at paintings if someone else organises it, for example on holiday. On those rare occasions he seems to enjoy it, is very observant and makes really interesting and perceptive comments. Regardless of any long term impact, visiting art galleries was a lovely thing to do together and was enjoyed by all of us at the time.

TELEVISION, CINEMA AND THEATRE

Television

Although Lydia (like most children) loved television, John would have been perfectly happy if our home had been a television free zone. When Lydia came home from school the first thing she did after eating was to relax by watching children's television. She found television an excellent way of 'unwinding' and it helped to keep her on the same wavelength as her peers. John *never* watched television when he came home from school. After growing out of his clock watching phase (see Chapter 13), John relaxed after school by reading a book on the loo. He would spend an hour or so reading parts of the book aloud and usually roaring with laughter at anything funny. You could have sworn there were two people in the loo, although given the size of the room that would have almost been a physical impossibility! The need or desire to keep on the same wavelength as his peers would have been a meaningless concept to him when he was younger and something he would have actively resisted as he grew older! Why did John watch so little television as a child? According to him:

It was a combination of several things:

– a smidgen of 'too much happening at once' (particularly in heavy social stuff that I could barely understand anyway)

– a lot of 'non-interactive, I can't go back and review bits I particularly liked'. Compare to my reading, which is *extremely* fractal: I hop backwards and forwards all the time. (Perhaps this is yet more signs of my peculiar lack of attentional control!)

– a *lot* of 'this is boring as hell'. Books or computers were generally a lot more interesting, and a lot more interactive.

John thinks that 'the imagination makes a better camera'. He found (and still finds) the pace of most documentaries on television far too slow and boring and would very rarely watch one, preferring to get his facts from reading. The only factual programmes John watched while he lived at home were some episodes of *Horizon* and *Panorama* when the content interested him. However recently he's acquired some boxed sets of the magnificent David Attenborough wildlife programmes and really loves these, although he says: '[Attenborough] takes things very slowly too, but that's all right because it's plainly an excuse to let the camera pan over some more fantastic shots of whatever-it-is.' Luke Jackson, who as a teenager with Asperger's syndrome wrote *Freaks, Geeks & Asperger Syndrome,* is also not particularly interested in television:

A television is like an extension of real life and real life is actually very difficult to work out sometimes. There are still people interacting with other people, facial expressions to work out, hidden meanings and plots to decipher. Not exactly something I want to spend my leisure time doing – I have enough of that the rest of the day.

John has never possessed a television since he left home. Soaps, reality TV, property and cookery programmes, sport, chat shows and most of the other fare to be found every day on our screens are of absolutely no interest to him. He's also never been much of a radio listener.

Although John enjoyed a few films with us in his teens and twenties, he became so involved and so scared that at times he would hover rather than sit, ready to hide behind the sofa or rush out of the room if he became too frightened. He was so absorbed that he couldn't protect himself from what was happening on the screen by staying slightly removed from the action. He seemed unable to separate reality from fiction. John believes:

> [At this age] I was finally starting to figure out the emotional states imparted by the plot (and displayed by the actors) at a level below intellect, and I couldn't really cope with my own emotions surging in concert. I'm more used to it now.

When he was 28 John wrote:

> If films are too realistic, it's very hard to control visceral responses… When I'm reading a book, I can detach myself emotionally from the unpleasant bits, and throw myself into the nice parts. I can't do that with TV or films, and I don't like things breaking my emotional stability (such as it is) like that.

However if he found the film funny, John didn't get upset. In his teens he would happily watch something like *Inspector Clouseau* with us. As in many of the books John loved as a very young child, the main character is physically clumsy and has all sorts of accidents but everything turns out satisfactorily in the end.

Ever since we moved to the north of England, when John was in his early twenties, he has come to stay with us between Christmas and New Year. There tend to be a lot of films on television at Christmas but for several years he routinely refused to watch any of these with us. He used to sit in the same room reading on my laptop, able to hear what was going on if he chose but not able to see anything. If he didn't like what he heard he would put his earphones on and listen to music. He didn't want to be excluded from the family as he enjoyed the 'cosy feel' of us all together in the sitting room with the Christmas tree and decorations and the wood-burning stove. He even removed the laptop from my study so that he could be with the rest of the family. However to my amazement things gradually started to change. When John was in his late twenties he wrote:

> I can *tolerate* superheroey escapist fantasy stuff; I can *tolerate* stuff like James Bond in which, to be honest, it's the action and the explosions and not anything else that's trying to grip you. Maybe I could tolerate other sorts of films too, or even enjoy them – I remember enjoying 'Eternal Sunshine of the Spotless Mind' – but it's unlikely, on present form, that I'll ever get the time or inclination to watch them. I'm just not a member of the consuming-media universe.

What I've found absolutely fascinating is, from the age of about 30 onwards, John has gradually begun to watch more and more films; when he stays with us he will watch whatever we're looking at. When he moved into a larger house, aged 37, he even turned one room into a home cinema! And it's not just science fiction themed films such as *Eternal Sunshine of the Spotless Mind, Groundhog Day* or *The Truman Show* that he enjoys these days. The person who just a few years previously had said: 'It's unlikely, on present form, that I'll ever get the time or inclination to watch [films]', has watched the entire boxed set of *Buffy* on his own at home, seven seasons containing 178 episodes in all! John has watched these repeatedly and it would appear that his improved ability to cope with the medium of film has resulted directly from watching *Buffy*. Although he says he still finds it 'a strain' he's learned to manage because the *Buffy* 'series runs on emotional roller-coasters, so it's a good set of training wheels'. Apparently the latter part of season five and all of season six are intensely social and emotional. John has managed to train himself to be able to handle his feelings by stopping the film when he gets overcome and replaying the action several times. According to John; 'The emotions in question are things like grief, as well – not easy to deal with, but things which I will alas eventually get hit with, so I'd better get some practice.' Stopping the film gives him time for the content to sink in and for him to think about what has happened. It also enables him to skip any emotionally intense bits which he can't bear to watch. He can dip in and out of the action repeatedly, watching his favourite bits in just the way he rereads books. Repetition leads to familiarity which has helped him to deal with his feelings. John said that he loves the *Buffy* series because of the interaction of the characters, the quality of the dialogue and the humour. He thinks the quality is very high and particularly appreciates the lack of a 'reset' button, which he describes as 'a very common device in episodic TV whereby nothing significant is allowed to change from episode to episode, let alone change *fast*, lest it throw off new viewers'.

John used to be very scathing about science fiction films writing to me in 2004:

> Book SF has completely spoiled me for film sci-fi. 'Good riddance to bad rubbish' *definitely* applies: Hollywood is stuck in the areas that book SF grew out of in the 40s or earlier... these days, much published SF is discussing things like the social consequences of mind uploading and pervasive nanotech, and the consequences of extreme lifespans for society...

> The only thing films *do* do right is stuff inherited from comics, e.g. superhero stuff. And that's not really my cup of tea except when I'm *really* down and *want* some total escapism. And even that is rare. I *can't* watch most sci-fi films now because I can predict essentially all plausible plot turns to a high degree of confidence within the first few minutes... and without the plot turns, what's there to watch? The acting quality? What acting quality?

> Where film sci-fi is concerned, I'm afraid I really do seem to have 'seen it all before'. In SF books.

However this was before he bought (in 2010) the full boxed set of *Babylon 5* (B5) which he thinks has superb plotting. One of the reasons he likes B5 so much 'is that it's so *literary*. B5 was conceived as 'a novel on TV' by someone familiar with the written SF oeuvre and also with a lot of other literature'. John said he really prefers series such as *Buffy* and *Babylon 5* to films, because the series are long enough to allow for sufficient complexity and for development of the characters. A few years ago John bought himself the complete boxed set of the *Yes Minister* and *Yes Prime Minister* series; he enjoys the dry humour enormously. Every time I stayed with John I used to watch a couple of episodes with him until we'd seen the lot and a few favourites more than once. We're currently working our way through the complete series of *The West Wing*, 154 episodes in all!

His preference for DVDs and boxed sets reminds me of Lorna Wing's comments in

1996 about the impact of video recorders on children and adults on the autism spectrum:

> Repetitive acting out of characters and sequences from television series has become fairly common among the children since video recorders have been generally available... Watching video recordings has had a marked effect on the behaviour of children with autistic disorders probably because a video repeats the same events every time it is shown without the slightest variation – the ideal entertainment for the person with autism.

Although I've never seen John engage in the 'repetitive acting out of characters', he does enjoy repeated quoting:

> *Buffy* is very good for quotable lines that can be dropped into random conversations without anyone noticing it. B5, less so: it is much more epic and theatrical, and unless you're a revolutionary or something you're unlikely to see many places in real life where its best lines can be used.

We didn't have a video when John was very young but I suspect that John would have preferred this to television alone. He could have replayed sections as often as he wished in the same way that he reads books and watches the boxed sets of *Buffy* and *Babylon 5*. If I had a child like John today I would encourage him to use DVDs and would watch some with him. I think judicious use of these *might* have helped John recognise and cope with his own emotions as well as those of others at a younger age.

Cinema

We didn't go to the cinema as a family very often because it was so difficult to find something that Lydia liked and John could cope with. He was so unpredictable and could easily ruin the outing for all of us. Although we tried hard not to let John's sensitivities spoil things for his sister Lydia, she certainly feels she missed out in some ways and the absence of cinema visits was a typical example. I remember that we found a few films in the cinema that we could all enjoy: *Beethoven* (a story about a large dog) and *ET* were reasonably successful. However a close childhood friend of our children, who saw *ET* with us, recalls: 'John was so upset by the sad part of the film he had to be taken out of the cinema.' Meanwhile our second au-pair, Ingrid, remembers:

> John could be very embarrassing when we were out at the cinema or theatre as he used to talk and comment all the time during the performance and scream loudly and jump up from his seat whenever anything exciting happened. It used to be a struggle to get him to sit down again. This used to annoy other people around us.

The day we went to see the film *American Beauty* stands out in my memory. John was now in his mid-twenties and we were spending time together as a family in order to celebrate Lydia's birthday. She particularly wanted us to see this film which she'd already seen once and loved. I was a bit concerned that John wouldn't like the film (as it didn't have a gripping plot with lots of action) and I didn't want him to make a scene and spoil the film for all of us. However it *was* Lydia's birthday and she really wanted us to see this particular film with her and wasn't feeling in a mood to accommodate her brother yet again. So in we went and sat with John on one side of me, Lydia on the other and my husband on the other side of Lydia, as far away as possible from his son! My normally tolerant husband couldn't bear the way John would constantly wriggle and shuffle in his seat and possibly talk. Although by that age John could sit very still when he was absorbed, you could never be entirely sure that he wouldn't get upset by something. By sitting next to John I could calm him down if he became too agitated and stop him moving just by putting my hand on his and possibly talking to him quietly. On this particular occasion I became very aware, after only a few minutes into the film, of John's increasing discomfort; he was wriggling and muttering angrily until I suggested that he might prefer to go into the foyer and read. He left his seat with great relief and was perfectly happy and relaxed sitting in the foyer reading until the film was over. For those who haven't seen this film, it concerns a man having a mid-life crisis, his teenage daughter and his unhappy wife. The social and emotional content was just too much for John at the time. When I asked him some years later why he'd been unable to cope with this film he wrote: 'It was a purely visceral reaction: intense formless fear and terror, and rapidly intensifying melancholia which took about a day to lift.'

The other films I remember going to see with John when he was older were *The Fellowship of the Ring* and *The Two Towers*. These are the first two of the three hugely popular films based on the Tolkien *Lord of the Rings* trilogy, which John loves and has read many times. He enjoyed the first film enough to be prepared to go to the second but this one proved to be quite another matter. John hated the changes made to the plot, muttering angrily much of the time. I thought he'd leave but he stayed in order to see just what the film maker had done with the script, or in his words: 'More a sort of fascinated horror at what corruptions they'd introduce next. Hey, let's twist the story.' He appreciated that 'you must have omissions in something that long, and I think the omissions were in general well-chosen throughout the film' but felt 'they actually went out of their way, including *adding* stuff, to destroy the motivations of major characters, to wreck the best scenes in the book'. He never went to see the third film, *The Return of the King*, although he says it is apparently 'superb, if you're not a flaming pedant like me'.

Theatre

For some reason the theatre never caused John the distress that films did. Perhaps it was easier for him to separate fiction from reality. Both our children really enjoyed the magical atmosphere of a theatre and the amazing way one can be transported into another world. Initially we went to afternoon productions which were written specially for children but when John and Lydia were in their teens we often took them with us to adult plays in the evening. We all enjoyed these evenings and I think it made our children feel quite grown up, as the absence of other people of their own age was noticeable.

To conclude: Music has always played an important role in John's life, whether it's going to concerts or listening to music while he works on the computer or reads. Much more surprising is the way John has developed from a child who rarely watched television (because he couldn't cope with it) into an adult who has turned one room in his house into a home cinema where he watches huge DVD series for pleasure. I believe the medium of film has played an important role in John's increasing ability to cope in the world of neurotypicals.

19
John's Sister, Lydia

Although John's voice is heard strongly throughout this book, almost everything has been written from *my* point of view. I don't think I ever truly appreciated how much Lydia was affected by having a brother on the autism spectrum. Her contribution to this book has been quite an eyeopener for me.

LYDIA'S RELATIONSHIP WITH JOHN

Lydia was born when John was 19 months old. I tried to keep (as far as possible) to the same routine that had worked so well before Lydia's birth and John seemed to take the arrival of a baby sister in his stride. When they were young, both children seemed to spend a great deal of time together, obviously enjoying each other's company. As mentioned in Chapter 12, they slept in the same room until John started school and John could often be found in Lydia's cot talking to her and showing her how his favourite toys worked. John was so affectionate and loving towards his sister when they were really young that we never guessed that he would have so much trouble relating to children of his own age. As John says:

> Well, yes, I definitely have all the normal human familial-bonding emotions in large quantities. Doesn't mean I know how to interact with peers who aren't automatically well-disposed towards me though.

After John started school the children had a room each and, as far as I'm aware, John never broke Lydia's toys or invaded her personal space. This can be a problem for some siblings of children on the autism spectrum, as Ozonoff, Dawson and McPartland (2002) describe:

> We've heard numerous children complain about their sibling with AS-HFA taking their belongings and failing to respect their personal space. Given the difficulties children with AS-HFA experience in judging personal boundaries and inferring the sentiments of others, it is important for you to intervene and make sure that your typical child has a 'safe' space where prized possessions or personal items can be kept away from prizing eyes and probing hands.

Lydia has many fond memories of playing with John as a child which have been described already in Chapter 12. She remembers John's passionate interests but this aroused no particular feelings in her one way or the other as she thought this was just him; she too had intense interests of her own, such as her Barbie dolls. When Lydia was young she thought 'John was a nice brother' whom she 'loved very much'. When she was six she wrote a sweet story at school (see Appendix 16) which really demonstrates how close she felt to her brother. She recalls that she didn't understand, when she was young, why each of them got a small present on the other child's birthday. Now she realises:

> [It was because John] couldn't cope otherwise when it was her birthday. He

wouldn't understand and think it was unfair. He had a very strong sense of fairness and justice... whereas other children could be told that they would get a present when their birthday came round, he couldn't wait.

In the early years, Lydia says 'John did not cause her a problem' but things got much more difficult for her as John grew older. Her mixed feelings start to show in the letter she wrote to John from Brownie camp when she was eight and a quarter years old: 'I am having a lovely time at camp, but I am missing you a lot. Are you alright, I am because I am not getting thumped.' It would also appear, from the piece of work Lydia wrote at school when she was eight and a half years old, that things had deteriorated. Of course she might have indulged in a degree of artistic licence in order to make the essay more interesting:

All about Myself:

... My brother is ten and his birthday is on... He has got brown eyes and brown hair (which is always messy). He has got brown glasses... His hobbies are going to youth club, playing with Harry, bullying me, shouting and humming to himself. He is very rarely nice to me and that is why I go mad when we are called twins... Altogether I have got a pretty nice family (except for John).

However in the same year Lydia also wrote about her favourite toy, a doll called Susan:

Another time, we were sitting in the garden when a wasp landed on Susan. My brother John thought Susan had been stung: he picked her up, came over to me and put the doll in my lap. Then he ran indoors. A few minutes later, John came out carrying some cream for Susan.

As an adult, John says he is 'very sorry that he was so awful sometimes to Lydia, but he didn't hit her often', and when he did she 'remembered it for ages and never let me forget it'. He also said that she liked to wind him up so that he would lose his temper. Lydia does admit:

Sometimes I would push him on purpose as I knew he would explode. I would wind him up when he was annoying me like a typical annoying brother... I felt quite frustrated at times with him, but don't know exactly why.

John can understand this: 'My explosions were mostly because I was frustrated with *me* and didn't know what to do about it.' Nevertheless, looking back as an adult, Lydia thought:

[They] usually got on really well and the majority of the time he was sweet, gentle, calm, relaxed, clever and funny. He is still extremely kind, with no hint of malice or manipulation – a real rarity. Also hilariously funny.

Although John was usually a very happy child, Lydia was aware of his anger and tantrums from a very young age. She can't remember any details clearly from that time but still retains the feeling of it: 'Chaos erupting and an awareness quite young that I had to be careful/cautious with John as he could suddenly explode, freaking out at unpredictable things.' John thinks:

'Chaos erupting' is exactly the right wording. However, the various panic-stricken newspaper reports that suggest that autistics are dangerous bombs waiting to explode at all times is entirely wrong: the explosions get rarer with time, and I at least took increasing care never to damage anything alive and never to damage anything expensive!

Lydia still remembers the meltdown on the day of my sister's wedding when John was six and she was four. She loved her bridesmaid's dress but John had an enormous tantrum when he was being dressed in his page boy's suit which he decided he wasn't going to wear. I don't remember how we eventually managed to persuade him to put these clothes on and you'd never know from the lovely photos of the wedding just how much effort had gone into dressing him. Recently I asked John if he remembered anything about my sister's wedding day. He still has a very clear recollection of hating the feel of the bow tie around his neck and the closely fitting waistcoat; he wasn't used to wearing either of these. I suppose (with hindsight) we should have allowed John to wear these clothes several times before the wedding but they would probably have looked the worse for wear by the time the wedding came. Lydia also 'vaguely remembers a humdinger of a meltdown in the street' but doesn't know why this took place. I suspect this may have been the incident (already described in Chapter 9) when the au-pair wanted to take John home from school by a different route. As Lydia grew older, she recalls:

[John would get] fearful, panicky and upset and his voice would get very, very loud. He'd go red in the face, his face would scrunch up, he'd look tearful and his whole body and face would seem to hold the most incredible amount of tension. He'd shake his fists and stamp his feet, yell and roar. When it happened in public everyone would turn to look and I'd want to disappear! Dad too I think. I think I was quite affected by the outbursts, and am very tuned into it in others, particularly in people who suddenly explode!... John would take a lot of talking down. Often the talking would make things worse and he'd get more and more wound up. It'd gradually die away – maybe because someone had said something that calmed him down but more likely because his fight or flight response started to die down (that level of response can't be maintained at a high level for too long). He often used the 'flight' bit and would run away from the 'threat', (e.g., during an emotional film or embarrassing TV programme). Sometimes he had enjoyed something (e.g... roller-coasters) until an aversive experience put him off (the aversive experience could be something very mild that most people wouldn't have been bothered by).

Lydia told me recently that she remembers desperately wanting John to watch television with the rest of us, all together as a family. She recalls, that even if he tried to watch something with us, at a certain point in almost everything a cushion would get thrown across the room, the spinning chair he often sat on would spin round and he would be off through the door which would slam shut. She remembers trying so hard to get him back but with little success. She believes that he couldn't cope with films and television where there was too much emotion or where something unpleasant was happening. She feels that he 'was overwhelmed by his emotions so that he couldn't cope any more and also became overwhelmed by other people's expressed emotions'.

Lydia isn't sure when she first noticed that John was 'different' from other children that she knew:

> [But] definitely by the time the au-pairs came, particularly when they struggled with him. Seeing John through the eyes of a stranger living in the family made some of his quirks more apparent, as we'd all just tended to get on with things and accept him for who he was.

Our first au-pair arrived when John was eight and Lydia, six and a half. Lydia says the 'difference' didn't trouble her unduly. Partly because John was born in the nineteen seventies he wasn't diagnosed with anything so we didn't have any diagnosis to explain to her and she never had any worries about 'catching anything'. Lorna Wing notes:

> The siblings, before they understand the nature of autism, may worry about the possibility of themselves developing autistic behaviour. They may have all kinds of alarming fears and fantasies and parents need to be sensitive to these feelings. They can help by their calm acceptance of all their children, their willingness to discuss and to explain and their love and reassurance.

Lydia feels John's appearance actually changed from being a cute young child, who didn't look different to others, to an older child with glasses, unkempt hair, tatty clothes and poor posture who stood out as different. She noticed how much John was excluded by some children. For example she remembers the incident at the airfield playground (described previously in Chapter 12) where other children seemed to size John up in seconds and decide he was too weird to play with. As far as John the adult is concerned:

> Nobody can ostracise like a child. I wouldn't have noticed the airfield thing though, I didn't want to go into that playground anyway, I wanted to go onto the roof of the car!

(The irony of children at a *flying display* deciding a child is too weird to play with, when their own parents are probably every bit as weird on flying-related subjects, is palpable.)

Lydia also recalls how John was excluded by the other participants during the one week summer camp they attended together one year and the drama week they attended at another time. Even some of the local children, who used a converted garden shed at the bottom of our garden as a club house, ostracised him (see Chapter 12). Lydia says this behaviour led to her ending the gang. Sometimes Lydia thought John was just being difficult and wished he would just get on with things instead of creating so much fuss and drawing so much attention to himself. Fortunately the children who had been coming round to our house to play for many years knew him well and accepted him as he was.

Lydia doesn't remember being embarrassed by John until he started secondary school. This was situated very near to the school Lydia had attended since she was seven. This meant she saw much more of him during the school day, particularly on the school bus. According to John:

> [This meant] she got to see high-tension me for the first time, with emergency pressure-relieving mechanisms on full blast, while *she* was nicely settled in. But nonetheless to admit to being related to *that* thing. What a dilemma.

As Lydia recalls:

I was very embarrassed at times, by the way he looked (dishevelled, slouched, odd posture/movements with arms/twitches), talked (loud, fast, boffin-y) and behaved (head in book, even when walking, laughing and talking to self, tantrums). I never talked about how I felt about being his sister and was very ashamed by my feelings. I didn't admit them to anyone (including myself) until I wrote that piece of coursework for my GCSEs. [see Appendix 17]. It was awful seeing people behaving cruelly to him and hearing them say some of the things I'd thought myself at times. I'd compensate by leaping to his defence and walking with him, listening to him and not reacting in an odd way. I guess this was partly compensation and partly a feeling of injustice. I still do it, to demonstrate to other people an alternative way to interact with him. I've noticed that people relax, stop staring and nudging each other and are much nicer and more patient with John when I go out of my way to demonstrate patience, kindness etc... However, there were times when I was too tired to walk with him and deal with him, and there still are... I never hid the fact that John was my brother, even though it led to some fairly excruciating moments where someone would be saying something nasty about him to me and I'd say 'he's my brother', in a very matter-of-fact way, thereby having the effect of cutting them completely dead. I notice people's reactions to John more than anyone (the rest of you have generally been utterly oblivious or not present in the situations in which things occur). I'm very sharp with anyone I notice talking about him, being rude to him or even looking at him strangely. This has happened in a number of countries, and my drop-dead glower and extensive knowledge of foreign swear-words has proved invaluable. There have been many times when I could have got into real trouble in the past for defending John, but people have always backed off. I think this is because they feel too ashamed of being caught out to carry on, and because I look like a 'normal', albeit a furious one.

As far as John was concerned though Lydia had no reason to be ashamed about her thoughts:

The difference is, she didn't say it, she didn't think it all the time, and she wasn't using it as a weapon to assist in social bonding. If she'd been attacking me as a way to ingratiate herself with others, *then* she would have been justified in being ashamed.

As for leaping to his defence, John says: '[It was] very much appreciated! I felt a bit less alone when I knew she was on the coach – also I knew her presence would stop people from doing anything *too* outrageously awful.' A friend of mine wrote that 'Lydia seemed part of John's support network'. John is very grateful that Lydia still leaps to his defence although as he says: 'I hope I am sometimes normal-seeming enough for normal interactions regardless, these days.' As for all the family being 'utterly oblivious' John wonders:

Gosh, could she be talking about me? I did increasingly notice people's reactions to me as I grew older – I just didn't think there was anything I could do to make people who were reacting like that like me at all. Best just to avoid them.

Lydia was a 'protective lioness' with him for as long as she can remember and it hurt her immensely to see John being ostracised and bullied. She thought it hugely unfair that people wouldn't give him a chance and see in him what she did. She could see that John was upset, confused and hurt by the way his peers and teachers treated him (particularly at secondary school) and she could also see that he had very few friends. She thinks he had more friends at primary school, especially girls, who probably found his gentleness and sensitivity appealing. Lydia remembers that the boys at his secondary school 'were brutal. It was bully or be bullied apparently.' As John sees it:

> The teachers' priority in a school like that is conformity: there are too few of them to deal with people as individuals. The children meanwhile, largely unmonitored by dint of sheer numbers, evolve their own society, and it's as nasty as uncivilized primate societies usually are. I suspect the really nasty teachers went to the same sort of school when they were young, and were still employing the same techniques, attacking one person who sticks out to ingratiate himself with the rest and that sort of thing, thus both integrating the rest and knocking down a nail that sticks out. If you care only about an easy life and people in the mass, and don't care at all about the children you are teaching as individuals, this technique probably seems quite reasonable. (Also, if you think like this you are a sociopathic monster. [This school] is the only place I've ever been where adults seemed to routinely treat children as the enemy.)

A few years ago John recalled the bullying problems on the school coach and how Lydia put a stop to them once and for all:

> I had a pretty much unchanging seat (a habit I retain to this day on the train), and it was near the front, near the front row where the teachers sat, so nobody dared act up too much there. (It helps that for at least three years my seat-mate had similar ideas, and an SF obsession to rival my own. Alas, I can't recall his name...)

> This is why I generally ran to the coach: to be sure of getting that seat!

> Things broke loose when those spaces were occupied; then I was forced backwards, into the middle strata of the coach, where the mob of boys was. That was unpleasant, but also very rare, because if necessary I'd stay late to avoid it.

> The most severe case [of bullying] I can remember came sometime in the 4th form, I think it was, when I was forced most of the way back, into the regions bordering the Domain of the Girls where I didn't dare sit for reasons of formless unease and because that Domain had a mass of complex cliques and interlocking friendships that I didn't understand at all. The little git who was sitting next to me tried to punch my lights out or something (he was a little fish in one of the groups that used to bully me, and I guess he thought that by beating me up he'd gain in stature, or perhaps just went for me opportunistically), and I'm afraid I hit him so hard in response that I bent his brace. He went crying to the teachers, who were much too canny to believe a word he said: they knew damned well that I wouldn't have been the aggressor.

> (Panic lends strength; it was my one effective defence against the bullies, and almost always stopped them getting physical, because they knew that when I

snapped, I didn't bother with limits...)

Afterwards, I seem to remember that Lydia had a word with him. I didn't hear what she said, but she told me afterwards that it was something along the lines of 'you do that again and I'll beat you up and then spread the word around the school that you were beaten up by a girl'. I never had *any* trouble on the coach again, from anyone. Not a whit!

I still think that was a lovely thing for her to do: valour far beyond the call of familial duty.

As a child, Lydia was always very advanced for her age and when we were out in the street people often thought our children were twins. In reality, John has often considered Lydia to be his older sister, because in so many practical ways she was much more capable than he was. In fact by the time Lydia was 18 months old, it was natural to treat her as the more responsible child. She was so organised, observant, sensible and willing to please and help, whereas John was rather unaware of the daily practicalities of life.

Our first au-pair, Anna, remembers Lydia as 'a very clever child, but calmer [than John] and interested in more 'normal' things for a 6 year old... A lovely little girl with strong opinions about things and also very mature for her age.' I remember thinking what a wonderful girl she was because she seemed so sensitive to her brother's needs. She was usually so adaptable and worked round him without any fuss. Unfortunately it never crossed my mind how this must be making her feel.

When Lydia grew older, she was the one who would take John aside and try and calm him down if he became very upset. John remembers this well: 'She was very good at it, not least because I felt guilty at responding to her calming overtures with anger.' Lydia recalls that all sorts of things could trigger a tantrum, including homework (the cause of numerous arguments between John and myself), being discovered not telling the truth, not wanting to do something he was supposed to do, not washing himself, being told that he was embarrassing us in public with his comments, and so on. He would listen to her when he wouldn't listen to me because my requests had usually been the cause of the tantrum in the first place. Lydia said she 'couldn't stand hearing him cry and being upset and wanted to make him feel better'. She talked to him about 'feelings and fairness', gave him 'the chance to vent' and then explained our point of view. She acted as a kind of mediator and 'loved being in that role'. Acting the 'older sister, looking after him and mothering him' made her 'feel good'. Although it was a lot of responsibility she feels there were 'huge gains as it helped with my empathy' and she was able to develop skills that she used later in her career as a child psychologist. This is quite a typical response to having a sibling with special needs, as Lorna Wing (1996) describes: 'Children with a sibling who is disabled in any way often develop a level of maturity beyond their years and many then go into caring professions in adult life.' Although Lydia comforted John when he was upset, he was unable to do the same for her. As he recalls:

If she was unhappy I'd want to make her feel better. The difference is, she knew how to go about it, while I didn't have the first clue. If I could have stopped her hurting by cutting some part of myself off I'd have done it in a second, but (unfortunately?) that sort of bargain doesn't exist outside of nasty fantasy works.

AUTISM, FAMILY LIFE AND THE IMPACT ON LYDIA

Although looking back Lydia says she didn't feel she missed out in terms of individual attention, I'm not sure that she felt the same at the time. When she was 13 she wrote me a very angry letter (see Appendix 18) in which she claims: 'I have been jealous of the attention he gets for as long as I can remember.' I can't recall what had happened to trigger such fury (which is perhaps just as well) but as a close friend wrote to me: 'It must have been remarkably difficult at times for Lydia particularly in the teenage years.' Bringing up strong willed, emotional and rebellious teenagers is rarely easy and as Wing (1996) wrote:

> Those with siblings with autistic disorders do face a number of special problems. Perhaps the hardest thing for them is that their parents have to give so much time and attention to the special child that there is little to spare for the rest of the family. This is particularly likely to affect a sister or brother who is close in age to the child with the disability. Parents need to be aware of this danger and do their best to set aside time for the rest of the family.

When John looks back at his feelings for his sister he remembers:

> I was mildly envious of her ability to ace exams without visible effort and acquire friends so easily, but I wasn't jealous of her as a whole because of all the visible pain problems and the like – and of course I didn't notice any differences in the amount of relative attention given to each of us. Also I don't think I'm much of a jealous sort, I loathe the emotion so much – the one time the emotion surfaced that I can remember, I crushed it flat and avoided situations which might cause it from then on.

The 'pain problems' that John refers to are the growing pains/cartilage/tendon problems Lydia suffered from in her early teens. In retrospect, Lydia feels she *was* listened to when she was on her own with me, especially when I listened to her daily music practice. She felt that some of her problems with friends and so on could be talked about but that big things to do with her brother were never discussed. Looking back she doesn't feel that we spent more time with John than her, believing that 'in a way you spent less time with him because he was so solitary'. I certainly remember spending time with Lydia on her own: for example taking her to watch the ballet in London, looking around second hand shops, jumble sales and fairs for Barbie dolls and dressing up clothes and so on. Lydia remembers John and his dad doing things together while she and I did things together. She recalls that I also spent time alone with John but feels:

> I missed out a bit with Dad because we didn't do stuff together after the age of five… It would have made it easier in my teens. I craved my dad's attention a lot and did things to try and get his attention. He was lovely, but distant. I felt more allied with dad at the table as we would both sit there and have the giggles… I loved it when he came to stay at my flat. We still do walks together.

Ozonoff et al (2002) provide wise advice when they write:

> A common perception of typically developing siblings is that brothers and sisters with autism or Asperger Syndrome receive disproportionate amounts of parental

attention. Very often this may be the case... Nevertheless, there are several strategies you can use to prevent siblings' feelings of neglect and potential resentment. In two-parent homes, divide and conquer, splitting up so that you can attend to two children simultaneously... During bedtime routines or other evening activities, make sure that you ask your typically developing children about their experiences, feelings and concerns.

Perhaps we should have done more with Lydia on her own and not quite so much as a whole family because Lydia felt that she got less attention when we were all together. Although we went out of our way to try to consider Lydia's needs and not let John be the centre of attention all the time, he was such a strong character and his needs so obvious that we weren't very successful. However John sees things differently:

When I think of Lydia I don't exactly think 'shrinking violet'. I tended to have my say forcefully without guilt because I assumed that if Lydia really cared about something she'd butt in and ride over the top of me.

We should have let Lydia have her say far more often. It wasn't easy though. On family occasions, such as a birthday for example, if John didn't want to do what Lydia wanted we fitted in with him and did something altogether as a family. Lydia felt:

Our range of activities/tastes/choices wasn't noticeably restricted when we were younger, but I definitely noticed it later on... I missed out on having someone around who enjoyed doing the things I enjoyed for, although John would let me choose what to do, when I did choose he didn't want to do it! This affected films we might see on a birthday, only eating out in places where he liked the food and wouldn't make a fuss, not having a birthday cake that he disliked even though it was my birthday, and so on, much of which I have blocked out. Things had to be organised around John and I had to squash a lot of my own desires and feelings about things, because I was told that John couldn't help it. I felt it was not acceptable to become stroppy about the situation, although on occasion I did say it was not fair.

As for 'missing out on having someone around who enjoyed doing the things I enjoyed', John's response was: 'Yeah, but if you had someone like that there could have been competition, which might have been destructive.' I remember the birthday cake situation clearly and think this is an excellent example of Lydia's needs coming second to John's. Lydia wanted a Pavlova on more than one occasion for her birthday but John hated meringue. As I wanted all the family to enjoy the cake together, we didn't have Pavlova. In retrospect I think I was wrong and Lydia should have had what she wanted, not just then, but on many other occasions. If I'd been more imaginative I would have had a Pavlova cake for the family and something else (or nothing?) for John instead. I'm not sure what I could have done about birthday films or eating out except leave John in someone else's care. However I'm not sure that Lydia would have been happy for her brother to be absent from her birthday celebration. Sometimes you just can't win! Lydia is absolutely right that family life was largely organised around John and I can see now just how difficult it must have been for her. As Ozonoff (2002) et al write:

Another common sentiment among siblings of children with AS-HFA, [is] the notion that the child's special needs will restrict the activities of the entire family... It is easy for a parent to avoid such activities to suit the needs of the family member with AS-HFA. However this practice can foster resentment in typical children. It also reduces the range of experiences encountered by your child with AS-HFA, and may reinforce his or her behavioural inflexibility.

Although I totally agree with these sentiments it's easier said than done. I was brought up in a household full of unhappiness, tension, quarrels, temper and upset; I suppose I just couldn't face the thought of our special family occasions being spoilt because of John's outbursts.

As mentioned already in Chapter 11, Lydia found family conversations very difficult, particularly at the dinner table:

Conversations as a family were very restricted and I didn't get to talk about the things I was interested in. It seemed to me that John talked a lot, very loudly and unrelentingly about things that I had no idea about. I could only understand about 10% of what he said! He was super-intelligent and it was intimidating... He was so keen on facts and always had things to say and did know more than all of us, which didn't help as none of us could hold our own half the time... I think you managed to hold your own very well, but Dad and I were in a different position. As the youngest member of the family with the smallest voice and in a position of least power, physically and literally/symbolically, yes it was difficult... You seemed to me to understand him very well and had a lot of patience with him in family settings... Dad was in a similar position to me, although he never seemed to want to talk about things that interested him. I did, and felt that John wouldn't let me get more than a sentence out. I also felt that you didn't have as much patience for listening to the things that I wanted to say as you did for John in those family settings. I really longed to have a 'normal' family who could sit round and talk about 'normal' things, and I felt very 'alien'. Despite the fact that John's much more of an 'alien' in a normative sense, I developed a feeling that's never gone away, of being different and not quite acceptable. I think that came from only having very short pauses in which to speak, and when I did speak, being shouted down and criticised [by John].

John now realises:

[This was] my fault. I didn't grasp that Lydia didn't like arguing for fun until long after we'd both left home: also I had no idea that anyone was having trouble following anything I was saying... I had to learn conversational grammar and strategies for drawing people in and what other people were interested in and so on, and then practise the whole mess enough that it become halfway automatic, and at this point I was ten years away from even learning that such a thing as conversational grammar *existed*, let alone that everyone else was following it so I had better do so as well.

Lydia said that she knew that we tried to explain to John that his sister was upset when she couldn't say what she wanted and when he rubbished her and she thinks it helped him understand. However she also knew he couldn't help it and in retrospect thinks the only thing that could have been done was for her to spend some time on her own with *both* parents without John, something we never managed to achieve. Lydia also feels:

> I missed out on having a normal brother a bit older than myself that I could sit down with and have normal conversations, and go out with which I would have liked... Having said all that I loved John very deeply and still do... he always wanted to talk to me and I was always aware that he wanted me around, whereas many older brothers would die rather than have their baby sisters around. He was always really proud of me and would say 'this is my sister'.

Although Lydia didn't blame John or get particularly angry with him about his behaviour, she believes that her feelings of frustration, of being very squashed and of guilt at having these feelings, were turned inwards. She revealed recently that she'd felt as a child that she was 'a bad person, selfish, mean, ungrateful and self centred' because whatever her problems at the time (such as being systematically ostracised for a year at school), those of John seemed so much more obvious. She felt that she couldn't burden us with what she considered to be minor issues in comparison to those of her brother. She didn't think that these feelings of hers were anything to do with what her parents told her; rather they arose from the situations she found herself in. What made the position far worse, was that her feelings and needs were not acknowledged by anyone, including herself. The habit of internalising her feelings and suppressing her own needs has had a long term impact on Lydia. Unfortunately, reading a draft of some of the chapters of this book has brought many of her feelings of being invisible while she was a child to the surface again, as she describes so movingly below:

> This invisibility has been a theme for me whilst reading parts of the book, and it has been a painful process at times. I'm sure that many siblings feel this way – certainly those who enter the helping professions. We have become so adept at making our needs (emotional or otherwise) smaller than those of our siblings (because of course they are, in comparison) that they become invisible from ourselves and others. What's left to burst through is then deep sadness, hurt, anger and frustration, as well as illness and pain, as we're so poor at self-care/asking for help. This behavioural style impacts on all of our subsequent relationships and life choices, both positively and negatively.

I think we really failed our daughter by not encouraging her to talk about her feelings. In retrospect, like so many parents, we were doing the best that we could at the time without any outside help and as a result were at times amazingly naïve and ignorant. If only we had been aware of the sort of wise recommendations made by Rogers et al (2012):

> Talk openly with your child about these fears and worries so you can provide facts and reassure your child. You will probably have these conversations many times, because it is unlikely that your child will understand everything that you say the first time you explain it. Different questions and concerns will arise over time. Make ASD an open subject in your household. If your child never asks about ASD, it's most likely because it seems to be an unacceptable topic. Bring it up yourself, the sooner the better, and the more frequently the better. Ask your child what scares him about his sibling's ASD, what worries him, what makes

him angry, what he thinks about, and how it affects his life... Help your child voice these feelings, and listen quietly, as you do with your partner. Acknowledge and restate the feelings rather than rejecting them, interrupting them, or denying them. (Some of them will be hard to hear, so be prepared.) Your child may have some painful observations about you – about your absorption in the sibling with ASD; about the lack of family time; about your increased expectations for your child for greater maturity, responsibility, child care, household care, or emotional support. Listen! Take it in. Try hard not to deny, not to become defensive, and not to get angry. Listen to what your child is saying; provide the information your child is asking for; correct any misconceptions; and reassure your child of your love, your acceptance of the child's feelings, and your appreciation for the child's honesty and trust in you.

Lydia now feels that being able to attend a sibling group for siblings of children on the autism spectrum would have been 'incredibly helpful' and made a 'huge difference' to her life while she was growing up. She felt very isolated and knew no one in a situation like hers. None of us realised how isolated Lydia felt, least of all John:

> My impression of Lydia was that she was surrounded by huge hordes of friends at all times... but, of course, none of those friends were in the same situation as she was. I didn't see that then at all, and didn't imagine that she could ever have been lonely.

Unfortunately I don't believe any sibling groups existed locally when Lydia was growing up and I think they are still all too rare. She believes that such a group would have helped her to understand what was going on, share some of her feelings, realise that these feelings were entirely normal for someone in her situation and that she wasn't a bad person. Hindsight is a wonderful thing and these days I would certainly go out of my way to find a sibling group for any child in my daughter's position. In the light of my own experience I would strongly encourage other parents to do the same. Lydia told me recently:

> In a departmental meeting at work, a presentation was given about siblings' groups for siblings of children with Aspergers, which made me cry. I don't think anyone saw, but I felt very emotional about it.

If there aren't any suitable groups in your area or if your child doesn't fancy the idea of a group, there are several excellent books and websites written for parents *and* children, some of which are listed in Appendix 28. Parents can use these as a trigger to help the sibling discuss their feelings. If I'd been able to read even *one* of these books I might have made fewer mistakes when dealing with Lydia but they hadn't been published when I needed them. There seem to be so many traps that parents can fall into unless they're aware of their children's feelings and I certainly fell into quite a few of them. Most of the books I've read recently emphasise the sibling's need to express their negative feelings about their brother or sister with special needs. These feelings may include fear, anger, jealousy, resentment, confusion, isolation, frustration, guilt, shame, embarrassment and concern for the future. Unfortunately I was blissfully unaware of any of this when Lydia was a child. Morell and Palmer (2006) hit the nail on the head when they wrote:

Siblings experience a wide range of emotions about living with a brother or sister on the autistic spectrum. They may feel angry and resent the amount of attention the sibling requires or the disruption they may cause to family life. Siblings may be embarrassed by their brother's or sister's behaviours. They may also feel protective of their sibling and defensive towards people who don't understand autism. These conflicting emotions can be difficult for a sibling to understand and handle.

Parents can help by being sensitive to the feelings of the siblings and by giving them the opportunity to complain, ask questions, or share their concerns... Siblings need to voice their feelings, both good and bad, about their brother or sister with autism. They may be reluctant to complain for fear they will anger or disappoint their parents. Siblings may be disappointed in themselves for having negative feelings about their brother or sister, making expressing these feelings out loud very difficult...

We can encourage the sibling to open up about their feelings by voicing our own... Parents sometimes choose to speak about living with autism only as a positive experience. We may want to hide our true frustrations or sadness from other children so as not to upset them... Our acceptance that life with an individual with autism is challenging is an important part of adapting to the stresses of our lives and learning from them. Siblings need to acknowledge this as well so that they, too, can recognise the difficulties and then appreciate the aspects of their lives with their autistic sibling that are positive and rewarding.

Sometimes initiating the discussion about the siblings' feelings is the hardest part... Sometimes discussing a book about the topic or watching a movie pertaining to autism is a good way to open communication with siblings.

I think I would have found reading a suitable book with Lydia the easiest way for me to open up the whole issue of 'feelings'. I agree with John's perceptive comment:

Another downside here is that, autism being a genetic condition, parents of autistics are *also* often quite bad at dealing with the whole expressing-feelings thing, so their more normal siblings are surrounded by multiple aliens in this respect.

One example of a book I would have found very helpful is called *Brotherly Feelings. Me, My emotions, and my Brother with Asperger Syndrome* by Sam Frender and Robin Schiffmiller. It has lovely illustrations and the characters are based on Robin's sons: Eric (age 13) who has Asperger's syndrome and Sam (age eight) who is 'neurotypical'. As Robin writes in her introduction:

The goal of this book is to provide the siblings of children with Asperger's Syndrome with an opportunity to explore their feelings and talk about their experiences. It is intended to reassure these children that they are not alone, and to let them know that there are many other children who face similar challenges and have similar feelings...

The experiences described in this book can be used to help initiate conversations between our children and the many important people in their lives... They will also help children explore conflicts within themselves; for example, the loving, yet resentful, feelings they have for their sibling; or the frustrations of being younger, yet feeling more mature...

By articulating these feelings, siblings of children with Asperger's Syndrome... will feel relieved to know that you are aware of their feelings, that their feelings are legitimate, and that you still love them.

How I wish I'd been able to use this wonderful book when *my* children were growing up; but it was only published in 2007.

Whenever Lydia, in her role as a clinical psychologist working with children and families, sees a child with a developmental disorder, she considers the other children, the 'lost' ones who aren't seen so much. She helps parents encourage siblings to communicate their feelings. In order to facilitate this process she suggests one of the following might be helpful: a row of faces on the wall so that the child can point to the one that most nearly matches their own feelings at the time; a large thermometer with different moods marked clearly on it which the child can point to; a post box into which a child can post a note saying how they are feeling so that these notes can then be discussed with parents. Indeed she believes that anything would be beneficial that makes it easier for siblings to discuss their feelings and to realise that it's normal to have feelings such as frustration and guilt. A professional may be needed to show parents how to help their child, as it can be similar to dealing with bereavement. Ives and Munro (2002) have some useful advice for parents:

Allow a grumbling time for the siblings, when they can moan and whinge and list all the complaints they have every right to have... Some children may be happier talking to someone who is independent and not part of the immediate family. Wherever possible, pragmatic solutions should be found to the problems expressed by the siblings. Things which cannot be changed can also be dealt with. Exercises where complaints and grudges are tied to the string of a balloon that is then popped is one way of helping the sibling let go of issues. Slipping the complaint into an empty glass bottle and then visiting the bottle bank can also be therapeutic.

In conclusion: Although there was room for significant improvement, I feel very happy about John's development and the way things have turned out. However I believe we failed Lydia in many ways, largely because we had no appreciation of the impact that living with a brother on the autism spectrum would have on her. We should have enabled her to talk about her feelings and helped her to realise how normal they were. We should have listened to her wishes more and not only done things to keep John happy and give ourselves an easy ride.

20

Assessments

DEVELOPMENTAL SCREENING

John's difficult start in life meant that his development was assessed regularly by paediatricians from both of the hospitals he stayed in as a baby. Almost all of the assessments were carried out in the rather artificial environment of a doctor's office. Unfortunately the assessments weren't at all helpful in delineating and addressing John's difficulties. This was probably due to a lack of comprehension of the ASD issue, inadequate testing and poor communication between the doctors and myself.

As part of the research for this book I obtained a copy of the letters sent to our GP by the doctors that examined John. Extracts from these can be seen in Appendix 19. It was a very strange experience reading these letters for the first time, so many years after the tests were carried out. When they were written, the doctors were obviously completely unaware that a Freedom of Information Act would ever be passed in the future – which meant their notes and letters might be read by the patient. I was quite surprised to see how poor the communication appeared to have been between myself and the doctor at our local hospital. For example, this doctor appeared to believe that John was good at jigsaws when he was actually very poor indeed at them. None of our concerns and worries, particularly about John's fine motor skills and visual perception, seem to have been extracted from the interviews with me. Although this doctor reported that John had lots of 'expressive jargon' at 18 months, at 22 months she doubted my reports about his language abilities. Two months later, a doctor from the hospital in London reported that John's speech was fluent and both the Denver screening tests (see below) showed that his language abilities were very advanced for his age. Why did our local doctor write that we had 'as yet not bothered' about John's toilet needs when he was only 18 months old? Perhaps I'm just being over sensitive and reading too much into the use of the word 'bothered'! The doctor from our local hospital also reported John's inability to build a tower of bricks at 22 months as 'would not cooperate' and didn't appear to register that this might indicate an underlying difficulty. She could easily have found out from us (but didn't seem to have done so) that John's coordination was too poor for him to be able to play with large Lego, stack bricks or draw. As it happens John was also unable to imitate a bridge made of three bricks when he was tested at 32 months.

Our local paediatrician seemed to think we were far too easygoing at home, so that the structured environment of the nursery school would be good for him. She didn't appear to have any idea whatsoever of the structured environment that actually existed in our home or how much we tried to stimulate John. Did she think pressurising a child was better than allowing a child to develop their strengths in a free and happy way? As John wrote to me: 'What happens if you pressurise something that's already under pressure? That's right, it explodes. I had enough frustration and over-stimulation tantrums as it was.' Interestingly enough the doctor from the hospital in London, who realised that I was aware of John's difficulties, was worried that I would push him too far!

Was the inability of the doctor at our local hospital to find out about John's difficulties *my* fault? Did I try to hide John's problems? Perhaps I was never asked the right questions or the doctor didn't hear what I was saying. A general question such as 'how are you getting on?' or 'are there any behaviour problems?' would have been very unlikely to elicit anything negative from me, unless I was having a major problem at the time of the appointment. I'm a positive person who tends to think a cup is half full rather than half empty. Once I've found a way round a problem I don't dwell on it any more and may well not think about bringing it up as an issue at a doctor's appointment, unless asked a specific question. As my psychologist daughter points out so accurately though: 'It would have been hard for the paediatrician to get a sense of your concerns if you didn't talk about them.' Although we had no detailed knowledge of a typical child's developmental milestones, it was quite obvious to us what John could and couldn't do compared to other children of the same age. Perhaps I should have made much more fuss about his difficulties as opposed to praising his strengths. However John was present at all the interviews and I've always tried to make him feel good about himself rather than moan about his difficulties. I don't think the doctors understood or appreciated that this is what I was trying to do. According to one doctor from the hospital in London (see Appendix 19) my behaviour was described as 'continuously showing off the things he could do', whilst the doctor at our local hospital wrote, when John was 22 months old, that she 'gave up because I think quite frankly, mother thinks he is a genius'. As it happens I've never thought of John as a genius but I *have* always thought (and still do) that he's very intelligent despite finding certain things difficult. According to a retired medical friend of mine:

> The above is quite a learning point for parents. You need to be prepared to be quite forthright about what the problems are and not stress how you are coping or people will not clock the difficulties. I've heard this with school professionals as well in the statementing process; they can talk themselves out of as much help as they need from the LA [Local Authority] by being too positive about how things are improving… It is quite difficult to make the switch from positivity to what seems negative but it is needed.

All these assessments would have been *much* more accurate if my husband and I could have filled in a screening questionnaire (say a week or two *before* the appointment) and given this to the doctor when we saw her. This would have given us some idea what to look out for, given us time to think about the issues that the doctor was interested in and enabled us to complete the questionnaire in a calm and unpressurised way. Potential issues could have been disclosed to the doctor without John hearing everything. Michèlle Lee (2004) has found a parental questionnaire to be 'a very useful tool. It enables parents to express in writing how they view the situation and to answer questions which they may have difficulty answering in front of the child.' As it was, most of the paediatric assessments by our local hospital seemed to be a waste of time. At the time I felt that the doctor was only interested to see if John had major disabilities such as cerebral palsy and anything less than this was of no interest to her. Perhaps it was for this reason that it never crossed her mind to refer John to a physiotherapist when he was eight and I was having terrible trouble finding someone to address his writing difficulties. If I'd known what I know now, I would have asked for such a referral in order to see if some of John's underlying motor problems could be improved. Instead this doctor referred John to an eye specialist. It was hardly surprising that this had absolutely no impact whatsoever on his writing. Interestingly enough she noted at this appointment that John 'concentrates on his own pursuits'. At that time this didn't raise any alarm bells, perhaps not surprisingly as Uta Frith's 1991 translation of Hans Asperger's 1944 paper had yet to be published. In effect, Asperger's syndrome didn't officially exist until the 1990s and looks as if it may be disappearing again with the advent of the fifth edition of the Diagnostic and Statistical Manual (DSM-5).

On the two occasions that doctors came to our home, the Denver Developmental Screening Test (DDST) was carried out. Screening tests in general are designed to identify potential problems and *not* to provide a diagnosis. The DDST is a very broad test, unlike more specific screening tests for autism, Asperger's syndrome, ADHD and so on. The test is divided into four parts, investigating gross motor function, fine motor function, social/personal skills and language ability. John passed all four parts of the test at two years eight months, although it was reported that he was unable to 'imitate a bridge made of three bricks'. At four years four months, although John passed the gross motor function part of the DDST, it was also noted that 'he can't catch a ball as yet'. This time he failed the fine motor section because, as one doctor wrote: 'He cannot imitate a square and is useless at drawing. In fact he cannot even hold a pencil properly let alone draw a face for me.' Strangely enough this doctor thought John 'has good coordination and I think this hand/eye coordination problem is obviously a mild one but one that may cause problems later at school'. That was all too accurate a prediction. I guess the reason the hand/eye coordination problem was called 'mild' is that this is precisely what it was compared to cerebral palsy, which can sometimes be a consequence of a very premature birth. Considering his fine motor difficulties, it isn't surprising that John was unable to manage his buttons and dressing was described as a battle every morning. John passed the personal and social parts of the test though and he sailed through the language section of the test with flying colours. The doctor thought his vocabulary was 'probably rather better than mine'. These tests are so broad that they didn't seem to trigger any alarm bells whatsoever and no help was offered or suggested. Certainly none of John's social problems were identified nor the underlying problems responsible for his inability to copy from the board or spell when he was a few years older. At the time I was unaware which tests were being carried out or what the findings were. They were carried out as part of research projects and no follow-ups resulted, even though letters *were* sent to our local hospital and our G.P. According to my medical friend:

> Denver screening was as you say meant to pick up the possibility of problems but was actually used as a full assessment perfectly interchangeably. It was never an effective set of tests though we were all taught to do them in clinics.

I find it interesting that some of the doctors had a feeling/suspicion that something wasn't quite right, although nobody did anything about it. They would have been unaware of the characteristics of children on the autism spectrum at that time. As a result the doctors' unease was expressed as a criticism of *my* understanding of John's abilities rather than a perception that here was a very bright child with some accompanying difficulties which should be investigated. When John was 32 months the doctor from the hospital in London wrote: 'I got the sneaking impression that he is perhaps not quite so clever as the rest of his family.' Similarly when John was three years old the doctor from our local hospital wrote: 'In many ways he is not as bright as she thinks he is.' However this was followed up in the same sentence by: 'But I think this is due to the fact that she has been very careful not to repeat history.' I find the connection between these two statements incomprehensible but my daughter thinks that what the doctor meant was that John was not doing as well as he could/should because I was trying not to pressurise him.

Some years after our experience, De Kleine and colleagues (2003) found (in their study of 431 very premature infants in the Netherlands) that 60% of those diagnosed with some form of developmental impairment using a set of standardised tests[69] had *not* been identified, by paediatricians, prior to these tests. The paediatricians had used a parental questionnaire, a physical examination, a test of neurological function (Touwen, 1989), the Denver Development Screening Test and a Dutch Language Screening Test (Gerritsen, 1988). Quoting from de Kleine's paper:

> Long term follow up studies of adolescents and young adults who were born preterm show that a developmental problem may impose a lifelong burden. Neonatal follow up should therefore aim to identify such problems at an early age and provide intervention therapy when needed... Follow up studies that do not include detailed, standardised tests for several domains will underestimate developmental problems in survivors of neonatal intensive care.

STATEMENT OF SPECIAL EDUCATIONAL NEEDS (SSEN OR STATEMENT)

As described in Chapter 16, when John was seven the headmistress of his infants' school asked us whether they could refer John to their 'educational psychologist in order to have his needs assessed'. Six months after the headmistress's original letter, an assessment of special educational needs took place. As John was now seven and a half and in the junior school, it was a different head teacher that completed the section on 'Educational Advice'. He wrote about John as follows:

> John is a very intelligent boy with a wealth of knowledge and understanding far beyond his years. The problem centres on his relative inability to adjust to the classroom environment allied to relationship with and attitude to other children.

> I feel that he requires individual help on a one to one basis or small group basis to nurture and develop his considerable abilities. At the same time however I feel that it is equally important that he receive individualised help in the classroom context to enable him to more readily undertake the standard pattern of classroom activities from which he is only partly benefiting at the moment. It may well be that a mixture of these strategies would enable John to achieve his potential.

As my medical friend wrote: 'That's quite a perceptive headmaster although as usual it takes the view that the child has to be fitted into the school rather than vice versa.' The whole process sounds wonderful, doesn't it? An educational psychologist would carry out an individual assessment of John's needs as a result of which his teachers would know what was required in order to achieve his potential. Hopefully John would receive individualised help and his difficulties would be a thing of the past.

We received the final 'Statement' several months later and this is reproduced in Appendix 20. At last, over a year after the initial letter from John's infant school, we had the magic statement. Except there was no magic. The Statement made no perceptible difference to John's progress at school. Did he get any individual help in the classroom once he was given a Statement? The simple answer is: 'No'. The class teacher was supposed to provide this individualised help in the classroom on top of dealing with about thirty other children – rather a tall order. The headteacher *did* spend an hour or so per week with John on his own but what they did in that time I've never discovered. Was the head given any professional advice or training as to what to do? Were any goals or targets set and reviewed? John would have enjoyed a one-to-one intellectual discussion with the head on a regular basis and it was indeed very good of the head to give up his time. However I've no evidence that any social skills training took place or any help with John's poor organisational skills provided. In fact neither of these difficulties were actually commented on in the Statement. I also doubt whether these sessions with the head were designed to improve John's fine motor skills as this requires specialist help and daily exercise. We were never asked to do any exercises with John and we're not aware that these were happening at school either. John *was* put on a cursive writing programme by his class teacher but he always maintained that this made his writing worse! I don't think this was true but the lack of skilled and specialised help meant that he was able to write reasonably legibly if he wrote slowly but he never learned to write legibly *and* fast. As described in Chapter 8, John used far too much pressure which made his hand hurt if he had a lot to write. According to John: 'If I pressed less hard, I sped up and the writing got worse.' There were no books or gadgets around (as there are these days) to help people with writing problems such as John's, so everyone was equally in the dark. Even though John received some occupational therapy as a result of the Statement, it was difficult to see what effect this had either in the short- or long-term.

If John's SSEN was ever reviewed we were never informed about the outcome and certainly weren't involved. We never had a meeting with anyone at John's junior school either about the Statement or about any remedial work that was being carried out with him. When John left his state primary school at 11 to attend a private secondary school, his Statement was never alluded to again. Looking back I can see just how naïve we were about the whole statementing process. We should have been far more proactive in dealing with John's schools in order to ensure that he got the help he needed. However, in those days, there was little help available, no internet to access for information and the whole process of identifying children with special needs and trying to provide help by means of a Statement was very new. I'm afraid we just trusted the professionals, always a dangerous thing to do! In those days there was no legal requirement to have individualised help in the classroom for a child with a Statement, there were no Individual Education Plans and Special Educational Needs Coordinators (SENCOs) didn't exist in either John's primary or secondary school. According to John:

> The primary message of my educators, from start to end of my life in the school system, was 'why don't you fit in your box and act just like everyone else rather than making our lives difficult?'

Many parents might consider we were lucky to have a SSEN but in reality the lack of funding and ongoing reviews meant it wasn't worth the paper it was written on. More recently, the extra funding and individual help that accompanied a SSEN meant that, in theory anyway, a Statement should be much more useful. However, precisely because the possession of a Statement always had cost implications, SSENs have been very difficult to obtain and the whole process has become somewhat adversarial. The NAS produced a report in June 2011 entitled *Great Expectations*[70] whose findings included:

- 7 out of 10 parents (68%) say it has not been easy to get the educational support their child needs;

- 48% of parents say they have waited over a year to get the right support for their child; over a quarter (27%) have waited more than two years;

- 18% of parents have had to go to tribunal to get the right support for their children. On average, they go to tribunal three to four times each.

After thirty years experience and the advent of School Action, School Action Plus and Individual Education Plans (IEP), one would expect far more help for children that are struggling at school. Not necessarily so, according to Ofsted in their publication *The special educational needs and disability review.*[71] They found:

Widespread weaknesses in the quality of what was provided for children with special educational needs...

The review team found that when a child was identified as having special educational needs at School Action level, this usually led to some additional help from within the school. When a child was identified as having special educational needs at School Action Plus, or especially with a statement, this usually led to the allocation of further additional resources from within and outside the school. However, inspectors found that this additional provision was often not of good quality and did not lead to significantly better outcomes for the child or young person...

Inspectors found poor evaluation by a wide range of public agencies of the quality of the additional support provided for children and young people. Too often, the agencies focused simply on whether a service was or was not being provided rather than whether it was being effective...

Despite extensive statutory guidance, the consistency of the identification of special educational needs varied widely, not only between different local areas but also within them.

Interestingly enough Ofsted found that *too many* children were being diagnosed as having special educational needs when what they actually needed was better 'day-to-day teaching and pastoral support'. They believed this was diverting attention and funds from those children who actually needed specialist help.

This isn't the only report to criticise the level of support provided for children with special educational needs. According to the foreword to the Green Paper, issued by the Department of Education in March 2011, and titled *Support and aspiration: A new approach to special educational needs and disability*:

Successive reports, such as the 2006 report of the Education Select Committee and Brian Lamb's report in 2009, have described a system where parents feel they have to battle for the support they need, where they are passed from pillar to post, and where bureaucracy and frustration face them at every step... Children and young people with SEN don't achieve as they could – by the time they leave school these young people are twice as likely to be out of education, training or employment as those without.

The outcome of this Green Paper was the Children and Families Act 2014. Section 19 of this act required that:[72]

Local authorities must pay particular attention to:

- the views, wishes and feelings of children and their parents, and young people;

- the importance of them participating as fully as possible in decision-making and providing the information and support to enable them to do so; and

- supporting children and young people's development and helping them to achieve the best possible educational and other outcomes.

In Part 3 of this act,[73] it can be seen that the SSEN is to be replaced by an *Education, Health and Care plan (EHC),* which is to be a single assessment process which will run from birth until the age of 25. The act also states: 'A local authority that maintains an EHC plan, or is securing the preparation of an EHC plan, for a child or young person must prepare a personal budget for him or her if asked to do so by the child's parent or the young person.' As I read this I wish I didn't feel so cynical. Would the progress of each child be monitored? Would the quality of extra support in schools suddenly magically improve? Would *all* teachers and teaching or classroom assistants at primary and secondary level be trained to understand what is needed to realise the potential of the children with special needs in their classes? Given the straitened circumstances of local councils these days, would there be ring-fenced budgets to ensure sufficient funding is available at a local level to pay for the services that children with an EHC plan require? What about Academies? If there's insufficient funding to meet children's needs, will the adversarial aspects of the previous system really be reduced? Will there be sufficient regulation and evaluation to ensure that *all* local authorities (and Academies) are equally willing to provide a good quality service for those with special needs in their area? I would still suggest that parents shouldn't follow the professionals blindly, trusting that everything will be fine in the end. Parents will still need to become powerful advocates for their children, a very wearing and stressful business. They need to become extremely knowledgeable and get as much help as possible from books and advice organisations in order to ensure that their child's special educational needs are continually met and their child's potential fully realised. A list of useful resources that could be particularly helpful can be found in Appendix 28.

COGNITIVE TESTING: THE WISC-R TEST

What type of assessments did John have when he was seven in order to provide the psychological advice for his SSEN? The only test John undertook was the WISC-R (Weschler Intelligence Scale for Children-Revised) which is now obsolete. It has been replaced by a newer version, the Wechsler Intelligence Scale for Children® – Fifth Edition (WISC–V®). The WISC tests are designed to reveal a child's cognitive strengths and weaknesses compared with a standardised sample of children of the same age. The WISC-R tests were divided into two groups: one called 'Verbal' tests (which gave rise to a 'Verbal IQ' and measured verbal and language-related abilities) and the other 'Performance' tests (which gave rise to a 'Performance IQ' and measured visual, motor and other non-verbal abilities). These tests were administered alternately; a brief description of each of the WISC-R tests taken by John can be found in Appendix 8. The WISC-R tests were designed so that the scaled score for an average population is 10 with a standard deviation of 3, giving rise to an average population IQ of 100 with a standard deviation of 15. What this means in practice is that about two thirds of the population from which the sample was drawn would have scaled scores between 7 and 13 and an IQ between 85 and 115, whilst approximately 95% would have scaled scores between 4 and 16 and an IQ between 70 and 130. Although these tests have been well standardised, they're very limited in what they measure and should never be used *on their own* either as a basis for a diagnosis or for ascertaining what help a child requires. As my clinical psychologist daughter explains: 'Observation and interview are key to good assessment practice, alongside testing.' They are definitely not the most appropriate tests for many of the problems that John experienced such as those relating to hand-eye coordination, motor skills, social abilities, working memory, concentration, organisational abilities and so on, although as my daughter says, they 'are the best place to start'. Additional testing is always required but this wasn't carried out when John was assessed for his Statement. These days there are many tests available but I suspect there were fewer in existence when John was tested in the first half of the 1980s. A list of some of the tests available in 2012 can be found in Appendix 21.

Many, many years after the Statement was issued, I contacted the local education authorities and acquired a copy of John's WISC-R test results which are summarised in the table in Appendix 22. This table also includes the results from the WISC-R test John took when he was 15 years old. The latter formed part of an assessment we paid for in order to support John's application for extra time when taking his GCSE exams. John needed (and was granted) extra time because of his continuing handwriting difficulties. Certain comments in the psychologist's report, which accompanied the WISC-R results when John was 15, are telling. She noted:

> [Although John] cooperated well, he showed quite marked symptoms of anxiety, with sarcastic comments on simple items and evidence of threat on things that he found hard… On the Verbal tests John was always more relaxed although throughout he tended to 'flap' and frequently accused himself of being stupid.

> [On the *Arithmetic* test John] kept up a constant chatter, with exclamations of 'Oh, I hate this sort of test'…

On the more practical Performance tasks John encountered difficulties on all of the sub-tests in comparison with the relative ease with which he approached the Verbal tasks. On the *Picture Completion* item (finding missing parts missing from pictures) he seemed to identify what was missing by a process of elimination. On the *Picture Arrangement* test (arranging cartoon pictures in order to tell a sensible story) having started off with sarcastic comments on the simpler items, it was quite evident that John was slow in processing visual information although he could use his strong verbal facility to overcome inherent difficulties... Overall, the results show a young man of very high Verbal potential, who has clear difficulties when faced with the more practical perceptual tasks. Because of his innate high level of intelligence experience has taught him strategies to overcome some of these difficulties, but inevitably there are problems in this area. The presence of soft neurological symptoms is strongly indicated.

It's interesting to note that the results of the WISC tests measured when John was seven and 15 look remarkably similar, even though they were carried out by different people many years apart. Although results from WISC tests are notoriously difficult to interpret, the table in Appendix 22 includes two very striking features. First of all there is a large scatter in the scaled scores, ranging as they do from 19 to 6. In fact scaled scores of 18 and 19 are so close to the ceiling of the test (19) that they may actually be an *underestimate* of John's capabilities on those particular tests. The other noticeable feature is that John's Verbal IQ is considerably greater (45 points at age seven and 40 points at age 15) than his Performance IQ. According to Martin Kutscher: 'On the WISC, a difference of more than 15 points between the Performance IQ and the Verbal IQ typifies a [specific] learning disability.' When there is such a large IQ difference it isn't appropriate to calculate a 'full scale' IQ, the measure normally used when we talk about a person's intelligence. According to Tony Attwood (2006):

There is no unique cognitive profile on an intelligence test that can be used to confirm a diagnosis of Asperger's syndrome. What we can say is that the overall profile of abilities on the intelligence test of a child with Asperger's syndrome tends to be conspicuously uneven, so one must exercise extreme caution in using a single IQ figure to represent the cognitive abilities of the child. The profile or pattern of intellectual abilities is more important than the overall or Full Scale IQ.

About 50 per cent of children with Asperger's syndrome have relatively advanced verbal reasoning skills, and may be colloquially be described as 'verbalizers'. If such a child has difficulty acquiring a particular academic ability in the social 'theatre' of the classroom, then his or her knowledge and understanding may be improved by reading about the concept or engaging in a one-to-one discussion.

Looking at the WISC-R results in more detail, it can be seen that on the Verbal part of the WISC-R, John's weaknesses were in the *Arithmetic* and *Digit Span* sub-tests. Meanwhile in the Performance part of the WISC-R, John's strength was in the *Block Design* sub-test and weaknesses were found in the *Picture Arrangement, Object Assembly* and *Coding* sub-tests. Kaufman (1979, 1995), who has written a great deal on WISC testing, has observed that children that are reading disabled or have other specific learning disabilities have relatively low scores on the *Arithmetic, Digit Span* and *Coding* sub-tests. It certainly makes me wonder whether John would have found it difficult to learn to read if I'd had left it up to the school and not taught him on a one-to-one basis. Kaufman also states that poor scores in *Arithmetic, Digit Span* and *Coding* have been associated with children diagnosed with attention deficit hyperactivity disorder and those suffering from anxiety.

Although the WISC-R cannot be used for diagnosis, Christopher Gillberg (2002) has some very interesting comments on the sub-tests, which seem to suggest that John might have Asperger syndrome. His analysis of the WISC-R results of many people with Asperger's syndrome describes John's results perfectly: excellent results for the information, comprehension, vocabulary, and similarities sub-tests; poorer results for the *Coding, Arithmetic* and *Picture Arrangement* sub-tests; good results on the *Block Design* sub-test and poorer results on the *Object Assembly* sub-test; a discrepancy between Verbal and Performance IQs of considerably more than 25 points. According to Gillberg:

> Correct solutions to the more complex tasks of the *Picture Arrangement* subtests of the WISC-R... require some understanding of the thoughts, wishes and feelings of other people. Pictures depicting various types of events – ranging from very 'concrete' to rather more 'mental' – have to be arranged in order so as to produce a coherent 'story'. Individuals with Asperger syndrome, like the majority of those with autism, have considerable difficulty solving these tasks...

> Individuals with Asperger syndrome have considerable problems with executive function, including, in certain cases some aspects of working memory, attention, and impulse control... The ability to plan ahead, motivation, sequencing and time concepts are often poorly developed...

> The... Wechsler scales of intelligence... include sub-tests that reflect executive functions. *Coding* and *Arithmetic* are examples of such sub-tests. Many individuals with Asperger syndrome... fail or perform less well on these. Seeing beyond detail and grasping the 'big picture' can be terribly difficult for individuals on the autism spectrum...

> In the WISC... there are two sub-tests, *Block Design* and *Object Assembly*, that can help tap problems in the field of visual central coherence. The *Object Assembly* test consists of cardboard pieces of a puzzle outlining a horse, hand etc. For anybody with a good sense of 'wholes' it is easy to see what they represent, but for somebody with a fixation on detail, this test can be extremely difficult. Quite a number of those with Asperger syndrome do poorly on this test. On the *Block Design* test, on the contrary, the individual is helped by not being distracted by the 'whole picture'. People with autism spectrum disorders often do very well on this subtest. A combination of good results on the *Block Design* subtest and poorer results on the *Object Assembly* is very common in Asperger syndrome...

> Verbal intelligence is often, though by no means always, better than so-called Performance intelligence. The discrepancy between Verbal IQ and Performance IQ can be very marked (25 points difference or more)...

> Every person seeking help and raising suspicions of suffering from Asperger

syndrome should be given a cognitive test... The Weschler scales often yield a characteristic profile with good or even superior results on sub-tests of 'information', 'comprehension', 'vocabulary', and 'similarities', and less good results or markedly inferior results on sub-tests of 'object assembly', 'arithmetic', 'coding', and 'picture arrangement'.

OTHER ASSESSMENTS

When John was eight and a half, our local county's educational research centre carried out some tests on John and reported:

- his level of reading is that which might be expected from a boy of his ability;
- it is nearly matched by his spelling;
- he possesses an excellent vocabulary;
- his score on the *Ravens Matrices* would suggest that he will learn new concepts easily;
- his written work is imaginative and interesting though his handwriting is evidently the area of difficulty;
- his visual sequential memory is at a very low level, this is his inability to hold a sequence of pictures, in the correct orientation, in his short term memory long enough to recall them accurately five seconds later;
- he also experienced some difficulty copying the abstract designs which, although these remained in front of him, he rearranged on the page.

The *Raven's Standard Progressive Matrices* (RSPM) tests are considered to be a purer test of an individual's intellectual capacity or abstract reasoning ability than the WISC tests because they're independent of language, reading and writing skills. In their study, Hayashi and colleagues[74] found that children with Asperger's syndrome performed significantly better in these tests than normally developing children. The RSPM tests involve non-verbal multiple choices in which, according to Wikipedia: 'The subject is asked to identify the missing element that completes a pattern'. The ability to see patterns has often been described as a particular strength of those with Asperger's syndrome so perhaps it's not really surprising that they perform well in the Raven's Matrices test. The findings of Michelle Dawson and colleagues, working with children diagnosed with autistic disorder (and not any other diagnostic categories in the DSM fourth edition such as Asperger's disorder), are particularly interesting.[75] Whereas the control (non autistic) children didn't show any significant difference between their WISC and *Raven's Matrices* scores, the autistic children had *Raven's Matrices* scores that were considerably higher than their WISC scores.

The county educational research centre recommended some books on visual perception which John really enjoyed doing with me. They also recommended a cursive handwriting programme for the school to adopt but this was less successful. Yet again, social difficulties and problems with organisation and concentration were not identified by means of their tests.

As part of John's assessment at 15, the educational psychologist also carried out the following tests whose findings are summarised below:

Bender Gestalt test: copying designs onto plain A4 paper

- work completed in an average time,
- although the work was not of a high standard there were no major deviations in the reproductions of the individual designs and fine detail was well noted,
- there was evidence of hand tremor on long lines.

Neale Analysis of Reading Ability – Revised – Form 2

Ceiling level of scoring in Rate, Accuracy and Comprehension.

Vernon Graded Spelling Test

Spelling Quotient above the ceiling of the test.

Free Writing

- John has great difficulty adhering to the line,
- the presentation is particularly untidy.

Laterality

Although there appear to be some elements of left handedness, John is predominantly right dominant in hand, foot, eye and ear.

AUTISM RESEARCH CENTRE SCREENING QUESTIONNAIRES

In *The Essential Difference* by Simon Baron-Cohen, a female brain is described as one that is good at empathizing and a male brain one that is good at systemizing. Baron-Cohen then suggests that people on the autism spectrum may have an 'extreme male brain': that is they may 'have a much *lower ability* to empathise, coupled with an average or even *talented* ability to systemize.' The book includes three questionnaires which can be used to evaluate one's Empathy Quotient (EQ), Systemizing Quotient (SQ) and Autism Spectrum Quotient (AQ), although Baron-Cohen emphasises that none of these tests are diagnostic.[76] When John was 32 he filled in all these questionnaires at my instigation; the results can be seen in Appendix 23, Appendix 24 and Appendix 25. Out of interest, and for comparative purposes, John's sister Lydia, father Tony and I also filled in the same questionnaires and the summarised results can be seen overleaf. The interpretation of the EQ, SQ and AQ scores are taken from *The Essential Difference*.

It's interesting (but perhaps not surprising) to note that for each of the quotients, John's results fall well within the range that Baron-Cohen attributes to 'most people with Asperger Syndrome'. Tony meanwhile scores well above average on the Autism Spectrum Quotient. I would certainly agree that Tony has many traits that can be found in someone with Asperger's Syndrome, such as his passion for aeroplanes and their statistics, dislike of crowds and social occasions and his difficulties with listening and paying attention to anything, unless it is aeroplane connected!

Empathy Quotient

Scores	Interpretation of EQ Score	Family Scores
0-32	low (most people with Asperger Syndrome or high functioning autism score about 20)	**John = 14**
33-52	average range (most women score about 47 and most men score about 42)	Tony = 42
53-63	above average	Charlotte = 60
64-80	very high	Lydia = 76
80	maximum	no one in the family

Systemizing Quotient

Scores	Interpretation of SQ Score	Family Scores
0-19	low	no one in the family
20-39	average (most women score about 24 and most men score about 30)	Lydia = 35 Tony = 39
40-50	above average (most people with Asperger Syndrome or high functioning autism score in this range)	Charlotte = 43 **John = 46**
51-80	very high (three times as many people with Asperger Syndrome score in this range, compared to typical men, and almost no women score in this range)	no one in the family
80	maximum	no one in the family

I found these results so intriguing that I thought I would fill in the Childhood Asperger Syndrome Test (CAST)[77] for John as I remembered him when he was about eight years old. The results can be seen in Appendix 26. When this questionnaire was completed (April 2009) the maximum score possible was 31 and scores above 15 pointed to a possible autism spectrum disorder or related social-communication difficulties. John's score was 25. Obviously, because of the passage of time, my recollections and hence my answers to this questionnaire can't be as accurate as they would be if John was a young child now; nevertheless I doubt if they are far from the truth.

Autism Spectrum Quotient

Scores	Interpretation of AQ Score	Family Scores
0-10	low	no one in the family
11-22	average (most women score about 15 and most men score about 17)	Charlotte = 11 Lydia = 12
23-31	above average	Tony = 29
32-50	very high (most people with Asperger Syndrome or high functioning autism score about 35)	**John = 40**
50	maximum	no one in the family

I would like to conclude this chapter with a quote from Mary Mountstephen's book, *How to Detect Developmental Delay and What to Do Next*:

Every child has a different story. They cannot easily be labelled, categorized or packaged in simple terms. It is possible, through careful analysis, to provide explanations for the child's presenting problems that will allow for appropriate intervention to ensue.

It can be hard for teachers and parents to locate the cornerstone of a child's difficulties. Even if they are able to do so, the child might be locked into patterns of learning or behaving that perpetuate his difficulties. For change to occur the child has to actually believe he has the potential and capability to change and improve his performance.

Children's problems are often compound and multifaceted. It can be hard to locate the crux of the matter and strip away the layers that cloud the situation. An assessment can be cathartic for the child and lead him to have a better understanding of his own strengths and weaknesses which in itself can promote change.

21
Diagnosis and Labels

Like many adults born in the nineteen seventies or earlier, John didn't receive a formal diagnosis of any kind as a child. Was this detrimental to his well being? I'm not sure that receiving a diagnosis in those days would have been beneficial, as little knowledge about developmental differences was widely available. According to Christopher Gillberg (writing in 2002): 'It is clear that many adult psychiatric patients presenting with major diagnostic difficulty actually have – previously undiagnosed – Asperger syndrome'.

If a child's condition is interfering with daily life, an *accurate* diagnosis, coupled with appropriate professional help and supportive teachers, is the gold standard to aim for. However it's really important to recognise, that even if a diagnosis has been received, the child hasn't changed and should still be treated as an individual, not as a set of symptoms. As Campito (2007) writes:

The special needs are something your child has. They are not the sum total of your child. Your child is still the same person she or he was before being diagnosed. Your child still has his or her same abilities, his or her same personality, and all the million and one other characteristics that make your child a unique person. The disorder should not define your child...

We need the focus to stay on the child, not on the disability or the special needs. The disability is only a part of the person who is my son.

Although John agrees that special needs are not the sum total of the child, he also believes:

If I didn't have the aspie cluster of symptoms I've got, my birth history, and so on, I would probably be a wildly different person, with different interests, a radically different (and likely more conventional) life to this point, and so on. So, though I am not my special needs, they have clearly been enormously influential.

However, no two children are alike. Just because a child behaves very differently from the majority of those around him, this does not *necessarily* mean a diagnosis/label has to be sought. If the child is thriving and happy and his parents/carers and teachers are able to treat him as an individual and provide all the support, help and encouragement that he needs, then a diagnosis may not be essential.

Of course I wish that the professionals we'd seen in the 1970s and 1980s had known as much about developmental differences/disorders as the corresponding professionals today and that many of the informative books and websites currently available had been accessible then. I feel sure we would have taken full advantage of all this knowledge. I wouldn't want to discourage anyone from seeking a diagnosis, as there can be many advantages associated with the possession of a label that explains why someone behaves in a particular way. However, receiving a diagnosis is not the same as waving a magic wand. For this reason I discuss the potential pitfalls associated with the process later in this chapter: as they say, 'forewarned is forearmed'. Nevertheless, as Ives and Munro (2002) point out to those parents who feel that a diagnosis of an autism spectrum disorder could be harmful to their child:

> If a professional told you that your child had diabetes, would you be reluctant to accept this 'label'? Knowledge and recognition of a particular disorder is incredibly important to the well-being and development of the child. It allows others to understand and to offer appropriate help. This should not change because we are talking about autism rather than diabetes. Ignoring or refusing to use a label will not change a child's problems, though it can make things worse.

Clare Sainsbury (2009) for example, has no doubt that receiving a diagnosis was the right thing for her:

> I've noticed that parents, teachers and other professionals are often reluctant to seek a diagnosis of Asperger's, or to talk openly about a child's diagnosis, for fear of 'labelling' them...

> Avoiding the label doesn't make the differences go away. Someone with undiagnosed Asperger's still has Asperger's. Sometimes parents in particular will react as if the diagnosis itself has harmed their child, and that if they could only get the diagnosis reversed, their child's problems would go away.

According to Simon Baron-Cohen (2008a), it may not be necessary for a person to retain a diagnosis for ever:

> A diagnosis is made at a particular snapshot in time, at a point in that person's life when things had got so difficult that they needed the diagnosis in order to access support and help.

> In the case of Asperger syndrome it may, for example, have been useful to have a diagnosis as a teenager, when they weren't coping with mainstream school and the social pressures that this implies. By adulthood, that same person may have found a niche in which they not only feel they fit, but in which they are thriving, and feel they no longer need the diagnosis. I have come across people who seek the diagnosis and I have come across people who seek to be undiagnosed. The latter are just as valid as the former, but will need just as thorough a reassessment of the individual. This is to check it is the case that they are coping sufficiently that the autistic traits that they have no longer interfere with their daily life. If this is the case, then they no longer meet the criteria for a diagnosis...

> The medium- and low-functioning individuals on the autistic spectrum will need their diagnosis all their lives, to ensure they obtain help with sheltered living, sheltered employment and protection as a vulnerable person.

John is puzzled by some of the above:

> What does 'interfere' even mean? I am functioning perfectly well, but clearly my ASD has caused my life to take a completely different shape than it otherwise would have had, to allow for its foibles. I guess massive resculpting of one's entire life doesn't count as 'interference', since I'm functioning OK?

ADVANTAGES OF RECEIVING A DIAGNOSIS

Explanation for a child's differences

I believe one of the most important benefits of a diagnosis is an awareness that there is an understandable *explanation* for the unusual behaviours that may have caused such unease and worry. According to Attwood (2006): '[This can lead to] greater acceptance of the child within the extended family and family friends.' A diagnosis makes it much easier for parents to change people's attitudes by explaining to them why their child behaves as he/she does. Again, as Attwood (2006) writes:

> Adults and other children will become increasingly aware that the child does not behave, play or think like other children. The initial opinion of adults within the extended family and school may be that the child is rude and selfish, while peers may think that the child is just weird. If there is no diagnosis and explanation, others will make moral judgements that will inevitably have a detrimental effect on the child's self-esteem.

A diagnosis can also mean that parents don't need to waste any more time looking for *reasons* for their child's problems or assigning blame. Macintyre (2001) found that many parents were relieved to get a diagnosis, for as one explained: 'Why worry about giving the child a label... surely the label 'Dyspraxia' is much better than being told your child is lazy, which is what I've been told again and again.' Hopefully a diagnosis would make it easier for parents to accept their child as they *actually* are, even though they may still be disappointed that their child won't turn out as they'd originally anticipated. I totally agree with Luke Jackson (2002) when he writes:

> The best advice I would give to parents that have found out that their child has AS is just to accept them as they are. Preconceived ideas are never a good thing. To be on the autistic spectrum is not the same as being on death row – it is not a death sentence, it is not terminal, it is merely a name for a lifelong set of behaviours. Your and your child's life may now take a different course than you would have expected, but it is just as important and may even be more fascinating and enlightening.

What it feels like to accept the fact that your child's life may 'take a different course' is expressed beautifully in the article *Welcome to Holland* written by Emily Perl Kingsley.[78] She compares the birth of a child with special needs to the arrival of their holiday plane in Holland, rather than Italy as expected. Quoting extracts from the article:

> The important thing is that they haven't taken you to some horrible, disgusting, filthy place, full of pestilence, famine and disease. It's just a different place.

> So you must go out and buy a new guidebook. And you must learn a whole new language. And you will meet a whole new group of people you would never have met...

> But everyone you know is busy coming and going from Italy, and they're all bragging about what a wonderful time they had there. And for the rest of your life you will say, 'Yes, that's where I was supposed to go. That's what I had planned.' The pain of that will never, ever, go away, because the loss of that dream is a very

349

significant loss.

But if you spend your life mourning the fact that you didn't get to Italy, you may never be free to enjoy the very special, the very lovely things about Holland.

Just as there's no point trying to make Holland feel like Italy so there's no point trying to change your child into someone they can never be. Realistic expectations are crucial if you are going to make the most of your child's potential and accurate information can help parents and teachers develop such realistic expectations. However, as my psychologist daughter Lydia points out (and I mention later in this chapter):

> [It's also important to] reiterate Emily's point about pain and loss, to normalise the grieving process that many parents reading this book will go through/be going through. Otherwise, there's a danger of glossing over it here and saying that parents 'should' just enjoy their child and accept them the way they are. There's a process that many/most people go through, of grieving for the child that they thought they had/were going to have and accepting the one that they do have. This process should be supported as much as possible, so that parents don't feel guilt and shame for experiencing the perfectly normal emotions associated with loss and grief.

Ideally when a child is given a diagnosis, it ought to help parents and teachers experience the world through the child's eyes. This world may look and feel quite surprising. According to Ozonoff and colleagues (2002): 'You will come to understand why your child does what he or she does… With a diagnosis comes some ability to share his or her perspective and see the world through the eyes of your special child.' If a parent or teacher has the ability to put themselves into a child's shoes, it makes it much easier to make the sort of decisions that will enable the child to develop in a positive way. It can help adults understand how to adjust their behaviour in such a way as to help the child fulfil their potential. This should help to reduce the level of frustration experienced by the child when trying to cope in what can often seem like a hostile and alien world.

In the perfect world, a diagnosis shouldn't be only doom and gloom. It should reveal the child's strengths as well as describe the difficulties. As Clare Sainsbury (2009) writes:

> It's important to be positive and not to paint a picture of Asperger's syndrome as a 'disease'… but it's also important not to deny the real difficulties that can be involved. Only when it has been acknowledged that a child is genuinely different from others and does have problems is it possible to go on to build a positive self-image based on acceptance and even celebration of differences.

With a true understanding and acceptance of a child's strengths as well as weaknesses, comes the opportunity to exploit the strengths so as to build up the child's self-esteem. Appropriate help, support or accommodations should be provided to overcome the difficulties.

Leventhal-Belfer and Coe (2004) describe the impact of a diagnosis from a child's point of view when they write: 'As children grow and begin to ask questions, having a diagnosis can also help them make sense of why they experience some things differently from their peers.' Giving a name to something and realising that it's no-one's fault can provide a huge sense of relief for parents and children. There's no longer any need for them to feel guilty; the child's difficulties aren't due to poor parenting and the child doesn't have to blame themselves when they can't do something as easily as their peers. As Gillberg (2002) wrote:

> Accepting a diagnosis can stop children feeling stupid about the things they are struggling with, can't do or just get wrong; they needn't feel as if they are going mad because there is now an explanation for their difficulties.

Other children in the family can also benefit from a greater understanding of their sibling's unusual behaviour. They could explain to their friends why their brother or sister behaves so oddly at times. As Attwood (2006) explains:

> Siblings may have known for some time that their brother or sister is unusual and may have been either compassionate, tolerant and concerned about any difficulties, or embarrassed, intolerant and antagonistic... parents can now explain to their children why their brother or sister is unusual, and how the family has had to, and will need to adjust and work cooperatively and constructively to implement the strategies. Parents and professionals can provide the siblings with age-appropriate explanations about their brother or sister, to give to their friends, without jeopardizing their own social networks.

Meanwhile many adults, who have found life difficult and couldn't understand why, find that a diagnosis, which provides an explanation for their problems, can come as a huge relief. Moreover a diagnosis can also reduce feelings of isolation when they discover that there are many other people in a similar position. As Gillberg (2002) explains:

> Many who have wondered over the years why so many things around them 'went wrong', find in the diagnosis itself the beginning of an explanation of so many difficulties that previously seemed to be incomprehensible. Reading about Asperger syndrome in a booklet, a book, or on the Internet can serve as an unexpected eye-opener, indeed quite often as a positive revelation. The insight that there are others with similar, almost identical, problems is often an enormous relief... Rather than being burdened by the diagnosis, the diagnosis itself takes a load off everybody involved. It paves the way for much more helpful attitudes and makes it possible to go on without constantly looking back, 'digging' hopelessly for more or less plausible explanations.

As well as acceptance by others, self-understanding and self-acceptance are crucial if a person is going to be equipped to make the best decisions in life regarding daily living, relationships or careers. For adults and children alike, forever struggling and pretending to be something you're not is exhausting, unlikely to be successful and could easily lead to depression. If as a result of a diagnosis comes a genuine acceptance of oneself 'warts and all', then hopefully it will be less likely that secondary psychological symptoms will develop and more likely that true happiness and fulfilment will be the outcome. We're all different and we should all be proud of who we are. Not quite, says John:

> We should all be *accepting*, but one should only be *proud* if one has done something one should be proud of. I'm not proud of 'who I am', just of some of the

351

things I've done (and some of the ways I've, now and then, made people happier).

Access to information, early intervention and support

A diagnosis can make it easier for parents and carers to access further information about their child's condition from a variety of sources including professionals, other parents, books, web sites, courses, information leaflets, magazines, interactive DVDs and so on. It's also to be hoped that access to appropriate professional support services would be made easier with a diagnosis. Ideally some useful interventions such as physiotherapy, occupational therapy, speech therapy, social skills groups, help with anxiety, stress and anger management and extra assistance in the classroom would follow on from a childhood diagnosis. Drug or dietary interventions may also be considered. Useful information can be accessed from a variety of sources: e.g. in the UK, the National Autistic Society and worldwide, those listed in http://www.autism-resources.com/links/organizations.html. Social services, supported living schemes, university and employment support may be easier to access after a diagnosis. It should make it simpler to obtain an Education, Health and Care plan in the UK, which can mean additional help and financial support are provided; it may also become easier to obtain some financial support in the form of disability benefits. In some countries, including the US, it's essential to have a diagnosis in order to get appropriate health insurance cover.

It may be possible to find and join an association created for those with the same label. These associations, which sometimes have local support groups, can provide useful ideas, practical help and moral support from others in a similar situation. As Eric Schopler (1995) found:

> One of the most overwhelming aspects of being a parent of a child with autism is the risk of intense isolation. Too few family members or friends understand what autism is and how it affects you, your child and your family. Your child feels so different. You feel so alone…
>
> I discovered that my best survival mechanism was to connect with other parents of autistic children. It was parents – the actual soldiers in the trenches – who knew the local resources and support services, and had the great ideas!

Local support groups may also enable children with special needs to participate in social activities. As Macintyre (2001) notes:

> [A diagnosis makes it easier for] parents and children to belong to a support group and this reduces isolation, means that children can meet other children with dyspraxia who know how they feel, allows parents to share strategies and helpful ideas, even just let off steam, means shared ideas can give everyone confidence in trying new moves.

There may be a social support network for siblings, providing the understanding and encouragement that can reduce feelings of isolation, hopelessness and guilt. Some adults who receive a diagnosis may also benefit greatly from joining a support group made up of people with a similar diagnosis. The group can make them feel as if they belong, on an equal footing, to a community with a shared culture and values. As Attwood (2006) explains:

An adult with a diagnosis of Asperger's syndrome may benefit from joining an adult support group that has local meetings, or an Internet support group or chat room. This can provide a sense of belonging to a distinct and valued culture and enable the person to consult members of the culture for advice.

A diagnosis ought to make it more likely that children will receive understanding and help from the adults around them rather than constant criticism which can have such a devastating effect on a child's self-esteem. As Attwood (2006) points out, it's important to realise:

> Children with Asperger's syndrome have no physical characteristics to indicate that they are different, and having intellectual ability may lead others to have high expectations with regard to their social knowledge. Once the diagnosis is confirmed and understood, there can be a significant positive change in other people's expectations, acceptance and support.

In theory a diagnosis (or diagnoses) should mean that parents, health and education professionals have a common understanding of the difficulties that the child is experiencing, are all striving towards the same goals and can work together productively to help the child as much as possible. Early intervention is very important as this can take advantage of the extraordinary plasticity of the young brain and reduce the incidence of unfortunate compensatory behaviours and secondary symptoms. According to Gillberg (2002):

> There is emerging evidence that early diagnosis, information, psychological support and educational interventions can reduce suffering and degree of handicap in the longer term, both for the individual and his/her affected family. This, to a considerable degree, is the effect of changed attitudes and better understanding among the closest members of the social network...

> Individuals with Asperger syndrome may react with severe psychiatric breakdown under conditions of even mild stress. It goes almost without saying that in such circumstances, many psychological problems should be seen as 'secondary' and that they would be potentially preventable through changes in the attitudes of people living or working with those affected by Asperger syndrome. One study in our centre showed that families, teachers and peers who 'know' what it is all about, are much more positive in their reactions than those who do not have a name for the problems. They make much more appropriate demands and have more realistic expectations. This means they can take the pressure off in some areas while having a more positive – and demanding – attitude in other fields.

Last, but by no means least, by naming a condition the door is opened to further research and knowledge.

Parents' role

It's crucial that parents don't think, once they've received a diagnosis, they can sit back and safely leave *everything* to the professionals. As Jan Campito (2007), who has two sons, one with Asperger's and one with attention deficit disorder, discovered:

I need to be able to describe my son's developmental disorder so that others can understand how it affects my child... I need to be able to talk to the person very specifically, about what they could/should do to help my child...

Frankly, I'm quite surprised by the extent to which I find that I need to take charge in this manner. I thought parenting a child with special needs would primarily entail finding the best experts available, and then just scrupulously following their advice. I was so wrong! Or at least so naïve! I've been amazed to discover how important it has been for me to become a guiding expert in my children's disabilities. I am very fortunate to live in a progressive, receptive school district, but even so, a significant proportion of the interventions and supports employed with my children have been instigated by me.

No one knows their child better than the parents and although I don't doubt that the experts always try to do what they think is best, mistakes are made and these same professionals don't have to live with the consequences. There's still a great deal to find out about developmental differences and disorders and new research continues to influence professional advice. Parents need to keep informed and may well have to fight to be heard and to make sure their child receives sufficient help. As Baron-Cohen (2008a) says, parents need to act as advocates for their children in order to make sure they receive the help they need:

The world is still not as autism- or Asperger-friendly as it could be. Until it is, parents and others continue to have a role in educating their local school, social services, GP or education authority about the nature of autism and Asperger syndrome and fighting on behalf of their child for appropriate support... Realistically, it is important to recognise that such parental involvement may be essential in helping a person with autism or Asperger syndrome get the right support. Joining a parent support group can make it feel less like having to fight alone.

Strong and persistent advocacy is particularly important because most children on the autism spectrum, with attention deficit disorder, dyspraxia, dyslexia or any other specific learning disability, look perfectly ordinary. It's hard to see, just by looking at them, that they may be finding certain aspects of their life extremely difficult. As the National Autistic Society points out:[79]

You can't tell that someone has autism just by looking at them. Some people with autism can appear to be very able, so you may need to tell social, education and healthcare professionals about your child's condition and their need of support.

Parents will need to keep explaining and fighting for whatever their child needs in order to succeed both at school and elsewhere. As Leventhal-Belfer and Coe (2004) point out: 'Advocacy is required in every setting in which the child participates in social relationships with peers.' A diagnosis should make it easier for parental advocacy to create a positive impact on the attitude of teachers and peers towards the child in question, thereby making their time at school less stressful. As Boyd (1999) explains:

[A diagnosis means] teachers can be informed, if they do not know already, of the symptoms of the diagnosed disorders as they relate to the child in question. Discussions could take place regarding which adaptations and accommodations would be most helpful in the classroom and playground. This ought to prevent children being punished for difficulties that are outside their control and enable them to achieve their full potential. Similarly, education of the other children in the school, plus positive action by teachers, may decrease bullying and even allow the diagnosed child to make some friends.

My daughter Lydia agrees that 'whole school approaches about ASD for example can be very useful (as long as they don't centre around or single out particular children)'. In order for parental advocacy in schools to have a chance of being successful it's important that a *cooperative* rather than a *confrontational* approach is used. This may be difficult when a worried parent feels that their child isn't getting the help they need and the school or teacher isn't sympathetic to these concerns. However a formal diagnosis ought to make it easier for parents to persuade the school that the child's difficulties are real and everyone would benefit from a change in approach. Although obtaining a diagnosis *should* make it more straightforward to advocate for one's child, it can still be both time consuming and challenging. As Missiuna and colleagues (2006) note:

> A number of parents clearly struggled with their role as an advocate for their child. They indicate that it took a lot of time and energy to be an advocate, and that they found it difficult to know the best approach to take at times.

In addition to undertaking an advocacy role, I think it's crucial that parents realise the difference *they* can make by the way they choose to parent their child. Children spend a large amount of time at home, even when they're of school age. The quality of parenting they receive can make an enormous difference to their future well-being. This is of course what this book aims to cover.

POSSIBLE ISSUES RELATED TO RECEIVING A DIAGNOSIS

Delays in receiving a diagnosis and advice

Unfortunately, obtaining a satisfactory diagnosis can be quite a difficult and time consuming process. The delays can be exacerbated by professionals encouraging parents to 'wait and see' because 'all children develop at different rates' and their child might 'grow out of' whatever the parents are anxious about. Ross and Jolly (2006) suggest:

> Parents should trust their instincts relative to the need for their child to have a formal assessment. Many times parents are encouraged to wait by professionals when they innately feel something is deviant in their child's developmental patterns.

Similarly Blakemore-Brown, writing in 2002, found:

> Despite increasing acceptance of the importance of early intervention in developmental disorders, many children may have been under a watching brief for years, if picked up at all, and then possibly placed on waiting lists for assessment and support for years.

> Families can become desperate to find out what is wrong and how to intervene to help their child. Instead they all too often have found themselves caught up in an inexorably slow process of diagnosis and in some cases intrusive surveillance.

Sophie Walker, writing in the UK in 2012, said:

[My daughter Grace] was formally diagnosed with Asperger's Syndrome only last year, after five years of waiting lists, inconclusive assessments, repeated questioning and a lot of shoulder shrugging.

These delays could mean that parental efforts to get their child diagnosed dominate family life; precious time and energy could be wasted when efforts could be focused on trying to understand their child's behaviour and needs. A diagnosis *per se* will not change the child or his behaviour. Children don't behave 'badly' or fail at their school work for no reason. It's important that parents and teachers try to understand as early as possible, regardless of whether any diagnosis has yet been made, why these children behave as they do. There's a huge amount of helpful information available on the web and in books which can provide insights into why a child might be acting in a particular way and offer suggestions as to how to work round the difficulties. As Amanda Kirby, writing in 2005 in Sugden and Chambers, points out:

Parents may have to wait months to access services then may need to go from one professional to another, first trying to find out what's wrong and then what to do. The wait may also increase the feeling that once the label has been given all help will follow and until it is given little can be done. Children with DCD [Developmental Coordination Disorder] by definition, using the DSM-IV... criteria, have difficulties in activities of living and learning on a daily basis. Many of these difficulties have functional impact and could often start to be addressed with or without a label at school or home with little risk of harm...

Growing waiting lists mean that some children may not receive any assessment or therapy. This is especially true for older children as health services for this group are often very limited beyond the age of 11 years.

While waiting for a diagnosis, parents and teachers should try to discover what the child finds easy and enjoys, what they find difficult if not impossible, what they find scary or overwhelming and so on. An awareness of which situations can trigger meltdowns or other difficult behaviours can provide useful clues to a child's needs as can the existence of any intense interests. This type of personalised understanding should help adults discover what sort of useful adaptations could be made both at home and at school. These interventions could reduce the stress experienced by all concerned and enable the children to have a happier childhood with less chance of developing secondary symptoms.

Reactions to a diagnosis

Since all parents are different, it isn't surprising that their reactions may vary when their child receives a diagnosis. As Baron-Cohen (2008a) writes:

People react differently to hearing the words 'I think your child has autism' or 'I think you have Asperger syndrome'. Some are relieved that finally there is a name for the condition that has always made them feel they, or their child are different; and relieved that finally they have a signpost for where to go for the most relevant help. Some react with a sense of shock that they, or their child, have a condition that is understood to be genetic, affecting brain development... The shock can sometimes turn to sadness if hopes turn to disappointments about the future. People vary in how long they take to adjust to the diagnosis.

Even though parents may have been aware that their child was different and may have been seeking a diagnosis for some time, they may still be overwhelmed by their emotional reactions when the diagnosis is actually received. Some parents will be pleased that at last they have official confirmation of what they'd already suspected and as a result hope that help and support will be forthcoming. Others may be shocked to hear that their child has something wrong with them, as Ives and Munro (2002) point out:

> Families unaware that autism was a possible outcome may find the news shocking. This is particularly likely when early suggestions from professionals indicated less pervasive conditions that the child could grow through (e.g. developmental delays or the 'terrible twos').

Before parents can fully accept the diagnosis and be capable of advocating for their child, they may need to work through feelings of shock, anger, denial and so on. It's crucial that emotional support is provided when parents are given a diagnosis and also at other key points in their child's life. Patricia Howlin (1998) writes:

> Additional support and guidance is particularly likely to be needed in the months following diagnosis; in the early years when behavioural problems may be at their most severe; when children first go to school...; when they move into adolescence and are unable to take part in any normal teenage activities; when they take their first holiday or period of respite care away from the family; when they go to college; or when they eventually leave home.

Adults, who may have struggled with life for many years, can also experience a range of strong emotions when they receive a diagnosis. As Attwood (2006) describes so vividly:

> I have noted that when an adult is diagnosed with Asperger's syndrome there can be a range of emotional reactions... There can be intense relief: 'I am not going mad'; euphoria at ending a nomadic wandering from specialist to specialist, at last discovering why they feel and think differently to others...

> There can also be moments of anger at the delay in being diagnosed and at 'The System' for not recognizing the signs for so many years. There can be feelings of despair regarding how their lives would have been much easier if the diagnosis had been confirmed decades ago. Other emotional reactions can be a sense of grief for all the suffering in trying to be as socially successful as others, and the years of feeling misunderstood, inadequate and rejected.

Grief

Many authors compare the stages of grief that many parents experience on receiving a diagnosis for their child, to that of a bereavement. The stages of grief include shock, numbness, denial, anger and despair or, as in Kübler Ross's[80] five stage model, denial, anger, bargaining, depression and acceptance. According to Ross and Jolly (2006):

Once parents receive a diagnosis it is very likely they may experience a grief re-action similar to when a death occurs. The grief response varies tremendously from family to family in terms of severity, intensity, and duration. Parents cannot be 'moved through' their grief reaction. It can be as short as a week or as long as several years in duration. In addition, a grief reaction can, and often does, reoccur as the child moves through predictable life stages and life events (e.g. entry into school, dating, proms).

Shock can easily be followed by, or accompanied by, denial and a refusal to accept the diagnosis. Parents may have hoped that they were worrying about nothing and can initially refuse to believe that their child really has something wrong with them. As Leventhal-Belfer and Coe (2004) wrote:

> For most parents the news that their young child has Asperger's Syndrome, or characteristics of AS, is shocking and they are overwhelmed with disbelief. Ex-ceptions to this are the parents who have another child or relative with an Autism Spectrum Disorder and see similarities between them, or the parents who have been insisting that something is different with their child since he was a toddler. For these parents the diagnosis, as frightening as it is, confirms that their parental intuition was on target. [Lydia would argue that these parents might still feel shock at their intuition being confirmed, even if they're not surprised.]

> The question for many parents, though, is: how can a child who is so bright, curi-ous, and connected with his parents have any similarities with a child who has Asperger's syndrome?...

> For parents who have not experienced any difficulty playing with their child, the idea of their child having difficulty engaging in reciprocal play with others seems unbelievable...

> They will struggle with understanding how their child could have an Autistic Spectrum Disorder since he is so very different from the stereotype they hold of what a child with autism looks like.

It's only natural that parents feel angry and frustrated and wonder why they should be the ones to have a child with problems while the children of their friends sail through life easily. They may feel they are to blame for not intervening and getting help sooner.

Chasing cures

It's perfectly natural for parents to feel a passionate need to search for a reason for their child's situation, for something or someone to blame. They can also, with the very best of intentions, become prey to the latest fads and fashions and spend a great deal of time researching possible 'cures' and then trying many of them out. Not only can this search be time consuming and expensive, it can subject the family to considerable stress and lead to unnecessary medication and continual disappointment, without the child's in-dividual needs actually being met. According to Bartram (2007):

> Diagnosis, much as it may be needed and wanted, exerts another pressure on par-ents which is hard to withstand. It brings the possibility of the child being eclipsed by the condition with which they are diagnosed. In the face of incurable

disability we easily feel helpless and useless. Some parents feel that in order to do their best for the child they must become experts in the condition. Access to the internet opens up infinite possibilities to read about conditions, therapies and even, it is hoped, cures. The danger of this response is that information about the condition might begin to replace first-hand knowledge of one particular child...

Schopler (1995) warns of the risks associated with trying out treatments for which there is no *independent* evidence of efficacy:

For a parent first encountering the diagnosis of autism, the possible choices of available treatments can present costly and overwhelming choices. Many such therapies and treatment concepts have appeared in the public press and professional journals...

These techniques are frequently heralded with great excitement by parents convinced that they have witnessed the miraculous improvement they have been searching for, or by professionals hoping for the fame and rewards of finding a cure. Unfortunately, the road to scientific progress is fraught with false hopes. Too often these techniques are only the product of successful marketing and media hype. The data do not support the technique's intended usefulness and often result in a short-lived fad.

Before trying any new intervention it would be wise to look at the web site of the charity *Research Autism*,[81] where a rating (independent of any commercial considerations) is given for many interventions.

Marital relationships

Receiving a diagnosis that implies that their child isn't 'normal' and won't 'grow out' of their difficulties can put a great strain on any marital relationship. If a child is given a diagnosis in an insensitive manner in the absence of sufficient support, the parents could easily experience significant worry and despair, given the type of depressing stories so often seen in the media. It's easy for parents to feel guilt that their child's problems are their fault in some way. Either parent may worry that they are responsible for passing on family genes that could cause the condition or that the mother did something wrong while she was pregnant. Blaming the other parent can easily threaten the relationship between the parents. As Leventhal-Belfer and Coe (2004) wrote, when parents receive a diagnosis for their child:

[This] may challenge an already stressed relationship if one of the parents, in our experience typically the mother, begins to wonder if the diagnosis fits their spouse. It is quite common that parents who may not be ready to accept the diagnosis for their child find that it sheds light on their partner and on their relationship.

If the parents can't agree on what is best for their child or if one of the parents becomes so obsessed with the condition that they neglect the rest of the family, this might also trigger the breakdown of the relationship. Too much time and effort devoted to the needs of the diagnosed child will inevitably be at the expense of a reasonably normal family life. It's important that the adults have the time and energy to look after any other children in the family as well as their own relationship.

Recognising the child's strengths

Worries that their child will be unable to grow up into an independent and happy adult are almost inevitable with any diagnosis of special needs. These fears will be strengthened if the diagnosis focuses on deficits and doesn't place enough emphasis on the associated strengths. As Sainsbury (2009) writes: 'Seeing children with Asperger's only in terms of deficits and deviations from the norm typically leads to an exclusive focus on attempting to remedy weaknesses, instead of developing strengths.' Because a 'disorder' is being diagnosed (as opposed to a difference), it is inevitable that it will be defined by features that are considered to be deficits. Even strengths are often defined in terms that make them look as if they are weaknesses. For example: the amazing ability of people on the autism spectrum to focus on details is defined as an inability to see the big picture, the extraordinary memory of so many on the spectrum is just ignored and the exceptional ability to focus on things of interest is disparagingly defined as obsessional. Many books on autism spectrum disorders, as well media coverage of the topic, are often quite depressing, painting as they do all the problems that people diagnosed with special needs might experience. No wonder parents worry so much about the future of their children. In order to give their children the best chance of leading a happy life and fulfilling their potential as they grow up, it would be far better for parents to concentrate on their children's strengths. Jan Starr Campito (2007) writes very movingly about her own experience:

> I don't know about you when you were faced with the initial, cold descriptions of your child's condition, but I wept. It was becoming painfully obvious to me that there was much I could not protect my child from, and I was terrified. The literature is going to try to provide a comprehensive list of all the things your child may need help with, and the problems your child may have to overcome. These confrontations are personally painful, so how do you accept this task of learning about your child's disability, while keeping the pain from overwhelming you?

> Although this may feel like small comfort now, keep in mind that children vary tremendously in how a particular disability manifests, and how that disability interacts with their personality and with their life experiences. Yet the literature often collapses all possible severities and all possible manifestations into a single discussion... The Internet fuels this, piling on article after article, some of which may not be accurate, and others may not apply to your child...

> The understanding in our home was that every person has things they can do well, and things they need to work on. The therapies were presented as things to make them 'even better' at whatever the activity was, or if the child acknowledged having difficulty with a skill, we would present the therapy as a way of getting others to help us learn.

My daughter points out the importance of 'watching and waiting', as parents don't need to know everything at once about their child's possible future:

> It can often be containing for parents to know that they don't have to know it all

now and actually couldn't possibly do this even if they wanted to! As each developmental trajectory is so different and unpredictable, it's never possible to know which criteria/experiences will apply to an individual as they develop. I would imagine that, post-diagnosis, thinking about the future and how to manage all of the years and challenges to come would feel like preparing to climb an impossibly tall mountain. It's important to think about this as a step-by-step process and, to continue with the metaphor, to climb a little of the mountain at a time, before pausing to review what has gone before and consider and prepare for the next leg of the journey. It is only at this point, when more is known about how the previous step has been negotiated, the current climate, the terrain that has now come into view and the internal and external resources that are available, that one can realistically hope to think about and take the next step. Just one step at a time.

What comes after the diagnosis?

Unless the child is profoundly disabled, lack of public funding may well mean, that despite obtaining a formal diagnosis, a child may have to wait a long time for any intervention. They may also find that when the intervention arrives there isn't enough of it or it doesn't do what 'it says on the tin'. As more children have been diagnosed in recent years with autism spectrum disorders (ASD) the pressure on limited funds has increased. As Rita Jordan pointed out in 2007:

> With an apparent increase in prevalence, the ASD category may also be seen as too broad to serve as the basis of resource allocation. This is resulting once more in arbitrary and unjust divisions of the spectrum so that some categories... are denied resources and support. Without that support, these individuals may be eventually 'pushed' into a situation where their difficulties increase and they are no longer able to manage unsupported, i.e. they become truly disabled.

According to Simon Baron-Cohen (2008a), there are horror stories of people diagnosed with Asperger's syndrome being passed around from one service to another with none of them willing to take responsibility and provide help and support:

> The local services sometimes pass the buck by saying that Asperger syndrome is the responsibility of the local mental health team. They in turn say that Asperger syndrome is not a mental health condition but a learning disability. The learning disabilities team then say that Asperger syndrome is not a learning disability because the person has an IQ above 70 and is an educational responsibility. The educational authority may then pass the buck by saying it is a social services responsibility, who pass the responsibility back to the mental health team.

Interestingly enough, Neihart (2000) points out:

> Unlike autistic children who often receive special assistance in schools, the bright AS student may be left to manage the best he or she can. Relationships with teachers and peers can be extremely difficult. Over time, such children may become depressed as a result of their social isolation. Severe anxiety states can also be present.

Shortage of resources can mean that parents find themselves continually battling for the help their child needs. Writing in the Dyspraxia Foundation Professional Journal in 2005, Weidner reported:

> The families in our survey expressed strong feelings of waging a battle on a daily basis to get help for their child. It is this struggle – with constant setbacks, small or large – that accumulate to wear the family down.

Walker (2012) writes movingly about the absence of help after her daughter Grace was diagnosed with Asperger's syndrome:

> So we had a diagnosis. With the diagnosis came a label.

> For a long time afterwards in that first year after being told, I felt as though the doctors had slapped a sticker on Grace – 'Fragile, This Way Up' – and left me to stagger off with her, with no destination and no map.

> Immediately after the initial shock wore off, I hoped that naming Grace's idiosyncrasy – awarding her the title of a person with Asperger's Syndrome – would present us with some allies, open some doors. Instead it became evident pretty quickly that we were on our own...

> Understanding and tolerance, it appeared, were no more on offer now than before we had a name for my daughter's condition.

Whereas relying on state funding may mean insufficient help, parents who pay for everything privately (or use health insurance) and see several professionals, may end up with far *too* much to do. Even if all the interventions are in themselves a good idea, one can have too much of a good thing. According to Bartram (2007):

> Few parents would subject their child to tests and other interventions unless they felt it was important to do so, but worries and anxieties can interfere with the capacity to distinguish between what is really valuable and what less so. So too, in the case of therapy and treatment in general, some parents assume that 'more is better' whereas this is not necessarily the case at all. In that way there can be a danger of placing themselves and their child under more pressure than is helpful...

> Parents sometimes feel that unless they have tried to help their child in *every way possible,* they have failed. Yet this frame of mind may not lead to well-being within the family. Driven by the fear of being found wanting, either by others or by themselves, parents may be in danger of taking on too much.

Once a child has received a diagnosis, with its emphasis on the child's deficits, there's the risk that everyone concentrates on what the child can't do rather than spending time on developing the child's strengths. It's very stressful for all concerned if every waking hour is spent trying to 'improve' the child and it's all too easy for the children who are being 'improved' to believe they're failures because they're always being faced with their difficulties. It doesn't leave enough time for the child to relax, just be themselves and enjoy some of their childhood. Kristine Barnett (whose extraordinary book *The Spark: A Mother's Story of Nurturing Genius* describes how her son Jake progressed from a diagnosis of autism at the age of two and a prognosis that he would never be able to read to attending college maths and science courses at the age of eight) wrote: 'The only compass I've ever followed is to let Jake do the things he loves and to make sure he gets to have a childhood.' Barnett had pulled her son out of special education classes as he wasn't deriving any benefit from them and allowed him to follow his passions with spectacular results. Because of her success with Jake, Barnett started a programme called *Little Light* for other children diagnosed with autism:

> From the beginning, I knew that I wanted to approach autism differently. Typical therapy focused on the lowest skills. Most of the parents who came to Little Light had spent years trying to get their kids to hop up to the next skill on the ladder, usually without much success. I had seen my share of these sessions, hours spent trying to get a kid to put three rings on a post or to feed a cookie to a puppet, all to no avail. I'd watched my own son nod off in a session, still holding a therapy putty ball. So instead of hammering away at all the tasks these kids *couldn't* do, I thought we'd start with what they *wanted* to do.

Even if the parents and experts believe there's a great deal that needs to be worked on, it's important to remember that 'Rome wasn't built in a day'. Moreover, trying to address problems before the child is ready or without suitably motivating them can be counter-productive. It's important to pick one's battles carefully and not try to sort everything out at once; prioritising is crucial. In practice this means only dealing with those issues which are the most important *and* amenable to improvement or those which are the most urgent. The most urgent ones are usually very obvious but the rest may be harder to identify. Instead of trying to 'improve' everything, why not accept that there are developmental differences between children, encourage the individual's strengths, find a way to use these strengths to help some of the weaknesses (when it's absolutely necessary) and use accommodations whenever possible? For example, the internet provided our son (who loved computers, could write well, was sociable but unfortunately unable to manage in live group situations) with the opportunity to be able to communicate easily with a group of like-minded people. There's no need to try and make these children like everyone else. What's important is to ensure that they grow up into happy and fulfilled adults able to live as independent a life as possible. As Sainsbury wrote so perceptively in her book *Martian in the Playground*:

> In schools, the impulse of teachers to try and make children with Asperger's behave in a 'normal' way often leads to a concentration on 'treating' harmless differences at the expense of actually educating the child in question. Teachers are unwilling to accommodate autistic styles of learning; instead all too often, when children develop strategies for themselves that increase their ability to learn and cope (such as pacing in order to think, or making drawings or talking to themselves in class in order to follow the lesson), teachers promptly suppress them as 'inappropriate' (and are then unable to understand why the child fails to learn or exhibits 'challenging behaviour').

Stigma and bullying

Parents may worry about the stigma attached to a diagnosis and as a consequence, isolate themselves from friends and family. Unfortunately, because many diagnoses focus on what children can't do and don't identify any accompanying strengths, a diagnosis can have very negative connotations. This can easily make parents and children ashamed and upset about what feels like a stigmatising label rather than proud of who they are and what they're good at. The child's self-esteem may be significantly lowered unless great care is taken to emphasise all the child's strengths and explain to them that their diagnosis hasn't changed anything. Labels in *themselves* are not the problem: it's unlikely that being labelled a genius, a prodigy or gifted would produce such feelings! It is the negative connotations associated with the particular label that cause the problem. For example, when I searched on freethesaurus.net for synonyms for 'autistic' I was appalled by the number of unpleasant entries such as emotionally dead, heartless, selfish etc. As Notbohm (2005) wrote:

> Those of us who live with and love a child with autism also live with the frustrating lack of knowledge and unfair stereotypes, assigned by the larger world. Whether we liked it or not, 'autistic' does not yet inspire general reactions of a favorable nature, does not yet stir the casual bystander to look beyond the label to see a whole person, splendidly full of both gifts and gaffs. The broader reaction, 'Uh-oh. Silent, withdrawn head-banger,' is still too common; the first assumption is one of limitations.

> I... abandoned the word 'autistic' in describing my son... What helped me out was a ridiculous website called www.hyperdictionary.com which pairs the word 'autistic' with the synonym 'unfit' and continues with... 155 'related terms' including anesthetized, catatonic, emotionally dead.

However, according to Ives & Munro (2002): 'Labels do not stigmatize, people do. Intolerance towards anyone different from the norm creates stigmas. Blaming the label is ignoring the underlying problem.' Sainsbury (2009), for example, describes what happened to her:

> Some people are afraid that having a label will stigmatize a child. But social stigma is attached to being disabled or different in any way, not to the label itself... Sadly, someone who is different will be stigmatized whether they have a label or not, and children with Asperger's who escape official labelling generally don't escape unofficial labelling. When I didn't have an official diagnostic label my teachers unofficially labelled me 'weirdo', 'nerd' and 'freak'; frankly, I prefer the official label. It's the stigma that's attached to being different which is the problem, not the label.

Sometimes a child labelled with a diagnosis can find themselves bullied *because* of the label. According to Attwood (2006):

> There can be disadvantages in having a diagnosis in terms of how the person and others perceive the characteristics. If the diagnostic news is broadcast widely, there will inevitably be some children or adults who misuse this disclosure to torment and despise the person with Asperger's syndrome. Care must be taken when using the diagnostic term Asperger's syndrome as some children may consider the condition is infectious (or tease the child that it is), or corrupt the term in a variety of ways – Asparagus syndrome, Hamburger syndrome or Arseburger syndrome, among others.

Walker (2012) describes a 17 year old boy, Harry, who was diagnosed in his early teens, wouldn't accept his diagnosis for more than a year and still keeps the diagnosis a secret because he is 'worried that his teenage peers would call him 'retarded' or something similar, and that any gossip about him would spread quickly through social networks like Facebook.' Unfortunately many children who receive a diagnosis may be bullied anyhow just for being different. As our son, who didn't have a diagnosis and was seriously bullied at secondary school, said: 'Exactly… teenagers do not need a diagnosis to detect difference.' In theory, education about difference plus a strong and rigorously enforced anti-bullying policy should minimise these problems but unfortunately bullying seems to be endemic in many schools as well as in the workplace.

How a diagnosis may be misused

Once a label is attached to a person in the form of a diagnosis, it's possible that the person will be pigeon-holed in some way rather than treated as an individual with their own personality and attributes; judging someone by a label is nothing more than pure prejudice. As Notbohm (2005) wrote: 'Every child deserves to start his or her life and education with a slate clean of preconceived notions. Labels are not necessarily malicious but they are seldom harmless.' One unfortunate side effect of this pigeon-holing is that teachers and parents *may* have unreasonably low expectations for the child, which in turn will influence the child's view of themselves. According to Attwood (2006):

> Having a diagnosis of Asperger's syndrome could limit the expectations of others, who may assume that the person will never be able to achieve as well as his or her peers with regard to social, academic and personal success. The diagnosis should facilitate realistic expectations but not dictate the upper limits of ability.

One of the most important influences on any child's development is the expectations of those around them. It's essential, that whether a child has a diagnosis or not, realistic expectations are maintained at all times, however difficult this may be to achieve. Unreasonably high expectations will lead to a feeling of constant failure, while low expectations may prevent the child from fulfilling their potential and taking advantage of whatever strengths they possess. If a parent or teacher believes that a child isn't capable of something because of some condition or other, then excuses of the type 'this child can't be expected to do so and so because he has disorder XXX', can ensure that everyone (including the child themselves) gives up on anything that is more challenging. When Campito's children (2007) tried to use excuses to get out of activities they found difficult:

> [She] simply told the boys that just because something was harder for them, that didn't mean they didn't have to do it. Their diagnoses just told us there was a logical reason why some things may be harder and might need a little extra attention and effort.

Low expectations can easily lead to a 'victim' frame of mind. This will make it far more difficult for the child to grow up into an adult who can work and live independently. Rather than giving up, the child should be encouraged, given suitable accommodations, extra time and assistance so that they can progress towards achieving whatever it was that proved so difficult. How will they ever learn otherwise? It could well turn out many years later that the 'experts' were quite wrong and people with this particular condition *could* learn to do something that was once thought to be impossible. For example, many years ago it was thought that someone who had lost the ability to speak as a result of a stroke would never be able to speak again and so no one tried to teach them. These days this is known to be false. 'Exactly', says Lydia who then adds:

> Similarly, individuals with a personality disorder diagnosis were considered 'untreatable' until relatively recently. However, therapies have started to be developed that have good evidence in terms of their efficacy for clients diagnosed with borderline personality disorder, for example.

With a formal diagnosis comes the possibility that a 'one size fits all' approach will be used. A diagnosis might lead a teacher, for example, to think they know exactly what will work best for the child because they have taught a child with the same diagnosis before; they fit the child into some narrow stereotype. According to Brenda Boyd (2009):

> There are always problems with stereotypes because by their very nature they tie things down too narrowly. People can easily get a fixed idea in their heads about what AS looks like, and not realise that their picture is far too narrow. It is worse than meaningless to make AS into a stereotype because it covers a wide range in the first place. Nevertheless it happens a lot.

> If you have one specific picture of AS in your head, and then you come across someone who looks completely different from that picture, you may find it hard to believe that other person also has AS.

Whatever the diagnosis, it is always best to look at each child individually and assess their individual strengths, interests and challenges when managing expectations and planning interventions. Gillberg (2002) puts it very clearly when he writes:

> Respect for the individual with Asperger syndrome must always take precedence in the planning of help and treatment for people with this variant of autism spectrum disorder. In spite of many superficial similarities, people with Asperger syndrome are all different, and there are no two people with the diagnosis who benefit from exactly the same kind of intervention approaches. As with other people, there is considerable variation in respect of the general intellectual level. The most highly intelligent are, of course, much better at abstractions than those who are of low normal intelligence... An intervention programme identical for all with the syndrome, be it psychological, educational or medical/pharmacological, should never be attempted.

Inadequate diagnosis

Unfortunately when it does arrive, the diagnosis may be quite inadequate. The children may be under-diagnosed, over-diagnosed or just misdiagnosed. How can this happen?

Symptoms rather than objective laboratory measures

When I was writing the first draft of this chapter, the definitions of developmental syndromes and disorders were to be found in the Diagnostic and Statistical Manual of Mental Disorders DSM-IV (1994), revised in 2000 and published by the American

Psychiatric Association, or in the International Classification of Diseases ICD-10 published by the World Health Organisation in 1993. These definitions, which are symptom based and decided on by a committee rather than by a truly scientific understanding of the underlying processes responsible for the 'disorders', are far from perfect and have to be regularly revised. So far there have been five revisions of the DSM since it was first published in 1952. Tony Attwood (2006) concluded that the results from a variety of research studies would suggest that 'a diagnosis of Asperger's Syndrome is almost impossible using current DSM-IV criteria'. In fact Asperger's disorder disappeared altogether as a separate label in DSM-5 (released in May 2013) where it's included in the category autism spectrum disorder. The problem is that we're currently hampered by our limited knowledge of how the amazingly complex structure called the brain actually works and how differences in its detailed activity will lead to an individual's strengths and weaknesses. All we can do at present is attempt to group certain symptoms together and give them a name, whether they actually result from the same underlying mechanisms or not. According to Thomas Insell, (now former) director of the National Institute of Medical Health:[82]

> The strength of each of the editions of DSM has been 'reliability' – each edition has ensured that clinicians use the same terms in the same ways. The weakness is its lack of validity. Unlike our definitions of ischemic heart disease, lymphoma, or AIDS, the DSM diagnoses are based on a consensus about clusters of clinical symptoms, not any objective laboratory measure. In the rest of medicine, this would be equivalent to creating diagnostic systems based on the nature of chest pain or the quality of fever. Indeed, symptom-based diagnosis, once common in other areas of medicine, has been largely replaced in the past half century as we have understood that symptoms alone rarely indicate the best choice of treatment.

For the majority of 'disorders' or syndromes defined by behavioural symptoms there is no blood test, scan or other medical test that can be used for identification. As Nally (1999) writes: 'There is still no medical test to diagnose autism, so professionals rely instead on observing the way your child behaves. Everyone observes behaviour differently and it is difficult to be objective.'

Disorders or variations in the human condition?

Are all the DSM diagnostic categories really 'disorders' or just variations in the human condition? Is it right to assume that the behaviour and capabilities of the majority are the gold standard and any deviation is a 'disorder'? Should these 'disorders' be 'cured' or should a true understanding and acceptance of difference mean that *everyone* learns to become more tolerant and flexible so as to accommodate these differences? The British Psychological Society[83] notes, in its DSM-5 consultation response:

> [Concern] that clients and the general public are negatively affected by the continued and continuous medicalisation of their natural and normal responses to their experiences; responses which undoubtedly have distressing consequences which demand helping responses, but which do not reflect illnesses so much as normal individual variation.

Any diagnosis might lead to medication and an inadequate diagnosis can lead to inappropriate medication. As my daughter points out:

> One of the downsides of labelling (cf. ADHD) is that it can then be linked to the use of medication for said condition – obviously people have their own opinions about this but medication often has serious side-effects and can damp down the very strengths and characteristics that make a person themselves (also see schizophrenia and creativity). Is it only a matter of time until there's a medication for ASD? Perhaps there already is.

Different professionals, different diagnoses

Receiving an accurate and unique diagnosis is further complicated by the fact that different names may be used to describe the same symptoms by professionals with different backgrounds, training, expertise and experience. Those who use different diagnostic criteria or methods of assessment, or come from different countries with different traditions of diagnosis, may well provide different diagnoses. As Blakemore-Brown (2002) wrote:

> Many parents can believe that a 'disorder' relates to a specific medical cause, linked to a very specific part of the brain or body. Many do not realise that the disorder or syndrome is actually a reference to a clustering of observed features... Different types of professionals can perceive the same cluster of symptoms but go on to use different terminology.

According to my daughter: '[There is also a] HUGE variance between professionals... from the same professional background and country in terms of diagnoses of the same person.' Dixon & Addy (2004), for example, point out (with reference to the diagnosis of dyspraxia):

> If the same child was presented to three different professionals for a diagnosis they may leave the surgery of each with a different diagnosis. That does not mean that one is right and two are wrong, but these professionals may have used different standardised tests to diagnose the child, and they may have a great deal of experience and interest in dyspraxia or very little... The diagnostician then should not only contribute a diagnosis or label (or lack of one) but they should explain exactly what they mean by that term at the time of assessment and diagnosis...

Lise Pyles (2002), describing her experiences with her son John who was born in 1984 in the US, wrote:

> I was glad to have the test results, but we, especially my husband, soon got the idea that we were living out the old adage, 'when you have a hammer, everything looks like a nail.' It seemed to us that every specialist found something wrong that was always conveniently right in his area of expertise. The physical therapist found motor problems. The language therapist uncovered language deficits. Nobody ever said, 'no problem here'. Between the school and the doctor, John had received the following labels: gross motor deficits, fine motor deficits, expressive language problems, sensory integration problems, poor muscle tone, mid-line problems, mild Tourette Syndrome, ADD with autistic traits, minimal brain disorder, and borderline mental retardation. How could all this get packed into one

kid?

Tanguey (2002) wrote about the problems that can arise diagnosing Non-Verbal Learning Disability (NLD):

Unfortunately, due to limited awareness of NLD, many children, especially when they are young, are commonly misdiagnosed. Because of their poor planning and organizational skills, their apparent problems with impulse control, and their inability to attend to tactile and visual information, educators and other professionals often misdiagnose NLD children as having ADD/ADHD.

Another common misdiagnosis within the NLD population is anxiety or panic disorder. It is true many of these children have very high levels of anxiety, however their anxiety is the result of their disability (NLD).

Depending on the background and experience of the professional carrying out the assessment, a child may be diagnosed with Developmental Coordination Disorder (DCD)/Dyspraxia (a condition characterised by poor coordination but often associated with social communication difficulties) or with Asperger's Syndrome (a condition characterised by social communication difficulties but often associated with coordination problems). According to the National Autistic Society website:[84]

As some of the characteristics of the two conditions overlap, meaning that both have many similar characteristics, it is important that the person making the diagnosis has the relevant experience and knowledge to make a thorough assessment.

Both conditions can occur to different degrees – they are on a spectrum – so every individual will have different areas of strengths and weaknesses. Some children are also able to develop strategies to help mask their difficulties.

This situation isn't helped by the fact, that according to Polatajko and Cantin (2006), a specific diagnosis of DCD 'remains a problem facing researchers and clinicians alike':

To date there is no gold standard for the measurement of motor coordination... One could argue that the Movement Assessment Battery for Children (M-ABC) and the Bruininks Oseretsky Test of Motor Proficiency have become de facto standards because of the frequency of their use in research and practice... results of a comparative study have shown that the M-ABC identifies more children with DCD than the Bruininks Oseretsky Test of Motor Proficiency.

Simon Baron-Cohen (2008a) makes an interesting comment about standardised tests:

When diagnosing a child, it is increasingly usual to use a standardized method...

Such standardisation of diagnostic methods was important to attempt, because previously all that was available was 'clinical judgement' or the doctor's opinion. However the latest research shows that these methods are not a gold standard in that they work best when combined with clinical opinion. That is, the original hope that they could replace the subjective opinion of the doctor has not turned out to be the case, because they miss some cases of Asperger syndrome.

According to Nally (1999) meanwhile:

Professional understanding of autism has changed during the years since it was first recognised. So you may well find out-of-date information in libraries or you may find that some professionals you consult have not kept themselves informed about the current understanding of autism or Asperger syndrome.

Some professionals believe that a child with autism or Asperger syndrome will shun social contact, and they assure enquiring parents: He's got good eye contact, so don't worry about autism. They fail to recognise the differences in the quality of the child's social interaction from that of other children.

Interestingly enough my daughter had a major difference of opinion with a psychiatrist on this very point when working as a trainee clinical psychologist in 2002. She believed one of the children she was working with to be on the autism spectrum, based on a thorough assessment. His parents and teachers also believed him to be on the spectrum. However the psychiatrist immediately ruled this out on the basis of a single short meeting where he observed that the child had 'good eye contact'.

Professionals may vary as to how strictly they adhere to the diagnostic 'rules' outlined in the DSM. Moreover if assessments and observations only take place in the unfamiliar clinical situation of an office, children's behaviour may differ quite significantly from that to be observed at home and at school with peers, possibly leading to an inadequate diagnosis. According to Pyles (2002):

> The really frustrating thing is that our kids often don't display their social deficits in the doctor's office. As wrong-footed as our kids are among their peers, they frequently are able to hold wonderful conversations with doctors, who often find our kids charming. It's almost funny... that many inexperienced doctors reject a diagnosis of Asperger Syndrome because the child is too sociable and talkative... Our kids can be quite sociable, just ineptly so. It's just one reason why you should make sure that any doctor who sees your child really understands Asperger Syndrome.

Comorbidity

One of the side-effects of the current diagnostic system is, if the DSM definitions are strictly adhered to, that many people appear to have more than one disorder at a time, an occurrence sometimes called comorbidity. According to Kutscher (2005):

> Autistic spectrum disorders such as Asperger's tend to be highly 'comorbid' – occur in conjunction with other conditions of the syndrome mix. ADHD, anxiety, obsessive-compulsive disorder (OCD) and sensory integration problems are common...

> Who says that kids have just one problem? Multiple issues often cluster together in combination... Not only does the same child tend to be born with multiple issues, but the issues may also *exacerbate* each other... Similarly, the problems can *imitate* each other.

Meanwhile Blakemore-Brown (2002) notes:

> Great confusion occurs when people try to blame one condition for all of a child's problems. This can lead to just one type of provision, which may be very limited and focused on one thread rather than the overall picture. If the child does not

improve as expected this could result in removal of any support... through understanding the complexities we are poised to apply more efficacious forms of support to each thread depending on a range of factors, including severity.

Whether comorbidity actually means someone has more than one condition, or just one condition that has been inadequately defined, isn't obvious though. As Mario Maj writes in The British Journal of Psychiatry in 2005 (in an editorial titled *Psychiatric comorbidity: an artefact of current diagnostic systems?*):

This use of the term 'comorbidity' to indicate the concomitance of two or more psychiatric diagnoses appears incorrect because in most cases it is unclear whether the concomitant diagnoses actually reflect the presence of distinct clinical entities or refer to multiple manifestations of a single entity.

For example: are difficulties with organisation and planning an intrinsic feature of Asperger's syndrome (AS) as well as of ADHD? If a child has AS and a significant weakness in this area do they have ADHD as well? According to DSM-IV it wasn't possible to have both ADHD and AS but a person may have both conditions in DSM-5. Similarly, does the inability to concentrate unless something is of great interest mean a child has ADHD, or AS, or both? Are problems with motor control so common in Asperger's syndrome that they count as a symptom or does the child also have Developmental Coordination Disorder (DCD)? According to DSM-IV no one could be diagnosed with both DCD and Asperger's syndrome. In DSM-5 they can be diagnosed with both conditions. Those involved in writing the Leeds Consensus Statement (2006)[85] would approve of the latter change:

We consider it important to acknowledge that overall, the evidence suggests that DCD is a unique and separate neurodevelopmental disorder which can, and often does, co-occur with one or more other neurodevelopmental disorders. Commonly, these include attention deficit hyperactivity disorder (ADHD), autistic spectrum disorder (ASD) and developmental dyslexia.

In Scandinavia, the diagnosis DAMP (which stands for Deficit in Attention, Motor Control and Perception), is applied to children and adults that show symptoms of ADHD and DCD. This suggests that the coexistence of these particular symptoms occurs so often that it can be worth giving one diagnosis rather than two.

Neihart (2000) also points out:

Children with AS share a number of characteristics with gifted children. It can be challenging to determine whether a child's unusual development is a result of gift-edness, a learning disability, or AS, especially among highly gifted children.

In the past few years, there has been a growing recognition among clinicians and teachers that gifted children with AS are sometimes not diagnosed because their unusual behaviours are attributed either to their giftedness or to a learning disability.

A government funded report, written by Snowling in 2008, describes problems co-occurring with dyslexia. According to Snowling:

Dyslexia often co-occurs with one or more other developmental disorders (e.g.

developmental coordination disorder or attention deficit hyperactivity disorder, with up to 40% so affected), and there is a 2.7 fold increase in the incidence of anxiety disorders in this population. The presence of such co-morbidities complicates the behavioural manifestations of dyslexia and affects outcomes.

The incidence of dyslexia depends on the criteria used to define the disorder.

It's easy to see why it can be so difficult to give a clear-cut diagnosis. To illustrate the extent to which symptoms *overlap* between 'disorders', I've constructed a list (see Appendix 27) which documents many of John's key characteristics. Against each one I've noted whether it is commonly associated with ADHD, autism spectrum disorder (including Asperger's syndrome), dyslexia, DCD/dyspraxia, NLD or giftedness. The sources used to derive the list are also recorded in this appendix. The list does *not* include *all* the symptoms associated with these labels, only John's. So, for example, depression, taking things literally and consuming a narrow diet are excluded, because these don't apply to John. Similarly, not everyone diagnosed with the 'disorders' listed in the appendix will exhibit all of John's symptoms because all children are different.

One of the many problems that occur when observing a set of symptoms is to identify which are the primary ones and which, if any, are secondary. Secondary symptoms can be thought to arise when difficulties arising from the primary symptoms aren't adequately addressed. As Blakemore-Brown (2002) writes:

> Children with significant problems whose needs remain unmet move into other defined populations over time. They develop very serious adolescent and adult disorders...

> Professional caution resulted in an earlier reluctance to label children, which has led to no support and in some cases disastrous irreversible outcomes...

> Knowing how to intervene early with support within the home and for the individual is more helpful than dismissing all problems by saying that the child will grow out of it or waiting until the child fits more serious sets of criteria.

It would also appear that diagnoses and labels follow fashions. As Dixon and Addy (2004) point out:

> [This can happen when a diagnosis is] made by someone who is not really in a position to give one, for example a teacher, a parent or a health visitor. It may be that they are perfectly correct in highlighting features of a child's performance that require observation and investigation but this is not a diagnosis...

However, according to Ozonoff et al (2002), trends and fashions may be due to the complexity of many developmental problems plus a desire for the clinicians to use whatever diagnosis will help their patients receive professional support:

> As the label of Asperger syndrome has become better known by professionals, both its use and misuse have increased. Every day, many children with multiple, difficult, complex developmental and behavioral problems are seen in clinics around the world, and the professionals who see them can occasionally be at a loss for a diagnosis. With the advent of the 'Asperger' label, some of these children have been diagnosed with Asperger syndrome. Some indeed have it, but

many do not...

Finally, to add to the confusion, not only is each child different but they will change as they grow older. That is, the balance of assets and deficits (whatever the diagnosis) will not only vary from one child to another but may alter for any one child over time, all of which could then make them appear to have a different disorder. What a minefield!

REVEALING A DIAGNOSIS

There are many ways that practitioners may reveal a diagnosis to a client but those that focus on diagnostic criteria will inevitably focus on the client's deficits. Anyone receiving such a diagnosis is bound to feel like a second class human being, defined by their failings. A much better way of communicating the facts about a diagnosis is one in which practitioners reveal the strengths as well as the weaknesses that may be attributable to the particular condition. I love Tony Attwood's (2006) description of the way he explains to a family that their child has a diagnosis of Asperger's syndrome:

> For children over the age of about eight years, I have developed the Attributes Activity to explain the diagnosis to the child and family... The first activity is to have temporarily attached to the wall of the room large sheets of paper, or to have the use of a large whiteboard with coloured pens. Each sheet is divided into two column, one column headed 'Qualities' and the other 'Difficulties'... [He then gets the rest of the family to identify and list their personal qualities and difficulties]. I ensure this is a positive activity, commenting on the various attributes and ensuring there are more qualities than difficulties. The child or adolescent with Asperger's syndrome is able to observe and participate, and understands what is expected when it is time for his or her turn.

> Sometimes the person with Asperger's syndrome is reluctant to suggest, or may not consider him- or herself to have, many qualities or attributes. The family are encouraged to make suggestions...

> I usually say to the child, 'Congratulations, you have Asperger's syndrome,' and explain that this means he or she is not mad, bad or defective, but has a different way of thinking... The Attributes Activity can be conducted by parents of young children without the presence of a specialist in Asperger's syndrome, but I have found that adolescents are more likely to accept the explanation of qualities and difficulties from a clinician rather than parents.

If the child receives the diagnosis from their parents, the latter probably need to feel comfortable with the diagnosis themselves before feeling able to talk about it in a constructive manner. Once this position has been reached, it's by no means obvious when and how a young child should be told. I would be inclined to follow the advice given by Sally Ozonoff and colleagues (2002) when they write:

> Parents often ask about sharing the news with their child. The first issue is usually '*Should* we tell him [or her]?' The answer to this question depends very much on the child's age, temperament, and other life circumstances, but usually the answer is 'Yes, at some point.' The next question, then, is *when*? The best way to determine if your child is ready to hear about AS-HFA is if he or she is expressing

awareness of his or her differences, particularly voicing concerns.

Sainsbury (2009) however, has a valid point when she writes that waiting until a child voices concerns is *too late* to tell them about any diagnosis:

Sometimes people decide that they will not broach the subject until the child spontaneously starts to ask about it; this seriously underestimates the degree to which children, especially children with Asperger's, can worry about a topic without approaching their parents about it...

Any child with Asperger's who is old enough to understand a simple verbal explanation of their condition is also old enough, if they don't get such an explanation, to notice that they are different from their 'normal' peers, and that they have difficulty doing things which seem to be easy for 'normal' children. Often they will infer that there must be something wrong with them. Many people with Asperger's concluded as children that they must be 'stupid', 'crazy', 'retarded', 'brain-damaged' or that what was wrong with them must be so awful that no-one would talk about it.

Attwood (2006) has some useful information regarding the explanation of Asperger's syndrome to a young child:

Children who are younger than about eight years may not consider themselves as particularly different to their peers, and have difficulty understanding the concept of a developmental disorder as complex as Asperger's syndrome. The explanation for younger children will need to be age appropriate and provide information that is relevant from the child's perspective. The main themes will be the benefits of programs to help the child make friends and enjoy playing with other children, and to help in learning and achieving success with school work. There can be a discussion and activities to explain the concept of individual differences.

Meanwhile Lydia suggests:

The idea of sharing an evolving and developing story about Aspergers as the child matures would be helpful here – starting very simply and developing over time. This idea is used with adopted children and HIV-positive children. Also in physics teaching I guess!

Telling your child about a diagnosis in a way that gives them a sense of relief, makes them feel good about themselves and doesn't give them a ready excuse to do less than their best, isn't an easy task for a parent. Sophie Walker (2012) gives a wonderful description of the difficult moment when she told her daughter Grace about her diagnosis of Asperger syndrome:

When I initially told Grace about her diagnosis her reaction was one of relief. I was very lucky. Staggering through a form of words that I had not sufficiently rehearsed, I realised, as I told her, that I wasn't well enough prepared to deal with an adverse reaction. I barely understood what I was telling her myself, and I hadn't done very much research...

She listened carefully as I stumbled through my speech. At first, her face bore a tight, anxious expression that I could see her attempting to flatten into carelessness. Then she brightened. 'So I'm like this because I can't help it?' she asked. 'All the things I get wrong are because I've got Asperger's Syndrome?'

I hesitated, with the sensation of having one foot above a landmine. 'Well, it's not about the things you get wrong,' I told her. 'It means there are some things that you find more difficult because of having Asperger's and that you are brilliant at some things because of it... And now that we know, we can figure out how to help you get better at the tough stuff.'

It was an absolutely terrifying conversation – just writing about it now makes the palms of my hands sweat... I was so scared that if I got this bit wrong, she would seize on the negatives of her diagnosis and define herself by them.

But, thank God, she was twinkling at me now. 'Does this mean I'm special?' she asked.

Apart from the child and their parents, who else needs to know? Every time a child goes to a new class, school, activity and so on, do those in charge have to know? What about the child's peers? As Ozonoff et al (2002) suggest:

If your child's differences would be obvious to others anyway, then providing an explanation for them by disclosing the diagnosis may well outweigh any perceived risks, such as stigma. On the other hand, if your child's symptoms have become so mild as to be mere 'quirks' or personality traits that do not impair functioning, then disclosing the diagnosis may not be beneficial.

On the other hand, Leventhal-Belfer & Coe (2004) believe:

There is no one set answer that fits every family, and the issue will arise every time you enroll your child into a new program or school. A lot depends on how the parents feel about the diagnosis and if they feel it will help others understand their child. Generally speaking, we feel that when the parents believe that the diagnosis is a vehicle for understanding their child and advocating for the services he might benefit from, they will feel more comfortable sharing the information with other adults in their child's life.

Surely there can't be any risk revealing a diagnosis such as an autism spectrum disorder to a child's school? Such a revelation should help the school understand the child's difficulties and help them give these pupils appropriate accommodations and support. According to Walker (writing in the UK in 2012) that isn't necessarily so:

You've now been set apart from the mainstream, and if your child goes to an academy or any school which prides itself on results and academic prowess, you may find that it is suggested you leave and go somewhere else more appropriate. Or you may just find that the school doesn't know what autism is and ignores the diagnosis.

I really like Attwood's (2006) approach to informing a child's peers about a diagnosis:

The child's opinion is respected regarding the question of whether or not peers should be told. If the child does want other children to know, there needs to be an agreement as to how widely the information will be disseminated, who will provide the explanation, how it will be done, and whether the child with Asperger's syndrome should be present.

When someone reaches adulthood with a diagnosis of Asperger's syndrome or is first diagnosed as an adult, the dilemmas regarding *who* to tell and *when* don't go away. Liane Willey has a very useful appendix in her book *Pretending to be Normal* which deals in some detail with the topic of disclosure as an adult. As far as I'm concerned, it's by no means obvious whether an adult should reveal a diagnosis when applying for a job. Although no one should be discriminated against because of any difference or disability, it could be hard to prove that discrimination has actually taken place if the diagnosis is mentioned on the application form and the applicant never gets to an interview. As Attwood (2006) writes:

> One of the concerns of adults with Asperger's syndrome is whether they should include reference to the diagnosis on a job application. If there is considerable competition for a particular vacancy, an applicant having a diagnosis that is unknown to the employer might lead to the application being rejected.

There are a few employers who are aware of the excellent qualities that can be associated with many 'disorders' and would provide any necessary accommodations required to make the person a productive employee. It was very heartening to read:[86] 'The German software giant SAP has declared that it intends to gain 'a competitive advantage' over its rivals by actively employing people with autism spectrum disorder.' Nevertheless I suspect there are plenty of employers who wouldn't offer a position to anyone they think will take up additional management time or will have trouble fitting in with their colleagues. Unfortunately, if a diagnosis isn't revealed and problems then arise during the employment because no allowances or accommodations have been made for a different style of working, then the employee could lose their job and forego any legal protection afforded by disability discrimination legislation. What a truly impossible situation this is. According to John, he has never revealed during the application process that he is on the autism spectrum, although without a formal diagnosis: 'I've never done it, but merely because it's never come up – it tends to get mentioned sooner or later... Not that having Asperger's is particularly unusual at any Silicon Valley-based software company!'

One thing I believe is crucial is that adults on the autism spectrum really understand and *accept* their strengths and challenges and try to avoid working in positions where their weaknesses are exposed. In addition, if they focus on their strengths so that they become very expert in a particular field, then employers might find it easier to overlook any eccentricities because their employee's contribution is so valuable. Our son has adopted this technique, becoming incredibly knowledgeable in the computing field and making sure he avoided any management roles. Although he received many annual appraisals where he was legitimately criticised for coping poorly under pressure, being easily distracted, poor organisational and planning skills, poor timekeeping and regular underestimation of how long a job would take, he was never sacked and also received comments on his appraisal such as:

> An extremely competent and valuable member of the team, with outstanding

technical skills. John is always willing to put his shoulder to the wheel in a crisis and performs an invaluable role as technical guru for his colleagues.

JOHN'S DIAGNOSIS

When John was a child, information about Asperger's syndrome, attention deficit hyperactivity disorder (ADHD), developmental coordination disorder (DCD) and specific learning disabilities wasn't widely available. Therefore, as just mentioned, John wasn't formally diagnosed, despite receiving a Statement of Special Needs and having all kinds of obvious difficulties. If John had been particularly disruptive at school or if I'd made much more fuss about his difficulties we might have received more help but as it was we had no diagnosis and were left to manage largely on our own.

We first became aware of the existence of DCD when John was 14 and we were searching (yet again) for someone to help him with his appalling handwriting. Someone we were put into contact with, thought that John may have DCD and sent us a leaflet briefly describing the condition. It was quite touching to see John read this pamphlet and hear him say in amazement: 'This is me.' There's no doubt that he was very relieved to find that he wasn't the only person on earth to have coordination difficulties and was very pleased to have a name for his problems. Although I was aware that the features of DCD described on the leaflet only addressed some of John's areas of difficulty, I joined the Dyspraxia Foundation and learned a lot more about the condition by attending conferences and reading their publications.

The first person to suggest that John may also have Asperger's syndrome was our daughter Lydia. In 1999, when Lydia was in her final year of a psychology undergraduate degree, she took a child development module which covered Asperger's syndrome and ADHD. As Lydia read the book *Autism. Explaining the Enigma* by Uta Frith (one of the recommended texts for the course), she had a moment of revelation. 'That's my brother', she thought and yet another piece of the jigsaw was in place. Although Baron-Cohen says that none of the Autism Research Centre screening questionnaires described in Chapter 20 are diagnostic, nevertheless *all* of John's results would certainly support a diagnosis of Asperger's syndrome. Everything about him seems to indicate such a diagnosis, from his inability to recognise body language and his poor social skills to his intense and passionate focussed interests and remarkable long-term memory. After Lydia's discovery I joined the National Autistic Society and learned an enormous amount from their publications, website and courses. I also found the excellent books published on the subject by Jessica Kingsley Publishers most informative. More important than *my* increasing knowledge about the autism spectrum though, has been John's discovery of a whole new world of human behaviour and understanding which he feels very comfortable with. It has been both exciting and interesting for him to see how similar some of his experiences are to those of others on the spectrum and equally just how different they can be. I think it has added greatly to his confidence to know that he's not a unique 'weirdo' and that he can be proud of his many strengths and abilities.

Lydia also suggested that John's problems with organisation, planning and concentration, his inability to sit still for long as a child and his tendency to interrupt might also be a sign of the attention deficit component of ADHD. Research studies have shown that very premature babies of low birth-weight are at an increased risk of developing ADHD

377

and DCD, and John weighed only two and a half pounds when he was born nearly 11 weeks early. If John had lived in Scandinavia he may well have been diagnosed with DAMP as he had DCD as well as the symptoms of ADHD.

The lack of a formal diagnosis when John was a child, the absence of any readily available information and the fact that we didn't know anyone else with a child like ours, meant that in some ways we felt quite isolated with our 'different' son. Having access to such information, knowing there were many children with similar problems and having a support organisation to ask for advice when things got tough would have made a real difference to our sense of isolation. These days, what organisations would we turn to for help and advice? Would we have to join every organisation that exists to help children with developmental problems, a time consuming and expensive option? It would seem that at present in the UK supportive organisations such as the National Autistic Society, the British Dyslexia Association, the ADD Information Service, the Dyspraxia Foundation and others operate quite independently. It would be wonderful if the separate organisations dealing with children's differences would cooperate in such a way that there was just one port of call for the concerned adult. Many of the difficulties experienced by parents, carers and teachers when trying to do their best for these children are very similar. *One* national organisation, with *one* advice line able to help parents whose children may have difficulties with social communication, bullying, concentration, coordination, managing their emotions, sensory perception, reading, writing, spelling, time management, homework and so on would be so helpful. If there was only one organisation it would be much easier to publicise it widely to the medical and teaching professions and to the public at large, thereby helping the largest number of children, their carers and teachers, *regardless of whether a diagnosis was in place or not*. This would make the most of available funding and of the time and expertise of willing volunteers. It may then be possible to support strong local groups throughout the country catering for *all* children with differences where parents and siblings could help each other and share their experiences. At present this network is very patchy in the UK, given that it's so dependent on willing volunteers with sufficient time and energy to run the groups and is split between various organisations. Perhaps it isn't surprising that many people with children diagnosed with Asperger's Syndrome for example or Dyspraxia have never even heard of the relevant support organisations.

In conclusion: Although we didn't have any diagnoses when John was a child, I believe our parenting methods (as described throughout this book) have been really successful and have enabled him to grow up into a very happy and fulfilled adult. Because we didn't expect (or receive) outside help or advice *we* took responsibility for trying to make our son independent and *we* took all the decisions about what was or wasn't an important issue to be dealt with and the timing of the intervention. We did our best to deal with both children as individuals (although Lydia didn't feel her feelings were catered for sufficiently), see the world through their eyes, cater to their specific needs and remain positive. In John's case this meant helping him with things he was struggling with as well as encouraging his strengths and interests and allowing him plenty of opportunity to develop them. There was plenty of early, tailored intervention carried out largely by me, based purely on the needs I could see with my own eyes. In fact there's been intervention throughout his life, always carried out very carefully when he was ready *and* willing to be helped. Whenever John wasn't ready to address a problem I would go out of my way to find ways round the situation so as to postpone actually addressing the difficulty until a more appropriate moment. All improvements were carried out in small chunks with loads of encouragement so that success rather than failure was the rule. I only dealt with what I felt to be the most important issues at the time and *never* tried to make him like everyone else. Yes, John has always been different from his peers but he was and still is a wonderful character, kind, affectionate to his family, friendly, funny, passionate, knowledgeable, interesting, full of integrity and so on. The importance of these excellent qualities can be lost so easily when one only looks at the labels. He's very aware how lucky he is to be living independently, with a challenging job which he loves, which makes the most of his skills and enables him to work from home. He's also happily occupied with several passionate spare time interests and, because of the internet, never feels lonely. John has even moved relatively recently to an area of the country where more 'geeky' people like himself live. He's done this so that he can have more *physical* contact with like-minded people as well as internet contact. He *does* struggle with certain things but with time has found ways to overcome, or at least minimise many of these difficulties. He continues to develop both personally and socially. What more could any parent want for their child?

Feedback

If you have enjoyed this book or found it useful please could you leave a brief review on Amazon. Your support really makes a difference.

If you would like to be informed when the author of this book publishes further books on autism, please contact Charlotte.Aldred1@gmail.com. Your email address will not be used for any other purpose.

Appendix 1

Extracts from John's Medical Notes

1. HOSPITAL A (IN LONDON)
Baby's condition at birth good. Apgar 6 at 1 minute, 7 at 5 minutes.
Problems:
1. <u>Prolonged rupture of membranes</u>
Mother's high vaginal swab – no pathogens isolated. Liquor clear. No evidence of infection in the baby, but antibiotics commenced because of respiratory problems later diagnosed as mild hyaline membrane disease.

2. <u>Prematurity</u>
Dates and gestational assessment both=30 weeks. Weight 1135g and head circumference 26.1cm. Both fell on the 25th centile. Child's temperature was 35°C on transfer, but remained satisfactory once on the open incubator. He was fed with mother's EBM initially via a nasojejunal tube and thereafter via a nasogastric tube and ultimately mixed bottle and n.g.feeding. Dextrostrix at all times satisfactory. He regained his birth weight within 10 days and then after losing weight during the third week he was gaining well at the time of discharge, reaching 1500g at 5 weeks.

3. <u>Mild hyaline membrane disease</u>
He developed tachypnoea, grunting and recession over the first 4 hours of life and a chest x-ray was consistent with mild hyaline membrane disease. A request for transfer to... was therefore made at 4 hours. He was treated with added oxygen via a head box and never required more than 45% oxygen. By 54 hours blood gases (radial artery monitoring) were satisfactory in air. Penicillin and Gentamicin were administered because of baby problem 1, although a septic screen subsequently proved to be negative.

4. <u>Jaundice</u>
Baby became clinically jaundiced from Day 2 with a maximum bilirubin on Day 4 at 240μmol/L. This then fell with phototherapy although rather slowly, but investigations as to causes of prolonged jaundice were negative.

5. <u>Patent ductus arteriosus with congestive heart failure</u>
On Day 15 he developed cyanotic episodes which responded quickly to stimulation. He was active and well, but had a loud systolic murmur maximal at the upper L.S.E. and bounding pulses, but no evidence of failure. A diagnosis of patent ductus arteriosus was made. The following day the apnoeic episodes became more frequent and pronged requiring intermittent IPPV with oxygen. Also signs of congestive cardiac failure – tachycardia, hepatomegaly, sacral-oedema and increasing heart size on chest X-ray developed. General condition deteriorated and he became hypotonic.

6. <u>Right lower lobe pneumonia</u>
At the stage where he developed P.D.A. with C.C.F. patchy shadowing in the right lower zone of the chest X-ray suggested right lower lobar pneumonia and Penicillin and Gentamicin were therefore recommended. Septic screen was again subsequently negative.

7. Hyponatraemia

(Medical treatment of P.D.A.) Digoxin and Frusemide were administered from Day 16 because of the signs of C.C.F. but resulted in no improvement of the heart failure and hyponatraemia. The serum sodium fell from 138 to 122 and the serum osmolality dropped as low as 257. A low urine osmolality (134) confirmed that the kidney was conserving sodium appropriately.

8. Surgical ligation of P.D.A

By Day 17 the baby's condition had deteriorated to such a degree that he looked pre-terminal. He was grey with very poor tone and his apnoeic episodes were so frequent and prolonged as to have become almost continuous. Because medical treatment of C.C.F. had failed and antibiotic therapy for R.L.L. pneumonia had produced no improvement, it was decided to close his P.D.A. surgically.

The ductus was approached extrapleurally via a left thoracotomy and found to be 4mm. in diameter. The vessels tied off proximally and distally but not divided. Post-operative course – he was ventilated for 24 hours and thereafter required added oxygen (maximum concentration at 45%) for a further 12 hours. Blood gases were again monitored via the radial artery punctures and were satisfactory in air at 36 hours post-operatively. His general condition was much improved. He was active, pink and vigorous. A repeat chest X-ray showed a normal heart size with clear lung fields.

9. Bradycardiac and apnoeic spells

On Day 24 he developed periods of apnoea and bradycardia from which he recovered after gentle stimulation. Although sepsis was suspected on the basis of a raised white cell count (total 26,000 neutrophils=63%) an infection screen was negative and a third course of antibiotics did not affect the apnoeic spells. Therefore continuous positive airways pressure (CPAP) of 3cm. of water was administered via a Bennett face mask using air. This terminated the attacks which did not return after the CPAP was discontinued at 24 hours.

2. HOSPITAL B (LOCAL HOSPITAL)

He returned... for 'fattening up'. He put on weight very satisfactorily over the next month. We repeated his Hb at weekly intervals and this remained at between 11-12g% until... when his Hb was then found to have dropped to 8.4g%. We repeated this taking a venous sample 2 days later when it was found to have dropped to 7.7g%. The blood film looked hypochromic and there was no evidence of haemolysis. The reticulocyte count was 3%. We thought this was due to an anaemia of prematurity even though he had been taking Folic acid 0.5 mg once weekly, Plesmet 10 drops t.d.s. and Abidec 2 drops t.d.s. We therefore decided to transfuse him and we gave him a top up of 50mls. The next day his post transfusion Hb was 14.4g%.

During all this time his mother had managed to maintain her supply of milk by expressing and we discharged him home the next day when he weighed 2.57kg. Mother was still breast feeding. His head circumference was 34 cm on discharge.

Appendix 2

References used for Prematurity Outcomes

Aarnoudse-Moens, C.S., Weisglas-Kuperus, N., van Goudoever, J.B. & Oosterlaan, J. (2009) 'Meta-analysis of neurobehavioural outcomes in very preterm and/or very low birthweight children.' Pediatrics 124(2), 717-728

Arnaud, C., Daubisse-Marliac, L., White-Koning, M., Pierrat, V., Larroque, B., Grandjean, H., Alberge, C., Marret, S., Burguet, A., Ancel, P., Supernant, K. & Kaminski, M. (2007) 'Prevalence and Associated Factors of Minor Neuromotor Dysfunctions at Age 5 in Prematurely Born Children. The EPIPAGE Study.' Archives of Pediatrics & Adolescent Medicine 161(11), 1053-1061

Bell, M. 'The Effects of Prematurity on Development,' & 'The Effects of Prematurity on the Social and Emotional Development of School Age Children.' http://www.prematurity.org/research/prematurity-effects1.html retrieved on 07/12/2011

Blakemore-Brown, L. (2002) 'Reweaving the Autistic Tapestry.' London: Jessica Kingsley Publishers

Foulder-Hughes, L.A. & Cooke, R.W.I. (2003) 'Motor, cognitive, and behavioural disorders in children born very preterm.' Developmental Medicine & Child Neurology 45, 97-103

Foulder-Hughes, L.A. & Cooke, R.W.I. (2003) 'Developmental Co-ordination Disorder in preterm children born ≤32 weeks gestational age.' Dyspraxia Foundation Professional Journal 2, 2-11

Gerhardt, S. (2004) 'Why Love Matters. How Affection Shapes a baby's brain.' London: Routledge

Hack, M., Flannery, D.J., Schluter, M., Cartar, L., Borawski, E. & Klein, N. (2002) 'Outcomes in Young Adulthood for Very-Low-Birth-Weight Infants.' New England Journal of Medicine 346, 149-157

Hack, M. (2006) 'Young adult outcomes of very-low-birth-weight children.' Seminars in Fetal & Neonatal Medicine 11, 127-137

Hille, E.T., den Ouden, A.l., Bauer, L., van den Oudenrijn, C., Brand, R. & Verloove-Vanhorick, S.P. (1994) 'School Performance at Nine Years of Age in Very Premature and Very Low Birth Weight Infants: Perinatal Risk Factors and Predictors at Five Years of Age. Collaborative Project on Preterm and Small for Gestational Age (POPS) Infants in the Netherlands.' Journal of Pediatrics 125(3), 426-34

Jongmans, M.J., Mercuri, E., Dubowitz, L.M.S. & Henderson, S.E. (1998) 'Perceptual-motor difficulties and their concomitants in six-year-old children born prematurely.' Human Movement Science 17, 629-653

Kesler, S.R., Reiss, A.l., Vohr, B., Watson, C., Schneider, K.C., Katz, K.H., Maller-Kesselman, J., Silbereis, J., Constable, R.T., Makuch, R.W. & Ment, L.R. (2008) 'Brain Volume Reductions within Multiple Cognitive Systems in Male Preterm Children at Age Twelve.' The Journal of Pediatrics 152, 513-520

Kessenich, M. (2003) 'Developmental Outcomes of Premature, Low Birth Weight, and Medically Fragile Infants.' www.medscape.com/viewarticle/461571 retrieved on 23/07/07

de Kleine, M.J.K., den Ouden, A.L., Kollée, L.A.A., Nijhuis-van der Sanden, M.W.G., Sondaar, M., van Kessel-Feddema, B.J.M., Knuijt, S., van Baar, A.L., Ilsen, A., Breur-Pieterse, R., Briët, J.M., Brand, R. & Verloove-Vanhorick, S.P. (2003) 'Development and evaluation of a follow up assessment of preterm infants at 5 years of age.' Archives of Disease in Childhood 88, 870-875

Limperopoulos, C., Bassan, H., Sullivan, N.R., Soul, J.S., Robertson, R.L., Moore, M., Ringer, S.A., Volpe, J.J. & du Plessis, A.J. (2008) 'Positive Screening for Autism in ex-preterm Infants: Prevalence and Risk Factors.' Pediatrics 121, 758-765

Malekpour, M. (2004) 'Low Birth-Weight Infants and the Importance of Early Intervention: Enhancing Mother-Infant Interactions. A Literature Review.' The British Journal of Developmental Disabilities 50 (part2 no 99), 78-88

Mills, M.D. (1999) 'The Eye in Childhood.' American Academy of Family Physicians 60(3), 907-18

Nadeau, L., Tessier, R., Lefebvre, F. & Robaey, P. (2004) 'Victimization: a newly recognised outcome of prematurity.' Developmental Medicine & Child Neurology 46, 508-513

Peters, K.L., Rosychuk, R.J., Hendson, L., Coté, J.J., McPherson, C. & Tyebkhan, J.M. (2009) 'Improvement of Short- and Long-Term Outcomes for Very Low Birth Weight Infants: Edmonton NIDCAP Trial.' Pediatrics 124, 1009-1020

Pineda, R.G., Neil, J., Dierker, D., Smyser, C.D., Wallendorf, M., Kidokoro, H., Reynolds, L.C., Walker, S., Rogers, C., Mathur, A.M., Van Essen, D.C. & Inder, T. (2014) 'Alterations in Brain Structure and Neurodevelopmental Outcome in Preterm Infants Hospitalized in Different Neonatal Intensive Care Unit Environments.' The Journal of Pediatrics 164, 52-60e2

Powls, A,. Botting, N., Cooke, R.W.I. & Marlow, N. (1995) 'Motor impairment in children 12-13 years old with a birthweight of less than 1250 g.' Archives of Disease in Childhood 73, F62-F66)

Raphael-Leff, J. (2007) 'Signs of Autism in Infants. Recognition and Early Intervention.' (ed. Acquarone, S.) London: Karnac Books

Schalij-Delfos, N.E., de Graaf, M.E., Treffers, W.F., Engel, J. & Cats, B.P. (2000) 'Long term follow up of premature infants: detection of strabismus, amblyopia, and refractive errors.' British Journal of Opthalmology 84, 963-967

Tessier, R., Cristo, M.B., Velez, S., Giron, M., Nadeau, L., Figuero de Calume, Z., Ruiz-Palaez, J.G. & Charpak, N. (2003) 'Kangaroo Mother Care: A method for protecting high-risk low-birth-weight and premature infants against developmental delay.' Infant Behaviour and Development 26, 384-397

Whitaker, A.H., Feldman, J.F., Lorenz, J.M., Shen, S., McNicholas, F., Nieto, M., McCulloch, D., Pinto-Martin, J.A. & Paneth, N. (2006) 'Motor and Cognitive Outcomes in Nondisabled Low-Birth-Weight Adolescents. Early Determinants.' Archives of Pediatrics & Adolescent Medicine 160(10), 1040-1046

Willacy, H.
In http://patient.info/doctor/premature-babies-and-their-problems Last Updated 9 Nov

2008, retrieved on 9 Sept 2009

Wong, H.S., Huertas-Ceballos, A., Cowan, F.M. & Modi, N. (2014) 'Evaluation of Early Childhood Social-Communication Difficulties in Children Born Preterm Using the Quantitative Checklist for Autism in Toddlers.' The Journal of Pediatrics 164,26-33

Appendix 3

Height, Weight and Head Circumference

Table 1 (Non-metric)

Date (yrs/wks from birth)[87]	Wt. (lb oz)	Ht. (ins)	Head (ins)
0wk (London)	2.8		10.28
5wk (London)	3.5		
10.5wk (Local)	5.10		13.39
15wk (Local)	7.9		
17wk (HC)	9.0		
21wk (HC)	11.6		
24wk (HC)	11.13		
26wk (HC)	12.7		
30wk (HC)	13.8		
35wk (HC)	14.14		
45wk (Local)	16.3		17.32
47wk (HC)	17.10		
1yr 2wk (Local)	18.2	17.6	
1yr 38wk (Local)	24.4		
1yr 46wk (HC)	26.8		
2yr 2wk (Local)	25.14	31.9	
2yr 40wk (Local)	28.7	34.8	
2yr 45wk (London)		35.4	19.57
3yr 10wk (Local)	30.9		

Table 2 (Metric)

Date (yrs/wks from birth)	Wt. (kg)	Ht. (cm)	Head (cm)
0wk (London)	1.135		26.1
5wk (London)	1,50		
10.5wk (Local)	2.57		34
15wk (Local)	3.20		
17wk (HC)	4.10		
21wk (HC)	5.20		
24wk (HC)	5.36		
26wk (HC)	5.64		
30wk (HC)	6.12		
35wk (HC)	6.75		
45wk (Local)	7.36		44
47wk (HC)	7.74		
1yr 2wk (Local)	8.25	44.75	
1yr 38wk (Local)	11.20		
1yr 46wk (HC)	12.02		
2yr 2wk (Local)	11.76	81	
2yr 40wk (local)	12.93	88.5	
2yr 45wk (London)		90	49.7
3yr 10wk (Local)	13.9		

Notes:
London: Measurements made at the hospital in London – no clothes
Local: Measurements made at our local hospital – no clothes
HC: Measurements made at our local Health Centre – fully clothed

Appendix 4

Hearing Test Results –
Extracts from Medical Records

March 1977

He was cooing and chuckling and I heard aah and ooh. Sheridan Stycar cup and spoon, bell and paper responded on right; left side very poor response, no response at all to high pitched rattle on either side.

In view of his history I think referral to Dr… [the consultant audiologist] is important.

May 1977

On testing with the Portable Freefield Audiometer I thought he was responding to:

500Hz 35 dBs
1,000Hz 25 dBs
2,000Hz 25 dBs
4,000Hz 35 dBs

When I came to do the baby's turning tests of hearing he was responding very poorly, but this may well have been because he was now tired. The tympanic membrane did look slightly inflamed and John was cutting teeth.

My impression was that there was a slight conductive hearing loss, but I wish to re-test him in 3 month's time.

July 1977

I was delighted to find that he is responding much better to sounds.

On 250, 500, 1000 and 2000 Hz he was responding at 25 dBs. At 4000 Hz I was sure of my response at 35 dBs, but a little doubtful at 25 dBs. Using the baby's turning tests of hearing he was responding on both sides to the conversational voice and whispered voice and the rattle, but he tired when I was using the cup and spoon and the paper.

I think John's hearing is normal, but have asked to see him when he is 3 years old so that we can obtain an audiogram.

[I do not know if any audiogram was obtained. If it was, no records were sent to the GP.]

Date not known, but between 1981 and 1987

Your child was one of several who were tested on the Pure Tone Audiometer in school today. I am pleased to inform you that the results of this routine test show that your child's hearing is satisfactory.

Appendix 5

Vaccinations and Immunisations

Table 1: Recommended Timetable in the 1970s

Approx Age *	Vaccine/Antigen
6mth	Diphtheria, Tetanus and Whooping Cough – 1
6mth	Poliomyelitis – 1
7.5-8mth	Diphtheria, Tetanus and Whooping Cough – 2
7.5-8mth	Poliomyelitis – 2
13mth	Diphtheria, Tetanus and Whooping Cough – 3
13mth	Poliomyelitis – 3
15mth	Measles
School Entry	Diphtheria and Tetanus – booster
School Entry	Poliomyelitis – booster

*Suggested dates given on the Personal Health Record Card. The card also noted that 'some family doctors prefer, however, to begin at three months of age'.

Table 2: John's Actual Vaccination and Immunisation Record

Age *	Vaccine/Antigen
7mth	Diphtheria and Tetanus – 1
9mth	Diphtheria and Tetanus – 2
9mth	Poliomyelitis – 1
12mth	Poliomyelitis – 2
16.5mth	Diphtheria and Tetanus – 3
16.5mth	Poliomyelitis – 3
2yr 2mth	Whooping Cough – 1
2yr 3mth	Whooping Cough – 2
2yr 3mth	Measles
2yr 4mth	Whooping Cough – 4
5yr 2mth	Diphtheria and Tetanus – booster
5yrs 2mth	Poliomyelitis – booster
15 yr	Tetanus
15yr	Poliomyelitis

*The ages were calculated from John's due date, not from his premature birth date.

Appendix 6

Paediatricians' Reports On Motor Development[88]

4 months (A):

Development is really quite good... starting to roll over and to take objects placed in his hand.

8 months (B):

He reached out and picked up a brick in either hand, transfers very competently, plays with paper and crumples it. He strikes the brick on the table chuckling. He finger feeds, drinks from a (special feeding) cup. Hypo-tonic. Quite able to put legs round neck and quite easy to dorsiflex feet parallel to legs. However I could not do this with his hands. There was no increased tone in his upper limbs. Loves playing with his toes. When pulled up to the sitting position there was no head lag. He is just starting to sit with a straight back and sits beautifully with forward support. Both lateral responses are present. Lifts head and chest clear. Moves legs and gets onto all 4s then is quite unable to move and literally collapses. I think that his next step will be that of crawling.

10 months (B):

He is now crawling (8.5months), pulling up, standing against the furniture (9 months) and personally I think he will start to cruise very shortly. He is still hypotonic, but there is no evidence of spasticity.

14.5 months (B):

Has been walking for the last fortnight.

18 months (B):

Walking about everywhere, crawling up and down stairs... feeds himself and sits at the table.

22 months (B):

He held a pencil for me and did free horizontal scribble. He would not co-operate and build a tower.

24 months (A):

I would have thought that he has more or less caught up his early developmental delay and he seemed a very normal child. Clinical examination was not of the easiest. His co-ordination seemed above average for his age.

2 years 7 months (B):

When he walked up the stairs for me I thought he was very immature, two feet to a step, and was unable to jump off the bottom step.

2 years 8 months (A):

He passed all elements of the Denver Developmental Screening Test. He was able to copy a vertical line and a circle, but didn't manage to imitate a bridge made out of three bricks.

3 years (B):

He is now able to go upstairs in an adult manner, right foot leading. He goes downstairs two feet to a step and is able to jump off the bottom step.

4 years 4 months (A):

I performed a Denver screening test on him and although he passed the gross motor section he can't catch a ball as yet. In the fine motor section he cannot imitate a square and is useless at drawing. In fact he cannot even hold a pencil properly let alone draw a face for me. In the personal and social section he passed this but is not managing his buttons yet and there are tremendous battles with dressing himself in the morning. I carefully went over his central nervous system and found no abnormality. He has good co-ordination and I think this hand/eye co-ordination problem is obviously a mild one but one that may cause problems later at school.

8 years 3 months (B):

Clinically mildly hypotonic. Clumsy, but latter improving. Very poor eye/hand co-ordination – mother very angry and thinks not having enough help with his appalling handwriting.

Appendix 7

Extracts From a Report written by a Paediatric Physiotherapist[89]

John was asked to sit at a table and write his name, date of birth, and address on a ruled sheet of paper. The following was observed:

1. He sat on the edge of the chair with rounded shoulders.
2. Positioned paper straight in front of him.
3. Used the non-writing hand to steady the paper.
4. Had a good tripod grip, but held it too close to the tip.
5. Due to point 4 he used excessive pressure for writing tool hold and for writing.
6. Due to points 2 and 4 he had to tilt his head and bend over to see what he was writing.
7. All his alphabets do not sit on the line.
8. Crowding of alphabets is present.
9. Inconsistency with formation, slant and spacing of his alphabets.
10. Overall there was no easy flow of writing.

He then did a few activities/exercises with me and the following difficulties were observed:

Control of smooth and slow movement.

Organisation and isolation of movement.

Girdle stability which is necessary for good posture, balance and co-ordination.

Scanning, observing detail and sequencing a 3-4 step movement from memory.

Balance and co-ordination.

Two handed activity and finer movement of fingers.

Eye-hand co-ordination.

Visual motor control.

Spatial awareness and motor planning.

Endurance of muscle control for structured movement is a weakness. In order to have good posture in standing and walking, good muscle power and good control of fine movement is essential. These features also contribute towards speed, fluency and legibility of good handwriting.

Appendix 8

Weschler Intelligence Scale For Children-Revised (WISC-R)[90]

These neurological tests are designed to reveal a child's cognitive strengths and weaknesses and to compare them with a standardised sample of children of the same age. The tests are divided into two groups, one called 'Verbal' tests, the other 'Performance' tests; they are administered alternately. The tests that were given to John are described briefly below.

Verbal Tests: these are all presented verbally and a verbal response is required.

Information:

This is a series of questions to ascertain the child's knowledge about common events, objects, places and people. It tests factual knowledge, long term memory and recall.

Similarities:

The child has to explain the similarity between pairs of words which represent everyday objects or concepts. It tests logical abstract thinking and reasoning and the understanding of verbal categories and concepts.

Arithmetic:

This comprises a series of arithmetic problems which the child solves mentally and responds to orally. This is the only test on the verbal scale to be timed and measures numerical problem solving and reasoning and computational skills. It can reveal sequencing difficulties.

Vocabulary:

The child has to define a series of words. It tests language development, word knowledge and verbal fluency.

Comprehension:

This is a series of questions that requires the child to solve everyday problems or to show an understanding of social rules and concepts. It tests the ability to evaluate and use past experience when responding to socially relevant questions, the ability to interpret or explain real-life problem situations, social and practical judgement and common sense.

Digit Span:

This is a series of number sequences which the child repeats verbatim for 'Digits Forwards' and in reverse for 'Digits Backwards'. This provides a measure of short-term auditory memory and concentration and 'Digits Backwards' provides some measure of working memory.

Performance Tests: these are presented visually and generally require a non-verbal response.

Picture Completion:

This comprises a set of pictures of common objects and scenes each of which is missing an important part which the child identifies. It requires virtually no coordination and can be answered vocally. It requires alertness to detail and visual discrimination.

Picture Arrangement:

A series of pictures, presented in a mixed-up order, have to be rearranged by the child into a logical story sequence. The test is thought to measure non-verbal reasoning and planning ability when dealing with social situations.

Block Design:

A set of two-dimensional geometric patterns are presented which the child replicates using two-colour cubes. Abstract visual problem solving, spatial analysis and good coordination are all required, but the individuals who do best on the test are more often those who are able to break the design up into its component parts.

Object Assembly:

This is a set of jigsaw puzzles of common objects, which the child assembles to form a meaningful whole. Non-verbal thinking is crucial although good coordination is required to assemble the pieces quickly.

Coding:

Simple shapes (Coding A) or numbers (coding B) are each paired with a simple symbol. The child draws the symbol in its corresponding shape (A) or under its corresponding number (B) according to a key. This is the only paper and pencil test and visual-motor coordination is the primary element for successful performance. Visual perception, visual memory, sequencing ability and concentration are all qualities measured by this test. Low scores on this test are related in many cases to reading difficulties.

Appendix 9

John's Explanation for his Difficulties with Social Interactions[91]

The background: H... invited me to go up to Golders Green in an email which I got about 1730. I thought, what the hell... and only when I was halfway there did he mention that it was a party (trepidation) with people he's known for years (more trepidation) and I don't know any of them (more trepidation) and some of them are female (massive trepidation).

Even though the pub we were meeting them in wasn't noisy, I coped with the situation for about 25 seconds before my soaring stress levels forced me to beat a retreat and head for home (missing the train by one minute, bah!)

This email is where I tried to explain to H... my rather bizarre behaviour, and how and why it was that I saw the party rather differently than everyone else probably did. There are lengthy digressions and it's typically verbose and convoluted: he might not bother to read it all. Oh well.

Subject: The cause of tonight's fiasco, or alien anthropology

I think you deserve an explanation of why I acted like I did tonight; you probably don't have a clue, because it's not remotely like an ordinary human would act.

But with regard to social modelling and interaction with other humans, it's best to regard me not as a human but as an alien studying the culture of Terrestrial bipeds.

Because I have little of the instinctive ability at social understanding that most people have, I've been forced over the past fifteen-odd years to derive consciously-applied replacements for them; conscious theories of how external effects modify the mind-states of humans, and of how those mind-states might affect their reactions to others.

Now this is one of humanity's special gifts, honed in most people by thirty million years or so of evolution as a social primate: and it's unconscious neural processing. Now unconscious neural processing is fast: it seems that you can keep your mental models of people updated in real-time, without effort. I've come to realise that my lack of this ability changes a lot about the way I perceive the world.

For me, running through my (much cruder!) conscious models takes vastly longer than real-time (perhaps fifty to a hundred times slower). So I can't use them in social interactions: instead, I have to run past interactions through them and try to find simpler rules of thumb that I can follow in real-time (I do this obsessively, hundreds of runs whenever I make a gaffe and spot it). These aren't very accurate, so at best I can rely on not screwing up about 50% of the time (and they're now more accurate than they've ever been). I can refine them for particular people as I learn how they think.

On first interaction with particular people, I have to rely entirely on generic rules-of-thumb, which work even less well, because I don't know the social protocols for determining common spheres of interest, or, hell, even for asking people what their names are. So it's so risky (and involves so much effort later on to refine specific models for those people) that I generally try to avoid meeting new people unless it's likely I'll meet them again: otherwise it's stress and ten to fifty hours of intense thought gone to waste.

I haven't yet come up with models that can handle everything, even with people I know and with whom I share interests. I can just about handle one-on-one conversations, but I still don't have any understanding of conversational grammar or multi-person conversations...; nor can I perceive most nonverbal signals. I'm working on conversational grammar now, stealing theories from Taylor in theoretical linguistics and trying to simplify them into something usable: it'll be several years before I have anything, I fear. (I only started using things from linguistics and psychology in the last year or so: my viewpoint is, if other people have done the work I need, why not nick it?)

I hypothesise that most people, when they come into a room crowded with lots of people they don't know (e.g. a party) feel the sort of exhilaration I'd feel when opening a new book by an author I know to be good: a feeling that systems that work will be exercised, that you can do something you're good at (and consequently enjoy).

But when I came into a room crowded with people I don't know, particularly if I'm expected to interact with them, it's at best trepidation and stress that I feel. Tonight it was much worse. I was simultaneously hit with:

— lots of new people, interests unknown, models unknown, names unknown

— no people who aren't new other than you, so I can't simply avoid the new people, or aim for conversational nexi where there is at most one new person

— they're in multi-person conversation (rules of thumb work even worse than usual, and detailed post-facto modelling almost impossible)

— they all have detailed models of each other; attention will be focused on me as a consequence (so they can build up models of me) and I'll be acting most unusually (as I'll be running on those kludgy rules of thumb and trying to handle conversational grammar and multi-person interactions and be stressed as hell and very distracted by all these internal processing streams as a consequence, and probably unable to concentrate on what anyone is actually saying)

— the consequences of failure are potentially catastrophic; you've known them for years and since it is almost certain that I'll commit a major social gaffe due to processing delays or failure of the rules of thumb, I might lose a friend: and since my count of people I account friends has never risen above about ten, I'll do almost anything to avoid that: stress level skyrockets some more

— let's be blunt, I have one standard human worry: some of them are attractive and female (→ instant terror unless I already know them.)

— I'd like to be able to handle these situations: I like people. But I can't cope with them. So the I'm-letting-you-down stress layer has the I'm-losing-opportunities layer and this-could-be-interesting-don't-miss-it layer piled on top of it. (And that last layer normally runs my life. Overriding it is hard.)

I'm normally in a state of considerable stress (it takes lots of quiet to de-stress me, and I almost never get that). In that situation, I was probably about a hundred times more stressed than you were. I was on the verge of shaking (itself not a good thing to do in early social interactions, as it's apt to be misinterpreted as fear of the other parties).

When I'm that stressed, it overwhelms normality: an autistic wave hits. My emotions deactivate themselves except for a low-grade fear/sorrow mixture underlying everything, objects in the visual field become outlined in invisible light [1] and freighted with vast significance, and obsessive analysis of every little detail in the external world takes over; I don't bother with nonphysical things like social interactions; they're almost impossible for me to detect in this state (all I can see is 'humans communicating': I can only comprehend the meaning of speech with effort). In this state I can literally spend an hour examining the grain of wood on a table. I hypothesise that this is the state that full-blown autistics spend their entire lives in. It's sort of like some drug highs, I think, but without the drugs, and not very pleasant. It wouldn't sell.

Today, everything was wrong: so I got out before the autistic wave hit: I'd rather everyone think I'm a coward than everyone think I'm a loony. Besides, it would have spoilt the evening for the rest of you, and that would never do.

Sorry, again.

[1] I get this when ill, as well: nobody else I've asked seems to. Corners and edges of objects seem to glow, but there's no extra light coming from them. I guess it's overactivity of the corner and edge-detectors in the visual cortex (probably located in regions V3, V4, or VP).

Appendix 10

Internet Communication and the Social Grapevine

As John describes it there are several reasons why he feels part of the grapevine on the net. These reasons apply mainly to the Usenet which has been John's primary social forum.

— lurking is easy, so you can listen in to what others say to each other and pick up info without being thought 'rude' or anything idiotic like that. Indeed, it's considered rude not to lurk for long enough that you know the social customs of a group before posting in it (except in purely technical groups).

— you can store what people say, or keep track of it; my... address-book-cum-spy-in-the-sky has little notes attached to most of the people I know with one line memory joggers...

— conversations can flow in multiple directions... every conversational fork can be followed... you can have a tree of replies-to-replies. For someone with a grasshopper mind like mine, this is a real boon.

— you can think as long as necessary before responding... this means you can re-search what you are saying... and helps to improve the tenor of the conversation. I usually think over even the shortest responses for multiple minutes: you just can't do that in a real time conversation.

— you can put off responding and nobody thinks anything of it

— even the rarest viewpoints are common on the net: the Usenet attracts a large number of geeks, being the oldest, most sophisticated, and hardest to learn of the various conversation systems out there. So you can always find a kindred soul of some sort.

— I have ludicrously over the top indexing systems that help me tell if I'm repeating myself or telling someone something that they've already been told by other people.

Appendix 11

Insights into John's Imaginary Life

Author: When did your imaginative games such as the battle against the 'Authority' start? Secondary or primary school? Did they arise because of the bullying at school by other pupils or something else?

John: They really got intense at secondary school, but there was certainly a lot of internal fantasy life in primary school. It's in secondary school that it acquired plotlines and a history and worldbuilding.

It was much less a reaction to bullying than an opportunity to explore ideas, and an opportunity to get back at the teachers in most of the universes (I think there were about six detailed ones in the end), the enemy was a faceless, bureaucratic authority: in more than one, said authority had sent specific agents after me to, well, to make my life hell (or try to send me to hell, or at least make me dead).

Author: What sort of things happened in this game?

John: I'm not sure 'game' was the right word. They were more like stories: I never actually wrote the plots down but I certainly revised them in my head, tweaked the worldbuilding and reran them endlessly with different assumptions to see what made a better story. (This is where I learnt about the importance of limitations: being all-powerful is very fun – for about six seconds, then it gets boring. Being downtrodden and having everyone against you and nonetheless winning, now that's entertainment – in part because I could be sure that nothing that bad was happening to me in reality!)

It's slightly hard to say what happened in any given universe, because I kept on revising the worldbuilding so much: they were more like sheafs of universes, really. The Authority universe was a sheaf started when I was perhaps 14 in which I was a member of a revolutionary underground, fighting against, not a Big Brotherish society, but a Big Faceless Bureaucracy (the Authority), whose sole interest was in maintaining stable living conditions for everyone come what may (their slogan was 'Stability. Conformity. Obedience.'). I was aware at the time that this was more than slightly ironic, given that I appreciate stable living conditions more than virtually anything else – but the methods the Authority was willing to employ were so nasty that, even as an ideological fellow-traveller, I'd been forced into clandestine opposition (though there were many occasions when my resolve wavered 'cos that makes the plotting more fun).

I had a lot of fun thinking of nasty things the Authority could do that would serve their goals (including sometimes intentionally being nice to lull us into a false sense of security), and ways to counter them, and ways in which societies could be damaged, and means to evade detection, and that sort of thing. Tiny cells were an important feature: there were normally three people in mine, with personalities oddly similar to Harry and Alison in hindsight! I was not the cell leader, although I came up with most of the ideas: that was the Harry-character. So all communications with other cells had to go through someone 'else'… which had the advantage of keeping the number of characters down.

I recall that one of the sneakiest things the Authority tried was a bioweapon that forced everyone to be happy all the time, thus ensuring a content population and distracting them from the fact that at the time the Authority couldn't even keep the power on let alone run the trains on time. That one succeeded and we had to figure out countermeasures in a happy daze, while knowing that we'd be condemning ourselves to misery again, and knowing that anyone we met would be against us: the Authority admitted our existence and put up posters saying 'these people want to bring back the doldrums' with a sizeable reward, so we had to try to fix things while hiding out in an abandoned house and sneaking out for food! Of course nobody was trying too hard to catch us because they were all in a happy daze too (the Authority tried to avoid being infected and screwed up). Even the Authority's pet assassin/bounty hunter, notably similar to Mr. C. in personality [author: a hated secondary schoolteacher] was happy and laughing all the time... but he thought killing people and earning a lot of money would make him even happier, so he didn't stop hunting us.

The location shifted quite a lot as it grew more complicated: it started out happening actually in the environment of the school, but ended up in a space habitat. There are more interesting ways things could go wrong in an environment as delicate as that, and the Authority had even more control: plus there was a good rationale for their existence in a delicate environment: I think their name changed to the Ecological Authority at the time. (I was distinctly amused to read Bujold's minor work 'Ethan of Athos' many years later and find that she'd had the same idea, only she'd made it the core of a novel: in a space habitat, dictatorial power would tend to accrue in the people who kept the ecology working...)

OK, so there was another reason for the space habitat thing. I was obsessed with closed environments at the time, and was hooked on the immortally brilliant computer game 'Elite' (like everyone else born in the 70s with any access to a BBC B). So at least one universe involved quite a bit of Elite-style space trading...

Probably the last universe I built was modelled on a fascinating pair of Daedalus articles from New Scientist: one talking about an 'ecologically sound human' (we're talking complete closed loop here, green hair, everything reused: this being Daedalus he'd actually done the maths and figured out how slowly such a human would have to move and so on), and one talking about large high-altitude balloons. So I invented a world in which I was the designer of a, well, a large high-altitude balloon. Permanently inhabited, of course, and very high altitude, 40-70km up, and enormous (the basket, if you could call it that, had a diameter of just over 2km). I had a pile of fun working out how to keep such a thing working (lots of advanced tech was needed just to keep everyone from suffocating!)... and then, well, we were staying up there for decades minimum, going down only for essential supplies, like a space habitat... and my attention was drawn by the places over which we were floating. We were so high up that any but minimal navigation was out of the question: we were blown at the whim of the winds – and a lot of the nations over which we were floating might not like that, and some of them might have the means to express their dislike, whether by direct action or by diplomacy or by more subtle means (we had a turnover of inhabitants, and several hostile nations smuggled secret agents on board and caused all sorts of havoc). I tried to keep this one sort of realistic, so a lot of the non-tech stuff was done by characters other than myself (trying to keep the characterizations from merging together was really difficult, what with this all being in my head). The political stuff was done by a committee, with perennial arguments over whether to do what the nations we overflew wanted, or not, and how to adjust our course, sometimes months in advance, to avoid dodgy places... (we dodged North Korea once, I remember, and found that the Chinese didn't much like us either, unless of course we agreed that they owned the balloon and all therein, including all the tech, most of which they didn't have themselves: i.e. they wanted to take it to bits or at least engage in a bit of asset denial).

Which has aged best? The Authority universe, certainly: I still revisit it now and again, and remember most of the details, because it had most narrative life. Most of the rest got bogged down in worldbuilding and tech tweaks and reruns, but the Authority universe had all the verve its bureaucracy lacked.

Appendix 12

Marbles and the Imagination

Author: Some time ago you said 'I was never interested in collecting marbles *per se*; I only collected them because their aggregate behaviour was fascinating, and because I could endow the marbles with personality and make up elaborate fantasies around that'. Please could I have an explanation/details about what you meant in this context by the words 'aggregate behaviour'?

John: The behaviour of the marbles as a group, i.e. not one marble but the collisional dynamics of the whole group were fascinating.

Author: Can you give me any examples of marble personalities you used and fantasies you created?

John: I used to think of it as a sort of composite living thing; the individual marbles had personalities (at least, the ones I could distinguish clearly: e.g. there was one very crotchety battered one which had, well, been through the wars, an 'old soldier' type; one with a very bright blue interior which of course had to be naively dashing everywhere, heedless of danger) but they were bonded together into this larger marble-swarm creature: they could leave but really preferred not to and got depressed if away for any length of time, and virtually everything they did they did as a group. Sometimes smaller groups got split off for special purposes. A sort of hive mind.

Appendix 13

John's Favourite Authors and the Reasons Why He Likes Them[92]

Ursula K. Le Guin: Bought because of the points she makes and her writing style. I doubt I need to describe her writing, you've read enough of it! Her 'A Wizard of Earthsea' was a GCSE set text and hooked me on adult SF. (She's eighty now and is still very active, publishing everything from fictional expansions of the life of minor characters in the Aeneid to a tirade against the Google Book Settlement.)

Poul Anderson: He grew up reading Norse sagas, and you can tell. A lot of his immense output is potboiler action stuff, and I'm not so interested in that: but some is quietly lyrical, and his knowledge of history was great enough that he pretty much owned the variant on time travel story where someone's made a tiny change in the far past and whoops now everything's different and we've got to figure out what it was and fix it so we can get our world back. The 'everything's different' was also well thought out: the world with no Protestantism, and a Holy Catholic American Empire, was notably disturbing (the change stemming ultimately from one minor knight leaving for the Crusades a day earlier than he otherwise would have, and living where in our world he died). He's even written updated Norse sagas and an entire four-volume historical fantasy set in the fifth century ('The King of Ys').

Lois McMaster Bujold: I put off reading her stuff for ages because they were published by Baen, which mostly publishes US-right-wing military blast-o stuff, and because their covers suggested that they were just the sort of appalling characterless laugh-as-your-enemies-die mankind-is-always-right-due-to-our-guns stuff that I've always avoided. Boy was I wrong. Yes, the Vorkosigan series does have a mercenary spacefleet at the centre of several books, but the 'mercenary admiral' is operating under an assumed identity, is a 4' hunchback, avoids action because his bones are so friable (and still spends a lot of time in hospital beds after action finds him anyway), and his real identity is widely-enough known that he has to pose as an illegal clone of, er, himself. What it's really about is politics. Bujold has described SF as 'fantasies of political agency', and certainly that's true in the Vorkosigan books (Barrayaran politics is horrendously complex and notably lethal, with three of the last five emperors overthrown in violence or intrigue). The plots (political and fictional) are often horrifically complicated, there's a lot of very dry humour, and the characterization is excellent as well. Oh, and also the books were written radically out of sequence and not pre-planned, but you can't tell because she slipped each book into the cracks between the others so well. Each book changes subgenre drastically, from a retelling of the Sorcerer's Apprentice with mercenary soldiers instead of brooms ('The Warrior's Apprentice') through studies of loss or romance which also happen to be whodunnits ('Memory' and 'Komarr' respectively) through to homages to Georgette Heyer which are so good that I couldn't stop laughing from one end to the other ('A Civil Campaign', perhaps her best work).

Her other works are remarkable as well: 'The Curse of Chalion' brings me to tears every time I read it, and her most recent series straddles the boundary between romance and SF, a most unusual combination given how appallingly badly most SF writers depict women. (Her intention was to have each side damn it because it was really an example of the other hated genre. She failed.)

Terry Pratchett: Surely I don't need to say why I read Pratchett. Half the country agrees with me! The satire, the dry humour, the characters (some very well drawn, some, um, less so), the underlying decency...

Neal Asher: Brain candy. Viciously complicated plots, very high technology, and lots and lots of often-violent action for very high stakes. The SF equivalent of an action movie, but nothing is ever quite as it seems because many of the players on both sides are transhuman: they just use humans as their agents. Quite why remains unclear...

Greg Egan: Brain bursters. The characterisation isn't much and neither are the plots but good grief the ideas. This is someone whose SF stories have frequently triggered multiple scientific papers (written entirely over the net: he's so reclusive that he's gone to great lengths to destroy all photographs of him, and only his agent has his address and is under strict instructions never to reveal it). 'Diaspora', for instance, starts with a world most of whose population has migrated into entirely virtual form (the first chapter covers the birth/construction of one of these: people, computer programs, what's the difference?). And that's just the start: by the middle of the book he's playing about with 5+1-dimensional space, an entire invented physics (with an appendix describing it in more detail), topology advanced enough that he needs an appendix to define his terms for those unfortunate readers who aren't topologists... and this is one of his simpler books. 'Schild's Ladder' took me five reads to comprehend (and I'm not sure I get it even now), and spends most of its time discussing the means by which physical laws are formed.

Kage Baker: Excellent time-travel novels, featuring a mysterious Company (Dr. Zeus, Incorporated), which has been meddling in the timeline since the start of human history: they take local humans who are about to die and make them immortal (and I mean literally immortal, absolutely unkillable, drop one into a nuclear blast and he'd survive) and then use them as local agents, stealing artworks which are about to be destroyed in fires, spreading diseases... hey, wait, why are they doing that? The same characters recur over and over again in different guises, for purposes unclear. Excellent plotting, excellent characterization, the only downside being that some of it is incredibly disturbing. Very dry humour.

James White: 'James Herriot set in space', only not quite, but definitely cut from the same episodic medical-problem mould. The patients are sentient, the staff mostly very nonhuman, and often they know nothing about the species they're treating other than what sort of air it breathes (if any). Sector Twelve General Hospital has to be one of the most impressive settings in all of SF. Much of it is 60s and 70s SF, and White was in his forties even then, so its treatment of women in particular is... off. But I can read past that. The fundamental decency and humanity of the stories gives me a lift whenever I reread them.

China Mieville: The opposite. Everything in Mieville's world is corrupt and decaying and probably oozing or grimy. The plots are nothing special, and he's notably fond of last-minute escapes and so forth. But the writing sometimes ceases to be pedestrian and hooks me and then I can't put the book down for hours.

Vernor Vinge: An ideas man at first, but his characterization and plotting has been getting better and better, and by 'A Deepness in the Sky' it carries the book. But his ideas are compelling enough that entire not-exactly-religious movements have been founded off the back of them (which he looks on with a certain suspicion). And his writing gets pretty impressive. But mostly he thinks things through. This is the opposite of Star Trek, where some amazing new thingy (maybe the ability to read minds at a distance) is invented for one episode and then forgotten even though it should radically change everything throughout the society. e.g. 'The Peace War' features one single simple invention (and we don't even learn what it is until halfway through the book: everyone involved thinks they know what it does, but they're wrong: annoyingly the blurb on the back of the book gives it away, argh): that single invention changes the course of human history, not once but repeatedly, and its consequences are very carefully worked out. He used to be a libertarian but I won't hold that against him: he's gone back on that recently because it's obvious to anyone as smart as he is that libertarians' ideal society would be neither stable nor a nice place to live.

Special mentions, being people which I'm hooked on for one book but hate the rest of their oeuvre:

Dan Simmons: The Hyperion cantos is an amazing set of four books: lots of people rave over the first book and damn the rest. I think the lot is amazing. Unfortunately most of the rest of what he's written is either horror (no thanks) or breaks my willing suspension of disbelief...

Susanna Clarke: I'm hooked on everything she's written, but so far that stands at one book (Jonathan Strange & Mr Norrell), even if it is an absolutely amazing one (mostly for the depth of its worldbuilding and its wonderful imitation of Austen).

Honourable mentions, being people I was hooked on once but no longer am: my tastes have matured and they frankly aren't terribly good writers. Most are excellent plotters, and back when interpersonal relations were too painful to read about or hard to grasp properly, that was what I was looking for:

Isaac Asimov: Excellent plotter, not afraid to steal from the best. Writing from the finest reinforced cardboard shop. Incredibly egotistical, and sometimes I'm afraid this came out in his writing. His extensive non-fiction writing is excellent (for its time: 60s science popularization, some of the first).

Peter F. Hamilton: Fun action stuff, but unfortunately he really really needs an editor: every book is hundreds of pages longer than the one before and introduces yet more characters and yet more plot threads to be tied up. I can't follow a book with hundreds of characters in, not least because most don't get enough characterization to keep them separate from each other.

Neal Stephenson: Wildly erratic: some of his stuff is excellent (e.g. 'Zodiac', a tale about ecoterrorists, very cynical) but he fell off the infodumping cliff a while back. A lot of his works are a lot of fun, but suddenly you'll hit two chapters in which the characters forget what personalities they have and talk about the history of Western philosophy or the right way to design a secure nanotechnological infrastructure... the digressions are all fun, but put me off buying his stuff after I made the mistake of buying the Baroque Cycle, three books in which he proves that he can't do historical fiction at all and lets his digressive tendencies go so insane that one entire book consists of nothing but one huge digression with no relevance to the plot at all. GAH.

Juvenilia, being the stuff that got me started and that I've never reread since:

Nick Fisk: The first SF author I ever read, deserves a mention here even if he's sub-B-list in writing skill. Cardboard characters, fun plots featuring a lot of frantic improvization (nowadays I recognise this as a sign of someone who hasn't quite got to grips with plotting yet). e.g. one of his series involved a bunch of kids who'd got a spacecraft and gone a-wandering in it having adventures... only they hadn't built it in their backyard as is traditional in bad SF, they'd stolen it from a junkyard, and it looked it and worked as well as you'd expect. Half the time they were more worried about their disintegrating ship than whoever was supposed to be after them. Notable for scenes of oh-crap madcap panic which are precisely like the scenes of madcap panic I've subsequently experienced when things go wrong on production sites at work.

Douglas Hill: I was hooked on one of this guy's series in secondary school. Typical action plot, guy given unbreakable bones by mysterious mentor goes after deeply-hidden evil conspiracy that... murdered his parents... but having unbreakable bones doesn't mean you can't be hurt. Quite a lot of fun, and I still remember it although I haven't read any of his stuff in fifteen years.

Appendix 14

Extracts From a Letter Written to John's Class Teacher

... it was discovered that there was something wrong with John's coordination (later affecting all manual skills, sports etc.) and with his visual sequential memory (affecting spelling, routine calculating, spatial presentation of work etc.). For example he couldn't hold scissors or a pencil at all in either hand when he was five which meant he didn't do any drawing, cutting or writing before he was five. This has caused great problems at school, from nursery school onwards, not helped by the fact that he is a very intelligent boy who, because of his handicap has often been given work of an inappropriate intellectual content. As an example of his intellectual capabilities he has been reading and understanding parts of my 'New Scientist' magazine since he was seven and a half, watching some of the Horizon programmes from the same age, reading widely on all scientific topics ranging from human biology to physical geography to astronomy etc. since he was six and displaying great understanding of computer programming since he was seven and a half. When the county educational psychologist tested him in the first year juniors it was found that he had a difference of approximately 47 points (on their measurement scale) between his verbal reasoning skills (~139) and his hand/eye skills (~92). This is of course, an enormous difference and has led to a great deal of frustration for John which has, quite possibly, been a contributory factor in his bad behaviour.

This is the first school year [now aged nine] that he has been physically capable of writing clearly. (For your interest he is only now able to do jigsaw puzzles that an infant school child could do). It is a top priority that he be allowed to develop this skill fully this year. As with all skills involving training of the neuromuscular system (e.g. piano practice) 'little and often' is far more effective than a great deal occasionally. It really is important that he do the cursive writing program EVERY DAY for say 10-15 minutes with the aim (1) to practice all the letters so that he can write them clearly and (2) to speed up so that by the end of the year, if possible, he can write clearly and at the same speed as other children of his age. This may not be possible, but we will never know if he isn't given a chance. This writing practice should not be treated as a punishment and I would be upset if he missed playtime or craft work (which is also important for his neuromuscular development) in order to do the writing. Equally if he has been trying hard at maths or writing his diary or a story etc. and he hasn't done as much as the others it is not his fault and he shouldn't be punished by missing craft or play. If he could write as fast as the others he wouldn't need the special program.

You must understand how frustrating it is for John and his parents to have to go through this whole procedure every year with a different class teacher until they understand (if ever) how to cope with John and help him as much as he needs.

... please be prepared to make allowance for his slowness in writing his diary etc. and doing routine mathematical calculations and in the case of the latter, if he can do the questions let him skip some of the repetitions so that he can get onto some maths commensurate with his ability.

Appendix 15

Letter Providing Reasons for Wishing to Transfer to the Local Mixed Secondary School

1. Location

This is the only school (apart from [...]) which is local, within walking or cycling distance and on an excellent bus route.

2. Journey to School

As both of us parents work full time and therefore rely on others for transport of our child backwards and forwards from school, this is a natural choice because several local children attend this school. We would be gravely concerned to see our son wandering around... on his own, particularly after school in the dark.

3. Child's Needs

Our child is badly coordinated and has had some difficulty learning in a classroom setting to the extent that the Infant School asked for an Assessment of Special Educational Needs under the 1981 Education Act. He works best in a well disciplined and enthusiastic atmosphere where there is plenty of work to do and no bullying. He is poor at sport and tends to get picked on by other boys. We feel that of all the schools we visited, this was the only one that would provide the well disciplined, enthusiastic, caring atmosphere that our son would be able to cope with. The strong attitude taken by this school towards bullying impressed us as well as the fact that there was not too much emphasis on sporting excellence.

4. Educational Achievements

We were most impressed both with the examination results and with the general education in the school. We feel that every attempt is being made to develop each child to its full potential, whether academic or otherwise, and to prepare them fully for a future career. Our son is very interested in science and computing and we particularly liked the first year science course, the setting of maths in the first year and the teaching of the computer language LOGO.

5. Denominational

Both parents are non-churchgoers and as such we do not wish for our son to go to a denominational school.

6. Summary

We feel that Mr P and his team at this school will provide the education most suited to our child's needs. Apart from [...] all the other schools in [...] would a) be too difficult for our son to travel to and b) not provide an appropriate education... although providing what we consider to be an acceptable education, would neither meet the criteria outlined in 3 above, nor, should the proposed reorganisation of secondary schools take effect, meet the criteria in 1 and 2 above.

Appendix 16

Story Written by Lydia when She was Six Years Old[93]

If I could choose a home I wold choose a hut by the sea I wold sew the seaweed into curtaintanis I wold have a seaweed floor and drift wood for a table I would decorate my house with sea shells I would paddle in the sea and make sand casles and I would pick flours and eat the poolen I would colect shells and I would draw words on my door it would say Lilly hut I would like my hut so would my brother we would have huts next to each other we would play ball on the beach we would have lots of fun in the sea at night we would kiss eatch other good night If it wasent to late we would tallk to eatch other or read to each other then we would sleep I would drem of the next day and John would drem of what it wold be like if we went to mouse school and he thout about the sums and the teacher and the work books and the calnders the next day we had our polen for breakfast then we playd with hoops and we... (rest missing)

Appendix 17

A Testament of Experience by Lydia (aged 15)

'How can you and your brother be so different?'

You wouldn't understand.

'Hey, your brother's really sad, I mean, what's his problem?'

Do you honestly want me to explain it to you?

'Why does your brother use a portable computer in school – why can't he just write like everybody else?'

Because he's not like everybody else.

'I feel sorry for you having to live with him!'

You feel sorry for me? I feel sorry for you.

'Haha. Someone spilt orange juice on your brother's computer and it packed up! Isn't that funny?'

Yeah. It's hilarious.

'Why's your brother so weird?'

You wouldn't understand.

Nobody seems to understand.

You just see what you see.

You see a misfit, who scurries from place to place, seemingly unaware of the rest of the world. The rest of the world who are, if I know them, probably laughing at him.

He knows he's being laughed at. Well it would be hard for him not to. Nobody will ever let him forget that he's different from the rest of the crowd.

Nobody will ever let me forget.

Do you think it doesn't hurt him?

Do you think he's immune, emotionless?

It hurts me.

I'm not immune. I have emotions.

Why can't you just accept him for what he is?

I do.

He's my brother, but I don't have to accept him.

I could disown him, be embarrassed by him, laugh at him, but I don't.

I don't.

I stand up for him.

But sometimes, just sometimes I act like you.

I laugh at him when he does something strange.

I tell everyone he's sad.

I'm embarrassed by him, and I hate myself for it.

I hate myself for being so cruel,

So uncaring,

So weak.
But there's a difference between you and me.
You laugh at him because you don't know any better.
You don't know why he acts the way he does.
    I do.
So why do I let myself behave like you?
    I know why.
    It's because I'm not strong enough.
I think that if I stand up for him, my friends will think I'm weird too.
When I laugh at him I feel so ashamed.
But it's easier to laugh than to explain.
    I should know.
I've been trying to explain for as long as I can remember.
    But it doesn't work.
I just want to shout 'Alright. So we all know he's different, but are any of you actually interested in why he acts like this? Are you? No, of course you aren't. Because if you knew you might feel guilty for taking the piss. So you just carry on as you are, in your own small-minded way, and what can I do to stop it? Nothing.'
Well now I want everyone to know. Then I can hate you all when you laugh at him because you'll have heard about his problems and you still laugh.
I'll know then that you're all bitter and cruel, not just stupid and igno-rant.
It's not his fault.
It's not really anybody's fault.
Things just didn't work out right.
There were problems with the birth – complications.
The doctors thought there was just one baby.
But there wasn't.
The contractions came two and a half months early and my brother was born. He was tiny.
Too tiny to be born – too young – underdeveloped.
The panic started.
The doctors realised there was another baby inside.
If they hadn't turned the machine off, the baby would have lived.
Maybe. But he wouldn't have been aware of this or anything else. He would have been a breathing toy.
Unable to do anything.
Aware of nothing.
So the machine was turned off.
That baby died, but my brother lived.
He underwent traumatic heart surgery and was left brain damaged by the premature birth.
He has no visual memory and severe learning difficulties.
Somehow, though, he's accepted these problems and has gone to [...]

school for six years.

His talent for computing has made him a few friends.

Why can't you be his friend?

I have so much love and respect for his friends, but it's only a few boys out of hundreds who have seen who he really is.

Nobody believes it when they find out who my brother is.

He's the joke of the school.

You used to tease me because of him and I just wanted to lash out. To hurt you like you were hurting me.

Why should he be made miserable by people like you after all the problems he's already had to conquer?

What have you had to struggle for?

If only you'd lived his life instead of him, then you'd know how he feels.

But I wouldn't wish that on anybody.

Appendix 18

Letter written to me in anger by Lydia when she was 13 and John 14½

Do not rip this up.

Mother

I want you to read this letter very carefully & consider what I am saying as I will not speak to you until you have.

I understand that you are angry with John – GREAT – at last I get a wee bit of attention around here. I deserve it a lot more than he does. I have been jealous of the attention he gets for as long as I can remember – that is probably why I started lying & stealing – to get some attention. I know you spend too much time with us and that you want to cut down on it so that you can do what you want – you definitely deserve that. However – instead of cutting down on the time you spend with me – how about cutting down on the time you spend with my stupid sod of a "brother"? He is shortening your life & he knows that he can get plenty of attention by behaving like a stupid bastard – which he is. I hope you realise that not only are you punishing him by removing his computer but you are also punishing me for something I haven't done. Think about it.

After saying all that – and I feel a lot better now – I still love you a lot and I hate seeing you treated like SHIT and taking it from silly Bugger.

Lydia

P.S. I am sorry this letter sounds so spoilt but I feel a bit truculent & sulky at the moment.

Have you considered my letter?

Can I use the computer?

Appendix 19

Extracts from Letters sent by Doctors

Age[94], [95]	Hosp	Comments
4w	B[96]	doing very well... no abnormal findings... weight 3.2 kg
15w	B	doing well... doing all that expected
7m	B	doing fine... transferring, chewing... upper respiratory infection
8m	B	head circumference 44cms – 1s.d. Nellhaus chart... reached out and picked up brick in either hand, transfers very competently, plays with paper and crumples it. He strikes the brick on the table chuckling and watched me scribbling on the paper... cooing and chuckling... heard aah and ooh... upper respiratory tract infection... finger feeds, drinks from cup, loves looking in the mirror, plays, smiles and laughs... perfectly normal on R.G. Scale... hypotonic... sits beautifully with forward support... both lateral responses present... lifts head and chest clear... gets onto all fours then quite unable to move and literally collapses... think developmentally normal – weight 7.36 kg
10m	B	head circumference 44.75- now crawling, pulling up, standing against the furniture... says Dad and is babbling... still hypotonic but no evidence of spasticity... yet another upper respiratory tract infection... weight 8.25 kg
14.5m	B	hearing normal... walking for last fortnight...
18m	B	lots of words and expressive jargon... walking about everywhere, crawling up and down stairs... loves looking at books, feeds himself and sits at the table... mother not as yet bothered about toilet needs... weight 11.2 kg
22m	B	held a pencil for me and did free horizontal scribble... would not cooperate and build a tower... mother says he speaks in sentences. I heard 2 word combinations. At this stage I gave up because I think quite frankly, mother thinks he is a genius!!... all systems were normal... height 81 cm... weight 11.76kg
2y	A[97]	has more or less caught up his early developmental delay and seemed a very normal child... clinical examination was not of the easiest, but I found nothing wrong... speech was fluent, though I didn't understand it at all... coordination seemed above average for his age...
2y 7m	B	mother not the slightest bit worried about John... she reported that he was very good at jigsaws... I heard him do preliminary counting...lan-

		guage appeared to be normal... walking up stairs very immature, two feet to a step and unable to jump off bottom step... attending nursery school at the FE college once a week... height 88.5 cm...weight 12.93 kg
2y 8m	A	(seen at home as part of a small follow up study of babies who had face mask ventilation.) Head circumference 49.7cm... general health seems very good... mother reported no behavioural problems... passed all four elements of Denver Developmental Screening Test (DDST) and in particular his language development was very advanced for his age... able to define three opposite analogies.. clearly knew colours, prepositions, and first and last name... able to copy a vertical line and a circle... didn't manage to imitate a bridge made of three bricks. Hearing and vision normal... no abnormality on detailed neurological examination.. seems to have normal developmental attainments and speech development in particular is excellent... have sneaking impression that he is perhaps not quite so clever as the rest of his family although certainly seems well within the range of normal... I also wondered whether his mother might also suspect this as she was continuously showing off the things that he could do. Height 90cm... not able to weigh him...
3y	B[98]	mother states now integrating with children after having been to the Further Education nursery... due to go to XX nursery in September 5 afternoons per week... Mother is not the slightest bit worried about John. In many ways he is not as bright as she thinks he is, but I think this is due to the fact that she has been very careful not to repeat history. Mother has a very unhappy childhood... and as a result I think she lets John do as he wishes, without any pressurising. This is why I think that the structured environment of XX will probably be good for him... now able to go upstairs in an adult manner, right foot leading... He goes downstairs two feet to a step and is able to jump off the bottom step... weight 13.9 kg
4y 4m	A	(seen at home as part of a low birth weight study). Height weight and head circumference are all in the middle of the normal range and in good proportion... I found him to be a very happy child, friendly and talkative and extremely well stimulated... wets bed every night... although passed Denver Screening test gross motor section can't catch a ball as yet... in the fine motor section he cannot imitate a square, is useless at drawing and in fact cannot hold a pencil properly let alone draw a face for me. He passed the language section with flying colours. In fact his vocabulary is probably rather better than mine. He passed the personal and social section but is not managing his buttons yet and there are tremendous battles with dressing himself in the morning. Vision and hearing completely normal... he has no squint. I carefully went over his central nervous system and found no abnormality. He has good coordination and I think this hand/eye coordination problem is obviously a mild one but one that may cause problems later at school.

		Obviously his mother has noticed these problems and I do hope she doesn't push him too far.
4y 4m	A[99]	You are a most exceptional family and John is truly a delightful child. It is very gratifying to see a child so physically and developmentally normal following the trauma in the neonatal period.
8y 3m	B[100]	Mother has always thought John a genius! Until recently!! clinically mildly hypotonic. Clumsy, but latter improving. Concentrates on his own pursuits. Very <u>poor</u> eye/hand coordination… hearing normal… Strabismus right eye. Mother very angry and thinks he is not having enough help with his appalling writing.

417

Appendix 20

Education Act 1981 – Statement of Special Educational Needs

II – Special educational needs

John has considerable academic ability in several areas of school work, which he generally enjoys. However, his poor hand/eye co-ordination and resultant writing difficulties, together with a weakness of concentration, have led to some underfunctioning below his true potential.

John therefore needs an individual programme of work specially planned by his class teacher, in consultation with other professionals (Advisory Teacher and/or Educational Psychologist) as appropriate, to help him overcome these particular difficulties.

III – Special educational provision

Special attention to John's difficulties with co-ordination and concentration in the mainstream primary school, where he should follow an individual and carefully monitored programme of work, which includes particular help with his handwriting.

This programme would be monitored in the normal way through continuous assessment by John's class teacher and in the regular review of his Statement by those professionals who are concerned with John's education at the school.

IV – Appropriate school or other arrangements

Continued attendance at... school... for the time being, subject to regular review.

V – Additional non-educational provision

None

Appendix E: Psychological advice

John is correctly placed in mainstream school and is a child of high ability in some areas of his development. However, there are significant differences between his verbal and visual spatial abilities, possibly as a result of perinatal difficulties. These assessment results have been discussed with both the school and Mrs A. It has been agreed that John's strengths should be encouraged and praised and that the school and home should continue to co-operate on a handwriting programme. At present objectives in this area would be that (1) the spacing of his words should improve, (2) the shape of his letters should become more consistent and (3) he should work to keep all writing on a straight line. He may continue to produce little in the way of quantity for some time to come.

Appendix 21

Some Childhood Screening Tests, Questionnaires and Checklists

From Roman (1998)

Measures of executive functioning:

Wisconsin Card Sorting Test (Berg, 1948); Category Test (Reitan, 1979); Tower of London (Shallice, 1982); Trail Making Test (Reitan, 1979); Progressive Figures and Color Form Tests (Reitan & Wolfson, 1985).

Measures of receptive vocabulary and expressive vocabulary:

Peabody Picture Vocabulary Test (Dunn & Dunn, 1981); Receptive One-Word Picture Vocabulary Test (Gardner, 1985); Expressive One-Word Picture Vocabulary Test – Revised (Gardner, 1990); Boston Naming Test (Kaplan, Goodglass, & Weintraub, 1983)

Measures of visual-spatial abilities:

Judgement of Line Orientation Test (Benton, Hamsher, Varney, & Spreen, 1983); Tactual Performance Test (Reitan, 1979); Test of Visual Perceptual Skills – Revised (TVPS-R; Gardner, 1996)

Sensory-perceptual and motor functioning:

Grooved Pegboard Test (Klove, 1963).

Educational and Academic measures:

Wide Range Achievement Test (Wilkinson, 1993); Woodcock-Johnson Tests of Achievement (Woodcock & Johnson, 1989); Test of Written Spelling – 3 (Larsen & Hammill, 1994)

From Blakemore-Brown (2002)

Questionnaires for ADHD:

Connors, (1986); Achenbach's Child Behaviour Checklist (CBCL) (1986, 1988)

From Lovecky (2004)

Tests of language and auditory processing:

Boston Naming Test; Test of Pragmatic Language; Expressive One-Word picture Vocabulary Test; Receptive One-Word Picture Vocabulary Test; Token Test for Children; Test of Auditory Reasoning and Processing Skills; SCAN-C: Test for Auditory Processing Disorders in Children - Revised; test of Language Development.

Tests of memory and learning:

California Verbal Learning Test – Children's; Children's Auditory-Verbal Learning Test; Wide Range Assessment of Memory and Learning; Test of Memory and Learning; Children's Memory Scale; Benton Visual Retention Test; Rey-Osterrieth Complex Figure – Delayed Memory.

Tests of visual-perception and visual-motor integration:

Bender-Gestalt Test; Beery-Buktenica Developmental Test of Visual-Motor Integration (VMI)-2; Developmental Test of Visual-Perception; Benton Facial Recognition Test; Benton Judgement of Line Orientation; Test of Visual-Perceptual Skills.

Tests of executive functions:

Wisconsin Card Sorting Test; Children's Category Test; Stroop Colour-Word Test; Verbal Fluency Test; FAS Test; d2 Test of Attention; Trail Making Test; Rey-Osterrieth Complex Figure Test; Benton Finger Localization test; NEPSY (includes the Tower of London Test); Continuous Performance Tests including Connors' Continuous Performance Test; Auditory Continuous Performance Test; Tests of Variables of Attention.

From Sugden and Chambers (2005)

Tests of developmental coordination disorder:

Movement Assessment Battery for Children Test (Henderson and Sugden, 1992); Gubbay's Test (Gubbay, 1975); The McCarron Test (McCarron, Bruininks, 1978); Southern California Sensory Integration Tests (Ayres, 1989); Developmental Coordination Disorder Questionnaire (DCDQ) (Wilson et al., 2000); Vineland Adaptive Behaviour Scales (VABS) (Sparrow, Balla and Cicchetti, 1985); Early Years Movement Skills Checklist (Chambers and Sugden, 2002).

From Williams et al (2005)

Screening tests for autism spectrum conditions with primary school age children:

Australian Scale for Asperger Syndrome (Attwood, 1998); Children's Social Behaviour Questionnaire (Luteijn et al., 2000); Pervasive Developmental Disorders Questionnaire (Baird et al., 2000); Asperger Syndrome Screening Questionnaire (Ehlers and Gillberg, 1993; Ehlers et al., 1999); Autism Behaviour Checklist (Krug et al., 1980); Gilliam Autism Rating Scale (Gilliam, 1995; South et al., 2002); Social Communication Questionnaire (Berument et al., 1999).

From Attwood (2006)

ASAS or Australian Scale for Asperger's Syndrome (Garnett and Attwood, 1998); ASDI or Asperger Syndrome Diagnostic Interview (Gillberg et al., 2001); ASDS or Asperger Syndrome Diagnostic Scale (Myles, Bock and Simpson, 2001); ASSQ or Autism Spectrum Screening Questionnaire (Ehlers, Gillberg and Wing, 1999); CAST or Childhood Asperger Syndrome Test (Scott et al. 2002,; Williams et al., 2005); GADS or Gilliam Asperger Disorder Scale (Gilliam, 2002); KADI or Krug Asperger's Disorder Index (Krug and Arick 2002); DISCO or Diagnostic Interview for Social and Communication Disorders (Wing et al. 2002).

From Martin et al (2006)

Measures for ADHD:

ATBRS or Australian twin behaviour rating scale (Levy et al., 1996); SWAN or strengths and weaknesses of ADHD symptoms and normal behaviour (Swanson et al., 2001).

Measures for developmental coordination disorder:

DCDQ or developmental coordination disorder questionnaire (Wilson et al., 2000); Bruininks – Oseretsky test of motor performance, Movement Assessment Battery for children (Wilson et al., 2000).

From Limperopoulos et al (2008)

Standardized developmental outcome testing:

M-CHAT or Modified Checklist for Autism in Toddlers (Robins et al 2001); CBCL or Child Behavior Checklist (Rescorla 2005, Achenbach & Rescorla 2000).

Appendix 22

Results of John's WISC-R Tests[101]

Verbal Tests	Scaled scores @ 7yrs 6 mths	Scaled scores @ 15yrs 9 mths
Information	17	15
Similarities	18	17
Arithmetic	12	13
Vocabulary	16	19
Comprehension	NM[102]	18
Digit Span	NM	13
AVERAGE VERBAL SCALED SCORE	**16**	**16**
Performance Tests		
Picture Completion	10	12
Picture Arrangement	NM	9
Block Design	13	13
Object Assembly	7	8
Coding	6	9
AVERAGE PERFORMANCE SCALED SCORE	**9**	**10**
VERBAL IQ	**137**	**141**
PERFORMANCE IQ	**92**	**101**
Difference between Verbal and Performance IQs	**45**	**40**

Appendix 23

The Empathy Quotient – John's Responses[103]

Characteristic	[104]	Pts
I can easily tell if someone else wants to enter a conversation.	STD	
I prefer animals to humans.	SLD	
I try to keep up with the current trends and fashions.	STD	
I find it difficult to explain to others things that I understand easily, when they don't understand it first time.	SLD	1
I dream most nights.	STD	
I really enjoy caring for other people.	STD	
I try to solve my own problems rather than discussing them with others.	STA	
I find it hard to know what to do in a social situation.	STA	
I am at my best first thing in the morning.	STD	
People often tell me that I went too far in driving my point home in a discussion.	SLD	1
It doesn't bother me too much if I am late meeting a friend.	STD	2
Friendship and relationships are just too difficult, so I tend not to bother with them.	STA	
I would never break a law, no matter how minor.	SLD	
I often find it difficult to judge if something is rude or polite.	STA	
In a conversation, I tend to focus on my own thoughts rather than on what my listener might be thinking.	SLA	
I prefer practical jokes to verbal humour.	STD	
I live life for today rather than the future.	STD	
When I was a child, I enjoyed cutting up worms to see what would happen.	STD	2
I can pick up quickly if someone says one thing but means another.	STD	
I tend to have very strong opinions about morality.	SLA	
It is hard for me to see why some things upset people so much.	SLA	
I find it easy to put myself in somebody else's shoes.	STD	
I think that good manners are the most important thing a parent can teach their child.	STD	

I like to do things on the spur of the moment.	STD	
I am good at predicting how people will feel.	STD	
I am quick to spot when someone in a group is feeling awkward or uncomfortable.	STD	
If I say something that someone else is offended by, I think that that's their problem, not mine.	SLA	
If someone asked me if I liked their haircut, I would reply truthfully, even if I didn't like it.	STA	
I can't always see why someone should have felt offended by a remark.	STA	
People often tell me that I am very unpredictable.	SLD	
I enjoy being the centre of attention at any social gathering.	STD	
Seeing people cry doesn't really upset me.	SLD	1
I enjoy having discussions about politics.	STA	
I am very blunt, which some people take to be rudeness, even though this is unintentional.	STA	
I don't tend to find social situations confusing.	STD	
Other people tell me I am good at understanding how they are feeling and what they are thinking.	STD	
When I talk to people, I tend to talk about their own experiences rather than my own.	STD	
I upsets me to see an animal in pain.	STA	2
I am able to make decisions without being influenced by people's feelings.	SLA	
I can't relax until I have done everything I had planned to do that day.	SLD	
I can tell easily if someone else is interested or bored with what I am saying.	STD	
I get upset if I see people suffering on news programmes.	SLD	
Friends usually talk to me about their problems as they say that I am very understanding.	STD	
I can sense if I am intruding, even if the other person doesn't tell me.	STD	
I often start new hobbies, but quickly become bored with them and move on to something else.	STD	
People sometimes tell me that I have gone too far with teasing.	SLD	1
I would be nervous to go on a big rollercoaster.	STA	
Other people often say I am insensitive, though I don't always see why.	SLA	
If I see a stranger in a group, I think that it is up to them to make an effort to join in.	SLD	1

I usually stay emotionally detached when watching a film.	STD	2
I like to be very organized in day-to-day life and often make lists of the chores I have to do.	STA	
I can tune in to how someone else feels rapidly and intuitively.	STD	
I don't like to take risks.	STA	
I can easily work out what another person might like to talk about.	STD	
I can tell if someone is masking their true emotion.	STD	
Before making a decision I always weigh up the pros and cons.	SLD	
I don't consciously work out the rules of social situations.	STD	
I am good at predicting what someone will do.	STD	
I tend to get emotionally involved with a friend's problems.	SLD	
I can usually appreciate the other person's viewpoint, even if I don't agree with it.	SLA	1
JOHN'S TOTAL SCORE ON THE EMPATHY QUOTIENT		**14**

Appendix 24

The Systemizing Quotient – John's Responses[105]

Characteristic	[106]	Pts
When I listen to a piece of music, I always notice the way it's structured.	SLD	
I adhere to common superstitions.	DD	
I often make resolutions, but find it hard to stick to them.	DD	
I prefer to read non-fiction to fiction.	SLD	
If I were buying a car, I would want to obtain specific information about its engine capacity.	SLD	
When I look at a painting, I do not usually think about the technique involved in making it.	DA	
If there was a problem with the electrical wiring in my home, I'd be able to fix it myself.	DD	
When I have a dream, I find it difficult to remember precise details about the dream the next day.	DA	
When I watch a film, I prefer to be with a group of friends, rather than alone.	DD	
I am interested in learning about different religions.	DA	
I rarely read articles or Web pages about new technology.	DD	2
I do not enjoy games that involve a high degree of strategy.	DD	2
I am fascinated by how machines work.	DA	2
I make a point of listening to the news each morning.	SLA	
In maths, I am intrigued by the rules and patterns governing numbers.	DA	2
I am bad about keeping in touch with old friends.	DA	
When I am relating a story, I often leave out details and just give the gist of what is happening.	DD	
I find it difficult to understand instruction manuals for putting appliances together.	SLA	
When I look at an animal, I like to know the precise species it belongs to.	DA	2
If I were buying a computer, I would want to know exact details about its hard drive capacity and processor speed.	DA	2
I enjoy participating in sport.	DD	

I try to avoid doing household chores if I can.	DA	
When I cook, I do not think about exactly how different methods and ingredients contribute to the final product.	SLD	1
I find it difficult to read and understand maps.	SLD	1
If I had a collection (e.g. CDs, coins, stamps) it would be highly organised.	SLA	1
When I look at a piece of furniture, I do not notice the details of how it was constructed.	SLD	1
The idea of engaging in 'risk-taking' activities appeals to me.	DD	
When I learn about historical events, I do not focus on exact date.	SLD	1
When I read a newspaper, I am drawn to tables of information such as football league scores or stock market indices.	SLA	1
When I learn a language, I become intrigued by its grammatical rules.	DA	2
I find it difficult to learn my way around a new city.	SLD	1
I do not tend to watch science documentaries on television or read articles about science and nature.	DD	2
If I were buying a stereo, I would want to know about its precise technical features.	DA	2
I find it easy to grasp exactly how odds work in betting.	DA	2
I am not very meticulous when I carry out D.I.Y.	SLA	
I find it easy to carry on a conversation with someone I've just met.	DD	
When looking at a building, I am curious about the precise way it was constructed.	SLA	1
When an election is being held, I am not interested in the results for each constituency.	DD	2
When I lend someone money, I expect them to pay me back exactly what they owe me.	SLD	
I find it difficult to understand information the bank sends me on different investment and saving systems.	SLA	
When travelling by train, I often wonder exactly how the rail networks are coordinated.	DA	2
When I buy a new appliance, I do not read the instruction manual very thoroughly.	DD	2
If I were buying a camera, I would not look carefully into the quality of the lens.	SLA	
When I read something, I always notice whether it is grammatically correct.	DA	2

When I hear the weather forecast, I am not very interested in the meteorological patterns.	DD	2
I often wonder what it would be like to be someone else.	SLA	
I find it difficult to do two things at once.	DA	
When I look at a mountain, I think about how precisely it was formed.	DA	2
I can easily visualise how the motorways in my region link up.	DD	
When I'm in a restaurant, I often have a hard time deciding what to order.	SLA	
When I'm in a plane, I do not think about the aerodynamics.	SLD	1
I often forget the precise details of conversations I have had.	DA	
When I am walking in the country, I am curious about how the various kinds of tree differ.	SLA	1
After meeting someone just once or twice, I find it difficult to remember precisely what they look like.	DA	
I am interested in knowing the path a river takes from its source to the sea.	SLA	1
I do not read legal documents very carefully.	DD	2
I am not interested in understanding how wireless communication works.	SLA	
I am curious about life on other planets.	DA	
When I travel, I like to learn specific details about the culture of the place I am visiting.	DA	
I do not care to know the names of the plants I see.	SLD	1
JOHN'S TOTAL SCORE ON THE SYSTEMIZING QUOTIENT		**46**

Appendix 25

The Autism Spectrum Quotient – John's Responses[107]

Characteristic	[108]	Pts
I prefer to do things with others rather than on my own.	DD	1
I prefer to do things the same way over and over again.	DA	1
If I try to imagine something, I find it very easy to create a picture in my mind.	DD	1
I frequently get so strongly absorbed in one thing that I lose sight of other things.	DA	1
I often notice small sounds when others do not.	DA	1
I usually notice car number plates or similar strings of information.	SLA	1
Other people frequently tell me that what I've said is impolite, even though I think it is polite.	DA	1
When I'm reading a story, I can easily imagine what the characters might look like.	SLD	1
I am fascinated by dates.	SLA	1
In a social group, I can easily keep track of several different people's conversations.	DD	1
I find social situations easy.	DD	1
I tend to notice details that others do not.	DA	1
I would rather go to a library than a party.	DA	1
I find making up stories easy.	SLA	
I find myself drawn more strongly to people than to things.	DD	1
I tend to have very strong interests which I tend to get upset about if I can't pursue.	DA	1
I enjoy social chit-chat.	DD	1
When I talk, it isn't always easy for others for others to get a word in edgeways.	DA	1
I am fascinated by numbers.	DA	1
When I'm reading a story, I find it difficult to work out the characters' intentions.	DD	
I don't particularly enjoy reading fiction.	DD	
I find it hard to make new friends.	DA	1
I notice patterns in things all the time.	DA	1

I would rather go to the theatre than a museum.	SLD	1
It does not upset me if my daily routine is disturbed.	DD	1
I frequently find that I don't know how to keep a conversation going.	DA	1
I find it easy to 'read between the lines' when someone is talking to me.	DD	1
I usually concentrate more on the whole picture, rather than the small details.	SLD	1
I am not very good at remembering phone numbers.	DA	
I don't usually notice small changes in a situation, or a person's appearance.	DA	
I know how to tell if someone listening to me is getting bored.	DD	1
I find it easy to do more than one thing at once.	DD	1
When I talk on the phone, I'm not sure when it's my turn to speak.	DA	1
I enjoy doing things spontaneously.	SLA	
I am often the last to understand the point of a joke.	DD	
I find it easy to work out what someone is thinking or feeling just by looking at their face.	DD	1
If there is an interruption, I can switch back to what I was doing very easily.	DD	1
I am good at social chit-chat.	DD	1
People often tell me that I keep going on and on about the same thing.	SLA	1
When I was young, I used to enjoy playing games involving pretending with other children.	SLA	
I like to collect information about categories of things (e.g. types of cars, types of bird, types of train, types of plant etc.).	SLD	
I find it difficult to imagine what it would be like to be someone else.	DA	1
I like to plan any activities I participate in carefully.	SLA	1
I enjoy social occasions.	DD	1
I find it difficult to work out people's intentions.	DA	1
New situations make me anxious.	DA	1
I enjoy meeting new people.	DD	1
I am a good diplomat.	DD	1
I am not very good at remembering people's dates of birth.	DA	
I find it very easy to play games with children that involve pretending.	DD	1
JOHN'S TOTAL SCORE ON THE AUTISM SPECTRUM QUOTIENT		**40**

Appendix 26

The Childhood Asperger Syndrome Test (CAST).[109]

QUESTIONS	COMMENT	Y/N	PTS
Does he join in playing games with other children easily?		N	1
Does he come up to you spontaneously for a chat?	Not sure		0
Was he speaking by 2 years old?		Y	
Does he enjoy sports?		N	
Is it important to him to fit in with the peer group?		N	1
Does he appear to notice unusual details that others miss?		Y	1
Does he tend to take things literally?		N	0
When he was 3 years old did he spend a lot of time pretending (e.g. play-acting being a superhero, or holding teddy's tea parties)?		Y	0
Does he like to do things over and over again, in the same way all the time?		Y	1
Does he find it easy to interact with other children?		N	1
Can he keep a two way conversation going?		N	1
Can he read appropriately for his age?		Y	
Does he mostly have the same interests as his peers?		N	1
Does he have an interest which takes up so much time that he does little else?		Y	1
Does he have friends, rather than just acquaintances?		N	1
Does he often bring you things he is interested in to show you?	Not sure		0
Does he enjoy joking around?		N	1
Does he have difficulty understanding the rules for polite behaviour?		Y	1
Does he appear to have an unusual memory for details?		Y	1
Is his voice unusual (e.g. overly adult, flat or very monotonous)?		Y	1
Are people important to him?		N	1

Can he dress himself?	Finds it hard		
Is he good at turn-taking in conversation?		N	1
Does he play imaginatively with other children, and engage in role play?		N	1
Does he often do or say things that are tactless or socially inappropriate?		Y	1
Can he count to 50 without leaving out any numbers?		Y	
Does he make normal eye contact?	Not after 7 yrs old	N	1
Does he have any unusual and repetitive movements?	Tics	Y	1
Is his social behaviour very one-sided and always on his own terms?		Y	1
Does he sometimes say "you" or "he" when he means "I"?	Only when much younger	N	0
Does he prefer imaginative activities such as play-acting or story-telling, rather than numbers or lists of facts?	Loves facts & very imaginative		0
Does he sometimes lose the listener because of not explaining what he is talking about?		Y	1
Can he ride a bicycle (even if with stabilisers)?		Y	
Does he try to impose routines on himself, or on others, in such a way that it causes problems?		Y	1
Does he care how he is perceived by the rest of the group?		N	1
Does he often turn conversations to his favourite subject rather than following what the other person wants to talk about?		Y	1
Does he have odd or unusual phrases?		Y	1
JOHN'S TOTAL POINTS			**25**

Appendix 27

John's Major Characteristics Compared with Various Conditions[110]

ADHD= Attention Deficit Hyperactivity Disorder
AS= Autism spectrum (including Asperger's Syndrome)
DCD= Developmental Coordination Disorder (or Developmental Dyspraxia)
NLD= Nonverbal Learning Disability

Some of John's key characteristics	ADHD	AS	Dyslexia	DCD	NLD	Gifted
Large gap between Verbal & Performance IQ on standardised intelligence tests		•	•	•	•	
Very uneven profile of abilities on standardised intelligence tests	•	•	•	•	•	
Finds change and transitions hard to cope with – likes order and routine	•	•	•	•	•	
Tendency to procrastinate	•	•		•	•	
Cautious with money						
Very strong, dry and unusual sense of humour including wordplay – not always easy to understand.	•	•			•	•
Very loyal	•	•				
Restricted range of intense interests		•				
Passionate interest in computers.		•				•
Strong interest in science, science fiction and fantasy		•				
Hyperfocus on things of special interest	•	•		•		•

JOHN'S MAJOR CHARACTERISTICS COMPARED WITH VARIOUS CONDITIONS

Characteristic						
Very hard working in areas of special interest and doesn't give up	•	•				•
Powerful imaginative world		•		•		•
Creative	•	•	•			•
Imaginary friends		•				•
Enjoys challenge of problem solving (in computing)		•	•			•
Enjoys helping others – especially with computing problems						
Good abstract reasoner		•				•
Good at pattern recognition in data	•	•			•	•
Thirst for knowledge		•			•	•
Curious as a child – asked lots of questions		•			•	•
Avid reader		•				•
Fascinated by words		•			•	•
Sophisticated and extensive vocabulary		•			•	•
Language different from peers	•	•			•	•
Good grammar		•				•
Good reading comprehension						•
Excellent long term memory – very good on detail		•		•	•	•
Very knowledgeable – 'little professor'		•		•	•	•
Underachieves academically	•		•	•	•	•
At school gets bored very easily – no motivation to complete tasks	•				•	•

Talks very fast	•	•	•	•	•	
Unusual prosody – flat pitch, stress wrong syllables, lack of normal speech rhythm		•		•	•	
Can talk very loudly	•	•		•	•	
Can be hard to understand – poor articulation	•	•	•	•		
Talks 'at' people – monologues – finds rules of conversation difficult	•	•		•	•	
Assumes listeners understand what is being said to them – doesn't notice their boredom	•	•			•	
Poor listening skills	•	•	•	•	•	
Can talk too much – dominates the conversation	•	•	•	•	•	
Slow processing speed	•	•			•	
Very blunt – can appear rude or commit 'faux pas' or social gaffes	•	•		•	•	
Reveals family secrets		•			•	
Interrupts	•	•	•	•	•	
Stammers (as adolescent and adult)			•			
Poor social skills and social communication	•	•		•	•	
Not good at social chit-chat or gossip	•	•			•	
Conversation free of hidden meaning or agenda		•			•	
Problem asking for help	•	•	•	•		
Copes poorly in groups	•	•		•	•	
Poor at team sports and unaware of rules	•	•		•	•	
Difficulties recognising body language and facial	•	•		•	•	

Characteristic						
expressions						
Difficulty, until an adult, watching TV and films						
Problems with eye contact	●	●		●	●	
On the Internet prefers communication that allows long delays such as e-mail	●	●			●	
As a child preferred adults or younger children	●	●		●	●	
As a baby did not experience separation anxiety		●				
As a child did not experience stranger anxiety		●				
Appears less mature than peers – naive	●	●		●	●	
Not accepted by peer group – appears very different to other children – may be thought of as weird, odd or eccentric	●	●		●	●	●
Unconcerned about his appearance – can look rather untidy	●	●		●	●	
Talks to himself	●	●			●	
Mutters under breath	●					
Hums to himself	●					
As a child made repetitive noises like that of a machine	●					
Few friends – loner by default	●	●		●	●	●
Has never had a romantic relationship (at time of writing when John aged 39)		●			●	
Bullied and teased as a child	●	●		●	●	
More interest in objects		●				

than people		•				
Low muscle tone – hypotonia	•	•	•	•	•	
Hand tremors on occasion				•		
Poor motor planning	•			•		
Poor gross motor skills – physically awkward	•	•	•	•	•	
As a child stuffed too much food into mouth				•		
As a child found chewing difficult		•		•	•	
Weaves around when walking – doesn't stay in a straight line		•		•		
Poor body awareness		•		•	•	
Clumsy – knocks into things	•	•	•	•	•	
Poor at sport e.g. poor ball skills, poor runner, difficulties hopping, skipping and jumping	•	•	•	•	•	
Stiff posture	•	•		•		
Unusual gait	•	•		•	•	
Late to establish hand dominance				•		
Poor fine motor skills e.g. problems with shoe laces, ties, belts, zips, buttons, scissors, cutlery, piano	•	•	•	•	•	
Difficulty cleaning teeth, combing hair, blowing nose, waving goodbye				•		
Poor hand-eye coordination		•		•	•	
Poor handwriting – slow or looks untidy and hard to read	•	•	•	•	•	
Hand hurts when writing			•	•	•	

Sometimes a slight hand tremor				•		
Poor spatial planning on paper			•	•	•	
Looks awkward when writing			•	•	•	
Difficulty organising thoughts when writing	•		•	•	•	
Limited written output				•	•	
Poor art skills – immature drawings	•	•		•	•	
Motor tics	•	•		•		
Chewed own clothes while wearing them		•			•	
Very short sighted						
Divergent Squint – strabismus – left eye wanders outwards						
Poor visual memory	•	•	•	•	•	
Problems with visual perception	•	•	•	•	•	
Took a very long time before able to cross the road safely				•		
Doesn't drive – would be very difficult to learn to drive safely				•	•	
Does not learn through observation or imitation		•			•	
Difficulty copying from the board		•	•	•	•	
Difficulty with jigsaws and construction toys			•	•	•	
Difficulty sorting shapes			•	•	•	
Excellent eye for detail, not for the large picture	•	•			•	
Difficulty controlling						

Difficulty controlling strong feelings, appears to overreact – explosive temper	•	•			•	•
Easily overwhelmed	•	•			•	•
Easily frustrated	•	•			•	•
Poor short term and working memory	•	•	•		•	•
Easily distracted	•	•	•		•	•
Can appear lazy	•	•	•		•	•
Needs one-to-one attention to finish work	•	•	•		•	•
Problems benefiting fully from a normal classroom environment – does better in a one-to-one situation	•	•	•		•	•
Could not listen and take notes	•	•	•		•	•
Poor at mental arithmetic	•	•	•		•	
Poor at rote learning e.g. alphabet	•	•	•			
Great difficulties learning to spell	•				•	
Problems with organisation	•	•	•		•	•
Lack of common sense		•				
Poor prioritisation	•					•
Great difficulty planning	•	•	•		•	•
Won't work hard for future goals and rewards – only if subject of sufficient intrinsic interest	•					
Forgetful/absent minded e.g. forgets to hand in homework	•					•
Loses things at school	•				•	•
Difficulty using locker at secondary school						•

Problems with sequencing	•	•	•	•	•	
Problems following sequence of instructions	•	•	•	•	•	
Poor time management	•	•	•	•	•	
Difficulty breaking tasks down	•				•	
Problems with homework and long term projects	•	•	•	•	•	
As a child would fidget and rock back in chair	•	•		•	•	
Moves around a lot	•			•		
Trouble staying in seat in classroom	•			•		
Always busy	•					
Very intense					•	•
Difficulty going to sleep – can't find the off switch and difficulty waking up	•	•			•	
Paces, moving hands and muttering	•	•				
Tense and anxious	•	•		•	•	
Panics easily	•	•		•	•	
Copes poorly with stress and pressure	•	•			•	
Under and over sensitive to temperature	•	•				
Under sensitive to pain as a young child	•	•				
Dislike of hair cutting, washing, bathing, cleaning teeth, cutting nails	•	•		•	•	
As a baby screamed when nappy changed						
As a baby screamed when bathed				•		
Very sensitive to smell and taste	•	•		•		

taste	•	•		•		
Upset by crowds and noise	•	•	1.	•	•	
Difficulties filtering out background noise	•	•	•	•		
Disliked children's parties		•		•	•	
Disliked clothes shopping		•		•	•	
Perfectionist – fear of making a mistake, doing badly or failing	•	•			•	•
Will not begin something if thinks will fail or quits if can't do task well	•	•	•	•	•	•
Dislikes competitive games and games of chance – poor loser	•	•			•	
Low self esteem particularly as a teenager	•			•	•	
Lies readily to avoid getting into trouble	•	•		•		
Tends to blame others when things go wrong	•					
Stubborn and determined – would argue or lose his temper if didn't want to do something	•	•				
Tendency to see things as black and white – obeys rules		•			•	
Very strongly held opinions – Finds it difficult to compromise	•	•			•	
Clarity of values/decision making unaltered by political or financial factors		•				
Cynical						
Treats all people equally regardless of position of authority, gender, race or age	•	•			•	

justice						
Kind and soft hearted – strong social conscience	•	•				
Doesn't hold grudges	•					
Fond of all animals, but scared to handle		?		?		
Very premature baby, low birth weight and breathing difficulties	•	?	•	•	•	
Bed-wetting for many years as a child	•					•
Hay fever		?				

This appendix has been compiled entirely from the references listed below, so if a symptom hasn't been specifically mentioned for a particular diagnosis in one of these references, then there won't be a tick in the appropriate column. However, this doesn't actually mean that this symptom cannot be found in someone with that particular diagnosis. Any other errors or omissions in this table are mine.

References used in compiling this table:

Attwood, T. (2006) 'The Complete Guide to Asperger's Syndrome.' London: Jessica Kingsley Publishers.

Attwood, T. 'The Discovery of "Aspie" Criteria.' www.tonyattwood.com.au downloaded 27/07/2010.

Barkley, R.A. (2000) 'Taking Charge of ADHD. The Complete Authoritative Guide for Parents.' New York: The Guilford Press.

Blakemore-Brown, L. (2002) 'Reweaving the Autistic Tapestry.' London: Jessica Kingsley Publishers.

Chinn, S. (2010) 'Addressing the Unproductive Classroom Behaviours of Students with Special Needs.' London: Jessica Kingsley Publishers.

Chivers, M. (2006) 'Dyslexia and Alternative Therapies.' London: Jessica Kingsley Publishers.

Elvén, B.H. (2010) 'No Fighting, No Biting, No Screaming. How to Make Behaving Positively Possible for People with Autism and Other Developmental Disabilities.' London: Jessica Kingsley Publishers.

Gillberg, C. (2002) 'A Guide to Asperger Syndrome.' Cambridge: Cambridge University Press.

Kirby, A. (1999) 'Dyspraxia The Hidden Handicap.' London: Souvenir Press.

Kutscher, M.L. (2005) 'Kids in the Syndrome Mix of ADHD, LD, Asperger's, Tourette's, Bipolar, and More!' London: Jessica Kingsley Publishers.

Kutscher, M.L. (2008) 'ADHD – Living without Brakes. 'London: Jessica Kingsley Publishers.

Lovecky, D.V. (2004) 'Different Minds. Gifted Children with AD/HD, Asperger Syndrome, and Other Learning Deficits.' London: Jessica Kingsley Publishers.

Syndrome, and Other Learning Deficits.' London: Jessica Kingsley Publishers.

Macintyre, C. (2001) 'Dyspraxia 5-11 A Practical Guide.' London: David Fulton Publishers.

Munden, A. & Arcelus, J. (1999) 'The AD/HD Handbook. A guide for Parents and Professionals on Attention Deficit / Hyperactivity Disorder.' London: Jessica Kingsley Publishers.

Neihart, M. (2000) 'Gifted Children with Asperger's Syndrome.' Gifted Child Quarterly, 44(4), 222-230.

Portwood, M. (1999) 'Developmental Dyspraxia. Identification and Intervention. A Manual for Parents and Professionals.' London: David Fulton Publishers.

Richards, R.G. (1999) 'The Source for Dyslexia and Dysgraphia.' New York: LinguiSystems, Inc.

Rubinstien, M.B. (2005) 'Raising NLD Superstars. What families with Nonverbal Learning Disabilities Need to Know About Nurturing Confident, Competent Kids.' London: Jessica Kingsley Publishers.

Selikowitz, M. (2009) 'ADHD (the Facts series).' Oxford: Oxford University Press.

Tanguey, P.B. (2001) 'Nonverbal Learning Disabilities at Home. A Parent's Guide.' London: Jessica Kingsley Publishers.

Tanguey, P.B. (2002) 'Nonverbal Learning Disabilities at School.' London: Jessica Kingsley Publishers.

Thompson, S. (1997) 'The Source for Nonverbal Learning Disorders.' New York: LinguiSystems, Inc.

Wing, L. (1996) 'The Autistic Spectrum.' London: Constable & Robinson Ltd.

Woliver, R. (2009) 'Alphabet Kids From ADD to Zellweger Syndrome. A guide to Developmental, Neurobiological and Psychological Disorders for Parents and Professionals.' London: Jessica Kingsley Publishers.

http://www.clubi.ie/dyslexia/charactr.html retrieved on May 25th 2009.

Appendix 28

Resources

Chapter 2: In the Beginning
A really useful free booklet entitled 'Look at me – I'm talking to you. Watching and understanding your premature baby' is published by the premature baby charity **Bliss**. It can be ordered from the web site http://www.bliss.org.uk or by phone from their free family support helpline on 0500 618140. Bliss is the 'UK charity working to provide the best possible care and support for all premature and sick babies and their families'.

Chapter 3: Food
Feeding premature babies:
http://www.babycentre.co.uk/baby/breastfeeding
http://www.breastfeeding-problems.com
http://www.kellymom.com/bf
http://www.preemies.about.com
'The best start – a guide to expressing and breastfeeding your premature baby.' can be obtained free of charge from http://www.bliss.org.uk/get-involved/shop
Eating problems:
Boyd, B. (2003) 'Parenting a child with Asperger syndrome. 200 Tips and Strategies: Chapter 3 – Common Problems A-Z.' London: Jessica Kingsley Publishers.
Ives, M. & Munro, N. (2002) 'Caring for a Child with Autism. A Practical Guide for Parents: Chapter 12 – Responding to Behaviour.' London: Jessica Kingsley Publishers.
Schopler, E. editor (1995) 'Parent Survival Manual. A guide to Crisis Resolution in Autism and Related Developmental Disorders: Chapter 7 – Eating and Sleeping.' New York: Plenum Press.
Williams, C. & Wright, B. (2004) 'How to live with Autism and Asperger Syndrome. Practical Strategies for Parents and Professionals: Chapter 13 – Feeding.' London: Jessica Kingsley Publishers.
The following information sheets can be downloaded free of charge from the **National Autistic Society** website:
'Dietary management for children and adolescents with ASDs: over-eating.' http://www.autism.org.uk/about/health/dietary-management/over-eating.aspx
'Dietary management for children and adolescents with ASDs: restricted diet.' http://www.autism.org.uk/about/health/dietary-management/restricted-diet.aspx

Chapter 4: Sleep
Durand, V.M. (2014) 'Sleep Better! A Guide to Improving Sleep for Children with Special Needs.' Baltimore: Paul H. Brookes Publishing.
Durand, V.M. (2008) 'When Children Don't Sleep Well: Interventions for Pediatric Sleep Disorders: Parent Workbook.' New York: Oxford University Press.
Ives, M. & Munro, N. (2002) 'Caring for a Child with Autism. A Practical Guide for

Parents: Chapter 12 – Responding to Behaviour.' London: Jessica Kingsley Publishers.

Jackson, L. (2002) 'Freaks, Geeks & Asperger Syndrome. A User Guide to Adolescence: Chapter 7 – A Word about Sleep.' London: Jessica Kingsley Publishers.

James, E.J. et al. (2008) 'Sleep hygiene for children with neurodevelopmental disabilities.' Pediatrics, 122, 1343-1350.

Pantley, E. (2002) 'The No-Cry Sleep Solution. Gentle Ways to Help Your Baby Sleep Through the Night.' New York: McGraw-Hill.

Quine, L. (1997) 'Solving Children's Sleep Problems: A Step by Step Guide for Parents.' Huntingdon: Becket Karlson Publishing.

Williams, C & Wright, B. (2004) 'How to live with Autism and Asperger Syndrome. Practical Strategies for Parents and Professionals: Chapter 16 – Sleeping.' London: Jessica Kingsley Publishers.

Some useful guides can also be downloaded free of charge from the Internet, including (in no particular order):

'Sleep and autism: helping your child.' from the **National Autistic Society**.[111]

'Helping your child's sleep. Information for parents of disabled children.' from **Contact a Family**.[112]

'Encouraging Good Sleep Habits in Children with Learning Disabilities.' from **Research Autism**.[113]

Chapter 5: Health

Visits to doctors and dentists could be made much easier if all health professionals were aware of the type of accommodations they could introduce to make the visits less traumatic for all concerned. Very useful advice can be obtained from a free leaflet called 'Patients with autism spectrum disorders: guidance for health professionals' published by the **National Autistic Society (NAS)**.[114] This is also a useful leaflet for parents to download and read as it might give them ideas to reduce their child's anxiety when visiting a health professional; if necessary, parents could provide a copy for the professionals concerned.

Chapter 6: Sensory Differences

Attwood, T. (2006) 'The Complete Guide to Asperger's Syndrome.' London: Jessica Kingsley Publishers.

Betts, D. & Patrick, N. (2008) 'Hints and Tips for Helping Children with Autism Spectrum Disorders. Useful strategies for Home, School, and the Community.' London: Jessica Kingsley Publishers).

Clements, J. & Zarkowska, E. (2000) 'Behavioural Concerns & Autistic Spectrum Disorders. Explanations and Strategies for Change.' London: Jessica Kingsley Publishers.

Kurtz, L. (2006) 'Visual Perception Problems in Children with AD/HD, Autism, and Other Learning Disabilities. A Guide for Parents and Professionals.' London: Jessica Kingsley Publishers.

Myles, B. and colleagues (2000) 'Asperger Syndrome and Sensory Issues. Practical Solutions for Making Sense of the World.' Kansas: Autism Asperger Publishing Co.

Notbohm, E. (2005) 'Ten Things Every Child With Autism Wishes You Knew.' Arlington: Future Horizons.

Chapter 7: Toilet Related

The Enuresis resource and Information Centre (ERIC) (http://www.eric.org.uk) is a good place to start if one's child is experiencing any toileting problems. As well as a telephone helpline they publish several booklets on the subject, full of excellent suggestions and advice.

'Toilet Training', a free leaflet produced by the **National Autistic Society (NAS)**[115]

Batts, B. (2010) 'Ready, Set Potty! Toilet Training for Children with Autism and other Developmental Disorders.' London: Jessica Kingsley Publishers.

Coucouvanis, J.A. (2008) 'The potty journey: guide to toilet training children with special needs, including autism and related disorders.' Shawnee Mission, Kansas: Autism Asperger Publishing.

White, M. & Rogers, J. (2002) "We can do it!' Helping children who have learning disabilities with bowel and bladder management: a guide for parents.' Bristol: The Enuresis Resource & Information Centre.

Wheeler, M.B. (1998) 'Toilet Training for Individuals with Autism & Related Disorders. A Comprehensive Guide for Parents & Teachers.' Arlington: Future Horizons

Williams, C. & Wright, B. (2004) 'How to live with Autism and Asperger Syndrome. Practical Strategies for Parents and Professionals: Chapter 14 – Toileting, Chapter 15 – Soiling.' London: Jessica Kingsley Publishers.

Ives, M. & Munro, N. (2002) 'Caring for a Child with Autism. A Practical Guide for Parents.' London: Jessica Kingsley Publishers.

A useful book called 'One Step at a Time' plus 13 tip sheets which deal with a range of toileting problems can be downloaded (free of charge) from the website http://www.continencevictoria.org.au/.

Chapter 8: Motor Related

Addy, L. M. 'Handwriting and Dyspraxia.' http://www.dyspraxiafoundation.org.uk/downloads/handwriting_and_dyspraxia.pdf

Boon, M. (2001) 'Helping Children with Dyspraxia.' London: Jessica Kingsley Publishers.

Dixon, L. & Addy, L.M. (2004) 'Making Inclusion Work for Children with Dyspraxia. Practical Strategies for Teachers.' London: Routledge.

Kirby, A. (1999) 'Dyspraxia. The Hidden Handicap.' London: Souvenir Press.

Kirby, A. & Drew, S. (2002) 'Guide to Dyspraxia and Developmental Coordination Disorders.' London: David Fulton Publishers.

Lee, M.G. (2004) 'Co-ordination Difficulties. Practical Ways Forward.' London: David Fulton Publishers.

Levine, M. (2003) 'A Mind at a Time. How Every Child Can Succeed.' London: Simon and Schuster.

Macintyre, C. (2000) 'Dyspraxia in the Early Years. Identifying and Supporting Children with Movement Difficulties.' London: David Fulton Publishers.

Macintyre, C. (2001) 'Dyspraxia 5-11. A Practical Guide.' London: David Fulton Publishers.

Macintyre, C. & McVitty, K. (2004) 'Movement and Learning in the Early Years. Supporting Dyspraxia (DCD) and Other Difficulties.' London: Paul Chapman Publishing.

Mountstephen, M. (2011) 'How to Detect Developmental Delay and What to Do Next. Practical Interventions for Home and School.' London: Jessica Kingsley Publishers.

Portwood, M. (1999) 'Developmental Dyspraxia. Identification and Intervention. A Manual for Parents and Professionals.' London: David Fulton Publishers.

Richards, R.G. (1999) 'The Source for Dyslexia and Dysgraphia: Chapter 12 – The Writing Process: Remedial and Bypass Strategies.' New York: LinguiSystems, Inc.

Ripley, K., Daines, B. & Barrett, J. (1997) 'Dyspraxia. A Guide for Teachers and Parents.' London: David Fulton Publishers.

Ripley, K. (2001) 'Inclusion for Children with Dyspraxia/DCD. A Handbook for Teachers.' London: David Fulton Publishers.

Tanguay, P.B. (2001) 'Nonverbal Learning Disabilities at Home.' London: Jessica Kingsley Publishers.

Tanguay, P.B. (2002) 'Nonverbal Learning Disabilities at School.' London: Jessica Kingsley Publishers.

Teodorescu, I. & Addy, L. (1998, 2001) 'Write from the start: Unique Programme to Develop the Fine Motor and Perceptual Skills Necessary for Effective Handwriting.' Carson Dellosa Pub Co Inc2001) or LDA (1998).

Williams, C. & Wright, B. (2004) 'How to live with Autism and Asperger Syndrome. Practical Strategies for Parents and Professionals.' London: Jessica Kingsley Publishers.

Suppliers:

> http://www.specialdirect.com
> http://www.taskmasteronline.co.uk
> http://www.peta-uk.com for special scissors
> http://www.sensetoys.com
> http://www.rompa.com

There is also an organisation called **'The Dyspraxia Foundation'** (http://www.dyspraxiafoundation.org.uk) which, as well as providing help and advice on its telephone help line, has a web shop with a list of useful books and leaflets, issues two newsletters a year plus one professional journal, runs conferences and has a number of local support groups.

The **Dyscovery Centre** also has a useful web site relating to dyspraxia with a discussion area and at http://www.boxofideas.org, suggestions for activities and resources.

The **National Handwriting Association UK** provides an information service and trains teachers to help children with handwriting difficulties. See http://www.nha-handwriting.org.uk

Chapter 11: Communication

Leventhal-Belfer, L. & Coe, C. (2004) 'Asperger's Syndrome in Young Children. A developmental guide for parents and professionals: Chapter 8 – Building Connections With Peers.' London: Jessica Kingsley Publishers.

Ozonoff, S., Dawson, G. & McPartland, J. (2002), 'A Parent's Guide to Asperger Syndrome & High-Functioning Autism: Chapter 8 – The Social World of Children and Adolescents with Asperger Syndrome and High-Functioning Autism.' New York: The Guilford Press.

Plummer, D.M. (2008) 'Social Skills Games for Children.' London: Jessica Kingsley

Publishers.

Pyles, L. (2002) 'Hitchhiking through Asperger Syndrome: Appendix 3 – Social Skills List.'

Baron-Cohen, S. (2008) 'Mind Reading: The Interactive Guide to Emotions.' London: Jessica Kingsley Publishers.

Williams, C. & Wright, B. (2004) 'How to live with Autism and Asperger Syndrome. Practical Strategies for Parents and Professionals: Chapter 10 – Developing Social Skills, & Chapter 11 – Developing Communication Skills.' London: Jessica Kingsley Publishers.

'The Transporters' at http://www.thetransporters.com

Another useful resource is the article 'Social skills in young children' which is written by **The National Autistic Society** and can be downloaded free of charge from the internet.[116]

Chapter 12: Play

These days there are several suppliers that have a range of excellent toys that would be suitable for children with special needs. For example:

Fledglings, http://www.fledglings.org.uk – a not-for-profit organisation for parents and carers of children with special needs.

The National Autistic Society http://**www.autism.org.uk/toys**

Sense Toys, http://www.sensetoys.com – focuses on resources that encourage interactive play.

Sensory Toy Warehouse, https://www.sensorytoywarehouse.com

Special Direct, http://www.specialdirect.com – provides a range of resources.

Chapter 14: Memory

Interesting suggestions to improve working memory can be found in the books written by:

Lovecky, D.V. (2004) 'Different Minds. Gifted Children with AD/HD, Asperger Syndrome, and Other Learning Deficits.' London: Jessica Kingsley Publishers.

Kirby, A. (1999) 'Dyspraxia The Hidden Handicap.' London: Souvenir Press.

Chapter 15: Reading and Spelling

Kutscher, M.L. (2005) 'Kids in the Syndrome Mix of ADHD, LD, Asperger's, Tourette's, Bipolar, and More!' London: Jessica Kingsley Publishers.

Chapter 16: School

Boyd, B. (2003) 'Parenting a Child with Asperger Syndrome. 200 Tips and Strategies.' London: Jessica Kingsley Publishers.

Kirby, A. (1999) 'Dyspraxia. The Hidden Handicap.' London: Souvenir Press.

Jackson, L. (2002) 'Freaks, Geeks, & Asperger Syndrome. A User Guide to Adolescence: Chapter 9 – The Problem with School, Chapter 10 – Bullying.' London: Jessica Kingsley Publishers.

Some helpful books for parents:

Attwood, T. (1998) 'Asperger's Syndrome. A Guide for Parents and Professionals.' London: Jessica Kingsley Publishers.

Barkley, R.A. (2000) 'Taking Charge of ADHD. The Complete Authoritative Guide for Parents.' New York: The Guilford Press.

Birnbaum, R. (2010) 'Choosing a School for a Child with Special Needs.' London: Jessica Kingsley Publishers.

Kozma, G. (2013) 'Secondary School. A Parent's Guide.' Peterborough: Need2know.

Lawrence, C. (2008) 'How to Make School Make Sense. A Parents' Guide to Helping the Child with Asperger Syndrome.' London: Jessica Kingsley Publishers.

Lawrence, C. (2010) 'Successful School Change and Transition for the Child with Asperger Syndrome.' London: Jessica Kingsley Publishers.

Leventhal-Belfer, L. & Coe, C. (2004) 'Asperger's Syndrome in Young Children. A Developmental Guide for Parents and Professionals.' London: Jessica Kingsley Publishers.

Morrell, M.F. & Palmer, A. (2006) 'Parenting Across the Autism Spectrum. Unexpected Lessons We Have Learned.' London: Jessica Kingsley Publishers.

National Autistic Society http://www.autism.org.uk/about/adult-life/transition-adulthood.aspx

Some helpful books for teachers and teaching assistants:

Ansell, G.D. (2011) 'Working with Asperger Syndrome in the Classroom.' London: Jessica Kingsley Publishers.

Boon, M. (2001) 'Helping Children with Dyspraxia.' London: Jessica Kingsley Publishers.

Chinn, S. (2010) 'Addressing the Unproductive Classroom Behaviours of Students with Special Needs.' London: Jessica Kingsley Publishers.

Dixon, L. & Addy, L.M. (2004) 'Making Inclusion Work for Children with Dyspraxia. Practical Strategies for Teachers.' London: Routledge.

Dyspraxia Foundation (2009) 'Classroom guidelines for schools and teachers.' can be found on the Dyspraxia Foundations's website http://www.dyspraxiafoundation.org.uk

Hannah, L. (2001) 'Teaching young children with autistic spectrum disorders to learn. A practical guide for parents and staff in mainstream schools and nurseries.' London: National Autistic Society.

Hewitt, S. (2005) 'Specialist Support Approaches to Autism Spectrum Disorder Students in Mainstream Settings.' London: Jessica Kingsley Publishers.

Hultquist, A. (2006) 'An Introduction to Dyslexia for Parents and Professionals.' London: Jessica Kingsley Publishers.

Kutscher, M.L. (2005) 'Kids in the Syndrome Mix of ADHD, LD, Asperger's, Tourette's, Bipolar, and More! The one stop guide for parents, teachers, and other professionals.' London: Jessica Kingsley Publishers.

Levine, M. (2003) 'A Mind at a Time. How Every Child Can Succeed.' London: Simon and Schuster.

Perepa, P. (2005) 'Classroom and Playground: support for children with autism spectrum disorders.' London: National Autistic Society.[117]

Sainsbury, C. (2009) 'Martian in the Playground. Understanding the Schoolchild with Asperger's Syndrome.' Bristol: Lucky Duck Publishing.

Stobbart, A. (2009) 'Bullying and autism spectrum disorders: a guide for school staff.' London: National Autistic Society.

Tanguay, P.B. (2002) 'Nonverbal Learning Disabilities at School. Educating Students with NLD, Asperger Syndrome, and Related Conditions.' London: Jessica Kingsley Publishers.

Thorpe, P. (2003) 'Moving from primary to secondary school: guidelines for pupils with autistic spectrum disorders.' London: National Autistic Society.[118]

Thorpe, P. (2004) 'Understanding difficulties at break time and lunchtime: Guidelines for Pupils with Autistic Spectrum Disorders.' London: National Autistic Society.[119]

Winter, M. (2003) 'Asperger Syndrome – What Teachers Need to Know.' London: Jessica Kingsley Publishers.

100% Awesomes[120]

The National Autistic Society[121]

The National Autistic Society (NAS)[122]

Kidscape[123]

Cyberbullying[124]

Chapter 17: The Computer

https://itunes.apple.com/gb/app/autism-apps/id441600681?mt=8

http://www.sheknows.com/parenting/articles/953661/best-ipad-apps-for-children-with-autism

http://www.b12patch.com/blog/autism/10-great-ipad-apps-for-autistic-children/

http://blog.friendshipcircle.org/2011/02/02/the-special-needs-ipad-app-series

Chapter 19: John's Sister, Lydia

For parents and carers:

Betts, D.E. & Patrick, N.J. (2008) 'Hints and Tips for Helping Children with Autism Spectrum Disorders. Useful strategies for Home, School, and the Community.' London: Jessica Kingsley Publishers.

Burke, P. (2004) 'Brothers and Sisters of Disabled Children.' London: Jessica Kingsley Publishers.

Cumberland, D.L. & Mills, B.E. (editors, 2010) 'Siblings and Autism. Stories Spanning Generations and Cultures.' London: Jessica Kingsley Publishers.

Harris, S.L. (1994) 'Siblings of Children with Autism. A Guide for Families.' Bethesda USA: Woodbine House.

Ives, M. & Munro, N. (2002) 'Caring for a Child with Autism. A Practical Guide for Parents.' London: Jessica Kingsley Publishers.

Morrell, M.F. & Palmer, A. (2006) 'Parenting Across the Autism Spectrum. Unexpected Lessons we have Learned.' London: Jessica Kingsley Publishers.

For children and their carers:

Bleach, F. (2001) 'Everybody is Different: a Book for Young people who have Brothers or Sisters with Autism.' London: The National Autistic Society.

Davis, J. (1994) 'Able Autistic Children- Children with Asperger's Syndrome. A Booklet for Brothers and Sisters.' Nottingham: The Early Years Centre.

Fairfoot, E. & Mayne, J. (2004) 'My Special Brother Rory.' London: The National Autistic Society.

Frender, S. & Schiffmiller, R. (2007) 'Brotherly Feelings. Me, My Emotions and My Brother with Asperger's Syndrome.' London: Jessica Kingsley Publishers.

Gorrod, L. (1997) 'My brother is different.' London: The National Autistic Society.

Hames, A. & McCaffrey, M. (editors, 2005) 'Special Brothers and Sisters. Stories and Tips for Siblings of Children with Disability or Serious Illness.' London: Jessica Kingsley Publishers.

Johnson, J. & Van Rensselaer, A. (2010) 'Siblings. The Autism Spectrum through our

Eyes.' London: Jessica Kingsley Publishers.

The **website https://www.sibs.org.uk** is full of excellent suggestions for parents and siblings alike.

The National Autistic Society (NAS) http://www.autism.org.uk/about/family-life.aspx

Chapter 21: Assessments

Organisations that can be of help to parents who have children with special needs include:

The **Advisory Centre for Education (ACE)**, 'a registered independent charity' which provides an advice line, free advice booklets, and written advice and information at http://www.ace-ed.org.uk

Contact a Family, 'a national charity which provides support, advice and information for families caring for children with disabilities or special needs' on a free advice helpline), fact sheets and information packs, written advice and information on http://www.cafamily.org.uk

Family Lives (formerly Parentline Plus), 'a charity which offers support to anyone involved in caring for children', with a 24 hour helpline, parent classes and workshops, information on http://www.familylives.org.uk

Independent Panel for Special Education Advice (IPSEA), 'a national charity which provides advice for parents of children with special educational needs' on a free advice line, a tribunal helpline, written advice and information at www.ipsea.org.uk

The **National Autistic Society Education Rights Service**, free phone from landlines and most mobiles and helpful information at http://www.autism.org.uk/services/helplines/education-rights-service.aspx;

Network 81, 'a national network of parents working towards properly resourced inclusive education for all children with special needs' offering advice on a helpline, a website http://www.network81.org

Information, Advice & Support Services Network, are a free 'statutory service offering information, advice and support to parents and carers of children and young people with special educational needs'. For further information see http://www.iassnetwork.org.uk

Books that parents could also find really helpful include:

Campito, J.S. (2007) 'Supportive Parenting. Becoming an Advocate for your Child with Special Needs.' London: Jessica Kingsley Publishers.

Hanks, R. (2011) 'Common SENse for the Inclusive Classroom. How Teachers Can Maximise Existing Skills to Support Special Educational Needs.' London: Jessica Kingsley Publishers.

Hope-West, A. (2011) 'Securing Appropriate Education Provision for Children with Autism Spectrum Disorders. A Guide for Parents and Professionals.' London: Jessica Kingsley Publishers.

Power, E. (2010) 'Guerrilla Mum. Surviving the Special Educational Needs Jungle.' London: Jessica Kingsley Publishers.

Row, S. (2005) 'Surviving the Special Educational Needs System. How to be a Velvet Bulldozer.' London: Jessica Kingsley Publishers.

Twachtman-Cullen, D. & Twachtman-Reilly, J. (2003) 'How Well Does Your Child's IEP Measure Up?' London: Jessica Kingsley Publishers.

Appendix 29

Abbreviations

ABA	Applied Behaviour Analysis
ACE	Advisory Centre for Education
ADD	Attention Deficit Disorder
ADHD or AD/HD	Attention Deficit Hyperactivity Disorder
AFE	Supporting Asperger Families in Essex
APA	American Psychiatric Association
APPGA	All-Party Parliamentary Group on Autism
AQ	Autism Spectrum Quotient
AS	Asperger's Syndrome or Asperger Syndrome
ASAP	Asperger Syndrome Adults and Parents
ASD	Autism Spectrum Disorder
Aspie	Someone with Asperger's Syndrome
Autie	An autistic person
B5	Babylon 5
BBS	Bulletin Board System
CBCL	Child Behaviour Checklist
CEO	Chief Executive Officer
CGI	Computer-Generated Imagery
CPAP	Continuous Positive Airway Pressure
CV	Curriculum Vitae
DAMP	Deficits in Attention, Motor control and Perception
DCD	Developmental Coordination Disorder, also known as Developmental Dyspraxia
DDST	Denver Developmental Screening Test
DMN	Default Mode Network
DSM	Diagnostic and Statistical Manual
DSPD	Delayed Sleep Phase Disorder

DSPS	Delayed Sleep Phase Syndrome
ECG	Electrocardiogram
EF	Executive Function
ELBW	Extremely Low Birth Weight
EQ	Empathy Quotient
gF	General Fluid Intelligence
GP	General Practitioner
HFA	High Functioning Autism
IEP	Individual Education Plan
IPSEA	Independent Panel for Special Education Advice
IRC	Internet Relay Chat
IRDS	Infant Respiratory Distress Syndrome
IV	Intra Venous
LA	Local Authority
LD	Learning Disability (USA) Specific Learning Disability (UK)
LP	Long-playing record
MABC or M-ABC	Movement Assessment Battery for Children
NAS	The National Autistic Society
NHS	National Health Service
NICU	Neonatal Intensive Care Unit
NIDCAP	Newborn Individualised Developmental Care and Assessment Programme
NLD or NVLD	Nonverbal Learning Disability or Non-Verbal Learning Disability
NT	Neurotypical – A person who is not on the autism spectrum
OCD	Obsessive-Compulsive Disorder
OT	Occupational Therapy
PC	Personal Computer
PDA	Patent Ductus Arteriosus
PE	Physical Education
RSI	Repetitive Strain Injury
RSPM	Raven's Standard Progressive Matrices
RSS	Rich Site Summary or Really Simple Syndication

SALT	Speech And Language Therapy
SEN	Special Educational Needs
SENCO	Special Educational Needs Co-Ordinator
SF	Science Fiction
SIDS	Sudden Infant Death Syndrome
SLD	Specific Learning Disability
SQ	Systemizing Quotient
SSEN	Statement of Special Educational Needs
ToM	Theory of Mind
VLBW	Very Low Birth Weight
WISC	Weschler Intelligence Scale for Children
WISC-R	Weschler Intelligence Scale for Children – Revised

Appendix 30

References

Achenbach, T.M. (1986) 'Child Behavior Checklist – Direct Observation Form'. Burlington, VT: University Associates in Psychiatry.

Achenbach, T.M. & Edelbrock, C. (1988) 'Manual for the Child Behavior Checklist and Revised Behaviour Profile'. Burlington, VT: University Associates in Psychiatry.

Achenbach, T.M. (1991) 'Manual for the Child Behavior Checklist'. Burlington, VT: University Associates in Psychiatry.

Acquarone, S. (editor, 2007) 'Signs of Autism in Infants. Recognition and Early Intervention'. London: Karnac Books.

Adams, L.W. & Mesibov, G.B. (2003) 'Narrow Interests in Autism'. Autism ■ Asperger's Digest Nov-Dec, 16-19.

Addy, L. M. 'Handwriting and Dyspraxia.' http://www.dyspraxiafoundation.org.uk/downloads/handwriting_and_dyspraxia.pdf

Allison, C., Baron-Cohen, S., Wheelwright, S., Charman, T., Richler, J., Pasco, G. & Brayne, C. (2008) 'The Q-CHAT (Quantitative Checklist for Autism in Toddlers): A Normally Distributed Quantitative Measure of Autistic Traits at 18-24 Months of Age: Preliminary Report.' Journal of Autism and Developmental Disorders 38, 1414-1425.

Alloway, T.P. (2009) 'Cognitive Training: Improvements in Academic Attainments.' Dyspraxia Foundation Professional Journal 8, 27-32.

All-Party Parliamentary Group on Autism. (2012) 'The Right Start: Reforming the System for Children with Autism. Report on Reform of the Special Educational Needs and Disabilities System.' www.appga.org.uk/news-and-reports/new-reports.aspx

Andron, L. (editor, 2001) 'Our Journey Through High Functioning Autism and Asperger Syndrome'. A Roadmap. London: Jessica Kingsley Publishers.

Ansell, G.D. (2011) 'Working with Asperger Syndrome in the Classroom'. London: Jessica Kingsley Publishers.

Arnaud, C., Daubisse-Marliac, L., White-Koning, M., Pierrat, V., Larroque, B., Grandjean, H., Alberge, C., Marret, S., Burguet, A., Ancel, P., Supernant, K. & Kaminski, M. (2007) 'Prevalence and Associated Factors of Minor Neuromotor Dysfunctions at Age 5 in Prematurely Born Children. The EPIPAGE Study.' Archives of Pediatrics & Adolescent Medicine 161(11) 1053-1061.

Attwood, T. (1998) 'Asperger's Syndrome. A Guide for Parents and Professionals'. London: Jessica Kingsley Publishers.

Attwood, T. (2006) 'The Complete Guide to Asperger's Syndrome'. London: Jessica Kingsley Publishers.

Attwood, T. 'The Discovery of 'Aspie' Criteria.' www.tonyattwood.com.au/index.php?option=com_content&view=article&id=79%3Athe-discovery-of-aspie-criteria

Ayres, A.J. (1989) 'Sensory Integration and Praxis Test Manual'. Los Angeles: Western Psychological Services.

Ayris, E. (editor 2011) 'Great Expectations'. London: The National Autistic Society.

Baddeley, A.D. & Hitch, G. (1974) 'Working memory'. In G.H. Bower (Ed.),'The psychology of learning and motivation: Advances in research and theory' 8, 47–89. New York: Academic Press.

Baird, G., Charman, T., Baron-Cohen, S., Cox, A., Swettenham, J., Wheelwright, S. & Drew, A. (2000) 'A Screening Instrument for Autism at 18 Months of Age: A 6-Year Follow-Up Study', Journal of the American Academy of Child and Adolescent Psychiatry 39, 694-702

Bancroft, K., Batten, A., Lambert, S. & Madders, T. (2012) 'The Way We Are: Autism in 2012'. London: The National Autistic Society

Barkley, R.A., Fischer, M., Edelbrock, C. & Smallish, L. (1990) 'The adolescent outcome of hyperactive children diagnosed by research criteria: An 8-year prospective follow-up study', Journal of the American Academy of Child and Adolescent Psychiatry, 29, 546-557

Barkley, R.A. (2000) 'Taking Charge of ADHD. The Complete Authoritative Guide for Parents'. New York: The Guilford Press.

Barnett, K. (2013) 'The Spark: A Mother's Story of Nurturing Genius'. New York: Random House.

Baron-Cohen, S. (2004) 'The Essential Difference'. London: Penguin Books

Baron-Cohen, S. (2008) 'Mind Reading. The Interactive Guide to Emotions'. London: Jessica Kingsley Publishers.

Baron-Cohen, S. (2008a) 'The Facts: Autism and Asperger Syndrome'. Oxford: Oxford University Press.

Bartram, P. (2007) 'Understanding Your Young Child with Special Needs'. London: Jessica Kingsley Publishers

Batten, A., Corbett, C., Rosenblatt, M., Withers, L. & Yuille, R. (2006) 'Make School Make Sense. Autism and Education: the Reality for Families today'. London: The National Autistic Society.

Batts, B. (2010) 'Ready, Set Potty! Toilet Training for Children with Autism and other Developmental Disorders'. London: Jessica Kingsley Publishers.

Beadle, D. (2008) 'Obsessions', Communication, Summer 2008, 24-25.

Bediz, L. (2009) 'Picky Eaters? Look to French childrens habits for guidance' http://theroadislife.blogspot.com/2009/09/picky-eaters-look-to-french-childrens.html

Bell, M. 'The Effects of Prematurity on Development,' & 'The Effects of Prematurity on the Social and Emotional Development of School Age Children.' http://www.prematurity.org/research/prematurity-effects1.html

Benford, P. (2008) 'The Use of Internet-Based Communication by People with Autism.' Thesis submitted to the University of Nottingham for the degree of Doctor of Philosophy. retrieved from http://etheses.nottingham.ac.uk/661/1/thesis_post_viva_version_2.pdf

Benton, A.L., Hamsher, K. de S., Varney, N.R. & Spreen, O. (1983). 'Contributions to Neuropsychological Assessment'. New York: Oxford University Press.

Berg, E.A. (1948). 'A Simple Objective Treatment for Measuring Flexibility in Thinking.' Journal of General Psychology, 39, 15-22.

Berument, S.K., Rutter, M., Lord, C., Pickles, A. & Bailey, A. (1999) 'Autism Screening Questionnaire: Diagnostic Validity.' British Journal of Psychiatry 175, 444-51.

Betts, D.E. & Patrick, N.J. (2008) 'Hints and Tips for Helping Children with Autism Spectrum Disorders. Useful strategies for Home, School, and the Community'. London: Jessica Kingsley Publishers.

Biggs, V. (2005) 'Caged in Chaos. A Dyspraxic Guide to Breaking Free'. London: Jessica Kingsley Publishers.

le Billon, K. (2012) 'French Kids Eat Everything: How our Family Moved to France, Cured Picky Eating, Banned Snacking and Discovered 10 Simple Rules for Raising Happy, Healthy Eaters'. London: Piatkus.

Birnbaum, R. (2010) 'Choosing a School for a Child with Special Needs'. London: Jessica Kingsley Publishers.

Blakemore-Brown, L. (2002) 'Reweaving the Autistic Tapestry'. London: Jessica Kingsley Publishers.

Bleach, F. (2001) 'Everybody is Different: a Book for Young people who have Brothers or Sisters with Autism'. London: The National Autistic Society.

Bleichrodt, N., Resing W.C.M., Drenth, P.J.D. et al. (1987) 'Intelligentie-meting bij kinderen: empirische en methodologische verantwoording van de geReviseerde Amsterdamse Kinder Intelligentie Test'. Lisse: Swets & Zeitlinger

Bliss (2012) 'The Best Start: A guide to expressing and breastfeeding your premature baby' www.bliss.org.uk/get-involved/shop

Boon, M. (2001) 'Helping Children with Dyspraxia'. London: Jessica Kingsley Publishers.

Boyd, B. (2003) 'Parenting a Child with Asperger Syndrome. 200 Tips and Strategies'. London: Jessica Kingsley Publishers.

Boyd, B. (2009) 'Appreciating Asperger Syndrome. Looking at the Upside – with 300 Positive Points'. London: Jessica Kingsley Publishers.

The British Psychological Association (2011) 'Response to the American Psychiatric Association: DSM-5 Development' http://apps.bps.org.uk/_publicationfiles/consultation-responses/DSM-5%202011%20-%20BPS%20response.pdf

Bruininks, R.H. (1978) 'Bruininks-Oseretski Test of Motor Proficiency'. Circle Pines, MN: American Guidance Service.

Burke, P. (2004) 'Brothers and Sisters of Disabled Children'. London: Jessica Kingsley Publishers.

Campito, J.S. (2007) 'Supportive Parenting. Becoming an Advocate for your Child with Special Needs'. London: Jessica Kingsley Publishers

Chambers, M.E. & Sugden, D.A. (2002) 'The Identification and Assessment of Young Children with Movement Difficulties.' International Journal of Early Years Education 10, 157-76.

Chinn, S. (2010) 'Addressing the Unproductive Classroom Behaviours of Students with Special Needs'. London: Jessica Kingsley Publishers.

Chivers, M. (2006) 'Dyslexia and Alternative Therapies'. London: Jessica Kingsley Publishers.

Clements, J. & Zarkowska, E. (2000) 'Behavioural Concerns & Autistic Spectrum Disorders. Explanations and Strategies for Change'. London: Jessica Kingsley Publishers.

Cohen, D.J. & Volkmar, F.R. (editors, 1997) 'Handbook of Autism and Pervasive Developmental Disorders'. New York: John Wiley & Sons, Inc.

Conners, C.K. (1986) 'How is a teacher rating scale used in the diagnosis of Attention Deficit Disorder?' Journal of Children in Contemporary Society 19, 33-52.

Contact a Family. 'Helping your Child's Sleep. Information for Parents of Disabled Children.' http://www.cafamily.org.uk/media/389272/helping_your_child_sleep.pdf

Coucouvanis, J.A. (2008) 'The Potty Journey: Guide to Toilet Training Children with Special Needs, Including Autism and Related Disorders'. Kansas: Autism Asperger Publishing.

Cumberland, D.L. & Mills, B.E. (editors, 2010) 'Siblings and Autism. Stories Spanning Generations and Cultures'. London: Jessica Kingsley Publishers.

Davis, J. (1994) 'Able Autistic Children- Children with Asperger's Syndrome. A Booklet for Brothers and Sisters'. Nottingham: The Early Years Centre.

Dawson, M., Soulières, I., Gernsbacher, M.A. & Mottron, L. (2007) 'The Level and Nature of Autistic Intelligence.' Psychological Science 18, 657-662.

Dendy, C.A.Z. (2011) 'Executive Function... What is this anyway?' www.chrisdendy.com/executive.htm

Dijkstra, E.W. (1975) 'How do we tell truths that might hurt?' http://www.cs.utexas.edu/users/EWD/transcriptions/EWD04xx/EWD498.html

Dixon, L. & Addy, L.M. (2004) 'Making Inclusion Work for Children with Dyspraxia. Practical Strategies for Teachers'. London: Routledge.

Dunford, C. (2007) 'Current thinking on Developmental Co-ordination Disorder (Dyspraxia).' Dyspraxia Foundation Professional Journal. Issue 6, 2-7.

Dunn, L. M., & Dunn, L. M. (1981). 'Peabody Picture Vocabulary Test- Revised'. Circle Pines, MN: American Guidance Service.

Durand, V.M. (2014) 'Sleep Better! A Guide to Improving Sleep for Children with Special Needs'. Baltimore: Paul H. Brookes Publishing.

Durand, V.M. (2008) 'When Children Don't Sleep Well: Interventions for Pediatric Sleep Disorders: Parent Workbook'. New York: Oxford University Press.

Durig, A. (2005) 'How to Understand Autism – The Easy Way'. London: Jessica Kingsley Publishers.

Ehlers, S. & Gillberg, C. (1993) 'The Epidemiology of Asperger Syndrome: A Total Population Study.' Journal of Child Psychology and Psychiatry, and Allied Disciplines 34, 1327-50.

Ehlers, S., Gillberg, C. & Wing, L. (1999) 'A Screening Questionnaire for Asperger Syndrome and Other High-Functioning Autism Spectrum Disorders in School Age Children.' Journal of Autism and Developmental disorders 29, 129-41.

Fairfoot, E. & Mayne, J. (2004) 'My Special Brother Rory'. London: The National Autistic Society.

Fitzgerald, M. (2004) 'Autism and Creativity: Is There a Link between Autism in Men and Exceptional Ability?' New York: Brunner-Routledge.

Fitzpatrick, M. (2008) 'A damaging delusion?' Communication, Autumn, 14-15.

Foulder-Hughes, L.A. & Cooke, R.W.I. (2003) 'Motor, Cognitive, and Behavioural Disorders in Children Born Very Preterm.' Developmental Medicine & Child Neurology 45, 97-103.

Foulder-Hughes, L.A. & Cooke, R.W.I. (2003) 'Developmental Co-ordination Disorder in preterm children born ≤32 weeks gestational age.' Dyspraxia Foundation Professional Journal 2, 2-11.

Frender, S. & Schiffmiller, R. (2007) 'Brotherly Feelings. Me, My Emotions and My Brother with Asperger's Syndrome'. London: Jessica Kingsley Publishers

Frith, U. (1989) 'Autism. Explaining the Enigma'. Oxford: Blackwell Publishers Ltd.

Frith, U. (editor, 1991) 'Autism and Asperger syndrome'. Cambridge: Cambridge University Press.

Gardner, M. F. (1985) 'Receptive One-Word Picture Vocabulary Test: Manual'. Novato, CA: Academic Therapy Publications.

Gardner, M. F. (1990) 'Expressive One-Word Picture Vocabulary Test (Revised): Manual'. Novato, CA: Academic Therapy Publications.

Gardner, M. F. (1996) 'Test of Visual Perceptual Skills (n-m) Revised'. Hydesville, CA: Psychological and Educational Publications.

Gardner, N (2013) 'All Because of Henry. My Story of Struggle and Triumph with Two Autistic Children and the Dogs that Unlocked their World'. Edinburgh: Black and White Publishing.

Garnett, M. & Attwood, T. (1998) 'The Australian Scale for Asperger's Syndrome', in Attwood, T. Asperger's Syndrome: A Guide for Parents and Professionals. London: Jessica Kingsley Publishers.

Gast, C. & Krug, J. (2008) 'Caring for myself'. London: Jessica Kingsley Publishers.

Gerhardt, S. (2004) 'Why Love Matters. How Affection Shapes a Baby's Brain'. London: Routledge.

Gerritsen, F.M.E. (1988) 'VTO Taalscreening 3-tot 6-jarigen: de ontwikkeling va een taalscreeningsinstrument voor gebruik in de Jeugdgezondheidszorg'. Amsterdam/Lisse: Swets & Zeitlinger.

Ghaziuddin, M. (2005) 'Mental Health Aspects of Autism and Asperger Syndrome'. London: Jessica Kingsley Publishers.

Gillberg, I.C. & Gillberg, C. (1989) 'Asperger Syndrome: Some Epidemiological Considerations: a Research Note.' Journal of Child Psychology and Psychiatry 30, 631-638.

Gillberg, C. & Coleman, M. (2000) 'The Biology of the Autistic Syndromes'. London: Mac Keith Press.

Gillberg, C., Gillberg, C., Rastam, M. & Wentz, E. (2001) 'The Asperger Syndrome (and High-Functioning Autism) Diagnostic Interview (ASDI): a Preliminary Study of a New Structured Clinical Interview.' Autism 5, 57-66.

Gillberg, C. (2002) 'A Guide to Asperger Syndrome'. Cambridge: Cambridge University Press.

Gilliam, J.E. (1995) 'Gilliam Autism Rating Scale'. Austin, TX: Pro-Ed.

Gilliam, J.E. (2002) 'GADS Examiner's Manual'. Austin, TX: Pro-Ed.

Gold, K. & Scassellati, B. (2006) 'Grounded Pronoun Learning and Pronoun Reversal.' http://www.cs.yale.edu/homes/scaz/papers/Gold-ICDL-06.pdf

Gorrod, L. (1997) 'My brother is different'. London: The National Autistic Society.

Grandin, T. & Scariano M.M. (2005) 'Emergence. Labelled Autistic'. New York: Grand Central Publishing.

Grandin, T. (2006) 'Thinking in Pictures. And Other Reports from my Life with

Autism'. London: Bloomsbury Publishing.

Grandin, T. (2008) 'The Way I See It. A Personal Look at Autism & Asperger's'. Arlington: Future Horizons

Gray, C. (2002) 'My Social Stories Book'. London: Jessica Kingsley Publishers.

Gray, C. (2004) 'Social Stories 10.0.' Jenison Autism Journal 15, 2-21.

Greenspan, S.I., Wieder, S. with Simons, R. (1998) 'The Child with Special Needs. Encouraging Intellectual and Emotional Growth'. US: Perseus Books

Gubbay, S.S. (1975) 'The Clumsy Child'. London: Saunders & Co.

Hack, M., Flannery, D.J., Schluter, M., Cartar, L., Borawski, E. & Klein, N. (2002) 'Outcomes in Young Adulthood for Very-Low-Birth-Weight Infants.' New England Journal of Medicine 346, 149-157.

Hack, M. (2006) 'Young adult outcomes of very-low-birth-weight children.' Seminars in Fetal & Neonatal Medicine 11, 127-137.

Hames, A. & McCaffrey, M. (editors, 2005) 'Special Brothers and Sisters. Stories and Tips for Siblings of Children with Disability or Serious Illness'. London: Jessica Kingsley Publishers.

Hanks, R. (2011) 'Common SENse for the Inclusive Classroom. How Teachers Can Maximise Existing Skills to Special Educational Needs'. London: Jessica Kingsley Publishers.

Hannah, L. (2001) 'Teaching Young Children with Autistic Spectrum Disorders to Learn. A Practical Guide for Parents and Staff in Mainstream Schools and Nurseries'. London: The National Autistic Society.

Harris, S.L. (1994) 'Siblings of Children with Autism. A Guide for Families'. Bethesda USA: Woodbine House.

Harris, G. (2011) 'Selective Eating in Children with Autism.' Google search for a pdf file to download.

Harvey, G. (2013) 'The Real Me.' Communication, Summer, 16-17.

Hayashi, M., Kato, M., Igarashi, K. & Kashima, H. (2007) 'Superior Fuid Intelligence in Children with Asperger's Disorder.' Brain and Cognition doi:10.1016/j.bandc.2007.09.008

Healey, K. (2008) 'Twin Brothers: Worlds Apart. Autism and Asperger's Syndrome From the Perspective of an Affected Person'. UK: Staffordshire Adults Autistic Society.

Heegaard, M. (2003) 'Drawing Together to Learn about Feelings'. USA: Fairview Press.

Heegaard, M. (2003) 'Drawing Together to Manage Anger'. USA: Fairview Press.

Henderson, S.E. & Sugden D.A. (1992) 'Movement Assessment Battery for Children'. San Antonio: The Psychological Corporation

Hewitt, S. (2005) 'Specialist Support Approaches to Autism Spectrum Disorder Students in Mainstream Settings'. London: Jessica Kingsley Publishers

Higashida, N. (2013) 'The Reason I Jump'. London: Sceptre

Hille, E.T., den Ouden, A.l., Bauer, L., van den Oudenrijn C., Brand, R. & Verloove-Vanhorick, S.P. (1994) 'School Performance at Nine Years of Age in Very Premature and Very Low Birth Weight Infants: Perinatal Risk Factors and Predictors at Five Years of Age. Collaborative Project on Preterm and Small for Gestational Age (POPS) Infants in the Netherlands.' Journal of Pediatrics 125(3),

426-34.

Hope-West, A. (2011) 'Securing Appropriate Education Provision for Children with Autism Spectrum Disorders. A Guide for Parents and Professionals'. London: Jessica Kingsley Publishers.

House of Commons Education and Skills Committee (2006) 'Special Educational Needs: Third Report of Session 2005-6: volume 1.' www.publications.parliament. uk/pa/cm200506/cmselect/cmeduski/478/478i.pdf

House-parents, C.S., Glass-blowers, N., van Overcloud, J.B. & Paternoster, J. (2009) 'Meta-analysis of Neurobehavioural Outcomes in Very Preterm and/or Very Low Birthweight Children.' Pediatrics 124(2), 717-728.

Howlin, P. (1998) 'Children with Autism and Asperger Syndrome. A Guide for Practitioners and Carers'. Chichester: John Wiley and Sons Ltd.

Hultquist, A. (2006) 'An Introduction to Dyslexia for Parents and Professionals'. London: Jessica Kingsley Publishers.

Humphrey, N. & Symes, W. (2011) 'Let me in.' Communication, Summer, 24-25.

Insell, T. (2013) 'The Four Kingdoms of Autism.' www.nimh.nih.gov/about/director/ 2013/the-four-kingdoms-of-autism.shtml

Ives, M. & Munro, N. (2002) 'Caring for a Child with Autism. A Practical Guide for Parents'. London: Jessica Kingsley Publishers.

Jackson, C. (2011) 'The Impact of Sensory Issues on Individuals and the Family.' Google search for a pdf file to download.

Jackson, L. (2002) 'Freaks, Geeks & Asperger Syndrome. A User Guide to Adolescence'. London: Jessica Kingsley Publishers.

Jamieson, A. (1980) 'The Old Fashioned Rules of Spelling Book'. London: Ward Lock Educational.

James, I. M. (2006) 'Asperger's Syndrome and High Achievement: Some Very Remarkable People'. London: Jessica Kingsley Publishers.

Jan, J.E., Owens, J.A., Weiss, M.D., Johnson, K.P., Wasdell, M.B., Freeman, R.D. & Ipsiroglu, O.S. (2008) 'Sleep hygiene for children with neurodevelopmental disabilities'. Pediatrics 122, 1343-1350.

Johnson, J. & Van Rensselaer, A. (2010) 'Siblings. The Autism Spectrum through our Eyes'. London: Jessica Kingsley Publishers.

Jongmans, M.J., Mercuri, E., Dubowitz, L.M.S. & Henderson, S.E. (1998) 'Perceptual-Motor Difficulties and their Concomitants in Six-Year-Old Children Born Prematurely.' Human Movement Science 17, 629-653.

Jordan, R. (2007) 'Does it Matter What We Call Autism?' Communication, Winter, 10-12.

Jordan, R. (2009) 'Values in Education'. Keynote speech in Autism Good Practice Conference http://www.educationscotland.gov.uk

Kaplan, E. F., Goodglass, H., & Weintraub, S. (1983) 'The Boston Naming Test (2nd ed.)'. Philadelphia: Lea & Febiger.

Kaufman, A. S. (1979) 'Intelligence Testing with the WISC-R'. New York: John Wiley & Sons.

Kesler, S.R., Reiss, A.l., Vohr, B., Watson, C., Schneider, K.C., Katz, K.H., Maller-Kesselman, J., Silbereis, J., Constable, R.T., Makuch, R.W. & Ment, L.R. (2008) 'Brain Volume Reductions within Multiple Cognitive Systems in Male

Preterm Children at Age Twelve.' The Journal of Pediatrics 152, 513-520.

Kessenich, M. (2003) 'Developmental Outcomes of Premature, Low Birth Weight, and Medically Fragile Infants.' www.medscape.com/viewarticle/461571

Kingsley, E.P. (1987) 'Welcome to Holland'. http://www.child-autism-parent-cafe.com/welcome-to-holland.html

Kirby, A. (1999) 'Dyspraxia: The Hidden Handicap'. London: Souvenir Press.

Kirby, A. & Drew, S. (2002) 'Guide to Dyspraxia and Developmental Coordination Disorders'. London: David Fulton Publishers.

de Kleine, M.J.K., den Ouden, A.L., Kollée, L.A.A., Nijhuis-van der Sanden, M.W.G., Sondaar, M., van Kessel-Feddema, B.J.M., Knuijt, S., van Baar, A.L., Ilsen, A., Breur-Pieterse, R., Briët, J.M., Brand, R. & Verloove-Vanhorick, S.P. (2003) 'Development and Evaluation of a Follow up Assessment of Preterm Infants at 5 Years of Age'. Archives of Disease in Childhood 88, 870-875.

Klin, A., Volkmar, F.R. & Sparrow, S.S. (editors. 2000) 'Asperger Syndrome'. New York: The Guilford Press.

Klove, H. (1963). 'Clinical neuropsychology'. In F. M. Forster (Ed.), The medical clinics of North America. New York: Saunders.

Kozma, G. (2010) 'Secondary School. A Parent's Guide'. Peterborough: Need2Know.

Krug, D.A., Arick, J. & Almond, P. (1980) 'Behaviour Checklist for Identifying Severely Handicapped Individuals with High Levels of Autistic Behaviour'. Journal of Child Psychology and Psychiatry, and Allied Disciplines 21, 221-9.

Krug, D.A. & Arick, J. (2002) 'Krug Asperger's Disorder Index'. Austin, TX: Pro-Ed.

Kurtz, L.A. (2003) 'How to Help a Clumsy Child. Strategies for Young Children with Developmental Motor Concerns'. London: Jessica Kingsley Publishers.

Kurtz, L.A. (2006) 'Visual Perception Problems in Children with AD/HD, Autism, and Other Learning Disabilities. A Guide for Parents and Professionals'. London: Jessica Kingsley Publishers.

Kurtz, L.A. (2008) 'Understanding Motor Skills in Children with Dyspraxia, ADHD, Autism, and Other Learning Disabilities. A Guide to Improving Coordination'. London: Jessica Kingsley Publishers.

Kutscher, M.L. (2005) 'Kids in the Syndrome Mix of ADHD, LD, Asperger's, Tourette's, Bipolar, and More! The one stop guide for parents, teachers, and other professionals'. London: Jessica Kingsley Publishers.

Kutscher, M.L. (2008) 'ADHD-Living without Brakes'. London: Jessica Kingsley Publishers.

Kynaston, L. 'Will my hair clean itself if I don't wash it?' www.menshealth.co.uk/style/hair-care/hair-self-cleaning-myths

Lamb, B. (2009) 'Lamb Inquiry: Special Educational Needs and Parental Confidence. DCSF.'
http://www.dcsf.gov.uk/lambinquiry/downloads/8553-lamb-inquiry.pdf

Larsen, S.C. & Hammill, D.D. (1994). 'Test of Written Spelling- 3'. Austin, TX: PRO-ED.

Lawrence, C. (2008) 'How to Make School Make Sense. A Parents' Guide to Helping the Child with Asperger Syndrome'. London: Jessica Kingsley Publishers

Lawrence, C. (2010) 'Successful School Change and Transition for the Child with Asperger Syndrome'. London: Jessica Kingsley Publishers.

Lawson, W. (2003) 'Build Your Own Life: A Self-Help Guide for Individuals with Asperger's Syndrome'. London: Jessica Kingsley Publishers.

Lawson, W. (2010) 'The Passionate Mind. How People with Autism Learn'. London: Jessica Kingsley Publishers.

Leach, P.J. (2010) 'The Essential First Year'. London: Dorling Kindersley.

Leach, P.J. (2010) 'Your Baby and Child'. London: Dorling Kindersley.

Lee, M.G. (2004) 'Co-ordination Difficulties. Practical Ways Forward'. London: David Fulton Publishers.

Leeds Consensus Statement (2006) on Developmental Coordination Disorder. http://www.pearsonclinical.co.uk/Psychology/ChildCognitionNeuropsychologyandLanguage/ChildPerceptionandVisuomotorAbilities/MABC-2/Resources/LeedsConsensus06.pdf

Leventhal-Belfer, L. & Coe, C. (2004) 'Asperger's Syndrome in Young Children. A Developmental Guide for Parents and Professionals'. London: Jessica Kingsley Publishers.

Levine, M. (2003) 'A Mind at a Time. How Every Child Can Succeed'. London: Simon and Schuster

Levy, F., Hay, D., McLaughlin, M., Wood, C. & Waldman, I. (1996) 'Twin Sibling Differences in Parental Reports of ADHD, Speech, Reading and Behaviour Problems.' Journal of child psychology and psychiatry, 37, 569-578.

Limperopoulos, C., Bassan, H., Sullivan, N.R., Soul, J.S., Robertson, R.L., Moore, M., Ringer, S.A., Volpe, J.J. & du Plessis, A.J. (2008) 'Positive Screening for Autism in ex-preterm Infants: Prevalence and Risk Factors.' Pediatrics 121, 758-765. http://pediatrics.aappublications.org/content/121/4/758.full

Lipsky, D. & Richards, W. (2009) 'Managing Meltdowns. Using the S.C.A.R.E.D. Talking Technique with Children and Adults with Autism'. London: Jessica Kingsley Publishers.

Lovecky, D.V. (2004) 'Different Minds. Gifted Children with AD/HD, Asperger Syndrome, and Other Learning Deficits'. London: Jessica Kingsley Publishers.

Luteijn, E., Luteijn, F., Jackson, S., Volkmar, F. & Minderaa, R. (2000) 'The Children's Social Behaviour Questionnaire for Milder Variants of PDD Problems: Evaluation of the Psychometric Characteristics'. Journal of Autism and Developmental Disorders 30, 317-30.

Macintyre, C. (2000) 'Dyspraxia in the Early Years. Identifying and Supporting Children with Movement Difficulties'. London: David Fulton Publishers.

Macintyre, C. (2001) 'Dyspraxia 5-11 A Practical Guide'. London: David Fulton Publishers.

Macintyre, C. & McVitty, K. (2004) 'Movement and Learning in the Early Years. Supporting Dyspraxia (DCD) and Other Difficulties'. London: Paul Chapman Publishing.

McCarron, L.T. (1982) 'MAND – McCarron Assessment of Neuromuscular Development (revised edition)'. Dallas, TX: Common Market Press.

Maj, M. (2005) 'Psychiatric Comorbidity: an Artefact of Current Diagnostic Systems?' The British Journal Of Psychiatry, 186, 182-184.

Malekpour, M. (2004) 'Low Birth-Weight Infants and the Importance of Early Intervention: Enhancing Mother-Infant Interactions. A Literature Review'. The

British Journal of developmental disabilities 50 (part2 no 99), 78-88.

Martin, N.C., Piek, J.P. & Hay, D. (2006) 'DCD and ADHD: a genetic study of their shared aetiology'. Human Movement Science 25, 110-124.

Mills, M.D. (1999) 'The Eye in Childhood'. American Academy of Family Physicians 60(3), 907-18.

Missiuna, C., Moll, S., Law, M., King, S. & King, G. (2006) 'Mysteries and mazes: Parents' experiences of children with developmental coordination disorder'. Canadian Journal of Occupational Therapy, 73 (1), 7-17.

Missiuna, C., Moll, S., King, S., King, G. & Law, M. (2007) 'A Trajectory of Troubles: Parents' Impressions of the Impact of Developmental Coordination Disorder'. Physical & Occupational Therapy in Pediatrics. 27(1), 81-101.

Montgomery, P. & Wiggs, L. (2007) 'Encouraging Good Sleep Habits in Children with Learning Disabilities'. Search for 'good sleep habits' in http://www.researchautism.net

Morrell, M.F. & Palmer, A. (2006) 'Parenting Across the Autism Spectrum. Unexpected Lessons We Have Learned'. London: Jessica Kingsley Publishers.

Mountstephen, M. (2011) 'How to Detect Developmental Delay and What to Do Next. Practical Interventions for Home and School'. London: Jessica Kingsley Publishers.

Munden, A. & Arcelus, J. (1999) 'The AD/HD Handbook. A Guide for Parents and Professionals on Attention Deficit / Hyperactivity Disorder'. London: Jessica Kingsley Publishers.

Myers, P. with Baron-Cohen, S. & Wheelwright S. (2004) 'An Exact Mind. An Artist with Asperger Syndrome'. London: Jessica Kingsley Publishers.

Myles, B.S. & Southwick, J. (1999) 'Asperger Syndrome and Difficult Moments. Practical Solutions for Tantrums, Rage, and Meltdowns'. Kansas: Autism Asperger Publishing Co.

Myles, B.S., Cook, K.T., Miller, N.E., Rinner, L. & Robbins, L.A. (2000) 'Asperger Syndrome and Sensory Issues. Practical Solutions for Making Sense of the World'. Kansas: Autism Asperger Publishing Co.

Myles, B.S., Bock, S.J. & Simpson, R.L. (2001) 'Asperger Syndrome Diagnostic Scale Examiner's Manual'. Austin, TX: Pro-Ed.

Nadeau, L., Tessier, R., Lefebvre, F. & Robaey, P. (2004) 'Victimization: a newly recognised outcome of prematurity'. Developmental Medicine & Child Neurology, 46, 508-513.

Nally, B. (1999) 'Diagnosis – Reactions in Families'. London: The National Autistic Society.

National Autistic Society. 'Dietary management for children and adolescents with ASDs: over-eating.' http://www.autism.org.uk/about/health/dietary-management/over-eating.aspx

National Autistic Society. 'Dietary management for children and adolescents with ASDs: restricted diet.' http://www.autism.org.uk/about/health/dietary-management/restricted-diet.aspx

National Autistic Society. 'Sleep and Autism: Helping Your Child'. www.autism.org.uk/10225

National Autistic Society. (2006) 'Make School Make Sense. Autism and Education:

the Reality for Families Today'.

National Autistic Society. 'Toilet Training'. http://www.autism.org.uk/about/health/toi let-training.aspx

National Autistic Society. 'Patients with Autism Spectrum Disorders: Guidance for Health Professionals'. http://www.autism.org.uk/professionals/health-workers.aspx

Neihart, M. (2000) 'Gifted Children with Asperger's Syndrome'. Gifted Child Quarterly, 44(4), 222-230.

Notbohm, E. (2005) 'Ten Things Every Child With Autism Wishes You Knew'. Arlington: Future Horizons.

Ofsted (2010) 'The Special Educational Needs and Disability Review'. www.ofsted. gov.uk/publications/090221

Oppezzo, M. & Schwartz, D.L. (2014) 'Give your ideas some legs: The positive effect of walking on creative thinking'. Journal of Experimental Psychology: Learning, Memory and Cognition. 40(4) 1142-1152 http://doi.org/sg8

O'Toole, J.C. (2012) 'Asperkids, An Insider's Guide to Loving, Understanding and Teaching Children with Asperger Syndrome'. London: Jessica Kingsley Publishers.

Ozonoff, S., Dawson, G. & McPartland, J. (2002) 'A Parent's Guide to Asperger Syndrome and High-Functioning Autism. How to Meet the Challenges and Help your Child Thrive'. New York: The Guilford Press.

Pantley, E. (2002). 'The No-Cry Sleep Solution. Gentle Ways to Help Your Baby Sleep Through the Night'. New York: McGraw-Hill.

Payne, S. (2009) 'Being a Parent of a Child with Developmental Coordination Disorder'. The Dyspraxia Foundation Professional Journal 8, 33-43.

Perepa, P. (2005) 'Classroom and Playground: support for children with autism spectrum disorders'. www.autism.org.uk/classroom-playground

Peters, K.L., Rosychuk, R.J., Hendson, L., Coté, J.J., McPherson, C. & Tyebkhan, J.M. (2009) 'Improvement of Short- and Long-Term Outcomes for Very Low Birth Weight Infants: Edmonton NIDCAP Trial'. Pediatrics 124, 1009-1020.

Pineda, R.G., Neil, J., Dierker, D., Smyser, C.D., Wallendorf, M., Kidokoro, H., Reynolds, L.C., Walker, S., Rogers, C., Mathur, A.M., Van Essen, D.C. & Inder, T. (2014) 'Alterations in Brain Structure and Neurodevelopmental Outcome in Preterm Infants Hospitalized in Different Neonatal Intensive Care Unit Environments'. The Journal of Pediatrics 164, 52-60e2.

Pinker, S. (1995) 'The Language Instinct'. London: Penguin Books.

Pinker, S. (1999) 'How the Mind Works'. London: Penguin Books.

Plummer, D.M. (2008) 'Social Skills Games for Children'. London: Jessica Kingsley Publishers.

Polatajko, H. J. & Cantin, N. (2006) 'Developmental Coordination Disorder (Dyspraxia): An Overview of the State of the Art'. Seminars in Pediatric Neurolgy,12, 250-258.

Portwood, M. (1996) 'Developmental Dyspraxia. A Practical Manual for Parents and Professionals'. Durham: County Council.

Portwood, M. (1999) 'Developmental Dyspraxia. Identification and Intervention. A Manual for Parents and Professionals'. London: David Fulton Publishers.

Power, E. (2010) 'Guerrilla Mum. Surviving the Special Educational Needs Jungle'. London: Jessica Kingsley Publishers.

Powls, A,. Botting., Cooke, R.W.I. & Marlow, N. (1995) 'Motor Impairment in Children 12-13 years old with a Birthweight of Less than 1250g'. Archives of Disease in Childhood 75, F62-F66.

Pyles, L. (2002) 'Hitchhiking through Asperger Syndrome'. London: Jessica Kingsley Publishers.

Quine, L. (1997) 'Solving Children's Sleep Problems: A Step by Step Guide for Parents'. Huntingdon: Becket Karlson Publishing.

Quinlan, D.M., (2000) 'Assessment of Attention-Deficit/Hyperactivity Disorder and Comorbidities. in Attention-Deficit Disorders and Comorbidities in Children, Adolescents, and Adults'. (Ed. Brown, T.E.) 455-508 Arlington: American Psychiatric Press.

Raphael-Leff, J. (2007) 'Signs of Autism in Infants. Recognition and Early Intervention'. (ed. Acquarone, S.) London: Karnac Books.

Reid, B. (2011) 'Great Expectations Report'. London: National Autistic Society (NAS).

Reitan, R. M. (1979). 'Manual for Administration of Neuropsychological Test Batteries for Adults and Children'. Tucson, AZ: Reitan Neuropsychological Laboratory.

Reitan, R. M., & Wolfson, D. (1985). 'The Halstead-Reitan Neuropsychological Test Battery'. Tucson, AZ: Neuropsychology Press.

Richards, R. G. (1999) 'The Source for Dyslexia and Dysgraphia'. New York: LinguiSystems, Inc.

Richardson, A. J. (2002) 'The Potential Role of Fatty Acids in Developmental Dyspraxia – Can Dietary Supplementation Help?' Dyspraxia Foundation Professional Journal 1, 31-50.

Ripley, K., Daines, B. & Barrett, J. (1997) 'Dyspraxia. A Guide for Teachers and Parents'. London: David Fulton Publishers.

Ripley, K. (2001) 'Inclusion for Children with Dyspraxia/DCD. A Handbook for Teachers'. London: David Fulton Publishers.

Roberts, B.L., Marlow, N. & Cooke, R.W.I. (1989) 'Motor problems among children of very low birthweight'. British Journal of Occupational Therapy 52(3), 97-99.

Robins, D.L., Fein, D., Barton, M.L. & Green, J.A. (2001) 'The Modified Checklist for Autism in Toddlers: an Initial Study Investigating the Early Detection of Autism and Pervasive Developmental Disorders'. J. Autism Dev. Disord. 31, 131-144.

Robison, J.E. (2008) 'Look Me in the Eye. My Life with Asperger's'. London: Ebury Press.

Roelfsema, M.T., Hoekstra, R.A., Allison, C., Wheelwright, S., Brayne, C., Matthews, F.E. & Baron-Cohen, S. (2012) 'Are Autism Spectrum Conditions More Prevalent in an Information-Technology Region? A School-Based Study of Three Regions in the Netherlands'. Journal of Autism and Developmental Disorders. Volume 42 (5), 734-739.

Rogers, S.J., Dawson, G., & Vismara, L.A. (2012) 'An Early Start for Your Child with Autism: Using Everyday Activities to Help Kids Connect, Communicate, and Learn'. New York: The Guilford Press.

Roman, M.A. (1998) 'The Syndrome of Nonverbal Learning Disabilities. Clinical Description and Applied Aspects'. Current Issues in Education 1, no 1.1 www.nld line.com/michaelr.htm

Rose, J. (2009) 'Identifying and Teaching Children and Young People with Dyslexia and Literacy Difficulties. An independent report to the Secretary of State for Children, Schools and Families'. http://webarchive.nationalarchives.gov.uk/20130401151715/http://www.education.gov.uk/publications/eOrderingDownload/00659-2009DOM-EN.pdf

Ross, D.S. & Jolly, K.A. (editors, 2006) 'That's Life with Autism. Tales and Tips for Families with Autism'. London: Jessica Kingsley Publishers.

Roth, I., Barson, C., Hoekstra, R., Pasco, G. & Whatson, T. (2010) 'The Autism Spectrum in the 21st Century'. London: Jessica Kingsley Publishers.

Row, S. (2005) 'Surviving the Special Educational Needs System. How to be a Velvet Bulldozer'. London: Jessica Kingsley Publishers.

Rubinstien, M.B. (2005) 'Raising NLD Superstars. What Families with Nonverbal Learning Disabilities Need to Know About Nurturing Confident, Competent Kids'. London: Jessica Kingsley Publishers.

Sainsbury, C. (2009) 'Martian in the Playground. Understanding the Schoolchild with Asperger's Syndrome'. Bristol: Lucky Duck Publishing.

Sassoon, R. (1999) 'Handwriting in the Twentieth Century'. London: Routledge.

Schalij-Delfos, N.E., de Graaf, M.E., Treffers, W.F., Engel, J. & Cats, B.P. (2000) 'Long Term Follow up of Premature Infants: Detection of Strabismus, Amblyopia, and Refractive Errors'. British Journal of Opthalmology 84, 963-967.

Schmidt, E. (2012) MacTaggart lecture 'Television and the Internet: shared opportunity'. http://www.mediaweek.co.uk/news/1087474/EDINBURGH-TV-FESTIVAL-Eric-Schmidts-MacTaggart-Lecture-full/

Schonell, F. (1979) 'The Essential Spelling List'. London: produced for W.H.Smith by Macmillan Education.

Schopler, E. (editor,1995) 'Parent Survival Manual. A guide to Crisis Resolution in Autism and Related Developmental Disorders'. New York: Plenum Press.

Scott, F.J., Baron-Cohen, S., Bolton, P. & Brayne, C. (2002) 'The CAST (Childhood Asperger Syndrome Test): Preliminary Development of a UK Screen for Mainstream Primary-School-Age Children'. Autism 6, 9-31.

Selikowitz, M. (2009) 'ADHD (the facts series)' Oxford: Oxford University Press.

Shallice, T. (1982).'Specific Impairments of Planning'. Philosophical Transactions of the Royal Society of London, Part B,(298), 199-209.

Siegel, B. (1996) 'The World of the Autistic Child. Understanding and Treating Autistic Spectrum Disorders'. Oxford: Oxford University Press.

Simons Foundation (2012) 'Proposed DSM-5 Criteria for Autism Spectrum Disorders'. http://sfari.org/news-and-opinion/news/2012/proposed-dsm-5-criteria-for-autism-spectrum-disorders

Sinclair, J. (1993) 'Don't Mourn for Us'. www.autreat.com/dont_mourn.html

Sinclair, J. (2010) 'Cultural Commentary: Being Autistic Together'. http://dsq-sds.org/article/view/1075/1248

Sinclair, J. (interviewed by Michael Ellermann) http://www.autism.se/RFA/uploads/ned ladningsbara%20filer/Interview_with_Jim_Sinclair.pdf

Snowling, M. (2008) 'State of Science Review: SR-D2 Dyslexia. Foresight Mental Capital and Wellbeing Project'. The Government Office for Science. www.foresight.gov.uk

Sparrow, S.S., Balla, D.A., & Cicchetti, D.V. (1985) 'Vineland Adaptive Behaviour Scales (VABS)'. Circle Pines: AGS.

Stanton, M. (2000) 'Learning to Live with High Functioning Autism. A Parent's Guide for Professionals'. London: Jessica Kingsley Publishers.

Stobbart, A. (2009) 'Bullying and Autism Spectrum Disorders: a Guide for School Staff'. London: The National Autistic Society.

Sugden, D. & Chambers, M. (editors, 2005) 'Children with Developmental Coordination Disorder'. London: Whurr.

Sunderland, M. (2007) 'What Every Parent Needs to Know: the Incredible Effects of Love, Nurture and Play on Your Child'. London: Dorling Kindersley.

Sunderland, M. (2008) 'The Science of Parenting'. London: Dorling Kindersley.

Swanson, J., Schuck, S., Mann, M., Carlson, C., Hartman, K. & Sergeant, J. (2001) 'The SWAN rating scale'. www.adhd.net

Tammet, D. (2006) 'Born on a Blue Day'. London: Hodder and Stoughton Ltd.

Tanguay, P.B. (2001) 'Nonverbal Learning Disabilities at Home. A Parent's Guide'. London: Jessica Kingsley Publishers.

Tanguay, P.B. (2002) 'Nonverbal Learning Disabilities at School. Educating Students with NLD, Asperger Syndrome, and Related Conditions'. London: Jessica Kingsley Publishers.

Teodorescu, I. & Addy, L. (1998 & 2001) 'Write from the start: Unique Programme to Develop the Fine Motor and Perceptual Skills Necessary for Effective Handwriting'. Carson Dellosa Pub Co Inc. (2001) or LDA (1998).

Tessier, R., Cristo, M.B., Velez, S., Giron, M., Nadeau, L., Figuero de Calume, Z., Ruiz-Palaez, J.G. & Charpak, N. (2003) 'Kangaroo Mother Care: A Method for Protecting High-Risk Low-Birth-Weight and Premature Infants against Developmental Delay'. Infant Behaviour and Development 26, 384-397.

Thompson, S. (1997) 'The Source for Nonverbal Learning Disorders'. New York: LinguiSystems, Inc.

Thorpe, P. (2003) 'Moving from Primary to Secondary School: Guidelines for Pupils with Autistic Spectrum disorders'. National Autistic Society (no longer available)

Thorpe, P. (2004) 'Understanding Difficulties at Break Time and Lunchtime: Guidelines for Pupils with Autistic Spectrum disorders'. www.autism.org.uk/products/core-nas-publications/understanding-difficulties-at-breaktime.aspx

Touwen, B.C. (1989) 'Examination of the Child with Minor Neurological Dysfunction'. Clinics in Developmental Medicine 11, 353-363.

Truss, L. (2003) 'Eats Shoots and Leaves: The Zero Tolerance Approach to Punctuation'. London: Profile Books.

Twachtman-Cullen, D. & Twachtman-Reilly, J. (2003) 'How Well Does Your Child's IEP Measure Up?' London: Jessica Kingsley Publishers.

Verhulst, F.C., van-der-Ende, J. & Koot, H.M. (1996) 'Manual for the Child Behavior Checklist'. (Dutch version) Rotterdam: Erasmus Universiteit.

Vermeulen, P. (2013) 'Putting Autism in Context'. Communication. National Autistic Society, Summer, 29-30.

Victorian Continence Resource Centre. 'One Step at a Time'. http://www.continence victoria.org.au

Walker, S. (2012) 'Grace Under Pressure. Going the Distance as an Aspergers Mum'.

London: Piatkus.

Webb, A. (2008) 'DASH – The Detailed Assessment of Speed of Handwriting: A Review'. Dyspraxia Foundation Professional Journal, 2-12.

Webster-Stratton, C. (1992) 'The Incredible Years. A Trouble-Shooting Guide for Parents of Children Aged 3-8'. Canada: Umbrella Press.

Weidner, W. (2005) 'Identification and Assessment of Children with Developmental Coordination Disorder: Textbook Fantasy vs. Real Life: A Snapshot of Families' Experiences'. Dyspraxia Foundation Professional Journal (4), 49-55.

Wheeler, M. B. (1998) 'Toilet Training for Individuals with Autism & Related Disorders. A Comprehensive Guide for Parents & Teachers'. Arlington: Future Horizons

Whitaker, A.H., Feldman, J.F., Lorenz, J.M., Shen, S., McNicholas, F., Nieto, M., McCulloch, D., Pinto-Martin, J.A. & Paneth, N. (2006) 'Motor and Cognitive Outcomes in Nondisabled Low-Birth-Weight Adolescents. Early Determinants'. Archives of Pediatrics & Adolescent Medicine 160(10), 1040-1046.

White, M. & Rogers, J. (2002) 'We Can Do It! Helping Children who have Learning Disabilities with Bowel and Bladder Management: a Guide for Parents'. Bristol: The Enuresis Resource & Information Centre.

Whitehouse, E. & Pudney, W. (1996) 'A Volcano in my Tummy: Helping Children to Handle Anger'. Canada: New Society.

Wilde, J. (1997) 'Hot Stuff to Help Kids Chill Out: The Anger Management Book'. US: Lgr Publishing.

Wilde, J. & Wilde, A. (2008) 'Hot Stuff to Help Kids Worry Less: The Anxiety Management Book'. US: Lgr Publishing.

Wilkinson, G. S. (1993) 'Wide Range Achievement Test Administration Manual'. Wilmington, DE: Wide Range.

Willacy, H. 'Premature Babies and their Problems'. http://www.patient.co.uk/doctor/premature-babies-and-their-problems

Willey, L.H. (1999) 'Pretending to be Normal'. London: Jessica Kingsley Publishers.

Williams, C. & Wright, B. (2004) 'How to live with Autism and Asperger Syndrome. Practical Strategies for Parents and Professionals'. London: Jessica Kingsley Publishers.

Williams, D. (2006) 'The Jumbled Jigsaw. An Insider's Approach to the Treatment of Autistic Spectrum 'Fruit Salads''. London: Jessica Kingsley Publishers.

Williams, J., Scott, F., Stott, C., Allison, C., Bolton, P., Baron-Cohen, S., Brayne, C. (2005) 'The CAST (Childhood Asperger Test) Test Accuracy'. Autism 9, 45-68.

Wills, J.' Toddling to Ten: Dealing with Fussy Eaters'. www.netmums.com/family-food/food-for-kids/dealing-with-fussy-eaters.

Wilson B.N., Kaplan B.J., Crawford S.G., Campbell, A. & Dewey, D. (2000) 'Reliability and Validity of a Parent Questionnaire on Childhood Motor Skills'. American Journal of Occupational Therapy 54, 484-493.

Wing, L. (1996) 'The Autistic Spectrum'. London: Constable & Robinson Ltd.

Wing, L., Leekham, S.R., Libby, S.J., Gould, J. & Larcombe, M. (2002) 'The Diagnostic Interview for Social and Communication Disorders: Background, Inter-Rater Reliability and Clinical Use'. Journal of Child Psychology and Psychiatry, 43, 307-325.

Winter, M. (2003) 'Asperger Syndrome – What Teachers Need to Know'. London: Jessica Kingsley Publishers.

Woliver, R. (2009) 'Alphabet Kids From ADD to Zellweger Syndrome. A guide to Developmental, Neurobiological and Psychological Disorders for Parents and Professionals'. London: Jessica Kingsley Publishers.

Wolman, D. (2008) 'The Truth About Autism: Scientists Reconsider What They Think They Know'. http://www.wired.com/2008/02/ff-autism

Wong, H.S., Huertas-Ceballos, A., Cowan, F.M. & Modi, N. (2014) 'Evaluation of Early Childhood Social-Communication Difficulties in Children Born Preterm Using the Quantitative Checklist for Autism in Toddlers'. The Journal of Pediatrics 164, 26-33.

Woodcock, R. W., & Johnson, M. B. (1989) Woodcock-Johnson Psycho-Educational Test Battery – Revised. Allen, TX: DLM Teaching Resources.

Wrobel, M. (2003) 'Taking Care of Myself. A Hygiene, Puberty and Personal Curriculum for Young People with Autism'. Arlington: Future Horizons.

Other Web Sites Referred to:

www.aettraininghubs.org.uk/training-hubs/

www.ace-ed.org.uk

http://apps.bps.org.uk/_publicationfiles/consultation-responses/DSM-5%202011%20-%20BPS%20response.pdf

www.asiam.ie/back-school-buddy-system

www.aspiesforfreedom.com

www.autismeducationtrust.org.uk

http://www.autism.org.uk/about/adult-life/transition-adulthood.aspx

http://www.autism.org.uk/about/family-life.aspx

http://www.autism.org.uk/about/health/dietary-management/over-eating.aspx

http://www.autism.org.uk/about/health/dietary-management/restricted-diet.aspx

www.autism.org.uk/circleoffriends

www.autism.org.uk/about/strategies/spell.aspx

www.autism.org.uk/professionals

http://www.autism.org.uk/services/helplines/Education-rights

http://www.autism.org.uk/toys

www.autismresearchcentre.com/arc_tests

http://www.autism-resources.com/links/organizations.html

www.autismspeaks.org

www.b12patch.com/blog/autism/10-great-ipad-apps-for-autistic-children/

www.babycentre.co.uk/baby/breastfeeding

www.bliss.org.uk/publications

http://blog.friendshipcircle.org/2011/02/02/the-special-needs-ipad-app-series

www.boxofideas.org

http://www.breastfeeding-problems.com/

www.businessballs.com/elisabeth_kubler_ross_five_stages_of_grief.htm

www.cafamily.org.uk

carolgraysocialstories.com

www.catphonics.pwp.blueyonder.co.uk/contents.htm

http://www.continencevictoria.org.au
www.cybermentors.org.uk
www.davidappleyard.com/english/spelling.htm
www.dyslexia.org/spelling_rules.shtml
www.dyspraxiafoundation.org.uk
www.education.gov.uk
http://en.wikipedia.org/
www.eric.org.uk
www.eurogamer.net/articles/vvvvvv-review
www.familylives.org.uk
www.fledglings.org.uk
http://www.froebel.org.uk
www.froebelweb.org/web2005.html
http://www.iassnetwork.org.uk/
https://itunes.apple.com/gb/app/autism-apps/id441600681?mt=8
www.ipsea.org.uk
http://jollylearning.co.uk/overview-about-jolly-phonics
http://www.k12reader.com/subject/vocabulary/fry-words/
www.kellymom.com/bf/
http://www.amazon.com/Toys-that-develop-motor-skills/lm/R2D7REK3V5P796
www.kidscape.org.uk
www.livesinthebalance.org
www.m-chat.org
http://media.education.gov.uk
http://medical-dictionary.thefreedictionary.com
www.merriam-webster.com/medical
www.nationalgallery.org.uk
www.ncbi.nlm.nih.gov/pubmedhealth/PMH0002527/
http://www.ncbi.nlm.nih.gov/pubmed/18240013
www.network81.org
http://neurowiki2012.wikispaces.com/
www.nha-handwriting.org.uk
www.nhlbi.nih.gov/health/health-topics/topics/cpap/
www.nhs.uk/start4life/Documents/PDFs/Start4Life_QA_acc.pdf
www.nimh.nih.gov/about/director/index.shtml
www.peta-uk.com
www.preemies.about.com
www.researchautism.net
www.rompa.com
www.sibs.org.uk
www.sensetoys.com
www.sheknows.com/parenting/articles/953661/best-ipad-apps-for-children-with-autism
www.specialdirect.com
www.taskmasteronline.co.uk
www.thefreedictionary.com

REFERENCES

www.thetransporters.com
http://uk.answers.yahoo.com
www.wikihow.com/Get-Self-Cleaning-Hair
http://www.winnicott.org.uk/

Acknowledgements

I'm deeply grateful to Jennie Carpenter who, despite being very busy, read every word of a previous draft of this book and came up with a large number of very helpful suggestions, the majority of which I used. I'm also hugely indebted to my son John, who read and criticised all the drafts of this book (as well as other books on autism that I asked him to comment on), proofread my final version of this book and cheerfully answered the large number of emails that I bombarded him with throughout the writing process. In addition I wouldn't have been able to publish my document either as an ebook or as a paperback without his programming skills and his perfectionist approach to everything he does. Special thanks are due to my daughter Lydia for the helpful comments she made on the chapters she read and her really honest input to the chapter on siblings. I would also like to thank Frances Cowan for her help with chapter 2, Penny Benford for her comments on chapters 11 and 17 and Angie Taylor and Ian and Helen Wand for their valuable comments on a previous version of chapter 19 which led to a complete rewrite.

I am really grateful to the following people for their encouragement, suggestions and support: Jessica Atkinson, Cherie Buckland, Carole Buckley, Richard Carpenter, Jane Dobson, Uta Frith, Christopher Gillberg, Cathie Jones, Rita Jordan, Katherine Snape and Elinor Tolfree.

I would like to thank my local library for all the books and journal papers they acquired for me: without this help I would have found it very difficult and expensive to carry out the reading required for this book, living as I do in a relatively remote location. I'm also immensely grateful to my surgeon Peter Lodge, without whose skill I wouldn't have been in a position to complete this book. Last, but definitely not least, I must thank my husband who has been totally supportive as I buried myself in my study every morning for many years. He has also had to listen to a great deal of talk about my book as I struggled with the early versions, much more than he would have chosen, I'm sure!

Permissions

I would like to acknowledge:

Extracts from Attwood, T. (2006) 'The Complete Guide to Asperger's Syndrome'. London: Jessica Kingsley Publishers. Reproduced by permission of Jessica Kingsley Publishers. Copyright © Tony Attwood, 2007.

Extracts from Gillberg, C. (2002) 'A Guide to Asperger Syndrome'. Cambridge: Cambridge University Press. Reproduced by permission of Cambridge University Press. Copyright © Cambridge University Press, 2002.

A Note on the Cover

The cover was prepared in Inkscape, using Raph Levien's Museum Bible (derived from Bruce Rogers' Centaur) for the main title, and Google's Noto Serif for the subtitle and author text; the back-cover text, like the rest of the book, is set in Liberation Serif.

Museum Bible and Liberation Serif are licensed under the SIL Open Font License, and Noto Serif under the Apache License 2.0.

[1] All names in this book have been altered in order to preserve anonymity.

[2] Retrieved on July 20th 2013 from *The Discovery of 'Aspie' Criteria* http://www.tonyattwood.com.au/index.php?option=com_content&view=article&id=79%3Athe-discovery-of-aspie-criteria

[3] Written on Feb 26 2013, retrieved on July 20th 2013 from http://www.nimh.nih.gov/about/director/2013/the-four-kingdoms-of-autism.shtml

[4] Website www.autismspeaks.org

[5] Retrieved on July 20th 2013 from http://www.wired.com/2008/02/ff-autism

[6] http://www.aspiesforfreedom.com

[7] Retrieved on July 2nd 2013 from http://www.autreat.com/dont_mourn.html

[8] Retrieved on July 2nd 2013 from http://www.autism.se/RFA/uploads/nedladningsbara%20filer/Interview_with_Jim_Sinclair.pdf

[9] Retrieved on July 2nd 2013 from http://www.autism.se/RFA/uploads/nedladningsbara%20filer/Interview_with_Jim_Sinclair.pdf

[10] Retrieved on July 20th 2013 from http://www.wired.com/2008/02/ff-autism

[11] http://www.autism.org.uk/about/strategies/spell.aspx

[12] Information about his approach can be found on www.livesinthebalance.org

[13] Retrieved on December 6th 2011

[14] Retrieved on December 6th 2011 from http://www.ncbi.nlm.nih.gov/pubmedhealth/PMH0002527

[15] http://www.ncbi.nlm.nih.gov/pubmed/18240013

[16] Retrieved on December 7th 2011

[17] Private communication Feb 2014

[18] Retrieved on December 14th 2011 from http://www.nhs.uk/start4life/Documents/PDFs/Start4Life_QA_acc.pdf

[19] Posted on September 22nd 2009 on: http://theroadislife.blogspot.com/2009/09/picky-eaters-look-to-french-childrens.html

[20] The National Autistic Society's Professional Conference, 2011.

[21] Retrieved on December 14th 2011 from http://www.netmums.com/family-food/food-for-kids/dealing-with-fussy-eaters

[22] The National Autistic Society's Professional Conference, 2011.

[23] See http://www.rcpch.ac.uk/child-health/research-projects/uk-who-growth-charts/uk-who-growth-chart-resources-0-4-years/uk-who-0

[24] For example, http://www.parentdish.co.uk/baby/cot-death-advice-how-to-reduce-the-risks

[25] Retrieved on July 8th 2014 from http://www.mayoclinic.org/diseases-conditions/egg-allergy/basics

[26] Retrieved on July 8th 2014 from http://www.ovg.ox.ac.uk/pertussis-whooping-cough

[27] 'The common way for writing myopia is to say how many dioptres your lens would need to be to correct your sight back to its normal level… The higher the number the more short sighted you would be: Mild myopia includes powers up to -3.00 dioptres (D), Moderate myopia, values of -3.00 to -6.00D, High myopia is usually myopia over -6.00D.' Retrieved on July 11th 2014 from http://www.rnib.org.uk/eye-health-eye-conditions-z-eye-conditions/myopia-and-high-degree-myopia

[28] http://www.autism.org.uk/professionals/health-workers/guidance.aspx

[29] SAFE (Supporting Asperger Families in Essex) and ASAP (Asperger Syndrome Adults and Parents)

[30] Retrieved in August 2011 from http://www.autism.org.uk/news-and-events/nas-conferences/previous-conferences/2011/professional-conference-2011.aspx

[31] Retrieved on March 19th 2013 from www.wikihow.com/Get-Self-Cleaning-Hair

[32] Retrieved on March 19th 2013 from www.menshealth.co.uk/style/hair-care/hair-self-cleaning-myths

[33] Retrieved on January 10th 2011 from http://en.wikipedia.org/wiki/Ray_Kurzweil

[34] Retrieved in August 2011 from http://www.autism.org.uk/news-and-events/nas-conferences/previous-conferences/2011/professional-conference-2011.aspx

[35] Retrieved on March 9 2012

[36] For further details see http://www.pearsonclinical.co.uk/Psychology/ChildCognitionNeuropsychologyandLanguage/ChildPerceptionandVisuomotorAbilities/MABC-2/Resources/LeedsConsensus06.pdf

[37] Taken from Dunford, C. (2007) *Current thinking on Developmental Co-ordination Disorder (Dyspraxia)*. Dyspraxia Foundation Professional Journal. Issue 6

[38] A review can be found on http://www.eurogamer.net/articles/vvvvvv-review

[39] Retrieved on 10/12/2012 from http://www.dyspraxiafoundation.org.uk/downloads/handwriting_and_dysprax ia.pdf

[40] www.nha-handwriting.org.uk

[41] Further details can be found (for example) at http://neurowiki2012.wikispaces.com/Default+Mode+Network

[42] http://carolgraysocialstories.com

[43] Quoted in Gold & Scassellati, downloaded from www.cs.yale.edu/~scaz/papers/Gold-ICDL-06.pdf on 22/03/2012

[44] A summary of the features underlying a Froebel education can be seen at http://www.froebeltrust.org.uk/ele ments.html

[45] *Cultural Commentary: Being Autistic Together* retrieved on 28th January 2013 from http://dsq-sds.org/article/ view/1075/1248

[46] Retrieved on 8th October 2012 from http://etheses.nottingham.ac.uk/661/1/thesis_post_viva_version_2.pdf

[47] Putting Autism in Context. *Communication. National Autistic Society.* Summer 2013 pages 29-30

[48] www.asiam.ie/back-school-buddy-system

[49] www.autism.org.uk/circleoffriends

[50] Commissioned by the UK government and developed with the Autism Research Unit at Cambridge University. Available from www.transporters.com

[51] For further information see www.carolgraysocialstories.com

[52] A radula is 'a horny band or ribbon in mollusks other than bivalves that bears minute teeth on its dorsal surface and tears up food and draws it into the mouth' – retrieved on May 16, 2012 from www.merriam-webster. com/medical/radula

[53] Retrieved on June 13th 2013 from http://sfari.org/news-and-opinion/news/2012/proposed-dsm-5-criteria-for-autism-spectrum-disorders

[54] 28th November 2015

[55] Retrieved on 13th July 2012 from http://medical-dictionary.thefreedictionary.com/executive+function

[56] Retrieved on July 13th 2012 from www.chrisdendy.com/executive.htm

[57] Retrieved on July 19th 2012 from http://media.education.gov.uk/assets/files/pdf/p/learn ing%20to%20read%20through%20phonics%20%20%20information%20for%20parents.pdf

[58] See http://jollylearning.co.uk/overview-about-jolly-phonics

[59] *Acanthostega* (meaning spiny roof) is an extinct labyrinthodont genus, among the first vertebrate animals to have recognizable limbs. It appeared in the Upper Devonian (Famennian) about 365 million years ago, and was anatomically intermediate between lobe-finned fishes and the first tetrapods fully capable of coming onto land. Retrieved on December 10th 2012 from www.babylon.com/definition/Acanthostega

[60] Retrieved from http://www.autism.org.uk/get-involved/campaign-for-change/campaign-resources/campaign-re ports/make-school-make-sense.aspx but no longer available on this web page

[61] The right start: reforming the system for children with autism. Report on reform of the special educational needs and disabilities system by the All-Party Parliamentary Group on Autism retrieved on August 31st 2012 from www.appga.org.uk/news-and-reports/new-reports.aspx

[62] For further details see www.aettraininghubs.org.uk/training-hubs

[63] This predates machines like the Raspberry Pi, BBC micro:bit etc. and is less of a problem now.

[64] Useful resources include: http://www.safekids.com/kids-rules-for-online-safety/; http://www.fbi.gov/fun-games/kids/kids-safety; http://www.microsoft.com/en-GB/security/family-safety/childsafety-age.aspx

[65] http://en.wikipedia.org/wiki/Gary_McKinnon

[66] Retrieved on October 8th 2012 from http://etheses.nottingham.ac.uk/661/1/thesis_post_viva_version_2.pdf

[67] Retrieved on October 13th 2012 from https://itunes.apple.com/gb/app/autism-apps/id441600681?mt=8

[68] www.nationalgallery.org.uk

[69] Tests used were the revised Amsterdam child intelligence test (Bleichrodt et al, 1987), the Movement ABC or the Movement Assessment Battery for Children (Henderson & Sugden, 1992) and the CBCL or full Child Behaviour CheckList (Achenbach, 1991 & Verhulst et al, 1996)

[70] This report can be retrieved by searching for National Autistic Society Great Expectations report

[71] See www.ofsted.gov.uk/publications/090221 published in September 2010

[72] www.councilfordisabledchildren.org.uk/media/554523/ChildrenAndFamiliesActBrief.pdf

[73] http://www.legislation.gov.uk/ukpga/2014/6/part/3/enacted

[74] Hayashi, M. et al., *Superior fluid intelligence in children with Asperger's disorder, Brain and Cognition* (2007), doi:10.1016/j.bandc.2007.09.008, retrieved on September 22nd 2012 from http://www.freewebs.com/adiscussion/Superior%20fluid%20intelligence%20in%20children%20with%20Asperger's%20disorder.pdf

[75] Dawson, M., Soulières, I., Gernsbacher, M.A. & Mottron, L. (2007) *The Level and Nature of Autistic Intelligence.* http://www.ncbi.nlm.nih.gov/pubmed/17680932

[76] These and other questionnaires can also be retrieved from http://www.autismresearchcentre.com/arc_tests

[77] Retrieved from http://www.autismresearchcentre.com/arc_tests

[78] http://www.child-autism-parent-cafe.com/welcome-to-holland.html

[79] In the NAS leaflet *After Diagnosis. Services and support for children with autism and their parents and carers.* Professionals can find out more at www.autism.org.uk/professionals.

[80] Retrieved on 18 May, 2013 from http://www.businessballs.com/elisabeth_kubler_ross_five_stages_of_grief.htm

[81] http://www.researchautism.net

[82] Retrieved on 9th April 2013 from http://www.nimh.nih.gov/about/director/index.shtml

[83] Retrieved on June 5th 2013 from http://apps.bps.org.uk/_publicationfiles/consultation-responses/DSM-5%202011%20-%20BPS%20response.pdf

[84] Retrieved on February 6th 2013

[85] http://www.pearsonclinical.co.uk/Psychology/ChildCognitionNeuropsychologyandLanguage/ChildPerceptionandVisuomotorAbilities/MABC-2/Resources/LeedsConsensus06.pdf

[86] New Scientist June 1st 2013

[87] Key:
London: Measurements made at the hospital in London – no clothes;
Local: Measurements made at our local hospital – no clothes;
HC: Measurements made at our local Health Centre – fully clothed

[88] All the dates calculated from due date, not premature date of birth. A=tests carried out by staff at hospital in London and B=tests carried out by one paediatrician at our local hospital.

[89] This assessment was made when John was 21.

[90] The details described above were obtained from *Intelligence Testing with the WISC-R* by Alan S Kaufman, where further information about these tests can be found.

[91] John sent this email to me when he was 28.

[92] John sent me this email in 2010.

[93] Lydia's original spelling is retained.

[94] w = weeks, m = months, y = years

[95] Age adjusted for prematurity, i.e. calculated from due date.

[96] Letters from our local hospital paediatrician to our family GP

[97] Letters from paediatricians at the hospital in London to our local hospital paediatrician and the family GP.

[98] Copy also sent to John's nursery.

[99] Letter sent to us following the home visit by the paediatrician from the hospital in London.

[100] Letter sent to the consultant at the specialist eye unit.

[101] The WISC-R tests were designed so that the scaled score for an average population is 10 with a standard deviation of 3, giving rise to an average population IQ of 100 with a standard deviation of 15. What this means in practice is that about two thirds of the population (from which the sample was drawn) would have scaled scores between 7 and 13 and an IQ between 85 and 115 whilst approximately 95% would have scaled scores between 4 and 16 and an IQ between 70 and 130.

[102] NM=Not Measured and so IQs were pro-rated by the educational psychologist at the time.

[103] For further details about this questionnaire including the scoring details see: Baron-Cohen, S (2004) *The Essential Difference.* London: Penguin Books

[104] Key:
STA = Strongly agree;
SLA = Slightly agree;
SLD = Slightly disagree;
STD = Strongly disagree.

[105] For further details about this questionnaire including the scoring details see: Baron-Cohen, S (2004) *The Essential Difference.* London: Penguin Books

[106] Key:
DA = Definitely agree;
SLA = Slightly agree;
SLD = Slightly disagree;
DD = Definitely disagree.
[107] For further details about this questionnaire including the scoring details see: Baron-Cohen, S (2004) *The Essential Difference.* London: Penguin Books
[108] Key:
DA = Definitely agree;
SLA = Slightly agree;
SLD = Slightly disagree;
DD = Definitely disagree.
[109] Results for John aged approximately eight years. The test details including the allocation of points were downloaded from http://www.autismresearchcentre.com/tests/default.asp
[110] This table only lists John's characteristics and therefore doesn't provide a complete list of all the symptoms that are frequently associated with these conditions. For this reason symptoms e.g. depression, taking language literally and problems with food have been excluded as these don't apply to John. As everyone is different, anyone with one of the above diagnoses won't necessarily exhibit all of John's symptoms: for example some children with Asperger's Syndrome are excellent at art.
[111] http://www.autism.org.uk/10225
[112] http://www.cafamily.org.uk/media/389272/helping_your_child_sleep.pdf
[113] Search for 'good sleep habits' in http://www.researchautism.net
[114] http://www.autism.org.uk/professionals/health-workers.aspx
[115] http://www.autism.org.uk/about/health/toilet-training.aspx
[116] Download from http://www.autism.org.uk/18453
[117] http://www.autism.org.uk/classroom-playground
[118] http://www.autism.org.uk/products/core-nas-publications/moving-from-primary-to-secondary-school.aspx (free publication)
[119] http://www.autism.org.uk/products/core-nas-publications/understanding-difficulties-at-breaktime.aspx (free publication)
[120] Available from http://www.autismeducationtrust.org.uk
[121] http://www.autism.org.uk/professionals/teachers/in-your-school/pack.aspx
[122] For parents about bullying and how to deal with it see http://www.autism.org.uk/bullying and for young people see http://www.autism.org.uk/bullies
[123] For advice about strategies to get away from bullies see http://www.kidscape.org.uk
[124] For help on cyberbullying see https://www.childline.org.uk/Explore/Bullying/Pages/online-bullying.aspx

Printed in Great Britain
by Amazon